Time Out

Mallorca
& Menorca

timeout.com

Mallorca & Menorca

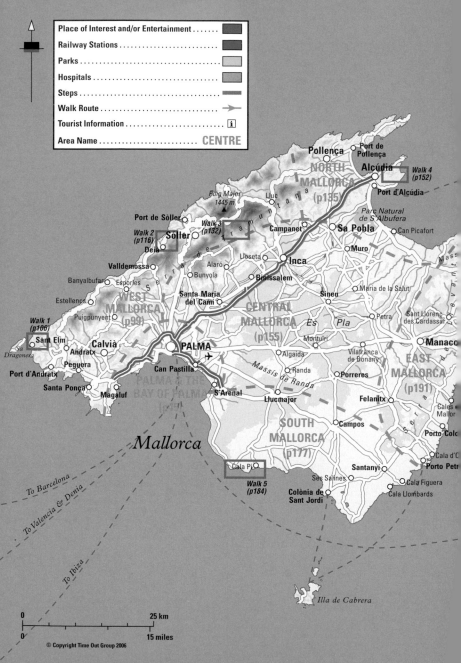

Place of Interest and/or Entertainment	
Railway Stations	
Parks	
Hospitals	
Steps	
Walk Route	
Tourist Information	i
Area Name	CENTRE

Pollença
Port de Pollença
Alcúdia
Walk 4 (p152)
Port d'Alcúdia

NORTH MALLORCA (p135)

Puig Major 1445 m

Walk 3 (p132)

Lluc

Parc Natural de S'Albufera
Can Picafort

Port de Sóller

Walk 2 (p116)
Sóller
Deià

Campanet
Sa Pobla
Muro

Valldemossa

Alaró
Lloseta
Inca

Bunyola
Binissalem

Maria de la Salut

Banyalbufar
Esporles
Santa Maria del Camí

Estellencs
WEST MALLORCA (p99)
Puigpunyent

Sineu
Petra
Sant Llorenç des Cardassar

Walk 1 (p106)
Sant Elm
Sa Dragonera
Calvià
Andratx
Peguera

CENTRAL MALLORCA (p155)
Es Pla

Manaco

PALMA

Montuïri

Vilafranca de Bonany
EAST MALLORCA (p191)

Port d'Andratx
Santa Ponça
Magaluf
Can Pastilla
PALMA & THE BAY OF PALMA (p79)
S'Arenal

Algaida
Randa
Porreres
Cales Mallor

Massis de Randa
Felanitx
Porto Colo
Cala d'O
Porto Petr

Mallorca

SOUTH MALLORCA (p177)
Llucmajor

Campos

Santanyí
Cala Figuera

Cala Pi
Walk 5 (p184)
Colònia de Sant Jordi
Ses Salines
Cala Llombards

To Barcelona
To Valencia & Denia
To Ibiza

Illa de Cabrera

0 — 25 km
0 — 15 miles

© Copyright Time Out Group 2006

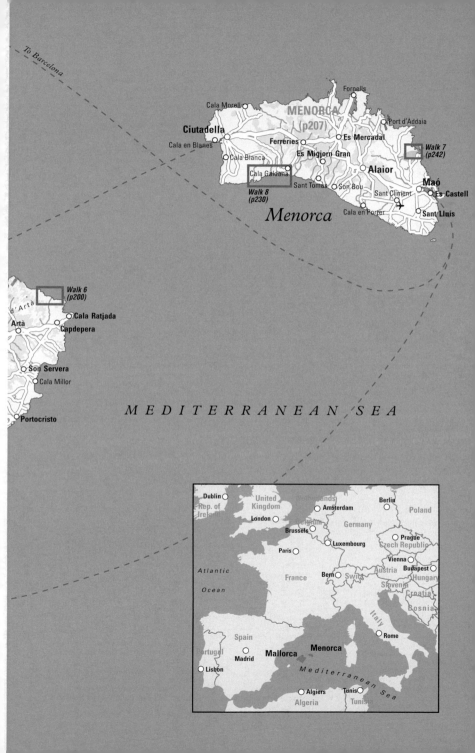

Published by Time Out Guides Ltd, a wholly owned subsidiary of Time Out Group Ltd.
Time Out and the Time Out logo are trademarks of Time Out Group Ltd.

© Time Out Group Ltd 2006
Previous edition 2004.

10 9 8 7 6 5 4 3 2 1

This edition first published in Great Britain in 2006 by Ebury Publishing
Ebury Publishing is a division of The Random House Group Ltd,
20 Vauxhall Bridge Road, London SW1V 2SA

Random House Australia Pty Limited 20 Alfred Street, Milsons Point, Sydney, New South Wales 2061, Australia
Random House New Zealand Limited 18 Poland Road, Glenfield, Auckland 10, New Zealand
Random House South Africa (Pty) Limited Isle of Houghton, Corner Boundary
Road & Carse O'Gowrie, Houghton 2198, South Africa

Random House UK Limited Reg. No. 954009

Distributed in USA by Publishers Group West
1700 Fourth Street, Berkeley, California 94710

Distributed in Canada by Penguin Canada Ltd
10 Alcorn Avenue, Toronto, Ontario, Canada M4V 3B2

For further distribution details, see www.timeout.com

ISBN 1-904978-03-7 (up to 31 December 2006)
9781904 978039 (from 1 January 2007)

A CIP catalogue record for this book is available from the British Library

Colour reprographics by Icon, Crowne House, 56-58 Southwark Street, London SE1 1UN

Printed and bound in Germany by Appl

Papers used by Ebury Publishing are natural, recyclable products made from wood grown in sustainable forests

Portals Nous. *See p93.*

Time Out Guides Limited
Universal House
251 Tottenham Court Road
London W1T 7AB
Tel + 44 (0)20 7813 3000
Fax + 44 (0)20 7813 6001
Email guides@timeout.com
www.timeout.com

Editorial

Editor Jonathan Cox
Deputy Editor Jan Fuscoe
Consultant Editor Lanny Aldrich
Listings Editor Alex Phillips, Alix Leveugle, Ian Collingwood
Proofreader Marian Moisy
Indexer Selena Cox

Editorial/Managing Director Peter Fiennes
Series Editor Ruth Jarvis
Deputy Series Editor Lesley McCave
Business Manager Gareth Garner
Guides Co-ordinator Holly Pick
Accountant Kemi Olufuwa

Design

Art Director Scott Moore
Art Editor Tracey Ridgewell
Senior Designer Josephine Spencer
Designer Henry Elphick
Digital Imaging Dan Conway
Ad Make-up Jenni Prichard

Picture Desk

Picture Editor Jael Marschner
Deputy Picture Editor Tracey Kerrigan
Picture Researcher Helen McFarland

Advertising

Sales Director Mark Phillips
International Sales Manager Ross Canadé
International Sales Executive Simon Davies
Advertising Sales (Mallorca) Margarita Calderón Blanco
Advertising Assistant Kate Staddon

Marketing

Marketing Director Mandy Martinez
Marketing & Publicity Manager, US Rosella Albanese

Production

Production Director Mark Lamond
Production Controller Marie Howell

Time Out Group

Chairman Tony Elliott
Managing Director Mike Hardwick
Group Financial Director Richard Waterlow
Group Commercial Director Lesley Gill
Group General Manager Nichola Coulthard
Group Circulation Director Jim Heinemann
Group Art Director John Oakey
Online Managing Director David Pepper
Group Production Director Steve Proctor
Group IT Director Simon Chappell

Contributors

Introduction Jonathan Cox. **History** Jonathan Cox (*Prehistory primer* Jonathan Bennett). **Mallorca & Menorca Today** Adam Coulter, Jonathan Cox. **Food & Drink** Jonathan Cox. **Wild Mallorca & Menorca** Chris Moss. **Festivals & Events** Chris Moss. **Palma & the Bay of Palma** Jonathan Cox, Sally Davies. **West Mallorca** Jonathan Cox. **North Mallorca** Sally Davies, Chris Moss (*Kid Stuff* Jonathan Cox). **Central Mallorca** Jonathan Cox. **South & East Mallorca** Sally Davies, Kirsten Foster, Tara Stevens (*Rafael Nadal* Jonathan Cox). **Menorca** Jonathan Bennett, Tara Stevens . **Directory** Jonathan Cox (*Golf* Jo Ditcham). **Walks** Jonathan Cox.

Maps JS Graphics (john@jsgraphics.co.uk). Maps are based on material supplied by Netmaps.

Photography by Jonathan Cox, except: pages 41, 67, 74 Fomento del Turismo de Mallorca; page 150 Fundación Yannick y Ben Jakober Collection; page 195 AFP/Getty Images.
The following image was provided by the featured establishment/artist: page 166.

The Editor would like to thank Tolo Llabrés, Anna Skidmore at the Fomento de Mallorca, Meno Cars (Avda. Vives Llull 128, Maó, 971 36 38 88, mobile 670 46 38 88, menocars@infotelecom.es).

Contents

Introduction

The Janus-faced Balearics are no longer solely the sand-and-sangria, sun-and-sombrero package-tour hedonist heaven of legend. Scarcely a Sunday travel supplement goes by without a feature on designer hotels in Palma or classy restaurants in the Mallorca interior.

Yet were you to holiday around the Bay of Palma, or in the north along the Bay of Alcúdia, or in some of the less salubrious east coast resorts, you'll find that the Little Britain- (and Kleine Deutschland-) on-Sea caricature still holds good. True, efforts have been made in recent years to spruce up some of the grottier vacation hotspots, and some of the most offensive concrete monstrosities have actually been demolished, but if your basic holiday wish is for Blackpool with sun, then you can still find it.

But such was the phenomenal success of the package tourism explosion of the 1960s and '70s (rocketing the Balearics from one of Spain's poorest regions to one of its wealthiest) that it's taken a very long time for most people to realise that this infamous image of the island is not, and has never been, the full story.

In the first half of the 20th century Mallorca was, in fact, one of the classiest holiday destinations going. The opening of the exclusive Hotel Formentor in 1929 brought in royalty and film stars, actors and writers, and there's a certain neat symmetry that the island is once again drawing in many of the world's biggest stars, many of whom have bought property in what has become just about the most expensive part of Spain (Michael Douglas, Claudia Schiffer and Michael Schumacher among them). And you can be sure that it's not the flamenco shows and bargain-priced chicken and chips that has brought them here.

Firstly, there's the island capital. With a population of a third of a million, **Palma** is by far the biggest settlement in the Balearics, and a truly cosmopolitan city that makes few concessions to the tourist industry. If you had a list of desirable attributes for any city, few ticks would be missing on Palma's checksheet – a seaside location, a labyrinthine old town, notable architecture, high-quality restaurants, bars and cafés of character, stylish shops, galleries and museums. It's got the lot.

And then there's the undeniable fact that Mallorca is a stunningly beautiful island, particularly in the west, which is defined by the massive rippling peaks of the **Serra de Tramuntana**. Here, the ruggedness of the landscape is such that large-scale holiday

Top ten · Biggest surprises

Sleeping and eating in style

No region of Spain has more classy hotels and fine restaurants than Mallorca. In an attempt to lure more upmarket, higher-spending visitors, the island is now covered by a network of sleek, stylish places to stay – from metropolitan designer hotels to luxurious-rustic *fincas*. And there are restaurants to match, both Michelin-starred temples of gastronomy and wonderful local joints. Expect to pay for the quality, though.

Menorca's rich prehistory

Nowhere in Europe has a greater concentration of prehistoric sites than Menorca. More than 100 are scattered over the tiny island, and most can be visited. Their typical structures of lookout tower (talayot) and T-shaped shrine (taula) are unique.

Hiking and high peaks

The Serra de Tramuntana mountain range, stretching down Mallorca's west coast, is the island's most spectacular natural asset, offering memorable climbing, hiking and birdwatching and little tourist development.

The Brits in Menorca

Menorca was ruled by Britain for most of the 18th century and there remain fascinating artefacts of the period, from the continued production of gin to the prevalence of bow windows and strange anglicisms in the Menorquí dialect. *See p216* **The British legacy**.

Subterranean stunners

The cave systems of Mallorca, particularly along the east coast, are astonishing. Dripping with multi-hued stalactites and lined with silent underground lakes, they make for an otherworldly experience, which even their thorough commercialisation can't spoil.

The perfect city break

Palma is a peach of a city. Despite sitting at the hub of the two pincers of grim development around the Bay of Palma, it remains resolutely in the hands of the locals. And with a mazy old town, an unforgettable cathedral, chic shops and characterful bars and restaurants, it amply repays a few days' visit at any time of the year.

Divine diving

The scuba diving off Mallorca is fairly dull, but the crystalline waters around Menorca are rich with wrecks, underwater caverns and marine life, providing some of the best diving in the Mediterranean, and there is no shortage of friendly diving schools offering try-dives for novices. *See p256* **Dive! Dive! Dive!**.

Timewarp interior

Holiday development is heavily concentrated around the coastlines of both islands, leaving their interiors to the locals and a slow-paced rural way of life that provides a window into the past. On Mallorca, the towns of Sineu and Artà, in particular, are full of charm yet remain unruffled by the packaging hordes nearby.

The monastic life

Mallorca is specked with spectacularly located monasteries, many of which offer some of the cheapest and most spiritually satisfying accommodation on the island. Don't expect frills; just simplicity, utter tranquillity and views to die for.

Life's a beach

Mallorca has its fair share of fine (if over-populated) beaches, but few can compare to the idyllic coves that crenellate the Menorcan coast. Many can only be reached on foot, and with their fine bleached sands and pellucid shallow waters, it doesn't take a great leap of imagination to fancy yourself in the Caribbean.

development is almost unknown (as are the sort of long sandy beaches that might attract it). It's certainly not free from tourists, but they tend to be of a rather more rarefied cast – keen to lose themselves in the anonymity of some of the most indulgent and discreet hotels in Europe, or else to head into the mountains to enjoy unforgettable, soul-cleansing hiking and the sort of solitude that you would have thought impossible on an island that welcomes ten million visitors a year.

Here, too, is where you'll find the expat successors to the writers and artists who have long been entranced by the coast's beauty and serenity. In particular, the village of **Deià**, popularised most notably by the poet Robert Graves, remains home to a thriving colony of (these days rather wealthy) arty types. Yet there are still likeable towns like **Sóller** (and **Pollença** to the north) which, though welcoming visitors during the day, revert

By numbers

Geography

Balearics
Area: 5,040 sq km (1,946 sq miles)
Mallorca
Area: 3,640 sq km (1,405 sq miles)
Length of coastline: 555km (347 miles)
Highest point: Puig Major (1,445m/
4,741ft; there are 37 peaks over 1,000m
in the Serra de Tramuntana)
Menorca
Area: 702 sq km (271 sq miles)
Length of coastline: 286km (179 miles)
Highest point: El Toro (357m/1,171ft)

Climate

Average daily max temp: 21.9°C (71.4°F)
Average daily min temp: 9.7°C (49.5°F)
Average daily hours of sunshine: 7.4
Average monthly rainfall: 35.3mm (1.4in)
Average humidity: 74.1%
See p277 **Weather**.

Population

Balearics
Total: 878,600
Mallorca
Total: 702,000
Palma: 346,700
Menorca
Total: 75,300
Ciutadella: 23,700
Maó: 22,900

Tourism

Mallorca
Tourist arrivals by air in 2004: 8,249,000
By nationality:
German 32%
British 32%
Spanish 16%
Menorca
Tourist arrivals by air in 2004: 1,043,000
By nationality:
British 54%
Spanish 23%
German 9%

back to the possession of the locals
at night when the tour buses leave.

Further north, the Serra terminates
in the dizzying precipices of the Formentor
peninsula, beneath which shelters the **Bay
of Pollença** and yet another type of holiday
experience. Port de Pollença is a relatively
low-key family-oriented resort that has

avoided the sort of excesses that have scarred
the Bay of Palma (and are threatening the
Bay of Alcúdia to the east).

On the east coast, too, you find a number of
popular family resorts that may lack character,
but are at least not as environmentally offensive
as they might be. In contrast, the wind-whipped
southern coast is largely undeveloped; though
flat and barren, it does possess a certain wild,
melancholic beauty.

And hemmed in by these foreigner-
dominated coastlines is the great rolling interior
– **Es Pla**, 'the plain'. For most of the island's
history, this agricultural heartland was
Mallorca's most important region, but the
coming of tourism turned centuries of tradition
on its head. Now a strip of barren rocky
coastline is worth vastly more than a fertile
field, and the interior is largely unknown and
ignored by the tourists who fear losing sight of
their nearest beach. This blessing has allowed
Es Pla to maintain its own distinct character,
and even though rural hotels are now appearing
across its unpopulated expanse, the absence
of scenic drama or major tourist attractions
is likely to ensure that this character is
maintained for the foreseeable future.

Such rural serenity is also common on
Mallorca's near neighbour. **Menorca** has always
been different. It lacks the dramatic geography
of the Tramuntana, but it is also largely free
from the frenzied overdevelopment that has
destroyed great swathes of Mallorca's shoreline.
There are holiday complexes and resorts, but
they're largely contained in relatively small
areas, leaving much of the island untouched.
It developed later than Mallorca, and with less
abandon, yet it too has suffered from image
problems. Or, rather, lack of image problems.
Tell anyone you're holidaying in Menorca and
chances are they'll either look blank or slightly
pitying, as if to say: 'Why? Isn't it rather dull?'
It's true that it is a touch more staid, and
a touch more British – perhaps a legacy of the
18th-century British occupation of the island
that UK holidaymakers make up by far the
largest block of foreign visitors (Germans come
joint top of the table in Mallorca. *See left*).

Yet Menorca offers just as many surprises
as Mallorca. There are the two delightful,
pint-size main towns at either end of the
island: **Maó** and **Ciutadella** – the former,
a commandingly located port overlooking one
of the Mediterranean's finest harbours (hence
the 18th-century British interest); the latter, a
seductive citadel filled with winding, mansion-
lined streets. The resorts, it is true, are largely
lacklustre, but they are concentrated on the
west and south-east coasts, leaving most of
the island largely unspoilt. The north coast,

in particular, is wild and often wind-ravaged, bringing to mind unlikely comparisons with some of the remoter parts of Ireland. The interior is littered with unique prehistoric sites, the origins and meanings of which are still subject to debate. They make a cultural counterpoint to the lazy pleasures of Menorca's prime beaches; though some are long strands, coves are more characteristic, with perfect crescents of ivory sand melting into azure seas.

So there you have it. Two small islands but a wealth of different possible experiences. Keep your expectations within reason (nowhere, for instance, is truly undiscovered) and you really can't fail to find the qualities you want in a holiday. And once you've caught the bug, believe us, you'll be back.

ABOUT TIME OUT GUIDES

Time Out Mallorca & Menorca is one of an expanding series of Time Out guides produced by the people behind London and New York's successful listings magazines. Our guides are all written and updated by experts who have striven to provide you with all the most up-to-date information.

THE LOWDOWN ON THE LISTINGS

Above all, we've tried to make this book as useful as possible. Addresses, telephone numbers, websites, transport, opening times, admission prices and credit card details were all checked and correct at the time we went to press. However, owners can change arrangements at any time. Before you go out of your way, we'd advise you to telephone and check opening times and other particulars. While every effort has been made to ensure the accuracy of the information contained in this guide, the publishers cannot accept responsibility for any errors it may contain.

Prices in restaurants

Within this guide you will see that we have denoted the price range of each restaurant we mention with between one and four euro symbols. These correspond approximately to the following price brackets for a full meal with drinks per person:

€	= under €20
€€	= between €20 and €30
€€€	= between €30 and €40
€€€€	= over €40

PRICES AND PAYMENT

We have noted whether venues such as shops, hotels and restaurants accept credit cards but have only listed the major cards – American Express (**AmEx**), Diners Club (**DC**), MasterCard (**MC**) – also known as EuroCard – and Visa (**V**). Many hotels and upmarket shops and restaurants may also accept travellers' cheques in all denominations.

THE LIE OF THE LAND

For the purposes of this guide we have divided Mallorca into six regions – Palma and the Bay of Palma, West, North, Central, South and East Mallorca, with a separate chapter on Menorca. Each of these has its own map and introduction at the start of the relevant chapter.

TELEPHONE NUMBERS

All telephone numbers in this guide include the code for the Balearics (971), which you always need to dial whether or not you are on the islands. The international dialling code for Spain is 34.

ESSENTIAL INFORMATION

For all the practical information you might need for visiting Mallorca and Menorca – including visa and customs information, advice for the disabled emergency telephone numbers, a list of useful websites and the lowdown on the local transport network – turn to the **Directory** chapter at the back of this guide. It starts on page 261.

LET US KNOW WHAT YOU THINK

We hope you enjoy Time Out Mallorca & Menorca, and we'd like to know what you think of it. In addition, we also welcome tips for places that you consider we should include in future editions, and take notice of your criticism of our choices. There's a reader's reply card at the back of this book – or you can email us at the following address: guides@timeout.com.

There is an online version of this book, along with guides to over 45 other international cities, at **www.timeout.com**.

Advertisers

We would like to stress that no establishment has been included in this guide because it has advertised in any of our publications and no payment of any kind has influenced any review. The opinions given in this book are those of *Time Out* writers and entirely independent.

In Context

Features

Banco de Sóller, **Sóller**. *See p124.*

Jaume 'the Conqueror'. *See p19.*

History

The Balearics have been attracting invaders for millennia – tourists are simply the latest wave.

PREHISTORIC BALEARICS

The Balearics, and Menorca in particular, are remarkably rich in prehistoric ruins. Humans first reached the islands some time before 4000 BC; just how long before is a matter of considerable controversy. Some archaeologists claim to have found evidence of human presence in Mallorca from around 5600 BC; others believe there's no reliable proof before the start of the fourth millennium BC.

Whatever the truth is, it seems that, for reasons unknown, man arrived relatively late in the Balearics – most of the Mediterranean islands had been settled by the seventh or even eighth millennium BC.

Equally, no one knows why the first settlers appeared. Perhaps the islands were happened upon by chance by fishermen or traders, who precipitated a larger migration of people driven from Iberia or the south of France by hunger.

These earliest inhabitants found shelter in caves, establishing what has become known as the Balearic cave culture. A major food source was undoubtedly *Myotragus Balearicus* – a stumpy, endemic goat-like animal – and it's possible that its extinction by 3000 BC was due to over-hunting by man. Some historians believe that the early islanders tried to domesticate *Myotragus*; they certainly made an attempt to establish primitive agriculture.

Given the islands' prominent position in the western Mediterranean, they inevitably attracted the attention of the sea-faring people of the region. From around 2500 BC to 1400 BC the first settlements outside caves appear – all inland, indicating the constant danger of pirate attack (a problem throughout Balearic history).

But not all interaction was violent. Ceramic technology came to the islands, domesticated animals were imported and, around the middle of the second millennium BC, the advanced Beaker culture (so named after their practice of burying distinctive bell-shaped ceramic beakers with their dead) was becoming influential. It also brought knowledge of metallurgical techniques to the islands.

The coming of the Beaker culture ushered in the Bronze Age. Gradually, a more sophisticated society developed with more efficient farming and improved metal-working, leading to population growth and social differentiation.

This era is known as the Talayotic Period (c1400-c800 BC) in the Balearics, after the distinctive talayots (from the Arabic word '*atalaya*', meaning 'watchtower'), unusual stone towers dating from this period that can still be seen scattered across the islands, especially in Menorca. The only similar structures have been found in Sardinia, suggesting that the two island cultures might share the same root.

Talayotic culture reached its apogee on Menorca. Here, and only here, are found the mysterious taulas (meaning 'tables' in Catalan) – huge T-shaped structures consisting of one stone lain flat on top of another upright stone. The other distinctive structures from this period are navetas – long, apsidal constructions, shaped like the prow of a boat with a large opening at one end and drystone walls that were possibly covered with twigs, leaves and dry mud.

For more on the design and possible functions of prehistoric structures, and where to find the best examples, *see p16* **Prehistory primer**.

Though trade increased in the Post-Talayotic Period (Iron Age, c800-c123 BC), this was generally a period of cultural and economic decline in the Balearics, with the quality of pottery, architecture and agricultural techniques all suffering. There was, though, greater contact with the outside world (evidence of bull cults on the islands provides a link with other islands, such as Sardinia and Malta, with similar cults), and the influence of other Mediterranean peoples on the Balearics during this period was becoming increasingly important.

PHOENICIANS, GREEKS, CARTHAGINIANS AND ROMANS

The Phoenicians (maritime traders from the eastern Mediterranean) established a presence on the Balearics around the turn of the first millennium BC, though they seem to have considered the islands as staging posts rather than places for settlement. They did, however, construct an outpost at Sanisera on northern Menorca, and some artefacts have been found at Alcúdia, but there is no evidence of other Phoenician towns.

From around 800 BC, the Greeks were dominant in the region, but, again, very little evidence of their presence in the Balearics has been found. The Greeks called the islands Gimnesias – alluding to the inhabitants' scant clothing (athletes in the Greek *gymnasion* exercised naked).

The city of Carthage had been founded by the Phoenicians in North Africa in the ninth century BC, and, as Greek influence waned in the seventh century BC, so the Carthaginians became the major regional power. They colonised Ibiza in 654 BC, but, like the Phoenicians and Greeks before them, seem to have regarded Mallorca and Menorca merely as stepping stones, founding no more than trading posts. (The small island of Cabrera off the south-east coast of Mallorca may have held one, and is a possible site of the birth of the Carthaginian general Hannibal.)

Both Greeks and Carthaginians valued the islanders as mercenaries – they were famed for their proficiency with the slingshot – and Balearic troops accompanied Hannibal on his journey over the Alps in the second Punic War. The collective name of the islands probably derives from the Greek verb *ballein*, meaning 'to throw'. They became known as the Balearides.

It seems that the islands faced little concerted external aggression throughout most of this period – there is no evidence of the fortification of settlements on Mallorca and Menorca from before 300 BC.

After Hannibal's defeat by the emergent Romans at the Battle of Zama in 202 BC, the Carthaginians withdrew from Mallorca and Menorca, ushering in a period of relative independence for the islanders, who were then free to develop a passion for piracy relatively unchecked.

'The togas of Alcúdia became famed throughout the Roman empire for their chic designs.'

Such was the menace that they posed to shipping in the region that the Romans were spurred to take Ibiza in 146 BC and then, under Quintus Metellus, Mallorca and Menorca in 123 BC, initiating 500 years of Roman hegemony. At this time the islands were dubbed Balearis Major (Mallorca) and Balearis Minor (Menorca).

The Romans rapidly introduced the infrastructure and trappings of their civilisation, founding towns at Pollentia (on the site of modern Alcúdia, not to be confused with modern-day Pollença, which appropriated the Roman name at a later date) and Palmeria (the name referring to the palm of victory) at present-day Palma. They also developed the old Phoenician settlement of Sanisera on Menorca as a port, and Port Magonum (Maó) as a bureaucratic centre. Roads, theatres, villas and temples were built; the interior was planted

Prehistory primer

Mallorca and Menorca have a rich and varied archaeological heritage, with dozens of sites all over the islands (but particularly on Menorca) dating from the first and second millennia BC. Many share common, distinctive features. Here's how to unravel the jargon...

Ruined talayot.

TALAYOTS

Talayots are conical, elliptical or quadrangular towers made from small and medium-sized rocks, tapering gradually as they rise. Sizes vary, as do states of dilapidation. The purpose of talayots is subject to debate, though they are believed to have been used as defensive towers or watchtowers, or perhaps a combination of both, since they are often found on high ground and, in some cases, form part of a settlement's defensive wall. Early Balearic islanders were renowned throughout the Mediterranean for their skill with a sling, and the talayots would have given a great height advantage for warding off marauders. It's also possible that the use of talayots changed over time, with some doubling as dwellings or storehouses.

Examples: Mallorca – **Capacorb Vell** (*see p183*), **Hospitalet Vell** (*see p204*); Menorca – **Torre d'en Gaumés** (*see p232*), **Torralba d'en Salort** (*see p223*), **Trépuco** (*see p222*).

TAULAS

Talayots are found on both Mallorca and Menorca, but a unique feature of Menorcan prehistoric sites is the taula, which is often found close to a talayot. This high, altar-like structure consists of two large rectangular rocks, one with a groove cut into it so that it can snugly balance on top of the other to form a 'T'. In some cases, a third, narrow rock stands behind the upright to act as a support, while in others this function is fulfilled, almost symbolically, by a narrow rib carved into the back of the upright.

Taulas undoubtedly had religious significance and are found at the centre of small, usually horseshoe-shaped walled sanctuaries. To the right of the entrance there is often an altar (though these are difficult to identify these days), and large amounts of ash, charred bones and broken amphorae have been found in many, indicating ritual of some sort. Whether the enclosures were covered with a roof or not is subject to some dispute, though, given the height of some of the taulas and the absence of any supporting evidence, this is unlikely.

Examples: Menorca – **Talatí de Dalt** (*see p223*), **Trépuco** (*see p222*), **Torralba d'en Salort** (*see p223*), **Torretrencada** (*see p257*).

NAVETAS

Dating from an earlier era than taulas, navetas are long stone chambers, shaped like the prow of a ship. Some were dwellings (central fireplaces and hearths have been found in many), while others served funerary purposes. This latter type often consists of two chambers, one on top of the other, with a small entrance hall connecting the two.

Taula.

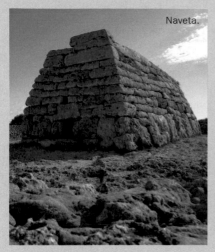

Naveta.

irregular-sized rocks, without mortar). A wall made in this manner often encircled settlements. Several villages also contain cisterns for rainwater collection carved into the rock. Another common feature is the hypostyle chamber, which may have been used for storage. Its name refers to the use of one or more pillars made of several individual rocks that increase in size from the bottom upwards, supporting a roof of stone slabs. This was probably then covered with sticks and vegetation to fill in the gaps.

Examples: Menorca – **Torralba d'en Salort** (hypostyle room; *see p223*), **Torre d'en Gaumés** (hypostyle room; *see p232*), **Son Catlar** (cyclopean encircling wall; *see p256*).

Examples: Menorca – **Naveta d'es Tudons** (*see p256*), **Rafal Rubí** (*see p223*).

HOUSES, CYCLOPEAN WALLS AND HYPOSTYLE CHAMBERS

Talayots and taulas are usually found at the centre of a settlement featuring one or more stone houses. These houses are generally small, low and little more than man-made caves, with cyclopean walls (made of

BARRACAS AND PONTS

On Menorca, and particularly at the western end of the island, you will spot circular and rectangular step pyramids specking the countryside. Yet more prehistoric structures, you may suspect, but these actually only date from the mid 19th century, and are (aesthetically rather pleasing) cattle shelters. The circular version is known as a barraca, while the rectangular type is called a pont.

Examples: They are numerous around Ciutadella, particularly heading towards Punta Nati.

Barracas.

with olive groves, fig trees, grain fields and vineyards; and the economy boomed. The togas of Alcúdia became famed throughout the Roman empire for their chic designs.

Throughout most of the Roman period, the Balearics formed part of the province of Tarraconensis (based around Tarragona on the Iberian mainland). In AD 404 the islands become a province in their own right, but by this time Roman dominance in Western Europe was crumbling before an onslaught of warlike tribes sweeping west and south.

VANDALS, BYZANTINES AND MOORS

One such tribe, the Vandals, led by Gesoric, brought a violent end to Roman rule in the Balearics in 425, obliterating almost all evidence of Roman civilisation. As adherents of Arianism (a Christian creed based on the distinctiveness of the figures of Christ and God, and thus denying their presence in the Trinity), the Vandals also made a point of destroying all signs of orthodox Christianity at the time. Hence the lack of Roman remains and early churches on the islands.

In 533 the Vandals were defeated in North Africa by the Byzantines under Belisarius, leading to Emperor Justinian I annexing the Balearics. But such a far-flung outpost of the Byzantine empire was never easy to maintain, and it had been all but abandoned by the end of the seventh century.

As Byzantine power in the Mediterranean diminished, so the dynamic forces of Islam swept in from the east. In 711 the Moors (Arab and Berber tribes) of North Africa crossed the Straits of Gibraltar and invaded the European mainland. Defeating the Visigoths under Roderic, they proceeded to overrun the Iberian peninsula with remarkable speed. Although there had been large-scale Moorish attacks on Mallorca in 707-8, and again in 798, the Moors regarded the Balearics more as a source of booty than as a potential part of their empire. After the latter raid the islanders appealed to the Holy Roman Emperor Charlemagne for protection, but this brought only temporary relief. As in the lawless preceding centuries, the Balearics continued to be a base for pirates and a target for marauders (they suffered an attack by Vikings in 859). It wasn't until almost 200 years after their invasion of Spain that the Moors finally decided to conquer the islands.

According to legend, a Moorish merchant, Isman al-Khaulani, was washed up on Mallorca after a storm. When he returned to Spain he extolled the beauty and potential of the island to the Emir of Córdoba and convinced him that it would be easy to annex Mallorca as part of al-Andalus. Khaulani himself headed the successful expedition in 902 and became   the first wali (governor) of Mallorca, building the Almudaina (government palace) by the sea in Palma, which the Moors named Medina Mayurka.

Agriculture and infrastructure on the islands was a shambles after centuries of raiding and neglect. The Moors' most important contribution to the Balearics was (as in the rest of their empire) to hugely improve irrigation, bringing water from the mountains to the fertile but parched plains. They also introduced almonds, apples, pears, apricots, peaches, pomegranates, cherries and new varieties of olive. Estates and grand houses were built in the foothills of the Serra de Tramuntana, and villages were founded across the plain (many still have names of Arabic origin: for example, Deià is from 'daia', meaning village; Algaida comes from the word for forest; Banyalbufar means 'vineyard by the sea'; and anywhere with an 'al-' or 'bini-' prefix derives from Arabic).

The 11th century was a period of peace, prosperity and relative cultural and religious harmony in the Balearics, with the islands too remote from the power centres of al-Andalus to play any part in the power struggles there. Palma, then known as Medina Maqurqa, contained 14 mosques, several synagogues and a couple of churches.

In 1076 al-Mu'tada proclaimed the independent Kingdom of the Balearics, breaking away from al-Andalus and ushering in the rule of the less tolerant Amortadha dynasty from North Africa. Christian islanders were persecuted and local shipping raided, prompting an invasion by Pisan, Genoese, Provençal and Catalan forces led by Ramón Berenguer III, Count of Barcelona, in 1114-15. The Christian armies took Ibiza and Palma, but Moorish reinforcements arrived from the mainland, forcing the Christians to evacuate the islands.

> **'When the Emir of Mallorca captured some of his ships in 1228, Jaume I was spurred to punish the insult and launch an invasion.'**

After this episode the more tolerant Almoravid tribe took over in the Balearics (and in al-Andalus), causing an improvement in the economic situation, with an increase in trade and decrease in piracy.

When the Almohad dynasty overthrew the Almoravids in North Africa and southern Spain in the mid 12th century, the Balearics were the

Roman remains at **Sanitja**. *See p246.*

only Almoravid kingdom to survive. In 1184 the Almohads attempted, and failed, to take Mallorca, sparking a period of unprecedented Mallorcan influence in North Africa as successive rulers of the islands rampaged through present-day Morocco, Tunisia and Algeria, proving to be a major thorn in the side of the powerful Almohad ruler al-Mansur, before his successor al-Nassir eventually succeeded in conquering the Balearics in 1203.

The pendulum of tolerance once again swung back – Christians were forced to convert to Islam, and piracy of shipping and raids against the mainland once again became major problems for other local powers. When the Emir of Mallorca captured some of his ships in 1228, Jaume (Jaime or James) I, king of the newly united Aragón and Catalunya, was spurred to punish the insult and launch an invasion (he also fancied harnessing the island's wine production and agriculture).

THE RECONQUEST AND THE KINGDOM OF MALLORCA

Jaume set sail in 1229 with 143 ships and landed at Santa Ponça in south-west Mallorca (a stone cross marks the spot where the first noble came ashore). He beat the Moorish force sent to meet his army and proceeded to besiege Palma. After three months, on 31 December, the

city fell, though it was another three years before the last of the Moorish resistance on the island was crushed. Pushed back to North Africa, the Moors continued to raid the Balearics for centuries afterwards.

The king's financial resources were limited, so he encouraged Don Pedro, Crown Prince of Portugal, the Count of Roussillon and the Archbishop of Tarragona to take on the invasion of Ibiza, which, while they were to acknowledge Jaume as overlord, they could then divide between themselves. This they completed successfully in 1235 (though Don Pedro passed his share of the spoils on to Jaume).

While Jaume took Mallorca by force (earning himself the sobriquet 'the Conqueror') and Ibiza by subcontracting the dirty work, he gained Menorca by guile. As another full-scale invasion was not financially viable, he sent bullish envoys to Menorca in 1232, while ordering the lighting of hundreds of fires across the north-east of Mallorca facing Menorca, creating the illusion of an immense army encamped just across the water. The trick worked and the Menorcan Moors capitulated. Their reward was a relatively tolerant regime for the next 50 years under which they were allowed to retain control of their own government while becoming vassals of Jaume.

> **'Alfons III proceeded to conquer Mallorca and Menorca with a violence and lack of compassion that was notable even for the times.'**

On Mallorca, however, the Moors received far harsher treatment. The island was divided up (the *repartiment*) between Jaume's supporters, and almost all traces of Moorish buildings were eradicated (accounting for the paucity of remains today – Menorca was initially spared this, but a similar policy was later introduced there too). However, at the same time, Jaume introduced the Carta de Població (People's Charter – a progressive decree guaranteeing equality before the law), exempted the island from taxation to encourage Catalan immigration and protected Jewish residents in an attempt to encourage trade.

Another of Jaume's innovations was the establishment of a form of Mallorcan government that lasted until the 16th century. It consisted of six *jurats* (adjudicators), made up of two knights, two merchants, one noble and one peasant, who elected their successors annually.

Before his death, Jaume made the fateful decision to divide his kingdom between his two

Local heroes Ramón Llull

The Balearics haven't been blessed by an abundance of internationally notable natives, leaving the field clear for the 13th-century scholar, writer, missionary and philosopher Ramón Llull to claim the undisputed title of most significant local son.

Born around 1235 into an aristocratic family, Llull devoted almost all his early energies to partying and pursuing women. He became a page at the court of King Jaume II, which provided him with endless opportunities for seduction (the fact that he had a wife and two kids was no barrier). Then, suddenly, he had his road-to-Damascus moment.

The legend of Llull's transformation from libidinous cad to ascetic saint recounts how, once again, he was in pursuit of a woman – this time a famed beauty called Ambrosia de Castellano. He pressured her into meeting with him, but when all she offered him at this rendezvous was prayers, he made clear that this was not what he had in mind at all. In desperation Ambrosia ripped open her bodice to reveal that her body was racked by leprosy and exclaimed: 'My lover is death!' Deeply shocked, Llull vowed to cast aside all earthly pleasures and devote himself to spiritual matters.

As unlikely as this story is, Llull clearly did have a transforming experience, probably involving visions of Christ. His dissolute lifestyle clearly lost its charm and he started to look for a more meaningful use for his life,

settling on the not unambitious goal of converting the Moors (and Jews) to Christianity and dying as a martyr. One of these aims he was to (possibly) achieve.

Llull joined the Order of St Francis, following studies in Montpellier and Paris, and immersed himself in religion. Having then visited all the key centres of pilgrimage in medieval Europe, he felt ready to tackle the unbelievers, but soon realised that he would only have limited success if the heathens didn't know what he was talking about. So Llull spent the next nine years learning Arabic and as much as he could of Muslim culture, philosophy and religion.

King Jaume II was impressed by the monk's missionary zeal and allowed him to set up a Franciscan monastery at Miramar on Mallorca in 1276, where monks could learn Arabic and Llull could work on his ideas. Patience was not a quality he was short on, and it was another decade of study and contemplation before he pulled together all these thoughts in his immense work, the *Ars Magna*.

What was unusual about Llull's ideas was that he attempted to prove the fundamental truth of Christianity not through assertion and calls to faith, but through reason. He believed that all knowledge and faith can be ascertained via reason.

'If understanding followed no rule at all, there would be no good in the understanding nor in the matter understood, and to remain in ignorance would be the greatest good.'

sons. Jaume II received the Balearics, Roussillon and Montpellier, while Pere (Pedro) II was given Aragón, Catalunya and Valencia. When their father died in 1276, it soon became clear that Pere had no intention of giving up part of what he saw as his rightful realm, bullying Jaume II into submission as his vassal and thereby throwing Jaume into the arms of the French.

When Pere discovered his brother's scheming he vowed to invade Mallorca, though his sudden death left this to his notoriously brutal son Alfons (Alfonso) III. Palma was captured in 1285, Jaume II deposed, and Alfons proceeded to conquer the rest of the island (and, in 1287, Menorca) with a violence and lack of compassion that was notable even for the times. On Menorca, he enslaved those

It was only now that Llull thought himself ready to properly begin his work, and he initiated a remarkable series of journeys all over the Mediterranean, the Middle East and North Africa. He was a tireless teacher and writer, and produced a vast number of works on diverse subjects. Although he ostensibly viewed the study of languages as a tool for the conversion of non-Christians, he fostered an interest in oriental languages (and founded a school for them in Rome) that was of importance to the development of European scholarship.

His interests were remarkably heterodox. He invented a type of compass and wrote almost 80 volumes of poetry, using, for the first time, standard Catalan rather than Latin, thereby founding the Catalan literary tradition.

Llull may or may not have been granted his wish for a martyr's death. One story tells of how he was stoned to death by an angry crowd of Muslims in 1315 while travelling to Bejaia in Algeria to preach against Islam. Others suggest he survived the attack and returned to Mallorca.

What is certain is that Llull is viewed as a local hero and/or a saint (though he has, to date, only been beatified) by many on Mallorca and Menorca, and in Catalunya. His enduring popularity has much to do with the breadth of his interests and scholarship. Catholic propagandists might find inspiration in his trumpeting of the natural superiority of Christianity and his missionary calling; Catalan nationalists and intellectuals admire his pioneering use of the Catalan language; ordinary Mallorcans celebrate Ramón Llull as a holy, distinguished son of the island.

On his name day (29 March), there is a pilgrimage to his grave in Sant Francesc church in Palma.

Moors who couldn't afford to buy their freedom and threw the old, the sick and the infirm into the sea. All traces of Moorish architecture were eradicated and the capital, Medina Minurka, was renamed Ciutadella.

Following his early death in 1291, Alfons was succeeded by his level-headed brother Jaume, King of Sicily, who had rather more respect for the settlement of Jaume I. In 1298

the partition was restored, with Jaume ruling over Aragón, Catalunya and Valencia, and his uncle Jaume II back in charge of Mallorca and Menorca. The latter made Sineu his residence and founded a number of towns, including Manacor, Llucmajor, Felanitx and Petra.

The islands prospered, developing their potential as a key trading post in the western Mediterranean and fostering home-grown textile and shipbuilding industries. Jaume II was also patron to the great Mallorcan poet and scholar Ramón Llull (*see p20* **Local heroes**). His chief architectural legacy is Palma's stunning cathedral (though it took 500 years to complete). There's some irony in the fact that, built as it was on the site of a demolished mosque, it actually faces Mecca rather than Jerusalem. He also commenced the building of the castle of Bellver outside Palma.

Jaume was succeeded by his sickly son Sanç (Sancho) I in 1311, and then Sanç's ten-year-old nephew Jaume III in 1324. Yet Aragón had a technically stronger claim to the Mallorcan crown than Jaume III, and relations gradually deteriorated until Pere IV of Aragón invaded the Balearics, driving Jaume III out to Roussillon on the mainland. When Jaume attempted to retake Mallorca, he was killed at the Battle of Llucmajor in 1349 and the Balearics lost their independence forever.

UNIFICATION WITH SPAIN AND A LONG DECLINE

It was not until the tourism boom of the last few decades that the Balearics were to again enjoy the level of prosperity they did under Jaume II. As the islands fell under the sway of the Crown of Aragón, so the focus for the nobility moved to the mainland. This, combined with shifting trading conditions (the Portuguese discovered the route to the Indies via the Cape of Good Hope just as the overland routes to the Far East via the Mediterranean became blocked by the growth of Turkish power), meant that the Balearics gradually regressed into a cultural and economic backwater. They became an even smaller cog in an ever bigger machine when the marriage of Fernando V of Aragón and Isabel I of Castilla in 1479 united Christian Spain, and then Columbus's voyages to the Americas in the 1490s meant the focus of European trade shifted almost immediately from the Mediterranean to the Atlantic. To compound the problem, the Spanish Crown forbade the Balearics and Catalunya from trading with the New World.

As the Balearics' wealth slowly evaporated and many of her more dynamic nobles and merchants moved elsewhere, so internal tensions within the declining islands simmered and bubbled. Often it was the Jews who were blamed, sometimes it was the ruling classes. High taxes and shortages of grain eventually ignited a peasants' rebellion in 1521 that led to the capture of Palma and a long period of instability before Charles V (King of Spain and Holy Roman Emperor) restored order. He negotiated the surrender of Palma, and then promptly reneged on his liberal promises, executing hundreds of the rebels.

'In the absence of anything better to do, many of Mallorca's noble families expended all their energies pursuing vendettas among themselves.'

The 16th century was also a time of renewed aggression from North African and Turkish pirates. The Moors had finally been expelled from Spain in 1492 and this, combined with the increasing presence of the Turks in the Mediterranean, meant that the Balearics were the victims of repeated attacks from Muslim raiders, particularly around the middle of the century. Menorca suffered even more than Mallorca. The notorious Barbarossa sacked Maó in 1535, and the Turks all but obliterated Ciutadella in 1558, taking away 1,000 of its citizens as slaves to Constantinople; such was the devastation that the official sent to rebuild the town initially had to live in a cave.

The defeat of the Turks at the naval Battle of Lepanto in 1571 reduced the frequency of the raids, but they continued on and off until the 18th century.

Economic matters didn't improve in the 17th and 18th centuries, with plague and emigration depressing the population, and, in the absence of anything better to do, many of Mallorca's noble families expended all their energies pursuing vendettas among themselves.

THE 18TH CENTURY AND THE STRUGGLE FOR MENORCA

The power vacuum in the Mediterranean came to be filled increasingly by the British, whose merchant and Royal Navy ships became more and more common around the Balearics in the latter half of the 17th century. Always on the lookout for promising harbours, they saw little of value in Mallorca, but the superb anchorage at Maó on Menorca did catch their eye.

When the Spanish throne fell vacant, the War of the Spanish Succession (1701-14) provided the excuse for the British to take Menorca in 1708, and the following century saw three periods of occupation, only ending when the British renounced their claim to the island in 1802. The Mallorcans had, unfortunately, picked the losing claimant to the throne, and the victor, Philip of Anjou, extracted his revenge by abolishing many of the island's historic privileges, including the right to call itself a kingdom.

For Menorca, however, the 18th century was a period of resurgent hope and prosperity, thanks to the island's importance to the British. True, a foreign power was in charge, but the changes wrought by the occupiers unquestionably improved living conditions for the islanders and brought them into the mainstream of European trade and culture.

The first period of occupation (until 1756) was dominated by the efficiency and benevolence of Menorca's British Governor, Richard Kane (see p238 **Local heroes**). He may have alienated the local aristocracy by moving the capital from Ciutadella to Maó, but he did much to stimulate economic and agricultural growth, as well as improving internal communications (particularly by building a new road between Maó and Ciutadella).

At the outbreak of the Seven Years War in 1756, thanks to a mix of complacency and timidity, the French took Menorca from Britain. (It was a profound shock to the British and led to the execution of Rear-Admiral John Byng, shot, as Voltaire put it, 'to encourage the others'.) During their occupation, the French founded the town of Sant Lluís.

The island returned to the British at the end of the war in 1763 and there followed a harsher, less productive period of occupation until Menorca was again invaded in 1781, this time by a French-Spanish army, and reverted to Spanish rule. A final (economically beneficial) period of British occupation from 1798 to 1802 ended with the Treaty of Amiens and the permanent reversion of Menorca to Spanish rule, and to the status of economic and strategic backwater.

Mallorca, meanwhile, had slipped into isolation and stagnation. Despite the frequent conflicts that convulsed much of the rest of Europe during the following two centuries, survival was the main concern for the desperately poor inhabitants of the Balearics, many of whom chose to emigrate to the Iberian peninsula or the Americas.

One such making the latter journey was the Franciscan friar Junipero Serra (1713-84; see p172 **Local heroes**), born in the central Mallorcan village of Petra, who played a major role in the settlement of California.

THE 19TH CENTURY

In the 19th century romantic travellers were 'rediscovering' Spain, captivated and repelled in equal measure by what many of them (rather patronisingly) saw as an unspoilt (read: primitive) pre-industrial society. An added dash of exoticism was provided by Spain's rich Moorish architectural legacy.

Less easily accessible, and notably lacking in Moorish remains, Mallorca and Menorca didn't feature on the itineraries of many 19th-century travellers. It's for this reason that the visit of the French writer George Sand and her companion, the composer Frédéric Chopin, in 1838-9 is still so loudly proclaimed in all of Mallorca's tourist literature (*see p113* **Local heroes**), despite the fact that they passed a miserable winter in Valldemossa, enjoying the scenery but railing against the ignorance of the natives and the poverty of the island.

> **'It wasn't until the end of the 19th century that the economic situation on the islands began to pick up.'**

In contrast, a foreigner held in far greater esteem locally is Archduke Ludwig Salvator (*see p24* **Local heroes**), the black sheep of the stuffy Austrian Habsburg dynasty, who fell in love with Mallorca on his first visit, barely 20 years old, in 1867. A pioneering ecologist and naturalist, he returned to live on the island's west coast and devoted 22 years of study to compiling his nine-volume *Die Balearen* ('The Balearics'), which detailed every aspect of life on the islands.

It wasn't until the end of the 19th century that the economic situation on the islands began to pick up. Agriculture slowly started to modernise, and almond production in particular became profitable, while awareness of Catalan culture (reflecting developments in Catalunya) grew, instilling a new pride in Palma's small bourgeoisie and intellectual community. The clutch of fine *modernista* (Catalan art nouveau) buildings in the city is testament to the growing reintegration of the Balearics into European trends in the arts.

But it was to prove a false dawn for the islands. In the last decade of the century phylloxera swept through the Balearics, destroying the emergent wine industry, while the loss of Spain's remaining colonies – Cuba, Puerto Rico and the Philippines – devastated local shipbuilding. Another wave of emigration followed.

THE EARLY 20TH CENTURY AND THE CIVIL WAR

During the first few decades of the 20th century, Mallorca and Menorca remained economically backward and deeply conservative. Mallorca did produce two nationally important figures during this time: the conservative politician and five times Spanish Prime Minister Antoni Maura (who spent all of his political life in Madrid), and the financier Joan March who, in true rags-to-riches fashion, was born into poverty yet rose to become the third richest man in the world.

The private Mallorca Tourist Board (Fomento del Turismo de Mallorca) was founded as long ago as 1905 (it still exists today), aiming not just to promote the island as a destination, but to improve its primitive internal communications. Its first project was building a road from Estellencs to Andratx. In 1908 it published the first tourist guide to the island, though tourism was to remain of only minor importance to Mallorca for some decades to come.

The Balearics came through the Spanish Civil War (1936-39) relatively unscathed, with very little fighting taking place on the islands. This was despite the fact that Mallorca and Menorca found themselves on different sides of the conflict. General Goded secured Mallorca for the Nationalist rebels, but General Bosch was not so lucky on Menorca; his troops refused to abandon the Republican government and mutinied. At the end of the war Menorca was isolated as the last outpost of the Republicans. A potential bloodbath was avoided, thanks in large part to the British, who helped negotiate the surrender of the island from HMS *Devonshire*.

THE TOURISM BOOM

Just before the start of the Civil War there appeared the first signs of what was to revolutionise the economy of the Balearics in the second half of the 20th century.

In 1929 the Argentine poet and dandy Adam Diehl opened the Hotel Formentor in north-west Mallorca, attracting socialites and celebrities from the outset, including Churchill, Edward VIII, F Scott Fitzgerald and Charlie Chaplin. Soon Mallorca was becoming well known as a luxury tourist destination – three classy hotels were built in Palma in the early 1930s, and a British presence began to develop on the Bay of Palma with the founding of an English school and British club west of Palma.

Between 1936 and 1945 tourism all but ceased. Then, in 1950, the UN lifted its sanctions on Spain; 100,000 tourists visited the island that year, the figure doubling during

Local heroes The Archduke

No one has enjoyed as passionate a love affair with the Balearics as the misfit cousin of the Austrian Emperor Franz I. For centuries the Habsburg dynasty had been the pre-eminent ruling family of central and eastern Europe, and few doubted that the Archduke Ludwig Salvator (often known as Luís, or Lluís, Salvador in Mallorca), the fourth eldest son of Grand Duke Leopold II of Habsburg-Tuscany, would pass a dutiful life in the solemn, formal, anachronistic courts of the Austro-Hungarian empire. But the Archduke had other ideas.

Born in 1847, he passed a relatively uneventful childhood in Florence, before Garibaldi's revolt forced his family out of Italy when he was 12. They settled at Brandeis near Prague, and Ludwig Salvator went on to study in Vienna and Prague, where he showed a talent for languages and wide-ranging interests, from philosophy and law to archaeology and the sciences. So far, so conventional.

Yet, to his family's disbelief, he then refused to go into the army, as was expected of the third in line to the imperial throne. In an attempt to make him take his dynastic duties seriously he was made Archduke of Bohemia and Moravia. However, in 1867, when his fiancée, Mathilde, burned to death in a freak accident (she set fire to her clothes when smoking a surreptitious cigarette, or, according to another version, the alcohol in her hair ignited when she went to show her ballgown to her cigar-smoking father), Ludwig Salvator decided that he couldn't keep the charade up any longer. The death of his father Leopold II in 1871 finally gave him the freedom (and money) he needed to live the life he desired.

The excuse of going to warmer climes to help his asthma led to his first visit to Mallorca when he was 20. He was immediately smitten, particularly by the wild Tramuntana mountains, and passed the next two years travelling around the islands writing a book on insects. Indeed, travel became something of an addiction for S'Arxiduc (as he was know in the Balearics), although from then onwards he was always drawn back to Mallorca.

He started to buy up land in the north-west of the Serra de Tramuntana (land thought virtually useless by local farmers), and built an Italianate home for himself at Son Marroig (now partially open to the public; see p118). He was to build two further houses – the brilliant white Moorish S'Estaca (now belonging to the actor Michael Douglas) and Miramar, a stone and marble confection that remains in his family.

The Archduke was a man out of place and time, and his views couldn't have been more out of step with the ethos of his era (most of his family considered him to be mad). While the swaggering self-confidence of the Victorian Age led the majority of his contemporaries to regard nature as something to be controlled and exploited, he had more in common with the environmentalists of the early 21st century. He saw man as but one humble part of nature, and nature as something that should be treated with profound respect.

At a time when charcoal burners were deforesting much of Mallorca, he forbade any cutting down of trees on his lands. Olive trees were particularly precious to him, and even when they had passed their best fruit-bearing

the following year. The boom in the tourism industry in the Balearics was, however, largely a 1960s phenomenon. One of the chief attractions for holidaymakers was that the islands were considerably cheaper than most European destinations. This coincided with the development of commercial air travel and all-in package holidays.

Palma's Son Sant Joan airport opened in 1960 and, almost immediately, the number of visitors arriving by air started to exceed the number coming by sea. Its growth was remarkable – two-thirds of a million passenger movements in 1960, a million by 1962, four million by 1969 and seven million by 1973.

This translated as a rise in little over a decade from a third of a million to almost three million annual visitors.

> **'For the islanders tourism has, inevitably, been a mixed blessing. Many have made fortunes out of it. '**

The global recession and oil crisis of 1974 came as a major shock. The tourism industry was devastated, and, for the first time, those involved in the all-but-uncontrolled expansion

years, he refused to uproot them. (Mallorca's first nature reserve, the Son Moragues park, was one of his legacies to the island.) He displayed a similar tenderness for the animal world, rescuing old dogs and horses on their way to the knacker's yard.

And walkers have good reason to thank him too. On the mountain tops between Valldemossa and Deià he had a series of wide paved trails laid out, forming a network of easily navigable footpaths, and directly above Son Marroig he had an ancient stone shelter restored for the benefit of trekkers.

The Archduke was fascinated by every aspect of the Balearics. His magnum opus *Die Balearen* ('The Balearics') was the result of 22 years of study. Within its nine volumes, he recorded in extraordinary detail every aspect of life on the islands, from comprehensive descriptions of flora and fauna to the dress and customs of the inhabitants.

Ludwig Salvator's domestic life was as unconventional as his intellectual views. He fathered children by numerous local women (all of whom he provided for). Although some sources claim that Watislaw Vyborni, a Polish fellow student in Prague, was the love of his life, the more commonly proffered candidate for this honour is an illiterate carpenter's daughter, Catalina Homar. He caused an immense scandal when, on one visit to Vienna, he took her along with him. Yet Catalina was an intelligent, capable woman who learned to read and write, mastered several languages and ran the Archduke's estates with great efficiency (she won a gold medal at a Paris exhibition for her malmsey wine).

Once again, though, tragedy intervened. Catalina caught leprosy on a long wished for visit to the Holy Land and died several years later in 1904.

At the outbreak of World War I, Ludwig Salvator was ordered to leave Mallorca by the Emperor and return to Brandeis. For once he obeyed, but having now lost the woman he loved and the land he adored, he also lost the will to go on, dying in 1915. But the reluctant Archduke had the last laugh, leaving everything he owned to the Mallorcans he loved most.

were given pause for thought. It slowly became clear that things couldn't continue as they had been. The economic boom wasn't sustainable indefinitely; environmental disaster was looming.

The last couple of decades (and particularly the last few years) have seen a slow acceptance of the need for more responsible development, for a less-is-more approach, encouraging higher-spending visitors with classier accommodation, and keeping a tighter lid on the boozed-up bucket-and-spaders.

For the islanders tourism has, inevitably, been a mixed blessing. Many have made fortunes out of it. For instance, what had once been the least valuable land on the islands – the often rocky and infertile coastal areas – suddenly became the most lucrative. And there is so much seasonal employment on the islands that many workers from mainland Spain spend their summers here. As a consequence, traditional life has inevitably been eroded, property prices are among the highest in Spain, and large swathes of the countryside have been permanently blighted by insensitive development.

Mass tourism made the Balearics and mass tourism threatens to destroy them. The key to the islands' future lies in trying to find a solution to this dilemma.

Key events

pre-4000 BC First inhabitants of Balearics arrive from Iberia or south of France, establishing the Balearic cave culture
c2500 BC-c1400 BC First settlements appear outside caves; agriculture and ceramics technology established; Beaker culture influential.
c1400 BC-c800 BC Talayotic Period sees development of more sophisticated society, with use of tin bronze, agricultural surplus and social differentiation.
c800-123 BC Post-Talayotic Period. Iron introduced; increase in trade; islanders involved as mercenaries in classical wars.
654 BC Carthaginians colonise Ibiza.
c300 BC First fortification of settlements on Mallorca and Menorca.
202 BC Romans defeat Hannibal at Battle of Zama; Carthaginians withdraw from Mallorca and Menorca.
146 BC Romans take Ibiza and raise Carthage.
123 BC Mallorca and Menorca conquered by the Romans, becoming part of the province of Tarraconensis (Tarragona).
AD 404 Balearics break from Tarraconensis to become province in their own right.
425 Vandals end Roman rule in Balearics.
533 Vandals defeated in North Africa by the Byzantines, who annex Balearics.
707-8 Extensive Moorish attacks on Mallorca.
711 Moors invade and overrun much of the Iberian peninsula.
798 Major Moorish raid on Mallorca.
859 Vikings attack Mallorca.
902 Moors settle Balearics, bringing prosperity to the islands.
1076 Independent Kingdom of the Balearics proclaimed.
1114-15 Pisans and Catalans take Ibiza and Palma, but later evacuate; more tolerant rule of Almoravids.
1203 Almohads reintegrate Balearics into the Moorish empire.
1229 Conquest of Mallorca by Jaume I of Aragón and Catalunya.
1230 Carta de Població decrees equality of Mallorcans before the law.
1232 Menorca capitulates, but keeps its Moorish government.
1235 Ibiza falls to Christian forces.
1269 Consecration of Palma Cathedral.
1276 Death of Jaume I 'the Conqueror'; his empire is split between his sons – Jaume II is first king of independent Balearics.

1285 Alfons III captures Palma and Mallorca from his uncle Jaume II.
1287 Alfons III takes Menorca from Jaume II.
1291 Death of Alfons III; succession of his brother Jaume, King of Sicily.
1298 Partition of Jaume I's empire restored; Jaume II returns as King of Mallorca.
1343 Pere IV of Aragón conquers Balearics.
1349 Jaume III defeated and killed at Llucmajor; Balearics lose their independence and are annexed by Aragón.
1479 Fernando V of Aragón marries Isabella I of Castilla, uniting Christian Spain.
1492 Columbus reaches the Americas; trade shifts from the Mediterranean to the Atlantic and the Balearics decline further; Moors finally expelled from Spain.
1521 Peasant uprising on Mallorca; put down by Emperor Charles V.
1535 Maó sacked by pirate Barbarossa.
1558 Ciutadella destroyed by Turks.
1571 Defeat of the Turks at the naval Battle of Lepanto reduces pirate raids on Balearics.
1701-14 War of the Spanish Succession; Mallorca picks the losing claimant and is stripped of many of its historic privileges.
1708-56 British occupy Menorca.
1756-63 French occupy Menorca during the Seven Years War.
1763-1782 Second British occupation of Menorca.
1785 Treaty of Algiers signed, ending North African piracy.
1798-1802 Third and final occupation of Menorca by British.
1808-13 The Peninsular War brings many refugees to Mallorca; increased social tension.
1820-22 Massive emigration to South America and Algeria.
1837 First regular steamship line opens between Mallorca and mainland Spain.
1879-98 Trade in wine and almonds brings a period of prosperity; the arrival of phylloxera and loss of Spain's last colonies curtail it.
1929 Hotel Formentor opens.
1936-39 Spanish Civil War; Mallorca sides with Nationalists, Menorca with Republicans.
1939-75 Dictatorship of Franco.
1960s Mass tourism is born in the Balearics.
1978 New Spanish Constitution approved, allowing for the creation of 'autonomies'.
1983 Statutes of Autonomy for the Balearics approved.
2002 Ecotax introduced, abolished in 2003.

Mallorca & Menorca Today

Tourism made the Balearics, and its uncertain future could break them.

Few local economies are as heavily dependent on tourism as those of Mallorca and Menorca. In the first half of the 20th century this was one of the poorest regions of Spain; by the end of the century it was one of the richest – and that change was almost entirely down to the rise of tourism. In 1950 annual visitor numbers were about 100,000; 16 years later the figure hit one million; by 2000, the high point, it was almost 12 million, with Menorca accounting for about a million of these. Tourism generates around £3 billion of revenue annually and accounts for 80 per cent of the islands' GDP.

Despite this huge reliance on tourists for so many years, by the mid to late 1990s islanders, particularly the Mallorcans, were starting to grow tired of the rowdy annual invasion of lager-fuelled Brits and Germans. At the same time, there was a resurgence of national pride and customs. This manifested itself in a number of ways: Catalan was made the official first language, the islands' Catalan names were adopted on tourist literature and local cultural, culinary and literary heritage was rediscovered.

Inevitably, the move of some locals towards Catalan nationalism led to further resentment of tourists (and also the many non-Catalan Spanish seasonal workers who flooded the island every summer) and what they were deemed to have done to the islands. The seemingly endless building epidemic spurred environmental groups, most notably the Grup Ornitològic Balear (GOB), to campaign against new hotels and golf courses, and the whole mass-market philosophy of quantity over quality began to be questioned.

In the mid 1990s, the Balearic government at last acted. The Partido Popular (PP), led by Jaume Mates, put in place legislation to restrict unchecked coastal development, eyesore hotels were torn down and fancy marinas and smart new convention centres sprang up. A subtle shift crept into the islanders' mentality towards tourism: for the first time the relentless pursuit of numbers was dropped for the pursuit of quality, as people began to realise that perhaps fewer tourists who spent more money was better for the islands in the long run.

Most of the major shift in outlook towards tourism during this period is applicable to Mallorca; Menorca was way ahead of the game.

FROM PACKAGE TOURISTS TO ECOTOURISTS

Menorca has never attracted the type of boorish tourist drawn to Magaluf or S'Arenal (and nor did it want to), restricting its mass-market tourism development to limited areas and promoting a 'family' image. This careful preservation of its rural and cultural heritage led in 1993 to UNESCO declaring the whole island a Biosphere Reserve in recognition of its extraordinary prehistoric heritage, the large number of plants and animals unique to the island and its largely unspoilt rural tradition. The idea behind the label is to limit the impact of mass-market tourism on an area – in Menorca's case, particularly its pristine beaches. Since then the Menorcan government has quietly and systematically created environmental areas that will eventually protect much of the island, including its precious *calas* (coves).

'Over the last decade there has been a major move to promote rural tourism.'

Mallorca, too, has belatedly realised that while large swaths of its coastline have been irreversibly scarred by development, much of the interior remains unspoilt and unruffled by mass tourism. Over the last decade there has been a major move to promote rural tourism on the island. This has a two-fold advantage: it eases the pressure on the coasts, and channels money into the relatively impoverished countryside. The result has been a boom in walking, mountaineering, golf, cycling, horse trekking and birdwatching, among other pastimes, and the appearance of 'boutique-style' quality rural hotels. It also means the island can market itself as a year-round destination. The figures speak for themselves; in 1994 there were 45 rural hotels and *agroturismos* in the Mallorcan interior; by 2004 that number had increased to 180. Whether tourist numbers can sustain so many places to stay in the interior, however, is a matter of current debate.

Menorca has been much slower in embracing the potential of the *agroturismo*; the first handful of classy rural hotels has only begun to appear in the last couple of years.

RISING TENSIONS, RISING PRICES

By the late 1990s, locals decided that the ruling PP had not gone far enough in curbing the excesses of mass tourism, and, in 1999, power swung back to the Socialists, but only with the help of a number of disparate parties, including the Green Party, which made up the 'Rainbow Coalition'. The Socialists went several steps further than the PP, pledging to introduce a tax on tourists that would be spent directly on the environment. They also made their aim to drag the islands upmarket explicit, with legislation banning any new-build hotels of fewer than three stars and organised pub crawls, and introducing a 3am closing time in many tourist areas.

At the same time Pla Mirall was launched, a European Union-funded project that involved a general sprucing up of the islands, but in particular Palma and specifically its old town. Old buildings were restored, roads fixed and streets smartened up. All this required labour, and a lot of it, so the islands brought in immigrant workers, mainly from Africa.

This was the first time that the predominantly white population had had such an influx of non-white faces, and inevitably this led to the usual tensions and covert racism. A corresponding rise in crime was conveniently blamed on these new workers, and as the works were gradually completed, no one had thought about what the immigrants would do next.

The general tarting up led, inevitably, to a matching rise in prices, fuelled by the introduction of the euro. Together this had a profound effect on the islands, leading to price rises in everything from restaurants to clothes and food. Designer shops, smart restaurants and boutique-style five-star hotels opened up. The islands were going resolutely upmarket and Palma, once considered a dull provincial town, began to take on a sophisticated air.

THE END OF THE RAINBOW

While the PP had not actually voiced its views on mass-market tourists, the Socialists did. The tourism councillor Celestí Alomar described the islands as 'full' and made it clear the overnment would prefer to have fewer tourists if the ones who came were high-spenders. This alienated both the mass market hoteliers who had built their livelihood on cheap but plentiful tourists and the biggest tourist bloc – the Germans.

At the same time, at the tail end of 2001, the Germans went on a spending spree in Mallorca and Menorca to get rid of the deutschmarks they had stuffed under the bed before the introduction of the euro. This resulted in inflated house prices and huge resentment from locals, many of whom could no longer afford to buy property. The combination was lethal – the Germans began to feel unwanted and their long love affair with the islands began to wane.

It was unfortunate that the Socialists' victory coincided with a gradual downturn in both the islands' and Germany's economies. The year 2000 was a high-water mark in terms of tourist receipts, employment and the economy, but by 2001 the economies of western Europe, most notably Germany, had begun to slide into recession. The introduction of the euro did not help matters, leading to a sharp rise in prices as Europeans chose to holiday closer to home or in cheaper destinations such as Turkey and Croatia.

'The islands are likely to undergo more profound changes as they adjust to a fledgling multiracial society'

So the ecotax was greeted with a certain degree of incredulity when it was pushed through in May 2002. It was the last thing the industry needed, and further fuelled the resentment hoteliers had been feeling. Some believe it was a deliberate attempt to antagonise Madrid, which was heartily opposed to it.

And so it came as little surprise when the Rainbow Coalition was defeated in the 2003 elections. What was a surprise was how close the vote was, and the PP is only in power thanks to the charismatic Maria Antònia Munar, whose Unió Mallorquina party made up part of the Socialist coalition, but who switched sides and gave the PP her support.

Again it was a different story on Menorca, which stayed with the left (the only Balearic island that did) and has Socialist mayors in five of its eight municipalities.

THE FUTURE

PP leader Jaume Mates, who lost the vote in 1999, led his party back to a sweet victory in 2003. Mates lost no time in describing the coalition's attitude to tourism as 'irresponsible' and stated his intention to restore relations with both central government and the tourism sector, while paying lip service to the Greens. Just weeks after the election Madrid rewarded the new government with a €24 million grant to plant trees – a prize it had denied the Socialists for their antagonistic stance.

Mates has put forward a number of proposals to improve the infrastructure on Mallorca, among them a second ring road round Palma, extension of the Palma-Manacor motorway to Alcúdia (currently being constucted) and, controversially, covering over the section of the Passeig Marítim that runs by the Parc de la Mar.

Rubbish. **Palma**'s eco-recycling bins.

The islands have gone through a sea change in the past few years and are likely to undergo more profound changes as they adjust to a fledgling multiracial society and, for the first time since the 1950s, experience falling tourist numbers, a stalling economy and rising unemployment. Figures in 2005 suggest that, although the Germans may be slowly returning to the islands, British mass market visitor numbers are dropping and profits in the tourist trade as a whole may be down by as much as 20 per cent on previous years.

With the tightening economic circumstances has come a rise in crime and delinquency, in particular the so-called *botellón*, or street drinking. For once this is not a problem blamed on tourists, but on local, under-aged drinkers who do not get served in bars so choose to drink on the street instead.

These changes are partly down to exterior economic forces and partly to political moves. Either way, they have left islanders aware of how reliant they are on tourism, and wary of upsetting this delicate relationship. The new government has made it clear that every tourist, however much they spend, will be welcome. Whether this policy puts the islands back on top as Europe's number one holiday destination, only time will tell.

Fresh fish at Palma's **Santa Catalina** market. *See p69.*

Food & Drink

Rustic tradition and contemporary style sit side by side.

The food of Spain reflects the country's complex history. The incursions of its many settlers – Phoenicians, Greeks, Romans, Moors – have all left their imprint on its cuisine. The further north you travel, the more northern European the influences; travel south and the flavours and ingredients become increasingly associated with North Africa, with the likes of aubergines, almonds, pine nuts, dried fruit and spices ever more prominent.

At first glance there doesn't seem to be much that is distinctive about the regional cuisine of the Balearics, and the built-up holiday areas can seem a dispiriting morass of tacky joints doling out pizza, bratwurst, burgers and full Englishes. If you scratch the surface, though, you'll find the islands' food to be rich and varied, with some surprising flavour combinations and a number of interesting, distinctive dishes.

BALEARIC CUISINE

La cuina mallorquina and *menorquina* has its roots firmly in rustic traditions, with a sprinkling of Arab influences, and is based around the classic trinity of Mediterranean ingredients – olive oil, garlic and tomatoes. Much of the islands' cuisine derives from 'peasant' food – local, simple and fresh. Unlike in much of southern Spain, where frying over high heat is ubiquitous, dishes here tend to be slow-cooked at low temperatures in a shallow casserole dish known as a *greixonera*.

For many years this so-called peasant food was derided by visitors and better-off locals, who tended to opt for international cuisine. But since Spain's autonomous regions began to rediscover their individual cultural heritages, island food has crept back on to the menu and you'll find it – sometimes given a contemporary gloss – at even the most upmarket establishments.

Standards across the islands are generally high, whether you are eating at the back of a nondescript bar or in an expensive seafood restaurant, and prices vary tremendously. Mallorca's top places rival the best in Europe (seven have Michelin stars), and have earned chefs such as **Marc Fosh** (at Read's, *see p161*) and **Koldo Royo** (*see p79*) international renown. You won't find a better range of superb contemporary restaurants in Spain outside Madrid and Barcelona.

(Note: where two spellings are given for ingredients and dishes below, the first is Catalan, the second Castilian. *See p278* **Language**.)

PORK

Meat usually means pork (*porc/cerdo*) and all its variations. Pigs were the staple meat on the islands for many years; roast suckling pig is the centrepiece of most island fiestas, and even today many villages celebrate their annual *matances* – pig slaughter. This ancient ritual, which brings together everyone in the community, all but died out as tourism took hold on the islands, but has now been revived. If you're not averse to gallons of blood and some hideous squealing, it's an event well worth catching. *Matances* take place in winter, after the pig has been fattened up all year, and historically are intended to provide food for the family until spring.

For this reason no part of the pig is left unused, and you'll find everything from offal to trotters and ears ending up in dishes, most famously in *frit mallorqui/frito mallorquín* – a flavoursome fry-up of potatoes, vegetables and a variety of pork (or lamb) unmentionables, spiked with wild fennel and mint. Another popular local dish is *llom/lomo con col* (pork loin stuffed with *sobrassada – see below –* and rolled in cabbage leaves). Pork lard (*saïm/ manteca*) and salted pork belly (*xuia/panceta*) are frequently used in Balearic dishes.

Various breeds of pig are raised on the islands, but the distinctive local porker is a black variety (*porc negre mallorquí*), and you'll find it served *fregit/frito* (fried) or *rostit/asada* (roasted), as *pilotes/albóndigas* (meatballs), *solomillo* (steak), *llom/lomo* (loin), *costelletes* (chops) and various types of sausage (*embotits/embutidos*), such as *sobrassada* (*see below*), *butifarra/butifarrón* (a black pudding-like sausage, flavoured with black pepper, fennel and allspice or cinnamon), *camaiot* (a less bloody, fattier *butifarra*, made with diced rather than minced meat) and *salxitxó/salchichón* (like chorizo, but with black pepper rather than paprika).

Sobrassada/sobrasada is one of the Balearics' best-known products. This spreadable, rich, chorizo-like sausage is made of cured pork, paprika, salt and seasoning. It comes in all shapes and sizes, and in spicy and mild versions; it can be eaten raw, simply slathered on crusty bread, or cooked, sometimes with honey. There are around 40 registered makers of *sobrassada* on Mallorca, qualifying for the quality mark of the *Indicació Geogràfica Protegida*. The best (and by far the most expensive) variety is labelled 'Sobrassada de Mallorca de Cerdo Negro' and is made from the island's indigenous black pig.

You'll also find every bar and restaurant with a leg of air-dried ham (*pernil salat/jamón*) on display, either on the bar or suspended in great shanks from the ceiling. It comes in a variety of forms and wildly different prices. The standard *serrano* ham (*pernil serrà/jamón serrano*) is the cheapest and is what usually ends up in baguette sandwiches (*bocadillos*). Ham from Jabugo in Andalucía is generally regarded as the finest and is the most expensive. This is the prized *pata negra*, or *jamón ibérico*, made from free-range black pigs fed only on acorns.

OTHER MEATS

Mallorcan lamb (*xai* or *be/cordero*) is another popular meat, often served in chunks, roasted with garlic and olive oil. Local breeds are small and sturdy animals, lending themselves perfectly to the slow cooking favoured locally. *Cordero lechal* (suckling lamb) is most commonly served as *palatillas* (shoulders) and *piernas* (legs), roasted over rosemary sprigs and garlic cloves in a gentle oven until tender.

Beef (*bou/buey*), particularly veal (*vedella/ ternera*), again comes in numerous forms, such as *solomillo* (steak), *estofat de vedella* (stew) and *fricandó* (casserole). It is likely to be imported.

> **'A classic Balearic dish is *caldereta de llagosta*... a simple but stupendously rich and flavoursome spiny lobster stew.'**

Game, such as rabbit (*conill/conejo*), pheasant (*faisà/faisán*), partridge (*perdiu/perdiz*) and quail (*guatllere/cordoniz*), is also popular, and you'll find classic dishes such as *conill alioli* (char-grilled rabbit smothered with garlic mayonnaise), *conill encebollado* (rabbit stewed with onions, olive oil and white wine), *perdiu a la vinagreta* (partridge in a vinegar-based sauce) and *guatllere amb figes* (quail with figs) served in the interior of both Mallorca and Menorca. Snails (*caragols/caracoles*) are also very popular locally.

Chicken (*pollastre/pollo*) is not a particularly favoured meat on the islands, but you will sometimes find it combined with seafood or stuffed with prawns and cooked in cava.

Restaurant prices

Elsewhere in this guide you will see that we have denoted the price range of each restaurant we mention in terms of between one and four euro symbols. These correspond approximately to the following price brackets for a full meal with drinks per person:

€	= under €20
€€	= between €20 and €30
€€€	= between €30 and €40
€€€€	= over €40

Queso mahón at Menorca's **Hort de Sant Patrici**. See p239.

FISH AND SEAFOOD

Seafood is, not surprisingly, enormously popular on Mallorca and Menorca. There is a local fishing industry, but it's small and demand is such that most fresh fish is imported, usually from Galicia. A classic Balearic dish is *caldereta de llagosta*, popular on both islands and originating from Fornells in the north of Menorca. It's a simple but stupendously rich and flavoursome spiny lobster stew, made with tomatoes and onions. (It's also ruinously expensive, with prices of €40 per portion not unusual.) The lobster for this dish is imported for most of the year, but if you order it from June to August you could be in luck and get a local creature: this is the legal fishing period, when you'll see lobster traps in all the fishing ports.

Local fish (*peix/pescados*) include dolphin fish (*llampuga/lampuga* – a great-tasting seasonal fish with only a very short season from late August to October), sea bass (*llop/lubina*), sea bream (*besuc/besugo*), monkfish (*rap/rape*), grouper (*anfós* or *nero/mero*), gilthead bream (*orada* or *daurada/dorada*), and red scorpion fish (*cap roig*), which you'll find served in a variety of ways, the most popular of which is simply *a la plantxa/a la plancha* (grilled on a hot metal plate), usually with a splash of olive oil, garlic and parsley. More elaborate methods include *al forn/al horno* (baked), which is usually confined to sea bass baked in salt. Other popular fish are anchovies (*boquerónes/anchovas*), sardines (*sardinas* or *alatxas/sardinas* or *alachas*), John Dory (*gall/gallo de San Pedro*) and red mullet (*molls/salmonetes*).

Octopus (*pop/pulpo*) is usually prepared Galician-style *a la feria*, lightly grilled and sprinkled with rock salt, oil and paprika and served on a wooden platter. Eels (*anguiles*), found in the S'Albufera marshes in northern Mallorca, are an island delicacy and pop up in a number of dishes, including *greixonera d'anguiles* (eel stew) and *espinagada*, an eel and spinach pasty-type delicacy from Sa Pobla. Mussels (*musclos/mejillones*) are usually *al vapor* (steamed) or *marinera* (in a light cream sauce). Crab (*cranc/cangrejo*) is not native, but is available in the more upmarket restaurants, as is lobster (*llamàntol/bogavante*). Cockles (*escopinyes/berberechos*) and clams (*cloïsses/almejas*) are also commonplace.

The most popular (and inexpensive) seafood is often squid (*calamars/calamares*), which comes *a la romana* (fried in batter), *en su tinta* (in its own ink) or *farcits* (stuffed), and prawns (*gambes/gambas*), which are cooked in a variety of ways – particularly *al ajilla/ajo* (in garlic) and *a la plantxa*. Also ubiquitous is salt cod (*bacallà/bacalao*), which, when served *a la mallorquina*, comes baked with layers of fried potatoes, tomatoes and swiss chard mixed with raisins, pine nuts, spring onions and olive oil.

VEGETABLES, RICE & PASTA

Compared with the rest of Spain, vegetables (*verdures/legumbres*) do at least play a part in local cuisine, rather than being consigned to a side dish as in many other parts of the country. Having said that, vegetarians and vegans are not well catered for and you'll find just a handful of vegetarian restaurants on the islands. It's also worth noting that many ostensibly vegetable-only dishes and salads come sprinkled with bits of *jamón*.

The tomato (*tomàquet* or *tomàtiga/tomate*), some of which are grown locally (a small, thick-skinned, sharply flavoured variety known as *ramellet*), is probably the most ubiquitous vegetable, used as the basis for many local dishes, as well as being smeared on bread in *pa amb oli* (*see below*) and as a staple in salads. The potato (*patate/patata*), also grown locally, is used in hearty *frito* dishes and crops up in *tumbet*, the characteristic local dish of aubergine (*albergínia/berenjena*), potato and courgette (*carabassó/calabacín*), lightly fried in olive oil, then layered with a freshly made tomato sauce and finished off in the oven. On Menorca it is often made with pumpkin.

Other commonly encountered vegetables include the onion (*ceba/cebolla*), artichoke (*carxofa/alcachofa*), mushroom (*xampinyons/champiñones*), asparagus (*espàrrec/espárrago*), cabbage (*col*), cauliflower (*colflori/coliflor*), carrot (*pastanaga/zanahoria* – the local variety is purple), red and green pepper (*pebre/pimiento*), Swiss chard (*bledes/acelgas*) and spinach (*espinacs/espinacas*). The latter is the basis of a number of dishes, including *espinacs a la Catalana* (spinach, raisins and pine nuts).

> **'Menorca's capital Maó (or Mahón) gave its name to mayonnaise.'**

A popular starter is *escalivada*, a grilled pepper and aubergine salad, while summer sees the appearance of *trempó*, a huge salad based on onion, pale green peppers and tomatoes and any number of other ingredients.

Northern Mallorca's S'Albufera marshes are famous for their rice (*arròs/arroz*). *Arròs bomba* is a round Spanish variety that has excellent cooking qualities and a robust flavour. It is perfect for *arròs brut*, a rustic dish of meat, game and vegetables flavoured with *sobrassada* and *butifarra*; *arròs negro*, a spectacular black rice dish flavoured with cuttlefish and coloured with its ink; or Spain's most famous dish, paella.

Pasta, traditionally cheaper than rice, became widespread on the impoverished islands before tourism transformed the economy of the Balearics, and remains a staple today. The most popular shape is *fideus*, looking like short bits of spaghetti.

FRUIT AND NUTS

Locals are more likely to end a meal with a bowl of fruit than a dessert. The islands produce excellent figs (*figas/higos*), oranges (*taronjas/*naranjas*), almonds (*ametlles/almendras*), apricots (*albercoces/albaricoques*), apples (*pomas/manzanas*), pomegranates (*magranas/granadas*) and melons (*melós/melones*).

CHEESE AND MAYONNAISE

The British left a lasting legacy on the Menorcan diet with the introduction of Friesian cattle. This breed produces, among other dairy products, Menorcan cheese (*formatge/queso*), a mixture of sun-ripened herbs and sea salt, coated with oil and paprika, and mixed with cream. Known generically as *queso Mahón*, its unique taste has been honoured with a *Denominació de Origen*, testifying to its quality. It comes in semi- and fully cured varieties. Mallorca produces a similar cheese in Campos, but it does not have the same piquancy as *queso Mahón*.

Menorca's capital Maó (or Mahón as it was previously known) also gave its name to mayonnaise, the classic emulsion of olive oil and raw egg yolks. It probably owes its origin to the culinary experimentation of the French occupiers of Menorca in the mid 18th century (*see p22*).

BREAD

Another classic island dish is *pa amb oli* (pronounced 'pámbolly'). *Pa amb oli* literally means 'bread and oil', and this is all it consists

Oranges are not the only fruit.

of in its purest, most basic form – a slice of dense, brown, richly flavoured local bread (*pa mallorquí*), liberally doused in island olive oil. To refine it slightly, the bread is rubbed with garlic and tomato, and in many places you'll find it served with a variety of toppings – such as *jamón*, chorizo and local cheeses – making a meal in itself.

Bread is also the centrepiece of another famed Mallorcan dish: *sopes mallorquines/sopas mallorquinas*. This typically robust winter stew made from stale bread and braised vegetables is, despite its name, not a soup, as the bread absorbs all the liquid. (In Catalan '*sope*' refers not to the soup, but to the slices of bread.)

PASTRIES AND DESSERTS

Ask a Mallorcan or Menorcan what foodstuff best represents the islands and they are likely to reply, the *ensaïmada*, Spain's answer to the croissant. This versatile, light, fluffy-textured spiral pastry is dusted with icing sugar and comes in a variety of sizes, from bite-sized portions to the cake-sized ones you see people lugging on to planes. Locals eat *ensaïmadas* at breakfast, spread them with *sobrassada* as a savoury snack or serve them stuffed with nuts and fruits and covered in cream as a dessert. Other popular sweet pastries are *bunyols* (doughnuts) and *robiols* and *crespells* (both particularly popular at Easter).

Savoury pastries include the pies found throughout Spain known as *empanadas*, which come with various fillings. The islands also have their own version of pizza (*coca*), differing from its Italian cousin in never having a tomato sauce base or cheese or meat toppings – its most popular form is covered in peppers. A sweet version of *coca* is made in Valldemossa.

Popular desserts include *greixonera de brosat*, a cream cheese tart, and *gató de almendra*, a light almond sponge cake. You might also want to try *granissats*, crushed ice flavoured with citrus fruit. Every *patisseria* and *xocolaterie* is stuffed full of local sweets such as chocolate and nougat.

Top five # Mallorcan restaurants

Internationally acclaimed chef **Marc Fosh** of **Read's** (*see p161*) is in the vanguard of Mallorca's ever-improving culinary scene, but where does a Michelin-starred maestro choose to chill out and chow down on his adopted island? Here are Fosh's favourites!

Bens d'Avall
Between Sóller & Deià. See p126.
The best restaurant terrace on the island, with sweeping views over the dramatic coastline. 'The Mallorcan guy called Benito who owns it and runs the kitchen is quite simply a bloody good cook. He's famed for his carpaccio of Sóller prawns, but he's also good on local lamb and fresh fish soups and stews.'

El Bungalow
Ciutat Jardí, Palma. See p80.
Little more than a fisherman's cottage, with a fantastic setting right on the beach. 'It's somewhere I can relax and eat an uncomplicated lunch. I always have *calamar* (grilled squid) and *escalivada* (roasted peppers and onions marinated in olive oil) to start, followed by *arroz negro* (rice cooked in cuttlefish ink), made creamy by a spoonful of *alioli* stirred in at the last minute.'

Molí de'n Bou
Sant Llorenç de Cardassar. See p196.

A homely Mallorcan restaurant in an old windmill. 'This guy produces some very modern Mallorcan cookery by updating traditional peasant dishes. He uses lots of local products, but keeps it fairly light. I've had sea bass here twice and both times it was exceptionally well cooked; simply grilled, with a nice crisp skin and slightly pink in the middle. Perfect.'

Es Passeig
Port de Sóller. See p129.
A seafront restaurant serving modern Med cuisine. 'The food doesn't try too hard to be clever; it is well presented, clean and the small menu is constantly changing. They do an excellent tuna carpaccio and an unusual selection of very simply grilled fish from local waters like Mallorcan *denton*.'

Es Raco d'es Teix
Deià. See p120.
'The German guy who runs this place got his first Michelin star at El Olivo – the restaurant of La Residencia – and recently won another one for Es Raco. He does everything obsessively well. Sauces are light and restrained, and there are no wasted ingredients. His star dish is local lamb in a black olive crust, served pink and juicy and sliced at the table.'

Grape expectations

If you've never been to Mallorca, you've probably never sampled Mallorcan wine. And, until recently, you weren't missing much. Its small-scale production and basic quality in the last century meant that little island wine was exported even as far as mainland Spain, never mind further afield.

During Moorish times, though, wine was produced extensively along the west coast of Mallorca (and, to a lesser extent, in the east too) and widely exported, right up until the islands' vines were wiped out by the phylloxera virus in the 1890s.

The first step in a local viticulture revival came with the founding in the 1930s of the José Luis Ferrer *bodega* in Binissalem. Progress was slow, however, and it was not until 1991 that the **Binissalem** area was bestowed a *Denominació de Origen* (DO), and the rebirth began in earnest. In 2000, a second DO was recognised: **Pla i Llevant**, covering parts of central and eastern Mallorca. Today, you'll find a surprisingly diverse and frequently excellent range of wines on offer in island restaurants and bars.

Some of the grapes used are familiar international varieties; others are indigenous. Mineral-nosed Callet is popular in red blends, though tannin-rich Manto Negro is the most commonly encountered local cultivar (all Binissalem DO reds contain a minimum of 50% Manto Negro). Indigenous white varieties include Giro Blanc, Gargollosa and aromatic Moll (or Prensal Blanc; Binissalem DO whites have at least 70% Moll).

Of the island's 20-plus producers, names to look out for among the Binissalem DO include the ubiquitous **José Luis Ferrer** (the reds shade the whites; try a *reserva*, resembling a light Rioja) and Consell's **Hereus de Ribas** (its

red-blend *Cabrera* is outstanding, if expensive). Among the most interesting Pla i Levant DO producers are **Miquel Gelabert** from Manacor (who isn't afraid to try unusual grape blends, though his straight Chardonnay is also a winner) and Petra's **Miquel Oliver** (who made his name with his *Muscat Original*, an exquisite dry Moscatel).

Don't be afraid to stray from DO bottles. Some of Mallorca's most interesting wines are labelled simply *Vin de la Terra*. The most celebrated example is multi-award-winning (and consequently pricey and hard-to-find) **Anima Negra**'s *An*, made with 100% Callet, previously thought to be a grape suitable only for blending.

José L Ferrer: Mallorca's best-known *bodega. See p159.*

Generally, though, you'll see the same unimaginative desserts in the Balearics as you will throughout Spain. Most establishments will offer *flan* (crème caramel), *arroz con leche* (cold rice pudding), *natillas* (cold custard), *helado* (ice-cream; the local Menorcan brand, sold all over Spain), fresh fruit and a plate of cheese with *membrillo* (quince jelly).

DRINK

Local wine has enjoyed something of a renaissance of late and, though most cannot match an established Rioja, they hold their own well. *See above* **Grape expectations**.

Mallorca has a long tradition of making anise-based herbal liqueurs (*herbes/hierbas*), with production centred on the town of Bunyola. There are three broad types – *dolces* (sweet), *seques* (dry) and *mesclades* (a mix of both).

Menorca is famous for its gin production, which was introduced by the British during their 18th-century occupation of the island. The most famous brand is Xoriguer, which comes from the distillery of the same name in Maó. It's served up in a variety of ways, the most popular being *pomada*, gin with cloudy lemonade; the perfect refreshing drink for a hot Balearic summer's day.

A life in a day at Natura Parc, near **Santa Eugènia**. *See p176.*

Wild Mallorca & Menorca

Think that Man long ago overwhelmed nature on the Balearics? Think again

From the air they might look small and parched, and from the beach just a bit too built up, but head away from the main holiday areas and Mallorca and Menorca reveal an unexpected profusion of bucolic landscapes and a wealth of flora and fauna waiting to be discovered.

THE LIE OF THE LAND

The islands are the visible high points of submerged mountains, a continuation of the Andalucian range in mainland southern Spain. Although wind, rain, time and tide have softened and levelled much of the islands, one dramatic range remains – the **Serra de Tramuntana**, a towering, craggy 90-kilometre (56-mile) long chain of mountains (several over 1,000 metres/3,280 feet) along Mallorca's west coast, cleft by deep gorges, forests of ancient oak and lush valleys. Criss-crossed by trails, this is nirvana for walkers, cyclists and climbers. Forests of holm oak are the typical dressing on the slopes, along with pines and,

further down, cultivated groves of gnarled 'olive trees, prickly pear, almond and fruit trees. The serra receives up to 1,500 millimetres (59 inches) of rain each year, as well as the force of hot and cold winds from every direction and the battering effect of the waves, providing the most dramatic, wild and often weird rock formations on the islands.

The other Mallorcan range, the eastern **Serra de Llevant**, is a drier, gentler landscape, reaching only 500 metres (1,640 feet); at its northern extremity it has a barren, lunar aspect.

The island's east coast is specked with sandy little coves and riddled with huge, meandering cave systems. The main ones at Porto Cristo – the Coves del Drac and the smaller Coves d'es Hams – and the Coves d'Artà are illuminated abysses, sparkling with stalactites and stalagmites.

Most of the largely featureless southern coastline of Mallorca is windswept and beach-free until you reach the huge sandy Bay of Palma. This is echoed in the north by the equally wide Bay of Alcúdia and the smaller Bay of Pollença. Most of Mallorca's most intensive holiday development is focused around these three bays (and, to a lesser extent, around the eastern coves). Rockrose and the native dwarf fan palm are the stalwarts of the coastal dunes in these areas.

In contrast, you have to search hard to find a tourist in the centre of the island, which ripples with the arid, undulating, agricultural plains of Es Pla (simply meaning 'the plane'), dotted with tilled fields, pretty orchards and the odd sanctuary-topped hill. Much of it remains rural and appealingly rustic; the agro-industrial revolution arrived late here, and even the farming lands have a bucolic, pre-19th century air about them.

Menorca, the north-eastern limit of the Balearics, covers just 700 square kilometres (270 square miles); it is less than a fifth the size of Mallorca, but has over 200 kilometres (125 miles) of coastline. Much of this is punctuated with sandy coves, while offshore are some of the clearest seas and best diving in the Med (see p256 **Dive! Dive! Dive!**).

Only El Toro, at 358 metres (1,175 feet), aspires (unconvincingly) to mountain status, but the jagged edges of the northern seaboard and the gently rolling rural hinterland – wetter and more fecund than elsewhere in the Balearics – are dramatic and beautiful. Geologically, Menorca consists of two distinct zones – the north is largely sandstone, while the south of the island is limestone, riven by narrow valleys in places and generally more sheltered than the north, which is frequently battered by the Tramuntana wind, its trees 'and bushes buckled into submission. Temperatures, though, are kind enough to allow islanders to label the autumn 'primavera d'hivern' (winter's spring).

BLOOMING BALEARICS

The islands are, in spite of their diminutive sizes and the fact that there are no rivers at all (the 'torrents' you see are dried-out streams that sometimes trickle with rainwater), home to a considerable range of landscapes and flora. These are best experienced on foot, though even drivers will find themselves pulling into lay-bys to gawp at a magnificent summit or an emerald-coloured meadow dotted with fruit trees set against a sheer cliff of rock.

Since Moorish times, the Balearics have been subjected to the taming will of farmers – the terraces and irrigation canals in the foothills of the Tramuntana hark back to the tenth-century pioneers. Orchards of citrus trees are common throughout the islands, especially in the lush meadows in the eastern foothills of the Tramuntana, as are almond groves and plantations of olive trees. Olives were introduced to Mallorca by the Romans and have prospered, especially near Sóller, sometimes described as the 'valley of gold' for the quality of the oils produced; oranges are also a major item in the central Tramuntana. Almond trees enjoy special affection in Mallorca, partly because of their economic importance, but also for their gorgeous white blossoms that come out early in the year, even before the snows have fully receded.

Es Pla remains the agricultural heart of Mallorca. Although it is naturally dry, thanks to human enterprise, the irrigated plain is packed with orchards of figs, melons, almond and carob trees as well as large stretches of caper crops and fallow fields. Rice does well around marshy Sa Pobla, as do hot pepper plants, while the grapes that supply Mallorca's wine industry thrive around Binissalem and Felanitx. Most of the windmills and waterwheels that once tapped into the artesian sources here are now devoid of sails or rotten, the ground water no longer available after decades of neglect.

'Keen twitchers tell of seeing up to 60 species of bird while on holiday.'

On both islands, but especially on Menorca, look out for wild flowers – orchids, poppies and gladioli – and patches of wild asparagus, heather, myrtle and bramble. In places like Menorca's Cala Galdana gorge – also a great birding environment – the air is filled with the sweet scent of flowers and plants, and species like the pig's ear and sawfly orchid are photogenic beauties, attracting hordes of butterflies and bees.

FUR, FEATHER AND FIN

In medieval times, falconry and game hunting – especially of wild boar, pheasant, roebuck deer and stag – were favourite pastimes among the nobility, the end result being the disappearance of all these animals; the '*coto privado de caza*' ('private hunting ground') signs you see everywhere in Mallorca nowadays simply mean 'Keep off – this is my land'. Moreover, as land was parcelled off into peasant farms in the days of Jaume III, there was no longer space for free-roaming game of any kind.

These days, you'll be lucky to spy a semi-feral goat, and even then it will be ringing a bell so that the owner can find it when milking or market day comes around. Inedible fauna has been almost wiped out, first by farmers and then by tourism-related schemes, and the best you can hope for is a field rat, maybe a weasel, or if you are really lucky, a genet (a small wild cat).

Birdlife, however, has to some extent managed to fly above and around much of the impact of *Homo sapiens turisticus* and, thanks to the diversity of geographies in the Balearics, is relatively abundant. On their swap-and-share websites, keen twitchers tell of seeing up to 60 species of bird while on two-week holidays.

As well as the unexciting European standards – sparrows, doves, ducks, shags and the like – there are also purple, grey and night herons, greater flamingos, several varieties of plover, egrets and reed warblers, all of them happy residents of, or migrants to, the remaining albuferas (marshlands). Carrion-eaters and birds of prey include honey buzzards, marsh harriers, kestrels, peregrine and Eleanora's falcon. This last is a birder's favourite, not least because it is impressive in flight, diving at speed to prey on small birds and large insects. Along the coast, the Mediterranean shearwater shares the thermals with ospreys, whiskered terns and a variety of noisome gulls.

Patient observers have reported sightings of Europe's largest bird of prey, the ultra-rare black vulture – especially around the highest peaks of the Tramuntana – as well as Audouin's gull, moustached warbler and marmora's warbler, all species hard to spot in Europe. The high points for serious birders are the spring and autumn migration cycles, when flocks of birds passing between northern Europe and Africa can be seen on high, some of them touching down to rest en route.

If you've only got time for one birding stop, Pollença on Mallorca is a wise option. The nearby S'Albufera marsh (*see p151*), the mountains of the Serra de Tramuntana and the cliffs and open seas off Formentor provide three typical habitats for Balearic birds. The small museum at S'Albufera is a useful introduction to the charms and challenges of the resilient Mallorcan wetlands.

In Menorca, the four-kilometre (two and a half-mile) stretch of waterland on the eastern coast – comprising S'Albufera des Grau (*see p241*), Illa d'en Colom and Cap de Favaritx – is an attractive setting for spotting birds.

To feed the airborne predators, but usually well hidden from humans, are martens, ferrets, weasels, rabbits, bats, hedgehogs and Mediterranean tortoises. In Formentor, look out for lizards darting up the vertical walls, and on Menorca and Cabrera you may spot the Lilford's wall lizard, which comes in several varieties, including a black and blue version; Menorca is also the unique Spanish habitat of the Italian wall lizard.

For all the empty rivers and trimming and pruning on terra firma, the oceans have remained to some extent native. As a visit

All creatures… at **Santa Eugenia**'s Natura Parc. *See p176.*

to Palma's Mercat del'Olivar will clarify, the waters off Mallorca and Menorca are awash with eels, sardines, tuna and Mediterranean sole, as well as lobsters, crayfish, spider crab and lots of common shellfish. Menu standards include swordfish, the little, see-through *jonquillo*, the *lluc* or sea pike and the *cap roig*, while rarities, after intensive fishing over many centuries, are the raor, a fish that buries itself deep down on the seabed, the *peus de cabra* barnacles and the gruesome-looking *rap* or sea devils. If you're not satisfied with encountering these in paellas, there is fairly good diving at Calvià and Port de Sóller in Mallorca and a fantastic scuba scene in Menorca (*see p256* **Dive! Dive! Dive!**).

BACK TO NATURE

Like other built-up corners of western Europe, the ecologies of the Balearic islands have been beaten and battered by roads, homes and humanity. Only recently have the Balearic governments shown an awareness of the fragility of the islands' ecosystems, prompted by a science and conservation NGO founded in 1973, GOB, the Grup Balear d'Ornitologia i Defensa de la Naturalesa (www.gobmallorca.com).

Menorca in particular is being pushed as a natural destination, helped by UNESCO declaring the island a Biosphere Reserve in 1993 – a scientific and conservation-oriented denomination that carries little legal weight.

In Mallorca, Alcúdia is being sold as an 'ecotouristic community' – six nearby reserves may not entirely compensate for the disastrous town and coastal planning on the Bay of Alcúdia, but the reinvention is a sign that some of the politicians who oversee Balearic tourism are at least trying to go green. Using a hierarchical system of designations, almost the whole of the western flank of Mallorca, as well as many small green spaces on the coast and inland, are protected; in Menorca, 19 near pristine areas, ranging from grassy coastal hills and beaches to marshes, are now under official protection. There are eight higher-status conservation areas, known as *Parcs Naturals*, seven of which are on (or just off) Mallorca (S'Albufera, the Península de Llevant, the Fonts Ufanes, S'Albufereta, Mondragó, the island of Sa Dragonera and the Cabrera Archipelago), plus S'Albufera des Grau (*see p241*) on Menorca. GOB wants the whole of the Tramuntana to become a *Parc Natural* too, but, there are conflicting interests in this tourism-dependent archipelago.

Iberian water frog. **Lluc**. *See p132.*

Pollença's **Moors and Christians** festival. *See p42.*

Festivals & Events

Traditional festivities still fill the Balearic calendar.

Having jumped almost overnight from isolated agricultural backwater peopled by pious peasants to mass market tourist destination, Mallorca and Menorca are not places people come to expecting a vibrant international cultural scene. The old seasonal cycles, tied to devotion to patron saints, still underlie most popular mass gatherings, and while Easter and New Year are the obvious major community celebrations, each village has its own busy calendar of activities. But so much foreign money has been drawn to the islands in the past decades that there is also a decent smattering of important musical events – the Pollença music festival in particular.

RELIGION

While not the passionate outpouring of devotion you might come across in Andalucia, **Semana Santa** (Holy Week, 10-16 Apr 2006, 2-8 Apr 2007) in the Balearics is still a major community highlight. Along with a rolling calendar of holy days, saints' days – Sant Antoni and Sant Sebastian are among the major players – and pilgrimages to selected monasteries and shrines, even those towns not named after a holy figure have a beloved patron saint or virgin to revere.

The warm-up is **Carnaval**, though this is usually closer in character to a popular fête than a Rio-style orgy of dancing and carnal delight – not least because Mallorcans like to include kids in such celebrations. During the four days before Lent begins, Palma,

Palmanova and Magaluf on Mallorca, and Maó and Ciutadella on Menorca organise parades of floats and colourful costumed performances in the streets. In Palma the procession, called **Sa Rua**, attracts as many as 25,000 spectators and 5,000 participants, who samba down the streets.

Palm Sunday marks the beginning of Semana Santa, when hooded penitents in coloured robes representing the island's 50 *confraries* (fraternities based on church congregations) file solemnly through towns, ostensibly celebrating the ride of Jesus into Jerusalem – though the atmosphere and music evoke the gloom of the coming crucifixion. There are processions in all the parishes, with Palma's endless march around the Rambla de los Duques de Palma prior to High Mass by far the most impressive. Ash Wednesday and Maundy Thursday celebrations have been taking place here since the 16th century, and the Palma event sees the public procession of **La Sang** (The Blood) – the Crucified Christ usually kept at the church of the General Hospital – from 7pm on the Thursday. On Good Friday, Christ figures in all the parishes are symbolically buried in sepulchres – Pollença's **Davallament** (Descent from the Cross) ceremony, performed since the Middle Ages, is probably the one to see, as the cadaver, draped in cloaks, is borne down the steps of the Via Crucis.

Christmas (Nadal) is the other obvious religious bonanza, a family affair when even backsliders and apostates make it to mass. There are nativity plays and carol services from mid December on, with children once again taking centre stage. On 6 January, Spaniards celebrate **Los Reyes Magos** (The Magi), and on the evening of the fifth, Palma heralds the event with the **Cabalgata de los Reyes Magos** (Horse Ride of the Magi) – three costumed figures arrive by sea into the harbour, lit up by flaming torches and fireworks, and lead a procession to Plaça Cort. Pollença is also the setting for a major **Corpus Christi** event (22 June) called the **Ball de les Àguiles** (Dance of the Eagles).

'Pilgrimages have long been central to Mallorcan life.'

As on the mainland, the **Mare de Déu dels Àngels** (2 Aug) in Pollença sees the Spanish traditional ritual fight between **Moors and Christians**, opening with the cry 'Moros a terra!' ('The Moors have landed!'). It's a lively affair – with the clash of wooden swords, scimitars and pitchforks, and turbaned pirates taking on heroic Christian Spaniards. On Menorca, Ciutadella's resistance against the Turks is celebrated in the town hall on 9 July with readings and re-enactments. There are also re-enactments on the dates of battles in Pollença (30 May 1550), Es Firó (11 May 1561) and at Andratx (2 Aug 1578), noted for the involvement of women in the defence of the faith.

Pilgrimages have long been central to Mallorcan life, and the **Lluc pilgrimage** to the Moreneta (Black Madonna; 12 Sept) is not only the biggest, but an ideal opportunity to visit the wonderful wild setting of the monastery amid the Tramuntana mountains.

Menorca's religious parties are characterised by the presence of horses, the symbol of *festes* on the island, with equestrian performances called *colcadas* set to the beat of a tambor and horse racing down the streets – **Corregudes des Cós** – marking the occasions of **Sant Joan de Missa** (23-24 June) and the **Dia de Sant Miquel** (29 Sept).

You could tire of saints and virgins in the Balearics. Every other day, one or more towns seems to be celebrating its patron or a holy figure of more general appeal. Among the most lavish in dress, dramatic effect and dance are **Beneides de Sant Antoni** (St Antony's Eve, 16 Jan) in Sa Pobla (also at Artà, Manacor and Sant Joan) – with bonfires to burn away sin, a greasy pole with a cock on top, pig sacrifices and brass bands; it's also a major event in Maó, where St Anthony is the patron saint. Two further sizeable religious occasions are the **Festa de Sant Sebastià** (20 Jan) in Pollença and the **Dia de la Beata** at Santa Margalida (1st Sun of Sept).

MUSIC AND THE ARTS

While most people associate the Balearic summer with intense heat and varying degrees of fairly brainless hedonism, some people are sweating over hot strings. The biggest classical festival is the **Festival de Pollença** (971 53 50 77, 971 53 40 12, www.festivalpollenca.org) during July and August at the Claustre del Convento Santo Domingo. Established in 1962 by violinist Philip Newman, under the patronage of Queen Sofia and the direction of Eugen Prokop, it has taken place every year since; past headliners have included Yehudi Menuhin, Viktoria Mullova and Montserrat Caballé, with the St Petersburg Philharmonic Orchestra topping the bill in 2005.

Chopin's stay in Valdemossa is recalled at the annual **Festival Chopin** (Aug) with shows by first-class virtuosi (www.festivalchopin.org); Gwyneth Chen was the star of the 2005 festival.

Another serious musical event is the **Deià International Music Festival** (971 63 91 78, mobile 678 98 95 36, www.dimf.com) from July to September, which features world-class orchestras and soloists. Since 2004, Deià has also hosted a long weekend (at the end of October) devoted to good talk, food, film, music and literature known as **Tertulia@Deià** (www.hayfestival.com/tertulia),

To see more earthy events, with more local sounds, there are regular folk fests – dance and music – in Palma, Maó, Ciutadella and in many villages. If you like religion with your roots music, check out Valldemossa's **Carro Triunfal** on 28 July – with the requisite country folk, donkeys and torch-bearing slaves; this is an occasion for the singing of the Sor (Sister) Tomaseta song to celebrate Mallorca's only home-grown saint (Catalina Tomás). The **Sant Llorenç celebrations** in Selva on 10 August provide a showcase for religiously inspired folk singing by the women of the Aires de Muntanya, formed in 1930 to preserve traditional music. Sóller's **International Folklore Festival** (end of July) has been going for over 20 years now, and Villafranca is a recognised centre for Mallorcan folk, with the scene given a lift by local folk artist-entrepreneur Tomeu Penya.

Menorca has its own folk traditions, and many religious and community events feature performances called *codolades* and *glosats*; the former satirical poetry readings, the latter poetic improv turns set to guitar. Ciutadella and Ferreries are the main centres for these.

A good number of globetrotting musical bands come to Mallorca. A hugely popular jazz-slanted event, the **Jazz Voyeur Festival** (971 90 52 92, www.jazzvoyeurfestival.com), was held for the first time in 2004 and was so successful it was extended over five months

Town fiestas & festivals

For public holidays, *see p274*.

January

Campos (9th); Algaida (16th); Maó (Menorca) and across Mallorca (Sant Antoni, 16-17th); Palma (19th); Pollença (20th).

February

Llubí (Sat before Shrove Tuesday); Sencelles (5th); Santa Eugènia (11th); Sencelles (27th).

March

Porto Petro (19th); Cala d'Or (31st).

April

Easter week – festivals all over the islands; Llubí, Montuïri (1st Tue after Easter); Muro, Porreres, Santa Eugènia (1st Sun after Easter); Ses Salines (23rd); Sineu (25th).

May

Ses Salines (1st); Sineu (1st Sun); Campanet, Felanitx, Sencelles (2nd Sun); Port de Sóller, Sóller (2nd week); Sencelles (3rd Sun); Manacor (last week); Pollença (30th).

June

Manacor (1st week); Artà (13th); Pollença (22nd); Menorca (23rd-24th); Cala Millor, Ciutadella (Menorca), Deià, Felanitx, Muro, Palma, Sant Joan (24th); Alcúdia, Andratx, Búger, Esporles, Port de Sóller (29th).

July

Campanet (1st week); Ciutadella (Menorca) (9th); S'Arenal (10th); Puigpunyent (15th); Cala Figuera, Port de Andratx, Port de Sóller, Porto Colom, Porto Cristo, Santa Margalida (16th); Sa Pobla, Santa María del Camí (20th); Petra (21st); Es Mercadal (Menorca) (3rd weekend); Es Castell (Menorca) (24-26th); Alcúdia, Algaida, Binissalem, Calvià, Llucmajor, Manacor, Muro, Sa Pobla, Santanyí, Valldemossa, Vilafranca de Bonany (28th); Inca (30th); Fornells (Menorca) (4th weekend); Es Migjorn Gran (last weekend).

August

Llubí (1st); Andratx, Petra, Pollença (2nd); Colònia de Sant Jordi (1st weekend); Alaior (Menorca) (1st & 2nd week); Santa Eugènia (1st Sun); Bunyola (5th); Campos (7-15th); Llucmajor, Petra (2nd Sun); Selva (10th); Alaior (Menorca) (1st weekend after 10th); Magaluf, Palma Nova, Santa Ponça (10-15th); Biniaraix (13-15th); Valldemossa (14th); Cala d'Or, Ca'n Picafort, Sencelles, Sineu (15th); Montuïri (15-24th); Alaró, Andratx, Porreres (16th); Sant Climent (Menorca) (3rd weekend); Alcúdia, Consell, Ses Salines, Sóller, Valldemossa (24th); Ferreries (Menorca) (25-26th); Felanitx (28th); Estellencs, Sant Joan (29th); Esporles, Felanitx (last Sun); Sant Lluis (Menorca) (end of month); Maria de la Salut (15 days during month).

September

Santa Ponça (1st 10 days); Vilafranca de Bonany (1st weekend); Santa Margalida (1st Sun); Maó (Menorca) (7-8th); Fornalutx (7-9th); Banyalbufar, Galilea, Lloseta, Maria de la Salut, Santa María del Camí (8th); Pollença (2nd Sun); Lluc (12th); Bunyola (21st); Petra (3rd weekend); Manacor (3rd Sun); Campanet, Llucmajor (29th); Binissalem (last week); Felanitx, Randa (last Sun).

October

Valldemossa (20th); Consell (3rd Sun); Porreres (last Sun).

November

Muro (1st Sun); Inca (3rd Thur); Llubí (1st Tue after 25th); Santanyí (30th).

December

Vilafranca de Bonany (4th); Montuïri (1st Sun).

(June-November) in 2005, featuring George Benson, Kool and the Gang, the Brad Mehldau Trio and the Roy Haynes Quartet. Concerts are held at venues such as Calvia's Casino and the Auditorium in Palma.

A longer-established **International Jazz Festival Sa Pobla** (971 54 41 11, Aug) drew in the likes of the Marcus Miller Band and the Miranda Jazz Sextet in 2005.

The Teatre Principal in Maó is the venue for Menorca's diminutive opera season (three or four performances in July and August), while Palma

Auditorium's ballet season (www.temporadade ballet.com) attracts major classical companies from overseas, as well as new and experimental dance troupes. The same venue hosts opera (971 73 47 35, www.auditorium-pm.com, Nov).

FOOD, DRINK AND BRIC-A-BRAC

Like so many things on the islands, food is treated in a businesslike manner. Palma's annual **Mallorca Food Fair** in April and Menorca's **Agricultural Food Festival** (see www.firesicongressos.com for these and other conferences and fairs) are more for trade than tasting, but admission to passers-by is allowed.

There are small-scale harvest celebrations across the islands, celebrating the prickly pears, oranges, loquats and figs that grow in the region, sometimes involving the election of a queen symbolising the fruit. In Vilafranca, there used to be a 'Queen of Melons' but, alas, prizes are now only given to the fruit and their growers. Other food fests respond to religious occasions. On the last Sunday before Easter, the congregation of Sant Joan, Palma, celebrates the **Festa del Pa i del Peix** (Festival of Bread and Fish), commemorating the feeding of the 5,000.

The **Festa d'es Vermar** in late September is Binissalem's main wine festival. The must is blessed, prizes are awarded to the biggest bunch of grapes, and local song and dance accompanies the opening of casks. As well as the obligation to honour Dionysus by quaffing quantities of the ever-improving *vino* from Mallorca's best-known DOC, goat meat dishes are served before fireworks and a singing, dancing street party.

Handicraft fairs often accompany food events, and many villages host agricultural-artisanal fairs, especially in September, when Manacor, Felanitx, Petra and Alaró all show off their wares. In the last week of March, Marratxi is the location for the **Fira del Fang** (Ceramics Fair), with displays of bowls, pots, pipes and the *siurells* – white figurines decorated with colourful dots – that inspired Miró.

Mallorcan markets

Listed below are Mallorca's general markets with the best picked out in **bold**. In addition, there's a daily crafts market in Palma's Plaça Major during the summer.

Monday
Calvià, **Manacor**, Montuïri.

Tuesday
Alcúdia, **Artà**, Campanet, Ca'n Picafort, Llubí, Porreres, Porto Colom, Santa Margalida.

Wednesday
Andratx, Capdepera, Colònia de Sant Jordi, Llucmajor, Petra, **Port de Pollença**, Santanyí, Selva, Sencelles, **Sineu**, Vilafranca de Bonany.

Thursday
Arenal, Campos, **Inca**, Lloseta, Sant Joan, Ses Salines.

Friday
Alaró, Algaida, **Binissalem**, Ca'n Picafort, Llucmajor, Maria de la Salut, Son Servera.

Saturday
Bunyola, Cala Ratjada, Campos, **Palma** (Avda. Gabriel Alomar i Villalonga), Porto Colom, Santa Eugènia, Santa Margalida, **Santanyí**, **Sóller**.

Sunday
Alcúdia, **Consell**, Felanitx, Llucmajor, Muro, **Pollença**, Porto Cristo, Sa Pobla, **Santa María del Camí**, Valldemossa.

BULLFIGHTS AND BOATS

The bullfighting season kicks off in March, and there is an irregular calendar of fights between March and October. There are bullrings at Palma (a 14,000-seater built in 1929; *see p84*), Muro (971 53 73 29), Alcúdia (971 54 79 03), Inca (971 50 00 87) and Felanitx (971 58 05 57), presenting both experienced matadors and *novilleros* (novices). Responding to the tourist market, Alcúdia hosts mock bullfights on Thursdays with no blood-letting.

Menorca's equestrian tradition is kept alive at the Maó Hippodrome and at the Torre del Ram in Ciutadella, with black horses taking part in trotting races and betting permitted (for information contact Federació Hípica Balear, 971 37 82 20).

The **Copa del Rey** (King's Cup) is arguably the most important regatta in the Mediterranean, running from late July into August, with its base at the Real Club Náutico in Palma (971 72 68 48, www.copadelrey.com). Second in the rankings is the **Regatta Princesa Sofia**, held every year during Easter week, also at Palma's Club Náutico (www.trofeoprincesasofia.org). The other major marine festival is the **Verge del Carme** (aka the feast of Nostra Senyora del Carme) on 15-17 July, featuring processions in honour of the patron saint of seafarers and fishermen in Palma, Maó, Port d'Andratx, Cala Bona, Porto Cristo, Port de Pollença, Cala Figuera, Cala Ratjada and Porto Colom. Port d'Andratx is the setting for arguably the most impressive, with hundreds of traditional *llaüts* bobbing in the harbour illuminated by torches.

The **Feast of Trinity**, the week before Whit Sunday, traditionally marked the beginning of the fishing season. In Port d'Alcúdia this is maintained with a festival honouring St Peter, the Galilean fisherman-disciple, and on 29 June in Maó, games, dancing and old sailing boats celebrate the same feast day.

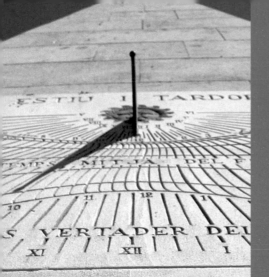

Palma

Plaça La Feixana, below Bastió de Sant Pere. See p69.

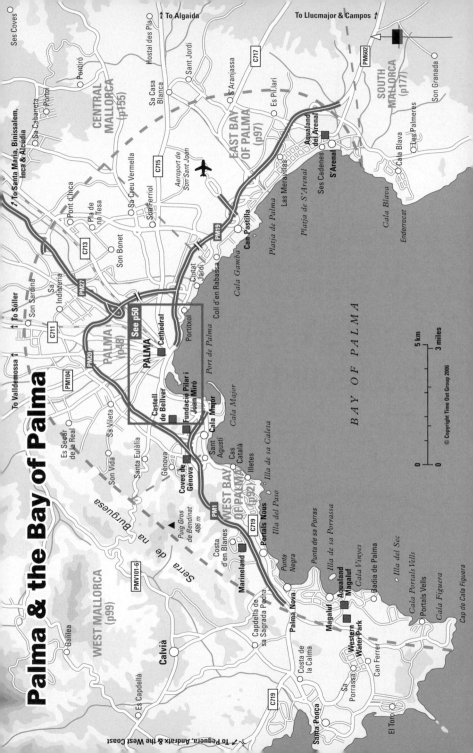

Palma &
the Bay of Palma

From the sublime to the ridiculous…

As your plane sweeps low over the sea coming into Son Sant Joan airport, the magnificent Bay of Palma is arrayed below you. With the jagged backing of the Tramuntana mountains and the towering bulk of Palma's cathedral glinting in the centre of the bay's arc of golden sand, it's an unforgettable sight. Forty years ago the city would have stood out in splendid isolation from the rural landscapes stretching all around it. Today, though, two long arms of intense development stretch from Palma around almost the entire bay, the result of the frenzied building boom of the 1960s and 1970s. Yet mercifully, although Palma and the bay are now physically one massive conurbation, in terms of culture, spirit and atmosphere they remain two utterly different worlds.

PALMA

The extraordinary thing about the cosmopolitan Mallorcan capital is how little the unchecked exponential development of the bay has affected its character. In fact, the city has positively benefited from the British and German tourist tide that laps all around it. Thanks to the tourist cash that has poured into the island over the past decades, the infrastructure of Palma has been hugely improved and the city – particularly the traffic-free old town – now gleams afresh. Yet there's been little compromise. In the majority of its characterful cafés, restaurants, bars and shops you'll find as many locals as visitors. And Palmesanos are a worldly, picky lot, ensuring that the quality of food and goods is high, while prices are relatively low (for this pricey island).

When you add in the fine museums and churches, markets and mansions, and the pleasure of simply wandering its ancient streets, it's easy to see why Palma is the perfect weekend break destination. And if you're staying elsewhere on Mallorca, it definitely warrants a couple of days of your time.

THE BAY OF PALMA

This is the Mallorca of boorish Brits and tanked-up Teutons, of full Englishes and chips with everything, of tattoos, tat and tacky holiday rep TV shows. The proliferation of just such an image in recent years has done serious

damage to the German tourism market (the Brits, it seems, aren't so fussy), and of late the island authorities have made serious attempts to reverse the bad PR with a major clean-up and renovation programme.

The featureless eastern side of the bay (more favoured by Germans) remains dreary and almost entirely unappealing, but the topographically more interesting western portion (dominated by the British) is at least now largely grot-free – even the most notorious offender, Magaluf, is just about presentable. There are also pockets of (relatively) more upmarket development, such as Portals Nous, and even unexpected oases, like Portals Vells at the far western end of the bay, that have miraculously escaped the high-rises.

The bay's one overwhelming draw, and the reason for all the development in the first place, remains unchanged – the best, longest, widest white-sand beaches on the island.

The best…

Aqueous attractions
Aqualand del Arenal (p88); Aqualand Magaluf (p95).

Art
Es Baluard (p70); Fundació Pilar i Joan Miró (p71); Museu d'Art Espanyol Contemporani (p67); Palau March (p62).

Beaches
Magaluf (p95); Palma Nova (p93); Portals Vells (p97).

Historic buildings
Can Marquès (p57); Castell de Bellver (p71); Palau de l'Almudaina (p61); Catedral de Palma (p59); Sa Llotja (p72).

Nightlife
Ca'n Barbarà (p83); Sa Llotja (p81); Passeig Marítim (p82); Santa Catalina (p82).

Palma

The Mallorcan capital has it all: character, atmosphere, a waterfront location and distractions aplenty.

To first-time visitors, Palma often comes as something of a revelation. On an island invaded by ten million visitors each year, this handsome, assured city of a third of a million people remains resolutely Spanish (or, as the locals would insist, *mallorquí*). Most tourists never set foot here – heading straight from airport to resort – but even the considerable number that do explore the Mallorcan capital are easily absorbed.

Dominating the wide Bay of Palma, this is a supremely liveable city – a sort of mini-Barcelona without the endemic street crime. Its heart is a pristine historic core, within which lie a clutch of compelling sights secreted among its (largely traffic-free) twisting medieval streets, including the all-dominant cathedral, a royal palace, art and historical museums, distinctive urban mansions and Gothic churches. Here too are buzzing shopping streets, lined with the sort of classy boutiques that chic *palmesanos* demand, as well as a varied bar and restaurant scene that caters to locals and tourists.

In contrast, the bland modern city fanning out inland from the old town offers few enticements for visitors. A bigger draw is the café-specked waterside, stretching from the Parc de la Mar in front of the cathedral east to the old fishing harbour of Portitxol, and west below the impressive Castell de Bellver to the city's old port of Porto Pi.

HISTORY

Although there were prehistoric villages in the vicinity of modern-day Palma (including Son Oms, which was scandalously bulldozed in the 1970s to build a second airport runway), there's no evidence of settlement on the site of Palma itself before the Roman invasion of 123 BC. The Romans founded the city of Palmeria on the hill now occupied by the Almudaina palace, which remained the centre of government ever after, but it wasn't substantially developed until the arrival of the Moors in AD 902. Renaming it Medina Mayurka, they constructed the first Palau de l'Almudaina, with a mosque next door on the site of the present cathedral. Other mosques were built, as well as public baths and a new city wall that enclosed a far greater area than that constructed by the Romans

(which, nevertheless, stood intact until the 13th century). This was to define the extent of the city right up to the 20th century.

Following the 13th-century Christian conquest of Jaume I 'the Conqueror', his son Jaume II built a new Palau de l'Almudaina, a cathedral on the site of the main mosque, the first docks close to the city and the Castell de Bellver to define the renamed Ciutat (city) de Mallorca (a direct translation of the Moorish name). Although the Moorish street plan was unaltered, almost all traces of Arabic architecture were eradicated as the city took on a Gothic appearance.

The Moorish walls were replaced by Renaissance fortifications in the 16th century, and these stood until the first decade of the 20th century, when population growth finally forced Palma out of its Moorish confines. A series of plans for the city's expansion were drawn up, though only adopted piecemeal, while in the centre some fine *modernista* buildings were constructed.

The 1950s and, especially, the 1960s were a period of major economic growth in Palma, chiefly fuelled by the rapidly expanding tourist industry. Zoning was introduced on the outskirts, creating two big industrial estates (Son Castello and Can Valero), one educational area (Son Rapinya), two dedicated to healthcare (Son Dureta and Son Llatzer) and the tourist developments along the bay to the west and east. The formation of a university in 1978 (which became the Universitat de les Illes Balears) ensured that the island's brightest young things weren't all lured to the mainland, and that Palma developed an agreeably youthful atmosphere.

Meanwhile, though, the fabric of the city centre had been neglected. It wasn't until the 1990s that the authorities finally acted, spending huge sums on restoring and cleaning up its medieval streets and diverting traffic around it. The result is as beguiling a city as you'll find on the Mediterranean.

Sightseeing

Apart from a couple of sights, almost everything of interest in Palma falls inside the jagged semicircle of roads, collectively known as the Avingudes ('Avenues'), that zig-zag their

Prosaically pedestrian(ised)
Plaça Major. *See p65.*

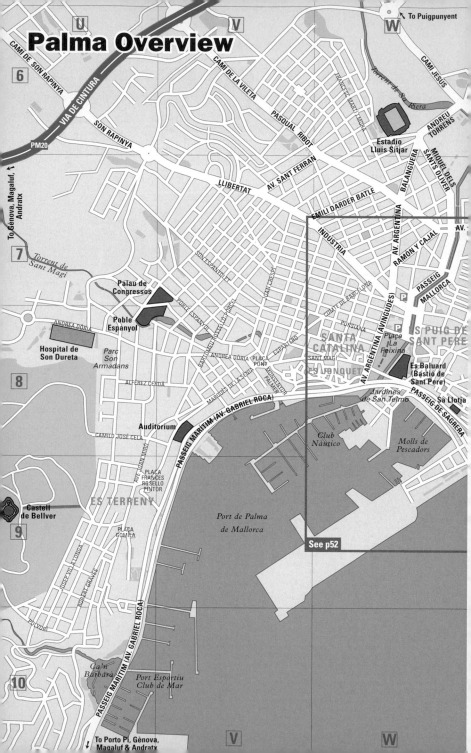

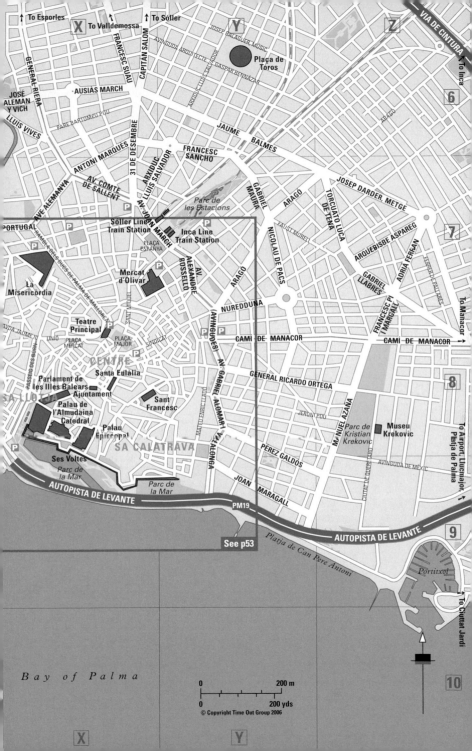

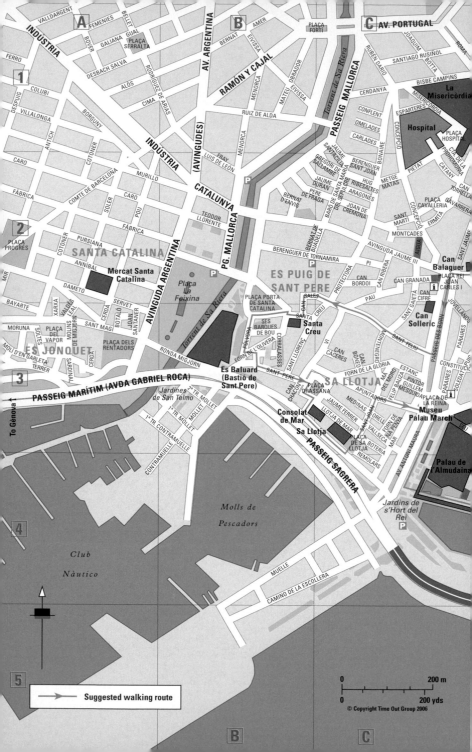

Central Palma

Palma Street Index

way along the course of the old fortifications. Starting from the cathedral, the following text takes you around all the chief points of interest in the old city, and can be followed as a walk (a suggested route is marked on the map, pp52-53; allow a whole day, or, preferably, two).

When you tire of the city, it's well worth hiring a bike and taking advantage of the cycle track that runs most of the way around the bay.

The Catedral & Sa Calatrava

Palma's two most significant and emblematic buildings sit side by side overlooking the sea. For almost 700 years the grand, towering form of the **Catedral de Palma** (known locally as La Seu; *see p58* **Temple of Light**) has loomed up from the harbourside, dominating the old town and providing a beacon for sailors. With an even longer pedigree, the **Palau de l'Almudaina** (*see p61*) started as a Moorish palace before being converted into a royal residence for Mallorca's Christian kings. A visit to the former is essential, but the latter is disappointingly lacking in atmosphere.

Nearby you'll find the specialist **Museu de Pepas** (Antique Doll Museum; *see p61*) and, around the other side of the cathedral, a posse of lurking horse and carriage drivers, keen to whisk you around the old town (the rates are fixed; ask before you jump aboard).

On the other side of the cathedral from the palace stands the **Palau Episcopal** (Bishop's Palace), started in 1238, finished in 1616 and currently undergoing a long-term restoration. Directly below the cathedral is a stylishly designed outdoor performance space, shaded by a suspended roof. This, together with the temporary exhibition space contained within the ramparts here (C/Dalt Murada s/n; 971 72 87 39, open June-Sept 10am-1.45pm, 5-8pm Tue-Sat, 10am-1.45pm, Oct-May 10am-5.45pm Tue-Sat, 10am-1.45pm Sun, free), is known as **Ses Voltes**. The walls themselves are part of the Renaissance fortifications begun in 1562, though this section wasn't completed until 1801.

Between the walls and the road running alongside the harbour is the **Parc de la Mar**, an artificial lake laid out in the 1980s in which the reflection of the cathedral shimmers (as it had in the sea before the harbourside was reclaimed). A café sits on the lake's far side and you'll see various pieces of sculpture dotted around its edges.

The narrow streets that meander eastwards from the cathedral are some of the city's most characterful. This district is known as **Sa Calatrava** and contains a number of diverting museums and mansions, including the island's most important museum, the **Museu de Mallorca** (*see p60*); if you have any interest in the island's rich prehistory, an hour here is well spent.

Further down the same street (C/Portella) you'll find the **Casa Museu J Torrents Lladó** (*see p57*), a well-designed museum dedicated to the eponymous painter, set within his evocative rambling house. Just around the corner on C/Can Serra is the only significant Moorish structure that survives in Palma, the **Banys Àrabs** (Arab Baths; *see p56*). Beyond their rarity value, the remains of the baths aren't very exciting.

It's worth ducking down C/Santa Clara to look at the charming **Convent de Santa Clara**, a largely 13th-century Mallorcan Gothic structure (though its façade was altered in the 17th century). There are still a few nuns here, and the public can only access the church.

As you wander the old town streets you'll gaze into the courtyards of numerous patrician mansions, most of which were built in Renaissance style in the late 17th and early 18th centuries. One such, **Can Oleza**, stands not far from the Museu de Mallorca at C/Morey 9; it became something of a model for what would be seen as a typical Mallorcan patio, with its external staircase, flattened arches, Ionic columns, loggia and iron railings.

Around the corner on C/Almudaina is a stretch of the Roman city wall, visible through a gateway on the right, while straddling the lane is the **Arc de l'Almudaina**. The origins of the arch are late Roman, though it was successively remodelled by the Moors and the Christians. At No.9 is another old mansion, **Can Bordils**, this one being medieval in origin (though it doesn't look it). It was altered by the Sureda family in the 16th century, and its patio dates from the 17th. Frustratingly, almost all of Palma's many mansions are closed to the public. The exception is the fascinating **Can Marquès** (*see p56*) just to the left on C/Zanglada, which offers guided tours around a grand house decorated much as it would have been in the early 20th century.

Emerging from the top end of C/Almudaina, handsome C/Palau Reial heads left back towards the cathedral and the Palau de l'Almudaina. At the palace end is **Palau March**, named after the phenomenally wealthy Mallorcan financier Bartomeu March, and now a permanent exhibition space (*see p62*). Further up the street is the **Círculo Mallorquín** building, now home to the **Parlament de les Illes Balears** (Balearic Parliament). Towards Plaça Cort is the neo-Gothic **Palau de Consell Insular de Mallorca**, built by local architect Joaquín Pavía in 1882 to house Mallorca's Island Council; it still meets here today.

Plaça Cort itself has been a key hub of the city since the 13th century. It is dominated by the elegant 16th/17th-century Renaissance-baroque **Ajuntament** (Town Hall), the roof of which juts over the façade. The building is open to the public on the last Thursday of the month, when the council is in session, and houses the pâpier-maché giants paraded around town during festivals. North-west of the *plaça*, a tangle of shop-lined pedestrianised streets wind down the hill towards Plaça Rei Joan Carles I.

The short street C/Cadena leads to Plaça Santa Eulàlia and back into the medieval town. Looming over the square is the blocky neo-Gothic façade of older-than-it-looks **Santa Eulàlia** (*see p65*), which you can peruse from one of the cafés scattered hereabouts.

Pedestrianised C/Convent de Sant Francesc leads eastwards from Santa Eulàlia to another of the old city's key churches, **Sant Francesc** (*see p65*), whose vast blank façade dominates the square of the same name. If you want to know more about Palma's many fine mansions, there's a map in the *plaça* (and at other locations around the city) that details the locations of most of the old town's best examples.

There's pleasant wandering to be had in the streets south of here. Take C/Pere Nadal and then turn left on to C/Monti-Sion, passing the elaborate baroque portal of the church of **Monti-Sion** (open times of services) before reaching Plaça Sant Jeroni and the 17th-century church of **Sant Jeroni** (the tympanum shows St Jerome's desert tribulations; open times of services). Running south from the square is C/Calders, on which you'll find the unexpectedly interesting **Museu Diocesà** (Diocesan Museum; *see p57*). Note that this is only a temporary home for the museum, while the Palau Episcopal is being renovated.

Just east of Sant Jeroni, bordering Plaça Porta d'Es Camp, is one of the very few remaining stretches of 10th- to 12th-century **Moorish Wall** (Murada Àrab), while C/Temple runs north from Plaça Sant Jeroni, past a gateway that leads off to the right to the **Temple** (Templar Chapel; open 10am-noon Tue-Thur, free). Once part of a compound belonging to the Knights Templar, and then taken over by the Knights Hospitaller in the early 14th century, this rather dingy church maintains certain Gothic and Romanesque features, though it was much altered in the late 19th century.

Continuing north from the Temple, through Plaça Pes de la Palla and along C/Bosc, brings you to one of the most recently refurbished areas of the old town: **Plaça de l'Artesania**. This somewhat self-conscious 'Centre Artesanal' (Artisans' Centre) is a focus for around 15 shops and workshops selling (and

sometimes making) pottery, glassware, jewellery, wood and paper products, leather goods, textiles, food and wine. (Most shops are open 10am-2pm, 4.30-8pm Mon-Fri, 10am-2pm Sat.) Not everything's wildly desirable, but there's enough quality here to make for a good half hour's browsing.

Around ten minutes' walk east of here into the new town is the **Parc Kristian Krekovic** and the **Museu Krekovic** (*see p60*), devoted to the Croatian-born painter Kristian Krekovic and to Peru, where he spent much of his life before passing his final years in Palma.

C/Morer runs from here west to Plaça Josep Maria Quadrado, which is bordered at one end by the back of Sant Francesc (*see p65*) and at the other, on a corner site, by the lively façade of **Can Barceló**, a large *modernista* mansion. Continuing west along C/Can Savella takes you past the huge courtyard and grandiose split staircase of **Can Vivot** (No.4), an impressive mansion built on medieval foundations by Valencian Jaume d'Espinosa for Joan Sureda i Villalonga around 1725. Its design was much copied elsewhere in Palma. It's worth detouring up parallel C/Can Sanç, where you'll find 300-year-old **C'an Joan de S'Aigo** (*see p76*), a classic Palman café.

Banys Àrabs

C/Can Serra 7 (971 72 15 49). **Open** *Jan-Mar* 9am-5.45pm daily. *Apr-Dec* 9am-8pm daily. **Admission** €1.50; free concessions. **No credit cards. Map** p53 D4.

Such was the zeal of the Christian conquerors of Mallorca in the 13th century that almost every architectural trace of the 300-year presence of the Moors in Mallorca was eradicated. A rare exception is the Arab Baths (Baños Arabes in Castilian), which date from the tenth century and probably once formed part of the palace of a wealthy official. Its layout is identical to that of bath houses in other Moorish cities of the time, with a tepidarium (warm room) alongside a grander caldarium (hot room). The latter is a square room topped with a half-orange dome supported by 12 pillars, the capitals of which all differ. (Many Moorish buildings made wide use of recycled materials.) In truth, you're unlikely to be inspired by the remains (the baths in the Palau de l'Almudaina are more evocative), but the small gardens are a shady spot to escape the heat.

Can Marquès

C/Zanglada 2A (971 71 62 47/www.canmarques.net). **Open** 10am-3pm Mon-Fri. **Admission** €6; €5 concessions. **No credit cards. Map** p53 D3.

The old city of Palma is littered with grand old mansions, many of which offer tantalising glimpses of their interior patios but allow no further access. Can Marquès is the exception. Admission isn't cheap, but the mandatory guided tours are excellent. The origins of the house are in the 14th century, but it attained its

Be inspired by the sculpture collection at **Palau March**. *See p62.*

current form when the wealthy coffee baron Don Martín Marquès bought it on his return from Puerto Rico in 1906. He renovated it in an intriguing blend of backward-looking, heavy duty dark furniture and furnishings, with light and playful contemporary *modernista* touches (the fluid lines of the doors are delightful). Piped sounds add life to the rooms, which include a reception room, ballroom, kitchen, family dining room (with art deco touches), private chapel, study and the lady of the house's bedroom, while some modern art exhibitions show that the current owners don't want Can Marquès to remain a static museum piece. Although parts of the original house are now private apartments, the rooms that have been restored offer a fascinating glimpse into the life of a wealthy family in Palma a century ago.

Casa Museu J Torrents Lladó

C/Portella 9 (971 72 98 35/www.torrentsllado.com).
Open *June-Sept* 11am-7pm Tue-Fri; 10am-2pm Sat.
Oct-May 10am-6pm Tue-Fri; 10am-2pm Sat.
Admission €3; free-€1.80 concessions. **Credit** MC,
V. **Map** p53 D4.
Open to the public since 2002, the former home and studio of the massively bearded painter Joaquin Torrents Lladó (1946-93), who lived most of his life on Mallorca, is well worth a visit, even if you're not a fan of his style (or if you've never heard of him). He achieved fame by the late 1970s for his precise, sober, baroque-influenced portraits (many of jet-eyed, dark-haired beauties gazing intently out of the canvas at the viewer). Yet his interests were far wider, encompassing the graphic arts, theatre set design, indus-

trial design and teaching (he founded three art schools that aimed to break the monopoly of the prevalent dry academic schools of art). Around 100 of his works are on display – among the best are his penetrating self-portraits, while his rather gaudy Mediterranean landscapes are more of an acquired taste. The real highlight, though, is his stunning studio, stretching over two storeys (with a library around the edges of the upper level). Lined in dark wood, with Persian rugs on the floor, floor-to-ceiling mirrors down one side and a snug sitting area under the staircase up to the library, it was designed for relaxing in as well as working. A grand player-piano tinkling away adds to the atmosphere. Elsewhere, look out for the piece of paper on which Robert Graves enigmatically wrote: 'Joaquin Torrents is a painter. Most painters think they are painters, but Joaquin Torrents really is a painter.'

Museu Diocesà

C/Calders 2 (971 21 31 00 ext 251). **Open** 10am-
1.30pm, 4.30-6.30pm Mon-Fri; hours vary Sat,
Sun, phone for information. **Admission** €2; €1
concessions. **No credit cards**. **Map** p53 E4.
Since 2001 a pared-down version of the Diocesan Museum has been temporarily housed in the chapel of San Pedro of the Casa de la Iglesia while the Palau Episcopal undergoes long-term renovation. It's likely to stay here until at least summer 2006, which is no bad thing (though it means the number of visitors has dropped radically); it's an atmospheric spot for a well-organised and enjoyable collection of religious art (an excellent English-language guide is

Temple of light

When Jaume I was ending more than three centuries of Moorish rule in Mallorca in 1229 he reportedly vowed to raze the city's Great Mosque and replace it with a Christian cathedral.

However, though the mosque was converted for Christian use by the king (and the minaret replaced with a belltower), its external structure remained largely intact until Jaume II commenced work on a new cathedral in 1306. It was to take 300 years before the completion of the façade in 1601 marked the end of the project. In subsequent centuries it became obvious (from the frequently collapsing masonry) that the great height of the nave was putting too much strain on the supporting structure, leading to a major reconstruction that resulted in the massive, soaring pinnacled buttresses that give the cathedral its distinctive profile.

Of the building's three doors, the finest is undoubtedly the Portal del Mirador, on the south façade, facing the sea. The design, by the cathedral's main architect at the time, Pere Morey, was executed between 1385 and 1430, and features wonderfully delicate, Flemish-inspired figures of Old Testament patriarchs and prophets and a tympanum of the Last Supper. The Mallorcan Guillem

Sagrera was one of the artists who worked on the door – he was in charge of works on the cathedral from 1420 to 1447, and the leading native 15th-century exponent of Gothic architecture (Sa Llotja was his masterpiece; see p81). In stark contrast, around the corner on the main façade is the inept Portal Major, a replacement for the door badly damaged in an earthquake in 1851. The third door, facing Plaça Almoina, is the no-nonsense Gothic Portal de l'Almoina (1498) at the base of the belltower (which can't, alas, be climbed). Beside it is the current entrance to the cathedral, through its small museum.

As you enter one of the finest Gothic church interiors in Europe, your eyes are drawn upwards into the thrillingly vast central space. The nave rises to 44 metres (144 feet), supported by delicate octagonal columns that culminate in cross-ribbed vaulting. The side aisles (lined by chapels) are a full 30 metres (98 feet) high, giving the interior an open, airy atmosphere that is enhanced by the light streaming through the huge rose window (with a diameter of more than 11 metres/ 36 feet) at the east end of the nave.

Much of the credit for the cathedral's ethereally light interior must go to Antoni Gaudí, the intensely religious Catalan architect, who supervised a major restoration between 1904 and 1914. There's little evidence here, though, of the iconoclastic eccentricities he displayed in many of his most famous works; instead Gaudí was largely concerned with returning the cathedral to its Gothic purity. He opened up the space by a number of modifications: moving the choir stalls from the centre of the cathedral to the walls of the Royal Chapel (in the apse of the nave), opening up the rose window and eight windows in the Royal Chapel (many had been closed or obscured by reredoses (ornamental screens)) and removing the baroque High Altar (replacing it with a plain Byzantine-era altar table). Over the altar hangs a decidedly odd baldachin (canopy) in the shape of an octagonal crown, decorated with symbols of the Eucharist. It was designed by Gaudí to add dynamism to the space, but looks less like an object of devotion and more like a left-over prop from a Terry Gilliam movie. Its somewhat tatty appearance is down to the fact that it is made from cardboard, paper and wood, and was only meant to be a provisional model. Gaudí never got around to making the real thing.

There are a few other signs of Gaudí's presence elsewhere in the cathedral – the contorted shapes of the metal railings in front of the altar are his work, as are the bright ceramic inlays framing the Bishop's Throne at the east end of the building. And for times when nature wasn't providing enough natural illumination, he installed electric lighting (very unusual in churches at that time).

The chapels running down the sides of the aisles are largely unthrilling, with the notable exception of the Chapel of Corpus Christi, to the left of the High Altar. Here you'll see a gilded polychrome baroque reredos (altar screen) of rare beauty and craftsmanship by local sculptor Jaume Blanquer. It dates from the first half of the 17th century and depicts in its three tiers the Temptations of St Anthony, the Presentation of Jesus in the Temple and the Last Supper.

The other chapel of interest is the Trinity Chapel, situated behind the High Altar and, unfortunately, not accessible to visitors. It was built by Jaume II in the early 14th century as a suitable resting place for the remains of his dynasty, but it was only in the 20th century that the chapel was finally used for

this purpose it now contains fine tombs to Jaume II and Jaume III by Frederic Marés (not visible from the nave).

The Museu de la Catedral is housed within three rooms – the lofty Vermells Sacristy (named after the red habits of those who once worked here) holds various ecclesiastical bits and bobs, including a giant gilded silver monstrance dating from 1585; the austere Gothic chapterhouse features some fine paintings (particularly the early 14th-century Santa Eulàlia reredos) and the tomb of Bishop Gil Sánchez Muñoz (who became the antipope Clement VIII during the Western Schism of the late 14th/early 15th century); and the exuberant, elliptical baroque chapterhouse, which was built at the beginning of the 18th century, contains some wildly over-the-top silver candelabra from that period, along with a piece of the Holy Cross and various saintly digits and pieces of bone.

Catedral de Palma

Plaça de l'Almoina s/n (971 72 31 30). **Open** *Apr, May, Oct* 10am-5.15pm Mon-Fri; 10am-2.15pm Sat. *June-Sept* 10am-6.15pm Mon-Fri; 10am-2.15pm Sat. *Nov-Mar* 10am-3.15pm Mon-Fri; 10am-2.15pm Sat. **Admission** €3.50. **No credit cards. Map** p53 D4.

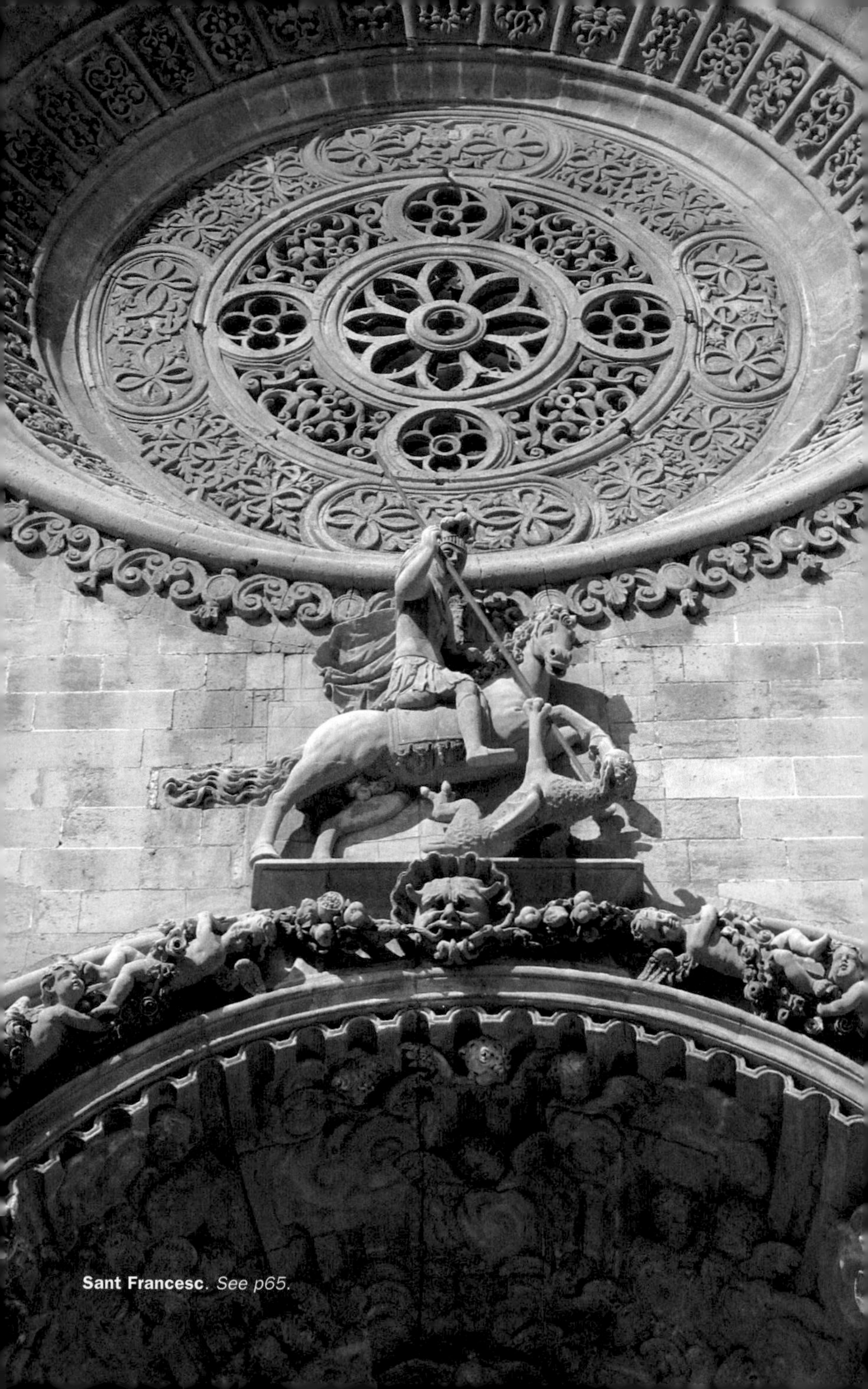

Sant Francesc. *See p65.*

included in the admission price). The chapel is a convincing, appealing piece of neo-Gothic, designed by Joan-Miquel Sureda y Veri and consecrated in 1894. In its ten small chapels are hung (by theme) some interesting paintings, notably a fine Flemish-style depiction of George slaying the dragon against the (idealised) background of late 15th-century Palma (1468-70) by Pere Niçard, a vivid 14th-century altarpiece by an unknown artist telling the story of St Paul from the Chapel of St Paul in the Bishop's Palace, and an anonymous altarpiece from around the turn of the 13th century recounting the tale of the Passion in 24 episodes.

Museu Krekovic

C/Ciutat de Querétaro 3 (971 24 94 09). **Open** 9.30am-1pm, 3-6pm Mon-Fri; 9.30am-1pm Sat. **Admission** €1.80. **No credit cards. Map** p51 Z8.
The Croatian-born artist Kristian Krekovic lived much of his life in Peru, before he moved to Palma in 1960, dying in the city in 1985. This museum holds around 150 paintings, as well as a variety of handicrafts and exhibits related to Peru and the Spanish presence in the country.

Museu de Mallorca

C/Portella 5 (971 71 75 40). **Open** 10am-7pm Tue-Sat; 10am-2pm Sun. **Admission** €2.40; free-€1.20 concessions; free to all Sat, Sun. **No credit cards. Map** p53 D4.
Created in 1961 (though it didn't open to the public until 1976), the Museum of Mallorca is the island's most wide-ranging museum, containing prehistoric archaeological finds, Roman and Moorish relics, and a decent spread of Gothic, Renaissance and baroque art, as well as paintings and some graphic work and industrial design from the 19th and 20th centuries. Disappointingly, though, it doesn't really tell the story of the island in any coherent way.

By far the most comprehensive and best thought-out section of the museum is that devoted to prehistory. It occupies the atmospherically lit basement and, although the English translation of the labelling can be somewhat tortuous, it gives a decent explanation of the earliest phases of human habitation of the island, including the mysterious, characteristic talayots (conical or quadrangular stone structures) and navetas (boat prow-shaped dwellings) that have been found all over the island, plus the controversial excavations of William Waldren in 1962 that appear to put human habitation of Mallorca at least 2,000 years earlier than was previously thought. The highlights are the skeleton of the tiny antelope-goat *Myotragus balearicus* that may have been driven to extinction by early human settlers and a room of tiny statues (most of nude male warriors with spear arm raised) that were probably used in cult worship. Particularly beautiful is the head of the 'Bull of Talapi', which looks more like a wistful gazelle.

On the ground floor is a rather piecemeal collection of Roman and Moorish artefacts, including the 'Almohad treasure' (a cache of Islamic coins and jewellery, hidden in a cave in 1229 when Jaume I and his troops arrived to claim the island, and unearthed only in 1984), a rare early Christian floor mosaic from the Basilica of Son Fadrinet near Campos, a partially recreated Roman domus (house) and some Roman tombstones. The first-floor exhibits kick off with some superb Gothic religious paintings by the Mallorcan Primitives, the finest being the depiction of the story of Santa Quiteria by the painter known as the Master of the Privileges (1330s). This room also contains a 14th-century Mudéjar doorway that was formerly in the church of Santa Eulàlia. Look out too for the sensitive works of Francesc Comes from around the turn of the 14th century. The Renaissance and baroque paintings on this floor are of far less interest.

The final floor of the museum was closed for renovation at the time of writing, and projected to reopen in 2006-7; in the meantime, some of its holdings will be shown on a rotational basis on the first floor. It contains some unexciting 19th-century Mallorcan paintings, some woodcuts and engravings, a room of *modernista* tiles, decorative objects and fittings, and paintings by some of the many foreign artists who moved to Mallorca after World War II (including a 1948 portrait of Robert Graves by Archie Gittes). The best-known native Mallorcan painter of the last century, Juli Ramis (1909-90), is represented by five powerful expressionist works.

The museum is housed within a superb mansion built in 1643 by Miguel Luís de Togores (whose coat of arms can be seen over the main entrance), and was once home to the Count and Countess of Aiamans; its popular name is Ca la Gran Cristiana.

Museu de Pepas

C/Palau Reial 27 (971 72 98 50). **Open** 10am-6pm Tue-Sun. **Admission** €4, free-€3 concessions. **Credit** MC, V. **Map** p53 D3.
By definition, a Museum of Antique Dolls (Museo Muñecas Antiguas in Castilian) is only likely to appeal to those with an interest in antique dolls. The private collection of Alicia García-German, on the first floor of an old house right by the cathedral, is more than the tacky tourist trap you might expect from the location. A couple of rooms are filled with more than 500 antique dolls, including many rare 19th-century specimens from France and Germany. The labelling is in Castilian only, but there's some information on the museum's leaflet and the assistant can usually explain more.

Palau de l'Almudaina

C/Palau Reial s/n (971 21 41 34/www.patromonio nacional.es). **Open** *Apr-Sept* 10am-5.45pm Mon-Fri; 10am-1.15pm Sat. *Oct-Mar* 10am-1.15pm, 4-6pm Mon-Fri; 10am-1.15pm Sat. Guided tours in English on request. **Admission** €3.20; €2.30 concessions; free Wed. Guided tours €4. **No credit cards. Map** p53 D3.
Ever since the conquering Romans built a fort on high ground overlooking Palma harbour in 123 BC, the site of the current Palau de l'Almudaina has been home to the island's rulers and key officials; it

remains the official royal residence in Mallorca today. The Vandals destroyed the Roman structure in the 5th century AD and built their own castle here. This was, in turn, converted into a Moorish alcazaba by the Emir Isam el Jawlani when North African Arabs conquered the island in the early tenth century. When the Christians wrestled Mallorca from the Moors in 1229, Jaume I used the palace as his main residence, though the building wasn't substantially altered until the reign of Jaume II, who remodelled it in Levantine Gothic style in the late 13th and early 14th centuries. Much of the palace's current appearance dates from this time, and, although it was altered on many subsequent occasions (and underwent a major restoration in the 1960s and 1970s), its glory days were really over when the Kingdom of Mallorca was annexed to Aragón in 1349. Today it is used for official functions and receptions.

The palace is centred around two linked, but essentially separate, wings: the King's Palace (and the adjoining Great Hall) facing the sea and the Queen's Palace (meeting it at right angles), with a number of other buildings – the Royal Cellar, St Anne's Chapel, the Arab Baths, the Royal Procurator's Office – making up the ensemble. The Queen's Palace and the buildings on the north and east side of the palace are closed to the public (they are partly occupied by the regional military HQ). It's definitely worth paying for one of the audio guides at the entrance – the rooms are largely bare and scantily signed, so additional explanation, albeit a rather floral and longwinded one, is useful in bringing the place alive.

The tour starts in the Paseo de Ronda corridor, with its black and white Mudéjar ceiling, only discovered during restoration in 1967, which leads into the first room within the former Great Hall. When the roof of the Great Hall collapsed in 1578, Philip II decided to partition the huge room into a series of smaller spaces. His master builder Pere Castany undertook the work, installing ribbed vaulting and bosses displaying the king's coat of arms. The first of these rooms is known as the Hall of Fireplaces after the three hearths here that once heated the entire Great Hall. The following smaller room, the Hall of the Kings, is hung with nine 20th-century portraits of the Kings of Mallorca by José Sancho de la Jordana. It leads into the largest of the chambers of the old Great Hall, the Council Hall, which is hung with some fine 15th- and 16th-century Flemish tapestries.

The four relatively small rooms that follow make up the ground floor of the King's Palace, and were largely used by servants and guards. From one of them, the Guard Room, you can access the Arab Baths, located between the King's and Queen's Palaces. These are thought to have originated as Roman baths, and were used by Arab and Christian rulers thereafter. Consisting of three diminutive rooms, they were clearly designed as private royal baths.

The ground floor of the King's Palace opens out on to a sizeable terrace which, thanks to the fine sea views it affords, is known as the Mirador de la Mar. Between the mirador and the sea you'll see the tenth-century Puerta de la Mar, the old sea gate to the palace, which continued in use until the 16th century, when the tide no longer reached the gate.

The tour then takes you out into the central courtyard (in the centre of which gurgles a fountain decorated with an 11th-century stone lion) and up the 16th-century Royal Staircase to the first floor of the King's Palace. Proceeding through a couple of anterooms you arrive at the chamber that is now known as the Queen's Study, though it was formally used for private royal meals and audiences with councillors. Of most interest here is a fine Mudéjar coffered ceiling (echoed in several rooms on this floor) and the remnants of a mural (date unknown) depicting knights on the march.

Heading back out of the study and right brings you to the Assistants' Office, which was formerly the King's Dressing Room, with another 16th-century coffered ceiling and a painted frieze alive with animals and human figures. Beyond here you enter the upper level of the old Great Hall, as you'll be able to tell by the great truncated Gothic arches that support the ceiling. This large room is now used for official receptions. Leading off the hall is the former King's Bedroom, now the King's Study, scene of the surrender of Mallorca's last Muslim emir to Jaume I in 1229.

The only other building that can be visited in the palace is the Levantine Gothic St Anne's Chapel, on the west side of the courtyard. Founded by Jaume II in 1310, this part of the palace is the least affected by change over the succeeding centuries.

The most prominent of the palace's towers is the Torre del Angel, topped by a bronze-covered wooden weather vane depicting the Archangel Gabriel. It was sculpted by Antoni Camprodón in 1310. The tower was originally built by the Moors in 1117 as a watchtower, and at one point (1395-1400) contained the workshop of the alchemist Jaume Lustrach, who the eccentric Juan I of Aragón hoped would discover how to turn base metals into gold. Inevitably, he didn't.

Palau March

C/Palau Reial 18 (971 711 122/www.fundbmarch.es). **Open** *Apr-Oct* 10am-6.30pm Mon-Fri; 10am-2pm Sat. *Nov-Mar* 10am-5pm Mon-Fri; 10am-2pm Sat. **Admission** €3.60; free under-12s. **Credit** AmEx, MC, V. **Map** p52 C3. **Photo** *p57.*

The Palau March is a deceptively recent construction, built in the 1930s and '40s under the guidance of Madrid architect Luis Gutiérrez Soto. In a deviation from his usual neo-Herreran style, and bowing to the tastes of his paymasters in the fabulously wealthy March family, Gutiérrez adopted a curiously historicist collection of styles. The grandiose result for many years the March residence, becoming a cultural foundation in the 1990s and, in 2003, a fully fledged museum.

The terrace at the entrance, in itself an appealing space with wonderful views, holds an exceptional collection of sculptures, representing different movements in the medium, and including works by Rodin,

Modernisme in Mallorca

George Sand may have ridiculed the poverty and insularity of 19th-century Mallorcan society in her scathing book *A Winter in Majorca* (*see p113* **Local heroes**), but by the end of that century a small but wealthy and increasingly outward-looking bourgeoisie had developed. The modernisation of agriculture and development of industry brought profits to the few, while a growing awareness of, and pride in, Catalan culture fuelled the monied classes with a desire to display their wealth and progressiveness in concrete form. In the early 1900s **Modernisme**, the Catalan take on art nouveau, came to Mallorca.

The most influential style in the applied arts and architecture in Europe from the 1890s, art nouveau was a Janus-faced movement, simultaneously looking into the past and the future. A love for decoration, for fluid, organic forms, was combined with a championing of new industrial techniques and materials, of concrete and iron and glass. The Balearics' linguistic and cultural links with Catalunya provided the great Catalan exponents of *Modernisme* (not to be confused with the ascetic, stripped-down Modernism movement that followed it) with a responsive secondary market for their architectural and decorative ideas.

The greatest name of *Modernisme*, Catalan architect **Antoni Gaudí i Cornet**, came to Mallorca in 1904 to oversee the restoration of **Palma Cathedral** (*see p58*). Lovers of Gaudí's extravagant creations in Barcelona might be disappointed by the restraint he showed in Palma. The deeply religious architect focused on restoring what he saw as the cathedral's lost Gothic purity, opening up the space and introducing more light. There are, though, characteristic flourishes in the baldachin (canopy) over the altar and the contorted shapes of the flowing railings in front of it, as well as the bright ceramic inlays framing the Bishop's Throne.

Prize for first *modernista* building in Mallorca, however, goes to Gaudí's rival, **Lluís Domènech i Montaner**. In 1903, on Palma's Plaça Weyler, he built the city's first luxury hotel, the **Gran Hotel**. It's a superb exercise in the balance of creativity and restraint, and the vibrant decorative stonework, ceramics and ironwork never threaten to detract from the building's structural integrity and discipline. Today, it is home to the **Fundació La Caixa** (*see p67*), which often puts on exhibitions exploring *Modernisme*'s links with later movements in art, architecture and design.

Opposite the Gran Hotel is a more modest incarnation of *Modernisme* in the lively façade of the little **Forn des Teatre pâtisserie**, while on Plaça Mercat stand **Casas Cassayas** – two identical *modernista* apartment buildings, designed in 1908 by Josep Cassayas.

The other key site in Palma for lovers of *Modernisme* is Plaça Marquès de Palmer, just south of Plaça Major. Here, side by side, rise two of the city's finest yet contrasting *modernista* buildings. **Can Rei** was built as a private residence and is the most Gaudí-esque structure in the city; a riotous explosion of floral motifs and polychrome ceramic mosaics, dripping down five storeys to a hanging balcony decorated with a scowling face flanked by dragons. Next door, former department store **L'Aguila** (by local architect Gaspar Bennàssar) is a far more measured and restrained work. Despite the coloured brickwork of its upper storeys (reminiscent of the style of the third great Catalan *modernista* architect, Josep Puig i Cadafalch), its strict geometry, metal frame and large windows provide a far clearer link than Can Rei to the more severe architectural movements that were to follow art nouveau.

When Gaudí came over to work on the cathedral in Palma, he brought with him his talented pupil **Joan Rubió i Bellver**. Rubío made his mark, however, not in the capital but in Sóller on the west coast. The town's successful citrus fruit export trade meant that there was plenty of money around to commission Rubió to give a *modernista* twist to the façade of the church of **Sant Bartomeu** on the main square. Later (in 1912), he built the **Banco de Sóller** next door – a rugged, fortress-like structure, lightened by playful iron window grilles – and his own house, **C'an Prunera** (1909-11) on nearby C/Lluna. There are a handful of other *modernista* mansions around Sóller, including one that now provides a home for the **Museu Balear de Ciències Naturals & Jardí Botànic de Sóller**. (For more on Sóller's *modernista* buildings, *see p124*.)

All aboard!

If you're staying in Palma and make only one foray out of the city, make it a journey on the **Ferrocarril de Sóller** (Sóller Railway). You'll be hard-pressed to find a local aboard this toytown-style service and, in truth, it's very unlikely it would still be operational were it not for the tourist trade, but this in no way detracts from what is a hugely enjoyable hour-long journey through the mountains.

This 27-kilometre (17-mile) length of track (with one of the narrowest gauges in the world at 914 millimetres/36 inches) opened in 1912, connecting the capital with Sóller on the west coast, and cutting journey times down from a day to just an hour and a quarter, thus allowing the citrus growers of Sóller to get to the Palma markets and back in a day.

Little has changed since then: the tiny station (marooned in the soulless expanse of the Plaça Espanya) is reached through a wrought-iron gate; the ticket office still dispenses old-fashioned paper tickets and the carriages are largely constructed from wood with banquette-style seats, brass fittings and gaslights.

The first part of the journey is not spectacular, and for the first ten minutes the track runs along the road like a city tram, before reaching the outskirts of Palma and then open countryside, with the peaks of the Tramuntana as a spectacular backdrop.

As you approach the first stop at Bunyola, olive fields give way to pine forests. Beyond the village the train enters the first of 12

tunnels, which become progressively longer, until it breaks through the mountains and emerges on the west side of the island. The views here are superb as the train wends its way over precarious bridges and across dry *torrentes*, high above a valley rutted with terraces and dotted with old farmhouses. In the distance you can spot Sóller and the villages of Biniaraix and Fornalutx.

The last part of the journey, the approach to Sóller, is delightful: citrus groves crowd round the carriages, close enough to pull off a ripe lemon or orange. From the station, you can jump on the equally atmospheric tram down to the sea at Port de Sóller (*see p128*).

Note that the services marked with an asterisk below make an additional stop at the Mirador del Pujol d'en Banya for five minutes to provide passengers with photo opportunities.

Ferrocarril de Sóller
C/Eusebio Estada 1 (Palma 971 75 20 51/ Sóller 971 63 01 30/www.sollernet.com).
Tickets €6.50 single, €11 return.
No credit cards. Map p53 E1.

Palma to Sóller *Mar-Oct* 8am, 10.50am*, 12.15pm*, 1.30pm, 3.10pm, 7.30pm daily. *Nov-Feb* 8am, 10.50am*, 1.05pm, 3.10pm, 7.30pm daily.
Sóller to Palma *Mar-Oct* 7am, 9.10am, 10.50am, 12.15pm, 2pm, 6.30pm (also 7pm Sat, Sun) daily. *Nov-Feb* 7am, 9.10am, 11.50am, 2.10pm, 6.20pm daily.

Eduardo Chillida, Henry Moore, Andreu Alfaro and Barbara Hepworth. The dynamic central piece by Xavier Corberó was created for Bartomeu March's residence in Cala Ratjada, with its dramatically positioned garden swooping down towards the sea, and loses a little of its impact in its new home.

The ground floor of the building houses some fascinating temporary exhibitions (in 2005 these included one exploring the relationship between Freud's ideas and Dali's), but the real highlight is the vast 18th-century Neopolitan nativity scene. Fantastically detailed, with scores of angels suspended overhead, the figures include three very varied and minutely observed retinues for the Three Kings, encompassing many ethnic groups and their respective forms of dress.

On the first floor are collections showing the skill and artistry of Mallorcan cartographers, regarded as among the best in the world in medieval times. Of equal interest are the murals of Catalan painter Josep Maria Sert (1874-1945), an artist whose public work tended towards the religious, as shown in the representations of Audacity, Reason, Inspiration and Work above the staircase, while his private work often reflected his love of circus and the music hall – as here with the gaily painted ceiling in the music room.

Santa Eulàlia

Plaça Santa Eulàlia 2 (971 71 46 25). **Open** times of services. **Admission** free. **Map** p53 D3.

You might not guess it from the outside, but Santa Eulàlia was one of the first churches to be built following the Christian conquest of Mallorca in 1229. A heavy-handed late 19th-century renovation altered the façade and added the belltower, but otherwise it's a remarkably harmonious 13th century Gothic structure – the only one on the island (other than the cathedral) to have a nave flanked by two aisles. Like the cathedral, it's airy and spacious within, and would undoubtedly be light were not most of the windows bricked up. As it is, the interior appears something of a symphony in grey until your eyes adjust to the gloom. Fifteen chapels run along the walls of the nave and round the apse. Most contain doom-laden baroque works – exceptions are the first on the right (as you face the altar), which features a delicate Gothic Flemish-style depiction of four saints, and the third on the left, which holds a similarly subtle Death of the Virgin.

Sant Francesc

Plaça Sant Francesc 7 (971 71 26 95). **Open** 9.30am-12.30pm, 3.30-6pm Mon-Sat; 9.30am-12.30pm Sun. **Admission** €1. **No credit cards. Map** p53 E3. **Photo** *p60.*

The largely blank façade of what was wealthy medieval Palma's church of choice is not at all what you'd expect fronting a late 13th-century Gothic structure. And when you learn that lightning damage caused the façade to be completely rebuilt in the baroque 17th century, its plainness seems even more anachronistic though the elaborate rose window and exuberant doorway do, perhaps, give the game away. It's also disconcertingly asymmetrical, with the left-hand side extending further than the right. Perhaps it's appropriate, though, that the statue standing to the left of the door is of the mercilessly severe and ascetic missionary Junipero Serra (and a Native American boy), who founded many of the missions that would become the major cities of southern California in the 18th century while attempting to convert the native population to Catholicism (*see p172* **Local heroes**).

To enter the church outside service times you have to pass through the convent to the right of the basilica, buy a ticket from the porter and turn left into the lovely 14th-century Gothic cloister, which is often filled with the chatter of the children at the attached school. Another left turn at the end of the cloister brings you into the Stygian darkness of the church. Hit the 'Illuminación del Retablo' switch on the right as you enter and you'll at last be able to gasp at the huge, overblown (even for the baroque) altarpiece. It's a tangle of gilt, polychrome statues and turquoise marbling, centred around a statue of St Francis (by Jaume Blanquer) flanked by Santa Clara and Santa Catalina. It's very difficult, however, to make out much detail in most of the 20 chapels spread around the nave and apse of the single-nave church. One of the better-lit is the first on the left behind the altarpiece. It contains the rather curious tomb of the theologian, poet, linguist and preacher Ramón Llull, one of Mallorca's most celebrated sons (*see p20* **Local heroes**). Llull's effigy is positioned high on the right-hand wall and turned on its side, as if it's about to topple to the floor.

Plaça Major & Centre

If you are following the walk marked on pages 52-53, you'll find that if you stroll up C/Carnisseria you'll come to Plaça Salvador Coll and, to the right, the pedestrianised shopping street C/Sindicat. To the left along C/Bosseria is a conjunction of narrow streets at Plaça Marquès de Palmer, where two of the city's finest *modernista* buildings sit side by side: private residence **Can Rei** and former department store **L'Aguila**. Both date from the first decade of the 20th century; the former is the more flamboyant and sinuous (in the style of *modernisme*'s greatest exponent, Antoni Gaudí), the latter more geometrically patterned in the manner of Gaudí's contemporary Puig i Cadafalch. The top half of Can Rei's five storeys drips with multi-hued ceramic mosaic and flower motifs, and features a corner gallery and a two-storey hanging balcony decorated with a fierce-looking face flanked by two dragons. L'Aguila's olive-painted metal frame, expanses of glass and fluid balconies give way to a more extravagant structure as it rises. Red, green and white brickwork run up either side, and a huge arched window is topped with gilded and polychrome floral designs and metal spikes.

There are more shopping opportunities in the tangle of meandering streets (many pedestrianised) south-west of here leading off C/Jaume II.

Although arcaded **Plaça Major** has a certain superficial grandeur, it's actually disappointingly prosaic on closer inspection, and the haunt of mime artists (the sort who paint themselves green and then stand still), crooning hippies (the sort who belt out limp John Lennon covers) and cafés (the sort where you're ushered to a seat by over-pushy waiters). Still, the small handicrafts market held here most days is worth a look.

Leading north from Plaça Major, C/Sant Miquel is Palma's primary pedestrianised artery. Here you'll find shops aplenty, as well as the **Museu d'Art Espanyol Contemporani** (Museum of Contemporary Spanish Art; *see p67*) and the nearby ancient church of **Sant Miquel** (C/Sant Miquel 21, 971 71 54 55, open 8am-1.30pm, 5-7.30pm Mon-Sat, 10am-12.30pm, 6-8pm Sun, free); particularly charming in the morning when the light falls through the rose window. Just north of here, the lovely little arcaded 18th-century oval courtyard of the church and hospital of **Sant Antoni** at No.30 is used as an exhibition space (hours vary).

Just past Sant Antoni, Plaça Olivar opens up to the right. Here you'll find central Palma's huge main food market, the **Mercat d'Olivar**, housed in a bright, airy new building. While it has had a lot of the character revamped out of it, and now feels like a giant, odour-free supermarket, complete with cashpoints and signposts, it does at least serve its purpose with efficiency.

Towards C/Sant Miquel's northern end, Plaça Porta Pintada branches off right and fans out into thoroughly prosaic **Plaça d'Espanya**, adorned only by an equestrian statue of Jaume I, conqueror of Moorish Mallorca in 1229. This utterly undistinguished modern square is essentially a transport hub, containing a clutch of bus stops and Palma's two stations (one for the **Ferrocarril de Sóller** – *see p64* **All aboard!** – and the other for services to Inca).

Running west from Plaça Porta Pintada is another wide pedestrianised shopping street, C/Oms, which eventually hits the Rambla dels Ducs de Palma de Mallorca at an angle. La Rambla apes its more famous counterpart in Barcelona in style, with a central strolling boulevard lined with plane trees and flower stalls, if not in liveliness (or length).

At the southern end of the Rambla, the road sweeps round to the right in front of the hill crowned by Plaça Major to emerge in narrow

Plaça Weyler, dominated by the majestic **Gran Hotel**. Designed by the Catalan architect Lluis Domènech i Muntaner, this was both Palma's first luxury hotel and the city's first *modernista* building when it opened in 1903. Despite its structural and decorative richness, polychrome ceramics, floral stonework and flowing ironwork, it's a highly disciplined work with not a touch of whimsy. It closed as a hotel in 1942 and is now home to the **Fundació La Caixa** (*see p67*).

There's more evidence of *modernisme* opposite the Gran Hotel in the façade of the little **Forn des Teatre** pâtisserie – a great place to pick up a *bocadillo* or an *ensaimada* – and on the conjoined Plaça Mercat, where stand two matching *modernista* buildings, **Casas Cassayas**, commissioned in 1908 by Josep Cassayas.

C/Unió continues westwards from here, past **Can Balaguer**. Commissioned by the first Marquis of Reguer in the first half of the 18th century, this was the largest mansion in the city, before being bought and partitioned by the Blanes family of merchants in the 19th century.

Further along is the pivotal **Plaça Rei Joan Carles I**. Locals and tourists congregate at the outdoor tables at long-established Bar Bosch (*see p75*) to catch up on the papers and indulge in some prime people-watching. Heading south from here in the direction of the sea is another tree-lined Rambla-like street, **Passeig des Born**, presided over by stone sphinxes and long Palma's premier promenading spot.

Just north of the passeig, on C/Sant Jaume, is the 14th- to 16th-century church of **Sant Jaume** (C/Sant Jaume 10, 971 72 43 75, open 11am-1.30pm, 5.30-8.30pm Mon-Fri, 11.30am-1.30pm, 5.30-9.30pm Sat, 9.30am-1.30pm, 7-9.30pm Sun, free), one of Palma's original four parish churches.

Running parallel to C/Sant Jaume is C/Concepció, worth a stroll for its eighth-century fountain – the awkwardly restored **Font del Sepulcre**, and the **Sa Nostra** exhibition space opposite (C/Concepció 12, 971 72 52 10, open 10.30am-9pm Mon-Fri, 10.30am-1.30pm Sat, free). As well as occasionally interesting exhibitions, it has a peaceful terrace-café on the first floor, open for lunch only.

Facing the Born, on the corner of C/Cifre, is **Can Solleric**, now a gallery showing temporary exhibitions (Passeig des Born 27, 971 72 20 92, open 10am-2pm, 5-9pm Tue-Sat, 10am-2pm Sun, free). Dating from 1763, this graceful mansion, with its five-arched loggia, is unusual in Palma in being a new construction (rather than being built on earlier foundations).

Discover Palma's past at **Castel de Bellver**. *See p71.*

Fundació La Caixa

Plaça Weyler 3 (971 17 85 00/www.fundacio. lacaixa.es). **Open** 10am-9pm Tue-Sat; 10am-2pm Sun. **Admission** free. **Map** p53 D2.

Run by the cultural foundation of the La Caixa savings bank, the former Gran Hotel now houses an exhibition space, café and bookshop specialising in design, travel and designer travel. Programming is organised in conjunction with the foundation's headquarters in Barcelona and, given the state of La Caixa's coffers, is normally excellent. On permanent display is a collection of important works, including vast, riotous oil paintings, by Catalan *modernista* Hermen Anglada Camarasa. Temporary shows often explore links between *modernisme* and other 20th-century movements in art, architecture and design.

Museu d'Art Espanyol Contemporani

C/Sant Miquel 11 (971 71 35 15). **Open** 10am-6.30pm Mon-Fri; 10.30am-2pm Sat. **Admission** free. **Map** p53 E2.

The Museum of Contemporary Spanish Art offers a potted history of 20th-century Spanish art, with 70 paintings from the March Collection representing 52 different artists. The Mallorcan financier Joan March Ordinas set up the March Foundation in 1955 to promote science and culture, and this elegant 18th-century mansion (where March was born) has been home to paintings and sculptures from the Foundation's modern Spanish collection since 1990. It was extended in 1996, and again in 2003, and now offers a pristine setting in which to brush up on the finer points of Spanish art over the last century.

Although the collection begins with works by the biggest names (Miró, Gris, Dalí and an important early painting by Picasso, *Tête de Femme*, from 1907), the focus is on four post-war movements: Dau al Set (Barcelona, 1948-53), Grupo Parpalló (Valencia, 1956-61), El Paso (Madrid, 1957-60) and the Grupo de Cuenca (Cuenca, 1960s). Many of the Dau al Set artists (such as Antoni Tàpies and Modest Cuixart) started out working in a 'magical realist' or surrealist style and evolved towards abstract expressionism. The Grupo Parpalló attempted to offer an alternative to formalist abstraction by reviving a more analytical, aesthetic style of abstraction (Eusebio Sempere's lovely *Four Seasons* is a fine example). El Paso artists, like Manuel Rivera and Manuel Millares, in contrast, were far more informal and dramatic in style. Some of them later joined with Fernando Zóbel, Gerardo Rueda and Gustavo Tomer to create the diverse Museo de Arte Abstracto Español, also run by the March Foundation, within the dramatically sited 'hanging houses' of Cuenca (between Valencia and Madrid). All in all it's a challenging, largely abstract collection, but enjoyable for anyone with an interest in 20th-century Spanish art. The museum also has excellent temporary exhibitions.

Palma

Es Puig de Sant Pere & Sa Llotja

The south-west quarter of the old town, stretching south of Avinguda Jaume III and west of the Passeig des Born and Passeig Antoni Maura, is one of the city's most atmospheric and appealing, containing both central Palma's main restaurant and bar area and quiet residential streets little altered in centuries. The higher part is known as **Es Puig de Sant Pere** (St Peter's Mount), and climbs up to the church of **Santa Creu** (one of Christian Palma's first four churches; C/San Lorenzo 4, 971 71 26 90, open Sept-June 10.30-11.30am, 6.30-7.30pm Mon-Fri, 6.30-7.30pm Sat, July, Aug 7.30-8.30pm daily, free) and the mighty 16th-century Renaissance **Bastió de Sant Pere**, now home to contemporary art museum **Es Baluard** (*see p70* **Es Baluard**).

Immediately west of here are the narrow streets and squares of the area known informally as **Sa Llotja** (or La Lonja in Castilian – meaning 'Exchange'), containing a wealth of bars and restaurants. The name comes from the magnificent 15th-century turreted building that faces the sea close by. Sa Llotja is the masterpiece of Mallorcan architect Guillem Sagrera (who also worked on the cathedral) and the high point in Mallorcan Gothic architecture. Commissioned by the Guild of Merchants as a commercial exchange, it was constructed between 1426 and 1448 and combines elegance with practicality. Light pours in through the huge windows, while six delicate spiralling columns (linking up to ribbing in the vaults and often compared to palm trees) provide for a spacious, uncluttered interior. The building is now used for temporary art exhibitions (and is closed to the public at other times).

Almost adjacent to it is the **Consolat de Mar**, founded in the 14th century as a centre for dealing with legal issues concerning maritime trade. The current building is 17th-century and is now the HQ of the Balearic Government.

As the Passeig des Born heads towards the sea, it changes name to Avinguda Antoni Maura (named after the Palma-born five-time Prime Minister of Spain during the first three decades of the 20th century). Alongside the road run the shady **Jardins de s'Hort del Rei**, once part of the Almudaina palace.

Your view of them might well be obscured by hoardings. At the time of writing, a massive construction project was underway to create a greatly enlarged car park under the Parc de la Mar, which will, hopefully, ease Palma's chronic parking problems. Expect disruption until at least the end of 2006.

Passeig Marítim to Gènova

The multi-lane Avinguda Gabriel Roca (more popularly known as the **Passeig Marítim**) sweeps along Palma's harbourfront. Once you've negotiated your way across the traffic, you can enjoy the waterfront walk and cycle track that follows the harbour edge past the ferry pier, the luxury yachts in the marina, a clutch of cool cafés, fishermen mending their nets, and, in the early mornings, a daily fish auction. If you want to get out on the water, Cruceros Marco Polo operates hour-long boat trips around the harbour from close to the foot of the ferry pier (mobile 659 63 67 75, trips at 11am, 1pm, 2pm, 3pm & 4pm Mon-Sat, €9, €5 concessions, free under-12s).

Inland from here, and west of the Bastió de Sant Pere, is the grid plan district of **Santa Catalina**, an area devoid of tourists but packed with good bars and restaurants; head here in the evening to eat and drink with the locals. The district's hub is the **Mercat Santa Catalina**, a fine food market.

Immediately south of Santa Catalina, sandwiched between C/Sant Magi and the Passeig Marítim, is the tiny district of **Es Jonquet**, a characterful tangle of little lanes and low houses that brings to mind Granada's Albaicín. There are a few places to sup here, particularly around the central Plaça del Vapor, plus a handful of restored windmills overlooking the marina.

West of Santa Catalina is the weird **Poble Espanyol** (*see p71*), an enjoyably tacky scaled-down re-creation of famous Spanish buildings.

More compelling, though, is the impressive **Castell de Bellver** (Bellver Castle; *see p71*), crowning a hill on the west side of Palma. You can drive up here, but there's no public transport and the castle is a good half-hour's walk from the cathedral, the latter part of which is steeply uphill (504 steps lead up to the castle). It's worth the effort, though: the views over the city from the castle are wondrous, and the **Museu d'Història de la Ciutat** (City History Museum) within is well worth a look.

Below the castle, the area known as **El Terreny** is currently one of the seediest parts of town though it was once the most fashionable nightlife district in Palma. As the city continues its inexorable rise it's entirely possible that history will come full circle and that within a few years El Terreny will again be the place to be seen after dark.

Further west around the bay from the castle is the workaday suburb of **Gènova** (about five kilometres/three miles from the old town), home to the **Coves de Gènova** (*see p71*), the **Fundació Pilar i Joan Miró** (*see p71*) and a number of good restaurants (*see p72*).

Es Baluard

'Palma' and 'art' are not two words commonly seen in the same sentence. Or, rather, they weren't until the last couple of years. True, the city has been home since 1990 to the 20th-century Spanish art collection of the Museu d'Art Espanyol Contemporani (*see p67*), but it has only been the opening of the Palau March's sculpture collection (*see p62*) and, particularly, the unveiling of the superb **Es Baluard, Museu d'Art Modern i Contemporani de Palma** in 2004 that have firmly placed the Mallorcan capital on the map for lovers of modern art.

The origins of the project were in 1997, when businessman Pere Serra offered to donate works from his collection to a new museum. Palma City Council, the Mallorca Island Council and the Balearic Government joined together to provide further works and to fund the development of the old Renaissance defences of the **Bastió de Sant Pere**, overlooking the marina, to house the collection.

Serra's collection of 20th-century art forms the core of the museum's permanent collection. The displays start with

Mediterranean landscape painting of the early 20th century, including works by artists with connections to the island, such as Joan Miró and Santiago Rusiñol (who wrote *Majorca: The Island of Calm*). In truth, much of it isn't particularly distinguished.

More interesting is the series of female portraits and nudes from around 1910 to the 1970s, which includes fine works by Kees van Dongen and Mallorcan artist Juli Ramis (there's also a Picasso and a Magritte). There then follows an examination of abstraction, with paintings by COBRA group artists Karel Appel and Asger Jorn of particular interest.

In addition to the permanent collection, there's always a temporary exhibition. A recent highlight was the retrospective of Icelandic artist Erró's often highly political, pop art-influenced work.

However, in truth, the main reason for visiting Es Baluard is for the building rather than the art it contains. It's a stunner. A team of architects that included Luis and Jaime García Ruiz, Vicente Tomás and Ángel Sánchez-Cantalejo have brilliantly incorporated the old fortifications within a thoroughly contemporary structure. It's a cool, soothing, harmonious blending of old stone, glass and white concrete. The three-storey structure incorporates the old cistern that once supplied water to boats in the port of Palma, and each level is connected by interior balconies, skylights and ramps. The linking of interior and exterior spaces is particularly clever, with the roof featuring wonderful sight lines and a walkway around the perimeter that allows visitors to fully appreciate the structure and purpose of the original fortifications.

Even if you don't want to go inside, don't pass by the chance to have a coffee or snack at the classy museum café; there are fine views from its wide stone terrace.

After the cathedral, this is the one 'sight' you should find time to see in Palma.

Es Baluard, Museu d'Art Modern i Contemporani de Palma

Plaça Porta Santa Catalina s/n (971 90 82 00/www.esbaluard.org). **Open** *Mid June-Sept* 10am-11pm Tue-Sun. *Oct-mid June* 10am-8pm Tue-Sun. **Admission** €6; €4.50 concessions. **Credit** AmEx, DC, MC, V. **Map** p52 B3.

Castell de Bellver & Museu d'Història de la Ciutat

C/Camilo José Cela s/n (971 73 06 57). **Open** *Apr-Sept* 8am-8.30pm Mon-Sat; 10am-7pm Sun. *Oct-Mar* 8am-8pm Mon-Sat; 10am-5pm Sun. Museum closed Sun. **Admission** €2; €1 concessions. **No credit cards. Map** p50 U9. **Photo** *p67.*

Erected on the 'Puig de sa Mesquida' (hill of the mosque) in the first decade of the 14th century by Jaume II as a royal residence, this unusual castle retains its original design (the only modifications were made in the 16th century to allow it to take artillery). It's essentially circular, with a two-storey galleried central courtyard. The castle was rarely used as a royal home, and from the 18th century was employed as a military prison (graffiti on the walls attests to its long use as such). It now houses the Despuig Collection of Classical Sculpture (acquired in the 18th century by Cardinal Despuig when he lived in Rome), the chapel of Sant Marc and the excellent City History Museum, which tells the story of Palma from prehistoric times to the present day.

Coves de Gènova

C/Barranc 45 (971 40 23 87). **Open** *July-Sept* 10am-1.30pm, 4-7pm Mon-Sat. *Oct-June* 10.30am-1pm, 4-6pm Mon-Sat. **Admission** €7; €3 concessions. **No credit cards. Photo** *p73.*

Guides take small groups down to a depth of 36 metres (118 feet) in these caves, discovered in 1906. If you have been to any of the east coast caves, these more modest caverns probably won't impress, but they have the advantage of not heaving with coach parties. Tours last about 40 minutes.

Fundació Pilar i Joan Miró

C/Joan de Saridakis 29, Cala Major (971 70 14 20/ www.a-palma.es/fpjmiro). Bus 6. **Open** *Mid May-mid Sept* 10am-7pm Tue-Sat; 10am-3pm Sun. *Mid Sept-mid May* 10am-6pm Tue-Sat; 10am-3pm Sun. **Admission** €4.80; free-€2.60 concessions. **No credit cards. Photo** *p74.*

Though born in Catalonia, Joan Miró was always intimately connected to Mallorca. His mother was from the island, he spent many childhood holidays here and married a native, Pilar Juncosa, before permanently settling at Son Abrines, near Cala Major (just west of Palma) in 1956 at the age of 63. Here you'll find the three main buildings that make up the Pilar and Joan Miró Foundation, two of which are interesting in themselves as rare examples of modern architecture in Palma.

Miró commissioned his old friend, the architect Josep Lluís Sert, to design a studio for him, and the result, the Sert Studio (completed in 1955), is supposedly a synthesis of Mediterranean materials and techniques in harmony with its environment; it was a milestone in Sert's architectural career. However, the uninitiated have to take this on trust – it looks more like a light industrial unit. More interesting is the interior, which is filled with unfinished canvases and gives an insight into the way Miró worked, often on a number of pieces simultaneously.

The second of the Foundation's buildings is Son Boter, a late 17th-century *possessió* (country house) that Miró bought in 1959 and used to work on extra large works and sculptures. Today, both studios are employed as venues for a range of courses, special projects and other pedagogic purposes.

In 1986, after Miró's death (in 1983), his wife determined to create an exhibition space and cultural centre in which to exhibit her late husband's work. She sold a few Miró gouaches and commissioned Rafael Moneo to build the low-rise, horizontal-lined structure that now provides the Foundation's headquarters. It opened in 1992 and displays a rotating (though often disappointingly limited) selection from the Foundation's 5,000 works, as well as some impressive temporary exhibitions from other artists (a recent highlight was a show of works by Louise Bourgeois).

Poble Espanyol

C/Poble Espanyol s/n (971 73 70 75). Bus 5 (to Son Dureta Hospital). **Open** *May-Oct* 9am-7pm daily. *Nov-Apr* 9am-6pm daily. **Admission** €5; €3 concessions. **No credit cards. Map** p50 U/V8.

Opened in 1967, the 'Spanish Village' was designed by the architect Fernando Chueca Goitia as an open-air architectural museum-cum-theme park. The idea was to reproduce many of the classic buildings of Spain in one place. Thus, visitors enter through the Bisagra Door (Toledo), passing Madrid's Hermitage of St Anthony on their right and the Alhambra's Patio of the Arrayanes (Granada) on their left before skirting around the church of Torralba de Ribota (Zaragoza) to reach the generic main square. Sound tacky? Well, it is (and the piped muzak floating from ubiquitous speakers doesn't help), yet it's also rather fun, particularly for kids, and some of the buildings are fairly convincing. Having recently changed ownership, the Poble has lost its quirky museums and artisans' workshops to an increasingly commercial selection of shops, bars and restaurants.

Portitxol & Ciutat Jardí

If you walk east along the harbourside from the cathedral, within 15 minutes you'll come to the hippest port on the Bay of Palma. **Portitxol** is unabashedly up-and-coming, friendly and peopled by a young, sophisticated crowd. It's the old fishing quarter and has retained its villagey feel, with old single- and double-storey fishermen's cottages lining a coast that alternates between narrow strips of sand and rocks. Sea-facing fish restaurants and cafés offer everything from designer restaurants to local *chiringuitos*. If you are staying in Palma, lunch or dinner here is a must.

As part of the makeover of Portitxol the seafront has been beautified and the walk from here to Ciutat Jardí – about 20 minutes – is lovely. Do as trendy locals do and stop at the small scallop-shaped beach east of the Hotel Portixol, known affectionately as **Es Portitxolet**. Fringed by rock pools and backed by wild olive trees, it's ideal for a little late afternoon sunbathing before a cocktail and a spot of tapas at one of the area's many bars prior to heading out for dinner around 10pm.

Further along, **Ciutat Jardí** is where Mallorcan families and laid-back groups of friends go to catch the rays. The beach's calm, clear waters make it ideal for kids and there's no shortage of beachfront cafés offering pizzas and sandwiches, cold beers and jugs of sangria.

Where to eat & drink

Culinarily speaking, Palma ranks highly compared with many Spanish cities, with an impressive number of high quality restaurants. There is a wide choice, too, from spit-and-sawdust establishments serving simple tapas to traditional Mallorcan restaurants and stylish modern eateries with prices to match. You'll also find a smattering of decent international restaurants including Chinese, Japanese, Indian and Thai.

Palma has a thriving café society, which takes in the opulence of the modern Cappuccino chain and atmospheric old places where the artists and intellectuals of Palma society once met – and where city workers and tourists now sip on their hot chocolates and nibble their *ensaimadas*.

In terms of food and drink, the city centre can be broadly divided into four distinct areas: **Sa Llotja** (west of the Palau de l'Almudaina) where you'll find the highest concentration of bars and pubs; **Centre**, which includes some of the more traditional restaurants in the streets of the old town and around Plaça Joan Carles I; **Santa Catalina** (west of the old city walls), with some of the best new restaurants and a favourite with locals; and **Passeig Marítim** (running along the harbourside), which is generally touristy, but has a few gems.

If you are in Palma for just a couple of days, you'll spend most of your time in and around these areas, but if you are staying longer you may wish to explore some of the outlying districts, including the harbour at **Portixol**, with its tiny marina and clutch of excellent restaurants, and **Gènova**, which lies in the hills on the city's west side and contains a number of good eateries.

Sa Llotja

Sa Llotja (or, in Castilian, La Lonja), named after the former stock exchange that dominates the square of the same name, is a clutch of streets stretching back from the seafront up to C/Jaume III and flanked on the east by Passeig des Born and on the west by the Passeig de Mallorca. Despite being the most touristy district of Palma, it offers up a number of superb restaurants, tapas bars and cafés.

Aramis
C/Montenegro 1 (971 72 52 32). **Open** 1-3.30pm, 8-11pm Mon-Fri; 8-11pm Sat. **Average** €€€€. **Credit** AmEx, MC, V. **Map** p52 C3.
This sophisticated yet relaxed restaurant offers a sleek, modern setting for first-rate international food with an Italian leaning. Starters are along the lines of beef carpaccio or an ethereally light, cappuccino-like caramelised onion soup with a single prawn. Move on to one of the pastas and risottos – including a delicate ravioli of chicken with saffron sauce – or something from the handful of fish dishes (such as bream with a red pepper sauce) or meat main courses (duck breast with potato gratin and date gravy is particularly good). The €13 lunch *menú* makes for a reasonably priced treat.

Es Baluard
Plaça Port de Santa Catalina 9 (971 71 96 09). **Open** 1-3.30pm, 8.30-11pm Mon-Sat. **Average** €€€. **Credit** AmEx, MC, V. **Map** p52 B2/B3.
From the same owners as the excellent Can Amer in Inca, Es Baluard specialises in traditional Mallorcan dishes. The decor is ineffably cool, with the restaurant done out like a typical Mallorcan kitchen, with big, brightly coloured plates, chunky furniture and earthy tones. The food is all market-fresh and served in a modern, uncluttered style. Try the *champiñones con mariscos* (mushrooms stuffed with seafood) and any lamb dish. The wine list is pretty impressive.

Bon Lloc
C/Sant Feliu 7 (971 71 86 17). **Open** 1-4pm Mon-Sat. Closed mid Aug-early Sept. **Average** €€. **Credit** MC, V. **Map** p52 C3.
Trading on its position as Palma's most established veggie restaurant, Bon Lloc charges a hefty €12 for its set lunch (there is no à la carte) of standard meat-free fare – carrot soup or lentil soup, courgette quiche or spinach tart and so on. Puddings are more creative and might include kefir with baked apple or a banana millefeuille. Service can be slightly frosty.

La Bóveda
C/Boteria 3 (971 72 00 26). **Open** 1-4pm, 8.30pm-midnight Mon-Sat. **Average** €€. **Credit** AmEx, DC, MC, V. **Map** p52 C3.
A hugely popular old tapas joint in the heart of touristville Sa Llotja, but the locals know it's too good to leave to visitors. With its rough stone floor, high ceiling (with lazily rotating fans), patterned wall tiles and galleried wine bodega, there's no shortage of character. Try a classic Mallorcan *pa amb oli*: the rich brown *pa mallorquí* is doused in olive oil, sprinkled with salt and rubbed with toma-

Playing with fire at **Plaça de Sa LLotja.**
See p69.

to – simple, perfect. There's also excellent seafood, the *fabes con almejas* (butter beans with clams) is a soupy, savoury delight, the *jamón* is as good as any you'll find in Palma (and so popular that one member of staff is employed solely to cut it), and house Rioja is a steal.

Caballito de Mar

Passeig Sagrera 5 (971 72 10 74). **Open** *July-Sept* 1-4pm, 8pm-midnight daily. *Oct-June* 1-4pm, 8pm-midnight Tue-Sun. **Average** €€€€. **Credit** AmEx, DC, MC, V. **Map** p52 C4.

A top fish restaurant in a great spot beside Plaça Sa Llotja and over the road from the harbour. It's formal, and certainly not cheap, but if you are after superb seafood dishes in an idyllic setting, it's worth the splurge. It's difficult to know what to choose – oysters or langoustines to start, or a towering *paradilla de mariscos*. As a main, you might want to try *lubina al sal* (sea bass in salt), *caldereta de llagosta* (spiny lobster stew) or paella. If it's warm, you can sit outside on the *terraza*.

Café d'es Casal Solleric

Passeig des Born 27 (971 72 61 22). **Open** 7am-3am daily. **Average** €. **Credit** AmEx, MC, V. **Map** p52 C3.

Smart office workers choose to meet in this small modern café attached to the art gallery at the top end of the street. There are croissants and *ensaimadas* for breakfast, along with excellent coffee, and *bocadillos* are available throughout the day.

Café Lírico

Avda. Antoni Maura 6 (971 72 11 25). **Open** 7am-midnight Mon-Sat. **Average** €. **No credit cards**. **Map** p52 C3/C4.

Don't be put off by the garish pictures of pizza outside – this is one of the city's oldest and most congenial meeting places. Inside it seems like little has changed since the 1920s (probably because it hasn't), with marble-topped round tables, old wooden chairs and big mirrors on the walls. This is where Deià's artistic community once met and where *palmesanos* of all ages still meet for a coffee. There's a *terraza* outside with views of the Almudaina palace.

Café La Lonja

C/Llotja del Mar 2 (971 72 27 99). **Open** 9.30am-1am Mon-Thur; 9.30am-3am Fri, Sat. Closed mid Dec-early Jan. **Average** €. **Credit** AmEx, MC, V. **Map** p52 C3.

This lovely, relaxed bar across from Sa Llotja is actually a very convincing fake – its *modernista* flourishes, dark wood fittings, revolving doors and luggage racks were actually put together 20 or so years ago. Still, it's a cosy spot to nurse a daytime *café con leche* or a night-time glass of wine. There's also a good range of tapas and *garrotins* (small, thin *bocadillos*).

Ca'n Carlos

C/Aigua 5 (971 71 38 69). **Open** 1-4pm, 8-11pm Mon-Sat. Closed 2wks Aug. **Average** €€. **Credit** AmEx, MC, V. **Map** p52 C2.

Miró's masterpieces at **Fundació Pilar i Joan Miró**. *See p71.*

For Mallorcan cuisine both traditional and creative, served in a civilised setting by agreeably old-school waiters, you can't better Ca'n Carlos. The menu is admirably short – start, perhaps, with a huge portion of earthy *sepias* (cuttlefish) cooked with *sobrassada* or broad bean stew, before sinking your teeth into a choice steak; turbot with *arròs negre* or aubergine stuffed with monkfish. A reassuring proportion of the clientele are locals.

La Cueva

C/Apuntadors 5 (971 72 44 22). **Open** noon-midnight Mon-Sat. Closed Feb. **Average** €. **Credit** AmEx, DC, MC, V. **Map** p52 C3.
A bright traditional tapas restaurant with *jamones* hanging from the ceiling, a stuffed bull's head on the wall and a fug of cigarette smoke. Specialities include *albóndigas* (meatballs), *riñones al jerez*, grilled sardines and rabbit stew with onions.

El Pilón

C/Cifre 4 (971 71 75 90). **Open** noon-midnight Mon-Sat. **Average** €€. **Credit** AmEx, DC, MC, V. **Map** p52 C2.
Another excellent tapas bar, just off the top end of Born, which is less smart than La Bóveda (*see p73*) but has a bewildering array of tapas on offer in a wonderful vault-like setting. You can watch it all

being prepared in the open kitchen. The seafood – *pulpo a la gallega, gambas, langostinos* – is particularly good and the prices are very reasonable too. Highly recommended.

Taberna La Bóveda

Passeig Sagrera 3 (971 71 48 63). **Open** 1.30-4pm, 8.30pm-midnight Mon-Sat. **Average** €€. **Credit** AmEx, DC, MC, V. **Map** p52 C4.
Bigger and brighter than its sister establishment on C/Boteria (*see p72*), this one has as its main draw a large terrace, wildly popular with the city's expat German population. The food is typical: *gambas al ajillo* (prawns with garlic), *jamón* and the very tasty *datiles con beicon* (dates wrapped in bacon), plus variations on *pa amb oli* (bread and oil). Prices are reasonable too.

Varadero

Moll Vell s/n (971 72 64 28). **Open** 9am-midnight Mon-Thur, Sun; 9am-2.30am Fri, Sat. **Average** €. **Credit** MC, V. **Map** p52 B5.
This is the place to meet for a pre-clubbing *copa* or two, where you can watch the sun set over the bay and enjoy a few plates of tapas. It's entirely surrounded by glass walls, giving views of the whole city, and on the cathedral side there's a terrace that juts into the sea. All-day opening means that

Varadero is popular for breakfast and lunch, and it transforms into a disco with good tunes on Friday and Saturday nights.

Xim's Bodeguita

Plaça de sa Llotja 3 (971 71 99 28). **Open** 11am-1am Mon-Thur, Sun; 11am-2am Fri, Sat. Closed Dec, Jan. **Average** €€. **Credit** MC, V. **Map** p52 C3.
One of a bunch of identikit tapas terraces on this square serving *pa amb oli* with ham, cheese or both; dates wrapped in bacon; *patatas bravas*; paellas and vats of sangria. It's a nice location, however, just in front of Sa Llotja, although it goes without saying that the clientele is 100% foreign.

Yate Rizz

Passeig des Born 2 (971 72 62 46). **Open** lunch Mon-Sat; phone for details. **Average** €. **No credit cards. Map** p52 C3.
To the horror of its highfalutin designer neighbours, the cheapest restaurant in Mallorca takes up prime real estate at the bottom of the Passeig des Born, just as it has for decades, since it attracted the likes of Errol Flynn. Get there as the doors open for a chance of beating Palma's grandmothers to the staggeringly cheap (€5.85) *menú del día*. A total gem.

Centre

This area runs east of Passeig des Born to the Avingudas and includes the old town, Plaça Major and the streets running off it up to Plaça Espanya. It's the oldest part of town, made up of tiny, winding streets, and full of little bars and simple restaurants where you can grab a tapa or a quick meal at a reasonable price; just don't expect anything too stylish or fancy.

S'Arc

Plaça del Banc de l'Oli 13 (971 71 17 20/www.sarc tapasyvinos.com). **Open** 9.30am-midnight Mon-Sat. **Average** €. **Credit** MC, V. **Map** p53 E2.
Clean and new-looking, despite its beams and painted wooden tables, S'Arc has keenly priced *bocadillos*, tapas and more substantial dishes such as duck with berries, cod with *alioli* and *greixonera de brosat* – a Mallorca grandmothers' favourite, similar to a baked cheesecake, with honey. There are plenty of decent wines available by the glass, a good €9 lunch *menú*, and, on Saturdays, a special *cocido* (a traditional, slow-cooked, *madrileño* stew).

Bar Bosch

Plaça Rei Joan Carles I 6 (971 71 22 28). **Open** 7am-2am Mon-Sat; 8am-2pm Sun. **Average** €. **No credit cards. Map** p52 C2.
Largely unchanged since it first opened in 1936, this is where *palmesanos* meet to talk politics and where tourists meet to people-watch. While the interior suffers from industrial lighting, its terrace is perennially popular and it can take an age to get served. Bar Bosch offers a limited range of reasonably priced tapas and *bocadillos*.

Bodega Bellver

C/Can Serinyà 2 (971 72 47 96). **Open** 7pm-midnight Mon-Sat. Closed Aug. **Average** €. **No credit cards. Map** p53 D2.
A diminutive and ancient bar, stuffed to the gunwhales with dusty bottles, football pennants and old wooden barrels, which somehow also manages to fit in a TV and a fruit machine. Peopled mainly by old men, it is nonetheless an unmissable and increasingly rare pocket of unreconstructed old Palma. Bellver serves meats and vegetables *a la plancha* (griddled).

El Burladero

C/Concepció 36 (971 71 34 59/www.burladero-restaurantes.com). **Open** 1-3.30pm, 8pm-midnight Mon-Sat; 8pm-midnight Sun. **Average** €. **Credit** MC, V. **Map** p52 C1/C2.
A great way to experience an authentic Spanish tapas bar without the ham and the smoke. As well as the cutesily painted wooden tables and chairs, it wants for nothing in the way of folkloric decor, but the music is downtempo and the atmosphere relaxed. Traditional tapas are here in spades, but best are the small earthenware bowls filled with green beans and ham or chicken with mushrooms, cumin, garlic and onion, all served with robust *mallorquí* bread.

Café Colonial

C/Palau Reial 3 (971 72 68 04). **Open** 7am-7pm Mon-Fri; 7am-3pm Sat. **Average** €. **No credit cards. Map** p53 D3.
Not especially atmospheric, this modern café is nonetheless usefully situated just up from the cathedral, offering a wide selection of coffees and teas along with *empanadas*, *bocadillos* and salads.

Café del Gran Hotel

Plaça Weyler 3 (971 72 80 77). **Open** *June-Aug* 9am-10pm Mon-Sat; 9am-2pm Sun. *Sept-May* 9am-9pm Mon-Sat; 9am-2pm Sun. **Average** €. **Credit** MC, V. **Map** p53 D2.
While its spartan bar and restaurant are at odds with the *modernista* splendour of the exterior of the Gran Hotel, its terrace is a nice spot for lunch, particularly in spring when the Judas trees are in blossom. As well as fancy tapas (tempura of langoustine and garlic shoots) there are main courses such as linguini with courgettes and gorgonzola, and chicken with aubergine ravioli.

Café Isla de Palma

C/Oms 32 (971 72 21 19). **Open** 8.30am-9.30pm Mon-Sat. **Average** €. **Credit** AmEx, DC, MC, V. **Map** p53 D1.
This Palma institution can be found on a pedestrianised street about ten minutes' walk north of Plaça Major. It's a tiny, unpretentious café-cum-pub, festooned with plant pots outside and tiny paintings of Palma inside. Within its cosy confines you can enjoy a pint of Guinness, Haagen Dazs ice-cream, excellent coffee and a slice of cake. Though probably not all at the same time.

Ca'n Joan de s'Aigo

C/Ca'n Sanç 10 (971 71 07 59). **Open** 8am-9.15pm
Mon, Wed-Sun. **Average** €. **No credit cards.**
Map p53 E3.

This wonderful old café, tucked away on a side street
between Santa Eulàlia and Sant Francesc, is one of
Palma's hidden gems. With more than 300 years of
history, a pretty tiled floor, green glass chandeliers,
and a tinkling fountain in a plant-filled mini-patio,
the atmosphere's a treat – as are the home-made ice-
cream, hot chocolate, iced *horchata* (tiger nut milk)
and pastries. There is another branch on C/Baró
Santa Maria del Sepulcre (971 72 57 60).

Ca'n Miguel

Avda. Jaume III 6 (971 72 49 09). **Open** 9.30am-
9pm daily. **No credit cards.** Map p52 C2.

A wickedly irresistible selection of home-made and
preservative-free sorbets and ice-creams – including
chocolate with Ceylon tea, date, and, weirdly, roquefort; try the basil, rose of Alexandria and rosemary.
The almond biscuits are also made in house and are
the perfect accompaniment.

Cappuccino Sant Miquel

C/Sant Miquel 53 (971 71 97 64). **Open** *June-Sept*
8.20am-2am Mon-Sat; 8.20am-1am Sun. *Oct-May*
8.30am-10pm Mon-Fri; 8am-2am Sat, Sun.
Average €. Map p53 E1/E2.

This is the most attractive branch of this fashionable
café chain, set in a former 18th-century palace and
boasting original fittings and a lovely courtyard, redolent with orange blossom and with a tiled fountain in
the centre. It does a huge selection of coffees and a
range of sandwiches, salads and pastries; expect to
pay premium prices. At night, despite the serried
ranks of tables, it has a youthful, clubby atmosphere
and has recently released its own lounge CD.

Celler Sa Premsa

*Plaça Bisbe Berenguer de Palou 8 (971 72 35 99/
www.cellersapremsa.com)*. **Open** noon-4pm, 7.30-
11.30pm Mon-Sat. **Average** €. **Credit** AmEx, DC,
MC, V. **Map** p53 D1.

Sa Premsa's vast, high-ceilinged dining room, open
since 1958, is lined with huge wine barrels, strings
of garlic, ancient bull-fighting posters and old photos. It is much loved by tourists for its comprehensive (and comprehensible) list of classic *mallorquí*
dishes at rock-bottom prices.

La Cuchara

Passeig Mallorca 18 (971 71 00 00). **Open** 1.30-
4pm, 8pm-midnight daily. **Average** €€€. **Credit**
AmEx, DC, MC, V. **Map** p52 B2.

This unassuming place (at the bottom of an office
block at the top end of this busy street) has garnered
an enviable reputation among those in the know.
The owner, Peter Newman, used to run the very popular English restaurant Samantha's in Gènova, but
the emphasis here is on cuisine described as '*cocina
castellana* with an international influence'. The menu
includes starters such as *chistorra* – superb chorizo-
style sausage from the island – delicious *croquetas*

and one of the best *pulpo a feira* (octopus with paprika) you'll ever taste. For mains, try the *lubina* (sea
bass) or the rack of lamb, both of which are superb.

Making Tapas

C/Can Brondo 5 (971 72 00 42/www.errepunto.com).
Open *Tapas* 11.30am-midnight Mon-Sat. *Restaurant*
1-4pm, 8.30-11.30pm Mon-Sat. **Average** €€. **Credit**
MC, V. **Map** p52 D2.

Perfect for the linguistically challenged, here the tapas
chug past your eyes on a raised conveyor belt, sushi
style. Tiny tartlets of goat's cheese, mini chicken brochettes, *pintxos* of black pudding with a fried quail's
egg or foie gras with kiwi fruit: all are tallied up at
the end according to how many saucers you have.
Downstairs is a restaurant, similarly creative, where
you can expect to find the likes of duck with mango
sauce, and cod lasagne with idiazabal cheese gratin.

Montenegro

C/Montenegro 10 (971 72 89 57). **Open** 1-4pm,
8.30pm-12.30am Mon-Sat. **Average** €€. **Credit**
AmEx, DC, MC, V. **Map** p52 C3.

Split into two smart spaces (its vaulted stone basement is wonderfully cool in summer) with tangerine
tablecloths and white moulded chairs, Montenegro
offers one of the best all-in lunch deals (€10) in town.
Starters range from courgette and bacon risotto to
broccoli and roquefort soup, and mains from roast
turkey to seared tuna on a bed of bulgur wheat, red
onion and tomato with a basil vinaigrette. Puddings
are equally excellent, particularly the apple carpaccio with goat's cheese.

Orient Express

C/Llotja de Mar 6 (971 71 11 83). **Open** 1.30-4pm,
8pm-midnight Mon-Fri; 8pm-midnight Sat. Closed
Nov & Dec. **Average** €€. **Credit** AmEx, DC, MC, V.
Map p52 C3.

Charmingly decked out as a 1920s dining car, complete with battered leather suitcases, mahogany mirrors and luggage racks, Orient is primarily a crêperie,
although you can also order risotto, stroganoff and
an ostrich carpaccio. Crêpes are tasty and varied: the
Trans Alpine is ham, cheese and tomato; the Porreras
Express holds spinach, béchamel, ham and egg.

Es Parlament

C/Conquistador 11 (971 72 60 26). **Open** 1-4pm,
8-11pm Mon-Sat. **Average** €€€. **Credit** MC, V.
Map p53 D3.

An old favourite with Palma's politicos, due to its
location right by the government buildings. In a candlelit setting with gilded mirrors, huge chandeliers
and high ceilings, it lost a lot of its former starchi-
ness under new ownership, and now serves dishes
such as beetroot gazpacho, breaded monkfish with
spiced apple and anchovy purée, and banana tatin.

El Refectori

*C/Missió 7A (971 22 73 47/www.conventdelamissio.
com)*. **Open** 1-3.30pm, 8-10.30pm Mon-Fri; 8-10.30pm
Sat. **Average** €€€€. **Credit** AmEx, DC, MC, V.
Map p53 D1.

'Burger 'n' shake, *por favor*.' **Diner**.

This is one of the finest restaurants in town. It's part of the Hotel Convent de la Missió (*see p87*), so the design is minimalist, with a moody black and white backdrop of the salt mines of Ibiza across the back wall, water rushing down a granite screen, and a red rose on every table providing the only splash of colour. The creative cuisine is modern European with Spanish influences, and although it is at the top end of the price scale, the food is superb, as is the service.

Tast

C/Unió 28 (971 72 98 78). **Open** 12.30pm-1am Mon-Sat. **Average** €€. **Credit** DC, MC, V. **Map** p53 D2.
A great place for lunch, though bright lighting and loud Spanish pop make it less ideal for dinner. If you are hungry, try the *chuleton a la piedra* – a selection of meats cooked on a hot stone at your table. There's a solid selection of tapas, such as *pulpo a feira, gambas al ajillo* and *jamón*. Leave space for pud – the *tocino de cielo* (a type of crème caramel) and the banana and white chocolate mousse are particularly moreish.

Santa Catalina

Until recent years Santa Catalina was somewhat run-down and shabby, but it's now enjoying a renaissance, fuelled by the large number of bars and trendy restaurants that have sprung up. Bounded on the east by Avinguda de la Argentina and to the west by C/Joan Crespi, the heart of Santa Catalina is the market of the same name and the streets running off it, notably C/Fabrica, where most of the best restaurants are located, Carrers Pursiana and Pou, and Plaça Progres.

Diner

C/Sant Magi 23 (971 73 62 22). **Open** 6am-4am daily. **Average** €. **Credit** MC, V. **Map** p52 A3. **Photo** *left*
A shrine to all that is good about the US of A, with juicy burgers, BLTs, Dixieland chicken, New York strip, bagels, peanut butter and jelly sandwiches and apple pie just like Mom used to make. The decor is everything it should be, too: red leatherette banquettes; a 1954 Seeburg jukebox; chrome bar stools and enamelled '50s adverts. Expect queues even at the most ungodly hours, such is Diner's deserved popularity.

Fabrica 23

C/Fabrica 23 (971 45 31 25). **Open** 1-3.30pm, 9-11.30pm Tue-Sat. Closed 2wks Christmas. **Average** €€€. **Credit** AmEx, MC, V. **Map** p52 A2.
Another stripped-down, funky modern restaurant that fuses traditional Mallorcan cuisine with European influences for a predominantly young crowd, courtesy of British chef Alexei Tarsey. It's all delicious (we especially recommend the sweet pota to salad with asparagus, watercress and hazelnuts), and not overly pricey. The set lunch is good value.

Sa Faxina

Avda. Argentina 39 (971 45 44 23). **Open** 6.30pm-3.30am Mon-Fri; 7pm-3am Sat, Sun. **Average** €. **Credit** AmEx, DC, MC, V. **Map** p52 B2.
It feels like a cross between a low-key gentlemen's drinking club and a pub: dimly lit, wood-lined and mainly male. Sporting events are shown on TV when its not organising its own, and there's the odd themed fiesta on Thursday nights.

Sa Llimona

C/Sant Magi 80 (971 28 00 23). **Open** 8pm-midnight Mon-Fri, Sun; 8pm-12.30am Sat. **Average** €. **Credit** MC, V. **Map** p52 A3.
Sa Llimona is one of the best-known places in Palma for Mallorca's signature dish, *pa amb oli*, a peasant snack of coarse brown bread rubbed with tomato and garlic and drizzled with olive oil. Here, it has been refined to include a wide selection of toppings – *pato* (duck), *jamón serrano, jamón ibérico* – and various salads, including a typical Mallorcan *lombarda*, which comes with apple, carrots and walnuts. There is another branch at C/Fabrica 27A.

Mangiafuoco

Plaça del Vapor 4 (971 45 10 72). **Open** 8-11.30pm Mon, Wed-Sun. Closed Jan. **Average** €€. **Credit** MC, V. **Map** p52 A3.

An unexpectedly upmarket Italian restaurant, tucked away on this atmospheric little square in Es Jonquet. While there are ticks in all the boxes – red gingham tablecloths, family photographs, pages of pasta followed by a decent sprinkling of veal and fish dishes – the ingredients are impeccably sourced, many of them imported from Italy, and cooked with flair by Italian chef Daniel.

Parrilla Asador Txakoli

C/Fabrica 14 (971 28 21 26). **Open** 1.30-3.30pm, 9-11.30pm Mon-Fri; 9-11.30pm Sat. **Average** €€€. **Credit** AmEx, MC, V. **Map** p52 A2.

An excellent Basque-run place where the emphasis is on fish: the *besugo* (sea bream) and *merluza* (hake) are particularly special. The cooking is straightforward, although not cheap, and is served up in a split-level wooden dining room with a friendly atmosphere. A tapas bar next door serves a fine selection of tapas, *raciones* and salads, and has a dining room at the back for sit-down meals.

Soho Urban Vintage Bar

Avda. Argentina 5 (971 45 47 19). **Open** 8am-2am Mon-Thur, Sun; 8am-3.30am Fri, Sat. **Average** €. **Credit** AmEx, DC, MC, V. **Map** p52 B2.

Opened in May 2005, the Vintage Bar has already become an essential stop on the night-time circuit thanks to its new wave retro look – '70s wallpaper, armchairs, still-functioning telly and album covers over the bar – and its cocktails and exceptionally friendly vibe. During the day there is mainly vegetarian food, and occasional happenings include open mic nights.

Passeig Marítim & around

This street (also known as Paseo Marítimo and officially Avinguda Gabriel Roca, but no one calls it that) is Palma's main waterside drag, running between Porto Pi and the cathedral. At the western end you'll find the city's main area for late nightlife with a number of *discotecas*, clubs and *discobares*; as you move east it's more restaurants, bars, pubs and cafés.

Bahía Mediterráneo

Passeig Marítim 33 (971 45 76 53/www.restaurante bahiamediterraneo.com). **Open** noon-midnight daily. **Average** €€€€. **Credit** AmEx, DC, MC, V. **Map** p50 U6.

The setting here is breathtaking. You take a lift up from the street and are met with over-the-top opulence in what was once the finest hotel in all Palma. In winter, dine below the chandeliers and huge mirrors; in summer, the *terraza* has perhaps the best views in the whole city, looking out across the bay to the cathedral. The food is of the highest quality, concentrating inevitably on fish, with lovely dishes such as *lenguado con gambas* (sole with prawns) and fresh *langostinos*. Superb service from old-school waiters.

Baisakhi

Passeig Marítim 8 (971 73 68 06). **Open** *Sittings* 8pm, 11pm Tue-Sun. **Average** €€€. **Credit** AmEx, DC, MC, V. **Map** p50 V8.

Palma's best-known and best-loved Indian restaurant offers a set menu (€28), including wine and lassi – and two sittings, at 8pm and 11pm. Wonderful surroundings – all tinkling music, wooden carvings and garlands of flowers – and a small army of friendly waiters.

Café Dàrsena

Passeig Marítim s/n (971 18 05 04). **Open** *July, Aug* 8am-3am daily. *Sept-June* 8am-1am Mon-Sat; 8am-2am Sun. **Average** €. **Credit** AmEx, DC, MC, V. **Map** p50 V8.

Located right on the harbourfront, with views of the yachts, this is a stylish spot to have a pre-dinner drink or a long, lazy lunch, with its glass walls and canvas canopies outside.

Café Port Pesquer. *See p79.*

Café Port Pesquer

C/Moll de la Llotja s/n (971 71 52 20). **Open** *July-Sept* 10am-2am Mon-Wed, Sun; 10am-3am Thur-Sat. *Oct-June* 10am-1am Mon-Wed, Sun; 10am-2am Thur-Sat. **Average** €€. **Credit** AmEx, DC, MC, V. **Map** p52 B3. **Photo** *p78*.

This chic harbourside café is certainly not one of the cheapest places in town, but its capacious decked terrace is a prime spot to while away a long sunny afternoon or evening. The *pa amb oli* with *jamón serrano* weighs in at a hefty price, but it's a very superior version, with olives and capers on the side, and is easily large enough for a light lunch for two. Good fish and seafood dishes are among the other options on the menu, and there's also a *menú del día* (Mon-Fri only).

Cappuccino Passeig Marítim

Passeig Marítim 1 (971 28 21 62). **Open** 8am 2am Mon-Fri; 8am-4am Sat; 8am-2.30am Sun. **Average** €. **Credit** AmEx, MC, V. **Map** p50 V8.

A prime spot on the harbourfront in which to see and be seen, with a large outdoor *terraza* and a glass-fronted area upstairs with great views across the bay.

Sa Cranca

Passeig Marítim 13 (971 73 74 47). **Open** 1-3.45pm, 8-11.45pm Tue-Sat; 1-3.45pm Sun. Closed Sept. **Average** €€. **Credit** AmEx, DC, MC, V. **Map** p50 V8.

Sa Cranca is an *arroceria*, which means that it specialises in rice dishes. There is a huge variety to choose from – seven different (and superb) paella dishes, including *valenciana* and *marisco*; *arròs a banda*, a Mallorcan speciality; and *arròs negre*, rice cooked in squid ink. Set on the first floor of one of the faceless office blocks that line this street, it has a great view of the harbour – reserve a table by the window.

Koldo Royo

Passeig Marítim 3 (971 73 24 35). **Open** *July, Aug* 8.15-11.30pm Mon, Sat; 1.15-3.30pm, 8.15-11.30pm Tue-Fri. *Sept, Oct, Dec-June* 1.15-3.30pm, 8.15-11.30pm Tue-Sat. Closed Nov. **Average** €€€€. **Credit** AmEx, MC, V. **Map** p50 V8.

Basque chef Koldo Royo served his apprenticeship with the masters of Basque cooking before opening his own place in Mallorca and has earned a Michelin star for his efforts. He is now the leading proponent of the *nueva cocina vasca* (new Basque cuisine). Dishes include such gems as roasted scallops with mushrooms, loin of rabbit stuffed with plums, wild pigeon with plum purée and shallot vinaigrette, and sea bass with black sepia pasta. Try to get a window seat with lovely views of the bay, and make sure you reserve well in advance.

Royal Siam

C/Camilo José Cela 10 (971 22 16 05). **Open** 1-4pm, 7-11pm daily. **Average** €€. **Credit** MC, V. **Map** p50 U8.

Royal Siam is the best Thai restaurant in town, serving outstanding dishes in lovely surroundings. The spring rolls with sweet chilli sauce and chicken satay are delicious. If you want something spicy, try the red chicken curry; the Thai beef salad is also excellent. Superb service and great value.

Saladet

C/Monsenyor Palmer 6 (971 28 82 09). **Open** 1pm-2am Mon-Fri; 6pm-2am Sat, Sun. **Average** €. **Credit** DC, MC, V. **Map** p50 V8.

Superb, cheap, home-made tapas courtesy of a Russian mother and daughter team in this tiny bar just back from the seafront. Try lamb's lettuce, clams and dates, mushrooms with walnut, mini vegetable crêpes or stuffed cabbage with rice and beef. Other reasons to come here include ham and mozzarella baked potatoes and an excellent wine list.

Samurai

C/Monsenyor Palmer 2 (971 73 78 37). **Open** 8pm midnight Mon; 1-4pm, 8pm-midnight Tue-Sun. **Average** €€€. **Credit** AmEx, MC, V. **Map** p50 V8.

A classily designed Japanese restaurant where the waiters sport traditional clothing and serve good sushi, tempura and sashimi. Sit at the bar around the *plancha* to enjoy the chefs putting on a show.

Shogun

C/Camilo José Cela 14 (971 73 57 48). **Open** 1-4pm, 7-11.30pm daily. **Average** €€. **Credit** MC, V. **Map** p50 U8.

Excellent Japanese cuisine served in stylish surroundings. Classic dishes employ market-fresh fish and good cuts of meat. The ambience is subtle and restrained, the service attentive and efficient.

Gènova

This area, a suburb just out of town to the west of the Castell de Bellver, is justly famous for its restaurants. If you are in Palma for more than a few days, it's worth the journey; about a 15-minute drive from the centre along C/Andrea Doria.

Sa Caseta

C/Martínez Vaquer 1 (971 40 42 81/ www.sacaseta.com). **Open** 1pm-midnight daily. **Average** €€€. **Credit** AmEx, DC, MC, V.

For high-end dining, this is one of the best eating spots in Gènova. There is a good-value tasting menu, consisting, perhaps, of snails, *frito Mallorquín* (generally offal), *bacalao*, suckling pig, almond cake, wine and cava.

Meson Ca'n Pedro 1

C/Rector Vives 14 (971 40 24 79/www.mesoncanpedro.com). **Open** noon-midnight Mon, Tue, Thur-Sun. Closed June. **Average** €€. **Credit** AmEx, DC, MC, V.

This spot is hugely popular, and one of the most famous of Mallorca's *asadores*, serving up huge piles of roast and grilled meats, such as suckling pig and lamb. Reportedly, it's the busiest restaurant on the island – the third busiest in Spain – so you may find that the focus is on quantity rather than quality. On

El Bungalow.

the same street, there's also a Meson C'an Pedro 2 (C/Rector Vives 4, 971 70 21 62, open July, Aug noon-midnight daily, Sept-June noon-midnight Mon-Wed, Fri-Sun), which specialises in fish.

La Rueda

C/Rector Vives 11 (971 40 34 60). **Open** July-Oct 7.30-11.30pm Tue-Sun. Nov-June 1-3.30pm, 7.30-11.30pm Tue-Sun. **Average** €€. **Credit** MC, V.
Across the street from Ca'n Pedro, La Rueda has a lovely garden terrace and specialises in South American cuisine. If you want *ceviche* (white fish 'cooked' in fresh lemon juice), you'll need to phone ahead to order; otherwise try the barbecued loin of beef for two.

Portitxol & Ciutat Jardí

Located around 15 minutes' walk east of the cathedral along the seafront, Portitxol's cutesy harbour and mix of the trendy and the trad is irresistible; there are more good seaside eateries further east in Ciutat Jardi.

Bar, Co

C/Vicari Joaquim Fuster 83, Portitxol (971 24 86 85). **Open** 1pm-midnight Tue-Sun. **Average** €€. **Credit** MC, V. **Map** p51 Z9.
Small, bright and smack in the middle of a noisy drinking strip, Bar, Co defies all expectations. Mexican owner Emilio Castrejón is passionate about sourcing and creating wonderful food and has consequently made this one of the city's most reward-

ing places to eat. Alongside an impressive list of wines, the Asian-influenced menu includes salads of seaweed and tofu or avocado, grapefruit and orange; Korean *tortitas* (made with potato, onion, fermented soy beans and oyster sauce); Thai soup – a whopping extravaganza of vegetables, shiitake, fish and chicken, and *solomillo con costra* (steak coated in breadcrumbs ground with pine nuts, parmesan, honey and mustard).

El Bungalow

C/Esculls 2, Ciutat Jardí (971 26 27 38). **Open** Apr-Oct 1.30-4pm, 8.30-11.30pm Tue-Sat; 1-4pm Sun. Nov-Mar 1.30-4pm Tue-Sun. **Average** €€€. **Credit** DC, MC, V. **Photo** above.
Set in a former fisherman's cottage separated by the coastal road from the modern apartment blocks behind, El Bungalow may offer simple food but it attracts an upmarket clientele. Even Michelin-starred chefs have praised its fresh fish and rice dishes, unobtrusive but efficient service and good prices. Waves gently lap up against the terrace.

S'Eixerit

C/Vicari Joaquim Fuster 73, Portitxol (971 27 37 81). **Open** 1-4pm, 8pm-midnight daily. **Average** €€. **Credit** MC, V. **Map** p51 Z9.
S'Eixerit is situated in an old house that has been converted into a delightful restaurant with plenty of cosy nooks filled with antiques, a gorgeous leafy garden and an open front terrace facing the sea. Locals flock here for the excellent value lunchtime *menú* and paella.

Minimar

C/Vicari Joaquim Fuster 67, Portitxol (971 24 86 04). **Open** *June-Aug* noon-midnight daily. *Sept-May* 1.30-4pm, 7.30pm-midnight Tue-Sun. **Average** €€. **Credit** AmEx, DC, MC, V. **Map** p51 Z9.

Owned by the ubiquitous Cappuccino group, Minimar is a cool spot with a terrace around two sides, while inside white chairs, minimalist decor and giant sheep portraits create the backdrop. Along with creative tapas – beef, guacamole and brie, cod gratin with alioli, or fried quail's egg, red pepper and chorizo – there are expensive salads and more typical fare, such as *calamares a la romana* and cod croquettes.

Portixol

C/Sirena 27 (971 27 18 00/www.portixol.com). **Open** 1-4.30pm, 8pm-midnight daily. **Average** €€€€. **Credit** AmEx, DC, MC, V. **Map** p51 Z9.

The restaurant at the stylish Hotel Portixol (*see p90*) is as gastronomically savvy as you'd expect from a place that has featured in more designer accommodation guides than you've had sashimi dinners. Chilled sounds provide a relaxing background as you gaze out over the swimming pool and decide, perhaps, to go for the red curry and lemongrass soup with king prawns, followed by duck breast cooked perfectly pink, with a side order of asparagus tempura. The quality and (inevitably) the prices are high, the service is spot on and the vibe is Zen.

Nightlife

Palma isn't blessed with the most exciting nightlife but it is reasonably active year-round and is particularly buzzing at weekends and during the summer months. In terms of pubs and bars, most of the action is around Sa Llotja, but many of these start closing at about 2am, so for late-night drinking and dancing you'll need to head to the Passeig Maritim where the city's glitziest *discobares* and *discotecas* are open until 5am or 6am.

For listings of what's going on and where, including live bands and the alternative scene, pick up a copy of the free mags *Youthing*, and the English-language *Digame*, both of which you'll find in clothes shops, hotels and bars. There is also a *Guia del Ocio* available at *kioscos*, which gives details of more mainstream entertainment such as theatres, cinemas, exhibitions and restaurants.

Sa Llotja

This is the traditional heart of the city's pre-clubbing nightlife, popular with locals and tourists, where you'll find Irish pubs next to flamenco clubs and lager and sangria drunk with equal vigour. It's all packed into a very small area concentrated around C/Apuntadors, where almost every doorway leads into a pub

or bar. Officially, most places are required by law to close at 2am, but you'll find that many will go on until 3am or 4am, particularly at weekends or in high season.

Abaco (C/Sant Joan 1, 971 71 49 39, open 9pm-2.30am daily, closed 7 Jan-13 Feb) is Palma's most over-the-top establishment, though you could quite easily walk past it if you didn't know it was there. Housed within an opulent mansion, it's an outrageously theatrical spot, with an indoor and outdoor patio full of flowers, cascading fruit, birds in cages, a fountain outside, classical music and an army of waiters to-ing and fro-ing with some of the largest (and most expensive) cocktails in Mallorca. The only pity is that tour groups regularly wander in for a gawp.

For some live music, **Café Barcelona** (C/Apuntadors 5, open 8.30pm-1am Mon-Thur, Sun, 8.30pm-3am Fri, Sat) is the place to find jazz, blues, flamenco and Latin dance every night from 10.30pm.

Atlántico (C/Sant Feliu 12, 971 72 28 82, www.atlanticocafe.com, open 6pm-2.30am Mon-Thur, Sun, 6pm-3am Fri, Sat) has a retro rock 'n' roll look, bedecked with memorabilia, and swings to the sound of Elvis and the Stones. **Agua** (C/Jaume Ferrer 6, mobile 607 54 32 77), is less predictable, thanks to the multifarious musical tastes of owners Richard and Lee, and you're as likely to hear soft metal as chillout or jazz. Nearby, **Duplex Lounge** (C/Jaume Ferrer 14, no phone, 6pm-1am Mon-Thur, Sun, 6pm-3am Fri, Sat) is an altogether more mellow place, French-owned and specialising in cocktails.

La Bodeguita del Medio (C/Vallseca 16, 971 71 78 32, open 9pm-1am Mon-Thur, Sun, 8pm-3am Fri, Sat) is an enjoyably tacky salsa dive; **O'Briens** (C/Sant Joan 7, 971 71 43 81, open 6pm-1am Mon-Thur, Sun 6pm-3am Fri, Sat) is a popular Irish pub, full of British and Irish visitors, with Guinness and Kilkenny on tap; **MacGowan's** (C/del Mar 18, 971 71 98 47, open 9pm-1am Mon-Thur, Sun, 9pm-3am Fri, Sat) offers more of the same, with pool and darts.

Santa Catalina

Some of Palma's alternative and rock clubs are concentrated in and around this area, including **Café Lisboa** (C/Sant Magi 33, no phone, open 11pm-2.30am Mon-Thur, 11pm-3.30am Fri, Sat) for rock and jazz, and **Rimanblu** (C/Fabrica 21, 971 28 85 77, open June-mid Sept 9pm-3am Mon-Thur, 9pm-4am Fri, Sat, mid Sept-May 4pm-3am Mon-Thur, 4pm-4am Fri, 10pm-4am Sat), whose name is a mangled version of 'rhythm and blues' and gives you an idea of the type of music on offer.

One day in Palma

The Mallorcan capital has more than enough distractions to occupy you for two or three days, but if you can't spare that long, here are our suggestions on how you can get the essential feel of this beguiling city in one day. (You could attempt the walk marked on the map on pages 52-53, but, frankly, this is probably too ambitious if you don't want to feel you're on a route march.)

So, for any easy, relaxed and realistic day out, we suggest you start with the **Cathedral** (*see p58*), Palma's most emblematic and important building. Get there when it opens at 10am or you'll feel you're drowning in a sea of tour groups. When you tire of craning your neck into the void above and puzzling over why Gaudí's contributions aren't more Gaudí-esque, then stroll along the front by the marina and have a coffee at one of the hip cafés that front the harbour (such as **Café Port Pesquer**; *see p79*).

While sipping, if you turn around you won't fail to notice the massive **Bastió de Sant Pere**, part of the city's fortifications. This huge bastion has recently been converted into Palma's newest art museum, **Es Baluard** (*see p70*). Its architecture is so stunning that it puts the art inside in the shade, but it shouldn't be missed. Head there next.

Lunch is probably beckoning now, and it's time to take your pick from Palma's many and varied restaurants. If you want to go local, you could try venerable tapas bar **La Bóveda** (*see p73*) or trad Mallorcan **Ca'n Carlos** (*see p74*); if you want somthing more fancy, sample the bargain-priced (for the quality) lunch *menú* at Michelin-starred **Koldo Royo** (*see p79*); then again, if your tastes are simpler and you've had enough stolid Mallorcan food, then sink your teeth into a quality all-American burger at **Diner** (*see p77*).

After your feast you probably won't fancy too energetic an afternoon, so take a slow stroll around the atmospheric and sparklingly restored old town. Patrician mansions line many of the streets, but the only one you can visit – and it's well worth a visit – is **Can Marquès** (*see p56*), which offers a fascinating glimpse into the lives of a wealthy Mallorcan family a century ago.

Stop off for a coffee and an *ensaïmada* at venerable café **Ca'n Joan de s'Aigo** (*see p76*), and, frankly, it's likely that you'll feel you've done enough for one day. Feel like you've only scratched Palma's surface? Well, that's because you have. Go on, head back for second helpings.

There are a number of clubs and bars along C/Industria. Try also **Zambizi** (C/Molina 3, 699 31 38 87, open 10.30pm-5.30am Fri, Sat).

Passeig Marítim & El Terreny

Passeig Marítim is popular with nightlife-loving tourists and locals, who have moved here since the Town Hall clamped down on late-night drinking in the Sa Llotja area. The area directly above Tito's (*see below*) is known as El Terreny, and used to be the trendiest part of town; it's centred on Plaça Gomila and Avda. Joan Miró, and is now pretty seedy. Around here is the centre of Palma's gay scene.

Palma's late nightlife begins at the eastern end of the Passeig Marítim at **Hogan's** (C/Monsenyor Palmer, 971 28 96 64, open noon-3.30am daily), an Irish-style pub popular with Brits; it screens big football matches and has occasional live music. If you are after more of a pre-clubbing atmosphere, you need to move west along the Passeig past the big hotels, where the bars and *discobares* are situated. Bear in mind that few open before 10pm and most won't

get going until midnight. One of the best is **Crazy Cow** (Passeig Marítim 33, 971 28 38 29, open June-Aug 9pm-5am daily, Sept-May 9pm-5am Wed-Sun), which has a *terraza* and plays house music and Spanish chart hits. For Latin sounds, lambada and cocktails try **Made in Brasil** (Passeig Marítim 27, 670 37 23 90, open 8pm-3.45am Mon-Thur, Sun, 8pm-4am Fri, Sat).

Palma's *discotecas* are not like Ibiza's, despite the presence of Pacha (*see below*), so don't expect uplifting house or cool garage and R&B – you'll find the music (perhaps with the exception of Pacha) predominantly safe, bland, bubblegum Spanish pop. The first of the big clubs is **Art Deco** (Plaça del Vapor 20, 971 73 34 95, open midnight-5.45am Thur-Sat), set back from Passeig Marítim and with a slightly older crowd. **Tito's** (Passeig Marítim s/n, 971 73 00 17, open June-mid Sept 10.30pm-5am daily, mid Sept-May 10.30pm-5am Fri-Sun) is the biggest in town, with glass lifts on the outside, six bars, a laser show, great views over the bay and commercial pop tunes. Opposite, **Level** (971 73 36 71, open 11pm-6am Fri-Sun) attracts well-heeled yachties to an outdoor setting with pool.

The legendary **Pacha** (Passeig Marítim 42, 971 45 59 08, www.pachamallorca.com, open June-Sept 11pm-6am daily, Oct-May 11pm-6am Thur-Sun), is the granddaddy of them all, and plays a mix of house, techno and trance. Dress up to get in – the doormen operate a ruthless dress code. Towards the end of the harbour is **Mar Salada** (Moll de Pelaires s/n, 971 70 27 09, www.marsalada.net, open 11pm-6am Fri-Sat, 11pm-2am Sun), another huge, late-night disco that plays current Spanish pop music.

Ca'n Barbarà

Beyond Pacha and just before Club de Mar, you'll find a handful of stylish places spread round the inner marina area of Ca'n Barbarà. These bars have only been open for a few years, but offer an excellent alternative to the frantic atmosphere of the Passeig Marítim. **Café Garito** (971 73 69 12, open 6pm-4am Thur, Sun, 6pm-4.30am Fri, Sat) is a laid-back place with a cool atmosphere that attracts surfer and hippie-chic types. Excellent music comes courtesy of big-name international DJs at weekends and occasional live music. It also puts on exhibitions and serves food (8pm-1am) and cocktails (until 2am). Just along, **113** (971 28 66 86, open 9pm-3am Mon-Thur, 9pm-4am Fri, Sun) is a more exclusive place, where the people are more designer cool and the house is easygoing. Inside, there is a huge central bar and two smaller ones, tiled columns and enormous comfy sofabeds. **Mosquito Coast** (971 73 77 88, open July, Aug 11.30pm-3am Mon-Thur, 11.30pm-4am Fri, Sat, Sept-June 11.30pm-3am Thur-Sat) is the biggest of the bars along here, with two floors reverberating to Spanish pop. Above here, Plaça Gomila is the destination for grungier sounds.

Gay

For information on the gay scene (though only in Castilian or Catalan), check out the **Ben Amics** website (www.benamics.com) or give them a call (971 72 30 58, 971 71 56 70) on Thursday evenings (6-9pm). The website has links to various bars, clubs, saunas and beaches.

Nightlife

El Terreny, below the Castell de Bellver, is at the heart of Palma's small gay scene, and you'll find a range of bars and clubs here and along the western end of Avda. Joan Miró, including: **El Sombrero de Copas** at No.26, **GE** at No.73 (mobile 639 30 40 08), **La Tasca** at No.41 (971 45 04 68), **Marcus Pub** at No.54 (971 28 61 44), **Dylan** at No.68, and **Status Pub** at No.38 (971 45 40 30). Bars on the streets off Avda.

Joan Miró include **Isidoro** (C/Alvaro de Bazan 2, 971 45 06 57) and **Café Lorca** (C/Federico Garcia Lorca 21), both of which are popular with gay women. You'll also find a couple of places on C/Industria, to the north-east, including **Room Service** and **NPI** (also popular with lesbians). Both hotels below have popular bars; the terrace bar at the **Rosamar** is the best place for outdoor people-watching. The majority of the gay discos are also situated along Avda. Joan Miró and include **Heaven** in Plaça Gomila and two which are attracting an increasingly mixed crowd: **Black Cat** at No.75, and **La Demence** at No.36. Tito's (*see p82*) has a gay night, Made For House, on Sunday. You'll find saunas at the **Hotel Aries** (see below) and, in the centre of town, **Spartacus** (C/Sant Espirit 8B, 971 72 50 07).

Where to stay

Hotel Aries

C/Porras 3 (971 73 78 99/www.ariesmallorca.com). **Rates** €42 single; €55-€75 double. **Credit** AmEx, DC, MC, V. **Map** p50 U9.
This gay hotel in the heart of El Terreny has a pretty roof terrace with jacuzzi, sunbeds and bar. Things can get a little hardcore in here, and the indoor bar (open 10pm-8am every night) features darkrooms and cabins, while the sauna area (open 4pm-midnight), has a whirlpool, wet and dry sauna, showers, cabins, darkrooms and a porn room.

Rosamar

Avda. Joan Miró 74 (971 73 27 23/www.rosamar hotel.com). **Rates** €45-€55 double; €65-€75 suite. **Credit** AmEx, DC, MC, V. **Map** p50 U9.
This privately run gay hotel in El Terreny is owned by gay couple Bill and Basilio. The atmosphere is laid-back and friendly, with an open-air evening bar used as a popular meeting place for gay crowds. There are two sun terraces with sunbeds and showers on the roof with views over the bay and the Castell de Bellver. There are 40 en suite bedrooms, some with balconies and views, other quieter ones at the back.

Arts & entertainment

Film

There are numerous cinemas in town, but the only one that shows films in their original language (VO) is **Multicines Renoir**, C/Emperatriz Eugenia 6 (971 29 73 01, www.cinentradas.com, tickets €4.50-€6).

Music

Live music can be seen in several bars and clubs across the city (*see p81* **Nightlife**). Classical concerts are usually performed in the **Auditorium** (*see below*). Rock bands and groups play in many of the venues in and around Plaça Gomila. For current listings, get hold of a copy of *Youthing* or *Dígame*.

Theatre

Palma has a thriving drama scene. For full listings of what plays are on get *Guia del Ocio* at a *kiosco*. The main venues are:

Auditorium
Passeig Marítim 18 (971 73 53 28/tickets 902 33 22 11/www.auditoriumdepalma.com/tickets www.servic aixa.com). **Tickets** €25-€45. **Credit** DC, MC, V. **Map** p50 V8.
Stages opera, dance, pop and classical concerts.

Teatro Municipal
Passeig de Mallorca 9B (971 73 91 48).
Performances Wed-Sun. Closed July, Aug.
Tickets €12-€20. **No credit cards**. **Map** p52 B2.
Features comedy, cabaret and small productions.

Sport

Bullfighting

Plaça de Toros
Avda. Gaspar Bennuzar Arquitecte (971 75 16 39).
Tickets phone for prices. **No credit cards**.
Map p51 Y6.
Palma's bullring, which dates from 1929, is in the north of the city. The bullfighting season runs from March to October but *corridas* are not frequent, with about one a month, and it's rare to see a poster advertising one in town. Bulls are not reared on the island and have to be shipped in from the mainland, and bullfighting does not take centre stage in the social calendar as it does in much of Spain. Tickets are not hard to come by: go to the ring itself and request *sol* (sun) or *sombra* (shade); *sol* is cheaper.

Football

Football does not command the same levels of obsession here as in the rest of Spain, despite the fact that the town's team Real Club Deportivo Mallorca, or **Real Mallorca**, has often finished in the top half of the Primera Liga and has won the national cup and reached the final of the European Cup Winners' Cup. *Palmasanos* are fair-weather fans – keen to support the team when it's riding high, but quick to abandon it when it slips down the league. It has 18,000 registered fans and a big stadium (**Son Moix**, in the north of the city by the Via Cintura), which has a capacity of 24,000. If you want to see a game, you shouldn't have too much difficulty getting a ticket. Most matches take place on a Sunday and you can buy tickets at the stadium.

Real Club Deportivo Mallorca
Son Moix, Camí dels Reis s/n (971 22 12 21/www.rcdmallorca.es). **Tickets** €20-€42; €7-€15 concessions. **Credit** AmEx, DC, MC, V.

Shopping

Palma's shopping is concentrated in two main areas that run into each other: along Passeig des Born and the mainly pedestrianised streets running east towards Plaça Major and bounded by C/Unio; and Plaça Major and the streets running east and north, including C/Sindicat, C/San Miquel and C/Oms.

On Born you'll find a number of fashion shops, including **Caroline Herrera** and **Corner**, the ever-popular **Zara** and **Massimo Dutti** and, at the top, **C&A**. The streets immediately east of Born, particularly those concentrated around Plaça Chopin, are where the upmarket clothes and shoes boutiques are situated, including **Elle** and **Escada**. Out on its own, in Sa Calatrava, **Modanostra** (C/Pont i Vic, 971 22 74 38) has gorgeous hip clothes for women, hand-stitched in the shop itself.

For trendy clothes and shoe shops head up to C/Sant Miquel, where you'll find a branch of **Camper** at No.17 (971 72 62 54), the groovy footwear brand based in Inca and sold all over the world (dirt-cheap end-of-lines can be picked up from the Camper outlets in Inca and at the Festival Park mall; *see p158* and *p166* **Shoes shine**) and a branch of supercool Barcelona designer **Custo** at No.15 (971 22 83 47). On C/Oms, the stores are more downmarket, with a couple of tattoo parlours at either end and various cheap clothes stores. There are two exceptions: **Xino's** and **Via 55**, both great for super-trendy jeans and clothes.

On C/Santo Domingo and the streets off it you'll find the best deals on high-class artificial **Majorica** pearls. Try **Sant Joan** (C/Jaime II 16, 971 71 16 15) for an excellent selection of bracelets, earrings and necklaces at good prices; for more pricey jewels try **Miro** on Plaça Rosari.

For traditional Mallorcan food and drink head for **Sobrasada** (C/Santo Domingo 1, 971 71 48 87), a tiny place where you'll have to duck to get in for the number of chorizos hanging from the ceiling. It has a great selection of *sobrassada* and other sausages, herb liqueurs from Bunyola and various breads. **Forno del Sant Cristo** (C/Paraires 2, near Plaça Frederic Chopin) is good for traditional Mallorcan *ensaïmadas* and liqueurs.

For an excellent selection of home-grown and international wines try **La Vinoteca** (C/Padre Bartolomé Pou 29, 971 76 19 32), which also has an export service and a second branch at Plaça Virgen de la Salud 3B, off C/Sant Miquel (971 72 88 29). Nearby, **La Favorita** (C/Sant Miquel 38A, 971 71 37 40) remains a reasonably priced deli specialising in *mallorquí* products. Opened in 1872, **La Pajarita** (C/Sant Nicolas 4, 971 71 18 44) is two shops in one, with gorgeous displays for both *xarcuteria* and sweets.

Fosh Food (C/Blanquerna 6, 971 29 01 08, www.foshfood.com) is an upmarket deli owned by Michelin-starred British chef Marc Fosh of Read's (*see p161*), and is worth the trip up here just for the chocolates alone. Marc and other chefs also give cooking classes here; see the website for details. There are food markets at Plaça Olivar (7am-2pm Mon-Sat) and Plaça Navegació (7am-2pm Mon-Sat).

For traditional hand-made crystal and glass try **El Vidrio** (C/Unio 13, 971 72 42 99). There is also a Saturday **flea market** (8am-2pm) on the lower Avingudes, to the east of the cathedral area.

You'll find a huge range of second-hand English books at **Fiol Llibres** (C/Oms 45A, 971 72 14 28), and **Book Inn** (C/Horts 20, 971 71 38 98) has a small but well-selected collection of new English and language-learning books.

The biggest shopping complex is **Porto Pi**, at the western end of Passeig Marítim, with more than 100 shops and a food court. There are also two big branches of department store **El Corte Inglés**, one at Avda. Jaume III 15 and another at Avda. d'Alexandre Roselló 15-16 (971 77 01 77, www.elcorteingles.com).

Craft markets are held at Plaça de les Meravilles (mid May-mid Oct 8pm-midnight daily) and Plaça Major (Jan, Feb 10am-2pm Fri, Sat, Mar-July, Oct-Dec 10am-8pm Mon, Fri, Sat, Aug, Sept 10am-8pm daily).

Where to stay

Palma has a limited number of budget places to stay, but you are spoilt for choice if you have a bit of spare cash and want to relax in one of its stylish, boutique-style hotels, most of which are located in sympathetically converted former *casa particulares*. The city is becoming increasingly popular as a year-round destination, thanks in no small part to the no-frills airlines, so you may find these places booked up well out of the traditional high season from June to September. From November to February you should be fine just turning up, but from Easter onwards and into October it's always worth ringing ahead. Most of the stylish accommodation is situated in the Old Town, with the bigger hotels strung along the Passeig Marítim.

Hotel Tres. *See p87.*

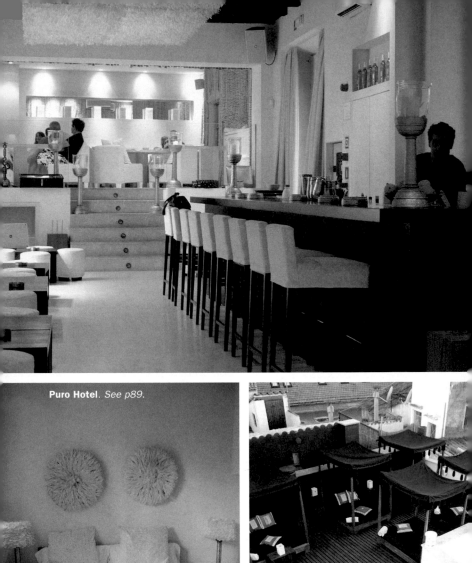

Puro Hotel. *See p89*.

Centre, Sa Llotja & Sa Calatrava

Convent de la Missió

C/Missió 7A (971 22 73 47/www.conventdelamissio. com). **Rates** (incl. breakfast) €210 double; €260-€320 suite. **Credit** AmEx, DC, MC, V. **Map** p53 D1.

Don't be discouraged by the discreet entrance on a dingy back street, for this is one of Palma's most stylish hotels. The Convent de la Missió is ferociously minimalist in a way that cleverly evokes the seminary (part of the adjacent convent) once housed here, and even the hotel logo espouses ecclesiastical chic, with a whimsical wisp of a crucifix. No expense has been spared on the comfort, however, and beds and pillows are of the best. The superior rooms and suites have hydromassage and Bulgari toiletries, while downstairs there is a Turkish bath and spa. Of the standard doubles, No.15 has the best view of the rooftops and the hills beyond. Video and DVD machines are available on request. The restaurant, El Refectori (*see p76*), is one of the finest in town.

Dalt Murada

C/Almudaina 6 (971 42 53 00/www.daltmurada. com). **Rates** €140 double; €236 suite. **Credit** AmEx, DC, MC, V. **Map** p53 D3.

None of the many town houses converted into luxury hotels retains as much character as this one, thanks to the efforts of the wonderfully welcoming Moragues family. They have left much of the antique furniture, tapestries and paintings (most by or of members of the family) just as they were, creating a uniquely intimate atmosphere. The penthouse suite is well worth splashing out on (and in – it contains an impressive jacuzzi). The lovely old dining room, with its original tiled floors, now serves as a breakfast and bar area, and sports an impressive library of DVDs – free to guests. There are plans afoot to extend the hotel from nine rooms to 14 in 2006.

Hostal Brondo

C/Ca'n Brondo 1 (971 71 90 43/www.hostal brondo.net). **Rates** €27 single; €45-€55 double; €55 triple. **Credit** MC, V. **Map** p53 D2.

Ten high-ceilinged rooms, decorated with putti, silk flowers and mahogany furniture, go for a song at the Brondo. Room 6 is especially nice, with a galleried balcony, as is the attic room with sloping ceiling. At the top there is also a studio flat for three or four people for a minimum of three nights; it has a well-stocked kitchen and a veritable library of videos and DVDs.

Hostal Ritzi

C/Apuntadors 6 (971 71 46 10). **Rates** €25 single; €38-€50 double. **No credit cards. Map** p52 C3.

If you are on a tight budget, want to be in the heart of the action and don't mind a bit of noise from the street then this place is ideal; just don't expect too many mod cons.

Hotel Born

C/Sant Jaume 3 (971 71 29 42/www.hotelborn.com). **Rates** €51-€65 single; €74-€91 double; €122 suite. **Credit** AmEx, DC, MC, V. **Map** p53 D2.

By far the best of the cheaper hotels in the centre, the Born occupies a great spot at the top of the main shopping drag. A former 16th-century palace belonging to the Marquis de Ferrandell, this has all the atmosphere of a four-star place, with a huge marble reception and its own palm-shaded courtyard where you eat breakfast. The clean, airy rooms all have baths, and some also have tiny balconies with views over the courtyard.

Hotel Regina

C/Sant Miquel 77 (971 71 37 03/www.hostalregina palma.com). **Rates** €39 single; €51 double; €60 triple. **Credit** MC, V. **Map** p53 F1/F2.

Useful for the train and bus stations, the Regina has clean and simple en-suite rooms, enlivened by colourful hanging baskets suspended in the windows. Rooms overlooking the street can be noisy, but there is a roof terrace for a little respite in the sun.

Hotel San Lorenzo

C/Sant Llorenç 14 (971 72 82 00/www.hotelsan lorenzo.com). **Rates** €107-€182 double; €246 suite. **Credit** AmEx, DC, MC, V. **Map** p52 B3.

A tasteful conversion of a 17th-century townhouse, with just six lovely rooms, each decorated differently, with comfy beds, wooden-beamed ceilings and big bathrooms; the suite has its own rooftop *terraza*. There's a pretty pool tucked at the back surrounded by trees, and the bar is a convivial place for a nightcap.

Hotel Saratoga

Passeig Mallorca 6 (971 72 72 40/www.hotel saratoga.es). **Rates** €106 single; €144 double; €161-€225 suite. **Credit** AmEx, DC, MC, V. **Map** p52 B2.

This big hotel has undergone a major refit in an attempt to be as cool as its tiny neighbours and in some ways it succeeds – the reception and patio area are stylish, and the rooftop pool and bar are worth a visit for the wonderful views – but the bedrooms don't quite live up to the hype. There's nothing intrinsically wrong with them; it's just you could be in any of Palma's huge hotels.

Hotel Tres

C/Apuntadors 3 (971 71 73 33/www.hoteltres.com). **Rates** (incl. breakfast) €118 single; €187-€241 double; €268-€482 suite. **Credit** AmEx, DC, MC, V. **Map** p52 C3. **Photo** *p85*.

The opening of the Tres in 2004 brought the total of Swedish-owned designer hotels in Palma to *tres*. There's no link between them, and while the Portixol goes for a maritime art deco vibe and the Puro opts for ethno-chic, the Tres (the biggest of the three, with 41 rooms) plumps for more of a classic contemporary look. There's an understated Scando-austerity to its clean lines and limited palette that's softened by the odd splash of colour and comforts such as luxuriant beds, sleek bathrooms and a DVD library.

Discover the most beautiful places on Mallorca and Menor
Immerse yourself in the world of Grupotel. In our hotels you will find modern facilities,
a fabulous gastronomy and a personalized service allways attentive with every detail.
Choose your favourite hotel and let yourself be seduced by the Islands.

Grupotel

There's a bar, but no restaurant, although snacks are available, and the breakfast is a treat. The two rooftop terraces, one with a plunge pool and sauna, offer stupendous views over the city, from the cathedral to the mountains.

Palacio Ca Sa Galesa

C/Miramar 8 (971 71 54 00/www.palaciocasa galesa.com). **Rates** €209-€292 double; €316-€410 suite. **Credit** AmEx, DC, MC, V. **Map** p53 D4.
For the ultimate in discreet refinement, you can't beat this gem of a hotel, located in a 16th-century mansion in the oldest part of the city, just a couple of minutes' walk from the cathedral. There are only 12 rooms (seven suites, five doubles) and each one is decorated with great panache and named after a famous composer (honeymoon favourite Schubert comes with an antique four-poster bed, while Gershwin is a duplex with its own sun terrace). Facilities include a roof terrace with fine views over Palma and a small heated indoor pool, which shares its atmospheric vaulted space with a sauna and mini-gym. Complimentary tea and cake is available from 4pm to 6pm in a replica of Monet's kitchen at Giverny, and the spoils of the honour bar (sherry is available free) can be enjoyed in the elegant lounge (with a log fire in winter) or around the fountain on the interior patio in hot weather.

Palau Sa Font

C/Apuntadors 38 (971 71 22 77/www.palausafont. com). **Rates** €104 single; €155-€179 double; €230 suite. Closed 3wks Jan. **Credit** AmEx, MC, V. **Map** p52 C3.
In a perfect location in the heart of town, the German-run Palau Sa Font blends classic Mallorcan architecture with ultra-modern design in a 16th-century former palace. The colourful designer touches of the entrance and the Gaudiesque look of the bar area belie the spartan nature of the rooms, though these are comfortable enough. On the first floor is a pretty terrace area with a plunge pool and sun loungers. Other attractions include an excellent breakfast and some of the friendliest staff we've met.

Pons

C/del Vi 8 (971 72 26 58). **Rates** €42-€45 double. **No credit cards**. **Map** p52 C3.
This simple one-star *hostal residencia* is in an old Palma house, with rooms arranged around a central courtyard just off the Passeig des Born. It's a lot less noisy than the similarly priced Ritzi (*see p87*).

Puro Hotel

C/Montenegro 12 (971 42 54 50/www.purohotel.com). **Rates** single €161; double €225-€251; suite €294-€428. **Credit** AmEx, DC, V. **Map** p52 C3. **Photo** *p86*.
The Puro is design mag heaven. Styling itself an 'urban oasis', it offers a blissed-out, ethno-hippy panacea to calm the weary metropolitan sophisticate. A chilled soundtrack wafts through the airy public spaces; strings of tiny shells cascade down the walls of the oriental-slanted restaurant; a massive white-feather light installation hovers over the

super-hip bar. The feather theme continues in the bedrooms, which come equipped with broadband access, yoga mats, a flash audio/TV system (with a small selection of free on-demand movies), and slate and dark-wood bathrooms boasting superb monsoon showers. If all this fails to relax you, there's also a plunge pool and huge double beds on the roof on which to recline and summon chilled bubbly from down below.

Passeig Marítim & around

Big hotels tend to dominate this part of town. You shouldn't have too much difficulty getting a room if you want to stay here at the weekend, even in high season, as they mainly cater for business travellers during the week and often give discounted rates on Friday and Saturday nights.

AC Ciutat de Palma

Plaça Pont 3 (971 22 23 00/www.ac-hotels.com). **Rates** €118-€155 double. **Credit** AmEx, DC, MC, V. **Map** p50 V8.
One of Palma's newer hotels is from the stylish AC chain, and it doesn't disappoint. The designers have gone for a minimalist look in the common areas, with a black, white and grey design, sliding Japanese-style doors and low, comfortable chairs. It's set around a simple, sun-drenched patio, with a small restaurant on one side and a bar on the other, which offers free drinks to residents. This theme is continued in the rooms, where even the minibar is free. The rooms don't quite achieve the same level of cool as the rest of the hotel, but they are a good size (especially the superior ones) and comfortable. The bathrooms are all marble, but with shower only.

Costa Azul

Passeig Marítim 7 (971 73 19 40). **Rates** €68-€74 single; €88-€109 double. **Credit** AmEx, DC, MC, V. **Map** p50 V8.
A cheaper alternative to its four-star neighbours and offering the same priceless views over the Bay of Palma and an indoor pool.

Hostal Cuba

C/Sant Magi 1 (971 73 81 59). **Rates** €28 single; €38 double. **Credit** MC, V. **Map** p52 A3.
An excellent, friendly budget option in a great spot one street back from the bay and flanking the Jardines de Sa Faixana. Spotless and airy rooms, with high ceilings, shutters and shower. The biggest and nicest rooms overlook the Avda. Argentina, but can be very noisy.

Hotel Mirador

Passeig Marítim 10 (971 73 20 46/www.hotel mirador.es). **Rates** €84.10-€96.10 single; €100-€124 double. **Credit** AmEx, DC, MC, V. **Map** p50 V8.
A comfortable high-rise hotel next door to the Tryp Bellver (*see p90*), which is slightly cheaper but offers the same views and similar amenities, including a

'Come on down; the water's lovely' at **Es Portitxolet**. *See p72.*

plunge pool (and indoor and outdoor pools, sauna and jacuzzi in an affiliated pool across the road) and good breakfasts. There are good deals to be had at weekends and out of season.

Hotel Tryp Bellver

Passeig Maritim 11 (971 73 51 42/www.solmelia. com). **Rates** €153-€170 single/double; €279 suite. **Credit** AmEx, DC, MC, V. **Map** p50 V8.

The best of the big seafront hotels in the area, with a shade more character than the rest, a funky white exterior and curved stone balconies. The rooms are a decent size and all have balconies – try to get one on a high floor as the views are stunning. Pool, gym and all the mod cons you would expect. Good rates out of season and at weekends.

Valparaiso Palace

C/Francisco Vidal Sureda 23 (971 40 03 00/ www.grupotel.com). **Rates** €152-€163 single; €248-€270 double; €321-€1,017 suite. **Credit** AmEx, DC, MC, V. **Map** p50 U8.

A plush five-star place set in its own grounds below the Castell de Bellver. Great views across the entire bay and superb amenities, with three pools – two huge ones outside and another smaller indoor one – gym, *terraza*, restaurant and bar, but rooms are of a three-star standard.

Portitxol & Ciutat Jardí

There are really only three noteworthy places to stay on the eastern Bay, all of them close-ish to the city in Portitxol and Ciutat Jardí.

Hotel Ciutat Jardí

C/Illa de Malta 14 (971 26 00 07/www.hciutatj.com). **Rates** €100 single; €140-€270 double. **Credit** AmEx, DC, MC, V.

The four-star Hotel Ciutat Jardí was built in 1921 and is now a 'national monument of tourist interest', whatever that means. Certainly, it's a lovely looking pad with a distinctive colonial air about it, an eye-catching dome dominating the centre and grand palm trees shading the pool. The rooms, especially those with huge sweeping terraces overlooking the sea, are oases of calm. Good for a romantic getaway.

Hotel Portixol

C/Sirena 27, Es Portixol (971 27 18 00/ www.portixol.com). **Rates** (incl. breakfast) €110 single; €190-€260 double; €350 suite. **Credit** AmEx, DC, MC, V. **Map** p51 Z9. **Photo** *above.*

A place for urban sophisticates, this Swedish-owned boutique hotel is typically Scando in design – minimal, calming and ultra-suave, with neat details like binoculars in your room for perusing the comings and goings at the port or the pool. Comfort is all in the bedrooms, while the brightly coloured mosaic-tiled bathrooms are a refreshing change from clinical white. Since the hotel is smack-bang in the middle of the marina it's worth paying extra for a room with a view. When the hotel opened in 1999, *Wallpaper** voted it one of its fave retreats. The owners opened Port de Sóller's Hotel Espléndido in 2005 (*see p130*).

Hotel Portofino

C/Trafalgar 24, Platja Ciutat Jardí (971 26 04 64/ www.hotel-portofino.net). **Rates** (incl breakfast) €58-€66 double; €78-€91 triple. **Credit** AmEx, DC, MC, V.

A basic, comfortable 75-room two-star hotel just a block from the beach and with its own swimming pool and snack bar. Request a balcony when booking as not all rooms have one. It's handy for the airport and the centre of Palma, and fine if all you want is an affordable beach holiday with no frills.

Son Vida

Son Vida is on the western outskirts of Palma, around 15 minutes' drive from the centre.

Arabella Sheraton Golf Hotel Son Vida

C/Vinagrella s/n, Costa d'en Blanes (971 78 71 00/ www.luxurycollection.com). **Rates** €227 single; €361-€379 double. **Credit** AmEx, DC, MC, V.

This beautifully designed, ultra-luxurious modern hotel is set in its own grounds below the Castillo Hotel Son Vida *(see below)*. It boasts huge rooms with comfortable beds, thick carpets, marble bathrooms and balconies with views across the grounds. A grand reception area leads to all the amenities: large pool, fitness centre, spa and 18-hole golf course. The restaurant Plat d'Or offers superb cuisine, while another less formal dining room serves Mallorcan and Spanish dishes.

Castillo Hotel Son Vida

C/Raixa 2, Urb. Son Vida (971 79 00 00/www.hotels onvida.com). **Rates** €145-€225 single; €195-€340 double; €665-€1,290 luxurious. **Credit** AmEx, DC, MC, V.

This hotel is regarded as one of the finest on the island. It is built around the remains of an old tower and set in extensive grounds overlooking the city. It's extremely luxurious in the old style – grand entrance hall, impeccable service, big wooden furniture and wall hangings – with an extraordinary *terraza* that affords breathtaking views over the city and harbour. Rooms vary: the best are high-ceilinged and have balconies, but those high up are without balconies and feel somewhat cramped. The hotel has an indoor pool, tennis courts, spa treatment and two 18-hole golf courses – one for exclusive use of guests and another it shares with the Arabella Sheraton *(see above)*.

Resources

Bike hire

Palma on Bike *Plaça Salvador Coll 8 (971 71 80 62/www.palmaonbike.com).* **Open** 10am-7pm daily. **Rates** €3 1hr; €10 1 day; €25 3 days. A deposit of €100, a credit card or a passport is required.

Internet

Big Byte *C/Apuntadors 6 (971 71 17 54/www.big bytepalma.com).* **Open** 9am-8.30pm Mon-Thur; 9am-7pm Fri; 1-8pm Sat, Sun. **Map** p52 C3.

Café Manamú *C/Concepció 5 (971 72 92 94).* **Open** 9am-2am Mon-Sat. **Map** p52 C2.

Xpace *C/Sant Gaietà 4D (971 72 92 10/ www.xpacecyber.com).* **Open** 10am-10pm Mon-Sat. **Map** p52 C2/3.

Police station

Avda. Sant Ferran 42 (971 22 55 00). **Map** p50 V7.

Post office

C/Constitució 6 (971 22 88 82). **Map** p52 C3.

Tourist information

General number 902 10 23 65/www.palmavirtual.es Casal Solleric, Passeig des Born 27 (971 72 96 34). **Open** 9am-8pm daily. **Map** p52 C3.

Plaça Espanya, Parc de las Estaciones (971 75 43 29). **Open** 8am-8pm daily. **Map** p53 E1.

Plaça de la Reina 2 (971 71 22 16/www.info mallorca.net). **Open** 9am-8pm daily. **Map** p52 C3. Regional tourist office, with (limited) information on the whole of Mallorca.

Getting around

By bike

If you're staying in Palma, it's well worth hiring a bike to explore the further reaches of the city, and to take advantage of the waterside cycle path that runs most of the way about the Bay of Palma.

By bus

A range of bus routes circumnavigate Palma's old town (almost all passing through Plaça Espanya) and run along the coastal roads either side of the bay. The city tourist offices have maps of bus routes, but the most useful is the No.1, which runs from the airport (journeys to or from the airport cost €1.85) to Porto Pi, via Plaça Espanya, Passeig de Mallorca and the Passeig Maritim. The No.2 passes through the centre of the old city. Among the useful routes going further afield are the No.4 to Gènova, the No.15 along the Platja de Palma to S'Arenal and the No.20 to Calvià. Within the Greater Palma area there's a flat fare of €1.10, or you can buy a ten-journey pass at news kiosks for €7.51. For more information call 971 21 44 44. Tourist buses (Palma City Sightseeing 971 22 04 28) run on two routes every 20 minutes around the city (and as far as the Castell de Bellver). You can jump on or off the buses as many times as you want within a 24-hour period and there's an audio commentary (€13, €6.50 concessions).

By car

Palma is a very easy city to get around on foot, so don't even think about driving in the centre – you are much better off leaving your car in one of the city's numerous car parks. The most convenient of these is underneath the Parc de la Mar, at the foot of the cathedral. At the time of writing it was being massively extended and, thus, not open (the work is expected to go on until the end of 2006). A central alternative is below Plaça Major, accessed along C/Unio at the bottom of the Rambla.

By taxi

Taxis are cheap and plentiful – there are ranks at the bottom of Avda. Antoni Maura, on Passeig des Born and in Plaça Weyler. Alternatively, simply hail one with its green light on or call Radio Taxi (971 75 54 40), Palma Radio (971 40 14 14) or Fono Taxi (971 72 80 81).

The Bay of Palma

There are unexpected oases in Mallorca's most notorious holiday zone.

East is least, west is best. That's what they say anyway, but in the case of the Bay of Palma it rather depends on your mood, your nationality and your pocket. It splits fairly neatly down the middle – the east for Germans and the west for Brits – with their two respective capitals, S'Arenal and Magaluf, facing off in a bid to outdo each other in tackiness and wet T-shirt competitions. Oh, the joys of package tourism.

But fear not, because between and beyond these two monsters there are pockets of loveliness (especially out of season) in the shape of secluded bays, like those found around Cala Portals Vells at the westernmost tip of the bay.

The Bay of Palma is heaven for yachters, with a marina every five miles and countless boat charters and sailing schools. Visit www.monalisacharter.com for just about any yachting need – from navigation charts to day charters.

Landlubbers can take full advantage of this 25 kilometre (16 mile) stretch of coastline by taking in some of the finest beaches, best dining and full-on nightlife on the island. It's all here, if you know where to look.

West Bay of Palma

The scary thing about the package tourism of the 1960s and 1970s was the way it spread like a disease, its far-reaching tentacles devouring everything it touched. The scars remain on the West Bay, which has been largely taken over by three- and four-star hotels, permanently block-booked by tour operators.

Mostly purpose-built for the onslaught of sunseekers from northern Europe, the West Bay, more so than the east, seems to have modelled itself on the success of the Costa del Sol. Marbella exists in the form of Portals Nous, while echoes of Torremolinos can be found in Magaluf, and with them you also get two extremes of clientele: lager louts and demented teenagers in Magaluf, shameless snobs and C-list celebrities in Portals Nous.

These dubious qualities aside, what you do get are some very affordable package deals (particularly out of season), some reasonable dining, excellent beaches and easy access to the spectacularly beautiful Tramuntana mountains and the west coast.

Cala Major, Sant Agustí, Ca's Català & Illetes

The first settlements you hit coming out of Palma heading west are **Cala Major**, **Sant Agustí**, **Ca's Català** and **Illetes**, none with any particularly outstanding features unless you savour the scenery of car rental offices, pizza joints and souvenir shops. (Cala Major, though, does contain an island of culture in the form of the **Fundació Pilar i Joan Miró** – see p71; to reach it coming from Palma, turn right just before the imposing walls of the Palacio Marivent.)

The only other place worth stopping is, perhaps, Illetes, which has a couple of decent sandy cove beaches, flanked by sloping, pine-studded but heavily populated banks. Keep your eyes peeled for signs to Illetes and a turning off to the beaches. Once off the main road, a right turn brings you to **Cala Comtesa**, with a substantial parking area and a small scoop of sand that's quiet out of season. A left turn takes you to **Platja Illetes**; there's not as much parking here but better facilities – a bus stop (No.3 from Palma to Port Andratx), massages on the beach and a couple of restaurants just across the road from the sand.

Where to stay, eat & drink

Most of the hotels along this stretch are block booked by English and French travel agencies. If you really must stay here, the best options are at opposite ends of the price scale.

In **Sant Agustí**, try **Hostal La Mimosa** (C/Suecia 5, 971 40 03 30, www.lamimosa. com, doubles incl breakfast €47), which offers clean, simple accommodation; its best feature is a swimming pool tucked away behind a walled garden.

Ca's Català is home to a better budget option, though: **Hostal Ca's Català** (Ctra. de Palma–Andratx, km7, 971 40 50 08, closed mid Oct-mid Apr, doubles incl breakfast €50). It's decorated with mix-and-match junky antique furniture and old maps hanging on yellow walls in the large lounge area, and has a pool.

Those looking for something more exclusive should head for the nearby **Hospes Maricel** (Ctra. de Palma–Andratx 11, 971 70 77 44, doubles €268-€360), a pocket of tranquillity

Portals Nous.

and elegance, with coolly designed but good-sized comfortable rooms, an infinity pool with chill-out area in the shade, a private jetty and coves cut into the rock where you can get a massage above the lapping water. The '*degustación*' breakfast is superb, though it comes at a price (€25.60).

In terms of eating, Avinguda Joan Miró, the endless road running around the west of the bay, is lined with English pubs and countless places dishing up pizzas, ice-cream and anything with chips. There are a few pockets of civilisation, however.

In **Cala Major**, **Casa Tauro** (C/Miguel Rosselló Alemany 1, 971 40 01 04, closed Mon Nov-Mar, €€) is one of the oldest (opened 1981) and friendliest bistros in the area, with a pretty terrace surrounded by geraniums and dragon trees. Grilled meats, island-style and paellas are the order of the day here, with a bargain daily special. The slipway down to the beach is old Torremolinos in miniature, with a couple of ersatz Spanish places, such as flamenco bar **Al Andalus** (C/Gavina 7, 971 40 58 03, €€), which puts on a dinner and show on Thursdays and Sundays. Next door, Danish-owned restaurant **Los Laeros Ca Na Christina** (Avda. Joan Miró 275, mobile 656 75 58 56, closed Mon, €€) is a break from the norm, offering Danish food served on a charming, rickety bamboo roof terrace.

In **Sant Agustí**, if you can't get through your holiday without a curry, try **Nawaab** (Avda. Joan Miró 309, 971 40 16 91, closed lunch Mon-Fri, €€), which has branches in Leeds, Huddersfield and Bradford. Nearby is a hip new lounge bar on the beach, **Mooncala** (Avda.

Joan Miró 305, 971 22 20 09), and **Bar Lucky** (Avda. Joan Miró 352, 971 40 59 71, closed dinner Sat and all Sun, €€), a decent spot for fresh grilled fish and English breakfasts.

Generally, things are a bit more refined in **Illetes**, though choices are fewer. Smart Mallorcan food can be found at **Restaurant Es Parral** (Passeig Illetes 75, 971 70 11 27, closed Dec & Jan, €€), which is a good dinner choice, but the menu is a little heavy for lunch. The stunningly situated **Virtual Club** (Passeig Illetes 60, 971 70 32 35, closed mid Oct-Apr, €€€) serves franco-*mallorquí* cuisine to celebs and the expat hip – with dishes such as turbot with hazelnuts and bacon, and lobster lasagne with star anise – on a terrace overlooking the sea. It also has a snack bar that knocks out club sandwiches for autograph hunters, a nightclub in a cave and a marvellously handy dinghy collection service should you rock up in a yacht. If you don't, you can still taste the high life by hiring a sunlounger for €9 – the price includes water and fruit provided at intervals.

Portals Nous & Palma Nova

Portals Nous has a jet-set reputation, but its reality is a little more economy than club class. The large marina, Puerto Portals, with its flashy restaurants and chic boutiques, does attract its share of celebrities, but they're more of the ilk of Peter Stringfellow and Anthea Turner than Michael Douglas and Claudia Schiffer. There are two beaches. The one to the right of the marina as you face the sea is a grubby town beach adjoining **Marineland,** which features kid-pleasing dolphin and seal shows. The other, to the left facing a rocky islet, is used more by locals.

By contrast, **Palma Nova** is quieter and less chi-chi than Portals Nous, with more low-key beachfront cafés and bars and a wide swath of sand shaded by mature umbrella pines. If you hop around the coast a little towards Portals Nous, you'll come across a couple of more secluded inlets, including the lovely **Son Caliu**, with its fat, pineapple-shaped palms, fine sand and gentle waters.

Marineland

C/Garcilaso de la Vega 9, Costa de'n Blanes (971 67 51 25/www.aspro-ocio.es). **Open** *July, Aug* 9.30am-6pm daily. *Feb-June, Sept-mid Dec* 9.30am-5pm daily. Closed mid Dec-Jan. **Admission** €12.25-€16.50; 3s-12s €11.40; free under-3s. **Credit** AmEx, DC, MC, V.

Where to stay, eat & drink

Portals Nous is definitely not the place to come if you're on a limited budget, unless you manage to bag a good package deal. The **Lindner Golf & Wellness Resort Portals Nous** (C/Arquitecte Francesc Casas 18, 971 70 77 77, www.lindnerhotels.com, doubles incl breakfast €160-€220) is an all-round four-star package in the style of a big-game hunting lodge, with something to please everyone – golf, spa, beauty salon, swimming pool, a kids' pavilion, crèche facilities, a snack bar and restaurant **Es Romaní** (closed lunch and all Tue, €€€). The Sunday jazz brunch attracts diners from all over.

Down on the waterfront, the four-star **Hotel Son Caliu** (Avda. Son Caliu 8, 971 68 22 00, www.soncaliu.com, closed 28 Nov-20 Jan, doubles incl breakfast €114-€159) has private access to a small, secluded cove, with mature subtropical gardens spilling on to the sand. Facilities include an indoor pool, sauna and tennis courts, and the large, comfortable rooms all have terraces or balconies.

A beautifully sited alternative is the 52-room **Hotel Bendinat** (C/Andrès Ferret Sobral 1, 971 67 57 25, www.hotelbendinat.com, closed end Oct-early Apr, doubles incl breakfast €190-€280) in neighbouring **Bendinat**, which perches over a rocky cove within lovely terraced gardens that include a pool.

You'll find one of the highest concentrations of high-class restaurants in the area in Portals Nous, with something to suit everyone, but beware of elevated prices. Top billing goes to the only double Michelin-starred restaurant on the island: **Tristán** (Puerto Portals, 971 67 55 47, www.tristan-restaurant.com, closed lunch all Mon mid Oct-Apr and all Nov-Feb, €€€€).

Housed in a marquee, decked out like a footballer's wedding and attracting a mainly German clientele, the restaurant produces the sort of accomplished, overblown dishes beloved of Michelin inspectors.

Tahini Sushi Bar & Restaurant (Puerto Portals 2, 971 67 60 25, €€€) is a Japanese restaurant that manages to make minimalism ostentatious with its decor of sleek black wood, bamboo canes and pebble and water features. Owned by the same chain, **Cappuccino Puerto Portals** (Puerto Portals 1, 971 67 72 93, www.cafe-cappuccino.net, €€) is a laid-back café, with a large sunny terrace crammed with wicker chairs and waiting staff in ankle-length white aprons. It's famous for its coffee, and also does good breakfasts, snacks and cocktails.

Blackpool? No, it's **Magaluf**. *See p95.*

The best Stuff for kids

Castles

Play at Moors and Christians on the parapet of the stunning circular **Castell de Bellver** (see p71), with memorable views down over Palma and the sea.

Caves

The mighty, miraculous **Coves del Drac** (see p203) will have kids' jaws dropping; almost as impressive are the other nearby cave complexes – the **Coves d'Artà** (see p203) and the **Coves d'es Hams** (see p204).

Sealife

Next to the Coves del Drac is the **Acuàrium de Mallorca** (see p203), with 115 tanks bursting with exotic fish, while **Marineland** (see p94) near Palma Nova features dolphin and seal shows.

Trains

The cute narrow-gauge **Ferrocarril de Sóller** (see p64), which once transported Sóller's bountiful citrus crop to Palma, now provides a memorable and fun hour-long journey up through the Tramuntana mountains.

Water parks

Aqualand Magaluf (see p95) and **Western Water Park** (see p96) in Magaluf, and **Aqualand del Arenal** (see p98) are massive watery fun palaces, packed with slides, rides and copious other splashing opportunities. Perfect for cooling off on a baking summer's day.

For low-key portside dining, **Wellies** (Puerto Portals 23-24, 971 67 64 44, €€) offers dressed-up pub grub, such as Caesar salad and club sandwiches, and more refined main courses like duck leg in a fruits of the forest sauce. Further along the main strip, **Pizzeria Diablito** (Puerto Portals s/n, 971 67 65 03, €€) has salads and pasta dishes, but the pizza is the thing.

Beautifully situated next to a tiny church high above all the glitz of the port, at the end of a narrow quiet road leading from the town, is **Port'Alt** (C/Oratorio 1, 971 67 61 79, closed dinner Sun and all Mon, €€). The menu centres around steaks, duck magret and the like, and there is a large, leafy garden terrace on the headland overlooking the sea. For takeaway, **Manuel's Gourmet To Go** (Ctra. de Palma–Andratx 30, 971 67 62 15) offers well-made

Asian and Spanish meals such as chicken tikka and meatballs; there are a couple of tables on the pavement in front if you can't wait to eat.

Pickings are poor in **Palma Nova**; almost all the hotels are booked up by tour operators and nowhere can be recommended for eating.

Magaluf

What first strikes you about Magaluf is its boorish personality – and that's following the recent clean-up, when the worst of the strip's hotels were demolished. What's left consists largely of high-rise three-star apart-hotels and depressingly English pubs and caffs, proudly declaring themselves 'Manchester owned and run' on the bunting and banners that fly above their beachside terraces. It's basically Blackpool with guaranteed sun, and its very notoriety has made it a 'sight' in its own right. You wouldn't want to stay here, but it's worth spending half an hour of your time observing the curious phenomenon of mass tourism up close.

Magaluf does, though, score highly on the theme park stakes, with **Aqualand Magaluf** and its tall cowboy brother the **Western Water Park** providing plenty of aquatic fun for the kids. Many of the hotels stage Vegas-style shows, or you could try the popular **Pirates Adventure** show, complete with 'Pirate Punch' and much swashbuckling. If your pockets are deep, you can climb aboard the **Nemosub**, a tourist submarine that operates underwater excursions; the whole experience lasts around two hours, though passengers are only underwater for around 45 minutes.

The beach here may be permanently packed, but it's a beauty, offering powdery white sand, clear blue water and, offshore, the tiny Isla de sa Porrassa waiting to be explored.

Just south of Magaluf is a relatively secret and unspoilt cove, **Cala Falcó**, with a makeshift beach bar and sunloungers.

Aqualand Magaluf

Ctra. Cala Figuera 1-23 (971 13 13 71/www.aspro-ocio.es). **Open** July, Aug 10am-6pm daily; May, June, Sept, Oct 10am-5pm daily. Closed Nov-Apr. **Admission** €17.50; €11.50 3s-12s; free under-3s. **Credit** AmEx, DC, MC, V.

Nemosub

C/Galeón 2 (971 13 02 44/www.nemosub.com). **Closed** Mon & Sun and all Nov-Mar/Apr. Trip times vary; reserve at least a day in advance. **Tickets** €59; €49 3s-12s; free under-3s. **Credit** AmEx, DC, MC, V.

Pirates Adventure

Ctra. Sa Porrassa 12 (971 13 04 11/www.pirates adventure.com). **Shows** Apr-Sept times vary; phone for details. Closed Oct-Mar. **Admission** €41-€45.50; €23.50-€25.50 concessions. **Credit** MC, V.

Western Water Park

Ctra. Cala Figuera 12-22 (971 13 12 03/www.western-park.com). **Open** *May* 10am-5pm Mon-Fri, Sun. *June-Oct* 10am-6pm daily. Closed Nov-Apr. *Admission* €18; €12 3s-12s; free under-3s. **Credit** AmEx, DC, MC, V.

Where to stay, eat & drink

Nowhere to stay or eat can be recommended in Magaluf, but if it's nightlife of a questionable quality you're after, there are pubs and bars galore and the biggest disco in Europe: the monster-sized **BCM** (Avda. de S'Olivera 14, 971 13 26 09, www.bcm-planetdance.com, closed Mon-Thur, Sun Oct-Apr), which packs in 4,000 people a night. The main plaça, BCM Square, is named after it and is filled with the 'trendiest pre-club bars in town' – Bubby's Tavern and Coyote Ugly, the US saloon-style theme bar that's currently taking Spain by storm. And local expats do say it's the best place in Mallorca to catch the match. And if that's not enough to keep you entertained, you can always try your luck at the **Gran Casino Mallorca** (Urb. Sol de Mallorca s/n, 971 30 00 00, www.casinodemallorca.com) up on the bluff.

Cap de Cala Figuera

The West Bay's best-kept secret is located at its westernmost tip; the two very pretty beaches here are a world away from the rammed sands of Magaluf. Follow the road out of town along the hard-baked, pine-studded landscape to **Cala Portals Vells** with its V-shaped inlets.

   El Mago is Mallorca's first official nudist beach, carved out of the sandstone cliffs and backed by aromatic pine forests and very little development. There's a small port and matchbox-sized boats, and out of season you could easily find you have the spot to yourself.

   From here you can walk around the cliffs to **Portals Vells** and on to the **Cove de la Mare de Déu** – a chapel built into the rock by fishermen in the 15th century to give thanks for a safe return home. The caverns are actually the mines from where the rock was hewn to build the chapel.

   Continue another mile or so along the road and you'll come to the headland, crowned by a lighthouse, of **Cap de Cala Figuera**, giving stunning views back across the bay.

Where to eat & drink

There are two *chiringuitos* on Cap de Cala Figuera, one on each bay. **Es Repòs** (Platja Portals Vells s/n, 971 18 04 92, closed lunch July & Aug and all mid-Oct-mid Mar) is the friendliest and best. You can spend anything

from €6 to €60 here depending on whether you are slumming it with fresh grilled calamares or going a bit more upmarket with a grilled spiny lobster tail slathered in alioli. **Restaurante Playa del Mago** on El Mago beach (971 18 07 66, closed dinner and Nov-Mar) offers paella and more basic meals.

Resources

Internet

Magaluf *Le Café, C/Punta Ballena 20 (971 68 10 16).* **Open** 10am-1am daily.
Portals Nous *Portality-Blue, C/de Palma–Andratx 32 (971 67 75 13/www.portalityblue.com).* **Open** 10am-9pm Mon-Sat.

Post office

Palma Nova *C/Na Boira 2 (971 68 00 06).*

Tourist information

Illetes *OIT, Passeig Illetes 4 (971 40 27 39/ www.calvia.com).* **Open** 9am-3pm Mon-Fri.
Magaluf *OIT, Avda. Pere Vaquer Ramis 1 (971 13 11 26/www.calvia.com).* **Open** 9am-6pm daily.
Palma Nova *OIT, Passeig de la Mar 13 (971 68 23 65/www.calvia.com).* **Open** 9am-6pm Mon-Fri; 9am-1.30pm Sat, Sun.

Getting there

By bus

From Palma, the No.1 runs to Porto Pi, 3 to Cas Català, 6 to Sant Agusti, and the 20 to Palmanova

East Bay of Palma

Favoured mainly by German package tourists, the East Bay starts well, having admirably retained some of its Mallorcan flavour – particularly around Portitxol and Ciutat Jardi (*see p71*), the area's saving grace. After that, it's downhill…

Can Pastilla to S'Arenal

Beyond Ciutat Jardi, **Can Pastilla**, the East Bay's biggest purpose-built resort has grown up along **Platja de Palma**, offering five and a half kilometres (three and a half miles) of white sand beach and watersports galore, especially of the blow-up banana variety. The sudden change in atmosphere and ambience is pronounced as you head into this well-chartered touristville.

   A footpath and cycle track stretches all the way to **S'Arenal** via encroaching apartment blocks and endless shops selling beach towels, cheap holiday clothes, sunglasses and suntan cream. If Magaluf points to Blackpool,

Can Pastilla. *See p97.*

Where to stay, eat & drink

In **Can Pastilla**, the two-star **Miraflores**
(C/Xabec 4, 971 26 31 00, reservations 902
40 06 61, www.miraflores.amic-hotels.com,
closed 20 Oct-20 Apr, doubles incl breakfast
€49-€89) and the **Hotel Gala** (C/Xabec 5,
971 26 08 16, reservations 902 40 06 61,
www.gala.amic-hotels.com, closed 20 Oct-
20 Apr, doubles incl breakfast €49-€79),
owned by the same people, supply clean,
no-frills accommodation. Most of the other
hotels in this area are block booked by
German tour companies.

If for some unknown reason you decide
that you want to stay in or near **S'Arenal**,
the classiest hotel is the **Mallorca Marriott
Son Antem Golf Resort & Spa** (Ctra.
Palma–Llucmajor, km3.4, 971 12 91 00,
www.marriott.com, doubles incl breakfast
€169-€209), a few kilometres out of town.
The villa-style resort is set in acres of rolling
countryside and offers two championship-level
golf courses, holistic spa treatments and
world-class dining.

A better choice if you want to party is the
aptly named four-star **Hotel Gran Fiesta**
(C/Marbella 28, 971 26 31 24, www.fehm/es/
pmi/granfiesta, doubles incl breakfast €62-
€104). Located just across the road from the
beach, it has a sauna, two swimming pools
and nightly entertainment. For something
cheap and cheerful, try the 30-room **Hotel
Las 5 Islas** (C/San Cristóbal 38, 971 44 11
20, www.milisa.com, doubles incl breakfast
€47-€55); all rooms have terraces, and a
handful of them have sea views.

Can Pastilla has some decent nightlife.
Head for the handful of Café del Mar-style
beach bars playing chillout grooves, funk
and house music around **Cala Estancia**.
Palma's hipsters come out here on balmy
summer evenings to watch a dramatic, blood-
red sun go down over the silhouette of the
Tramuntana mountains. **El Cielo** (C/Pajel 1,
971 74 32 42, www.elcielocafe.es, open 2pm-
3am daily) is one of the best places.

Resources

Tourist information

S'Arenal *OIT, Plaça Reina Maria Cristina s/n (971
44 04 14/www.llucmajor.org).* **Open** *Apr-Oct* 8am-
2.30pm Mon-Fri. Closed Nov-Mar.

Getting there

By bus

From Palma, the Nos.15 and 23 run to S'Arenal, and
the 17 runs as far as Can Pastilla.

so S'Arenal is Frankfurt-on-Sea, albeit a
sunny one. Tapas translates to *biergarten* and
bratwurst, the signs are in German and you'll
be hard-pressed to find a Spanish-speaking
waiter. The beach may be long and wide, but
there's little joy to be had in coming here, unless
you're planning to visit **Aqualand del Arenal**
– the area's waterpark.

Aqualand del Arenal

*Autovia Palma–S'Arenal, km15, Exit 13 (971 44 00
00/www.aspro-ocio.es).* **Open** *July, Aug* 10am-6pm
daily. *May, June, Sept, Oct* 10am-5pm daily. Closed
Nov-Apr. **Admission** €20.50; €14.50 3s-12s; free
under-3s. **Credit** AmEx, DC, MC, V.

West Mallorca

Lluc. *See p132.*

West Mallorca

West Mallorca

The further you travel from the Bay of Palma, the wilder the island becomes.

West Mallorca provides some of the Balearics' most memorable scenery. At its south-west fringes, overspill resorts from the Bay of Palma try their hardest to neutralise the spectacular backdrop, but as soon as you round the island's westernmost point, you enter another world. With the slopes of the southern Tramuntana mountains dropping almost directly into the sea, there are no beaches and no room for extensive holiday development. Just stunning natural beauty.

THE SOUTH-WEST

The tone becomes more measured as the coast road heads west from Magaluf towards the family-oriented resorts of Peguera and Santa Ponça. These are the quintessence of mass tourism: solid, efficient and almost entirely devoid of character. The coast in this area is the most jagged on Mallorca, marked with numerous bays and coves, and fringed by tiny islands. The best-known of these islands is Sa Dragonera, a nature reserve and birdwatcher's paradise. There are a few pretty spots, including Camp de Mar with its sheltered bay and small beach; Port d'Andratx, an increasingly trendy alternative for the moneyed crowd; and tiny Cala Fornells, a low-key resort set in a tiny bay.

Inland is a complete contrast, almost untouched by tourism and hiding some of the prettiest villages in this part of the island. The seat of local government is Calviá, once one of the poorest towns in Spain; now, thanks to tourism, one of the richest. The surrounding area is characterised by dense pine groves, torrentes and soaring peaks. Among them lie the villages of Puigpunyent and Galilea, tiny places less than half an hour from the coast but part of a Mallorca from another era.

WEST COAST

The coast from Andratx to Sóller is isolated from the rest of the island by the Serra de Tramuntana, which falls steeply into the Mediterranean in a series of jagged cliffs and surf-battered coves. The spectacular precipices, pine-forested hills and shimmering blue of the sea give it an air of almost unworldly beauty that, thanks to the absence of sandy beaches and unsuitability of the terrain for building, is almost pristine; tiny villages are all that dot the mountainsides. The majesty and peace of the mountains have drawn foreign writers and artists to this bit of the coast for years, particularly to the lovely village of Deià, where Robert Graves was a pioneering expat.

Further along the coast, Port de Sóller offers a complete contrast to the brash resorts of the south, while inland the town of Sóller and the villages nearby – Fornalutx, one of Spain's prettiest, and Biniaraix – have managed to retain their calm and character.

In contrast, the once-tranquil hamlet of Valldemossa, briefly home to Frédéric Chopin and George Sand, is too close to Palma and the Bay of Palma's bucket-and-spade resorts for its own good. Its setting is still beautiful, but this is one spot that has been overwhelmed by tourism.

NORTHERN SERRA

The jagged peaks, wide-open spaces and tortuous roads that creep through the northern Serra endow this part of Mallorca with a majestic scale that doesn't really belong to the island. The road that snakes its way from Sóller to Pollença must be one of the island's slowest, if most dramatic. Thrill-seekers shouldn't miss the nerve-jangling side road off to the coast at Sa Calobra, which provides the only road access to the sea between Port de Sóller and Cala Sant Vicenç. There is superb hiking throughout the northern Tramuntana, including the ascent of Massanella, Mallorca's highest climbable peak. It overlooks the island's most famous monastery at Lluc, the hub of the northern Serra

The best...

Hotels
Hotel Espléndido, Port de Sóller (*p130*); **Sa Pedrissa**, Deià (*p123*); **La Residencia**, Deià (*p123*); **Son Net**, Puigpunyent (*p108*).

Resorts
Port d'Andratx (*p104*); **Port de Sóller** (*p128*).

Restaurants
Bens d'Avall, near Sóller (*p126*); **Es Port**, Port de Valldemossa (*p115*); **Es Racó de Teix**, Deià (*p120*); **Restaurante Es Guix**, near Lluc (*p134*); **Es Vergeret**, Cala Tuent (*p133*).

Villages & towns
Banyalbufar (*p110*); **Deià** (*p118*); **Fornalutx** (*p127*); **Sóller** (*p124*).

The South-west

The best resorts lie in the west, while inland tourists are a rare breed.

Peguera.

Santa Ponça, Peguera, Cala Fornells & Camp de Mar

The autopista becomes the C719 just west of Magaluf. From here you can go south to thus-far unspoiled Portals Vells (*see p97*). Alternatively, you can head west, passing **Son Ferrer** and **El Toro** – two lifeless *urbanizaciones*, the latter of which has a small marina, **Port Adriano**, and a luxury hotel (Vista Port Adriano; *see below*) – before running along a wild stretch of coast and reaching **Santa Ponça**, where Jaume I stepped ashore in 1229, planting his flag and marking the start of the Reconquest of the Balearics. The event is marked by a tall stone cross, carved with reliefs at its base, which stands on the headland at the southern tip of the bay, and the **Capilla de la Piedra Sagrada**, where the first Christian mass was held.

But no one comes to Santa Ponça for its historical significance – this is a resort plain and simple, favoured by Brits, dominated by a number of characterless package tour-packed

hotels and some truly hideous places to eat. Santa Ponça's saving grace is its beach, which is long, with fine white sand leading out into a clear, shallow bay.

Santa Ponça sprawls into Peguera, but to get there you will need to get back on the C719. **Peguera** is less depressingly downmarket than Santa Ponça, with almost entirely German-run shops, restaurants and bratwurst stalls. The three beaches here (one disfigured by the high-rise hotel looming behind it) are well kept and there is a pleasant promenade and a part-pedestrianised main street, El Bulevar de Peguera, lined with tacky shops.

If you fancy a (tiny) beach, take a left at the roundabout just after the Bulevar and head to **Cala Fornells**, a pint-size and unexpectedly delightful little place on the other side of the bay. The road threads through **Aldea Cala Fornells**, where cute private villas tumble down the hillside in a picturesque, colourful jumble, before reaching Cala Fornells, with its postage stamp-sized sandy beach, some concreted rocks on which to sunbathe and two big hotels.

From Cala Fornells it's a short drive back on the C719 to **Camp de Mar**, nestled in a perfect little bay, with a small slice of beach and clear, calm waters. The idyllic setting is disfigured somewhat by three enormous hotels right on the seafront and, sprinkled over the pine-forested hills behind, a number of large private villas – Claudia Schiffer and Michael Schumacher are among their owners. There's little to do here other than laze around, which is, of course, why people come. A row of small shops on a pedestrianised street leads down to the sea and a number of decent restaurants, which, though mobbed during the day, are appealing at night as many people eat in their hotels.

Where to stay, eat & drink

In **El Toro**, the five-star **Hotel Vista Port Adriano** (Urb. El Toro, Port Adriano, 971 23 73 23, www.hotelportadriano.com, doubles €260-€315 incl breakfast) has 56 doubles and 11 suites beside the marina. The rooms are a good size, simply designed with large beds, big balconies and lovely coast views, and all come with marble bathrooms and separate showers. There's a pool and a good restaurant.

The best choice in **Santa Ponça** is the **Hesperia Playas de Mallorca** (Gran Via del Puig Major 2, 971 69 33 66, www.hoteles-hesperia.es, closed Nov-Apr, doubles €85-€120), a bright, modern hotel over the road from the beach. It's set around a large swimming pool and has good-sized rooms (all with balconies, and most with pool or sea views).

The nicest spot to stay in **Peguera** is the three-star **Hotel Bahía** (Avda. Peguera 81, 971 68 61 00, www.hotelbahia.com, closed Nov-Mar, doubles €76-€81 incl breakfast), a very pretty place in its own grounds. It's great value for what you get: smartly designed air-conditioned rooms, indoor and outdoor pools, sauna, putting green and pool bar.

In **Cala Fornells**, **Hotel Petit Cala Fornells** (971 68 54 05, closed 2 Nov-19 Dec, doubles €90-€156) is a delightful spot with an upper *terraza* for drinks and views, and a lower one for dining. It has classily furnished rooms, some with four-poster beds and all with balconies.

There are a couple of good restaurants in **Aldea Cala Fornells**: **La Gran Tortuga** (971 68 60 23, closed Mon in Jan & Feb, all Dec) boasts a stunning setting, with a balcony and *terraza*, set round a swimming pool and with priceless views towards Cala Fornells. The pool bar serves light snacks (€); upstairs is the restaurant (€€€), which has some fine main dishes, including *bacalao gratinado* (baked salt cod with garlic) and a delicious *merluza a la Mallorquina* (Mallorcan-style hake). Diners can

use the pool. **C'an Luís Mi Bodega** (C/Cala Fornells, 971 68 60 35, closed Wed and Dec & Jan, €) serves tapas on a shaded terrace, and specialises in meat dishes, such as *cochinillo al horno* (roast piglet), as well as good-value paella.

The best place to stay in **Camp de Mar** (by some distance) is the **Dorint** (C/Taula 2, 971 13 65 65, www.sofitel.com, doubles €270-€385), set beside an 18-hole golf course, just back from the beach. This is real five-star luxury, with extremely comfortable and very big rooms, all with large balconies and views either of the golf course or the sea. There is a lovely pool and two superb restaurants, one serving traditional Mallorcan and Spanish cuisine, the other 'international'. It also has a large gym, an indoor pool and a spa.

On the beach you can choose from two hotels: **Grupotel Playa Camp de Mar** (971 23 50 25, www.grupotel.com, closed Jan-Apr, doubles €104-€208), popular with British tourists and offering comfortable, characterless (mainly) sea-facing rooms, a large pool, jacuzzi and tennis court. The other option is the **Hotel Riu Camp de Mar** (Avda. de la Platja, 971 23 52 00, www.riu.com, closed Oct-mid Jan, doubles €142-€183 incl breakfast). It's mainly used by German tourists and has a large swimming pool and sports centre with tennis and squash, games room, kids' playground, bike hire and scuba diving. In July and August, both these hotels are likely to be block-booked by tour operators, so ring ahead.

Eating options in Camp de Mar include the **Petit Ambassador** (Camí de Salinar 1, 971 23 58 18, closed Nov-mid Jan, €€), which has a shady terraza affording great views of the beach and the bay, and specialises in fresh fish. **La Siesta** (C/Ses Dunes 5, 971 23 58 41, closed Nov-Feb, €€) offers traditional meaty Mallorcan cuisine; it has a pretty vine-covered terrace, again with pleasant views. **Arco Iris** (C/Salinar s/n, 971 23 51 61, closed Nov-Feb, €, lunch *menú* €7) is the best-value place along this stretch, with a more relaxed feel and lower prices that don't reflect any dip in the standard of the food. It specialises in paella of the Valencian and *marisco* (seafood) variety. The aptly named **Bar-Restaurante Illeta** (no phone, €), occupies the rock in the middle of the bay, and is reached by a walkway from the beach. Although the food isn't the best (though it does serve a decent selection of reasonably priced fish and shellfish), it wins hands down for location.

Resources

Internet
Santa Ponça *Ciber, Puig d'es Teix 7 (971 69 73 24).* **Open** 10am-10pm Mon-Fri; 4-10pm Sat, Sun.

West Mallorca

Post office

Peguera *C/Pins 5 (971 68 63 95).*
Santa Ponça *Avda. Puig Major s/n (971 69 15 56).*

Tourist information

Peguera *OIT, C/Ratoli 1 (971 68 70 83/ omtpeguera@calvia.com).* **Open** 9am-6pm daily.
Santa Ponça *OIT, Via Puig de Galatzo s/n (971 69 17 12/omtsantaponsa@calvia.com).* **Open** 9am-6pm Mon-Fri; 9am-1.30pm Sat, Sun.

Port d'Andratx

The coastal road (PM102) wends gently west from Camp de Mar, up through the pine-forested hills pock-marked with huge villas, before reaching **Port d'Andratx**, a snug place built round a bay that is home to a marina, a working fishing fleet and a large number of restaurants and bars. This was once a quiet fishing village, but its proximity to Palma and picturesque setting have transformed it into one of the most popular spots along this part of the coast. Despite this, it retains an old-fashioned charm and a stubborn resistance to the worst of the horrors that have been inflicted on towns further east. However, horrifyingly speedy development in recent years now scars the hills that encircle the bay with identikit villas (though their twinkling lights look pretty at night).

The town's main artery is the harbourside road, which starts as Avda. Mateo Bosch and ends up as Avda. Almirante Riera Alemany. Most places of interest are along here, on parallel C/Isaac Peral and on the streets leading between the two, particularly around the tiny pedestrianised Plaça Almirante Oquendo. Port d'Andratx has plenty of small shops and a scattering of designer boutiques, reflecting the well-heeled clientele it attracts; look particularly on C/Isaac Peral and C/Cristófal Colom.

A boat service (mobile 639 61 75 45) runs to Sant Elm hourly every day from 10.15am until 1.15pm, with boats returning on the hour (last at 3pm).

Where to eat & drink

Port d'Andratx is packed with places to eat. The café-pâtisserie **Consigna** (Avda. Mateo Bosch 19, 971 67 16 04, closed Nov, €), near the start of the harbourside road, is popular with locals and tourists for coffee and pastries, while a little further along you can enjoy the excellent coffee and salads at the town's branch of sleek café chain **Cappuccino** (Avda. Mateo Bosch 31, 971 67 22 14, €).

The restaurants specialise in seafood and there is not a great deal to choose between them. **Miramar** (Avda. Mateo Bosch 18, 971

Camp de Mar. *See p102.*

67 16 17, €€€€) is perhaps the best (though a line of parked cars out front mars the view of the fishing fleet), but with prices to match; the shellfish is superb, but you'll have to dig very deep indeed to enjoy the house special: spiny lobster stew (around €60). **Rocamar** (Avda. Almirante Riera Alemany 27, 971 67 12 61, closed Wed in Oct and all Nov-Jan, €€€, lunch *menú* €16), a bit further on, is a more affordable alternative that also majors in shellfish. **Marisquería Galicia** (C/Isaac Peral 37, 971 67 27 05, closed 7 Jan-7 Feb, €€) is a Galician seafood restaurant where the atmosphere and prices are less touristy than those on the front; try the *pulpo à la Gallega* (Galician-style octopus).

There are four neighbouring late-night bars about two-thirds of the way along the harbourfront, after the Hotel Brismar; most

West Mallorca

Port d'Andratx.

Sant Elm. *See p106.*

West Mallorca

have terraces on the front overlooking the bay. First up is **Tim's** (no phone), a small drinking den that serves home-made pizzas at lunch; **Valentinos Bar & Art Café** (no phone) is next, which offers snacks and home-made cakes during the day (you can't miss the painted life-size horses on its first-floor balcony); next is **Mitj y Mitj** (no phone), which plays club sounds until late and serves up pizzas, salads and *pa amb oli*; and lastly there's **L'Havana** (971 67 26 08) – it doles out Cuban-inspired cocktails and a small selection of tapas.

Where to stay

Surprisingly, Port d'Andratx has few places to stay. Built against the hill overlooking the bay, the German-managed **Hotel Villa Italia** (C/San Carlos 13, 971 67 40 11, www.hotel villaitalia.com, doubles €171-€213), as its name suggests, resembles a Tuscan *palazzo*, complete with stucco ceilings, Italianate marble fittings and Roman columns – it's all a touch Liberace. All rooms have balconies and great views; there are ten doubles and six suites – with round, tiled baths – and a split-level room at the top with views across the bay. Facilities include a pool, gym and good restaurant with a terrace.

The simple, old-style **Hotel Brismar** (C/Almirante Riera Alemany 6, 971 67 16 00, www.fehm.es/pmi/brismar, closed mid Nov-mid Dec, mid Jan-mid Feb, doubles €80-€95) enjoys a great location overlooking the marina, with its own private sundeck by the beach. It's clean and friendly, and half the rooms have

Walk 1 La Trapa

Distance: 9km (6 miles). Circular.
Time: 3hrs (with possible extension).

The south-western tip of Mallorca is a wild and beautiful spot, and this walk, up to the ruined monastery of La Trapa, is one of the island's most popular hikes (so don't expect to be doing it alone). A reasonable degree of fitness is required, as there's a long upward climb and then a descent that involves a fair amount of rock scrambling, but the phenomenal views of the coastline and the offshore island of Sa Dragonera more than compensate.

Start at the rough car park around two kilometres (one and a quarter miles) before you reach Sant Elm on the road from Andratx. (You'll pass a smarter car park at a cemetery 200 metres before the one you want.) Here you'll see a sign marking the Camí Sa Font dels Morers by a map showing the route to La Trapa. Head off on the wide track that leads gently downwards in the direction of Sant Elm – you'll be sticking to this easy-to-follow track all the way to La Trapa.

After around ten minutes, the path splits at a sign saying 'Camí de Can Bolei'; you bear round to the right. The path winds sedately through the valley, with rocky hills rising on both sides, until, after a further quarter of an hour, you come to a T-junction in front of a couple of houses. You will return along the left-hand path to this spot later, but take the right turn now (marked 'Camí Coll dels Cairals'), looping around the back of the houses and then starting to climb the hill beyond. This is the beginning of a steady but tiring 45-minute ascent.

After about 20 minutes you reach a sign that says 'Reserva Natural La Trapa' and, usually, a chain across the road, barring anyone foolish enough to have brought their vehicle this far. Continue, and, when you reach the top of the climb, you are rewarded with superb views in two directions – down towards Sant Elm and west along the coast. It can be very windy up here, but the hardy mountain goats that you may see clearly aren't fazed by a bit of a breeze. It's worth scrambling up the rocks to your left for an even better vantage point, and a black vulture's-eye view of the jagged little island of Sa Dragonera.

Down below you'll also see the ruins of La Trapa, to which you descend in five or so minutes. Trappist monks, fleeing from the chaos of the Peninsular War, arrived here in 1810, but were moved on by the Spanish government after only 14 years.

You can extend the walk at this point by continuing along the west coast (at the first hairpin bend as you come down to La Trapa,

balconies and views; those at the front can be a bit noisy on summer nights though, as the town's late-night bars are right next door.

Set in its own grounds one street back from the main drag in a quiet location, the **Hostal Catalina Vera** (C/Isaac Peral 63, 971 67 19 18, closed Dec & Jan, doubles €58) is an excellent, friendly budget option, with loads of character. The breakfast room is filled with ceramic pots and pictures, the rooms are very clean and comfortable and all have their own shower room.

Resources

Internet
Port d'Andratx *Cyber, C/Sa Fàbrica (971 67 10 10).* **Open** 10.30am-2.30pm, 6-11pm Mon-Sat; 6-11pm Sun.

Tourist information
Port d'Andratx *OMT, C/Sa Fàbrica 12 (971 62 80 19).* **Open** 8.30am-3.30pm Mon, Tue, Fri; 9.30am-4pm Wed, Thur; 9.30am-2pm Sat, Sun.

Andratx, Sant Elm & Sa Dragonera

Four kilometres (two and a half miles) inland from Port d'Andratx is **Andratx**, a sleepy place nestling among slopes of olives and almonds. It's a common arrangement in Mallorca to find towns set back from the coast, with their associated 'Port' nearby, and reflects the threat of pirate attack that has plagued the island through most of its history (pirate sorties were common in this area until the 18th century). Andratx's origins are Roman, when it was known as Andrachium. After the Reconquest, Jaume I made it his base, eventually ceding the area to the Bishop of Barcelona.

The town is dominated by the fortress-like church of **Santa Maria**, with huge walls built to deter would-be marauders. Clamber to the top for great views of the Port. The **Castell Son Mas**, an oft-fortified tower dating from the 15th century, was similarly constructed – there's a relief of one wild-haired pirate staring

there's a narrow path off to the right, marked with a sign to S'Arracó and Sant Elm pointing in the direction you've just come from).

Down at the monastery you'll probably see evidence of the restoration of the buildings being undertaken by the GOB environmental organisation, which has owned the La Trapa reserve since 1980. The reserve covers 75 hectares (187 acres). If you're a twitcher, you should look out for Marmora's warbler and Yelkouan shearwater (two species endemic to the Balearics), and also peregrine falcons and booted eagles. You'll probably have noticed the bent and broken skeletons of many trees in the area, the legacy of a major fire in 1994 that burned 1,300 hectares (3,241 acres) of land. GOB has done a great deal of work since then to replant the slopes.

Walk down past the monastery's restored mill house to the viewing area for more wonderful, precipitous views over to Sa Dragonera, and down to the rocky cove of Cala Basset (overlooked by a watchtower). An inscribed stone here tells a cautionary tale – a young Mallorcan fell to his death at this spot in 1985.

When you've had your fill, climb back to just above the monastery and take the path to the right signed to Sant Elm, climbing up and over the headland, following the rough path marked by cairns and crimson paint splodges. It's a pretty tough, steep scramble.

Around 45 minutes after you set off from the monastery you reach a T-junction in the path. To the right, through two concrete posts, a walk of around a quarter of an hour will bring you down to Cala Basset, where you can swim off the rocks on calm days. If you don't fancy a dip, take the left turn and continue on towards Sant Elm on a track that becomes wider and easier.

After seven or so minutes you come to another T-junction where a sign marks the Camí Punta de sa Galera. If you feel in need of refreshment, turn right and then immediately left after the abandoned, mural-spattered house C'an Tomeví, and within 20 minutes you'll be in Sant Elm where you can get a meal or a drink at one of a number of seafront restaurant-bars. (From here, you can then either retrace your steps to the T-junction of the paths or walk the couple of kilometres up the road towards Andratx to return to the car park.)

Otherwise, take the left turn, and within ten minutes you're back at the point by the two houses where you turned right just before beginning your ascent of the hill. Turn right here and retrace your steps to the car park. It should take around 25 minutes.

out to sea on the outer wall. It's also worth popping in to the **Centre Cultural Andratx**, lying just outside the town on the road to Es Capdellà, to check out one of the three annual contemporary art exhibitions and to see the modest but growing permanent collection; German artists feature heavily, and much of it is challenging stuff. It's worth timing your visit to Andratx for a Wednesday so you can catch the local market.

The PM103 twists and turns westwards from Andratx through pretty countryside of pines and rocky outcrops, passing through the nondescript hamlet of **S'Arracó**, before reaching **Sant Elm** and the coast. Despite its promising location on the map as the westernmost point on Mallorca, Sant Elm is a unprepossessing little resort, with two small, grey sand beaches that get very crowded on summer weekends. The setting, though – surrounded by forested hills and looking out towards the island of Sa Dragonera – is a treat, and there is a decent choice of places to eat.

Perhaps the biggest draw, however, is the chance to take a boat trip to virgin **Sa Dragonera** (Crucero Margarita, mobile 639 61 75 45, mobile 696 42 39 33, €10, €7 under-12s); boats leave from the far end of Avda. Rei Jaume I, near El Pescador restaurant (first boat at 10.15am and hourly thereafter, last back Oct-Apr 3pm, May-Sept 4pm). This uninhabited four kilometre- (two and a half-mile-) long island, named after its supposed similarity to the jagged back of a dragon, is an extension of the Tramuntana, and well known for its birdlife. Among the species you may spot are Eleanora's falcons, cormorants, Audouin's gulls, shags and petrels; it is also home to a large number of lizards. In the 15th century one of the Balearics' most notorious pirates, Redbeard, used it as his base; today, it's a nature reserve and the protected area includes two smaller islands, Illa Mitjana and Es Pantaleu (the public can use the beach on the latter). You'll need to get permission to visit from the reception centre in Cala Lladó, where the boat drops you. You can't wander at will; the centre will give you details of permitted itineraries, which include hiking up the 312 metre- (1,024 foot-) high Puig de Na Popia and walking to the lighthouse at Cap des Llebeitx, the southernmost point of the island. **Parc Natural de Sa Dragonera** (971 18 06 32), based in Sant Elm, has information about the island.

A German-run scuba diving centre, Scuba Activa (Plaça Monsenyor Sebastian Grau 7, 971 23 91 02, www.scuba-activa.com, closed Nov-15 Mar), offers dives around Sa Dragonera.

To the north-east of Sant Elm rise steep, rocky hills. Here lies the **Reserva Natural La Trapa**, centred on the ruined monastery of **La Trapa**. The reserve is only accessible on foot and the one and a half-hour walk up to it is one of the island's most popular hikes. One path starts out at the northern end of Sant Elm; another one is detailed on *p106* **Walk 1**.

Centre Cultural Andratx

Ctra. Andratx–Es Capdellà, km1.5 (971 13 77 70/ www.ccandratx.com). **Open** 10am-6pm Tue-Sat; 10am-4pm Sun. **Admission** €5; €3 concessions. **No credit cards**.

Where to stay, eat & drink

There are two accommodation options in **Sant Elm**. The unattractive **Hotel Aquamarín** (C/Cala Conis 4, 971 23 90 75, www.universalhotels.org, closed Nov-Apr, doubles €43-€53 incl breakfast) sits between the two beaches; its rooms are basic and clean; all rooms have balconies and most have sea views. The alternative is the **Hostal Dragonera** (Avda. Rei Jaume I 5, 971 23 90 86, hostaldragonera@teleline.es, closed Dec and Jan, doubles €49-€58) which offers simple, clean en suite rooms with tiled floors and views towards the island, and a decent restaurant with a lovely *terraza*.

The best place to eat is right at the end of the street that runs up from the beach. **El Pescador** (Avda. Jaime I 48, 971 23 91 98, €€) serves the freshest of catches from its own fishing boat, the *Caladent II*. Try the house special, a delicious light *lenguado* (sole), or the *paella de mariscos*. There are a number of other decent places along Avda. Rei Jaume I, including **Vista Mar** (No.46, 971 23 90 44, closed Mon, €€), which, true to its name, offers great sea views, and excellent fish dishes, and **Na Caragola** at No.23 (971 23 90 06, closed Wed and Nov-Jan, €€), which occupies a prime spot at the end of the street with a fine terrace affording views across to Sa Dragonera; it specialises in paellas and fresh fish dishes at reasonable prices.

Resources

Police station

Andratx *C/Curia 1 (971 62 80 08)*.

Post office

Andratx *Avda. Joan Carles I 20 (971 23 53 44)*.

Calvià, Galilea & Puigpunyent

The regional capital of **Calvià** lies in the foothills of the mountains, just ten minutes' drive inland from Santa Ponça and the coast, and yet is completely untouched by tourism – that is, other than growing fat on tourist euros; its gleaming, outsize town hall is proof of this. Calvià now has one of the richest town councils in the whole of Spain – 40 years ago it was one of the poorest in Europe.

The town was founded in the 13th century, and the church that tops it, **Sant Joan Baptista** (open 10am-1pm daily) was begun in the same century, but not completed until 1896, after numerous remodellings. The exterior is notable for its slender belltowers and large Gothic window, and a Romanesque-style façade with a depiction of the Garden of Gethsemane; the interior has an enormous cockleshell emblem carved into the ceiling over the red marble altar. Outside in Plaça Església is a fountain, a shaded terrace looking out over the valley to the coast, and a mural depicting the history of the town.

Four kilometres (two and a half miles) west of Calvià is tiny **Es Capdellà**, from where the PMV103-2 road follows a spectacularly winding course north-east up into the mountains. After around 20 minutes of driving you reach the village of **Galilea**, which spills dramatically down the slopes. This is one of the loveliest unspoiled spots in the area, with extraordinary views across the countryside and down to the coast. Galilea is topped by the **Parroquía de la Immaculada**, a chunky little church with a sundial carved into its outside wall.

From here, it's a further 20 minutes' drive to **Puigpunyent** (meaning 'pointed peak'), another sleepy little place with an appealingly isolated feel (yet it's only 20 minutes from Palma). The village is spread along a small valley and dominated by the thrusting 1,027-metre (3,369-foot) peak of **Galatzó** – hence its name. It's best known for being home to one of the finest hotels on the island, **Son Net** (*see p109*), a former private mansion owned by Count Ramón Zaforteza that dominates the village from a plateau above it. In Puigpunyent itself there's little to see, beyond the 17th-century parish church and its outsize belltower in Plaça Leon XIII.

The source of the **Torrent Sa Riera** (at 23 kilometres/14 miles one of the longest on the island), which extends all the way to Palma, lies a couple of kilometres north from here.

From Puigpunyent, you can either head east along the PMV104-1 to Palma, or north along the PMV110-1 to Esporles, Sa Granja and the west coast (*see p110*).

Where to stay & eat

If you want to stay near **Calvià**, a kilometre south of the town is **Son Malero** (Camí de Son Malero s/n, 971 67 03 01, www.sonmalero.com, doubles €100 incl breakfast), boasting a pool and magnificent views; it has four double rooms, a suite and an apartment with its own terrace.

Calvià has several good restaurants, including **Restaurant Sant Joan** (Plaça Església 5, 971 67 09 27, closed Mon, €€€€). Located beside the church, it's a smart place with a pretty *terraza* and excellent – albeit very expensive – French cuisine, courtesy of chef Eric Lymberis; his specialities include snails with mushrooms, red mullet, and lemon sorbet with vodka. **Mesón C'an Torrat** (C/Major 29-31, 971 67 06 82, closed lunch May-Sept, all Tue and 20 Nov-20 Dec, €€), specialises in suckling pig. **Ses Forquetes** (C/C'an Vich s/n, 971 67 06 13, closed dinner, all Sat & Sun, €€) occupies a lovely spot below the town hall and offers smart surroundings and very reasonable prices; try the paella, rabbit or langoustines.

In **Galilea**, **Scott's Galilea** (971 87 01 00, 0871 717 4227 in UK, www.scottsgalilea. com, €187-€289 for two people incl breakfast, minimum four-night stay) is not exactly a hotel, but more a luxurious collection of private studios and houses, refurbished and redesigned by George and Judy Scott, who run Scott's Hotel in Binissalem. Each of the seven studios and houses has a sitting room and kitchen, most have a fireplace and all enjoy south-facing terraces. The three houses are split-level, classily fitted and very private, and one can accommodate four people. The views from all the properties are some of the best on the island. There is also an outdoor pool and sauna.

Puigpunyent is home to the outstanding **Son Net** (971 14 70 00, www.sonnet.es, closed 9 Jan-9 Feb, doubles €193-€353). The reception area looks out to the internal patio, with a small well at its centre (the hotel still uses water from it). Around the patio run corridors hung with original Chagall, Hockney and Warhol paintings, a small bar, fitness centre and the original chapel. The grounds are extensive and perfectly kept, with terraces, fountains, huge old cypresses, a clay tennis court and an enormous pool surrounded by private cabañas

Galilea.

and a poolside bar and restaurant. There are just 25 rooms, all luxuriously fitted with big, comfortable beds and soft pillows, antique wooden furniture and marble bathrooms. The bedrooms at the back, though comfy, are best avoided as they have no views; if you can afford it, go for a deluxe double (or one of the extraordinary suites, the choicest of which will set you back €1,284). **L'Orangerie** restaurant (€€€€) occupies a beautiful old olive pressing room, complete with original press, and has an outdoor *terraza* overlooking the village. The food is refined stuff: the likes of gazpacho with rock fish and octopus, and sea bass with pineapple chutney.

If your budget is slightly more modest, there's a good *agroturismo* a couple of kilometres from Puigpunyent; **Son Pont** (Ctra. Palma–Puigpunyent, km12.3, 971 71 95 27, www.sonpont.com, double €98 incl breakfast) is a restored 17th-century Mallorcan house set in its own grounds, with four rooms and priceless mountain views.

Resources

Post office
Calvià *C/Serral 1 (971 67 06 27).*
Puigpunyent *C/Na Beltrana s/n (no phone).*

Getting there

By bus
Hourly buses run from Palma around the western Bay of Palma and on to Santa Ponça, Peguera, Camp de Mar, Andratx and Port d'Andratx. There is 1 bus (Mon-Fri) runs from Peguera to Valldemossa via Andratx, Estellencs and Banyalbufar.

West Coast

The west really is the best of Mallorca.

Estellencs, Banyalbufar & Esporles

A drive along the twisting C710 coastal road from Andratx to Sóller is one of the great Mallorcan experiences. You won't find any more dramatic and sublime landscape in Europe than the dizzying, pine-clad slopes of the Tramuntana plunging hundreds of metres down into an azure sea.

There are a number of places to admire the view, the first of which (coming from Andratx) is the **Mirador de Ricardo Roca**, which is marked by a restaurant with a terrace and a viewpoint beyond it.

A further four kilometres (two and a half miles) brings you to the first settlement you encounter on this hostile coastline: **Estellencs**. It's a diminutive place of chunky stone houses scattered across the terraced mountainside and centred on the small church of **Sant Joan Baptista**. A two kilometre- (one and a quarter mile-) long track (marked 'Platja') leads down from the main road to a postage stamp-sized shingly beach. There are a handful of good places to stay in the village and a couple of decent restaurants. A stunning walk to the next village along, Banyalbufar, is indicated by a sign off the main road on the Banyalbufar side of the village – it's a five-hour trek there and back, and you'll be rewarded by staggering views all the way.

A few kilometres further along the main road is another stunning spot, often known as the **Mirador de Ses Ànimes** (Viewpoint of the Souls) but signposted as **Mirador Torre del Verger**. The watchtower (which you can climb up) was built in 1579 as a lookout point to spot pirates and provides one of the finest views along this stretch of the coast. There's a plaque here commemorating the Habsburg Archduke Ludwig Salvator (*see p24* **Local hero**).

Banyalbufar lies just beyond the next bend (six kilometres/four miles from Estellencs), and is similarly formed from a series of terraces created by the Moors, who built an elaborate series of channels, pipes and cisterns that still irrigate the fields. They named the village 'bany al buhar', which means 'vineyard by the sea', and produced wine, despite being forbidden to drink it. Vines were cultivated here until the 1870s, when the phylloxera virus wiped out

the vineyards across the island, forcing the inhabitants to turn to tomatoes (which are still grown here today – the reservoirs on the lower slopes provide the fruit with water all year round). On the small square on the way into the village is the town hall and a squat church, the **Església de la Natividad**, which dates from the 15th century but whose twin domes were completed some 200 years later. On the other side of the road is the **Baronia**, a beautiful mansion, once the feudal seat of the nobles who governed this region and now a hotel. Have a peek inside the old stone courtyard, below the main entrance to the hotel, for an idea of its former splendour.

The C710 becomes increasingly winding and narrow as it leaves Banyalbufar, rising towards the junction with the PM104. Just before here is a turning to **Port d'es Canonge**, which is made up of a nondescript *urbanización*, a handful of exquisitely restored private fincas (one owned by Richard Branson) and a couple of restaurants ranged around a shingly beach, but it's not really worth the half-hour hairpin drive to discover.

From here you can continue on for a further ten kilometres (six miles) along the C710 to Valldemossa (*see p112*) or head south on the PM104 to Esporles and **La Granja**, a one-time Moorish farm that became a convent and then home to the Fortuny family. Today, it's an unsatisfying mishmash of everything from tedious collections of farm implements via children's toys and musical instruments to (for reasons unknown) torture equipment. There's precious little explanation, it's often heaving with coach parties, and, frankly, is not worth the hefty admission price. If you'd hoped for a glimpse into how a wealthy Mallorcan family once lived, you're far better off heading for Els Calderers in the centre of the island (*see p171*). The gardens are nice though.

From La Granja you can head south-west to Puigpunyent (*see p108*) or south-east for a couple of kilometres to **Esporles**, a likeable village, just 20 minutes' drive from Palma, but with a refreshing middle-of-nowhere feel to it. The old quarter is centred on a sizeable church dating from the 13th century; opposite is tiny Plaça d'Espanya and the town hall. The newer part of Esporles stretches south beside the raised pavement along the Passeig del Rei, which is home to numerous cafés, bars and restaurants.

La Granja

Ctra. Esporles–Puigpunyent, km2 (971 61 00 32/
www.lagranja.net). **Open** 10am-7pm daily (last entry
6pm). **Admission** €9-€11; €4.50-€5.50 concessions.
Credit AmEx, DC, MC, V.

Where to stay, eat & drink

At the Mirador de Ricardo Roca, you'll find
the restaurant **Es Grau** (971 61 85 27, closed
Thur and 15 Nov-15 Dec, €€), which serves
standard fare such as grills and fresh local
fish on a terrace with breathtaking views.

In **Estellencs**, the two-star **Maristel**
(C/Eusebi Pascual 10, 971 61 85 50,
www.hotelmaristel.com, doubles €110-€140
incl breakfast) has unremarkable en suite
rooms, but wondrous views and two pools;
the **Hotel Nord** (Plaça Triquet 4, 971 14 90
06, www.hotelruralnord.com, closed Nov-Jan,
doubles €95-€120 incl breakfast) is a pleasant
alternative, with eight air-conditioned rooms
(three with terraces) decorated in trad *mallorquí*
style; or try the friendly family-run five-room
Sa Plana Petit Hotel (C/Eusebi Pascual s/n,
971 61 86 66, www.saplana.com, doubles €85-
€95), which offers home cooking washed down
by the owner's own wine, and there's a pool too.

For eating out, try friendly newcomer **Son
Llarg** (Plaça Constitució 6, 971 61 85 64, closed
Tue, €), which offers Mallorcan classics like
tumbet and *pa amb oli* alongside excellent
salads, home-made pizzas and fresh pasta.

Alternatively, head next door to **Montimar**
(Plaça Constitució 9, 971 61 85 76, closed
Mon and Dec & Jan, €), a traditional place
in a grand house with a pleasant terrace serving
unadorned Mallorcan cuisine.

There are plenty of places to stay in
Banyalbufar. The choicest is **Son Borguny**
(C/Borguny 1, 971 14 87 06, www.sonborguny.
com, doubles €90-€120 incl breakfast),
signposted on the steps leading up from
the main road. This 15th-century building
has been tastefully converted into a hotel with
eight rooms, each individually designed in
Mallorcan style, with light fabrics, wooden
furniture and floors, exposed beams and iron-
framed beds. The 'Sol' and 'Luna' rooms are
the best, with jacuzzis and stunning views.
Dinners on request. **Mar i Vent** (C/Major 49,
971 61 80 00, www.hotelmarivent.com, closed
Dec & Jan, doubles €98-€128 incl breakfast)
is a good alternative, with 29 pretty rooms,
all with great views, a lovely *terraza* for an
evening drink and a pool. **Baronia** (C/Baronia
16, 971 61 81 46, www.hbaronia.com, closed
Nov-Mar, doubles €60 incl breakfast) occupies
a former *palacio*, but is marred by the ugly
modern extension stuck on the back. The
en suite rooms are basic, but there's a large
pool and lovely views. Down the hill from
the main road you'll find the stylish hotel-
restaurant **Ca Madò Paula** (C/Constitució 11,
971 14 87 17, www.camadopaula.com, doubles
€100-€135, restaurant closed Wed and Nov-

Vineyard by the sea... the wine terraces of **Banyalbufar**. *See p110.*

Feb, €€€), which has crisp rooms, and serves both classic and more adventurous dishes like ostrich steak with Cassis mustard. Right at the bottom of the village, the rooms at **Sa Coma** (Camí des Molí 3, 971 61 80 34, www.hotelsacoma.com, closed Nov-Jan, doubles €101) are nothing to write home about, but the uninterrupted sea views are.

There's plenty of choice for eating places in Banyalbufar. **Restaurante Son Tomás** (C/Baronia 17, 971 61 81 49, closed dinner Mon, all Tue and Nov, €€€) is the best and most popular spot in town, located at the far end of the village as you approach from Estellencs. The emphasis is on fish: try the house special *peixado a la mallorquí* (a type of paella) while gazing out at the view from the *terraza*. **Café Bellavista** (C/Comte Sallent 11, 971 61 80 04, closed Sun and Dec & Jan, €), at the other end of town, has similarly wonderful views from a lovely terrace, and serves sandwiches and snacks. The slope here is so steep that the table legs are cut to different lengths to compensate. **Ca's Cosi** (C/Baronia 1-3, 971 61 82 45, closed Tue and Dec-Mar, €) is a pleasant place halfway along the main street that serves simple pastas and local meats such as lamb. There's also a cute pizzeria, **Pegason** (C/del Puente, 971 14 87

13, €) just across the main road from the town hall (look for the sun and 'Restaurante Mediterrània' painted above its door), which serves good pizza and pasta dishes.

In **Port d'es Canonge**, **Ca'n Toni Moreno** (971 61 04 26, closed Mon and 20 Dec-20 Jan, €€€) is a prime spot for fresh fish; the *zarzuela* (fish stew) is particularly fine.

In **Esporles**, the former Hostal Esporles has changed hands recently and been converted into a lovely, chic rural hotel. Now known as the **Hotel Rigel Esporles** (Plaça d'Espanya 8, 971 61 02 02, www.rigelesporles.com, closed mid Jan-mid Feb, doubles €110-€130 incl breakfast, restaurant €€€), it has 11 tranquil rooms (including a suite and a junior suite), plus a sauna, gym, jacuzzi and massage room. There's also a sleek restaurant offering Mallorcan/Mediterranean cuisine.

For other eating options, wander along Passeig del Rei to **Es Brollador** (No.10, 971 61 05 39, closed Tue, €€), which has a lovely patio and fine local meats, including *cordero con miel* (lamb with honey) and *lec hona frita* (suckling pig). **Café Passeig** (No.13, 971 61 92 44, closed Mon, €) is an old-style café, good for a tapa or pastry.

Four kilometres (two and a half miles) from Esporles is the classy **Posada del Marqués** (Es Verger, 971 61 12 30, www.posadamarques. com, doubles €193 incl breakfast, restaurant €€€, restaurant closed lunch Nov-Feb), a handsome 16th-century stone house that's been converted into a four-star hotel, with 17 air-conditioned rooms (some with terraces), a pool and restaurant. It's signposted from the main road on the south side of the village.

Resources

Police station
Esporles *Plaça Espanya 1 (686 94 48 26).*

Post office
Banyalbufar *Plaça de la Vila 2 (no phone).*
Esporles *C/J Riutort 45 (971 61 91 37).*
Estellencs *C/Síquia 4, Baixos (no phone).*

Valldemossa

Valldemossa is a town totally dedicated to tourism – almost every building seems to be either an overpriced restaurant or tacky souvenir shop. Its proximity to Palma (18 kilometres/11 miles) and ease of access from the coastal resorts have made it an essential excursion for the package tour market and, as a result, it heaves with day-trippers and coach parties all day long. By night a semblance of normality returns, but 30 years of such

Mirador Torre del Verger. *See p110.*

Local heroes Sand and Chopin

In November 1837 the French writer George Sand arrived in Palma on a stinking ferry full of pigs. With her were her two children and her companion, the ailing Frédéric Chopin. They hoped that a winter of sun on a beautiful, balmy Mediterranean island would restore the composer's health. The reality turned out to be rather different.

Their problems started immediately: they couldn't find anywhere to stay. No one visited Mallorca for pleasure in the mid 19th century, and initially they had to make do with two barely furnished rooms in an unsavoury district of Palma. After a week they found a scarcely more appealing villa to rent outside the town. Meanwhile, Chopin's piano had been impounded by customs, who were demanding a sum almost equal to its value to release it. At least the weather hadn't disappointed them. Yet.

After three weeks of unbroken sunshine it started to rain, and barely stopped raining for the following two months. The damp exacerbated Chopin's illness, which the locals assumed to be consumption, though Sand believed it was a nervous condition that developed from bronchitis. Their landlord, convinced that they would infect his villa, forced them to leave.

A few years previously the Spanish government had suppressed the monasteries, and Sand learned that a suite of cells could be rented up in the Tramuntana mountains at Valldemossa for a trifling sum. And so the foursome lumbered over terrible roads up to the Real Cartuja de Jesús de Nazaret (see p113), where they were to spend the remainder of their time on Mallorca.

Sand was entranced by the monastery and its location, calling it 'the most romantic dwelling place on earth'. She was, though, less enamoured of the continuously awful weather and, most particularly, the natives. In isolated, deeply conservative rural Mallorca the unconventional Sand famille were the object of great curiosity and suspicion. A forceful female writer speaking a foreign language, refusing to go to mass, dressing her daughter in male clothing and living with a man who wasn't her husband was a strange and alarming phenomenon.

The uncompromising Sand had little time for such prejudices and railed against what she saw as the laziness, stupidity, deviousness and mendacity of the locals (who she semi-jokingly referred to as 'monkeys'): 'The Mallorcan peasant does not consider the foreigner a human being, so he will cheat him, make him pay over the odds, lie to him, insult him and pilfer from him without the least scruple'.

She couldn't stomach the food ('infernal concoctions, cooked by the Devil in person') and hated the wine ('harsh, black, caustic'), the inefficiency of the agriculture and the island's social and economic stagnation. Just about the only positive words she could muster concerned the landscape, and specifically that of the Tramuntana mountains. 'Majorca is an El Dorado for painters,' she declared. 'There is Helvetian green, under a Calabrian sky, amidst the solemnity and silence of the Orient.'

The trip wasn't an utter disaster. Although Chopin's health 'worsened to an alarming degree', he composed a number of works while in Valldemossa (including, tellingly, his 'Raindrop' Prelude), while upon their return to France in March 1838, Sand wrote a hugely entertaining and 'perhaps unintentionally unfair account' of their sojourn, A Winter in Majorca. At the time of its first publication the book was, unsurprisingly, denounced by the Mallorcans, provoking a diatribe against the 'immoral writer' by 40 Palman lawyers. There's no little irony that the very same book is now prominently on sale in a number of editions and languages all over the island, and that the Sand/Chopin connection is proudly trumpeted.

invasions have changed its delicate character irrevocably; it's a great shame as it is still one of the prettiest settlements on the island.

The village's origins date from Moorish times; its name 'Vall d'en Musa' means 'valley of Musa', the Moorish owner of the original estate. By far its biggest draw for visitors is the **Real Cartuja de Valldemossa**, best known as the place where Frédéric Chopin and George Sand spent an infamous, bitter winter in 1838-9. Sand immortalised their stay in her book A Winter in Majorca (see above **Local heroes**), the thrust of which could be summed up as 'love the landscapes, hate the natives (and the weather)', and, despite its less than complimentary viewpoint, you'll find it for sale all over the island, and all over the monastery too.

The Cartuja's origins stretch back to 1399, when it was founded by Carthusian monks, who lived here until they were expelled in 1835 (hence the fact that cells were going cheap when Sand and Chopin showed up). Visits start at the church, an uninspiring neo-classical structure tacked on to the main complex, notable only for a few frescoes painted by Goya's brother-in-law. Head straight through to the cloisters where you'll find the pharmacy, a pleasingly chaotic collection of potions preserved in delicate jars and painted wooden boxes, which the monks doled out to parishioners; it continued as the village chemist's until 1896. Next door, the Prior's Cell is reached through a small private chapel dedicated to Santa Catalina Tomás (*see below*). Inside, there is a library where the monks would break their silence for a once-a-week chat, and the audience chamber, where the Prior would meet guests, hung with numerous oil paintings and containing various penitential objects used for self-flagellation.

Cells two and four are where most visitors head; these were the ones inhabited by Chopin and Sand. They're a curious mishmash of objects: locks of hair, original scores, the piano on which the sickly Chopin composed one of his most famous works, the 'Raindrop' Prelude, love letters and a signed manuscript of *A Winter in Majorca*. But it's all curiously unsatisfying, and you get little insight into how the pair led their lives here. Wander out into the beautiful terrace gardens outside the cells for some lovely views down the valley towards Palma.

Next door, the **Museu Municipal** gives a brief history of Archduke Ludwig Salvator (see *p24* **Local heroes**) on the ground floor; upstairs is dedicated to a small but impressive display of modern art, including paintings by Joan Miró, sketches by Picasso and etchings by Francis Bacon and Max Ernst. Double-back to get to King Sancho's Palace, which has several rooms to explore, full of paintings and knick-knacks; Nicaraguan poet Ruben Dario stayed here in the early part of the 20th century.

Adjoining the monastery complex is the pretty **Jardí de Joan Carles I**.

Valldemossa's other (though certainly lesser) tourist draw is the curious **Costa Nord** centre, initially funded by Michael Douglas, who has a house nearby (S'Estaca, one of the Archduke Ludwig Salvator's properties). The actor hoped that the centre would create 'a cultural bond between the island's inhabitants and those who visit it'. It's part restaurant-bar, part audio-visual show; the latter consists of a 15-minute history of Mallorca, followed by a less cursory and more interesting look at Archduke Ludwig Salvator, his life and contribution to Mallorca. Frankly, it's a bit pricey for what you get.

Douglas sold the centre to the Balearic Island Government in 2003, although he keeps involved, not least in promoting the island at international tourism trade fairs.

In the lower part of the village is the church of **Sant Bartomeu**, dedicated to the life of Mallorca's only saint, **Santa Catalina Tomás**. She was born in Valldemossa in 1533 and worked on an estate near Bunyola, where she performed various miracles, before joining the Church at the age of 21. Throughout her life (she died of natural causes in 1574) she experienced countless mystical experiences and strange phenomena, and according to *The Book of Saints*, 'during the last years of her life she was in continual ecstasy'. She was canonised in 1930, and lies in a shrine in the church of Santa Margalida in Palma, where celebrations dedicated to her take place on 28 July each year.

To escape the crowds, take the long, narrow and winding road down to diminutive **Port de Valldemossa** (Michael Douglas's fabulous estate S'Estaca is off this road), which is little more than a stony beach, a scattering of houses, a couple of beach bars in season and a great and long-established fish restaurant on the quay, **Es Port** (*see p115*).

Six kilometres south of Valldemossa, heading towards Palma, is the **Lafiore** glass factory, which specialises in hand-blown reproduction

Valldemossa. *See p112.*

antique Roman glassware. Visitors can watch glass-blowing demonstrations and spend their euros in the factory shop.

Costa Nord

Avda. Palma 6 (971 61 24 25/www.costanord.com). **Open** 9am-5pm daily. **Admission** €7.75; €4.75-€6 concessions. **No credit cards.**

Lafiore

Ctra. Palma–Valldemossa, km11, S'Esgleieta (971 61 01 40/www.lafiore.com). **Open** *Shop* 9.15am-8pm Mon-Fri; 9.15am-2pm, 3-6pm Sat. *Workshop* 9am-1pm, 2-5pm Mon-Fri; 9.15am-1pm Sat. **Admission** free.

Real Cartuja de Valldemossa

971 61 21 06. **Open** *Jan, Dec* 9.30am-4pm Mon-Sat. *Feb* 9.30am-4.30pm Mon-Sat; 10am-1pm Sun. *Mar-May, Oct* 9.30am-5.30pm Mon-Sat; 10am-1pm Sun. *June-Sept* 9.30am-6.30pm Mon-Sat; 10am-1pm Sun. *Nov* 9.30am-4pm Mon-Sat; 10am-1pm Sun. **Admission** €7.50; free under-10s. **Credit** AmEx, DC, MC, V.

Where to eat & drink

The eating places in the centre of Valldemossa are much of a muchness. You're best off walking past the main gaggle of shops and cafés on the main road in the direction of Deià, where, beyond the main bus stop, you'll find

two friendly restaurants side by side. **Can Pedro** (Avda. Arxiduc Lluís Salvador s/n, 971 61 21 70, closed dinner Sun & all Mon, €€) offers largely traditional food and Mallorcan wines; **Vesubio** (Avda. Arxiduc Lluis Salvador 23, 971 61 25 84, closed Wed and Jan, €) serves up good pizzas and pastas.

A little further along this road you'll see a sign pointing the way to **Son Moragues** (Valldemossa, 971 61 61 11, closed Mon & dinner Sun, €€€), which offers a great dining experience in an old *finca* (one of the Archduke's old properties) on the edge of the village. It serves up traditional Mallorcan food with, perhaps, a little more ceremony than it deserves, but the surroundings are wonderful.

The best place to drink when night falls is the bar and restaurant at the **Costa Nord** (Avda. Palma 6, 971 61 24 25, €€€).

A wonderful spot to eat fresh fish, pulled out of the sea on to the quay, is long-serving **Es Port** (971 61 61 94, www.geocities.com/ restaurantesport, closed Wed in Feb, dinner Sept-June and all Nov & Dec, €€€) in **Port de Valldemossa**, seven kilometres (four miles) from Valldemossa. Tucking into a vast paella on the terrace while taking in the sea views is one of the great Mediterranean dining experiences.

Another enjoyable restaurant, on the road between Valldemossa and Deià, is **Ca'n Costa** (Ctra. Valldemossa–Deià, km2.5, 971 61 22 63, closed Tue, €€), another of the Archduke's numerous former properties along the coast. The interior is a wonderful old *tafona* (olive press room), within which decent, if not outstanding, Mallorcan food is served. The wine list is excellent and the family welcome warm. This place is a big favourite for Sunday lunch with Mallorcan families from Palma.

Where to stay

The most luxurious hotel in the area is undoubtedly the **Hotel Valldemossa** (Ctra. Vieja de Valldemossa s/n, 971 61 26 26, www.valldemossahotel.com, doubles €261-€417 incl breakfast, restaurant €€€€), located in a former private house just outside Valldemossa on the old Palma road. (You'll see billboards advertising it all over the island; perhaps something to do with the fact that its owner also owns all Mallorca's billboards.) It has just 12 rooms, all with private *terrazas* or patios, tiled floors, marble bathrooms and refined design; one has a four-poster bed. The views from the pool area and the dining room terrace are extraordinary. One note of caution: the lofty prices in the restaurant aren't always justified by the quality of conception and execution of the dishes.

Walk 2 Around Deià

Distance: 16km (ten miles). Circular.
Time: 6hrs.

There are some very popular walks around the famously chic village of Deià, but the following long and fairly strenuous hike avoids the crowds for most of its length, climbing high above the village, then following the contours of the hills through coniferous forests before descending to the sea and returning to Deià along the cliff tops. It makes a fine day's walking, and has refreshment stops at the halfway point and at the end, where you can swim on fine days at the Cala de Deià. Parking in Deià is nightmarish, which is why this walk starts in the sizeable car park down by the sea at Cala de Deià (if you don't have your own transport, start in Deià). This does mean that the first hour and a half or so is almost all climbing, but at least you get all the uphill out of the way at the beginning. If you want an easier, clearly signposted and more populated stroll, take the path to Sóller from the hamlet of Lluc-Alcari, a few kilometres north of Deià.

From the car park, walk up the road you've just come down, and turn right on to the path signed to Deià. It's a steep but beautiful 40-minute climb up to the village.

On reaching the main road through Deià, turn left and then take a right in front of La Residencia hotel (between the bus stop and the sign to the hotel and El Olivo restaurant).

Follow this road, going sharp left in front of the huge drystone retaining wall of a house, through a pair of metal gates, then on upwards as the road changes from metalled to rough concrete to track, then back to concrete. As it bends round to the left below another villa (about 20 minutes after setting off from Deià), take the wide track leading off to the right.

Five or so minutes later you pass a sculpturally twisted tree trunk on your right, then, after another five minutes, take the track to the right of the highest of the villas that you'll come across, bearing left around the back of the property and climbing over a low drystone wall, before continuing along the path with a wire fence to your right.

You'll come to a drinking fountain with a brass tap. There's a route downwards here, indicated by red marks, but ignore it and continue upwards following the cairns and a set of red paint splodges.

After six or seven minutes you pass through a wire gate between two trees, and then, soon after, through a gap in a stone wall.

At this point, you'll see a viewpoint towards the sea to your left (next to a stone hut), but the path continues straight on (marked by a cairn). Follow the cairns upwards, past another hut and up a succession of terraces.

Around 15 minutes later the path starts to level and you can enjoy precipitous views down to Deià and the sea as you walk into coniferous woodland. Pass through another gap in a stone wall, and bear round to the left (ignoring a steep uphill path).

The route becomes a little tricky to make out after this point, but around a quarter of an hour after passing through the stone wall you should find yourself walking along the top of a terrace. After a couple of minutes you come to a fork in the path, with the left fork heading downwards and the right gently upwards. There are purple splodges on a tree and a rock here. Take the right upward path.

Eight minutes later, just past a flat mossy area supported by a stone wall, the path swings left. One branch heads up, but continue on downwards on the main one to the left, past another raised mossy area. You may spot goats darting between the holm oaks. After five minutes you'll come across a huge pile of rocks and various stone foundations.

After this point the trail becomes wide and clear and heads generally downwards, supported by a wall, with fine views down towards the sea.

Around 15 minutes after passing the big pile of rocks you'll come to a T-junction. The right path goes upwards, but take the left branch downwards, by another mossy-topped spot, some stone foundations and a huge boulder with a fissure running through it, and then through a wide gap between stone pillars, under a curious wooden construction over the path and round a metal gate with spikes on top of it.

The track is now wide enough for a four-wheel drive. Ignore an offshoot heading upwards and continue down. About a quarter of an hour after the T-junction you'll find yourself walking down through a series of terraces, punctuated by gnarled old olive trees and massive boulders. The track goes through a stone wall and you can enjoy the great views towards the mountains surrounding Sóller.

Pass through a large metal gate and immediately cross the signed Deià–Sóller footpath (you may well meet the first other walkers you've come across on this hike here). After a couple of minutes you'll arrive at a huge 300-year-old house, from which excellent quiche and fresh orange juice is dispensed to walkers (at a price).

From here, take the cobbled path downwards, turn sharp left by a ruined chapel (not towards Sóller) and continue down to the main Deià–Sóller road. Turn left along the road and after one minute, as the road bends left at a right angle, go right down the side road marked to 'Restaurant Bens d'Avall'.

Keep heading downwards, following signs to the restaurant (ignoring a turn-off to the right). Eventually, you'll come to the restaurant (see p126), the terrace of which, looking down the coastline towards Deià, makes a welcome spot to take a break with a drink.

Most of the rest of the walk is back along the coast. Walk back up the road until you're above the restaurant car parking, looking for a place to scramble down to the right into the rainwater run-off trench and up on to the footpath on the other side. Turn right and head towards the sea.

Around ten minutes later, as the track bends right to go down to the cove below the restaurant, you take the path to the left, where you'll see a red paint splodge, and continue up to walk alongside a wire fence. After five minutes go left up a wider track with a gate on the right, then climb over a stile in front of where the track has a chain across it.

The rest of the walk consists essentially of following the cairns and paint marks along the coast. Much of the ground is fairly rough, and a fair amount of scrambling is involved, particularly around the many fallen trees.

You should arrive at Cala de Deià (where you can swim on calm days and get a meal and/or drink) around two hours after leaving the restaurant.

Alternatives in the area include **Cases de Ca's Garriguer** (Ctra. Valdemossa–Andratx, km3, 971 61 23 00, www.vistamarhotel.es, closed Oct-Mar, doubles €161-€171 incl breakfast), a lovely old house that contains ten spacious, elegant rooms, seven with terraces and three with balconies; there's a pool, sauna and gardens too. Another pleasant place to stay, a couple of kilometres south of Valldemossa, is **Finca Son Brondo** (Ctra. Palma–Valldemossa, km14.3 & km15.2, 971 61 22 58, www.fincasonbrondo.com, €150 incl breakfast), which has been in the same family since the 16th century and now offers six bedrooms, a pool and even a chapel.

A first-rate mid-range option in the heart of the village is the friendly **Es Petit Hotel de Valldemossa** (C/Uetam 1, 971 61 24 79, www.espetithotel-valldemossa.com, doubles €120-€160 incl breakfast), offering eight individually decorated air-conditioned rooms (two with terraces) within a carefully restored townhouse; there's a big communal terrace with great views too. Along the same street, bargain-hunters should be satisfied by the attractive **Hostal Ca'n Mario** (C/Uetam 8, 971 61 21 22, closed 15 Dec-15 Jan, doubles €50 incl breakfast), which is reassuringly old-fashioned, centrally located and has a good and good value restaurant (closed dinner Mon-Sat, €).

Resources

Police station
Valldemossa *C/Rei Sanxo I s/n (112).*

Post office
Valldemossa *C/Pintora Pilar Muntaner 3 (no phone).*

Tourist information
Valldemossa *OIT, Avda. Palma 7 (971 61 20 19/ oficinaturismevalldemossa@yahoo.es).* **Open** 10am-2pm, 3-6pm Mon-Fri; 10am-1pm Sat.

Deià

The C710 continues along the coastline from Valldemossa, passing (after about eight kilometres/five miles), **Son Marroig**, the favourite estate of Archduke Ludwig Salvator (*see p24* **Local heroes**). This impressive pile is just one of a number of properties the Archduke bought to preserve this part of the coastline (another, S'Estaca, is now owned by Michael Douglas; *see p24*). Only part of it is open to the public and, though visitors can admire the Archduke's voluminous library and hundreds of photos and paintings, there's no English labelling and no attempt to tell his fascinating

Port de Sóller. *See p128.*

life story. Outside, sculpted gardens lead to cliff-edge, and include Ludwig Salvator's favourite spot for thought, the white marble rotunda. From here you can see down to **Sa Foradada**, which means 'pierced rock' – it's just that, a jagged rock rising from the sea with a big hole through it.

A couple of kilometres back towards Valldemossa is another of the Archduke's old properties, the one-time monastery of **Miramar**, founded in 1276 by King Jaume II on the prompting of Ramón Llull as a missionary school. Both Miramar and Son Marroig passed to the family of his secretary Antoni Vives on the Archduke's death in 1915, and remain in their ownership today. A museum tells the story of the building.

Four kilometres (two and a half miles) further on from Son Marroig is one of the most celebrated villages on the island, **Deià**. It's an extraordinarily pretty place, and knows it. Honey-coloured houses nestle on the precipitous terraced slopes of the mountain, the **Puig des Teix**, which drop dramatically down to a tiny cove below.

Despite its renown, and being packed with (largely upmarket) hotels and restaurants (mostly along the main road, which doubles as the village high street), Deià stubbornly

maintains its own character. Little further concession is made to tourists; car parking, for example, is minimal, and coaches are banned from stopping. (If you can't park in the village and you fancy a swim as well as a peruse of the village, it's worth driving down to the cove, parking in the ample pay-and-display car park there, then braving the half-hour hike back up, rewarding yourself with a dip and a drink at the beach bar when you return.)

Deià's history dates back to Moorish times, the Arabic name 'ad-daia' simply meaning 'hamlet', and the Moors cultivated the slopes and terraced the land here, growing grapes and olives. The Reconquest saw the extension of farming to the higher slopes with the growing of citrus fruit and keeping of sheep and pigs. Like so many villages along this stretch of the coast, Deià grew with its back to the sea: protection against pirates and the north winds.

Today, the village has around 700 inhabitants, more than half of whom are foreigners. It has been attracting artists and writers for decades, the most famous being **Robert Graves** (*see p122* **Local heroes**), who lived here for most of his life. It was largely Graves's presence here that drew in a stream of famous writers and actors to Deià, including Anaïs Nin, Kingsley Amis, Anthony Burgess, Gabriel Garcia Márquez, Mario Vargas Llosa, Ava Gardner and Alec Guinness. But Graves wasn't the first foreigner to fall for the village's charms – DH Lawrence, Arthur Rackham and composer Manuel de Falla all preceded him. Graves's widow Beryl lived in Deià until her death in 2003, and three of his sons still have homes here, including Tomás, a printer, bookbinder, writer and rock musician (look out for gigs featuring 'Sleepy Tom').

There's still a vague air of bohemianism to the place, albeit of a moneyed, Notting Hill kind these days, and, though some visitors find Deià a little precious, its easygoing confidence continues to seduce many. It makes a great holiday base.

It doesn't take long to wander around. Head up the hill to the church of **Sant Joan Baptista**, where you'll see Graves's headstone under a tree towards the back left-hand corner of the churchyard as you enter, marked simply 'Robert Graves, Poeta, EPD' (*'En Paz Descanse'*, 'Rest In Peace'). The views from here are marvellous. Adjoining the church is a tiny museum (open July-mid Sept 10am-1pm, 5-8pm Tue-Sun, free), which has a few bits of Graves memorabilia. A nose around the tiny graveyard reveals ample evidence of Deià's bohemian heritage, with a corner on a lower terrace devoted to foreign artists and writers who were so captivated by the village that they never left it.

If you're interested in Mallorcan prehistory, the **Deià Archaeological Museum** is worth a visit. Founded by American archaeologist William Waldren in 1962, it contains finds from several local sites, in particular that at Muleta near Sóller.

There are a good number of appealing shops in the village, such as **Nexus** (C/Arxiduc Lluís Salvador 9, 971 63 93 10) and **Islas** (C/Arxiduc Lluís Salvador 17, 971 63 91 44, closed Jan, Feb), whose long-term expat owners bring back some lovely clothes from their forays to Latin America and South-east Asia (some of which they design themselves). Tasteful Mallorcan clothing, crafts and art are sold at **Galeria Deià** (C/Arxiduc Lluís Salvador 3, 971 63 91 42), and there are further classy shops on the hill between the church and the main road. The **Tafona Gallery** within La Residencia hotel (*see p123*) has year-round shows of work by local artists. For rare books, art and photography books, prints and arty objects, check out **Zembla** (C/Porxa 5, 971 63 60 86), next to the Town Hall.

To get down to the small beach (a mix of stone, shingle and a tiny patch of sand) of **Cala de Deià**, head along the road out of town towards Sóller, and turn left at the sign saying 'Depuradora' (there's a small sign to Cala de Deià too). It's a five-minute drive or 25-minute walk down to the cove, which has a couple of beautifully situated seasonal bar-restaurants.

Deià's arty heritage has left it's mark on the village's cultural calendar. The **Deià International Music Festival** (971 63 91 78, mobile 678 98 95 36, www.dimf.com) was born nearly 30 years ago and offers a progamme of classical performances from local and international artists from March to September. A newer arrival is **Tertulia@Deià** (www.hayfestival.com/tertulia), a long weekend of events in English, Catalan and Spanish to celebrate literature, music, film, food and good conversation. The first Tertulia was in 2004, and was such a success that a second was held in 2005; it is now intended to be an annual event over four days at the end of October.

Deià Archaeological Museum

C/d'es Clot 4 (971 63 90 01). **Open** *June-Sept* 5-7pm Tue, Thur, Sun. *Oct-May* by appointment. Times tend to vary; phone to check. **Admission** free.

Miramar

Ctra. Valldemossa–Deià s/n (971 61 60 73). **Open** 9.30am-7pm Tue-Sun. **Admission** €3. **No credit cards.**

Son Marroig

Ctra. Valldemossa–Deià s/n (971 63 91 58). **Open** *Apr-Sept* 9.30am-8pm Mon-Sat. *Oct-Mar* 9.30am-6pm Mon-Sat. **Admission** €3; free under-10s. **No credit cards.**

Where to eat & drink

There are a remarkable number of eating and drinking options in Deià, most of them excellent and most towards the pricey end of the scale. Probably the pick of the restaurants is **Es Racó d'es Teix** (C/Sa Vinya Vell 6, 971 63 95 01, closed Tue and Dec, Jan, €€€€), run by Josef Sauerschell, the chef who earned El Olivo a Michelin star (which it no longer has) and then set up on his own, achieving the same feat at Es Racó. Expect perfectly conceived and executed modern Mediterranean and Mallorcan dishes (such as grilled sea bass with pak choi, rhubarb chutney and curry oil), served in a lovely old stone building or on a series of elegant terraces in summer.

Another classy (if very expensive) dining spot is **El Olivo** (971 63 90 11, closed Nov-Jan, €€€€), within the mega-cool La Residencia hotel. This is a thoroughbred restaurant, from the slickly professional yet friendly staff and lushly romantic decor (candelabras abound) to the verve and quality of the imaginative modern European cooking. If you can stretch to the €80 five-course (plus 'surprise' dessert) Chef's Menu, you will be rewarded by the likes of asparagus cream with lobster ravioli.

Among the other local gems is **Sebastián** (C/Felipe Bauzà s/n, 971 63 94 17, closed Wed, 1 Nov-20 Dec and mid Jan-early Feb, €€€), which offers superb meat dishes (including lamb and wild boar in season) in elegant surroundings with a rustic touch (try the grilled foie gras with sweet peas), and **Restaurante Jaime** (C/Arxiduc Lluís Salvador 22, 971 63 90 29, closed Mon and Jul, €€€); Jaime died in 2002, but his son Biel Payeras reinvented this Deià institution across the road from the original, serving a refined, modernised version of traditional Mallorcan food. Lovely terrace.

Up a narrow lane from the main road in a delightful tree-shaded setting is **Sa Vinya** (C/Sa Vinya Vella 3, 971 63 95 00, closed Tue and mid Nov-mid Feb, €€€). The food is good and well presented in a clean, uncluttered style, somewhere between contemporary and traditional Mallorcan (breast of pigeon and fillet of rabbit with spring garlic sauce, for example), and the relaxed, friendly service is lovely.

Other possibilities are **Sa Dorada** (971 63 95 09, €€), which offers the likes of honey-glazed duck, chicken with almonds and various types of steak, and **Restaurant Deià Ca'n Paco** (C/Felipe Bauzà 1, 971 63 92 65, €€€), where you'll find traditional Mallorcan dishes alongside sashimi, Caesar salad and chicken brochette.

If you don't want a major blow-out at major prices, try **Patricia's Bar** (C/Felipe Bauzà 1, 971 63 91 99, closed Wed, €), owned by the same

Local heroes Robert Graves

Today, around one in four of the residents of Mallorca is a foreigner. Such a figure would have horrified the island's best known 20th-century expat, the writer and poet Robert Graves (1895-1985).

When Graves first arrived on the island in 1929 it was already known as a desirable and unspoiled holiday spot in certain rarified artistic and moneyed circles (the famous Hotel Formentor had opened the previous year), but few foreigners chose to actually live on Mallorca.

Graves, though, was after more than a break in the sun. He already had a reputation for his poetry, and his fiery, engaging personality and popular but intelligent writing made him famous at an early age. In 1929 he published *Goodbye to All That*, a sharply observed and lucidly written autobiography covering the period before, during and immediately after World War I. It was hailed as a classic. Yet Graves's life at the time was a mess: he was unhappily married, broke and suffering shell shock.

The idea of leaving England for Mallorca was suggested to him by Gertrude Stein (who described it as 'Paradise, if you can stand it'). He followed her advice, abandoned his wife Nancy Nicholson and his four children, and with his lover, American writer Laura Riding, came to live in Deià (which he referred to as 'Binijiny'), building his own house, Canellûñ.

And Mallorca was a kind of paradise for Graves. Here he found the peace and inspiration he needed to write, producing more than 120 books in his 90 years, including the historical novels *I, Claudius* (1934) and *Claudius the God* (1943).

He also became famed as a literary exile, attracting a stream of celebrity visitors – Ava Gardner, Alec Guinness, Peter Ustinov, Gabriel García Márquez and Kingsley Amis among them. Graves charmed them all and played wild practical jokes at the parties he hosted.

But if his VIP guests were impressed, his Mallorcan neighbours were generally bemused by the eccentric, stink bomb-loving writer and his flamboyant friends. Graves was 'Mr Roberto', the keen swimmer and joker. He spoke Spanish, admired the Mallorcan character and revelled in the food and drink, but he was never one of the locals.

And he was not keen on others following in his footsteps. In *Mallorca Observed* (1954), he writes: 'Tourists are good animals, though they vary according to nationalities. The most

people as Sebastián, which serves excellent falafels, baguettes, simple salads and ice-creams at very reasonable prices, or **El Barrigón Xelini** (C/Arxiduc Lluís Salvador 19, 971 63 91 39, closed Mon, €€), a great modern tapas bar with bags of atmosphere, a wide range of reasonably priced dishes and a small *terraza*; it puts on live jazz every Saturday from 9pm. Also on the main drag, **Las Palmeras** (C/Arxiduc Lluís Salvador 11, 971 63 90 16, €€) offers Mallorcan dishes and tapas, and has a vine-covered terrace. For all-day drinks and snacks, head for **Senset & Senseta** (C/Vinya Vella 1, 971 63 61 09, €), which overlooks the main drag.

Down in the cove are a couple of wonderfully located restaurants that have been operating for decades. **Ca's Patró March** (971 63 91 37, closed Nov-Mar, €€€) is an informal, though certainly not cheap, fish restaurant and bar (where you'll struggle to get a table for lunch in summer, thanks to all the luxury yachts mooring in the cala). It has been run by three generations of the March family and the present owner, Juan, often goes out before dawn to catch the fish for that day's meals. The other spot is the cheaper **Restaurante C'an Lluc** (mobile 649 19 86 18, closed Wed and Nov-Mar, €€), run by Francisca and her husband Jordi, whose cave-located kitchen knocks out great, simple Mallorcan home cooking and fish.

Ca'n Quet (Ctra. Valdemossa–Deià s/n, 971 63 91 96, closed Mon and Nov-Apr, €€€€), part of Es Molí hotel (*see below*), enjoys a sublime position, tucked into the side of the hill overlooking a stream, and the food is exceptional – lots of fresh local produce and a wide selection of fish, such as *rape asado con jamón* (roast monkfish with ham) and *merluza* (hake) with local mushrooms. Treat yourself to the cold white chocolate soup with fruits of the forest to finish.

In terms of drinking, there's the cool, contemporary **Al Bar**, owned by Simon Finch, who played a key role in creating Tertulia@ Deià (*see p121*). It's a clean, modern space, where the decorative focus is two great discs made up of pieces of glass found on beaches. There's also a big terrace and good, simple food. Look out for frequent events here.

easily domesticated, the Majorcans agree, are my English compatriots.' The pioneering expat, he wanted it all for himself, but for all its snobbish attitudes to the masses, the book provides a fascinating portrait of an old Mallorca on the cusp of changing forever.

Graves was very much the Brit abroad – he liked the fact that Mallorca wasn't far from the Greenwich meridian, was hot and was cheap. But there is no doubt that the rural Mediterranean lifestyle suited him – he began to think of Laura Riding as an ancient Mediterranean moon goddess, until she left him for another writer in 1939. By then Graves was back in the UK, having left Mallorca in 1936 when Palma became a Francoist base during the Spanish Civil War.

Ten years later he returned to the island for good, this time taking Beryl Pritchard, who was to be his partner until his death. Graves had by now formulated a personal mythology of a matriarchal White Goddess – an idea that pervades all his later work. By the 1950s, he had won international reputation as a poet, novelist, literary scholar and translator, and in 1962 WH Auden described Graves as England's 'greatest living poet'.

Mallorca's influence on the Graves opus is oblique. The island's climate, colours and the topography of its fig and citrus trees no doubt fed his imagination for the Roman works he wrote in Deià, and some of his poetry is notably set among rocks, crags and islands. But for the most part, there's little evidence of his surroundings giving direct inspiration.

Graves's influence on Deià, however, is still huge, though it's probable that few of the people who visit 'Graves's Deià' today have read any of his works. And that's a pity, for there's something in his versatile writings to appeal to everyone, whether it's the lyricism of his poetry, the vivacity of his historical novels or the authority of his entertaining works on Greek and Hebrew myths.

A more personal legacy is the continuing presence of his family in the village – Beryl lived here until her death in 2003, and three of their sons are still resident. Every year on 24 July (Graves's birthday), locals gather at Deià's amphitheatre across the road from Canelluñ to hear Graves's family and friends read selections of his poetry, under the direction of the 'keeper of the flame', his daughter Lucia.

Sa Fonda (C/Arxiduc Lluís Salvador 3, 971 63 93 06) is the hub of village nightlife. Owned by local legend Tomao, it is *the* place to come for sunset drinks and late-night partying; there's lots of live music in summer, and those in the know travel from all over the island to be here on Saturday nights.

Where to stay

Although Deià is known for its luxury hotels, there are places to stay to suit every budget and taste. Possibly the most celebrated hotel on Mallorca, the super-chic **La Residencia** (Son Canals s/n, 971 63 90 11, www.hotel-laresidencia.com, doubles €241-€471 incl breakfast) is a haven of indulgence and recuperation for the rich and (discretion-craving) famous, offering low-key luxury and an informal, thoroughly relaxed vibe. The decor of the 59 rooms (including 22 suites, three of which have their own private swimming pools) is contemporary-rustic with immense traditional Mallorcan dark wood beds and wardrobes, tiled floors, white linen,

earth-toned bathrooms and paintings by local artists. There are three swimming pools (one indoor), sauna and steam room, outdoor jacuzzi, beauty salon, gym and two tennis courts. Note that there's a five-night minimum stay between April and October.

For all its charms, La Residencia can't promise much in the way of rooms with views. Not so **Es Molí** (Ctra. Valldemossa–Deià s/n, 971 63 90 00, www.esmoli.com, closed Nov-Apr, doubles €188-€304 incl breakfast), another exceptional hotel,offering some of the choicest vistas on this stretch of coast. It's set in luxuriant grounds, with a pool, tennis court and bar with picture windows overlooking the bay. There are 75 rooms, the best of which are sea-facing and have their own private terrace.

If you want somewhere more intimate, but with views that are, if anything, even better, try **Sa Pedrissa** (Ctra. Valldemossa–Deià, km74.5, 971 63 91 11, www.sapedrissa.com, €128-€289 incl breakfast), just outside the village. Owner Sebastià Artigues's beautifully restored former olive mill is a five-star luxury haven in immaculate taste. The eight rooms and suites, all with views either to Deià or the coast, are wood-beamed and fitted to an extremely high standard, with soft pillows, big beds, comfy armchairs, terraces or balconies and marble-tiled bathrooms. The pool is at the edge of the grounds and looks across to the village, with a barbecue area behind. The kitchen is superb, serving local meats and fish, and you can choose to eat in the house itself, in an atmospheric dining room with original fittings, or on the *terraza* outside, which on a warm night is sublime.

A cheaper option is **S'Hotel d'es Puig** (C/Es Puig 4, 971 63 94 09, www.hoteldes puig.com, closed Dec-Feb, doubles €101-€120 incl breakfast), located in the heart of Deià on the road up to the church. This former *hostal* was where Anaïs Nin and Manuel de Falla would stay when holidaying in the village, and it also appears in one of Graves's works. Today, it has been tastefully refurbished and upgraded, with eight comfortable rooms with en suite showers, while retaining its original character. There's also a pool.

Hostal Villaverde (C/Ramón Llull 19, 971 63 90 37, www.hostalvillaverde.com, doubles €60-€80 incl breakfast), a very pretty budget option tucked below the church, has simple, clean rooms (some with terrace), an open courtyard and a lovely tree-covered *terraza* looking out to the coast.

If there is no room in Deià itself, try the **Hotel Costa d'Or** (C/Llucalcari s/n, 971 63 90 25, www.hoposa.es, closed Nov-Apr, doubles €100-€220 incl breakfast), a gorgeous hotel a couple of kilometres towards Sóller in the hamlet of Llucalcari. It's set in a pretty pine grove in a stunning position overlooking the sea. The rooms are simple (the ones to go for are at the front with the views), and there's an outdoor pool, tennis court and bar.

Resources

Police station
Deià *Porxo 4 (971 63 90 77).*

Post office
Deià *Via Arxiduc Lluís Salvador 29 (971 63 91 93).*

Sóller

Sóller, the major settlement on Mallorca's west coast, lies 11 kilometres (seven miles) north-east of Deià. With a magnificent backdrop of encircling high peaks, this relaxed town of little over 10,000 inhabitants makes both a fine base for exploring the coast and the mountains, and an enjoyable day-trip destination.

Until the four kilometre- (two and a half mile-) long tunnel between here and Palma opened in the mid 1990s, the only way to get to Sóller was along the **Coll de Sóller**, a 14-kilometre (nine-mile) series of hairpin bends that winds over the top of the mountain, or by train on ancient rolling stock (*see p64* **All aboard!**). And before the rail line opened in 1912, the journey from the capital – just 30 kilometres (19 miles) away – took the best part of a day. As a result, Sóller has historically turned its face to the west and the sea, setting up trade agreements for its lucrative citrus business with Barcelona and France in preference to Palma.

The citrus fruit groves that line the valley floor – the **Valle de los Naranjos** (Valley of the Oranges) – made its inhabitants rich in the late 19th and early 20th centuries, and account for the fanciful architecture and grand mansions dotted around the town. Citrus fruits, olives and hand-made sausages are still produced here, and it's well worth spending some time exploring its winding streets, followed by a leisurely lunch in the central square, Plaça Constitució.

The square is dominated by the towering church of **Sant Bartomeu** (open 10.30am-1pm, 2.45-5.15pm Mon-Thur, 10.30am-1pm Fri, Sat, free), which was begun in the 13th century but is largely baroque in style, with a neo-Gothic tower and a *modernista* (Catalan art nouveau) façade by a pupil of Gaudí's, **Joan Rubió i Bellver**. Rubió came over with Gaudí from Barcelona in 1904 when the great architect was invited to work on Palma Cathedral. Rubió busied himself in Sóller, finishing the church façade (in 1904), designing the building next door, the **Banco de Sóller** (in 1912; now the Santander Central Hispano bank – its rugged, rusticated exterior is lightened by the wonderfully intricate metalwork of its window grilles) and his own house **Ca'n Prunera** (1909-11) (C/Lluna 90), which has more striking ironwork and is alive with floral motifs.

There is not much else in Sóller with regard to sights, but at the edge of town on the main road from Palma is another *modernista* mansion that is now home to the **Museu Balear de Ciències Naturals & Jardí Botànic de Sóller**, a small museum and botanic garden dedicated to the study and conservation of Balearic palaeontology and the evolution of native flora and fauna.

Sóller is good for shopping. C/Lluna, off Plaça Constitució, offers some of the best shop ops; for classy, imaginative jewellery, try **Arte Artesania** (C/Lluna 43, 971 63 17 32, www.arte artesania.com) or for genuine *albarcas*, sandals made with old car tyres (check the tread on the soles), go to **Ben Calçat** (C/Lluna 74, 971 63 28

West Mallorca

74). You can pick up some interesting second-hand clothes and accessories at **La Bohème** (C/Bauza 11, no phone) and cute kids' toys at **Cavall Verd** (C/Bon Any 5, 971 63 35 17). **Ceràmica Castaldo** (Ctra. de Deià s/n, mobile 653 48 94 52), located at the start of the Deià road on the outskirts of town, has desirable ceramics, artily displayed.

The municipal **market** (8am-1pm Mon-Sat), just north the main square, isn't big on atmosphere, but you can find good meat, fish, fruit and veg here. Opposite is **Sa Fàbrica de Gelats** (Plaça Mercat, 971 63 17 08, www.gelatsoller.com), where more than 40 flavours of ice-cream are made, some using the valley's oranges and lemons. Market day is Saturday, when the centre is cordoned off from traffic and shops spill into the streets to join countless market stalls.

If you want to explore the spectacular mountains in the area, Tramuntana Tours (C/Lluna 72, 971 63 24 23, mobile 649 03 47 59, www.tramuntanatours.com) organises guided hikes and mountain bike tours, or you can hire a bike and head off on your own.

Sóller celebrates a number of fiestas: Nit de San Antoni (16 Jan), Fira i Es Firó (2nd Sun and Mon in May), San Pere (29 June) and Sant Bartomeu (24 Aug).

Museu Balear de Ciències Naturals & Jardí Botànic de Sóller

Ctra. Palma–Port de Sóller, km30 (971 63 40 64/ www.museucienciesnaturals.org). **Open** 10am-6pm Tue-Sat; 10am-2pm Sun. **Admission** €3. **No credit cards. Map** p126.

Where to eat & drink

Sóller has an abundance of small bars and cafés, concentrated on and around Plaça Constitució. One of the less touristy is **Es Planet** (No.3, 971 63 45 70, €), where locals sip their morning coffees and later munch on *pa amb oli*, pizzas, salads, and hot and cold baguettes. **Café Sóller** (No.13, 971 63 00 10, €) is great for well-above-average salads and pasta dishes, and is pretty cool (in both senses) inside. Even hipper is **Bar España** (No.1, no phone, €), in front of the Banco de Sóller. Once a grimy old spot, it has been taken over by the original owners' children and transformed into a sleek Barcelona-style joint that serves basic snacks.

For cheap fare and fresh fruit juices, try **Bar La Union 'Sa Botigueta'** (C/Jeroni Estades 9, 971 63 01 63, €), just off the main *plaça* (there's also an entrance on C/Born). If juice is your thing, check out the tiny Brazilian juice bar **Açai Café** (C/Rectoria 3, 971 63 18 18, www.acai-cafe.com).

Surprisingly, the town isn't great for restaurants – most people head down to the Port (*see p128*) or to the handful of excellent places just outside Sóller (booking is advisable for all of them).

Sa Teulera (Ctra. Lluc–Pollença s/n, 971 63 11 11, closed Wed and Feb, €€) is a delightful, informal, rustic restaurant that packs out with locals at weekends who come to enjoy great steaks, rabbit, quail and particularly *lechona* – suckling pig roasted over fires made with almond shells. If you're coming from the Deià road, turn right at the war memorial between Sóller and the Port, and the restaurant is on the left after a couple of kilometres.

More formal is **Ca'n Ai** (Camí Son Sales 50, 971 63 24 94, closed Mon, €€€), an old country house with a garden, where first-rate Mallorcan and international dishes can be enjoyed. Look out for the signs close to the Sóller roundabout. You can also stay here (*see below*).

Back five or so kilometres towards Deià a road leads off towards the coast and has a sign to **Bens d'Avall** (Urb. Costa de Deià s/n, 971 63 23 81, closed Sun dinner, Mon and Nov-Feb, €€€€). This classy place enjoys a spectacular coastal setting; its terrace is a dreamy spot for a long lunch or dinner. The food is contemporary and superb, but be prepared to pay heftily for it.

Where to stay

Recent years have witnessed an explosion of wonderful places to stay in and around Sóller, though most are towards the top end of the price scale.

Prize for poshest spot in town goes to the five-star **Gran Hotel Sóller** (C/Romaguera 18, 971 63 86 86, www.granhotelsoller.com, doubles €214-€332), a splendidly restored late 19th-century building that was a hotel in the 1960s and '70s, but reopened in its current incarnation in 2004. The 38 rooms are decorated in a clean, modern style, with plenty of local stone in evidence. Top selling points include a spa with indoor pool, and a rooftop pool with bar and fabulous views, and a superior Mediterranean restaurant, **Can Blau** (€€€).

Ca'n Roses (C/Quadrado 9, 971 63 22 99, www.canroses.com, closed Nov-mid Dec, doubles €150-€235 incl breakfast) is a supremely tasteful and relaxing hideaway, secreted down a side street close to the main square. A huge wooden door gives on to a patio around which there are eight light-filled rooms (some with terraces), beautifully designed, with steel beds, exposed wood beams and wooden floors. But it's the garden that will take your breath away: palms and orange trees shade a huge swimming pool.

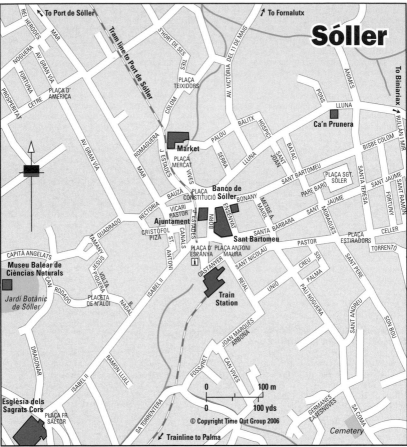

A further classy addition to central Sóller's accommodation options is Siobhan and Brian Kearney's **Hotel Salvia** (C/Palma 18, 971 63 49 36, www.hotelsalvia.com, closed Nov-Mar, doubles €251-€353 incl breakfast), an effortlessly stylish conversion of an 18th-century townhouse to a slick six-bedroom hotel (the whole place can be rented too). It's got a pool, and Siobhan serves up an excellent dinner a couple of times a week. No children under 14.

C'an Quatre (Cami de Villalonga 16, 971 63 80 06, www.canquatre.com, doubles €120-€130) is yet another delightful place, just off the main square, but feeling like it's out in the countryside. There are six rooms (five with terrace) and a suite, all designed in rural style. It's set within its own grounds, with a pool and wonderful views of the mountains.

Other options include four-star **Ca'l Bisbe** (C/Bisbe Nadal 10, 971 63 12 28, www.hotelcalbisbe.com, closed 15 Nov-15 Jan, €106-€126 incl breakfast), in the heart of the town, but with a big pool, and, more modestly, four-room **Ca'n Isabel** (C/Isabel 13, 971 63 80 97, www.canisabel.com, €112-€139 incl breakfast), which, nevertheless, offers plenty of modern comforts (air-con, satellite TV, classy bathroom products).

Typically of Mallorca, once you veer away from the classy end of the accommodation scale, pickings are lean. Sóller does have a number of passable *pensiones*. **Margarita Trias Vives** (C/Reial 3, 971 63 42 14, www.sollernet.com/casamargarita, doubles €27-€36) is a basic budget option in a central location handy for the square and the station; it has seven rooms, one with a terrace. Another possibility is

El Guía (C/Castanyer 2, 971 63 02 27, closed Nov-Mar, doubles €75 incl breakfast), just behind the station, which has a large courtyard and simple rooms.

On the road to Deià, **C'as Xorc** (Ctra. Sóller–Deià, km56.1, 971 63 82 80, www.cas xorc.com, closed Nov-Feb, doubles €160-€290 incl breakfast, restaurant €€€) is a stunningly located oasis of indulgence that enjoys some unforgettable views of the valley and the mountains. The bedrooms are large, airy and not over-designed, and there's a fine restaurant and a lovely pool.

There are a number of other good *agroturismos* and *hoteles rurales* around Sóller. Among the best are **Ca n'Ai** (Camí Son Sales 50, 971 63 24 94, www.canai.com, closed Nov-mid Feb, doubles €225 incl breakfast), **Can Coll** (Camí de Can Coll 1, 971 63 32 44, www.cancoll.com, closed Nov-Jan, doubles €155-€262 incl breakfast) and **Ca's Sant** (Camí ses Fontenelles 34, 971 63 02 98, mobile 649 91 11 94, www.cas-sant.com, doubles €165-€180 incl breakfast).

Resources

Internet
Sóller *Forn de Campos, Avda. Jeroni Estades 9 (no phone/www.forndecampos.com).* **Map** p126.

Police station
Sóller *Plaça de Constitució 1 (971 63 41 41).* **Map** p126.

Post office
Sóller *C/Rectoria 7 (971 63 11 91).* **Map** p126.

Tourist information
Sóller *OIT, Plaça Espanya s/n (971 63 80 08/ ma.mintour08@bitel.es).* **Open** *Mar-Oct* 10am-2pm, 3-5pm Mon-Fri; 10am-1pm Sat. *Nov-Feb* 9am-3pm Mon-Fri; 10am-1pm Sat. **Map** p126.

Fornalutx

A couple of kilometres east of Sóller, in the foothills of some of Mallorca's highest mountains, lies **Fornalutx**, once voted the prettiest village in all Spain. It's quite a responsibility, and one that the town burghers take seriously: there are strict planning and parking laws. With that sort of billing, the reality is a minor letdown (though there are a handful of lovely places to stay). The village itself is tiny, with a small central square with a fountain and a set of steps where the residents celebrate the festival of Reyes Magos on 6 January by giving every child in the village a present. Beyond climbing the steps and having a drink in a café to recover, there's not actually anything to do here, and it's a well-worn stop-off on the tourist trail, so you'll have plenty of company.

From Fornalutx, it's about a 20-minute walk or a short drive to the even tinier, but equally pretty, hamlet of **Biniaraix**. There's a memorable walk from Biniaraix up the vertiginous *barranc* above the village by way of a cobbled path to the rounded, iron cross-topped peak of **L'Ofre** (1,090 metres/3,576 feet).

Where to stay & eat

Despite its diminutive size, **Fornalutx** contains four excellent places to stay. The most chic is **Ca'n Verdera** (C/de Toros 1, 971 63 82 03, www.canverdera.com, closed Nov-Feb, doubles €160-€180 incl breakfast), a strikingly beautiful hotel set in a 150-year-old house, tucked into a side street off the main *plaça* (you'll need to park at the car park just beyond the square and walk up). The rooms are all individually decorated in light tones with stylish fittings and the odd splash of colour from original contemporary artworks. The highlight is the huge penthouse suite, with its own *terraza* and views from the picture windows across the village and valley. (Note that most rooms don't have views.) The small grounds include a shaded patio and a pool looking over towards the mountains.

Petit Hotel (C/Alba 22, 971 63 19 97, www. fornalutxpetithotel.com, closed Nov, doubles €133 incl breakfast) is a former convent, sympathetically and stylishly converted, with just 11 rooms. All are individually designed in a modern style with space and light as key features. Bathrooms are a good size, with marble floors and fluffy towels. The suite is particularly lovely, with views over the terrace and valley. There's also a jacuzzi, sauna and swimming pool.

Near neighbour **Ca'n Reus** (C/Alba 26, 971 63 11 74, www.canreushotel.com, doubles €110-€125) occupies a characterful old townhouse, that has been sympathetically restored. Its seven comfortable, sleek rooms have been sensitively designed; five of them have stunning views of the mountains. The garden room is particularly lovely: secluded, homely and leading straight out to the garden. Other pluses include a small pool, decked terrace, living-room area and the reputation for the best breakfast in town.

If you fancy self-catering (though with breakfast thrown in), then the Marroig family's **Sa Tanqueta** (971 63 85 20, www.sa-tanqueta. com, closed mid Nov-Jan, 2-person apartment €128-€150, 4-person apartment €223-€255, incl breakfast) on the outskirts of the village offers

14 bright, contemporary one- and two-bed apartments sharing a communal pool; most have terraces and all have awesome views.

There aren't many eating options in Fornalutx. On the road leading up out of the village, you'll find **Ca'n Antuna** (C/Arbona Colóm 4, 971 63 30 68, closed Mon and mid Nov-mid Dec, €€), where King Juan Carlos and Queen Sofia have been known to pop in for simple, traditional Mallorcan cooking at its best: soups, hunks of lamb or pork and wine served in *jarras* (terracotta jugs). Sit outside on the vine-covered *terraza* for priceless views of the valley and village.

Es Turó (C/Arbona Colóm 6, 971 63 08 08, closed Thur and mid Jan-mid Feb, €€), a bit further down, offers more good, honest home cooking, with similar views.

On the road through the village, just beyond the main *plaça* is **Bella Vista** (C/Sant Bartolomé s/n, 971 63 15 90, closed Wed and 15 Nov-15 Jan, €€), which, true to its name, offers marvellous views of the valley and excellent Spanish/Mallorcan dishes, such as roast suckling pig and grouper with baked vegetables.

If you need a change from Iberian cuisine, try **Café Med** (C/Sa Plaça 7, 971 63 09 00, closed Sat and Dec & Jan, €€€). Brummie Neil Wilson opened this smart place in 2004 and has secured his niche by offering essentially simple international dishes cooked to perfection. The beef carpaccio with capers and parmesan is as good as you'll find in Italy; the crab risotto with pan-fried salmon, a perfect summer dish.

Resources

Police station
Fornalutx *Vicari Solivellas 1 (971 63 19 01)*.

Post office
Fornalutx *Bellavista 2 (971 63 05 05)*.

Port de Sóller

Four kilometres (two and a half miles) from Sóller, **Port de Sóller** is the antithesis of the brash resorts in the south-west and around the Bay of Palma. Family-oriented, slightly old-fashioned, slightly scruffy, it's a lovely place to spend some time.

The port is spread in an arc around a pretty harbour, protected by cliffs either side, with a naval base at the north end and a couple of sandy beaches. Historically, it has always been Sóller's gateway to the rest of the world, acting as a departure point for boats laden with citrus fruits making their way to France and mainland Spain. It was also a magnet for pirates; in 1561 the port was razed in an attack, forcing the

Sóller. *See p124.*

Sóllerics to fortify the harbour with huge stone jetties and lighthouses; hence, the bay comes almost round on itself. The whole episode is re-enacted with the chaotic, alcohol-fuelled *moros i cristianos* (Moors and Christians) fiesta in the second week of May.

Port de Sóller was never intended as a resort and only began to be developed after 1913, when the tramline from Sóller was built. The same open tram (€2 one way) makes the 20-minute journey today, terminating at the eastern end of the bay by the harbour and the best restaurants. From here the town beach is a few metres away, flanked by numerous bars and eating places.

The second beach, **Platja d'en Repic** (better, bigger but more touristy) is on the bay's western side. If you want to head for this beach, get off the tram at its first stop when it reaches the Port and walk left along pedestrianised, restaurant-lined Passeig de sa Platja. From here, you can walk (or drive) the couple of kilometres up to the lighthouse; the views across the bay from here are glorious, and there's an excellent restaurant, Es Faro (*see p130*).

There are more wonderful views to be had around the other side of the bay from the recently opened **Museu de la Mar Sóller**, which explores the importance of the sea in the history of Sóller; it's located in the old fisherman's district of **Santa Caterina**. To reach it, walk up restaurant-lined C/Santa Caterina d'Alexandria, just beyond the tram terminus, and then go right up some steps as C/Mallorca bears left.

Barcos Azules (971 63 01 70, www.barco sazules.com), based at the kiosk at the harbour, runs glass-bottomed boats and catamarans to Sa Calobra and Cala Tuent. Divers can get kitted out at Octopus (C/Canonge Oliver 13, 971 63 31 33, mobile 608 631 756, www.octopus-mallorca.com, closed Nov-May), near the tourist office, while a range of watersports, including sailing, canoeing, water-skiing and windsurfing, can be organised by the Escola d'Sports Nautics (Passeig Platja d'En Repic s/n, 971 63 30 01, mobile 609 35 41 32, www.nauticsoller.com, closed Nov-Apr).

The tourist office is on C/Canonge Oliver, which runs parallel to the bay, one street back from the tram terminus.

If you're driving, the best place to park is in the car park on your left just before you reach the bay.

Museu de la Mar Sóller

Oratori de Santa Caterina d'Alexandria (971 63 02 00). **Open** *June-Sept* 10am-2pm, 5-8pm Tue-Sat; 10am-2pm Sun. *Oct-May* 10am-1.30pm, 3-6pm Tue-Sat; 10am-2pm Sun. **Admission** €3. **No credit cards.**

Where to eat

The best of Port de Sóller's restaurants are near the harbour and the tram terminus. **Sa Llotja des Peix** (Moll Pesquer s/n, 971 63 29 54, closed Jan-mid Feb, €€) is possibly the pick, and certainly enjoys the prime location, in a building right on the harbour's edge with a first-floor terrace. Its fresh fish and paella are faultless, and served with panache; the meat dishes are good too.

On the street running up the hill from behind Sa Llotja des Peix, C/Santa Caterina d'Alexandria, are a number of other excellent fish restaurants. Informal **Es Racó** (No.6, 971 63 36 39, closed Wed mid Nov-end Jan, €) has a good selection of paellas, meat dishes, salads and tortillas at low prices. **El Pirata** (No.8, 971 63 14 97, closed Mon and 15 Nov-15 Jan, €€) may be adorned with kitsch shiver-me-timbers memorabilia but offers first-rate fish, such as hake, sea bass and gilthead, and specialities like *rape con salsa 'Pirata'* (monkfish in 'Pirata' sauce). Neither of these two places has outdoor seating.

If you want to eat al fresco, bag a table outside one of the next three places on this strip. Popular **Restaurant Balear** (No.14, 971 63 15 24, closed Wed and Dec, Jan, €€) has plenty of toothsome piscine offerings, such as the flavoursome, meaty local fish *denton*. Next is **Ca'n Ribes** (No.22, 971 63 84 93, closed Tue and Dec, Jan, €€), a stylish place with first-rate paella, good salads and quality meat dishes, like shoulder (*palatilla*) of lamb. The last restaurant on the street is also the trendiest: **Lua** (No.1, 971 63 47 45, closed Mon, €€€) offers a more varied menu than most spots in town, with classics like *cogollos con anchoas* (lettuce with anchovies) alongside simple seafood and loosen-the-belt extravagances such as veal sirloin steak with foie gras and a reduction of Pedro Ximenez sherry.

If you're not bothered about sea views, and would rather eat with locals than tourists, try the excellent, family-run **Cellar des Port** (C/Antoni Montis 17, 971 63 06 54, closed Wed and Jan, €€), opposite the entrance to the Hotel Es Port. Its delicious Mallorcan food includes *llom con col* (pork with cabbage), which is a lot more tasty and interesting than it sounds.

Many of the restaurants along the Passeig de sa Platja, by the Platja d'en Repic, aren't as good, but there are exceptions. **Es Passeig** (No.8, 971 63 02 17, closed Wed and Jan, €€€) excels in simple, smartly presented modern Mediterranean cuisine. **Es Canyis** (No.32, 971 63 14 06, closed Mon and Dec, Jan, €€) is a prime spot for first-rate fish. **S'Atic** (No.15, 971 63 81 13, closed Mon, lunch Tue

West Mallorca

and all Dec, €€€) is a superb contemporary restaurant with splendid harbour views in the unlikely location of the fourth floor of the modest Hotel Los Geranios. **Agapanto** (Camí des Faro s/n, 971 63 38 60, www.agapanto. com, €€), on the road to the lighthouse, is a cool bar-restaurant with a terrace, offering the likes of linguine with pesto and prawns, and Asian-style guinea fowl, and a lively programme of live music, flamenco, tango and art exhibitions.

Best location in town has to go to **Es Faro** (Punta de Jrossa, 971 63 37 52, closed Tue, €€€) at the end of the road to the lighthouse, with stunning views over the bay; it serves superb but pricey fish dishes.

Where to stay

Port de Sóller has numerous places to stay, mainly along the bayside Passeig Es Través or just behind it, but until recently none were outstanding. The rebirth of the **Hotel Espléndido** (Passeig Es Través 5, 971 63 18 50, www.esplendidohotel.com, doubles €140 incl breakfast), which reopened in July 2005 (though not all 84 rooms will be complete until 2006), has brought some class to town. The Swedish owners of the super-chic Hotel Portixol in Palma have breathed fresh life into this classic seaside hotel dating from the 1950s and it now sparkles with a harmonious blend of modern and classic detailing. Most rooms have views over the bay, there's a chic cocktail bar, bistro, health club and a pool behind the hotel up the hillside offering more fine vistas.

Another welcome arrival is the **Aimia** (C/Santa Maria del Camí 1, 971 63 12 00, www.aimiahotel.com, closed Dec, Jan, doubles €139-€203 incl breakfast), which was thoroughly revamped in 2004 by the Alcover family in a sleek, contemporary style. Many of its 43 good-value rooms have balconies and look out over the sizeable pool, surrounded by wooden decking. There's also an indoor pool, jacuzzi, sauna, Turkish bath, fitness centre, bar and restaurant.

Situated just 200 metres back from the beach, but seemingly in a different world, the **Hotel Es Port** (C/Antoni Montis s/n, 971 63 16 50, www.hotelesport.com, closed Dec, Jan, doubles €84-€88 incl breakfast) is a lovely old family-owned hotel within extensive grounds. It boasts indoor and (huge) outdoor pools, tennis courts, gym, massages, jacuzzi, sauna and plenty of old-fashioned charm.

The above three hotels are certainly the prime places to stay in the Port. Other options include the **Aparthotel Generoso** (C/Marina 4, 971 63 14 50, www.hotelgeneroso.com,

closed Nov-mid Jan, doubles €56, apartments €117), in a good spot behind the town beach, with clean, comfortable, old-fashioned rooms; the apartments have sea views. If you are here for any length of time, or are with kids, you should consider the apartments, which are a good size and include a kitchen and two balconies; there's also a large swimming pool. **Hotel Miramar** (C/Marina 12-14, 971 63 13 50, www.hotelmiramarsoller.com, closed Nov-Jan, doubles €38-€42) is a more basic option with plain rooms, some with a sea view, and a decent restaurant.

Hotel Marina (Passeig de la Platja, 971 63 14 61, www.hotelmarinasoller.com, closed mid Nov-end Jan, doubles €64-€120 incl breakfast) is a two-star place backing Platja d'en Repic, which has been completely refurbished. Rooms have a sea or mountain view, and there's a large pool and a kids' play area. At night the *terraza* in front of the hotel has live music. **Hotel Los Geranios** (Passeig de la Platja 15, 971 63 14 40, www.hotel-losgeranios.com, doubles €110-€150 incl breakfast) offers comfortable rooms with balconies and air-conditioning; some have jacuzzis. No pool, but there's a sauna and great restaurant S'Atic (*see p129*) on the top floor.

High on the hillside overlooking the bay (you'll need a car to reach it) is the gorgeous **Muleta de Ca S'Hereu** (Camp de sa Mar s/n, 971 18 60 18, mobile 649 82 13 33, www. muletadecashereu.com, doubles €148-€193), an ancient building that now houses spacious air-conditioned bedrooms kitted out with antique Mallorcan wooden furniture; there's also a pool and a restaurant.

Resources

Tourist information

Port de Sóller *OIT, C/Canonge Oliver 10 (971 63 30 42/ma.mintour09@bitel.es).* **Open** *Mar-Oct* 9am-12.50pm, 2.40-4.50pm Mon-Fri. Closed Nov-Apr.

Getting there

By bus

From Palma, hourly buses Mon-Fri (3 Sat, 2 Sun) run direct to Sóller and Port de Sóller, with a further 7 Mon-Fri (3 Sat, 3 Sun) to Sóller and Port de Sóller via Valldemossa and Deià. There are 5 buses Mon-Fri (3 Sat) to Esporles, 2 buses Mon-Fri to Estellencs via La Granja and Banyalbufar, and 2 buses daily between Port de Sóller and Fornalutx. For services from the west coast to Pollença and the north, *see p147.*

By train

For details of the Palma–Sóller train, *see p64* **All aboard!**

Northern Serra

Wilderness, wind and wonders.

Before the advent of tourism, the northern Serra de Tramuntana – named after the northerly Tramuntana winds that buffet it year round – was Mallorca's least desirable and least populated landscape. Precipitous and mostly barren, it is of little use for agriculture and was – and can still be – hazardous for any transport other than the mule. It is the only region of the island to get anything close to a winter; snow often falls in February and March on the highest peaks. Lluc, meanwhile, is the wettest, and possibly the greenest, spot on Mallorca.

Only one road passes through the mountains of the northern Tramuntana. The craggy, soaring peaks hinder access to the coast, but the C710 is a wonderful winding route, linking Sóller to the monastery at Lluc and then to Pollença.

Heading north-east from Sóller, there are fine views down to Port de Sóller and the sea from the **Mirador de ses Barques** (a kilometre after the turn-off to Fornalutx). Continuing onwards, you're soon among the loftiest peaks of the range. The two highest – **Puig Major** (1,445 metres/ 4,741 feet) and **Massanella** (1,352 metres/4,436 feet) – straddle the road across the stunning **Gorg Blau** (Blue Gorge), which is now home to two reservoirs. A wonderful walk around Tossals Verds, another 1,000 metre-plus mountain, starts from one of these reservoirs, the **Embassament de Cúber** (*see p132* **Walk 3**).

There are plenty of other fine hikes to be enjoyed in this area – it's often simply a matter of taking a short stroll from wherever you have bedded down and heading up a path through the farmlands. Puig Major is topped by a military radar station, so Massanella is the highest climbable summit in the Balearics (for a route up Massanella from Lluc, *see p132*).

Just north of the second of the reservoirs, the **Embassament de Gorg Blau**, the C710 passes through a tunnel and emerges near a turn-off on to the only road to fight its way to the coast between Port de Sóller and Pollença: the narrow and precipitous 13-kilometre (eight-mile) route to the coves of Sa Calobra and Cala Tuent. Dealing with the sheer drop-offs and oncoming coaches on steep single-lane hairpins is only for confident drivers (the road turns through 270 degrees at one point), but the open views across the mountains and down to the sea are splendid, and there are quite a few stopping and passing places to break the journey.

Depending on the season, the narrow inlet of **Sa Calobra** can be trying; in summer it is packed with coach parties most of the day. The main draw lies ten minutes' walk from the parking area along the shoreline (follow the crowds). A path passes through a narrow, paved tunnel hewn out of the rock before emerging at the bed of the **Torrent de Pareis** (Torrent of the Twins), an impressive canyon with sheer vertical walls that opens into the sea. After heavy rainstorms, the water coming down from the Torrent de Lluc and the Torrent de Gorg Blau streams builds up and the usual trickle of water becomes a genuine torrent. You can swim off the small pebbly beach here. If you want to enjoy the experience in relative peace, it's worth making the effort to come first thing in the morning or in the evening.

Another way to avoid the coach-party hordes is to take the side road a kilometre back from Sa Calobra that winds down to the beach at **Cala Tuent**. Though it's stony, this is one of the most uncrowded and serene beaches on this part of the island, with great swimming in crystal water. There's little more here than a smattering of villas, a small 13th-century church, the **Ermita de Sant Llorenç**, overlooking the cove, and a wonderful bar-restaurant (Es Vergeret, *see p133*), up the hillside on the cove's south side.

After the Torrent de Pareis, the second obligatory stop for coach parties to this part of the island is the monastery of **Lluc** (36 kilometres/22.5 miles north-east of Sóller and 20 kilometres/12.5 miles south-west of Pollença). Stunning for its location over its architecture, which mostly dates from the 18th and 19th centuries and is austere in the extreme, the **Monestir de Nostra Senyora de Lluc** (Monastery of Our Lady of Lluc) is the most visited site in the north of Mallorca (though whether its popularity is justified is debatable). Once a place of peace and contemplation, the monastery – also known as the **Santuari de Lluc** – now has a busy daytime scene of incoming tour coaches and resting cyclists. Most people choose to descend on the site between 11am and 5pm (when canny travellers are out exploring the mountains) and at dusk the monastery is almost eerily calm again.

The location of Mallorca's most important Christian shrine, Lluc was already a significant spiritual site in pagan times. Prehistoric

Walk 3 Tossals Verds

Embassament
de Gorg Blau.

Distance: 13km (8 miles). Circular.
Time: 4hrs 30mins.

A network of trails criss-cross Mallorca's
high mountains, and the area around the
two reservoirs Cúber and Gorg Blau, in the
shadow of the island's tallest peak, Puig
Major (1,445 metres/4,741 feet), is one of
the most spectacular and popular with hikers.
The following walk offers unbeatable views
and great variety of terrain. There's a steepish
descent close to the beginning, which passes
through a series of tunnels (a small torch
is very useful here) down into a serene valley,
and then a longish, rocky ascent before
the walk levels out for its last hour or so.
If you want just a short hour-long stroll (4
kilometres/2.5 miles), then there's a road
and path that circumnavigate Cúber reservoir.

Park your car in the Fonts de Noguera
car park, 100 metres or so beyond Cúber
reservoir (there's another car park here) on
the main road from Sóller to Pollença. Walk
back to the reservoir and through a wooden
swing gate by a low green gate across the
road, and then head along the metalled road.

After 15 minutes you'll come to a dam.
Immediately before it, take a rocky track
that leads down to the left towards a gorge.
Within another 15 minutes you'll have fine
views down the gorge, and the rough, rock-
strewn path will turn steeply downwards.

Ten minutes later you'll reach the bottom
of this part of the gorge. Cross the stream
here (it may be dry in summer) and bear left,

continuing along for a few minutes and
then upwards following a water pipeline.

Fifteen minutes on and the rough path
by the pipe bends sharply downwards again.
Within five minutes you come to the first
of a series of tunnels through which the pipe
passes. This is your route too, and is where
that torch comes in handy. There's plenty of
room to walk through, though the rocky floor
of the tunnel can be slippery. Ten minutes
later and you arrive at the second tunnel.

It dips and rises towards its end, so you
probably won't be able to see the other
end. This emerges by a rusty old cement
mixer and a tall concrete water tank.

The path continues steeply down and after
another quarter of an hour you'll come to
the third tunnel. There's then a mini-tunnel
and the fourth and last of the longer variety.
This may well be waterlogged at one end,
requiring you to either walk along the top
of the pipe or get your feet wet.

The path now descends more gently
and swings left at the bottom of the valley,
ringing you to a fork. Take the left, lower
option, and within five minutes you reach
a stile by a metal gate with a bridge over a
stream beyond it. A little further downstream
from here is a great spot to stop for a picnic
lunch, sitting on the rocks and cooling
your toes in the mountain water (though
in midsummer it may be dry).

At the bridge, a right turn takes you
downwards through a gorge towards Lloseta,
but you should turn left and follow the
metalled road as it snakes upwards along

a series of terraces for 25 minutes. Eventually, you'll arrive at the Tossals Verds refuge, where you can get food and drink (and there's a toilet too). There are often sizeable crowds of walkers congregated here.

Walk up the left side of the refuge and follow the signed path upwards towards Cases Valles and Font des Noguer (your destination). After 15 minutes of climbing a steep rocky path you'll come to a junction, with paths to left and right both heading towards Font des Noguer. Take the right branch (also signed to Cases Velles), which tells you that you're one hour 50 minutes from the end of the walk.

Within 15 or so minutes you'll find that the steepest climbing is over and the path starts to level out. Soon you come to another sign – carry on towards Font des Noguer (one hour 35 minutes away). Below to your left are terraces and the remains of some abandoned buildings. A few minutes later you'll see, high above you to your left, a dramatic bare crag (with a shape like an arch eroded into it).

The path now starts to descend a little, and then roughly follows the line of the contour, sometimes dipping, sometimes rising. Soon, on your right, superb views open up down through a precipitous gorge to the plain beyond. After another ten or so minutes you pass through a wooden gate and the gorge you're walking along starts to narrow; you may hear the stream below. You come to the stream, cross it on stepping stones, turn left, and then almost immediately recross it on a log bridge before continuing upwards on the path.

Ten minutes on, the path splits and you take the left branch, which tells you that Font des Noguer is now an hour away. Another ten minutes and you start to descend, passing through a wooden gate over an aqueduct. When this is coursing with water you'll wish there were an old inner tube lying around and you could leap in it, for it runs all the way back to the car park. The rest of the walk is easy and largely flat. You turn left and follow the aqueduct all the way back to the car park (which should take around 45 minutes), gasping at the sheer, barren mass of Mallorca's tallest peak Puig Major, topped by its military radar station, in front of you.

Mallorcans visited a cave here – now known as **Sa Cometa dels Morts** – probably to perform a ritual to the dead. They also deified the holm oak woods, a belief that was later embraced by polytheistic Roman settlers. The first theory of the origins of the name 'Lluc' is that it comes from lucus, the Latin for 'sacred wood', and there are still dense swaths of holm oak and cypress on the road leading to Lluc and in the foothills of the rocky slopes that line the wide valleys here. After the 13th-century Reconquest, monks migrated to the then remote spot, building a chapel and reworking the historic holiness of Lluc into a miracle.

Today, Lluc remains a site of pilgrimage for religious Mallorcans, who make their devotions to the dark-skinned statue of the Virgin, **La Moreneta**, also known as Our Lady of the Mountains. The legend of the statue's origin is that a young shepherd called Luke ('Lluc' in *mallorquí*, and thus the second theory about the name of the monastery) found a vividly coloured statue in the woods – perturbed, he sought a monk who was in turn startled when the tiny statue began to glow and play heavenly music.

To see the Virgin, go in through the main doors, walk past the accommodation reception entrance, head down the corridor and cross a small courtyard – in the next, larger courtyard, follow the hand of Bishop Campins (the priest who refurbished Lluc in the 1900s) into the main church, the **Basílica de la Mare de Déu de Lluc** (8.30am-8pm daily, admission free). This plain Renaissance church (built 1622-91) has an elegant façade hemmed in by sober residential buildings. During special services, the Virgin – a small, unprepossessing figure carrying a plump Jesus holding the Book of Life – sits atop a swivelling platform above the high altar. Most of the time, however, this platform is turned to face a small chapel behind the altar where the faithful can kiss the base of the statue. The **Escolania de Lluc** boys' choir, founded almost 500 years ago, sings at mass in the church every day. The choirboys are known as **Els Blauets** (The Blues), after the colour of their cassocks.

With its complex arrangement of buildings and annexes, it takes some time to get your bearings at Lluc. There are two main restaurants (one in the monastery, one at the entrance) and two cafés (one close to the main entrance and another, far quieter one at the rear of the main car park). There are outhouses, an open-air basilica and a small botanical garden (10am-1pm, 3-6pm Mon-Sat, admission free) on the east side of the monastery. A narrow trail runs through the latter, taking visitors through pungent patches of herbs (mint, sage, ginger), exotic and native montane trees, and a frenzy of croaking frogs and bees slurping nectar.

Behind the monastery complex is the **Camí dels Misteris del Rosari** (Way of the Mysteries of the Rosary) – a broad, winding footpath up to a crucifix; continue down the far side of the hill and the path curves back round to the monastery. The views out west across the pastoral idyll of the Albarca valley are lush.

On the first floor of the main building is the **Museu de Lluc**, with one floor dedicated to Talayotic and Roman archaeological finds and an assortment of ecclesiastical items, and an upper floor featuring some dimly lit paintings and modern abstract sculptures. The main rooms hold an important collection of coins, ancient bronze items and a sizeable display of ceramics and fans. A beautiful 18th-century four-poster bed, draped in local lacework, is the outstanding item of furniture, while the most popular attraction, a Talayotic sarcophagus from the fourth century BC, found in Sa Cometa dels Morts, has regrettably had its skeleton removed reportedly because it upset visitors.

If you want to spend a few days exploring the mountains, Lluc makes the best base. One popular walk from here is up to the top of **Massanella**, the island's highest accessible peak (1,352 metres/4,436 feet). The monastery staff will tell you how to get to the road – about 20 minutes' walk – where the hike begins. The owner of the land through which it passes usually charges a small fee for access. Take water and give yourself six to seven hours for the return trip. Red arrows and dots mark the trail where it passes over hard to make out rockscapes. The view from the summit on a clear day is as breathtaking as you'd expect, and you get the full force of the energising Tramuntana wind.

Museu de Lluc

971 87 15 25. **Open** 10am-1.15pm, 2.30-5.30pm daily. **Admission** €2.60. **No credit cards**.

Where to stay & eat

Es Vergeret (C/Cala Tuent s/n, 971 51 71 05, closed dinner and Nov-Jan, €€), the wonderful restaurant at **Cala Tuent**, is smart yet thoroughly relaxed and keenly priced, and has just about the best paella and most gracious service on the island; the view from its spacious stone terrace is magnificent.

The monastery at **Lluc** is the only place to stay in the area – 129 cells are available for one, two, three, four or six people; there are also more commodious apartments available (971 87 15 25, www.lluc.net, doubles €31). You get an authentically spartan space, with a single bed, a desk and a picture of the crucified Christ – no television and you also have to make your own

View from **Es Vergeret**.

bed, but it's quite wonderful and utterly peaceful when the day's coaches have all departed.

As well as two cafés selling *empanadas*, sandwiches and drinks, there are two restaurants at Lluc. **Ca S'Amitger** (971 51 70 46, closed Fri, €€€) is at the entrance to the monastery complex and serves up seafood starters, meaty main dishes plus the likes of paella, sole, hake and the local *emperador* fish. Wines are good and the service is friendly, family-style and a bit slow.

The main dining experience is inside the monastery at **Sa Fonda** (971 87 15 25, €€€), where the impressive columned and arched room formerly used by the monks has been turned into a serious, efficient restaurant with a long bar. Plenty of local dishes are on offer, such as kid in tomato sauce, plus some fine wines from Mallorcan and Riojan bodegas and superb strong coffee to round off a day of hiking or meditation perfectly.

By far the finest and best situated restaurant in the area, however, is outside the monastery. Follow the signs to **Inca** (a half-hour walk or five minutes' drive) to **Restaurante Es Guix** (971 51 70 92, closed Tue and Jan, often closed dinner, phone to check, €€€). At lunchtimes – it rarely opens in the evenings – its secluded terraces are deservedly packed. It's partly the isolation, but above all the fabulous creative approach to peasant cooking; its *frito mallorquín* with lamb's liver and *arròs brut* (somewhere between a broth and a paella) are superb and well priced. A good list of mainly Mallorcan wines, too, presents excellent value. The flower-filled entrance and kids' playground are further pluses, as is the (usually freezing cold) natural rock swimming pool in which diners are allowed a dip.

Getting there

By bus

One bus a day runs from Can Picafort to Sa Calobra via Port d'Alcúdia, Alcúdia, Port de Pollença, Cala Sant Vicenç, Pollença, Lluc (1hr stop). There are 3-4 buses from Palma to Lluc via Inca. For buses from Port de Sóller to Pollença/Alcúdia via Lluc, *see p147*.

North Mallorca

Features

Maps

Beyond **Colònia de Sant Pere**.
See p151.

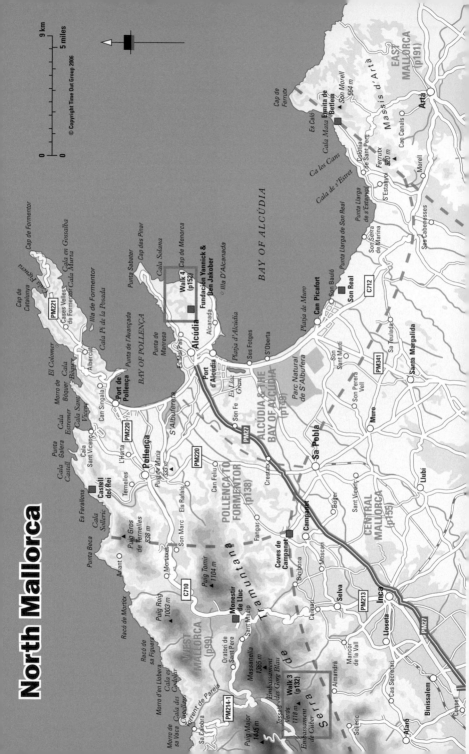

North Mallorca

© Copyright Time Out Group 2006

9 km

5 miles

EAST MALLORCA (p191)

Massís d'Artà

Artà

Son Morell
Ermita de Betlem
▲ 564 m
Cap de Ferrutx
Es Caló
Cala Mata
Cap de Menorca
Cala Estremer
Cala Murta
Cala en Gossalba
Cases Velles de Formentor
Cap de Formentor

Can Canals
Colònia de Sant Pere
Ferrutx ▲ 520 m
Morell
Ca los Cans
Cala de s'Estret
S'Estalvol
Ses Cabenèsses

Walk 4 (p152)
Fundación Yannick & Ben Jakober
Alcúdia
Alcanada
Cap de Menorca
Cala Solana
Cala des Pinar
Punta Sabater
Punta de Manresa
Punta de l'Avançada
Illa d'Alcanada

Punta Llarga de s'Estanyol
Punta Llarga de Son Real

BAY OF ALCÚDIA

Cap de Catalunya
Cala Figuera
PM221

Illa de Formentor
Cala Pi de la Posada

BAY OF POLLENÇA

Morro de El Colomer
Cala Bóquer
Cala Sant Vicenç
Albercutx
Can Singala
Port de Pollença

El Mal Pas
Port d'Alcúdia
Ses Fotges
S'Oberta
Platja d'Alcúdia

Platja de Muro

Son Bauló
Son Real

Can Picafort

C712

Es Farallons
Punta Galera
Cala Castell
Punta Beca
Castell del Rei
Cala Estremer
Cala Sant Vicenç
Sant Vicenç
PM220

L'Horta
Pollença
Puig de Maria ▲ 330 m

El Lluc Gran
Son Fe
S'Albufereta

ALCÚDIA & THE BAY OF ALCÚDIA (p149)
Parc Natural de S'Albufera

Son Sant Martí
Son Sant Martí

PM341
Sa Taulada

Santa Margalida

Cala Sóller
Els Rafals
Ternelles
Son Marc
PM220
Can Feliu
Crestatx

POLLENÇA TO FORMENTOR (p138)

PM27
Sa Pobla

Son Perera
Son Perera Vell

Muro
Llubí

Puig Gros de Ternelles ▲ 838 m

Fangar
Búger
Sant Vicenç

Racó de Mortitx
Mortitxet
Son Marc
Puig Tomir ▲ 1104 m

Coves de Campanet
Campanet
Búgiبona
Moscari

CENTRAL MALLORCA (p155)

Morro de sa Figuera
Racó de sa Vaca
C710
Puig Roig ▲ 1003 m

Monestir de Lluc
Sant Madip
Selva
PM213
Inca

Campanet
Ciutajat

Selva

Inca

Morro d'en Llobera
Cala des Coloirs
Morro de sa Vaca
Cala es Coloirs
Torrent de Pareis
Sa Calobra

WEST MALLORCA (p99)
Oratori de Sant Pere

Massanella ▲ 1365 m

Mancor de la Vall

Lloseta
PM27

Puig Major ▲ 1445 m
Embassament des Gorg Blau
Verds ▲ 1118 m
Walk 3 (p132)
Embassament de Cúber

PM214-1

Tossals das Gorg Blau
Serra de Tramuntana

Almandrà
Cas Secretari

Binissalem
Consell

Alaró
Sóller

North Mallorca

The island in microcosm: wild scenery, characterful towns and mass tourism.

The northern reaches of the craggy Serra de Tramuntana mountain range offer the most dramatic and beautiful landscapes in all Mallorca. The rugged terrain and scarcity of roads to the coast mean that there are very few hotel developments – in fact, few settlements of any kind – between Sóller and Pollença. It is only where the land flattens out around the sweeping bays of Pollença and Alcúdia that mass tourism has become established. The historic towns of Alcúdia and, particularly, Pollença retain much of their original character, thanks in part to being physically separate from their namesake resorts.

POLLENÇA TO FORMENTOR

One of the Mallorca's most delightful towns, Pollença, reclining in the squat foothills of the Tramuntana, is packed with cafés and restaurants. A short drive and you find yourself in the better known Port de Pollença, a smallish but extremely popular family-oriented seaside development, with rather more tasteful and topographically sensitive buildings than other

The best…

Art
Fundación Yannick y Ben Jakober, near Alcúdia (p150).

Beaches
Bay of Alcúdia (p151).

Hotels
Ca'n Cap de Bou, Port de Pollença (p146); **Es Convent**, Alcúdia (p149); **Hotel Llenaire**, Port de Pollença (p146); **Nou Hotelet Cas Ferrer**, Alcúdia (p149); **Son Brull**, outside Pollença (p143); **Son Sant Jordi**, Pollença (p142).

Resorts & towns
Cala Sant Vicenç (p145); **Pollença** (p138); **Port de Pollença** (p143).

Restaurants
Ca'n Cuarassa, outside Port de Pollença (p145); **Genestar**, Alcúdia (p150); **Ristorante Il Giardino**, Pollença (p141).

Step right up: **Port de Pollença**. See p143.

Balearic beach resorts. Close by is tiny Cala Sant Vicenç, with its two thriving beaches, while stretching away east of here is the narrow and impossibly dramatic Formentor peninsula and the cape that marks Mallorca's northernmost point.

ALCÚDIA AND THE BAY OF ALCÚDIA

Tiny fortified Alcúdia offers one of the more touristy versions of Mallorcan small town life, while the long strip of Port d'Alcúdia teems with German- and Brit-friendly bars and restaurants. It's easy to escape the throng, though – Alcúdia sits at the neck of an undeveloped peninsula criss-crossed with a number of walking trails. Echoing in size and sandiness the Bay of Palma, the Bay of Alcúdia isn't quite as built up – but it's heading that way. Though the beach is attractive, it fills up with evacuees from the endless strip of sea-view apartments and faceless high-rise construction that lines the wide coastal road. Only a short distance inland, however, there are emerald green pasturelands, pretty fruit groves and tracts of ecologically important wilderness.

Pollença to Formentor

There's something for everyone on Mallorca's northern tip.

North Mallorca

Plaça Major, **Pollença**.

Pollença

The prettiest town in the north-west of Mallorca, **Pollença** (sometimes written 'Pollensa') is tucked into the low foothills of the northern Tramuntana (61 kilometres/38 miles north-east of Palma and 55 kilometres/34 miles from Sóller – the former route is vastly quicker). resort of Port de Pollença, just six kilometres (four miles) away, Pollença's character has been little affected by the major tourist developments nearby and is, thus, a great base for exploring the region.

There's a Roman stone bridge across the Torrent de Sant Jordi here (built around AD 120), but the town wasn't founded until the 13th century (when its inhabitants confusingly appropriated the name of the Roman town of Pollentia, on the site of today's Alcúdia; *see p148*). It's a small, compact settlement of 14,000 people, built inland from its harbour, as so many Mallorcan towns were, in an attempt to deter pirate raids. Nonetheless, it was attacked – most forcibly in 1550 by the Turkish corsair Dragut. A local hero, Joan Mas, led the resistance and finally overcame the invaders – a victory celebrated every 2 August during the festival of **Mare de Déu dels Àngels** (*see p149*).

The centre's labyrinthine streets – most of them devoid of pavements – are almost the only remaining traces of the medieval town; most of the houses here date from the 17th and 18th centuries. Three imposing churches dominate the skyline. On Plaça Major rises the vast, austere **Nostra Senyora dels Àngels**; although its origins are in the 13th century, the church was largely rebuilt in baroque style between 1714 and 1790. It dominates Pollença's pleasantly irregular main square, which buzzes with chatter from its al fresco bars and restaurants in fine weather.

South of Plaça Major lies **Nostra Senyora del Roser**. The baroque interior of this deconsecrated church contains a superb organ from 1732. In the adjacent cloister of the 16th-century baroque **Convent de Sant Domingo** is the **Museu de Pollença**, holding a collection of miscellaneous items of archaeological, ecclesiastical and folkloric interest, with some decent Gothic art also on display. The landscapes and depictions of local customs by Argentine artist Atilio Boveri – who visited Pollença in 1912-15 and was also responsible for one of the Via Crucis paintings in the church – are also worth a look.

North of the main square stands the Jesuit church of **Monti-Sion** (completed in 1738), and between it and Plaça Major are clusters of cafés, restaurants and some interesting shops. C/Ombra leads out of Plaça Major to Plaça dels Seglars, with its terrace eateries, and to the foot of the **Via Crucis**, Pollença's most treasured landmark. This steep, straight, 365-step, cypress-lined stairway leads up to a simple chapel on the hilltop of **El Calvarí** (Calvary), from which there are panoramic views of Pollença and its setting between the mountains and the coast. On Good Friday, a figure of Jesus is borne down the Via Crucis in a procession known as the **Davallament** or 'Lowering' (*see p41*).

An even more dramatic vantage point is the top of **Puig de Maria**, the summit of a 333-metre (1,093-foot) hill on the southern edge of town. You can drive the horrendous zigzagging road to the top of Puig, where an old, now monkless 18th-century monastery provides cheap, simple lodgings, or, alternatively, climb the same route on foot in about 45 minutes. To reach it on foot from the centre of Pollença, follow C/Alcúdia and Avinguda Pollentia until you hit the main road; turn right and the start of the Puig road is 100 or so metres away on the opposite side of the road.

Apart from Christianity, Pollença is also known as a good shopping town, and there is a lively food and crafts market on Plaça Major and the surrounding streets on Sundays. Among the notable shops are **Ceràmiques Monti-Sion** (C/Montesión 19, 971 53 35 00), with its irresistibly colourful selection of hand-painted jugs, tiles, mugs and plates. **Aina** (Plaça Vella 1, 971 53 06 86) stocks wonderfully quirky kids' clothes, from embroidered dresses for parties to stripy Victorian-style swimming costumes with built-in floats, much of it in technicolours. (It has a branch in Port de Pollença at C/Joan XXIV s/n, 971 86 67 81.) **Enseñat** (C/Alcúdia 5, 971 53 36 18) isn't cheap, but it's the smartest place in town to pick up all those edible Med goodies (some produced on the shop's own estate nearby) – from unusual Binissalem wines to fine olives and oils, hams, sausages, local pulses and delicate sweets. Come on Sunday mornings for the regular tasting of trad Mallorcan food and wine.

North Mallorca

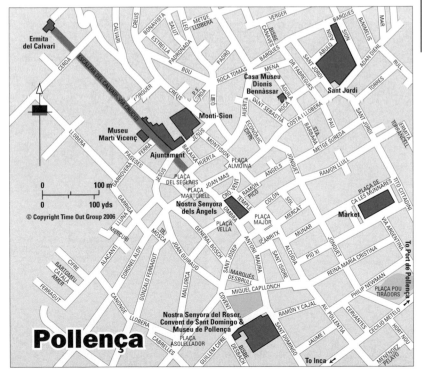

Pollença's also an artistic hub – the shared legacy of Catalan painter Hermenegild Anglada-Camarasa, who settled in Port de Pollença in 1914 and died there in 1959, and renowned Pollençan intellectual and oil painter Dionís Bennàssar (1904-67). The **Casa Museu Dionís Bennàssar** is the latter's old home and exhibits some of the best of his early academicist and modernist works, as well as figurative studies of everyday life in Pollença.

Other arty distractions worth taking in are the beautiful contemporary textiles and sculpture in the **Museu Martí Vicenç**, a small museum in a 300-year-old building towards the lower end of the Via Crucis that showcases the work of Martí Vicenç (1926-95), an innovative local weaver. A range of modern art, some of it on sale, is on view at the **Galeria Maior** (Plaça Major 4, 971 53 00 95, www.galeriamaior.com, open 10.30am-1.30pm, 5.-8pm Tue-Sat, 11am-1.30pm Sun, free) on the main *plaça*.

Pollença doesn't slack in music either – the annual **Festival de Pollença** (971 53 50 77, 971 53 40 12, www.festivalpollenca.org), established in 1962, takes place in July and August, with concerts in venues around the town, and attracts international classical musicians and ensembles.

A popular walk from the town is towards the coast and the ruined **Castell del Rei**, passing through the village of **Ternelles** before heading up behind the diminutive **Serra de Sant Vicenç** mountains. The Ternelles valley is popular with birdwatchers, and the seven-kilometre (four and a half-mile) hike from Pollença to the Castell del Rei has long been a favourite with walkers (ask at the tourist office for directions). There are great views from the castle, a coastal fortification established by the Moors in the 11th century and further strengthened by Jaume I; this was the last fort to surrender to Pere of Aragón when Jaume III's short-lived Kingdom of Mallorca came to an end in 1343. You can swim here at the shingly coves of **Cala Castell**. The castle is on a private estate and vehicle access is restricted; it should be possible to drive part of the way down the road and then leave your car at a gate, but it's wise to check with the tourist office first.

Casa Museu Dionís Bennàssar

C/Roca 14 (971 53 09 97). Open *Apr-Nov* 11am-1pm Tue-Sun. **Admission** €2. **No credit cards. Map** p139.

Son Brull hotel. *See p142.*

Top ten

Mallorcan must-dos

Capital idea

Palma is a Mediterranean stunner. She's got it all: good looks (a pristine old town, a waterfront location), intelligence (first-rate art museums), and she knows how to have a good time (great shops, bars and restaurants). *See p82* **One day in Palma**.

Going underground

The island's most famous sight is hopelessly over-commercialised and hideously rammed with tour parties from dawn to dusk, but the **Coves del Drac** (*see p203*) are simply an extraordinary natural phenomenon and shouldn't be missed.

All aboard

Its days of transporting oranges from Sóller to Palma may be long past, but the toy town-cute narrow gauge **Palma–Sóller railway** (*see p64* **All aboard!**) has never been busier, transporting tourists on a memorable journey through the mountains.

Going back to their roots

There may be more of them on Menorca, but the prehistoric site of **Capocorb Vell** (*see p183*) in the south of Mallorca is one of the largest and most complete in the Balearics; it provides a fascinating insight into the lives of the islands' earliest inhabitants.

Feet first

Mallorca heaves with factory outlets, many of them unimpressive. The one shop op that shouldn't be missed, though, is a trip to the outlet store on the outskirts of Inca of something-for-everyone shoemaker **Camper**. *See p166* **Shoes shine**.

Virgin islands

The **Parc Nacional de Cabrera** (*see p189* **Virgin Islands**) lies off the south-east tip of Mallorca. Take a boat trip to these untouched and evolutionarily unique islands for the completest possible escape from the tourist hordes.

To the manor born

A more recent past is brought to life in the beautifully restored grand country seat of **Els Calderers** (*see p171*) in the centre of the island; it gives a palpable sense of how the other half lived in the 19th century.

Mountain excitement

Drive the **coastal road** from Port d'Andratx to Sóller. Nowhere in Europe will you experience more dramatic scenery than on Mallorca's west coast, and this spectacular and hair-raising route makes it dangerously difficult to keep your eyes on the road. *See p110*.

A walk on the wild side

The lofty Tramuntana mountains offer some of the most exhilarating hiking you'll ever experience. Devote at least one day to walking – a good introduction would be the classic route up to the ruined monastery of La Trapa in the south-west (*see p106* **Walk 1**).

Heads in the clouds

If you want a new perspective on Mallorca, in the fullest sense of the word, spend a night in one of the island's hill-top former monasteries, such as the **Santuari de Sant Salvador** (*see p194*) or the **Santuari Nostra Senyora des Puig** (*see p143*).

North Mallorca

Museu Martí Vicenç

C/Calvari 10 (971 53 28 67/www.martivicens.org). **Open** 10am-2pm, 5-7.30pm Mon; 10am-7pm Tue-Sat; 10am-1.30pm Sun. **Admission** free. **Map** p139.

Museu de Pollença

Convento Santo Domingo, C/Guillem Cifre de Colonya s/n (971 53 11 66). **Open** 10.30am-1.30pm, 5pm-midnight Tue-Sat; 10.30am-1pm Sun. **Admission** €1.50 (free Sun and after 7.20pm). **No credit cards. Map** p139.

Where to eat & drink

Pollença's Plaça Major doesn't want for classic cafés where regulars meet to scan the newspapers, share gossip and sip on wake-up *cortados* and *solos*, with a pastry and a fresh orange juice on the side. **Ca'n Moixet** (No.2, 971 53 42 14, closed 15-31 Jan, €) is one of the oldest, and also does very good, hefty *bocadillos* with *jamón* and toasties. **Bar Juma** (Plaça Major 9, 971 53 32 58, €€), part of the eponymous hotel (*see p142*), is another good breakfast bar, which also does a brisk trade at lunch with seafood and meat tapas, and has a nice terrace out on the *plaça*.

The most popular restaurant on the square is **Ristorante Il Giardino** (Plaça Major 11, 971 53 43 02, closed Nov-15 Mar, €€), and understandably so. The staff are delightful, as is the Italian food, which employs high-quality ingredients in classic tricolore salads and carpaccios, pizzas, meat and fish dishes, and great pastas, such as an unusual black fettucine with king prawns in a rich, tomatoey sauce; the house Penèdes red is excellent and good value too.

For simpler Italian lunch fare, **Ristorante La Piazzetta** (Plaça dels Seglars 5, 971 53 44 82, closed Mon Mar-June, Sept, Oct and all Nov-Feb, €€) is a good choice. The French and Italian couple running this tiny restaurant on Pollença's second square specialise in bruschettas and simple but tasty pasta dishes, and there's great tartuffo and pannacotta to round off the meal.

For Mallorcan food, try the traditional and popular **Bar Nou** (C/Antoni Maura 13, 971 53 00 05, closed Tue and mid Dec-mid Jan, €€), which specialises in hams, cheeses and *pa amb oli*, all prepared with love and care; for bigger appetites, sample the paellas, *chipirones* (baby squid) and outstanding *navajas* (razor clams).

Cantonet (C/Montesión 20, 971 53 04 29, closed lunch, all Tue and Nov-Jan, €€) offers Mallorcan and Italian dishes, including outstanding home-made ravioli – with fish, cheese or guinea fowl. Eat outside on the lively street in fine weather against the backdrop of Monti-Sion church.

Named after the bright red flowers on its patio, **Clivia** (Avda. Pollentia 5, 971 53 36 35, closed lunch Mon & Wed in summer, all Wed in winter, 12 Nov-20 Dec, €€€), set in an old townhouse, is well loved for its Spanish and Portuguese-influenced cuisine, with good veal and exceptional fish dishes. Expect welcoming staff and generous portions of cod, monkfish, eel, squid, sea bass in white wine and great spicy fish soups.

At **La Font del Gall** (C/Montesión 4, 971 53 03 96, closed Nov-Feb, €€€), owners have come and gone over the years – and quality has wavered at times – but in its latest incarnation the restaurant shows Scottish influences, with cock-a-leekie soup sitting next to sardines with ginger on the menu.

Another restaurant serious about its food is **Ca'n Costa** (C/Miquel Costa i Llobera 11, 971 53 12 76, closed lunch, all Tue and Oct-Apr, €€€), set in an old cinema off the main square. Dishes include *queso Mahón* parcels, seared tuna with chilli mash, and lovely lemon sorbet and raspberry mousse.

The Hotel Son Sant Jordi's **La Placeta** (*see below*, closed Mon, €), is a beautifully located terrace café-restaurant in a quieter part of town, with a short, simple menu of international and Mediterranean dishes.

Where to stay

Most visitors to this part of the island stay near the beach at Port de Pollença, but slowly the town is opening up. The pioneer was three-star family-run **Hotel Juma** (Plaça Major 9, 971 53 50 02, www.hoteljuma.com, closed 15 Nov-15 Dec, doubles €108 incl breakfast), founded in 1907, which remains a great spot to lay your head right on the town's main square. Immaculately clean, and in tip-top condition decor-wise, this friendly place has a very Mallorcan feel to it, with simple, spruce (though not cheap) rooms over a bar. Ask for a room with a view of the square (though be prepared for some noise from the nightly gathering of tourists and locals below).

Just around the corner (enquire at the Juma if the doors are locked), the same family has recently opened the excellent and great value **L'Hostal** (C/Mercat 18, 971 53 52 81, www.hostalpollensa.com, closed 15 Nov-15 Dec, doubles €85 incl breakfast), with six stylish and modern rooms, two of which connect for those staying *en famille*.

In a similar vein, if slightly more minimalist, is the **Desbrull** (C/Marquès Desbrull 7, 971 53 03 89, www.desbrull.com, closed mid Nov-mid Dec, doubles €75-€91 incl breakfast), which opened in 2003.

The **Son Sant Jordi** (C/Sant Jordi 29, 971 53 03 89, www.sonsantjordi.com, doubles €156 incl breakfast) is a beautifully restored townhouse hotel, decked out with rough stone walls, cream linen, feng shui-influenced draperies and old Mallorcan touches. The hotel has its own terrace café-restaurant and a swimming pool in the back garden. Located five blocks from the main *plaça*, it's a charming and serene spot, and the staff are happy to advise on walks, golf, cycling and nature trips.

The **Posada de Lluc** (C/Roser Vell 11, 971 53 52 20, www.posadalluc.com, closed Dec-Jan, doubles €95-€140 incl breakfast) was built in the 15th century as a nobleman's mansion; the building was donated to the monks of Lluc, so that they had a place to rest when travelling through. It's now a fairly luxurious *hotel del interior*, with eight rooms decked out with Mallorcan furniture and mod cons like satellite TV and minibar. There's a lovely pool too.

For the ultimate in luxury, head to **Son Brull** (Ctra. Palma–Pollença, km49.9, 971 53 53 53, www.sonbrull.com, closed Dec, Jan, doubles €303-€413 incl breakfast, restaurant €€€€), which opened within a former 18th-century convent just outside Pollença in 2003. Owned by the Mallorcan Suau family (who also run the Hotel Cala Sant Vicenç; *see p146*), this oasis of indulgence has 23 sparkling rooms, indoor and outdoor pools, a health spa with Turkish bath, sauna, jacuzzi, treatment rooms and a classy restaurant.

The cheapest but most breathtaking accommodation around Pollença, up a death-defying road, is at the **Santuari Nostra Senyora des Puig** (Puig de Santa Maria, 971 18 41 32, €11 per person). It is an utterly peaceful and truly spiritual place to visit, with magnificent views, not to mention the excellent paellas and lentil-and-pork stews the kitchen turns out on request, with fruity sangria on the side. Rooms are rough and ready, with three beds per cell, no curtains on some windows and little to do except read and reflect.

Port de Pollença & Cala Sant Vicenç

Between Pollença town and its port is **Albufereta**, a botanically rich wetland area far smaller than the S'Albufera park south of Alcúdia (*see p241*), but, since 2001, designated as Mallorca's first nature reserve and enjoying a high level of protection. Popular with bird enthusiasts, it is an important stopover on the Europe–Africa migration highway and home to over 100 species, including egrets, herons, bitterns and ospreys.

While the inland town grew to prominence, its nearby beach and fishing port, seven kilometres (four and a half miles) away, went about its low-key business undisturbed (apart from the odd pirate raid) until the late 19th century, when it began to become popular with artists and aristocrats for a spot of R&R. The gracious Hotel Miramar opened in 1912 and stood more or less alone until the 1960s when serious tourist development began.

Today's resort of **Port de Pollença** (Puerto Pollensa in Castilian) stretches for three kilometres (two miles) around the curved **Bay of Pollença**, straying inland for just four blocks of bright, white, medium-height hotels, villas and busy back streets, set against the dramatic backdrop of the Formentor peninsula. The town may be a tad disorderly in appearance but, as an easygoing family destination, it's less brash than other Mallorcan resorts and deservedly popular, not least for the range and quality of its restaurants, which range from classic Mediterranean and Mallorcan, to Chinese, Japanese and Indian.

The northern end of the beach has a pedestrianised promenade, the pine tree-lined Passeig Anglada Camarasa, along which stand some smartish hotels and good bars and restaurants. This is also the most popular

North Mallorca

Port de Pollença.

Out to lunch at one of **Cala Sant Vicenç**'s restaurants. *See p143.*

end for bathers, so if you want a bit of space it's best to walk towards the southern (Alcúdia) end, beyond the windsurf hire firms.

Diving is well established in the resort, with Scuba-Mallorca (C/El Cano 23, 971 86 80 87, www.scubamallorca.com, closed Nov-Apr) among the reliable operators – look out for Turkish wrasse, groupers, barracudas and lovely low coral walls. The Port is also home to the Real Club Náutico as well as a busy marina, and there are a number of sailing opportunities, ranging from chilling out on a lavish yacht while people service your every whim to chartering your own unguided boat. There are also half a dozen places to rent a bike near the centre.

A popular walking trail (six-kilometre/three and three quarter-mile round trip) from Port de Pollença heads inland to the **Vall de Boquer** ; it starts from the end of Avinguda Bocchoris.

One of the more attractive resorts in the area is diminutive **Cala Sant Vicenç**, four kilometres (two and a half miles) off the Pollença–Port de Pollença road. It comprises three tiny sandy beaches (and a rocky cove), a handful of hotels, and a few touristy restaurants and bars. It's a pity that the Hotel Don Pedro hogs the seafront, but it's still

a choice spot for a swim (though the sea can get pretty rough here and the red flag is frequently hoisted). Looking right from the main car park you see the rocky hills of the **Serra del Cavall Bernat** and the Formentor peninsula behind it. There are more fine views from the **Puig de l'Àguila** hilltop a few kilometres out of town.

Where to eat & drink

Port de Pollença has its Irish theme pubs and fish and chips, but also offers local cuisine and a range of restaurants you'd only normally expect from a far bigger town. One of the best is the **Ivy Garden** (C/Llevant 14, 971 86 62 27, €€€), where dishes such as calf's liver with bacon and sautéed apple, and duck breast with ginger, honey and soy sauce are served in a pretty interior courtyard.

There are plenty of lunch places on the long prom and a block into the town. A good choice is **La Goleta** (Passeig Saralegui 118, 971 86 59 02, closed 15 Nov-15 Feb, €); it sits below a nondescript hotel block, but its steaks, paellas and fish dishes are simple, tasty and cheap, and it's popular with locals.

locally where possible, and the vast wine list is a joy. Presentation is verging on art, but the food is honest and tasty, and there are terrace tables out on the quay.

For something different, go to bamboo-lined **Fujisan** (C/Formentor 38, 971 86 44 21, €€€), which despite the off-putting glossy Kodak pics of its food, serves decent sashimi, maki rolls and miso soup.

A bucolic option just a couple of kilometres from Port de Pollença, is **Ca'n Cuarassa** (Ctra. Port de Pollença–Alcúdia, 971 86 42 66, www.cancuarassa.com, €€€), which has great views over the bay, a lovely shaded terrace, and a gourmet menu of Mediterranean specials and pastas – the rabbit with potato alioli is a treat, and the calf's liver ultra-succulent; skewered prawns is a lightweight alternative. Tiramisú and home-made ice-cream wrap up meals here, and there's a long wine list to explore.

Cala Sant Vicenç concentrates on providing quick lunches for bathers – there are plenty of cafés and snack bars at the top of the bluff and down near the beaches, and many do beans on toast, pizzas, chips and the like. For something more exciting, go along to the restaurants at the Hotel Cala Sant Vicenç (*see p146*) or try the high-quality meats at barbecue restaurant **Modesto Grill** (Avda. Torrent s/n, 971 53 38 49, closed lunch and Nov-Apr, €€).

Pizza is not always top notch in the Balearics, but **Little Italy** (Passeig Voramar 59, 971 86 67 49, closed Nov-Apr, €) has the correct Italian idea about dough thickness, oil, tomato and cheese.

Going up a grade, give **A Punt** (C/Templer Fielding s/n, 971 86 40 10, closed lunch July-Sept, €€€) a punt. Lovely out on its leafy terrace, trad and a bit stuffy inside, this is probably the best meat restaurant in Port de Pollença, with a wood-fired oven full of shoulders of lamb and T-bones, as well as a variety of fish. Upstairs there are fresh pastas, pizzas and other Italian standards – and a gorgeous balcony – with a good wine and cava list, and jazz on Wednesdays and Fridays.

Monied folk also eat at the **Real Club Náutico** (Moll Vell s/n, 971 86 56 22, €€€€) on the jetty. This is where you go for goose liver pâté, the house special of lobster casserole and a good vantage point from which to keep a close eye on your yacht.

Popular with well-heeled locals is **Stay** (C/Moll Nou s/n, 971 86 40 13, www.stayrestaurant.com, €€€€), which specialises in salmon, lamb, roast duck, pork in apple and calvados sauce, beef with foie gras and port, and a dessert of fresh fig and almond strudel. Stay's aim is to be international with a Mallorcan twist, sourcing

Where to stay

Much of **Port de Pollença** is made up of boring-looking hotel blocks and villas. The beachside hotels are slightly better, and the older establishments tend to feel more sophisticated, but many are block-booked by travel companies.

The *grande dame* is the **Hotel Miramar** (Passeig Anglada Camarasa 39, 971 86 64 00, www.hotel-miramar.net, closed Nov-Mar, doubles €78.50-€138 incl breakfast). Opened in 1912, the Miramar prides itself on its pedigree – check out the photos in the lobby, showing when it stood alone on the beautiful beach. Artists hung out here in the 1960s and now, for all the package rep folders you see around, there's still a certain grace to the place. Air-con and double-glazing throughout make it cool and serene, and the terrace café is a people-watchers' fave.

At the posher, eastern end of the pine walk, the smart four-star **Hotel Illa d'Or** (Passeig de Colón 265, 971 86 51 00, www.hoposa.es, closed 23 Nov-7 Feb, doubles €93.50-€172 incl breakfast) looks newish but has actually been here, at least in name, since 1929. It's particularly popular with families and those who want everything near to hand – including

North Mallorca

a gym, nice terrace restaurant, indoor and outdoor pools, sauna and jacuzzi. Apartments are available in the same complex.

For those on a tighter budget, there's the basic **Hostal Bar Corró** (C/Joan XXIII 68, 971 86 66 83, www.hostalcorro.com, doubles €30), with an internet café downstairs or the **Hostal Residencia Paris** (C/Magallanes 18, 971 864 017, www.pollensa.net, doubles €45). Both are located in ugly medium-height towers but are central and friendly.

An original alternative to beachside hotels, the finca **Ca'n Cap de Bou** (Bay of Pollença, 971 27 21 59, 971 86 74 03, mobile 696 90 15 12, www.cancapdebou.com, closed Nov-Feb, house for up to 8 people €180-€190, apartments for 2/3 people €90-€95) is a lovely old rural building with room for 28 guests. With tennis courts, a pool and boats to rent, it has all the services, but come dusk is a refuge from the neon naffness of the town. The sea is less than a kilometre away and you can even travel there by donkey cart on request.

Another superb rural hotel is the luxurious **Hotel Llenaire** (Camí de Llenaire, km3.8, 971 53 52 51, www.hotelllenaire.com, closed Nov-Jan, doubles €282), just south of Port de Pollença, which opened in 2003. It sits within its own estate, offers eight huge suites and three superior doubles, plus facilities that include a pool, solarium and sauna.

There are several package-type hotels at **Cala Sant Vicenç**, but the most eye-catching is easily the five-star **La Moraleja** (Urb. Los Encinares s/n, 971 53 40 10, www.lamoraleja.net, closed Oct-Apr, doubles €259-€294 incl breakfast), which, despite its rather showy faux opulence (note the vintage cars in the folly-cum-showroom and Dallas ranch approach to furnishings) is extremely friendly, has deceptively few bedrooms (17) and is much loved by its guests.

Alternatively, stay at the more elegant **Hotel Cala Sant Vicenç** (C/Maressers 2, 971 53 02 50, www.hotelcala.com, closed Dec-Jan, doubles €136-€263 incl breakfast), where you get to indulge in the excellent cuisine at this locally revered **Cavall Bernat** (€€€€) restaurant, as well as a trattoria and a poolside grill. The hotel is owned by the same family as the sleek Son Brull near Pollença (*see p143*).

To stay or eat right on the waterfront, try the friendly, simple and comfortable **Hotel Niu** (Cala Barques s/n, 971 53 01 00, www.hotel niu.com, closed Nov-Mar, doubles €60-€130 incl breakfast), owned by a British-Mallorcan couple. Rooms vary according to the view and whether they have a terrace or balcony. A separate building, C'an Franc, houses four smart suites (€130-€180), and there are three different restaurants with varying degrees of formality.

Formentor.

Tucked away among the pine trees above the next beach along, Cala Molins, is the **Hostal Los Pinos** (971 53 12 10, www.hostal-lospinos. com, closed Nov-Apr, doubles €60-€72 incl breakfast), which makes a reasonable stab at looking Mediterranean – with plenty of cats and geraniums – despite its size. There is a decent-sized pool and the views are unbeatable.

Formentor

From Port de Pollença, it's half an hour's drive (21 kilometres/13 miles) up and round the switchbacks of the steep, narrow road to Mallorca's most northerly cape, **Cap de Formentor**, celebrated by poets and artists for its pine forests, its peace and its superlative, dizzying panoramas. It's an essential trip if you're in the area, but make it early or late in the day if you don't want to be part of a tourist convoy. The main stops are at the **Mirador des Colomer**, a short pathway on the edge of a 232 metre- (760 foot-) high sheer vertical cliff, and the lighthouse. Further fine views can be had from side journeys up the **Atalaya d'Alberutx** and at **Can es Faro**, but you'll need good nerves and suspension to take on the old, beaten-up roads here.

Like the rest of the Tramuntana, the unwieldy topography of this slender promontory was of little interest to Mallorca's earliest conquerors, though its name (*forment* means wheat) suggests that it was valued at some stage in history by farmers. The first record of a proprietor dates from 1231, two years after the conquest of Jaume I, and from then until the 20th century the whole of the peninsula changed hands only a few times and development was scant – a few houses, barns, a lighthouse, a single road.

In 1928 Adam Diehl, an Argentine art-loving dandy who'd made his fortune in the meat trade, bought the whole of the peninsula for half a million pesetas and built a stylish, modernist hotel here for artists and aristocrats (*see below*). Non-residents can visit the **Hotel Formentor** as they drive through and stroll along the lovely public beach, the **Platja de Formentor**.

But there is a more public heritage that the hotel has bequeathed. Neither Diehl nor subsequent owners were keen to downgrade the hotel by allowing large-scale tourist development to take place on their exclusive strip of wilderness. The happy consequence of this has been the preservation of Formentor's ecologies, particularly the seabirds – twitchers report sightings of honey buzzards, black kites and booted eagles as well as Mallorca's star bird of prey, the Eleanora's falcon. The rocky outcrops also provide homes for lizards and smaller birds like martins and swifts, especially at the northern tip

Where to stay & eat

Literally the only place to stay on Formentor is the legendary **Hotel Formentor** (Platja de Formentor s/n, 971 89 91 01, www.hotel formentor.net, closed Oct-Mar, doubles €262-€452 incl breakfast). It opened in 1929, and early guests included the Duke of Windsor, the Maharajah of Papurtala and writer Ramón Gomez de la Serna. Later on Hollywood icons such as Elizabeth Taylor, Ava Gardner, Audrey Hepburn and Gary Cooper would add further lustre, putting Mallorca on the classy tourist map and creating a legacy that, frankly, the hotel can no longer quite live up to. Nowadays, summits of suits are the closest the place comes to reviving former glories, and there's a rather dated, sunken *Titanic* feel in the endless corridors of this vast 127-room complex, though staff work hard to be welcoming. Check out the hairdressing salon, the boutiques and the dining balconies to get a feel for how the other half used to live. There are three in-house restaurants.

The only other option for a bite to eat is the café (mobile 619 74 85 91, open 10am-6pm daily, closed dinner and Nov, €) at the very end of the promontory, near the lighthouse. Here you can get filled baguettes, pizza and ice-cream while you admire the stunning view.

Resources

Internet
Pollença *Café 1550, Avda. de l'Argentina 1 (971 53 13 30/www.cafe1550.com)*. **Open** 7am-2am daily.
Port de Pollença *Café Caramba, C/Mestral 7 (971 86 66 46)*. **Open** 10am-2am Tue-Sun. **Map** p139.

Police station
Pollença *C/Munar 16 (971 53 04 37)*. **Map** p139.

Post office
Pollença *C/Jonquet 61 (971 53 11 25)*. **Map** p139.
Port de Pollença *C/Levant 15 (971 86 69 71)*.

Tourist information
Cala Sant Vicenç *OIT, Plaça Sant Vicenç s/n (971 53 32 64/oitcsv@ajpollenca.net)*. **Open** *June-Sept* 9.15am-2pm, 3-5pm Mon-Fri; 9.15am-1pm Sat. Closed Oct-May.
Pollença *OIT, C/Guillem Cifre de Colonya s/n (971 53 50 77/oit@ajpollenca.net)*. **Open** 8am-3pm Mon-Fri; 9am-1pm Sat. **Map** p139.
Port de Pollença *OIT, Passeig Saralegue s/n (971 86 54 67/oitport@ajpollenca.net)*. **Open** *Mar-June* 8am-3pm Mon-Fri; 9am-1pm Sat. *July-Sept* 9am-2pm, 4-6pm Mon-Fri; 9am-3pm Sat. *Oct-Feb* 8am-3pm Mon-Fri.

Getting there

By bus
Autocares Mallorca runs 1 bus (Line 11) Mon-Sat from Palma (departing at 10.15am) to Formentor via Inca (10.50am), Alcúdia (11.20am) and Port de Pollença (11.30am), arriving at Formentor at 11.50am, and setting off from Formentor for the return journey at 3.30pm.

Line 3 buses run twice a day Mon-Sat from Can Picafort (9am, 2.15pm) to Formentor (arriving 10.20am, 3.20pm) via Port de Alcúdia (9.30am, 2.40pm), 3 times Mon-Sat from Alcúdia (9.45am, 11.15am, 2.50pm) to Formentor and 4 times Mon-Sat from Port de Pollença (10am, 11.30am, 3pm, 4.30pm) to Formentor.

Line 4 buses run twice a day Mon-Sat between Port de Sóller (leaving 9am, 3pm) and Can Picafort (arriving noon, 6pm) via Sóller (9.10am, 3.10pm), Lluc (10.20am, 4.20pm), Pollença (10.45am, 4.45pm), Cala Sant Vicenç (10.55am, 4.55pm), Port de Pollença (11.10am, 5.10pm), Alcúdia (11.30am, 5.30pm) and Port d'Alcúdia (11.35am, 5.35pm). Return buses leave Can Picafort at 9am and 3pm.

For information on buses to Sóller, Port de Sóller, Lluc and Sa Calobra, *see p134*. For information on other buses to Alcúdia and around the Bay of Alcúdia, *see p153*.

Alcúdia & the Bay of Alcúdia

A characterful Mallorcan town and characterless tourist development.

The **Bay of Alcúdia**, beyond Colònia de Sant Pere. *See p151.*

See p151.

Alcúdia

Alcúdia's winding streets, dotted with Renaissance mansions, coupled with a recent explosion of boutique hotels and great restaurants, make it the perfect base for those whose idea of a beach holiday does not include bingo or burgers. While it sees its fair share of tourists, most are daytrippers in from the coast who have melted away by nightfall.

The town's location on a rise – its name is of Moorish origin, 'al-kudia' meaning 'on the hill' – at the foot of a stubby peninsula between two huge bays made it a strategically key site for most of the island's history. The Phoenicians established a trading post here, and then, following the successful invasion of 123 BC, the Romans built their island capital on this spot.

Levelled by the Vandals, it was the Moors who re-established a fortress and settlement, and their Christian successors further developed Alcúdia as an important centre of trade. Today, this neat, trim town of 14,000, 14 kilometres (nine miles) south-east of Port de Pollença and a fast 60-kilometre (38-mile) journey from Palma, remains the main hub of northern Mallorca.

For visitors, the main draw of the place is the compact old centre, contained within the thick, low-slung town wall. This was first erected between 1298 and 1362, by order of Jaume II, though most of what you see now was reconstructed in recent decades. Some 26 six metre- (20 foot-) high turreted towers and three gates punctuate the wall. Inside is a network of spruced-up narrow streets, replete with cafés, restaurants and souvenir shops, leading off the central axis of C/Major–Plaça Constitució–C/Moll-Plaça Carles V.

There are few specific sights to admire, but the shady lanes make for an enjoyable wander, particularly on Tuesdays and Sundays when there's a fruit and vegetable, clothes and handicrafts market. Not many visitors venture into the church of **Sant Jaume**. The building originated in the 13th century, but most of the present structure dates from a neo-Gothic remodelling in the 1880s; the Sant Crist chapel is all that remains of the original church – the Sant Crist image is an object of devotion for Alcúdians. The church's organ dates from 1559.

The Romans named their town Pollentia (meaning 'power'; the name was, confusingly, later appropriated by the founders of modern Pollença). To mug up on the town's Roman past, visit the **Museu Monogràfic de Pollentia** – funerary objects, coins, tombstones and marble fragments form the bulk of the collection, garnered from excavations since the 1920s. The town was located just south of the later walled settlement and covered a considerable area. Disappointingly little has survived of Pollentia, but what there is still constitutes the most important Roman remains on Mallorca. There are some scant ruins just south of the church of Sant Jaume over the main road, but the one stand-out is the remains of the amphitheatre, the **Teatre**

Romà (open Apr-Sept 10am-7pm Tue-Fri, 10.30am-1pm Sat, Sun, Oct-Mar 10am-5pm Tue-Fri, 10.30am-1pm Sat, Sun, free). Built in the first century AD, with eight tiers and a small stage embedded in the rock, it is still used for al fresco performances today. To reach it, walk up C/Santa Anna. Nearby are the ruins of the Roman **Fòrum**.

To counterbalance the culture of consumption of its coastal outpost, Alcúdia now boasts the impressive **Auditori d'Alcúdia** (Plaça de la Porta Mallorca 3, 971 89 71 85, www.alcudia. net), a huge theatre and arts space, which houses a library, café and radio station. The whole gamut of the performing arts is explored each season, from Catalan singing stars to David Hare dramas, with a dance programme for those who can't follow the local lingo.

Despite the weight of tourist development in this part of the island, it's remarkably easy to leave it all behind and escape into nature. Take the minor road that leads from the town north-east along the northern edge of the peninsula (signposted to El Mal Pas, Bonaire, Manresa and El Victoria) towards the **Cap d'es Pinar** (the Cap itself is a military zone and out of bounds to the public). You'll take in fine views across the Bay of Pollença towards Port de Pollença and Formentor, passing the turning for the art collection and sculpture garden of the **Fundación Yannick y Ben Jakober** (*see p150* **Kid stuff**) and a few little beaches before coming to a large car park at the **Ermita de la Victòria**. This 17th-century shrine, situated seven kilometres (four and a half miles) from Alcúdia, provides a home to a revered image of the Virgin – viewable above the baroque altar inside this dark, sombre church. Every year, on 1 and 2 July, the **Mare de Déu de la Victòria** is celebrated here and *bunyols* (potato doughnuts) and *mistella* – a Mallorcan alcoholic drink – are served at midnight; on the following day the local band gives a concert and almonds are ritually showered on everyone.

For visitors, though, the Ermita is most notable as a starting point for some superb walks into the peninsula's wild hills, chiefly to the peaks of **Penya Rotja** (315 metres/1,033 feet) and **Talaia d'Alcúdia** (444 metres/1,457 feet); for the latter, *see p152* **Walk 4**.

Museu Monogràfic de Pollentia

C/Sant Jaume 30 (971 54 70 04). **Open** 10am-4pm Tue-Fri. **Admission** €2; free concessions. **No credit cards**.

Where to stay, eat & drink

Alcúdia's smaller, more characterful hotels are within the walled town; most are conversions of 18th- and 19th-century townhouses. Newest

of these and most fun is the **Nou Hotelet Cas Ferrer** (C/Pou Nou 1, 971 89 75 42, www.nouhotelet.com, doubles €117-€149 incl breakfast), a favourite with sophisticated thirtysomethings, who lounge on its decked terrace flicking through coffee-table books, while its design mag credentials are lent a real warmth by the effervescent Tolo Llabrés, a mine of information on the town. Honeymooners should ask for Botticelli, complete with four-poster and splashes of red velvet, while Sappho is painted Mediterranean blue and has a gorgeous candlelit terrace with double sun-lounger for watching the stars.

Another graceful conversion is the **Hotel Sant Jaume** (C/Sant Jaume 6, 971 54 94 19, www.hotelsantjaume.com, closed Dec-Jan, doubles €90-€111 incl breakfast), an elegant, traditional place with much of its original furniture and mosaic flooring, and a pretty Andalucian-style patio where breakfast is served around an old well. Its six rooms are all different, and all have generous bathrooms.

Across the road is **Ca'n Simó** (C/Sant Jaume 1, 971 54 92 60, www.cansimo.com, doubles €85-€115 incl breakfast), with smart, comfortable rooms, a small plunge pool, jacuzzi and sauna. Its recently redecorated restaurant (€€) serves good-value Mediterranean dishes, along with lighter snacks such as *pa amb oli*.

The three doubles and one suite (€115) at the stylish, friendly 14th-century **Es Convent** (C/Progrés 6, 971 54 87 16, www.esconvent.com, closed Dec-Feb, doubles €95 incl breakfast, restaurant €€€€, closed Mon) are decorated in immaculate less-is-more chic, and the hotel has a superb restaurant serving imaginative dishes such as monkfish with oxtail, salsify and wild mushrooms, and braised lamb with a broad bean cassoulet.

At the other end of the scale, the **Fonda Llabrés** (Plaça Constitució 6, 971 54 50 00, www.fondallabres.com, doubles €34-€36) is an extraordinary bargain, and the oldest hotel in town. It has 21 pristine, simple but attractively furnished rooms above a convivial restaurant and tapas bar (€).

Son Siurana (Ctra. Palma–Alcúdia, km45, 971 54 96 62, www.sonsiurana.com, doubles €112-€171 incl breakfast), just out of town, is the most lavish of the local finca-type lodgings; its vast pool and wide-ranging views make Mallorcan *agroturismo* seem very desirable. Its restaurant closes one month in the winter, usually between January and February

It is now possible to stay at the **Ermita de la Victoria** (Ctra. Cap des Pinar, km6, 971 54 99 12, www.lavictoriahotel.com, doubles €66) itself, if breathtaking views and complete tranquillity appeal. The 12 rooms are all en

North Mallorca

Kid stuff

Port d'Alcúdia may have fallen prey to some of the crassest tourist development on the island, but within a lager can's throw of all the tat is proof of just how much the image of Mallorca is changing. Hidden away on the Alcúdia peninsula is the unique art collection and sculpture garden of the **Fundación Yannick y Ben Jakober**.

Yannick Vu, the artist daughter of a Vietnamese sculptor and a French pianist, first came to Mallorca in 1963 with her then husband, the Italian painter Domenico Gnoli. They lived near Valldemossa at S'Estaca (which was built by the Archduke Ludwig Salvator and is currently owned by Michael Douglas) until Gnoli's death in 1970. Two years later Yannick married Gnoli's friend Ben Jakober, who came from a family of art-lovers of Hungarian descent and, encouraged by his new wife, he started working as an artist himself. Since 1992 the couple have worked together to create sculptures that can be seen in a number of locations around the island, including the Parc de la Mar in front of Palma cathedral, the Anfora at Palma Airport and the gardens around the Finca Sa Bassa Blanca.

Over 40 years ago Yannick saw a painting by Mallorcan artist Joan Mestre i Bosch of a young girl holding some cherries, in a shop in Palma. She bought it and as a result unwittingly started what was to become the **Nins Collection** – a remarkable collection of more than 140 portraits of children ('*nins*' is the Mallorcan word for children). Tragedy turned what began as a hobby into an obsession when their daughter Maima died in 1992; the following year they created the Foundation in her memory.

Housed in a former subterranean water cistern, and beautifully lit, the collection offers a fascinating window on to the privileged yet stifling lives of the offspring of royal and noble families. Dating from the 16th to the 19th centuries, the paintings illustrate how relatively recent the concept of a childish childhood is; most of these stern-faced infants are dressed and portrayed as miniature adults. Around 50 paintings are on display at any one time, with the exhibition changing a couple of times a year.

The Jakobers had Finca Sa Bassa Blanca largely rebuilt in the 1970s by well-known Egyptian architect Hassan Fathy. It was his only commission in Europe, and he created for them a *ribat* or classic North African fortified house, constructed around a courtyard, cleverly making it seem far older than its actual years. The house itself will soon also be open to the public in a space being prepared to display their contemporary art collection.

The Foundation is tricky to find. Heading towards Port d'Alcúdia from Alcúdia you come to traffic lights and a left turn before you leave Alcúdia, with signs pointing left to El Mal Pas, Bonaire, Manresa, La Victòria and, enigmatically, 'Fundació'. Take this left and drive for a couple of kilometres before turning right at the Bodega del Sol (there's a further small 'Fundació' sign on its wall). It's then another two kilometres to stone gate posts and an unmade road beyond. Two more kilometres along this brings you to the gates of the Foundation, which open automatically and beckon you onwards to one of Mallorca's least expected and best hidden attractions.

Note that the collection is only open on Tuesdays unless you prebook a guided tour for a group of four or more people.

Fundación Yannick y Ben Jakober
Finca Sa Bassa Blanca, Alcúdia (971 54 98 80/www.fundacionjakober.org). **Open** 9.30am-12.30pm, 2.30-5.30pm Tue; 9am-6pm Wed-Sat by appointment only for guided tours for groups of 4 or more. **Admission** free Tue. Guided tours (Wed-Sat) €9; free under-10s. **No credit cards**.

suite and though simply decorated, are far from ascetic. The **Restaurante Mirador de la Victòria** (Ctra. Cap des Pinar, 971 54 71 73, €€, closed Mon and 4wks Jan-Feb) is nearby, and serves gutsy Mallorcan fare on a covered terrace with a stunning view across the bay.

In addition to the hotel restaurants mentioned above, a swath of recent openings has considerably increased the town's gastronomic opportunities. At the cutting edge of the scene is **Genestar** (Plaça Porta de Mallorca 1, 971 54 91 57, closed Wed, €€); small, bright, monochrome and achingly modern, with food to match. A laughably low-priced *menú degustación* (€22 plus wine) might include a salad with *botifarra* sausage and Mallorcan cheese; truffle ravioli; local *cap roig* fish with baby vegetables; slow-braised pork cheeks with a red wine reduction; and similarly stunning desserts. A short wine list is expertly put together – try Divins, from a tiny bodega in Selva.

Sa Romana (C/Pollentia 81, 971 54 94 28, €€€€) is built on the site of a Roman villa (parts of which are visible behind glass), out near the Teatre Romà. Beautifully presented meat and fish dishes show a perfect balance of quality and creativity.

Restaurante Sa Plaça (Plaça Constitució 1, 971 54 62 78, closed Wed, €€€) is a slightly frilly restaurant, with tables out on the square, serving Italian and Mallorcan cuisine. The €15 *menú* at lunchtime is good value.

For something simpler, **Sa Portassa** (C/Sant Vicenç 7, 971 54 88 19, closed Mon in Winter, €) has a long list of Mallorcan tapas and a popular interior courtyard.

The most relaxing place for a drink and a snack, meanwhile, is **Es Canyar** (C/Major 2, 971 54 72 82, €). Walk straight through the unexceptional-looking bar to a gorgeous candlelit, vine-covered terrace, with sofas lining the walls. Food varies from *pa amb oli* to pizzas to the odd North African speciality.

Port d'Alcúdia & the Bay of Alcúdia

For all the maritime merchant traffic that plies the Alcúdia–Barcelona line, there's really nothing very port-like about **Port d'Alcúdia**, except for one major ugly building in the middle of the only slightly more attractive Sol-this and Playa-that package hotels. Already far larger than Port de Pollença, this strip of high-rise hotels and villas, immediately south of Alcúdia town, seems intent on extending right around the 15-kilometre (nine and a half-mile) shoreline of the Bay of Alcúdia. Tens of thousands of tourist beds are already made

up each morning, and though the local authority optimistically rebranded the region as an 'ecotouristic municipality' (whatever that might mean) in 1992, the damage has been done. Out of peak season, though, strolling along the prom can feel remarkably pleasant – somewhere between Miami and Margate – and the beach is a treat. There's money in the coffers here, so the paving and wooden walkways are kept spruced up, and there are almost as many smartish coffee shops as burger bars and Brit-style pubs.

Every arrow on the main C712 points towards the 'platja', 'playa', 'strand', 'beach'… that's the only reason for the coast road between Alcúdia and Artà. Follow them and you are soon in a dispiriting corridor of multi-storey hotels, expat villa developments, fast food outlets and tat-dispensing shops. Early maps of Mallorca show no road around the Bay of Alcúdia, and even today there's a feeling of pointlessness to the route, unless you own a place here – or know someone who has gone into exile at one-time fishing port **Can Picafort**, favoured by older people and families, despite the proliferation of 'fun pubs', or the smaller **Colònia de Son Serra**. The beaches are nice enough – the **Platja de Muro** is perhaps the best, though **Son Bauló** is quieter, but there aren't even resorts of any coherence – just the usual services, petrol stations and basic eateries.

Many people go for a ramble over the dunes at Can Picafort to take a look at the **Son Real** necropolis – the walk itself is pleasant when it's not too hot, but the burial site, dating from the seventh century BC to the first century AD and containing 109 tombs, is in a sorry state of disrepair. Since excavations during the 1960s and the prompt removal of the skeletons from the 100-plus tombs, the sea and weather have been allowed to erode the walls of the artificial caves, and the protective fence is rusted and ruinous.

At the eastern limit of the Bay of Alcúdia, beyond the final resort development of **Colònia de Sant Pere**, is the **Ermita de Betlem**, a tiny monastery founded in 1805 in what remains a blissfully pristine location. The walk up here takes in woods and a steep hill climb; the stunning views make the effort worthwhile.

The only other bright spot in all this man-made monotony is the incongruous presence of the wonderful **S'Albufera** nature reserve between Port d'Alcúdia and Can Picafort. The **Parc Natural S'Albufera de Mallorca** (to give it its full name) covers 1,708 hectares (4,221 acres) and is the largest and most important wetlands in the Balearics; nowhere on the islands will you find greater biodiversity. Among its riches are 66 species of funghi,

29 of fish, eight of bat, 300 of moth and 200 of bird. It's the latter that provide the greatest draw for visitors, with warblers, egrets and sandpipers commonplace. There are raised observation platforms and circuits of trails (you can hire bikes at the visitors' centre) and, in spring, wild flowers brighten up the yellows, greens and browns of the reed beds. Be sure to take binoculars with you if you want to see rather than merely hear the flourishing wildlife.

Parc Natural S'Albufera de Mallorca

Ctra. Alcúdia–Artà (971 89 22 50/www.mallorca web.net/salbufera). **Open** *Apr-Sept* 9am-6pm daily. *Oct-Mar* 9am-5pm daily. **Admission** free.

Where to eat & drink

Not only is there little attraction for the independent traveller in staying in **Port d'Alcúdia** and along the bay (particularly as Alcúdia town has so many great places to stay), but many of the hotels are block-booked by tour operators and you won't be able to get a room even if you wanted to.

Eating options aren't great either, though **Pizzeria Roma** (Avda. Pere Mas i Reus 4, 971 89 22 27, closed Nov-Easter, €) serves up the best pizzas and steaks in town and **Restaurante Jardín** (C/Tritones s/n, 971 89 23 91, www.restaurantejardin.com, closed Mon, €€€) is classier than most, with tables in a leafy garden and dishes including magret of duck in port, and roast suckling pig with baked apple.

As a major resort, Port d'Alcúdia's nightlife scene is the liveliest in the north – clubs like the Roman-themed **Menta** (Avda. Tucan 5, 971 89 19 72, www.mentadisco.com, closed Oct-Apr), which boasts its own swimming pool, is still the biggest and the best in town.

Walk 4 Around the Talaia d'Alcúdia

Distance: 10km (6.25 miles). Circular.
Time: 4hrs 15mins

The cute little town of Alcúdia, site of Roman Pollentia, sits at the flat base of a peninsula that rises dramatically to the 444 metres (1,457 feet) of the mini-mountain of the Talaia d'Alcúdia. The stiffish climb up here affords 360-degree views that stretch from the Formentor peninsula to the north, down to the highest peaks of the Tramuntana mountains to the west, south-west across the plain, south-east to the cliffs around the Cap de Ferrutx at the far side of the Bay of Alcúdia, and even as far as Menorca. On the descent, there's the chance to scramble down to a fine beach and plenty of peaceful walking that feels a world away from the major tourist developments just a few kilometres away.

Pass through Alcúdia, heading towards the Ermita de la Victòria. The road skirts along the northern coast of the peninsula, past the marina at Bonaire, before climbing and ending in a large dirt car park. Park here. You'll see the tall, plain stone-built Ermita de la Victòria church, and a complex of buildings (including the Mirador de la Victòria restaurant, 971 54 71 73, which offers wonderful views and good-quality food).

Walk up the steps to the right of the church and continue up past a block containing some public toilets where you'll meet a wide dirt track. Turn left (upwards).

After a steady climb of around 20 minutes you'll see a sign pointing sharp left to Penya des Migdia. If you are willing to add 50 or so minutes on to the walk, take this path up to its end – the viewpoint at Penya Rotja – and then retrace your steps. Otherwise, continue on the track, admiring the increasingly impressive views towards the Formentor peninsula as you climb. You'll also see plenty of dwarf palms, a species native to Mallorca.

Around ten minutes after passing the sign to Penya des Migdia the path starts to level and straighten as it passes along a ridge. You can now see down over the huge Bay of Alcúdia, as well as the Bay of Pollença. Five minutes further and you'll spot a sign pointing in the direction you're walking to the Talaia d'Alcúdia (which you can see rising before you) and a green plastic water tank (used for fighting forest fires) on your right, before the track narrows below the crag and starts to climb steeply. Bear to the right before swinging round to the left as you ascend.

Ten or so minutes after starting this climb you'll pass a huge cairn and a sign pointing down left to the Platja des Coll Baix. You'll take this path on your way down from the summit of the Talaia d'Alcúdia, which is only five minutes' climb away. The views from the top are as fine as any you'll enjoy in Mallorca.

Resources

Internet
Port d'Alcúdia *Eu Moll Games, Passeig Saralegui 114 (971 86 69 44)*. **Open** *Apr-Oct* 10am-10pm daily. *Nov-Mar* noon-10pm Tue-Sun.

Police station
Alcúdia *Bastió de Sant Ferran s/n (971 54 50 66)*.

Post office
Alcúdia *C/Pollentia s/n (971 54 54 40)*.

Tourist information
Can Picafort *OIT, Plaça Enginyer Gabriel Roca 6 (971 85 03 10)*. **Open** *May-Oct* 9am-1pm, 4.30-7.30pm Mon-Fri. *Nov-Apr* 9am-1pm Mon-Fri.
Platja de Muro *OIT, Avda. de S'Albufera 33 (971 89 10 13)*. **Open** *May-Oct* 8.30am-3pm Mon-Fri; 9am-1pm Sat. *Nov-Apr* 8am-3pm Mon-Fri.

Port d'Alcúdia *OIT C/Major 17 (971 54 80 71)*. **Open** 8am-3pm Mon-Fri. *OIT, Ctra. Artá 68 (971 89 26 15)*. **Open** *May-Oct* 10am-1.30pm, 3-5.30pm Mon-Fri; 9am-1pm Sat. *OIT, Passeig Maritim s/n (971 54 72 57/turismepm@alcudia.net)*. **Open** *May, June, Sept, Oct* 9am-8pm Mon-Sat. *July, Aug* 10am 9pm Mon-Sat.

Getting there

By boat
There are regular ferry services between Alcúdia and Menorca and Menorca and Barcelona. *See p262.*

By bus
Autocares Mallorca runs 16 buses (Line 1) daily from Palma to Port d'Alcúdia (1hr 15mins) via Inca (30mins) and Alcúdia (1hr). There are buses every 15 minutes around the Bay of Alcúdia from Alcúdia to Can Picafort via Port d'Alcúdia. For information on buses to Sóller, Port de Sóller, Lluc, Sa Calobra and Formentor, *see p147.*

When you've had your fill, return down the same path and take the narrow rocky path (now to the right) to Platja des Coll Baix. You'll soon see the rounded head of the Puig d'es Boc ahead of you. After around 30 minutes of walking along this path, you skirt the right-hand side of the Puig and start to descend steeply in zigzags until a refuge you'll notice below you. The descent takes around half an hour, and on it you'll have a vertiginous view almost directly down over the pristine brown-sand beach of Coll Baix.

At the refuge you'll find picnic tables and a water fountain. If you fancy going down to the beach, it'll take you around 25 minutes to reach it from here. Otherwise, turn right as you face the refuge and walk down a wide track. After five minutes you meet a chain across the track, then, five minutes later, another chain across a track to the left. A couple of minutes after this you'll see a sign pointing right to the Coll de ses Fontanelles; take this path.

The landscape now becomes far more intimate as the path rises slowly along a valley through light woodland; the wild flowers are stunning in spring. Around eight or so minutes after starting on this path it narrows before a rockface. Turn sharply right here before the rockface, climbing upwards and then left along the top of it. You now skirt the right-hand side of the valley.

For the next ten minutes you cross and re-cross a dried-up stream bed, looking carefully for the cairns that mark the path, before being led by cairns sharply up to the left along a side valley littered with fallen trees. Around ten or so minutes after starting climbing the path levels out and you find yourself walking (largely gently downwards) along the left side of the main valley. You traverse a gully, go over a ridge and then continue down the side of the valley, which slopes away to the right towards the Bay of Pollença.

Towards the end of the valley a wide track forms a T-junction with the path (by a little dam on a dried-up stream; it should have taken you around 40 minutes to reach this point from the time you started climbing the side valley with the fallen trees). Turn left and continue on this track, ignoring turn-offs, past a clutch of holiday villas on your left until, after around 15 minutes, you come to another T-junction at a clump of trees. Here, turn right, and then left after a minute, following a sign to Ermita de la Victòria.

Follow the wide track, which narrows as it descends and, after ten or so minutes, arrives at the road you drove along to reach the Ermita. Up to your left stands an ugly multi-storey youth hostel. Cross the road and you'll see a little beach where you can soothe your feet in the sea (there are some picnic tables here), before tackling the half-hour climb back up the road to the car park.

North Mallorca

Central Mallorca

Jardins de Alfàbia. *See p162*.

Central Mallorca

Rural life continues unruffled in the island's peaceful interior.

It comes as a surprise to many visitors to find that most of Mallorca is made up of a great central plain, logically called Es Pla ('The Plain'), which remains remarkably untainted and unruffled by the massed holiday developments around its edges.

This is the agricultural heart of the island, a vast, gently undulating swath of wheat, fruit and vegetable fields, with vines on its eastern and western edges. Its role as the bread basket of the island means that Es Pla has some of Mallorca's largest, most vibrant and historic markets. These add much-needed bustle to its somnolent towns and villages – diffuse settlements with identical sandstone houses, green shutters and a few abandoned windmills. Many of Es Pla's old farmhouses and manor houses are now beautiful, luxurious rural hotels, and a few modest peaks, topped with sanctuaries, break up the landscape and offer memorable views.

Note that the towns on Es Pla's eastern edge (Felanitx, Manacor and Artà) and southern rim (Llucmajor, Campos and Santanyí) are covered on pages 180-181.

ES RAIGUER

The area known as Es Raiguer hugs the gentle eastern slopes of the Serra de Tramuntana; its focus is the main route between Palma and Alcúdia via Inca. This is the most fertile land on the island, with almond trees, vineyards, olive groves and sheep and pig breeding aplenty. Each town and village is characterised by its industry, the most famous of which is Inca, famed for its leather. Binissalem and Santa María del Camí are the centre of wine production; Consell is known for its *pa moreno* (unsalted dark bread) and for its blood sausage; Lloseta produces cloth and shoes; Alaró prides itself on its ceramics.

Though much of Es Raiguer is only minutes away from Palma and the coast, it is a world away in terms of outlook; the small towns and villages on this part of the island are only just getting used to tourists. You may be surprised not to be met with open arms or by someone able to speak English: *mallorquí* is spoken here with fierce pride and a foreigner speaking Spanish will often be replied to in *mallorquí*.

ES PLA

The vast central plain is bisected by the C715 Palma–Manacor road, which runs through farmland overlooked by the sanctuary-topped minor peaks of the Serra de Randa. A handful of mildly diverting towns – Algaida, Randa, Montuïri, Porreres, Petra – and a couple of worthwhile tourist attractions lie on either side of the main road. Away from it, the only noises you're likely to encounter are the sounds of birdsong and the swish of a passing phalanx of German cyclists.

Sineu is historically the most important town in the northern Pla, its long-standing importance marked by its direct connection by road to Palma. It's also the most rewarding and lively base in the region. The countryside is criss-crossed by winding roads, lined with honey-stone walls; it's a model railway landscape of spongy green trees, isolated farm buildings and terraces of citrus groves and vines. Yet the Bay of Alcúdia sands are 15 minutes' drive away.

The best...

Hotels
Ca's Comte, Lloseta (*p161*); **Finca Sa Rota d'en Palerm**, Lloret de Vista Alegre (*p170*); **L'Hermitage**, Orient (*p163*); **Monnàber Nou**, Campanet (*p167*); **Es Passarell**, Porreres (*p174*); **Read's**, Santa Maria (*p161*).

Markets & shops
Festival Park (*p158*); **RECamper** (*p166*); **Sineu** (*p169*).

Restaurants
Ca'n Calco, Campanet (*p167*); **Es Celler**, Petra (*p173*); **Es Réco de Randa**, Randa (*p176*); **Es Verger**, Alaró (*p162*); **Sa Penya**, Sineu (*p170*); **Read's**, Santa Maria (*p161*).

Sights
Coves de Campanet (*p167*); **Els Calderers** (*p171*).

Towns
Binissalem (*p158*); **Petra** (*p171*); **Sineu** (*p169*).

Views
Santuari de Cura (*p176*); **Santuari de Monti-Sion** (*p173*).

Es Raiguer

The foothills of the Tramuntana hide some of the island's finest places to stay.

Santa Maria del Camí, Binissalem & Lloseta

Santa Maria del Camí (17 kilometres/11 miles north-east of Palma) is not a particularly appealing place, but it does hide a number of architectural gems, including the **Convent del Minims** (Plaça dels Hostals), a beautiful convent and cloisters just off the main square. You can't go inside, alas, but you can look in through the gates at the exquisite 17th-century architecture. South of here is the oldest and prettiest part of town, which has a clutch of 17th-, 18th- and 19th-century buildings in a delightful square, Plaça de la Vila. The 17th-century town hall, with its delicate arches and columns, has a stunning Gothic altarpiece inside from 1384, the work of Mallorcan painter Joan Massana, and part of the original parish church. Just around the corner is the impressive baroque pile of the church of **Santa Maria** (Plaça Caidos), with its distinctive blue-tiled spire and Churrigueresque-style interior.

There are a number of small bodegas in town, including **Can Vinagre** (C/Paborde Jaume 17A, 971 62 03 58) and **Jaume de Puntiró** (Plaça Nova 23, 971 62 00 23), and on the road just outside town, **Bodega de Macià Batle**, which is regarded by many as producing superior wines to the better-known José Luis Ferrer (*see p159*).

By far the biggest draw for visitors to Santa Maria is the huge, and hugely popular, Sunday morning open-air market. The clothes won't set many pulses racing, but the caged birds and furry animals are certainly a spectacle, and the fresh fruit and veg, sausages and cheeses are superb. Look out for the woman serving up sobrassada sandwiches, made with fresh *pa mallorquí*.

Possibly the best one-stop shop op on the island lies just west of Santa Maria. **Festival Park** (Ctra. Palma–Inca, km7.1, 971 14 09 25, www.festivalparks.com, closed Sun Nov-Feb) is an American-style mall of fast food outlets, cinemas, bowling alleys, Europe's largest reptilarium, shops and almost 30 factory outlet stores. These include groovy footwear brand Camper (971 22 60 01), Menorcan high-class shoemaker Jaime Mascaró (971 22 65 66) and high-street staples like Mango (971 22 96 94). Most shops are open 10am-10pm Monday to Saturday. Bus IB20 between Palma and Inca via Santa Maria, Binissalem and Lloseta stops at Festival Park.

The C713 (which runs parallel to the motorway) continues north-eastwards from Santa Maria through **Consell**, an ugly little place with nothing to recommend it beyond one nice restaurant (*see p160*) and the immense antiques and bric-a-brac market held on the outskirts, also on a Sunday morning.

Press on to **Binissalem** (ten kilometres/six miles north-east of Santa Maria), an architectural delight, dominated by its church and packed with 17th- and 18th-century mansions – the highest concentration on Mallorca outside Palma. All this conspicuous wealth was thanks to a couple of industries: stone, from which the church was built, and wine. The town was originally a Muslim settlement known as Robines. It was later refounded in 1300 by Jaume II and has long been a focus for powerful, wealthy, landed families. It is also the centre of the island's wine industry, home to all the big names.

All roads lead to Plaça Església, where the Friday market (not the most exciting on the island) is held. The square is dominated by the church of **Nostra Senyora de Robines**, which has an enormous multi-layered base, started in the 15th century and topped by a triple-levelled arched spire that was added in 1908. The cockleshell patterns in the walls represent St James; the town now uses the shell as its emblem.

The real architectural delights of Binissalem lie to the east along C/Pere Estruch (just off C/Concepció, which runs south from the main *plaça*) and its extension, C/Vicenç de Paul, where you'll find a string of baroque mansions. Unfortunately, none is open to the public and you'll have to make do with admiring their exteriors, characterised by wrought-iron balconies and green wooden shutters.

There are others dotted around town, two of which can be visited. **Can Gelabert de la Portella**, a *casa señorial* converted into a cultural centre, dates originally from the 1500s, though the current structure was built between 1664 and 1837. Inside, over two doorways, are depictions of the destruction of Pompeii. This was home to writer, poet and playwright **Llorenç Moyà** (1916-81), a leading light

Santa Maria del Camí. *See p158.*

in the island's rediscovery of its Catalan literary heritage, who spent much of his life immortalising the house in verse.

Can Sabater was home to another writer, **Llorenç Villalonga** (1897-1980), best known for his novel *The Dolls' Room*, about the decline of a noble family at the end of the 19th century, which is often interpreted as an allegory of the fate of the Mallorcan nobility. It is now the **Fundació Casa Museu Llorenç Villalonga**, a museum and cultural centre, and has preserved some of the rooms in which the writer lived and worked.

The best-known wine producer on Mallorca, the **Bodega de José Luis Ferrer**, is on the southern edge of Binissalem. The vineyard has a small shop selling wine and glasses, and offers a 25-minute tour and tasting. It's not exactly inspiring – the bulk of the wine is kept in huge steel containers or cement stores – but you do learn about the production process and visit the mildewed old cellar where barrels are lined up floor to ceiling. There are also a couple of smaller bodegas in town where you can sample and buy, including **Vins Ripoll** (*see below*).

Lloseta, a couple of kilometres north-east of Binissalem and the same distance west of Inca, is a dusty little place with little to detain you except a couple of good restaurants and the **Palau d'Aimans**, now a sumptuous hotel (Ca's Comte; *see p161*). The palace was constructed by the Aimans family in the mid

18th century and later enlarged by Joan March, the wealthy banker. It's a stunning building, blending traditional Mallorcan architecture with Italian Renaissance style. Outside in the square are the sculpted gardens and parish church, to which the Aimans' private chapel is adjoined, with a crypt containing their bones. Just outside the village, the 19th-century **Ermita es Cocó** sits in a delightful spot on a rise by the Almadra torrent. The building was paid for by the Count of Aimans, and a pilgrimage takes place here from Lloseta on the first Wednesday after Easter.

Bodega de José Luis Ferrer

C/Conquistador 103, Binissalem (971 51 10 50/ www.vinosferrer.com). **Tours** 11am, 4.30pm Mon-Fri; 11am Sat. **Admission** €6. **Credit** MC, V.

Can Gelabert de la Portella

C/Portella s/n, Binissalem (971 88 65 31).
Open 4-9pm Mon-Fri; 5-9pm Sat. **Admission** free.

Fundació Casa Museu Llorenç Villalonga

C/Bonaire 25, Binissalem (971 88 60 14/971 88 65 56/www.cmvillalonga.org). **Open** *Jan-July, Sept-Dec* 10am-2pm Mon, Wed, Fri, Sat; 10am-2pm, 4-8pm Tue, Thur. Closed Aug. **Admission** free.

Vins Ripoll

C/Pere Estruch 25, Binissalem (971 51 10 28/ www.vinsripoll.com). **Open** 7am-3pm Mon-Fri. **Admission** free. Reservation essential.

Where to eat & drink

The restaurant at **Read's** hotel in **Santa Maria** (*see p161*; €€€€) is a treat. The cathedral-like dining room with its startling trompe l'oeil has become a Mallorcan gastronomic temple, thanks to Michelin-starred chef Marc Fosh and his inspired but consciously healthy cooking. Expect the unexpected: the likes of foie gras with green apples and pollen, and fillets of hare with elderflower, anise and caramelised pumpkin. Sounds wacky; tastes sublime. Meanwhile, the wonderful Jaime Cácares has got 21st-century maître'd-ing down to a fine art.

There are a few places to eat on Santa Maria's main square, none of them amazing. **C'an Calet** (Plaça dels Hostals 26, 971 62 01 73, €) is perhaps the best, with a pretty patio and a good selection of reasonably priced dishes including fillet of *cap roig* (a native Mediterranean fish), duck and rabbit.

Consell boasts one good restaurant, **Los Pinos** (Plaça del Pou, 971 62 20 58, closed Wed, €), in a pretty square with a waterwheel in the centre. Don't expect style – it doesn't get much more local than this, with rock-bottom prices and traditional Mallorcan peasant-style food and decor; try the snails alioli followed by *llom con col* (pork loin with cabbage).

Binissalem has a handful of simple bars and pizzeria-type eateries and one good restaurant, **Scott's Bistro** (C/Pou Bo 20, 971 87 00 76, closed lunch daily, €€€), an offshoot of the eponymous hotel (*see p161*). It caters primarily for a British clientele who want simple, tasty, fresh food, such as chargrilled pepper stuffed with spiced prawns, and medallions of monkfish with fresh tagliatelle and spinach.

Singló (Plaça Església 5, 971 87 05 99, €) is a smart place in the main square that serves a small selection of tasty and reasonably priced dishes, such as paella, gazpacho and *bocadillos*; it also does a very reasonable lunchtime menu. Also on the main square, **Restaurant Robines** (No.25, 971 51 11 36, €€), offers decent Mallorcan staples, including various tasty lamb dishes and *sopas mallorquins*, which, loaded with meat and veg, provides a hearty meal in itself.

There's not much night-time bar action in Binissalem. What there is takes place in the main square and the streets just off it. One of the best spots is **Café Ca S'Hereu** (C/Pere Estruch 1, no phone, €€), which attracts a mixture of resident Brits and locals, drawn by its stylish decor, ambient music, roof terrace, patio and occasional live bands; it serves a small selection of simple dishes, but food is not its

Binissalem. *See p158.*

forte. **Pub P'dal** (Passeig d'es Born 8, 971 51 10 61, €) has bags of atmosphere, a pool table, table football, excellent music until very late and good pizzas from a wood-fired oven at the back.

There are two excellent places to eat in **Lloseta**. **Can Carrossa** (C/Nou 28, 971 51 40 23, closed dinner Sun & all Mon, €€€), enjoys a pretty setting, with a small terrace leading out on to the town gardens. Chef Joan Abrines, who teaches at the island's catering school, runs this place at night, serving a superb three-, four- or five-course set menu at very reasonable prices. A further good bet is **Santi Taura** (C/Guillem Santandreu 38, 971 51 46 22, www.restaurants antitaura.com, closed Tue and dinner Sun Sept-June, all Tue and all Sun in July, all Aug, €€), where chef Santi offers an accomplished modern take on Mallorcan cuisine on his five-course no-choice menu.

Where to stay

This largely unsung corner of the island contains a few excellent places to stay. In **Santa María**, **Read's Hotel & Restaurant** (Ctra. Vieja s/n, 971 14 02 61, www.readshotel. com, doubles €214-€385 incl breakfast) is an opulent, sometimes excessive, but always entertaining five-star manor house that indulges just about every luxury you can imagine. From the beamed ceiling of the barn-like indoor swimming pool overlooking a still larger outdoor version to the beautifully laid-out grounds, courtyards and terraces, all taking in views of the Tramuntana, to the dramatically decorated communal rooms (featuring the theatrical frescoes of Tim Bramhill), it's all the vision (and eclectic design sense) of owner and former lawyer Vivian Read. Amazingly for a place of this ilk, the family-run atmosphere endures. The restaurant is one of Mallorca's best (*see p35*).

A more affordable, but still splendid, alternative near Santa Maria is the seven-bedroom *agroturismo* **Torrent Fals** (Ctra. Santa Maria–Sencelles, km4.5, 971 14 45 84, 696 50 80 03, www.torrentfals.com, doubles €125-€145 incl breakfast), located within a 15th-century *finca*. It's been converted with impeccable less-is-more taste and features a fine restaurant and a swimming pool in the midst of a pine forest.

The place to stay in **Binissalem** is **Scott's** (Plaça Església 12, 971 87 01 00, www.scotts hotel.com, closed 15 Dec-15 Jan, doubles €161-€219 incl breakfast). George and Judy Scott have transformed this 18th-century house on the main square into a delightful hotel, which has the look and feel of a private home. The 17 rooms (six of them suites) are decorated in a

homely style, with supremely comfortable beds and well-stocked bathrooms (though no TV, unless you request one); they look on to a pretty patio full of flowers and running water, with a sundeck above and a small heated indoor pool. Welcome touches include the honour bar in the cosy drawing room and small kitchens stocked with tea, coffee and biscuits. George is also author of crime fiction and has written two novels, both set on the island; you'll find a complimentary copy of *The Bloody Bokhara* awaiting you in your room when you check in.

Lloseta's **Ca's Comte** (C/Comte d'Aimans 11, 971 87 30 77, www.cascomte.com, doubles €120 incl breakfast, restaurant closed lunch, €€) is a surprising stunner in a low-profile village; the conversion of this 18th-century townhouse could grace a *Wallpaper* feature. Juxtaposed with cool stone walls and wooden beams are great sheets of glass and minimalist vases, ornaments and light fittings. There are four doubles and four split-level suites, which come with a lavish lounge and views down over the central *plaça*. The breakfast is an indulgent banquet of fruits, pastries and hot bites. Family-run, this *hotel rural* is ultra-friendly, amazingly helpful for local information and an absolute steal at the price. Its restaurant (for guests only) is also first-rate.

Resources

Police station

Binissalem *C/Concepció 7 (971 51 11 26)*.
Lloseta *C/Guillem Santandreu s/n (971 51 94 39)*.
Santa Maria del Camí *C/Mn Josep Calafat 1A (mobile 608 83 05 37)*.

Post office

Binissalem *Passeig del Born 11 (971 51 10 51)*.
Lloseta *C/Junípero Serra 1 (971 51 40 51)*.
Santa Maria del Camí *C/Bernat de Santa Eugènia 41 (971 62 00 26)*.

Alaró, Orient & Bunyola

North of Santa Maria and Binissalem is the prettiest part of Es Raiguer, where tiny villages nestle in the foothills of the Tramuntana. Five kilometres (three miles) north-west of Consell and the C713 is **Alaró**, which makes a pleasant lunch stop. The village is centred on its main square, Plaça de la Vila, with a pretty town hall (with some tourist information) and church at the south end and a scattering of restaurants, bars and cafés on or just off it.

Alaró is framed by two molar-shaped outcrops of rock, the **Puig d'Alaró** and the **Puig de s'Alcadena**, which act as the gateway to the higher slopes. The road heading north out of the village passes between the twin peaks, before coming to the turning to the **Castell d'Alaró**, whose ruined battlements appear to grow out of the cliff face. The first part of the journey up to the castle is not too bad (except on a Sunday, when a snake of traffic heads up to Es Verger restaurant; see p162). Once you arrive at the restaurant, you can park and hike up the rest of the way (about an hour and a half to the top). The castle's history dates back to Moorish times, but it was beefed up by Jaume I, and although there's not a great deal left, the views from here are quite breathtaking: to the west the valley of Orient, to the east the plain and to the south Palma and the coast. Carry on up to get to the small restaurant and bar for equally stunning vistas.

The PM210 rises up from Alaró towards the mountains for a few kilometres through pine groves and almond trees, before dropping into the sheltered valley in which **Orient** lies, surrounded by acres of luxuriant olive and almond groves. This almost cloyingly beautiful hamlet has just 26 inhabitants, a very pretty church and one of the best hotels on the island (L'Hermitage; see p163). Its origins date back to the 13th century and its name probably derives from the Latin aureus, meaning 'golden'. Its high point in terms of population came in the 18th century, when 100 souls lived here, drawn by the extremely fertile land. Sightseeing is limited to the 17th-century church of **Sant Jordi** on a tiny square reached via steps from the main road. Inside, Sant Jordi (St George) is depicted on the high altar, which is made of gold, donated – so legend has it – by the womenfolk of the village. The church's most significant artefact is the crucifix to the right of the altar, made of cypress wood; it's one of the oldest on the island.

From Orient, it's a winding 11-kilometre (seven-mile) drive west to **Bunyola**, a rather nondescript place of note only as a stop on the Palma–Sóller railway and for its lethal home-brewed liqueur, Tunel.

A few kilometres from town, just before the entrance to the tunnel to Sóller, lie the prettiest gardens on the island, the **Jardins de Alfàbia**, a blissfully shady oasis of water, lush palms and citrus groves radiating out from an old manor house. Several airy rooms in the house can be visited – there's a splendid ceiling in one, and another in the gatehouse that has the distinction of being the only Mudéjar coffered ceiling in Mallorca. Don't neglect to buy a glass of fresh lemonade or orange juice from the bar in the gardens.

Jardins de Alfàbia

Ctra. Palma–Sóller, km17 (971 61 31 23). **Open** *Apr-Sept* 9.30am-6.30pm Mon-Sat. *Oct-Mar* 9am-5.30pm Mon-Fri; 9.30am-1pm Sat. **Admission** €4.50. **No credit cards**.

Where to eat & drink

Regarded as the best restaurant in **Alaró**, **Traffic** (Plaça de la Vila 8, 971 87 91 17, closed Tue, €€€) specialises in hearty cooking, but with a bit of style. There's the usual selection of tapas and traditional meat and fish concoctions (as well as pizzas), but also less commonly encountered dishes like octopus with onions. Inside, it's all wood beams and stone, but if it's warm you'll want to be out on the pretty patio. Next door is **Ca'n Punta** (Plaça de la Vila 9, 971 87 94 40, closed Thur and Nov, €€), which also knocks out quality Mallorcan cooking, though in a slightly less formal setting. Good dishes include the *ensalada de gambas* (prawn salad) and the *cabrito monañas a las finas hierbas* (goat with herbs). You can sit outside on the *terraza*, inside in the rather stuffy *comedor* (dining room) or out the back on a private patio. **Sa Fonda** (C/C'an Ros 4, 971 51 05 83, closed Mon, €€) has a heavy German influence, but whips up some good local fare, including fresh fish such as *dorada* (gilthead) and *lubina* (sea bass) and various rice dishes at reasonable prices.

Drinking options include **Acros** (Plaça Església, no phone, €), which has a small terrace, and **Maio Café** (Plaça Mercat s/n, no phone, closed Tue, €), on a pretty tree-lined *plaça* up from the main square, which attracts old men playing cards and young lads playing video games and serves a selection of cheap *pa amb oli* dishes.

On the road up to Alaró's ruined castle, **Es Verger** (971 18 21 26, €) is one of the island's worst-kept secrets; convoys of 4x4s head up the precarious mountain track every Sunday lunchtime. It's a real spit-and-sawdust place, serving traditional food at low prices in a spectacular setting. Its popularity hasn't changed its (very) basic character. A walk up to the castle to build up your appetite followed by a plateful of shoulder of lamb, slow-cooked in deep cave-like ovens (fired by whole branches of olive wood) is a memorable experience.

In **Orient**, the restaurant at the hotel **Dalt Muntanya** (see p163, closed Nov-Jan, €€€) has a delightful *terraza* looking out to the mountains and serves meaty local dishes like *pierna de cordero* (leg of lamb), *cochinillo asado* (roast suckling pig) and *conejo* (rabbit), served without fuss in a simple, traditional style. Starters are fancier – the ravioli stuffed with mushrooms and crawfish smothered in Mallorcan cheese is particularly tasty. **Mandala** (C/Nueva 1, 971 61 52 85, closed lunch Fri & Sat and all Mon in Jan-May, Oct, Nov, closed lunch daily and all Sun June-Sept, closed all Dec, €€) is an excellent restaurant tucked up at the top end of the village and offers a selection of international dishes such as Thai prawn curry. There's also a first-class restaurant at **L'Hermitage** hotel (*see p163*; €€€€).

Adjacent to the Jardins de Alfàbia (*see p162*) is **Restaurante Ses Porxeres** (Ctra. Palma–Sóller 17, 971 61 37 62, www.sesporxeres.com, closed Mon, dinner Sun and all Aug, €€€), a very classy establishment in a wonderful setting that serves excellent Mallorcan cuisine, including pheasant and lamb dishes.

Where to stay

Can Xim (Plaça de la Vila s/n, 971 87 91 17, www.canxim.com, doubles €80-€100) on **Alaró**'s main square has eight clean, fresh rooms, all en suite and air-conditioned, and with a good-sized pool.

A few minutes outside the village, on the road to the castle, is the pleasant *agroturismo*, **Son Penyaflor** (Camí del Castell, 971 51 00 71, www.sonpenyaflor.com, doubles €98), with seven simple rooms in its own grounds, nestling below the mountains.

A further accommodation alternative nearby, located between Alaró and Orient, is the classy *hotel rural* **S'Olivaret** (Ctra. Alaró–Orient, km3, 971 51 08 89, www.solivaret.com, doubles €164-€176 incl breakfast), which has indoor and outdoor pools.

In the diminutive hamlet of **Orient**, the *agroturismo* **Son Palou** (Plaça de l'Església s/n, 971 14 82 82, www.sonpalou.com, closed Dec, doubles €126-€144 incl breakfast) is a fine spot to lay your head, with clean-lined, airy rooms, a pool and great views.

The most celebrated place to stay in this area, though, is the wonderful **L'Hermitage** (971 18 03 03, www.hermitage-hotel.com, closed Nov-Feb, doubles €169-€219 incl breakfast, restaurant €€€€), just outside Orient. Whether you go for the (four) older rooms in the monastery or the (20) suite-chalets built out the back – the latter are newer but more spacious and more private – there's little to do here but stare at the fruit trees, play tennis, take a dip in the outdoor pool, detox in the sauna and then tuck into the great food at the hotel's posh rustic-style restaurant.

A much cheaper alternative in Orient is the **Dalt Muntanya** (Ctra. Bunyola–Orient, km10, 971 61 53 73, www.daltmuntanya.net, closed Nov-Jan, doubles €96), which has been completely refurbished from the original *hostal* into a modern, stylish and extremely

Immerse yourself in a pool of gastronomic delights: **Read's Hotel & Restaurant**. *See p161.*

Central Mallorca

comfortable three-star hotel in its own grounds. The design is rural chic, so it's big beds, soft duvets, airy rooms, marble bathrooms, stone tiles and wooden shutters. Many of the 18 rooms have great views of the mountains and all are different: No.16 is split-level with a bathroom on the upper floor; No.18 has a tiny skylight; No.1 has a kidney-shaped bath; and No.8 looks out on to the patio. For the quality, this place is a bargain. It's worth opting for half-board: for €18 extra per person you get to eat in the excellent restaurant (*see p162*).

If you want to stay near **Bunyola**, try **Finca Sa Màniga** (C/Afores s/n, 971 61 34 28, www. fincasamaniga.com, doubles €104-€128 incl breakfast); it has four spacious, air-conditioned rooms and bikes for the use of guests.

Resources

Police station
Alaró *C/Petit 1 (971 51 00 02).*
Bunyola *C/San Jose 2 (mobile 609 35 81 65).*

Post office
Alaró *Avda. Constitució 37 (971 51 03 09).*
Bunyola *C/Mare de Déu de les Neus 8 (no phone).*

Inca

If you want proof that Mallorca hasn't entirely fallen prey entirely to tourism, come to **Inca**, the island's third largest town in both population and industrial output (Manacor is the second). And then beat a hasty retreat… for the truth, even acknowledged by Mallorcans, is that Inca isn't, to put it politely, a very prepossessing place. This is a working town, first and foremost, with a long tradition of shoemaking and leather-working. The leather industry continues to act as a magnet for migrant workers, many of whom come from North Africa.

Tourists, though, rarely get beyond the town's beltway of roundabouts and junctions for Palma (35 kilometres/22 miles to the south-west), the northern resorts and the roads out into Es Pla. Even those who swoop on the town's factory outlets to buy cut-price shoes, jackets and other items of leatherware (Inca has dubbed itself 'city of leather') have only to drive into the town's eastern fringes and park up at the US-style lots to go bargain-hunting in the warehouse stores.

Es Parc restaurant, Selva. *See p167.*

The weekly market (Thursday morning) draws a few intrepid foreigners, but the goods are pretty mundane. The biggest and best market is on Dijous Bo (Good Thursday), the first Thursday in November. The rest of the time, there's a laid-back bustle to the commercial centre, and some good cellar restaurants.

The one absolute must-visit in Inca, however, is the **RECamper** outlet of funky-but-comfy shoemaker **Camper** (*see p166* **Shoes shine**); you can't miss it on the main bypass. The company's HQ is in Inca, and it's immoderately proud of its Mallorcan heritage. There's another Camper outlet store at **Festival Park** (*see p158*).

Where to stay, eat & drink

Inca might be short on charm but it has plenty of good restaurants, many located in old wine cellars. One of the most famous is **Celler Can Amer** (C/Pau 39, 971 50 12 61, closed Sat & Sun June-Oct, closed dinner Sun Nov-May, €€), which has a good reputation, despite some of its dishes being stuck in a old-style haute cuisine timewarp of gloopy reductions and overblown combinations. Look for lighter

or simpler-sounding dishes, such as quail roasted in honey and orange or salt cod marinated with peppers and tapenade.

The old town's pedestrianised central artery C/Major is as pleasant as Inca gets, and is topped and tailed by two good spots for a drink and a snack. **Cafetería Bar Antonio** (Plaça Santa Maria la Mayor 10, no phone, €) has been around for more than 35 years and is housed in a splendid, massive arcaded building facing the town's main church; its tables in the *plaça* are the nicest spot in town to sit. **Café Espanyol** (Plaça Espanyol 5-6, 971 50 00 00, closed Sat afternoon and all Sun, €) is even older (it opened in 1937) and is popular with a more local crowd, who hide in the shade indoors, leaving the sunny tables on the square to the tourists.

In the summer heat, a pleasant outdoors alternative is to head out of town to **Celler Son Aloy** (Ctra. Inca–Sencelles, km3, 971 50 23 02, closed dinner Mon, Sun and all Tue, €€), which supplies some of the grapes used by the famous Bodegas Santa Catarina. Various meats, including *gazapo* (young rabbit), lamb chops, sausages and belly of pork, are barbecued on a rather spartan patio surrounded by acres

Selva. *See p167.*

Central Mallorca

Shoes shine

If you want evidence of just how cool Mallorca is these days, look no further than the proud presence of the HQ of one of the hippest international brands on the island. **Camper**, based in the otherwise unfashionable town of Inca (between Palma and Alcúdia) is one of the hottest shoemakers of the past decade. Selling around three million pairs each year, and with an annual turnover of over 130 million euros, Camper has made its name with funky, chunky yet comfy and practical footwear that somehow floats above the vagaries of fashion.

The designs may be innovative and irreverent, but the company insists its success is rooted on a bedrock of quality Mallorcan shoemaking tradition. Although Camper started up in 1975, it traces its origins to a Mallorcan craftsman shoemaker, Antonio Fluxà, who journeyed to England in 1877 to learn all about the new industrial methods of shoe manufacturing, and, on his return, introduced the first mechanised production of shoes to the island. It was Antonio's grandson Lorenzo who created Camper 30 years ago, reflecting a new and decidedly modern post-Franco philosophy of 'freedom, comfort and creativity'.

It wasn't until the 1990s that the international expansion of the brand began. Camper now has stores in 46 countries and has diversified into super-cool hotels (a Casa Camper, designed by Rafael Moneo, is due to open in Alaró in 2006) and restaurants (named FoodBALL – based on the frankly rather bizarre idea of food served within balls of rice). Rolling out these concepts is keeping the Camper creatives busy for now, but when asked about what the next project might be, a representative said enigmatically: 'We are like a free spirit – who knows what will come next.'

An essential shopping excursion is a trip to Camper's outlet store **RECamper** (971 50 71 58, www.camper.com), which sells end-of-line and one-off shoes at irresistibly low prices. Heading from Palma to Alcúdia on the main road you'll see the store to your left as you skirt the edge of Inca. There's a further outlet store at the Festival Park mall back towards Palma (*see p158*).

of vines. Or if you're just thirsty rather than hungry, you can indulge in a tasting of some of the very reasonably priced Santa Catarina wines.

There's no real reason for staying in Inca. However, just outside town there's a very pleasant four-star country manor, which also has an excellent restaurant. **Casa del Virrey** (Ctra. Inca–Sencelles, km2.4, 971 88 10 18, www.casavirrey.com, doubles €107-€139 incl breakfast) presents a gracious front to the world, with mature palms and white-cushioned garden furniture in its spacious forecourt. Mature gardens hide a lovely swimming pool. The hotel's 16 rooms are smartly comfortable, with lots of antiques and rich fabrics, and you will feel just as at ease in the welcoming public rooms. The chef at the hotel's **Restaurante Doña Irene** (closed Mon, €€€) produces wonderfully rich dishes, such as quails stuffed with foie gras and truffle sauce.

Another agreeable accommodation option in the area is **Son Vivot** (Ctra. Palma–Alcúdia, km34, 971 88 01 24, www.sonvivot.com, double €100 incl breakfast), a functioning agricultural estate that offers four bright guest rooms, a pool and al fresco dinner on request.

Resources

Internet
Inca *Net Games, Gran Via Colóm 141 (971 50 33 21).* **Open** 11am-11pm Mon-Sat.

Police station
Inca *C/Artà 11 (971 88 08 18).*

Post office
Inca *Plaça Àngel 12 (971 50 04 23).*

Selva, Caimari, Binibona, Moscari & Campanet

North of Inca, in the foothills of the mountains, lies a patchwork of industrious small towns and appealing, uneventful villages, linked by winding lanes that are popular with cyclists.

The main settlements are the leather-working town of **Selva** (four kilometres/two and a half miles north of Inca) and the farming community of **Campanet** (six kilometres/four miles east of Selva). The former is topped by a massive fortress-like church, and is worth a visit for the wondrous views from the terrace of the restaurant **Es Parc** beside it (*see below*).

The latter is close to the area's only real 'sight': the **Coves de Campanet**. This karst cave complex of 3,200 square metres (34,400 square feet) was discovered by workers in 1945 and opened to the public three years later. Several chambers go down as far as 300 metres (984 feet), and the Sala de la Palmera (Palm Tree Chamber) and Sala del Llac (Lake Chamber), which surrounds a crystalline lake, are quite beautiful.

This tiny portion of Es Raiguer takes in the handsome stone-built village of **Caimari**, more run-of-the-mill **Moscari** and the pretty hamlet of **Binibona** (a great base for walking). For reasons unknown it has, in recent years, became a focus for some great hotels and *agroturismos*.

Coves de Campanet

Ctra. Palma–Alcúdia, km39, Campanet (971 51 61 30/www.covesdecampanet.com). **Open** *Apr–Oct* 10am-7pm daily. *Nov–Mar* 10am-6pm daily. **Admission** €9. **No credit cards.**

Where to stay & eat

In **Selva**, the six-room **Sa Bisbal** (Plaça Santa Catalina Tomás 1, 971 51 57 24, www.hotelsabisbal.com, closed Nov, Dec, doubles €110 incl breakfast) is located in a lovely 17th-century building at the top of the town. The pick of the rooms is room 6 on the top floor, with a beamed ceiling, massive windows looking out towards the mountains and its own terrace. There's a pool too. The prime spot to eat and drink in Selva is **Es Parc** (Parque Recreativo, 971 51 51 45, noon-5pm, 7pm-midnight daily), an unexpectedly chic restaurant-bar atop the hill in the centre of the town, with a huge terrace offering wondrous views of the mountains

Just north of Selva, the villages of **Caimari**, **Binibona** and **Moscari** are the focus for a clutch of rural hotels and fincas. One of the prettiest and most friendly is **Finca Es Castell** (C/Binibona s/n, 971 87 51 54, www.fincaescastell.com, closed Jan, double €128-€150 incl breakfast, restaurant closed lunch and all Sun, €€), run by a lovely Italian/English couple; it has three terraces, a bar and a good restaurant (open to non-residents).

Other fine choices in the area include **Finca Albellons** (Parc Natural, Binibona, 971 87 50 69, www.albellons.com, double €75-€82),

Finca Binibona (C/Binibona s/n, 971 87 35 65, www.binibona.com, double €150-€171), **C'an Beneït** (C/C'an Beneït s/n, 971 51 54 16, www.canbeneit.com, double €140-€155), **C'an Furiós** (Camí Vell Binibona, 971 51 57 51, www.can furios.com, double €161-€214 incl breakfast), **C'an Casetes** (C/Horitzo 14, 971 87 35 62, www.cancasetes.com, double €95-€109 incl breakfast) and **C'an Calco** (C/Campanet 1, 971 51 52 60, www.cancalco.com, closed mid Jan-mid Feb, double €108 incl breakfast). The latter also has an excellent restaurant, run by two chaps from Alcúdia who own their own boat and are happy to take guests fishing (expect a 6am wake-up call) to catch their own dinner. Non-fishermen are also welcome to enjoy their no-choice four-course menu (€€€). Booking advisable.

One of the nicest hotels in the area is located just outside **Campanet**. **Monnàber Nou** (971 87 71 76, www.monnaber.com, doubles €176) is an immaculate, luxurious converted farmhouse, set in beautiful countryside, with every conceivable facility and a fine restaurant, **Es Mirador de Monnàber Nou** (€€€€).

A cheaper option in the area is the lovely, stylish finca **Monnàber Vell** (Monnàber Vell s/n, 971 51 61 31, www.monnabervell.com, closed Jan, Dec, doubles €98-€138 incl breakfast), set in a 200 hectare (494 acre) estate.

A further possibility nearby for small groups and families is **Fangar** (Ctra. Antigua de Campanet–Pollença, km5, 971 45 70 44, mobile 610 23 80 55, www.fangar.com, 2 people €90-€121, 4 people €143-€159), which offers four two-bedroom air conditioned cottages with kitchenettes, and a shared pool.

Resources

Police station

Campanet *C/Major 25 (971 51 60 05).*
Selva *Plaça Major 1 (971 87 52 69).*

Post office

Campanet *C/Major 34 (971 51 60 05).*
Selva *C/Llevant 5 (971 51 52 56).*

Getting there

By bus

From Palma there are 8 buses Mon-Fri (4 Sat, 3 Sun) to Inca via Santa Maria, Consell, Binissalem and Lloseta, as well as 6-8 buses Mon-Sat (5 Sun) from Palma to Bunyola.

By train

There are 29 trains Mon-Fri and 26 on Sat & Sun between Palma and Inca (36mins), via Marratxi (14mins), Santa Maria (20mins), Alaró-Consell (24mins), Binissalem (28mins) and Lloseta (32mins).

Es Pla

Long ignored by tourism, the central plain now offers some blissful rural retreats and an unhurried pace of life.

The perfect cure for those seeking rest, views and a bargain: **Santuari de Cura**. *See p176.*

Sa Pobla, Muro & Maria de la Salut

The motorway and the old C713 between Palma and Alcúdia effectively divides the towns of the mountains from the towns of the plain. Sizeable **Sa Pobla**, a few kilometres west of hilly Campanet, and just a ten-minute drive from the coast, has the unmistakable feel of a rural, agricultural Es Pla settlement. Laid out on a grid plan, it sits amid fields that were reclaimed by draining the salt marshes; a monument in the centre of the town pays tribute to those who took part in this Herculean task. Three harvests a year – of potatoes, haricot beans and a variety of veg – attract seasonal workers. Surprisingly, Sa Pobla boasts two museums (in the same building), the **Museu d'Art Contemporani i Jugeta Antigua de Sa Pobla** features two collections: one of contemporary works by Mallorcan artists, and the other of toys. It also has its own winery, **Bodegas Crestatx**, which can be visited.

Five kilometres (three miles) south-east of Sa Pobla lies **Muro**, declared a town in 1300 by Jaume II (which explains why its street plan has a more organic feel than that of its near-neighbour). The small, oblong central *plaça* is dotted with fine townhouses, terrace cafés and restaurants; the imposing church of **Sant Joan Baptista** and the 15th-century La Sang chapel are definitely worthy of a peek. The **Museu Etnològic**, a miscellaneous collection of jars, tools, folk music instruments and an old waterwheel, attracts few visitors. There's also a bullring (971 53 73 29) that was chiselled out of the rocky landscape in 1910; it occasionally welcomes big-name matadors. Round the back of Muro is a beautiful raised promenade with benches looking over the fields and out to sea.

Other towns of the northern Pla, like **Llubí** and **Santa Margalida**, are pleasant for a drinks stop but otherwise contain little of interest. **Maria de la Salut** (eight kilometres/five miles south of Muro) is a small, pretty village, its streets surrounded by terraced gardens of cacti and citrus groves, with the odd gamboling sheep adding to the Arcadian air. It's worth passing through (unless you're a vegetarian) in order to visit **Embotits Artesanals Matas** (C/Artà s/n, 971 52 56 21, www.embotits-matas.com, closed Sat and Sun). This is one of only a few artisanal sausage and cured meat makers in the whole of Spain, never mind the Balearics. Among its products are *sobrassada* (mild or spicy), *llonganissa* and *botifarra sin sangre* (without blood), made using high-quality pork from Girona in Catalunya on the mainland, natural seasonings and no artificial colourings, flavourings, preservatives or additives of any kind. Only vitamin A is used as an antioxidant. (This means you may get some mould on your sausage skin, but it can be scraped off.) On your visit you can see the processes involved in making these delicious products, and get a taste at the end. The *sobrassada* covered in pimiento (pepper) and the *camaiot* (pork meat stuffed into skin rather than a stomach) are both Matas-patented products unavailable anywhere else.

Bodegas Crestatx
Joan Sindia s/n, Sa Pobla (971 54 07 41/www.bodegas crestatx.com). **Open** 9am-1pm daily. **Admission** free.

Museu d'Art Contemporani i Jugeta Antigua de Sa Pobla
C/Antoni Maura 6, Sa Pobla (971 54 23 89). **Open** 10am-2pm, 4-8pm Tue-Sat; 10am-2pm Sun. **Admission** (combined) €4; €2.70 concessions. **No credit cards.**

Museu Etnològic
C/Major 15, Muro (971 86 06 47). **Open** 10am-3pm Tue, Wed, Fri, Sat; 10am-3pm, 5-8pm Thur; 10am-2pm Sun. **Admission** €2.40. **No credit cards.**

Where to stay

Between the village of **Búger** and Sa Pobla is a lovely finca: **Son Pons** (Ctra. Búger–Sa Pobla s/n, mobile 649 45 37 76, www.son pons.com, doubles €90-€170 incl breakfast). It's a characterful 16th-century building that now contains six bedrooms, with a pool outside and a drive of around ten minutes to reach the beach.

A very good reason for staying in **Maria de la Salut** is to hang out at **Casa Girasol** (Casa Son Roig, 971 85 80 07, www.casa girasol.de, doubles €134-€144), which offers home comforts in charming surroundings with a rich past. The farmhouse was in the hands of the Font i Roig family from the 14th century to 1989. Some of the house's original features are still put to good use, such as the wood-fired bread oven, the well and the tiny chapel, where marriages and christenings can still be held. There are eight tasteful rooms and plenty of space for lounging around the patios, shady gardens and pool.

Another fine place to unwind, located between Sineu and Maria de la Salut, is **Son Fogueró** (Ctra. Sineu–Maria de la Salut, km2, 971 52 53 43, www.sonfoguero.com, closed Nov & Dec, doubles €199-€289), a gorgeous 300-year-old finca. Owned by interior designer Maria Antonia Carbonell and her husband Pere Alemany, Son Fogueró is a super-private haven that attracts arty types like Catalan artist Jaume Plensa. The design of its five suites encompasses natural stone walls, beamed ceilings, antique furniture and striking modern art. There's an honour bar, a restaurant, a pool and pretty gardens, specked with modern sculptures by the owners' sculptor son.

A few kilometres inland from unappealing Can Picafort on the Bay of Alcúdia, off the road to Muro, is the unexpectedly classy **Finca Son Serra** (Predio Son Serra, Ctra. Muro–Can Picafort, km6.5, 971 53 79 80, www.finca-son-serra.de, closed Nov-Apr, doubles €120-€140). This 18th-century house is set in parkland lush with palms, fruit trees and flowering climbing plants, and has a big pool and views out to sea.

Resources

Police station
Muro *Plaça Comte d'Empúries 1 (971 53 76 49).* Sa Pobla *Plaça Constitució 1 (971 86 22 86).*

Post office
Muro *C/Gran 99 (971 54 00 85).*

Sineu

Located 33 kilometres (21 miles) east of Palma and almost midway between Inca and Manacor, **Sineu** is right at the geographical centre of Mallorca and the heart of the central plain. This smartly preserved town of steep cobbled streets and spruce sandstone townhouses is the best base for exploring Es Pla, and has a couple of lovely hotels and restaurants (many within historic wine cellars). Though it welcomes its fair share of tourists during the day, few stay the night.

Sineu comes alive on Wednesdays when the whole island seems to visit its historic outdoor market. Dating from the 13th century, it's the only remaining livestock market on the island (though one suspects that the few piglets, kids and ducks it attracts are there more to amuse the tourists than attract the farmers). Arrive early and breakfast on traditional hot chocolate and *churros* (long, thin doughnuts) before foraging among the clutter of stalls selling wrinkled fragrant olives, Day-Glo jellied fruits, pungent local cheeses, dodgy watercolours, 1,001 different types of knife and some beautifully creative jewellery. Like Inca, Sineu is particularly notable for one annual market (and also its spring festival) – the Sa Fira – which takes place on the first Sunday in May.

During the Middle Ages, Sineu was the key town of the interior, and Jaume II built a royal palace here, though nothing remains. The cute little main square, simply called Sa Plaça, is dominated by the church of **Santa Maria de Sineu**, dating from 1549, with its unusual seven-storey pyramidal spire. It's a huge structure, indicating the town's historical significance, with a recently restored interior that is pleasingly simple and light-filled, with modern stained glass. Entrance is via the adjoining Plaça de Sant Marc, where you'll see a bombastic statue of the town's emblem, the winged lion of Sineu, honouring the town's patron St Mark.

Just down from here is Plaça El Fossar, the liveliest part of town by day and in the evening (though Sineu is very quiet at night out of high season). During the day you'll find the cafés here are particularly popular as refuelling stops for the legions of cyclists who patrol Es Pla's network of quiet country roads. It's not a recent phenomenon: there's a monument here to cyclist Francesc Alomar.

In an old railway station building, the **Centre d'Art S'Estació** art gallery shows an eclectic collection of work by local artists, all for sale.

A few kilometres south-west of Sineu, **Lloret de Vista Alegre** is a village of pretty walled gardens, with a *mirador* tucked away behind the church, offering views over the dappled green valley dotted with palms and almond trees.

Centre d'Art S'Estació

C/Estació 2 (971 52 07 50/www.sineuestacio.com). **Open** 9.30am-1.30pm, 4-7pm Mon-Fri; 10am-1pm Sat. **Admission** free.

Where to stay

The **Hotel Son Cleda** (Plaça Es Fossar 7, 971 52 10 38, www.hotelsoncleda.com, doubles €80-€95 incl breakfast) is 300 years old and retains its original features, including an impressive marble staircase, ornate glass chandelier and Mallorcan antiques. Guests have use of a walled terrace at the back of the house and all the comforts of four-star accommodation (air-con, minibar, internet access) at three-star prices, plus lovely friendly service. Located on the other side of the hill, the **Hotel León de Sineu** (C/dels Bous 129, 971 52 02 11, www.hotel-leondesineu. com, doubles €115-€132 incl breakfast) has a beautiful, leafy walled garden with a sauna and a small pool. The rooms are light and airy,

with white walls and linen and original period tiles on the bathroom floors (ask for one overlooking the garden).

Heading south out of **Lloret de Vista Alegre** towards Montuïri, you'll see a sign for **Finca Sa Rota d'en Palerm** on the left (Ctra. Lloret de Vista Alegre–Montuïri, 0.8km, 971 72 69 34, mobile 617 22 52 84, www.sa-rota.com, apartment for 2 or junior suite with terrace €137-€146, house for 4 €212-€227). This beautiful, friendly, family-run old finca has apartments, junior suites and a house for four with its own private entrance, all kitted out with antique furniture (the owner restores it herself). You can see all the way to the Tramuntana from the secluded apartments' terraces. There are hammocks slung between orange trees and a sheltered outdoor pool. Guests and visitors can eat good home cooking at the finca if they reserve in advance.

Another good place to stay near Sineu is **Sa Casa Rotja** (Ctra. Sineu–Muro, km3, 971 18 50 27, www.sacasarotja.com, doubles €69-€80 incl breakfast), located just off the Sineu–Muro road, which offers a variety of cottages with one, two and three double rooms, and a communal pool.

Where to eat & drink

Of Sineu's *celler* restaurants, you won't do better than **Celler Es Grop** (C/Major 18, 971 52 01 87, closed dinner Mon & Sun, €€) which knocks out authentic Mallorcan cooking, including lots of offal and fried things, in an old-fashioned bodega lined with giant barrels strung with chilli peppers and cluttered with ancient wine bottles. The owner speaks no English, which adds to the authentic experience.

Moli d'En Pau (Ctra. Santa Margarita 25, 971 85 51 16, closed Mon, €€) is located in a 16th-century flour mill, over the rail tracks on the road to Maria de la Salut. Traditional seasonal Mallorcan cuisine is on offer, including earthy tongue and tripe concoctions, fresh fish, such as turbot and bass, and steaks and chops. You can dine next to an aviary of songbirds, parrots and a duck on the garden patio.

The only Basque restaurant in Es Pla, **Sa Penya** (Ctra. Montuïri 9, 971 52 03 64, closed lunch Mon and all Sun in June-Aug, dinner Sun and all Mon in Sept-May, €€€) is a stylish spot with large landscape paintings on the walls, picture windows overlooking the surrounding wheatfields and smart, rustic-chic decor. The menu features a range of cod dishes – the staple of Basque cuisine – and richly creative desserts.

In terms of drinking, there's little to choose between the cafés of Plaça Es Fossar, with the notable exception of the terrace of the **Son Cleda** hotel (*see p170*, €), which is by far the

chicest spot in town to sip a beer. It also offers
an eclectic and keenly priced selection of
excellent snacks and light meals – the likes
of imaginative salads, provençal-style hake,
lasagne and even Cornish pasties.

Resources

Police station
Sineu *C/Sant Francesc 10 (971 52 00 27/mobile
639 15 00 15).*

Post office
Sineu *C/Carril 4 (971 52 02 04).*

Petra, Sant Joan & Vilafranca de Bonany

Between Sineu and Manacor lie three pleasant
villages. Ten kilometres (six miles) south-east
of Sineu is **Petra**, a tightly knit, quiet-bordering-
on-comatose village with a grid of unfeasibly
narrow streets and one big claim to fame. In
1713 Miguel José Serra was born at C/Barracar
6. Better known as the missionary **Junípero
Serra** (*see p172* **Local heroes**), he went
on to found a series of missions in California
(including the future cities of San Francisco
and San Diego), and is seen by many as the most
important European pioneer of the southern
American Pacific coast. Petra takes considerable
pride in the Serra connection, and a small
museum (hours variable, donation requested)
and his birthplace are worth a peek. The
museum's three rooms contain a range of
Serrabilia. There are models of the nine missions
he personally founded, plus Native American
arrowheads, pictures and documents. A leaflet
is available in (idiosyncratic) English. Three doors
down from the museum is the humble Serra
family house, which was bought by the Rotary
Club of Mallorca and given over to the City
of San Francisco in 1932, which returned it to the
keeping of Petra in 1981. If the museum is closed,
a plaque at its entrance tells you which door
to knock on to arouse the custodian. On the little
street facing the museum are a series of Majolica
panels depicting Serra's missionary foundations.

Take a hike up to the **Ermita de Bonany**,
a couple of kilometres south-west of Petra. This
is where Serra preached his last sermon before
heading off to the Americas. It's one of the easier
hermitages to reach on foot, but it's still a bit of a
climb, rewarded by wonderful views over Es Pla.

Seven kilometres (four and and a half miles)
west of Petra lies the typical, tiny Es Pla
settlement of **Sant Joan** – all squat sandstone
houses and green shutters. There's a sanctuary
here – the **Santuari de la Consolació** – built

A sleepy, one-pooch village: **Petra**.

on a knoll overlooking the town. It's in pristine
condition, thanks to a restoration undertaken
by Sant Joan residents in the 1950s and 1960s.

Just outside Sant Joan is **Els Calderers**
(signposted at Ctra. Palma–Manacor, km37).
This gorgeous old house used to belong
to the noble Veri family, who employed 38
people at one point to oversee the vineyards
that surrounded it until the 1870s phylloxera
epidemic wiped out the vines. The house, which
dates from 1750, has been restored to its late
19th-century condition and the well-organised
self-guided tour takes you through more than
20 rooms around a light-filled central courtyard.
The restoration is exquisite. Among the rooms
are a private chapel and atmospheric wine
cellar (where you can sample *vino tinto* from
the barrel), a vaulted reception room and the
master of the house's office. Outside there are
pens containing the types of animals that the
family would have kept – a cow, goats, pigs,
sheep, hens and turkeys. A café serves snacks;
take them outside and enjoy this lovely spot.

The first settlement of any size on the C715
Manacor–Palma road, coming from Manacor,
is **Vilafranca de Bonany**. Its shops are
famed for their colourful displays of fresh Es
Pla produce; look out for curvaceous gourds, the
wrinkled deep rust-red tomatoes (*tomatigues de*

ramallet) and melons. This is the melon capital of Mallorca and the harvest is celebrated with a festival on the first weekend of September.

Els Calderers

Ctra. Palma–Manacor, km37 (971 52 60 69/ www.todoesp.es/els-calderers). **Open** *Apr-Oct* 10am-6pm daily. *Nov-Mar* 10am-5pm daily. **Admission** €7. **No credit cards**.

Where to stay & eat

For a good, honest lunchtime *menú*, **El Cruce** (Ctra. Palma–Manacor, km41, 971 56 00 73, closed dinner Mon-Fri, €) on the main C715 near **Vilafranca**, will come up with the goods.

If you're after something a notch higher in the culinary stakes, one of the best *celler*

Local heroes Junípero Serra

The unremarkable village of Petra was the birthplace in 1713 of the remarkable missionary and traveller Junípero Serra, who was to play a significant role in the Spanish settlement of California. Though Serra's background was humble, he was intellectually gifted and hugely determined. At 15 he enrolled in a Franciscan school in Palma and, within a couple of years, was ordained as a priest (and changed his name from Miguel José to Junípero). Such was the young man's talent that he was appointed a professor of theology at the age of 24.

However, after a dozen or so successful years as an academic and preacher, Serra craved a new challenge. In 1749 he and a group of fellow Franciscans sailed off to pursue missionary work in Mexico. After a gruelling journey, the priests landed at Vera Cruz in the Gulf of Mexico and, despite ill health, then walked more than 300 kilometres (190 miles) to Mexico City. This was the first of a series of improbable journeys for which Serra became renowned (particularly because his asthma and a permanently swollen leg made walking difficult for him).

For the next 18 years he wandered around remote parts of Mexico engaged in missionary work. When, in 1767, the Spanish Crown expelled the Jesuits from Spain's colonies, Serra and the Franciscans were asked to take over the missions in Baja (lower) California. The following year Carlos III claimed the west coast of America for Spain, and Serra and a small group of soldiers and priests trudged north to stake their claim in Alta (upper) California. After another mammoth trek they arrived at the Pacific coast in 1769 in the area of the current US–Mexico border.

During the next 15 years Serra and his priests attempted to convert the natives to Catholicism (claiming to have succeeded, with 5,000 conversions in this time) and founded a series of missions along the Pacific coast, including San Francisco and San Diego. Serra died at the age of 71 at the Mission of San Carlos Borromeo at Carmel, near Monterey, in 1784. He was beatified in 1988.

His closest friend and fellow Franciscan missionary Palou left an account of Serra that makes it hard to like the man even if you admire his zeal and willpower. He frowned on pleasure in any form, eating little, smiling never and indulging in frequent self-mortification. And while he did oppose punitive expeditions against the natives, it is also true that he was central in establishing the European foothold in California that was (albeit unknowingly) to bring disease, death and eventual destruction to the native population.

restaurants in Es Pla, **Es Celler** (C/Hospital 46, 971 56 10 56, closed Mon, €€), can be found in **Petra**. Don't expect fancy creations, just reliably good wood oven-roasted meat in a hearty country style. The complimentary local black olives and rustic brown bread are worth the visit alone. From here, head down the slope and take a right to come to Plaça Ramón Llull, the main square for bars. **Café Ca'n Tomeu** (No.47, 971 56 10 23, €€), established in 1945, has terrace tables shaded by umbrellas where you can eat tapas, salads and *pa amb oli*.

Probably the best place to eat, drink and then sleep it off is the hotel-restaurant **Sa Plaça Petra** (No.4, 971 56 16 46, www.saplacapetra. com, doubles €109, restaurant closed Tue, €€). The restaurant has a pretty garden terrace with lemon trees and serves dishes such as suckling pig, cod in garlic mayonnaise and paella, as well as inventive desserts including cheese ice-cream. There's a wine cellar stocked with quality local wines, and three beautiful, antique-filled rooms with luxurious marble-lined bathrooms. Ask for the large double with a view of the *plaça*.

You can also stay in one of the plain double rooms at the hill-top **Ermita de Bonany** (Puig de Bonany, 971 56 11 01, doubles €20), outside Petra. For something a little more luxurious, try **Son Torrat** (Camí de Bonany, km2, 630 01 78 58, www.sontorrat.com, apartments for 2 €60-€80), a 16th-century house on the road between Petra and the Ermita that's been converted into six apartments with wonderful views. There's a pool, and a jacuzzi within an ancient *aljibe* (stone water tank) that makes you feel you're bathing inside a cave.

Resources

Police station

Sant Joan *C/Major 61 (971 52 60 03/971 33 30 03)*.
Petra *C/Font 1 (659 49 15 50)*.
Vilafranca de Bonany *Plaça Major 1 (971 83 21 06)*.

Post office

Petra *C/Sol 5 (no phone)*.
Sant Joan *C/Consolació 18 (971 52 60 75)*.
Vilafranca de Bonany *C/Principal 8 (no phone)*.

Montuïri & Porreres

Montuïri, just north of the Palma–Manacor road (eight kilometres/five miles east of Algaida and 11 kilometres/seven miles west of Vilafranca), is an unusually laid-out village; its main street runs along a ridge, with steeply sloping alleys running off either side. Considering the volume of traffic pounding

down the C715, it's also remarkable for its ghost town-like emptiness and silence, broken only by the occasional old lady, clad in traditional smock and headscarf, puttering through the streets on an ancient moped with a crate of tomatoes strapped to the back. The village is transformed on 24 August during the Feast of San Bartomeu, when *cossiers* (dancers) dress up in traditional costume; their curious dancing represents the triumph of good over evil.

On the edge of town, the **Museu Arqueológic de Son Fornés** is housed in an old restored flour mill and focuses on the nearby Son Fornés archaeological site, where megalithic talayots and evidence of a medieval settlement have been found (no information in English). The forlorn **Son Fornés** site itself is situated a couple of kilometres west of the town on the PM320 Pina–Sencelles road. There's not a lot left of the talayot, though it is of interest in being hollow, and clearly used as a living space or storage room, unlike most of the normally solid talayots on Menorca.

Ten kilometres (six miles) south-east of Montuïri, **Porreres** sits in pretty countryside, amid pine and almond trees. It's an attractive, somnolent little village, centred on a main street that runs between its church (with a distinctive crenellated spire) and the main square, Plaça de la Vila. A general market is held around the *plaça* on Tuesdays. That Porreres once amounted to more than this is apparent with one look at its cathedral-sized church of **Nuestra Señora de la Consolació**. If it's open, take a peek into its dark (there's only one window), barrel-vaulted interior. Here you'll find a multi-storey gilded baroque altarpiece and a side chapel as big as most churches.

Just outside Porreres (take the road to Llucmajor then turn left soon after), the small **Santuari de Monti-Sion** (971 64 71 85) perches on top of a low hill, its slopes bristling with pines. The current two kilometre-long road up to the Santuari was built by the inhabitants of Porreres in just one day in 1954; along it are the Stations of the Cross, dating from 1497. A school was founded up here by Franciscan monks in 1551, which was home, at one time, to more than 500 pupils; it was closed during the 19th century and the buildings fell into disrepair, before being renovated in the 20th century. Only groups can stay overnight, but all visitors can use the picnic area outside the sanctuary walls. There's a procession up to the Santuari from Porreres on the Sunday after Easter.

Museu Arqueológic de Son Fornés

C/Emili Pou s/n, Montuïri (971 64 41 69/www.son fornes.mallorca.museum). **Open** 10am-2pm, 4-8pm Tue-Sun. **Admission** €3; €1.80 concessions. **No credit cards.**

Central Mallorca

You'll be blown away at the glass factory at **Gordiola**. *See p175.*

Where to stay & eat

Near **Montuïri**, *hotel rural* **Es Figueral Nou** (Ctra. Montuïri–Sant Joan, km0.7, 971 64 67 64, www.esfigueralnou.com, closed Nov-Feb, doubles €140 incl breakfast) is a converted winery on a five-hectare (12-acre) *possessió* with 25 large, crisply elegant rooms (some have four-poster beds) and views clear across the plain to the Serra de Tramuntana. There are pleasant gardens, a small golf course, tennis courts and a chic swimming pool bordered with wooden decking.

Its younger, funkier sister hotel, **Son Manera** (Ctra. Montuïri–Lloret, km0.3, 971 16 15 30, 971 64 67 64, www.sonmanera.com, €140-€198 incl breakfast), just down the road, opened in 2003 and offers full spa facilities.

Another choice spot to stay in the area is **Puig Moltó** (Ctra. Pina– Montuïri, 971 18 17 58, www.espuigmolto.com, closed Nov, Dec, doubles €128-€161 incl breakfast), one of the oldest estates on Es Pla, surrounded by fig and carob trees, and with ten bright, light suites, and a pool.

The most authentic eating option in Montuïri is **Bar d'Hostal** (C/Constitució s/n, 971 64 60 49, closed Mon, €€), a converted glassworks, which only serves *pa amb oli* – bread and oil with various toppings; coming from Palma, take the first signposted turning to Montuïri on your left and then the first tarred road to the right.

The **Ermita de Sant Miquel** (Puig de Sant Miquel, 971 64 63 14, closed Mon, restaurant €), near Montuïri, has been nicely renovated and houses an excellent café-restaurant.

There are a handful of fincas offering accommodation in and around **Porreres**. **Es Passarell** (Ctra. Porreres–Felanitx, km5.5, 971 18 30 91, www.espassarell.net, doubles €91-€118, apartment €96-€139), just outside Porreres on the road to Felanitx, is the pick. This cosy yet elegant finca is owned and run by Lola, a warm, exuberant woman with wonderful taste in art, decor, pets and people. The rooms and apartments have the air of relaxed luxury, with rich fabrics, lots of books and an air of do-as-you-please. There are six apartments, all with fireplace, garden and terrace, three double rooms with bath, terrace and stove, and one double with a shower. A communal dinner is available three times a week. There's a pool too.

In the other direction, towards Llucmajor, you'll find **Finca Son Sama** (Ctra. Llucmajor– Porreres, km3.5, 971 12 09 59, www.sonsama. com, doubles €92 incl breakfast, restaurant closed Sun, €€), a secluded farmhouse dating back to 1531 and stuffed with island antiques. Rooms are large with terracotta-tiled floors. The restaurant, Es Mirador, has endless views of the plains and does bargain-priced suckling lamb and pig. The rather wild garden and sense of isolation make staying here only for those who really want to feel they're away from it all.

Further possibilities include the luxurious **Sa Bassa Rotja** (Finca Son Orell, Camí Sa Pedrera s/n, 971 16 82 25, www.sabassa rotja.com, doubles €158-€182 incl breakfast, restaurant €€), set within a sizeable estate at the foot of the hill crowned by the Monti-Sion sanctuary. It has 25 big rooms, a restaurant, two pools and tennis courts.

Cheaper and more homely is the seven-room **Finca Son Mercadal** (Ctra. Porreres–Campos, Camí Son Pau s/n, 971 18 13 07, www.son-mercadal.com, doubles €100 incl breakfast), which also has a pool, and can be found five kilometres (three miles) south of Porreres on the road to Campos. Guests are free to make use of the owners' bicycles, horses and even donkeys.

For eating in Porreres, **Restaurant Centro** (C/Obispo Campins 13, 971 16 83 72, closed Sun night, €€€, lunch *menú* €8.50 Mon-Fri, €15 Sun) has a hearty lunchtime *menú* that distinguishes between 'fish' and 'fresh fish' (much of the fish served up on Mallorca is frozen, but the Centro has its own fishing boat, the *Pala Llonga*). The elegant and bustling colonial-style dining hall is a great place to gawp at Es Pla's hearty yeomen. On the main square, **Café Sa Plaça** (Plaça de la Vila 4, 971 64 74 84, €) has decent tapas.

Resources

Police station
Montuïri *Plaça Major 1 (971 64 41 25/47).*
Porreres *Plaça de la Vila 17 (971 64 72 21).*

Post office
Montuïri *C/Corregudes s/n (971 64 61 68).*
Porreres *C/Veiet 17 (971 64 73 19).*

Algaida & Randa

Algaida (21 kilometres/13 miles east of Palma and eight kilometres/five miles west of Montuïri) is the first place you come to heading out from the capital along the Palma–Manacor road. A typical small Es Pla town, it isn't much of a draw in itself, though it does have a good hotel and some popular Mallorcan restaurants.

By the main road on the west side of the town, you won't fail to spot a massive mock castle, looking like a set from a cheesy Hollywood movie. This is the factory, museum and shop of glass-makers **Gordiola**, who have been producing the stuff since 1719. It may look like a hideously kitsch tour party magnet (which it is), but it really is worth a stop. It's quite something to see the glass-making boys, clad in shorts and T-shirts (with a couple of old masters lending some sense of decorum), producing the goods in front of your eyes. The setting itself – the heat, the darkness, the dramatic Gothic setting – is like something out of Dante. Upstairs, in a series of grand rooms, is the Gordiola's glass collection from around the world. In the shop you can pick up a souvenir – much of the glassware is a touch gaudy, but there are some beautiful (and pricey) modern chandeliers too.

Those whose interests lie more with the natural world, might want to detour a few kilometres north-west of Algaida to **Natura Parc**, just outside **Santa Eugènia**. This compact, shady nature park boasts mammals (deer, goats, llama), birds (most notably black vultures) and butterflies (in Spain's biggest enclosed butterfly garden). It's a worthwhile detour for kids.

The pretty little village of **Randa**, seven kilometres (four and a half miles) south-east of Algaida, rises like a vision beneath the surrounding mini-peaks of the **Massís de Randa**. It has a storybook air, with bright, blooming flower gardens, alive with the murmur of bumblebees and the sound of gurgling water trickling through the still-functioning Moorish irrigation system. Traditionally, this was a stop-off point for pilgrims on their way to the monasteries of Gràcia, Sant Honorat and Cura, sited at the bottom, middle and top, respectively, of the neighbouring table mountain called **Puig de Randa**.

Visitors in search of a couple of days of quiet contemplation can still stay at the **Santuari de Cura** (*see p176*). You'll be plagued by coach parties by day, but at night it'll be just you and the 360-degree view over the plains, with, to the south, the island of Cabrera looking like it's floating in the sky. The only blot is a group of large radio masts next to the monastery.

The illustrious Mallorcan scholar, preacher and linguist **Ramón Llull** (*see p20* **Local heroes**) founded the island's first hermitage here in the 13th century (most of the current buildings, however, are faceless and modern). The monastery later became an important seat of learning, and you can see artefacts from this period and from Llull's own lifetime in the former grammar school hall, including Llull's original manuscripts and empty bottles of monk-made liqueur. The current chapel was built bit by bit throughout the 17th and 18th centuries. There's a crib here all year round, according to Franciscan tradition. Because of the monastery's position looking down over acres of farmland, a 'blessing of the fruits' ceremony is held here every year on the fourth Sunday after Easter.

Gordiola
Ctra. Palma–Manacor, km19 (971 66 50 46/www.gordiola.com). **Open** *May-Sept* 9am-8pm Mon-Sat; 9am-1pm Sun. *Oct-Apr* 9am-7pm Mon-Sat; 9am-1pm Sun. **Admission** free. **Photo** *p174.*

Natura Parc
Ctra. Palma–Sineu, km15.4, Santa Eugènia (971 14 40 78/www.mallorcaweb.net/naturaparc). **Open** *May-Sept* 10am-6.30pm daily. *Oct-Apr* 10am-5.30pm daily. **Admission** €7; €4.50 concessions. **No credit cards.**

Where to stay & eat

In the centre of **Algaida**, **Apartaments Rurals Raïms** (C/Ribera 24, 971 66 51 57, www.finca-raims.com, suite €105, apartments €115-€130), offers one suite and four apartments in a 17th-century manor house and bodega. Wine is still made here under the Oliver Moragues label and guests can learn about the process (and taste the results). Rooms are light and chic, with white walls and white linen. There's a beautiful garden, where you can sit or even have a massage, and a pool. Bikes are available free to guests.

Many Palma residents head out this way for Sunday lunch at one of Algaida's traditional restaurants, such as **Cal Dimoni** (Ctra. Palma–Manacor, km21, 971 66 50 35, closed Wed, €€), for meat *a la brasa*, or **Ca'n Mateu** (Ctra. Palma–Manacor, km21, 971 66 50 36, closed Tue, €€) for suckling pig.

North-west of Algaida, in **Santa Eugènia**, is the lovely agroturismo **Sa Torre de Santa Eugènia** (C/Alqueries 70, 971 14 40 11, www.sa-torre.com, apartments for 2 €123), which has apartments with kitchens and terraces, plus two pools and a hugely atmospheric cellar restaurant.

A few kilometres north-east of Algaida, close to the hamlet of **Pina**, **Son Xotano** (Ctra. Pina–Sencelles, km1.5, 971 87 25 00, www.sonxotano.com, doubles/suites €173-€231) is a terribly grand *possessió* that has been in the hands of Don Pedro Ramonell's family since the 13th century (the current house dates from the 16th century). However, its grandeur is tempered with a real homely feeling; Son Xotano isn't as modern or overstyled as some *hoteles rurales*. Its gardens are rambling, its rooms filled with a jumble of antiques and family memorabilia, and there are plenty of nooks and crannies for relaxing in the shade and for children – who are made extremely welcome here – to explore. Rooms are large and comfortable and some have terraces. You are stuck out of the way here, but there's plenty to do: swim in the pool, ride the estate's own pure-bred horses, rent bikes or just walk around the estate. The restaurant in the former wine cellar, **Es Menjador des Canonges** (open to non-residents, €€€) is a treat too.

There's also a fine place to eat in the village of **Pina**: **Es Molí de Pina** (C/Sant Plácid 3, 971 12 53 03, closed dinner Sun, all Mon & Tue and Aug, €€) is, as its name suggests, in an old windmill, and offers up classic seasonal Mallorcan dishes and first-rate desserts and cakes.

A couple of kilometres north of Pina, in the tiny village of **Ruberts**, is **Son Jordà** (Ctra. de Sineu, km22, 971 87 22 79, www.sonjorda.com, doubles €100 incl breakfast, restaurant closed Thur), a sizeable 16th-century finca consisting of three wings, 21 bedrooms, a chapel, restaurant, swimming pool and tennis court.

In **Randa**, **Es Recó de Randa** (C/Font 13, 971 66 09 97, 971 12 03 02, www.esrecoderanda. com, doubles €145, restaurant €€) is a rambling collection of buildings within a 17th-century convent, and has one of the most beautiful gardens on the island, with spectacular views. This is a cosy spot to stay and/or eat if you happen to be on the island in the winter, with its open fires and oil lamps. The restaurant serves up first-rate Mallorcan fare, such as wood-roasted suckling pig. There's a pool too.

Other eating options in Randa include **Ca's Beato** (C/Tanqueta 1, 971 12 03 00, closed Mon, €€), which offers classy versions of Mallorcan dishes, such as cuttlefish stuffed with *sobrassada* or pork steak stuffed with giant prawns in sweet wine, within an old stone-walled dining room and out on the sunny rear terrace; it's very popular with groups visiting the nearby sanctuary. For more space and cheaper, simpler dishes try **Celler Bar Randa** (C/Església 24, 971 66 09 89, closed Wed and mid June-mid July, €) further down the slope, a lively, informal bar-restaurant serving the likes of quail, snails, tortilla, and egg and chips.

If funds are tight and you have a taste for fine views, you can overnight in the recently refurbished accommodation at the **Santuari de Cura** (Puig de Randa, 971 12 02 60, www.santuariodecura.com, €40). Alternatively, you can just stop by for a cheap lunch of traditional *pa amb oli* bread rubbed with tomato and topped with either ham or cheese, with local pickles; the restaurant (971 66 11 83, closed Mon, €) is incongruously stuffed full of Mallorcan football team memorabilia.

Resources

Police station
Algaida *C/Rei 6 (971 12 53 35/mobile 639 68 11 70).*

Post office
Algaida *Sa Plaça 2 (971 12 53 43).*

Getting there

By bus
From Palma there are 5 buses Mon-Fri (4 Sat, 2 Sun) to Muro via Inca and Sa Pobla. Between Palma and Petra 4 buses run Mon-Fri (3 Sat, 2 Sun) via Montuïri, Sant Joan and Vilafranca. There are 9 buses Mon-Fri (6 Sat, 5 Sun) between Palma and Felanitx via Algaida and Porreres.

By train
There are 13-14 trains daily between Palma and Sa Pobla (53mins) via Muro (49mins) and Inca, and 13-14 trains daily between Palma and Manacor (1hr 4mins) via Sineu (48mins) and Petra (56mins).

South Mallorca

Cap de Cala Figuera. *See p97*.

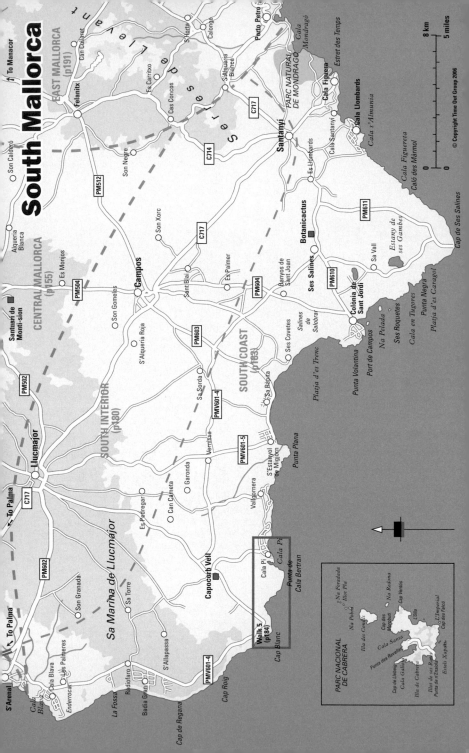

South Mallorca

Wedged between the Bay of Palma tower blocks and the resorts of the east coast is the island's little explored, little developed empty quarter.

As the last of the Bay of Palma's resort high-rises fades out of view, there's an abrupt change in landscape. Horizontal lines replace vertical, and the heaving holiday hordes suddenly vanish. Locals are as scarce as tourists on the wind-scoured southern plains, while the coastline is only fitfully marked by half-hearted resorts, which become more appealing as you round the island's south-eastern tip.

SOUTH INTERIOR

For such a densely populated island, the sparsely settled south comes as a surprise and a relief. True, it's a relatively harsh, flat, scrubby place, but it provides a welcome window on to a rural Mallorca little affected by decades of tourism. The main towns of Llucmajor and the more attractive Campos and Santanyí have a languid, likeable air, and some of the island's loveliest and most isolated rural hotels provide stylish oases of utter peace that you might have thought impossible to find on the Mediterranean's most popular holiday island. The quiet of the country roads is disturbed only by the swish of massed groups of lycra-clad cyclists.

Cala Santanyí. See p188.

The best...

Beaches
Cala Mondragó (*p188*); **Platja d'es Trenc** (*p183*).

Hotels
Son Bernadinet, Campos (*p180*); **Son Cosmet**, Campos (*p180*); **Son Marimón**, Santanyí (*p182*).

Resorts & towns
Cala Figuera (*p188*); **Cala Llombards** (*p188*); **Santanyí** (*p188*).

Restaurants
Bar Tropical, Cala Llombards (*p188*); **Bar-Restaurant Sa Font**, Santanyí (*p181*); **Ca'n Pep**, Sa Ràpita (*p186*); **Restaurant Es Brot**, Campos (*p180*)

SOUTH COAST

The relative paucity of long sandy beaches (Platja d'es Trenc is a notable exception), together with the almost constant wind and uncompromisingly flat landscape, means that tourist development along the south coast has been relatively ragged, intermittent and unconvincing. Cala Pi enjoys probably the best site, and there's a fine coastal walk from here, but none of the other resorts in the area are enticing. Colònia de Sant Jordi is undoubtedly the liveliest coastal base in the summer, and it's from here that must-do boat trips leave for the pristine islands of the Cabrera national park. Things pick up when you round the tip of the Cap de Ses Salines, with a scattering of munchkin-sized fishing villages, intimate coves, sapphire waters and secluded farmhouse hotels.

South Interior

Little to see, but some lovely places to stay.

Llucmajor & Campos

As you head east on the main road from S'Arenal and Palma the first place you come to is the unremarkable, dusty settlement of **Llucmajor** (27 kilometres/17 miles south-east of Palma), long a centre of the island's shoe-making industry. The town today is dominated by the handsome 17th-century church of **Sant Bonaventura**.

Despite its medieval origins there's little of note to the town today, though its main square, Plaça Espanya, is attractive and has a couple of decent high-ceilinged old bars, populated by old men in berets and checked shirts swatting flies and playing on fruit machines. A fruit and vegetable market takes place here on Wednesdays, Fridays and Sundays – its Friday incarnation also features clothes and bric-a-brac stalls.

In 1349 one of the most decisive events in Mallorcan history took place just outside the town, when the last independent king of Mallorca, Jaume III, was killed at the **Battle of Llucmajor** by the forces of Pere IV of Aragón. The island was never to be independently ruled again.

A further 13 kilometres (eight miles) south-east on the main road is another typical – but distinctly more attractive – rural town, **Campos**. Founded in 1300 by Jaume II on the site of earlier Roman and Arab settlements, it now serves as the market garden for the coast (there's a good fresh produce market on Thursdays and Saturdays). Its narrow streets, lined by huddled, honey-hued houses, make for an enjoyable short wander.

Fans of the Sevillian artist Murillo can check out his painting of Christ in the **Museu Parroquial** (C/Bisbe Tellades 17, 971 65 00 03, santjulia@terra.es, €2, usually group visits only, but open to public 1st Sat of month; phone to check) attached to the church of **Sant Julià**. There is also a famed pâtisserie, **Pastisseria Pomar** (C/de sa Plaça 20, 971 65 06 06), which was founded in 1902, the super cool 'lifestyle store' and art gallery **Alina** (C/Santanyí 12, 971 65 15 94, www.alina.com, call for opening hours), the excellent Es Brot restaurant (*see below*) and some superb and seriously off-the-beaten-path places to stay in the surrounding plains.

Where to stay, eat & drink

In **Llucmajor**, there are plenty of cafés for light snacks around Plaça Espanya. Just outside town, on the road to Campos, you'll find a reasonably priced, rustically decorated restaurant offering traditional Mallorcan cuisine, **Ca'n Tià Taleca** (C/Campos 115, 971 66 02 79, closed Wed, €€). The restaurant was founded in the 1970s, and menus from the period hang on the walls; the current vast menu includes sea bass baked in salt, rabbit with shellfish, suckling pig, pastas and pizzas.

In **Campos**, **Restaurant Es Brot** (C/Ràpita 44, 971 16 02 63, closed dinner Sun and all Mon, €€€) has been featured in a number of magazines and won the Mallorcan national gastronomic competition three years in a row. The secret of its success? Artistically presented dishes created with the finest ingredients and an obsession with quality. The menu offers specialities like duck liver, *solomillo de ternera bearnesa* (steak in a béarnaise sauce) and *fava de varada* (a typical Mallorcan bean dish). Unusually for Spain, all desserts are home-made and include a wonderful *biscuit glace de almendra con chocolate caliente* (almond ice-cream wafer with a hot chocolate sauce).

In terms of places to stay, here is where rural tourism really comes into its own. Time stands still at the country manor of **Son Bernadinet** (Ctra. Campos–Porreres, km5.9, 971 65 06 94, www.sonbernadinet.com, closed 1 Dec-10 Jan, doubles €188-€214 incl breakfast), which you'll find at the end of a long pine-wooded lane. The farm has been in the family for 200 years and the owners go all out to make you feel like one of them. With a cool, spacious interior and vast lawns, vegetable gardens and aromatic herb beds outside, the place exudes calm. Not to be missed is the home-produce breakfast, and the nightly changing three-course dinner for guests.

South of Campos, **Son Cosmet** (Ctra. Campos–Sa Ràpita, km2, 971 65 16 43, www.soncosmet.com, doubles €148-€188 incl breakfast) is another bucolic idyll; a stunning old manor house in splendid isolation, set amid gardens dotted with terracotta urns of geraniums and fields of grazing horses, where nothing cuts through the silence but birdsong and the tinkle of goat bells. There are no TVs or minibars, but the house is stuffed with antiques, many of them museum pieces, and

there are enough quiet corners and terraces
to spend a long weekend here without setting
eyes on a soul. Seemingly invisible staff restock
a wonderful breakfast buffet and magically
replace used beach towels with clean by the pool.

Just south of here, **Es Palmer** (Ctra. Campos–
Colònia de Sant Jordi, km6.4, 971 18 12 65, www.
espalmer.com, doubles €70-€114 incl breakfast)
has ten rooms dotted around a palm grove, each
with a terrace and slightly eccentric touches;
nicest are the rooms in an old windmill. The
restaurant provides simple home cooking and
is cosy in winter, when there is a log fire and a
wood-fired oven for roast lamb and suckling pig.

Santanyí

Around 14 kilometres (nine miles) south-east
of Campos along the C717, and the same
distance north-east of Colònia de Sant Jordi
on the coast, is the attractive small town
of **Santanyí**, founded in 1300. A massive
golden sandstone gateway (Sa Porta Murada)
gives on to narrow streets lined with squat
townhouses and cottages, which centre on the
elongated main square and hilltop church of
Sant Andreu Apostel. The local honeyed
sandstone is much in evidence throughout
the town; it was also used in the construction
of Palma's cathedral and Sa Llotja.

Saturday is market day and the best time
to visit Santanyí. Its streets throb with life and
colour, and Plaça Major bursts with nature's
bounty. As well as stalls selling everything from
ironmongery to jewellery and cloth (look out
for the traditional Mallorcan fabric, the 'cloth of
tongues'), there are some interesting shops here,
such as **Ceramiques de Santanyí** (C/Guàrdia
Civil 22, 971 16 31 28), which produces artisan
ceramics and specialises in a unique metallic
glaze; all the objects are hand-made and are
original designs. **Reina Rana** (Plaça Major
15, 971 64 20 75) is a German-run jewellery
and accessory shop, dripping with crystals
and semi-precious stones. **Vinos Artesanos
Binissalem** (C/Pau s/n, mobile 636 40 15 02)
is a small, friendly shop with a well-chosen
selection of Mallorcan wine at decent prices.

From Santanyí, the beaches and small-scale
resorts of the south-east coast are just a few
kilometres away (*see p183*).

Where to stay, eat & drink

Santanyí's Plaça Major has several cafés and
tapas bars, the best of which is the funky **Bar-
Restaurant Sa Font** (Plaça Major 27, 971 16 34
92, €), with young, friendly staff serving *pa amb
oli* topped with cheese, ham and so on, alongside
crêpes and Galician cider served in traditional

Sant Julià church in **Campos**.

ceramic bowls. **Sa Cova Galeria Bar** (Plaça
Major 30, 971 16 31 46, closed Nov, €€) has
salads and sandwiches, internet access, twice-
weekly live music sessions in summer (Wed and
Sat from 9pm) and a free-for-all singalong music
session from 5pm on Sundays (providing 'food
for the spirit', according to co-owner Jean).

For something more substantial, or simply
an atmospheric drink, **Sa Gripia** (C/Obispo
Verguer 26, 971 65 38 52, closed Tue, €€€) has
an excellent selection of Mallorcan specialities,
such as *rodet* (stuffed cabbage leaves) and
quails with raisins, cabbage and pine nuts,
along with baked fish, paella and steaks.
Enter through an art gallery of the same name
and emerge into a charming courtyard, where
tables are laid out in the shade and the only
irritating feature is the piped music.

There's nowhere to stay in Santanyí,
but off the C714 heading north towards
Ca's Concos you'll find **Sa Galera** (Ctra.
Santanyí–Ca's Concos, km6.3, 971 84 20
79, www.hotelsagalera.com, closed 1 Nov-10
Jan, €169-€212 incl breakfast). This lovely
13th-century manor stands within an estate
that includes 5,000 almond trees and one

of the island's most important centres for the breeding of thoroughbred Mallorcan horses. There are 16 smart, fresh rooms, a big pool and a restaurant.

Off the C717 between Santanyí and Alqueria Blanca is another good *agroturismo*, **Son Marimón** (Ctra. Santanyi–Alqueria Blanca, km1.4, 971 18 17 04, www.sonmarimon.com, closed Dec-mid Jan, doubles €110-€136 incl breakfast). Outside it resembles a cute storybook castle, with its mini-crenellated tower; inside it's more fairytale farmhouse (dating from 1832), with white coverlets, fresh flowers and rough stone walls. All five rooms/suites have a view and most of them have terraces.

Resources

Police station

Campos *Ctra.Campos–Felanitx s/n (971 65 16 26).*
Llucmajor *C/Andalucia s/n (971 66 90 00).*
Santanyí *Plaça Major 12 (971 65 30 02).*

Post office

Campos *C/Sa Siquia 15 (971 65 01 64).*
Llucmajor *C/París 45 (971 66 05 07).*
Santanyí *C/Centre 28 (971 65 30 48).*

Getting there

See p190.

The Saturday market in **Santanyí**. *See p181.*

South Coast

Tourism is low-key in Mallorca's empty quarter.

Cala Pi, Es Trenc & Colònia de Sant Jordi

South of the main C717 road running through Llucmajor and Campos to Santanyí is Mallorca's empty quarter – a largely flat, hypnotically desolate, sparsely populated swath of country that is edged by a smattering of unconvincing little resorts.

Coming from S'Arenal by the coast road the first settlement you arrive at is **Cala Blava**, a pleasant enough *urbanización*. From here to **Cap Blanc** it's a wilderness drive, with long tracts of desert-like scrub stretching into the distance among a patchwork of almond and citrus orchards and wild olive groves. You can't access the lighthouse and old watchtower at the cape itself as the area is part of a flyblown military facility, looking much like a neglected holiday camp.

The road turns inland here and, after five or so minutes' driving, sweeps past **Capocorb Vell**, one of the most important prehistoric sites in the Balearics. Spread over an extensive area (though the original village was far larger) are the remains of no fewer than five talayots (two quadrangular, three conical) and 28 dwellings. The settlement was probably founded around 1000 BC, and continued in use into Roman times. A marked trail takes you around the village, while a leaflet in English explains what you are seeing. Buy tickets at the rustic outdoor bar, which keeps the same hours as the ruins and in itself makes a pleasant roadside stop for a beer or an ice-cream.

Heading back towards the coast, a finger-shaped gorge nuzzles its way into the plain from the turquoise bay of **Cala Pi** – the OAP of Mallorca's tourist developments. There's little going on here, but this is its charm, and the largely low-rise villas and hotels have been sensitively landscaped to lessen their environmental impact. From the small beach, walled in by tall limestone cliffs, you can walk to even smaller, more private inlets (*see p184* **Walk 5**). Climb up the cliffs that rise behind the boathouses, walk around the point and across shallow cliffs dotted with wild flowers for sweeping views across the sea to the island of Cabrera and, on clear days, the hazy outline of Ibiza; it's a fabulous picnic spot.

Continuing along the coast, there's nothing much to detain you in **S'Estanyol de Migjorn** and **Sa Ràpita** – dusty, windswept, low-rise developments that wouldn't look out of place in a western movie – unless you're going to eat at the memorable Ca'n Pep (*see p186*).

The main draw in this part of the island lies east of here – **Platja d'es Trenc**, the only lengthy stretch of sand on Mallorca that has escaped heavy development. To reach it, head out of Sa Ràpita towards Campos, and you soon come to a badly signed right turn down a bumpy road through flower-filled meadows, passing old windmills and farmhouses, with chickens on the road and poppies on the verges. At the next junction turn right to **Ses Covetes**. Park on the road or pay for the car park near the beach. At the end of this road a rocky coastline is bordered by a few battered holiday homes and a couple of beach bars.

Turn right for a small, relatively quiet beach upon which the only building is the expensive but unbeatably located Sa Copinya bar-restaurant (*see p186*). Alternatively, follow the coast round to the left as you face the sea and you'll come to one of the island's most amazing beaches. Now a nature reserve, it is backed by gently undulating sand dunes sprung with elephant grass and squat pines, and offers a three and a half kilometre- (two mile-) long, gently curving expanse of soft sand served by a single beach bar with shady tables and great *pomadas* (Menorcan gin with lemon ice).

Behind the beach lie the **Salines de Llevant**, salt pans that attract around 170 migratory bird species. The other main access to Es Trenc is from the Campos–Colònia de Sant Jordi road, a couple of kilometres north of the latter – there is no development at this end of the beach and fewer tourists.

Colònia de Sant Jordi is the main settlement on this stretch of coast and the best base. The outskirts of this one-time fishing village are undistinguished: a grid of chunky apartment blocks that border the salt pans (good for birdwatching and a gentle stroll, but otherwise not wildly interesting). The port, however, has some charm; modest fishing craft bob in the sheltered bay in front of an arc of bistros and cafés.

Walk 5 Cala Pi to Cap Blanc

Distance: 13km (8 miles). Linear.
Time: 3hrs 30mins.

The southern coast of Mallorca is far less developed than the Bay of Palma and the northern and eastern shorelines. While this has much to do with its lack of beaches, its reputation as an often bleak, wind-whipped wilderness probably doesn't help. This clifftop walk, however, reveals a wild and ruggedly beautiful side to the south that few visitors see (yet it's little more than 30 minutes' drive from Palma). It has a (very) short climb at the beginning, and some scrambling over rocks, but is otherwise pretty level and easy. As it's a linear walk, you can obviously cut it short at any point. Cala Pi offers plenty of dining and drinking opportunities.

Park in Cala Pi and follow the signs to the beach ('Platja'). Descend the steps to the small strand sitting snugly at the end of an inlet, sheltered by cliffs on either side. A great setting, though marred a little by the smelly seaweed that sometimes clogs up the beach. On the far side is a line of boathouses. Walk in front of them, in the direction of the sea, and at the last of the row of six solidly built houses turn immediately right and walk up some steps (not easy to see) at the back of the house and on to its flat roof. From here it's a steep but short climb of less than a minute up the rocks (with some rough-hewn steps) to the path at the top of the cliff.

Turn left, and follow the path as it dips into a little gulley, then rises through a gap in a stone wall. As you walk along, take in the views back down the inlet and across to the *atalaya*, one of many 16th-century watchtowers that still stand sentinel over Mallorca's coastline and once warned the islanders of the approach of Muslim pirates. You walk for a while with a drystone wall on your right, bearing left at its end to stay close to the clifftop, before coming to a wider track that heads inland (with a largely broken-down stone wall on its right).

Continue on this path to get around the narrow, snaking Cala Beltrán inlet, where you'll meet a wide gravel track. After a couple of minutes on this track, take a rough path to the left (marked by two cairns) for less than a minute before coming up to a clear track leading back towards the cliffs; turn left on to this.

You soon hit the open rocky clifftops at Punta de Capocorb. (You should be about half an hour into the walk by this point.) Locals often fish from the rocks. In the distance, on a clear day, you can see the islands of Cabrera. From here, it shouldn't be possible to go wrong, providing you keep the sea on your left, though the rock scrambling can be punishing on the ankles. Cairns mark a route higher up, which is perhaps easier than picking your own way. The cliffs gradually rise to more impressive heights as you continue. You'll need to head upwards as they become more sheer, fortified by the tang of the wild rosemary scattered among the rocks.

You may get as high as an unexpected stretch of gravel road. Follow this a short distance and then take a left back on to the cairn-marked path, where someone has helpfully made a big arrow with stones.

It's easier on the feet from here on. Continue along the ever-higher cliff edge, bearing left at a 'gateway' made by two wind-sculpted bushes and a ruined stone building as the path heads around the bay of Es Carril. For some time you'll have been able to see the *atalaya* that marks (just beyond) the walk's furthest point on the headland opposite. Follow the cliffs around the bay and then go through a gap in a stone wall which is topped with barbed wire. Ten minutes later you'll arrive at another barbed wire-enhanced stone wall, but, alas, this time there's no gap, just a sign saying 'Stop – Zona Militar'. This is the turnaround point, somewhat frustratingly – the watchtower is only a further five minutes away.

Retrace your steps back to Cala Pi.

From here you can take day-long boat trips to the offshore nature reserve of **Cabrera** (*see p189* **Virgin islands**), or spend long, lazy days exploring nearby virgin beaches.

From the **Platja d'es Port**, with its thatched parasols, sun loungers and Hobie Cats (fun-size catamarans), you can walk around the rocks eastwards to the aptly named **Es Dolç**

('Sweet Beach') and, if you have the energy, all the way to Cap de Ses Salines (about seven kilometres/four and a half miles one way; *see p185*), taking in magnificently secluded beaches en route, such as **Platja d'es Carbó** and **Platja d'es Caragol**. Allow a day to walk to the Cap and back, and bring plenty of water and a picnic; there are no refuelling stops.

South Mallorca

A less touristy place than Colònia de Sant
Jordi to stop for a break and a meal is **Ses
Salines**, a sleepy village five kilometres (three
miles) inland. It's dominated by its church and
named for the nearby salt flats; the marshes
are a birdwatcher's paradise, and home to
species such as cranes, kestrels and ospreys.

Just outside the village is **Botanicactus**,
a large but somewhat tired and desultory
botanical garden containing a lake, lawns,
palms, bamboo and more than 400 species
of cactus; one specimen is over 300 years old.

Botanicactus

*Ctra. Ses Salines–Santanyi s/n (971 64 94 94/
www.botanicactus.com).* **Open** *May-Sept* 9am-7pm
daily. *Oct-Apr* 9am-5pm daily. **Admission** €6.50;
€4 concessions. **No credit cards.**

Capocorb Vell

Ctra. Llucmajor–Cap Blanc, km23 (971 18 01 55).
Open 10am-5pm Mon-Wed, Fri-Sun; 10am-2pm
Thur. **Admission** €2. **No credit cards.**

Where to stay, eat & drink

After a visit to Capocorb Vell, get back with
the living at the bustling roadside diner **Cas
Busso** (Ctra. Cap Blanc, km24, 971 12 30 02,
closed Tue and Jan-Feb, €€); it specialises
in meats roasted in the wood-fired oven,
or you can book a day in advance for paella.
In **Cala Pi**, the €7 weekday lunchtime *menú*
at **Sa Terrassa** (Passeig Cala Pi 391, 971 12
31 65, closed Sat, €€) is good value, but it's
the *piedras* (meat cooked on a hot stone)
that everyone comes for. In terms of where
to stay, you're much better off heading further
round the coast as most of Cala Pi is devoted
to timeshares and private villas.

Just about the only reason to visit **Sa Ràpita**
is to eat at **Ca'n Pep** (Avda. Miramar 30, 971
64 01 02, closed Tue and Feb, €€€), a wonderful
seafood restaurant that exudes delicious odours
from its justly renowned bouillabaise and great
selection of fish. It's incredibly popular at
weekend lunchtimes, so book ahead.

Near **Es Trenc** beach, secluded **Can
Canals** (Ctra. Campos–Sa Ràpita, km7, 971
64 07 57, www.cancanals.com, junior suites
€120-€150 incl breakfast) offers 12 junior
suites, a restaurant (in the evening) and (from
2006) a spa. Located just a minute's walk from
the southernmost end of the beach, four-star
El Coto (Avda. Primavera 8, 971 65 50 25,
www.elcoto.de, closed Nov-Feb, doubles
€90-€146 incl breakfast) has all the usual
trimmings, including minibars, air-conditioning
and a large pool set in splendid gardens.

At **Ses Covetes**, refreshment can be had
at **Restaurant-Café Noray** (C/Murters s/n,

Cap de Ses Salines. *See p188.*

mobile 607 98 26 35, closed Oct-Feb, €), or
on the small beach to the west at **Sa Copinya**
(Platja de Ses Covetes, 971 64 10 57, closed
Nov-15 Mar, €€€).

In terms of accommodation (and food) in
Colònia de Sant Jordi, a good bet is the
Hostal & Restaurante Playa (C/Major
25, 971 65 52 56, www.rcstauranteplaya.com,
closed lunch Mon, €€€, doubles €72-€80 incl
breakfast), a converted fisherman's cottage
cluttered with Mallorcan rustic bric-a-brac,
china and glassware, overlooking a secluded
beach on the north side of town; ask for a room
with a balcony overlooking the sea. Opened
in 1921, it's the oldest hotel in town, with
a quiet whitewashed terrace scattered with
flowers. Specials here are spanking fresh, salt-
baked fish and a fine paella, but prices reflect
the lovely location.

Just around the corner, **Hostal Colonial**
(C/Ingeniero Gabriel Roca 9, 971 65 52 78,
www.hostal-colonial.com, closed Nov-Feb,
doubles €46-€54 incl breakfast) has been
in the same family for three generations and
is one of the best bargains in town for good-
value, no-frills accommodation; all rooms
are immaculate and have a small balcony
or terrace. The owners run a taxi company

La Reseva Rotana · Golf · Hotel · Restaurant
Cami de s'Avall km 3 · 07500 Manacor
Tel: +34 971 845685 · Fax: +34 971 555258
info@reservarotana.com · www.reservarotana.com

A private paradise on Majorca

At LA RESERVA ROTANA the authentic undisturbed Majorca has been conserved where golfers enjoy the luxury of a private 9-hole golf course. The golfers can play **without any stress and as many times as they desire at their own rhythm. There is no need of any tee time!** As the course is exclusively reserved for the guests of the hotel with its 21 rooms, it is impossible that the players suffer from an overcrowded course or any waiting periods.

LA RESERVA ROTANA is a paradise of **tranquility and relaxation** on the island. The hotel is located on a hill, the heart of a private 300-acre Finca surrounded by the own vineyard, olive plantations and flocks of sheep.
The 17th century mansion has been transformed to a charming hotel where with love to the detail the typical Majorcan style has been preserved. All this with the hospitality and personalized service of a great team.
At the restaurant a charming team serves delicious creations made of only fresh products from the own Finca or market. Enjoy with it the Merlot of the own bodega or wines from best Spanish vineyards.

No better location: sapphire waters and golden sands at **Cala Santanyí**. *See p188.*

and can pick up and drop off at the airport, and have made a name for themselves with their home-made ice-cream.

In the centre of town, the modern three-star **Hotel Martorell** (C/Cervantes 2, 971 65 50 30, closed Nov-Mar, doubles €62 incl breakfast) has a mainly German clientele and is another good-value place, with 24 comfortable rooms – all with balconies – and a swimming pool.

Between the beaches of Es Dolç and Es Port, the **Pensión Es Turó** (Plaça Es Dolç, 971 65 50 57, closed Nov-Apr, doubles €42-€52 incl breakfast) has pristine, spartan rooms with balconies in a squat block; prices vary according to the view – street, port or sea. There is a simple restaurant (€) with a comfy seaside terrace too.

If you had something more rural in mind, **Ses Rotes Velles** (Ctra. Campos–Colònia de Sant Jordi, km8.7, 971 65 61 59, www.ses rotesvelles.com, closed Dec-Jan, doubles €110-€140 incl breakfast) is a stone's throw from the bustle of the town, and very popular among German tourists. Villa-style accommodation gives added privacy, while the pool and shady terraces provide a pleasant focal point for drinks and meeting your neighbours.

The **Hotel Balneario San Juan de la Font Santa** (Ctra. Campos–Colònia de Sant Jordi, km8.2, 971 65 50 16, www.balneariodelafont santa.com, closed Nov-Mar, doubles €109 incl breakfast), the only *baños* (spa) in the Balearics,

feels more like an old people's home than a place to relax and revitalise. A pity because the 38-degree waters are apparently excellent, but here they are siphoned into clinical bath cubicles (19 in all). The spa is open to the public 9-11am and 4-5.30pm Mon-Fri (€10.50 per session).

For breakfast and picnic fodder in Colònia de Sant Jordi, head for **Panaderia Pons** (C/Major 29, 971 65 51 71, closed Mon) for dreamy *ensaïmadas* and other local pastries. On the port, the **Port Blau** (971 65 65 55, closed Tue and Nov-Mar, €€€) knocks up a fine *mariscada* (a decadent platter of lobster, giant shrimp, prawns, clams, mussels, razor clams and fresh fish) for €32. A couple of blocks back from the port, to the east end, is **Es Carbó** (C/Ingeniero Gabriel Roca 123, 971 65 64 96, closed Tue, €€€) a restaurant specialising in high-quality seafood with prices to match, but largely frequented by locals.

Ses Salines is a good place to lunch. Of the various tapas bars on the main drag, the best is tiny **Casa Manolo** (Plaça Bartomeu 1, 971 64 91 30, closed Mon and Sept, €€), with 50 superbly fresh and simply cooked choices. Photos of its customers, running the A- to Z-list celebrity gamut from the crown prince of Spain and his new bride to German soap actors, are testament to its mythical status on the island.

Just outside the village, **Es Turó** (Camí de Cas Perets, 971 64 95 31, www.esturo.com, doubles €110-€146, closed Nov-Dec) has ten large and peaceful rooms in buildings that have been owned by the same family for 200 years. The colourful gardens and pool area offer plenty of quiet corners to read or contemplate the view across the plain and beyond to the island of Cabrera.

Also on the outskirt of Ses Salines is **Finca Sa Carrotja** (Sa Carrotja 7, 971 64 90 53, www.sacarrotja.com, closed Dec-Jan, doubles €90-€140 incl breakfast), part of which dates back to the 16th century. There are six inviting bedrooms, with air-con and period furniture; five have their own terraces. Genial hosts Guillem and Pilar will rustle you up a fine dinner on request. There's a pool too.

Calas Llombards, Santanyí, Figuera & Mondragó

From the Colònia de Sant Jordi–Ses Salines–Santanyí road (PM610), a long, straight road heads south for ten kilometres (six miles) through bush and burr to the lighthouse at Mallorca's southernmost point, **Cap de Ses Salines**. This is one of the windiest parts of the island, as the countless fallen trees in the area testify. The lighthouse here is of no great size, age (built in 1993) or beauty (and there's no public access to it), but it's worth making the journey to enjoy the wildness of the spot and to walk the rocky shoreline and gaze out towards Cabrera. The wide shelf of rock and reef makes swimming tricky, but the area is beloved by windsurfers who gather here in droves. Keep walking around the headland to your right when facing the sea and after about 25 minutes you'll come to the beautiful **Platja d'es Caragol**.

You could easily spend a day losing yourself around the laid-back *calas* a few kilometres south-east of Santanyí, which are particularly popular with German tourists. The most westerly, **Cala Llombards**, is a mellow, secluded bay with a funky beach bar that has a penchant for 1970s rock music (*see p188*), unnatural blue water and high cliffs folding gently over themselves; you could almost be in Jamaica.

If things are a little too chilled here, continue on to family-oriented **Cala Santanyí**, the closest these tiny coves get to a resort town. The beach isn't quite so idyllic here, thanks to the hotel that rises along one side of it, but the location is splendid, with sapphire waters lapping on to golden sand through a canyon carved into the limestone. There are plenty of good walks up to the cliffs and the giant natural arch of Portals, created by millennia of persistent waves. Follow signs from the top of the town just above the Hotel Pinos Playa.

When you reach the end of the tarmac, bear left down a dirt track until you arrive at an obelisk of sandstone blocks. Continue down the cliff on the footpath and you'll come out just above the arch.

Beyond this, tourist development is far from unknown in **Cala Figuera**, but has yet to completely dominate. There's no beach as such, but you could easily clamber into the sea from the boat slipways, and you often see sunbathers toasting themselves on the weathered quay. With a thriving café scene in the summer months, there's no shortage of places to eat and drink; it's a romantic spot come nightfall. To find the picture-perfect fishing port, with its whitewashed, green-shuttered cottages tumbling down towards the sea, take the unmarked left turn just before town.

If you feel the need for a complete break from tourist development, head across parched, ochre plains from here to the 785-hectare (1,940-acre) **Parc Natural de Mondragó** (Ctra. Alquería Blanca–Mondragó s/n, 971 18 10 22, open 9am-4pm daily, free). The park can be accessed either from the Cala Figuera side or from the north. Once you've parked, set off on foot to explore pine forests criss-crossed by dusty paths (there are several marked trails, from 20 to 40 minutes long). You'll see plenty of birdlife and, if you're lucky, frolicking hares, rabbits and genets (spotted cat-like relatives of the mongoose), and, on the rocky headlands, sunbathing Balearic lizards – the park's mascot. The rocky coves that protect the southernmost tip of the park are good for sunbathing and snorkelling, though most visitors head for the park's two magnificent white sand beaches. The south beach is the less crowded of the two, but the north beach tends to be more sheltered on a blustery day and has the advantage of a couple of *chiringuitos* for ice-cold beer and snacks.

For the east coast resorts north of Mondragó, *see p187*.

Where to stay, eat & drink

In **Cala Llombards**, look no further than **Bar Tropical** (mobiles 649 41 63 49, 608 43 76 95, closed Nov-Mar, €€), the quintessential beach bar – a dying breed, alas, on this island. There is probably nowhere finer on all Mallorca to eat the freshest, best-quality fish these waters have left to offer, charred on the griddle and served with nothing but a squeeze of lemon juice and maybe some garlic. Up on the hillside, **Casa Poesia** (Avda. Cala Llombards, 971 64 20 62, www.casa-poesia.com, closed Jan, doubles €50) has 17 en-suite rooms and a good-value, creative restaurant (€€) in a modern block.

Virgin islands

With the abolition of the controversial ecotax in 2003, the future of Mallorca's natural spaces looks ever more shaky, vulnerable to the seemingly unquenchable thirst of golfers for new courses. It's all the more reason to visit one of the best-preserved nature reserves in the whole of the Mediterranean, let alone the Balearics – the offshore islands of the **Parc Nacional de Cabrera**.

By far the largest of the archipelago's 17 islands and islets, Isla de Cabrera, lying about 15 kilometres (nine miles) south-west of Cap de Ses Salines, is the only one that can be visited, and then only from March to October (except for groups). Excursions A Cabrera (971 64 90 34, ww.excursionsacabrera.com, €29, lunch €7) runs daily boat trips from Colònia de Sant Jordi harbour, leaving at 9.30am; they're pricey, but worth it. Note that pre-booking (online, by phone or at the booth on the harbourside) is essential. You can also take a boat from Porto Petro harbour (971 65 70 12, €35, lunch €2), which leaves at 9.30am on Sundays in June, and at 9.30am on Mondays and Fridays from July to September; again, pre-booking is essential.

The Excursions A Cabrera trip consists of an hour's spray-lashed boat ride past seabird-laden smaller islands and into Cabrera's large, peaceful natural harbour, where there's a tiny information centre with leaflets in English and a small bar selling drinks and snacks. However, it's best to bring along your own picnic to have on the beach or the large covered picnic area. (The lunch offered by the boat company is not recommended.)

You're restricted to wandering on the island along two fairly short paths. One takes you to a castle perched on a cliff, with sweeping views across to the Bay of Palma. It was built in the late 14th century to stop pirates using the island as a base for raids on Mallorca, and in the 19th century held French prisoners from the Napoleonic Wars. You can still see the soldiers' graffiti on the walls.

The island's other path leads to two wonderful, peaceful beaches – one sandy, the other full of richly teeming rock pools, and both with beautifully clear, enticing waters for swimming.

Because the archipelago is made up of a number of different micro environments, it's an evolutionary hotspot, with different creatures displaying various adaptations. For instance, Cabrera has 80 per cent of the world population of the Balearic lizard, and around ten different subspecies have developed on these islands. You'll see hundreds of them darting frantically across your path. Further interesting discoveries have been made in one of the island's caves, where scientists have found several unique species of crustacea.

This is also a wonderful spot for birdwatching, with many native species of birds, as well as others that stop here on their annual migration or to breed. You could see shags, shearwaters, petrels, the rare Audouin's gull, and birds of prey such as ospreys, kestrels and falcons.

You have about four hours to explore and sunbathe on the island, then, on your even wetter return journey to Mallorca (we recommend you sit inside the boat on the way back), there are stops in Sa Cova Blava (Blue Cave), where the water glows a particularly jewel-like blue and you can have a swim. The boat arrives back in Colònia de Sant Jordi at about 5pm.

Cala Figuera. *See p188.*

Despite its unprepossessing exterior it has some colourful touches, and is run with enthusiasm by young Germans.

Cala Santanyí caters largely for (German) families. Accommodation choices include the **Pinos Playa Hotel y Apartamentos** (Costa d'en Nofre 15, 971 16 50 00, www.pinosplaya. com, closed Nov-Apr, doubles €29-€76.50), which manages to maintain a personal service despite its size. Rooms are large (around half have fine views), and facilities include a diving centre, kindergarten (free), two pools (one heated), squash and tennis courts, a sauna, jacuzzi, three bars and a disco. For somewhere more basic, though on the beach, try the **Hostal Playa** (C/Cova d'es Drac s/n, 971 64 54 09, closed Apr, doubles €45 incl breakfast), which has an attractive little beach restaurant opposite.

In **Cala Figuera**, the two-star **Hotel Villa Sirena** (C/Virgen del Carmen 37, 971 64 53 03, www.hotelvillasirena.com, closed Nov-Mar, doubles €55-€61) sticks out on the promontory (from here the houses fall away exposing slate grey cliffs with well-worn paths for strolling – it's a perfect suntrap). The USP of this otherwise fairly ordinary hotel is the way it has made its own beach by carving platforms into the rock and inserting a ladder into the water to make access easy.

The **Restaurante Hostal Cala** (C/Virgen del Carmen 56, 971 64 50 18, apartments €56) is a real bargain, offering apartments with kitchenettes, wicker furniture and fab balconies over the jewel-like gorge, affording excellent views of the small man-made caves chiselled out of the cliffs. Next door, the **Hostal Ca'n Jordi** (C/Virgen del Carmen 58, 971 64 54 59, closed Nov, doubles €44, apartments €51-€63), run by a family from Yorkshire, is smaller and cheaper, but with similar views and rooms with balconies.

Several bars and restaurants line a pedestrianised stretch of road, where you can dine in the shade of the pines to the sound of gently breaking waves. **Café L'Arcada** (C/Virgen del Carmen 80, 971 64 50 32, closed Nov-Mar, €€) offers a good range of Mallorcan dishes along with pizzas and other safe fare. Nearby, **Es Port** (C/Virgen del Carmen 88, 971 16 51 40, €€) also has pizzas, pastas and a handful of basic Spanish dishes.

For somewhere special, head for **Villa Lorenzo** (C/Magallenes 11, 971 64 50 29, www.villalorenzo.com, closed Nov-Jan, restaurant €€€€, doubles €58 incl breakfast), a great place for top-notch Mallorcan cooking. It's located just a few hundred metres from the port and has a beautiful garden terrace dominated by an old-fashioned brick stove and a pleasant pool for a swim before lunch. The attached *hostal* is great for some quality R&R.

Hostal Playa Mondragó (Platja Mondragó s/n, 971 65 77 52, www.playamondrago.com, closed Nov-Apr, doubles €25-€34), set back from the pristine beach, is a sad example of how to blight a beauty spot. The interior is as uninspiring as the outside (and often booked out by package companies), but if you want to stay in the Parc Natural there's no other option.

Resources

Police station

Colònia de Sant Jordi *C/Doctor Barraquer 5 (971 16 60 35).*
Ses Salines *Plaça Major 1 (971 64 93 11).*

Tourist information

Colònia de Sant Jordi *OIT, C/Doctor Barraquer 5 (971 16 60 05).* **Open** 8am-2pm Mon-Fri.

Getting there

By bus

From Palma, there are 7 buses a day (5 Sat, 2 Sun) to Colònia de Sant Jordi (1hr), calling at Llucmajor and Campos. Also, 5 buses Mon-Fri (3 Sat, 2 Sun) run to Cala d'Or, calling at Llucmajor, Campos and Santanyí. There are 4 buses Mon-Fri (2 Sat) between Colònia de Sant Jordi and Manacor (1hr) via Campos (25mins) and Porreres (35mins). One bus runs Mon-Sat between Palma and Cala Pi.

East Mallorca

Artà. *See p196.*

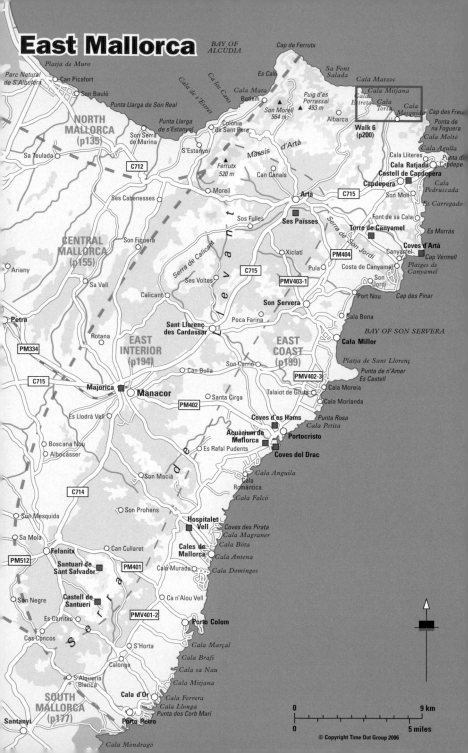

East Mallorca

Less frenetic than the Bay of Palma and Bay of Alcúdia, the east of the island offers a gentle, family-friendly alternative.

The modest peaks of the Serra de Llevant ripple down Mallorca's east flank, providing a faint echo of the lofty Tramuntana range in the west. Although this is the third of the island's major tourism hubs (together with the Bay of Palma, and the north around Pollença and Alcúdia), development here is less intrusive, and the pace of life slower and more relaxed. Consequently, it's particularly popular for family holidays.

EAST INTERIOR
Away from the coast, the Serra de Llevant's hills descend gently into the vast central plain, Es Pla. The east's major artery, the C714/C715, connects the area's main settlements, including Manacor, Mallorca's second largest town and centre of the artificial pearl-making industry, and the far more appealing Artà, which makes a great base for exploring the region.

EAST COAST
The coastline, once marked by pristine coves and specked with fishing villages, has now largely been swallowed up by Daz-white

Pull up at **Porto Colom**. See p204.

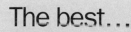

The best...

Beaches
Cala Mesquida (p200); **Cala Mitjana** (p199); **Cala Torta** (p199).

Caves
Coves d'Artà (p203); **Coves del Drac** (p203).

Hotels
Hotel Restaurante S'Abeurador, Artà (p197); **Hotel Sant Salvador**, Artà (p198); **Son Gener**, between Artà and Son Servera (p198); **Son Mas**, near Porto Cristo (p204).

Resorts
Porto Colom (p188); **Porto Petro** (p204).

Restaurants
Finca Es Serral, Artà (p197); **Es Molí d'en Bou**, Sant Llorenç de Cardassar (p196); **Ses Rotges**, Cala Ratjada (p199).

Towns & villages
Artà (p196); **Capdepera** (p199).

holiday complexes, low-rise but land-hungry. However, the resorts here can vary dramatically – from the old-fashioned calm of Porto Colom to the nouveau riche, nouveau Ibiza flash of Cala d'Or and the all-inclusive monster complexes of Cala Millor. The wild north-east, beyond Cala Ratjada, has yet to be (and hopefully never will be) developed. Barren it may be, but here's where to head if you want virgin beaches. The east coast is also home to the biggest and most spectacular of Mallorca's cave systems. (For the laid-back resorts in the south-east between Cala Mondragó and Cala Llombards, see p188.)

East Interior

The modest Serra de Llevant hills form the backbone of the east.

Felanitx & Manacor

The island's main eastern artery, the C714/ C715, runs from Santanyí (*see p188*) through Felanitx and Manacor to Artà. **Felanitx**, the most southerly of the latter three, is crowned by its main attraction, the 16th-century church of **Sant Miquel**, decorated in florid Churrigueresque style, with an impressive organ. An outer wall of the church was rebuilt after it collapsed on a Palm Sunday procession in 1844, killing 414 people. The town's other claims to fame are the local wine (this is Mallorca's junior wine region, after Binissalem) and 'green pearls' – capers, produced in the surrounding farmland – both of which can be purchased, along with local ceramics, at the Sunday morning market.

It's also claimed locally that Felanitx is the birthplace of Christopher Columbus, that he learned to sail in nearby Porto Colom, and that he named the first land he discovered San Salvador after the **Santuari de Sant Salvador** nearby. This sits on the highest peak (516 metres/1,693 feet) at the southern end of the Serra de Llevant. The hair-raising road up to it runs off the Felanitx–Porto Colom road, and the view from the top is certainly amazing enough to inspire world-conquering ambitions. There's a picnic area at the foot of the monastery car park – a wonderful spot for sunsets. You can also spend the night up here in the sanctuary (*see below*).

To the south, on the neighbouring peak (408 metres/1,339 feet), are the ruins of the **Castell de Santuari**, a 14th-century fortress on the site of an earlier Moorish castle. Ask at the monastery for directions to the footpath (it's about a three-kilometre/two-mile walk) or, alternatively, you can drive up to the castle from a minor road off the main C714. Frustratingly, you have to make do with gazing up at the ramparts as there's no access to the ruins from the road.

Located 18 kilometres (11 miles) north of Felanitx, and 48 kilometres (30 miles) east of Palma, **Manacor** is Mallorca's second largest town (though a distant second: 34,000 inhabitants as opposed to a third of a million), its size mainly due to its status as a centre of industry. It's an ugly, sprawling place, centred on the church of **Nostra Senyora dels Dolors**, an effective piece of late 19th-century neo-Gothic, with an impressive belfry and altarpiece. Just north of the church is the late 13th-/early 14th-century **Torre del Palau**, the only remaining part of a royal palace built by Jaume II. A couple of minutes' walk north-west of here on Plaça de Convent is the **Convent de Vincenç Ferrer**, with its late 17th-century baroque church and cloister.

There's a scruffy weekday morning market on Plaça Constitució and a Saturday morning crafts market on Plaça de sa Bassa, but most visitors to the town come for the pearls. Manacor is famed internationally as a centre for the manufacture of **Majorica** pearls, a high-quality artificial pearl that is suppoesdly all but indistinguishable from the real thing. If you want to learn more about how they are made (it involves an awful lot of fish scales), join the coach parties who pile into the Majorica factory. But don't expect to pick up a bargain here – this is a classy product that sells at a classy price. There are other factory outlets on the main Palma road, peddling furniture, ceramics and olive wood products.

A kilometre out of town, on the road to Cales de Mallorca, the **Torre dels Enagistes** is a 14th-century fortified enclosure that has been converted into Manacor's archaeological museum, the **Museu de Manacor**.

Majorica
C/Pere Riche s/n, Manacor (971 55 09 00/ www.majorica.com). **Open** 9am-7pm Mon-Fri; 10am-1pm Sat, Sun. **Admission** free.

Torre dels Enagistes – Museu de Manacor
Ctra. Cales de Mallorca, km1.5, Manacor (971 84 30 65/www.manacor.org). **Open** *Mid June-mid Sept* 9.20am-2pm, 6-8pm Mon, Wed-Sat. *Mid Sept-mid June* 10am-2pm, 5-7.30pm Mon, Wed-Sat; 10.30am-7pm Sun. **Admission** free.

Where to stay & eat

Just outside **Felanitx**, off the road to Manacor, **Sa Posada d'Aumallia** (Camí Son Prohens 1027, 971 58 26 57, www.aumallia.com, closed Dec & Jan, doubles €134-€161 incl breakfast), at the end of a fragrant, tree-lined lane, is a sociable alternative to an *agroturismo*, with al fresco piano suppers every night. The decor is smart, if a bit fusty, but staff are unbeatably friendly. Felanitx itself is short on restaurants, but there are plenty of cafés for tapas or *bocadillos*.

Local heroes Rafael Nadal

Not many things of beauty have come out of Manacor. Mallorca's third city is home to Majorica pearls, granted, but otherwise the gritty, grimy centre of the east doesn't enjoy the most glamorous of reputations.

Enter **Rafael Nadal**, the dashing, fist-pumping Duracell bunny of Spanish tennis. Born in Manacor in 1986, Rafa was given his first tennis racquet aged four and showed immediate promise. At the tender age of 12 he reached the final of Europe's most prestigious under-14s tournament; at 15 he turned professional; in 2000 he was a member of Spain's Davis Cup winning team; in 2003 he became the youngest man since Boris Becker to reach the third round at Wimbledon; in 2004 he won his first ATP title and was again part of the winning Spanish Davis Cup team. But it was 2005 that was truly Rafa's *annus mirabilis* and saw him take his place among the tennis world's elite. At the time of writing, with 2005 only just over half through, he had already bagged eight ATP titles, including the French Open (beating Roger Federer in the semis) and climbed to number two in the world rankings. A star was born.

With his penchant for clothing in fiery oranges and yellows, his flowing locks, his prodigious talent, his hyper-athleticism and

frequent cries of '*Vamos!*' on court, Rafa ticks all the boxes of tennis bratdom. Yet, off court he's quiet, modest and polite, largely thanks to the powerful influence of his tightly knit family.

The final of the French Open was watched live on a big screen in Manacor's main square, with the cheering led by Rafa's namesake grandfather. The family patriarch was so keen to keep his five children around him that he bought land at Porto Cristo for them all to live on. It's here that Rafa still lives with his parents, sister and extended family, which includes his uncle Miguel Angel, a formidable defender who was part of Johann Cruyff's mighty Barcelona team of the 1980s and '90s, and whose uncompromising nature earned him the nickname, the 'Beast of Barcelona'.

His nephew might have followed him into football were it not for the influence of another uncle, Toni, a former tennis pro, who persuaded the precociously talented youngster that he'd go further with a racket than with a football. His hero, and fellow Mallorcan, Carlos Moyá (who also won the French Open, in 1998) was another important influence on the rising star.

So where does he go from here? Toppling Federer from the world number one spot will be as formidable a challenge as exists in sport, and, despite being a clay court specialist, Rafa yearns to win Wimbledon. But not before he's tidied his room.

As his mum recalls, 'I watch him on court and the way he behaves is the way he behaves in life – all heart, very responsible, hard-working and much more mature than most boys his age. But he is very untidy and disorganised. On the day of the French Open final I went into his room and I was shocked... it was a complete mess.'

For all you want to know, and possibly a lot you don't, from the tension of Rafa's strings to his current girlfriend situation (situation vacant at the time of writing), check out unofficial fan site www.vamosrafael.com.

East Mallorca

Ascetics and/or those on minimal budgets can stay in one of the 14 spartan cells at the **Santuari de Sant Salvador** (Puig de Sant Salvador, 971 82 72 82, doubles €30); the views make up for the lack of comforts.

If you need a little more luxury, about five kilometres (three miles) north of **Manacor** on the road to Artà you'll find the **Hotel Rural Son Trobat** (Ctra. Manacor–Sant Llorenç, km4.8, 971 56 96 74, www.sontrobat.com, closed Dec & Jan, doubles €120-€150 incl breakfast), with 25 huge bedrooms and bathrooms, including a suite with a bed tucked under a brick archway. There are charming gardens and patios and a swimming pool.

Even grander is **La Reserva Rotana** (Camí de S'Avall, km3, 971 84 56 85, www.reservarotana.com, €300 incl breakfast), also just north of Manacor (take the PMV 332-1). This rather aristocratic 17th-century *possessió* is furnished with stag's heads and hunting prints and boasts its own nine-hole golf course (use of which is included in the room price) in addition to a swimming pool and tennis court. If you can live without the grandeur and the golf, then at the same location you'll find the far cheaper *agroturismo* **Es Mayolet** (971 84 56 85, www.mayolet.com, €110 incl breakfast).

Another lovely country hideaway is a similar distance from Manacor on the road to Cales de Mallorca. **Son Amoixa Vell Hotel Rural** (Ctra. Cales de Mallorca–Manacor, km5.4, 971 84 62 92, www.son amoixa.com, closed 1-25 Dec, doubles €182-€289 incl breakfast) is a light, airy, elegant and extremely comfortable German-owned finca. Facilities include a secluded pool, tennis court, small sauna and exercise room. Breakfast is a generous buffet and new guests are warmly welcomed with a complimentary bottle of cava in their room.

Between Manacor and Artà, **Sant Llorenç de Cardassar** is an unremarkable spot except for one great restaurant, the Michelin-starred **Es Molí de'n Bou** (C/Sol 13, 971 56 96 63, closed Mon all year, 2wks mid Jan, 2wks mid Nov, €€€€), housed within an old windmill, which serves up perfect, simple Mallorcan peasant dishes with a contemporary twist and has a 200-strong list of Spanish wines. A €30 lunch *menú* provides a reasonably priced alternative to eating à la carte.

Artà

As you head northwards out of Manacor the C715 runs through picturesque orchards and pastureland until, after 20 kilometres (12.5 miles), you come to the pretty and prosperous

town of **Artà**. Sitting at the north-eastern edge of the island, it is surrounded by the ancient hunting grounds of Mallorcan royalty to the south and the Toblerone-shaped peaks of the northern Serra de Llevant to the north. The town is rarely troubled by the coastal package tourists and, consequently, makes a great base for exploring the region, particularly as it boasts a handful of excellent hotels and restaurants, and the region's most secluded beaches are close at hand (*see p199*).

The literal high point of the town is the **Santuari de Sant Salvador d'Artà**. It's ringed by metre-thick walls that have stood since Moorish times, giving protection against pirate raids, though the sanctuary itself is a 19th-century neo-classical structure; there's a good café up here.

On the way back down the hill towards town you'll pass the late 16th-century church of the **Transfiguracio del Senyor**. Its museum (C/Sant Salvador s/n, 971 83 60 20, open 10am-2pm, 3-5pm Mon-Sat, closed 4wks Dec-Jan, €1.30) has displays of religious artefacts, as well as a video showing the unusual celebrations of the **Festa de Sant Antoni Abat** (16-17 January), when revellers in traditional dress fill the square and behave more like football fans than church-goers, chanting and jumping around. Other townsfolk dress up as horned and hairy devils, ride horses backwards and generally terrorise the rest of the populace with big sticks. Somehow all this is supposed to protect both the local livestock and local population from harm. A bigger regional museum in the Plaça Espanya is closed for the foreseeable future while the space is being renovated.

There's not much more to see or do in Artà, other than eat, drink and shop (it's at its most lively on Tuesday market day), but it's a great place to do these. The main drag – C/Antoni Blanes and C/Ciutat – is a wide pedestrianised street lined with bars, restaurants and shops, like baker **Can Matemales** (C/Antoni Blanes 5, no phone, closed Mon), selling wonderful breads, pastries and pies.

Two kilometres (one and a quarter miles) south of town, the megalithic settlement of **Ses Païsses** sits surrounded by woods and almond groves. The extensive (but not easily understandable) ruins date from 1000-800 BC; the main entrance portal, built from three massive stone blocks, is perhaps the most impressive of the remains.

Ses Païsses

Camí de sa Corbaia (619 07 00 10). **Open** *Apr-Oct* 10am-1.30pm, 4-7.30pm Mon-Sat. *Nov-Mar* 9am-1pm, 2-5pm Mon-Fri. **Admission** €1.50; €0.40-€0.75 concessions. **No credit cards.**

Hit the high spots: **Santuari de Sant Salvador**. *See p194.*

Where to eat & drink

Artà is by far the best place to head for a meal and/or a drink in north-east Mallorca. The main drag C/Antonio Blanes–C/Ciutat is lined with numerous bars and restaurants. The bistro-style **Café Parisien** (C/Ciutat 18, 971 83 54 40, closed Sun, €€) has an enchanting courtyard, fragrant with roses, jasmine and lemon trees and shaded by vines. The waiters are entertainingly eccentric and diners are entertained by live jazz on Saturday evenings. Across the street **C'an Balaguer** (C/Ciutat 19, 971 83 50 03, €€) offers classic Mallorcan and Catalan specialities, such as *paella de bacalao* (salt cod) and *fideuà* (a kind of noodle paella), and has children's menus. **S'Esquit** (C/Ciutat 25, 971 83 67 80, closed Sun, €) has a new age look and a decent list of Mallorcan tapas, such as *tumbet* and *frito*.

   Bar Mateu (Plaça de s'Aigua 6, 971 83 67 30, €) is an intriguing little bar (between the main street and the sanctuary) with a friendly owner and lots of pictures depicting locals dressed as devils for the *festa major*. It has tables outside – in the middle of a roundabout. Young, cheery staff serve popular local specialities such as roast lamb and stuffed aubergines at **Na Creu Restaurant** (C/Maria Ignaci Morey 12, 971 83 63 50, closed lunch Sat in July & Aug and all Nov & Dec, €€), hugely popular for its bargain-priced lunch *menú*; an interior patio is used in the summer.

   Down a winding country lane just outside Artà is one of the region's most wonderful restaurants, **Finca Es Serral** (Ctra. Cala Torta, km5, 971 83 53 36, closed Mon, lunch in July & Aug and all Nov-Feb, €€). It's run by a charming couple, Sebastián Amorós and Margarita Lliteras (he toils the land, she cooks its bounty), who are as passionate about saving the planet as they are about their organic produce. Their meat and vegetables are reared and grown within sight of the kitchen window to produce dishes tried and tested by generations of their ancestors. Try the almond soup, tender spring lamb and home-made desserts such as *greixonera dulce* – a sort of bread and butter pudding that really only exists in old-fashioned Mallorcan farmhouse kitchens. The decor is surprisingly contemporary and hip, but always in keeping with the bucolic ethos.

   The restaurant in the **Hotel Restaurante S'Abeurador** (*see p198*, €€€, closed Wed) is wonderfully atmospheric, serving Spanish and Moroccan dishes and tapas. **Ca'n Epifanio**, the restaurant at Hotel Sant Salvador (*see p198*, €€€€) is slightly stuffier, but offers rich, gamey dishes like Barbary duck with chocolate sauce and venison wrapped in tramazzini.

   The bar-café next to the sanctuary, **Cafetería Sant Salvador** (C/Costa Sant Salvador s/n, 971 83 61 36, closed Mon, €), has hearty, simple lunch dishes, *bocadillos*, toasted sandwiches and tables in the sun.

East Mallorca

Artà. *See p196.*

Where to stay

In Artà, there are a handful of excellent hotels. The prime choice is the **Hotel Sant Salvador** (C/Castellet 7, 971 82 95 55, www.santsalvador. com, €150-€225 incl breakfast). This small hotel is set within an unusual mansion built in 1890 by a rich textile merchant; locals claim that the wonderful curving interior façade was designed by Gaudí, though there's no written evidence to back this up. Each of the eight spacious rooms is individually designed and combines an inspired mix of the contemporary and traditional, with no holding back on the use of bold, bright colours. There's a small garden and a pool, a cool bar, Ca'n Epifanio restaurant (*see above*), weekly concerts (spring to autumn) and art exhibitions.

Ca'n Moragues (C/Pou Nou 12, 971 82 95 09, www.canmoragues.com, closed 2wks in Jan, €123) is a tastefully converted 19th-century townhouse, still in the same family and with much of its original antique furniture; it has an honesty bar, outdoor plunge pool, sauna and sun terrace. The family also owns a farm outside the town and can organise hiking and hunting excursions.

Another first-rate place to stay is the **Hotel Restaurante S'Abeurador** (C/Abeurador 21, 971 83 52 30, doubles €72 incl breakfast), a townhouse hotel of great charm, replete with old farm furniture and cobblestone floors. Towards the rear are rambling terraces with fountains, fruit trees and the scent of herbs and flowers. Individually decorated rooms lead off this secret garden; one is a 100-year-old converted chapel. The restaurant (*see above*) is first-rate.

A further option is the **Hotel Casal d'Artà** (C/Rafael Blanes 19, 971 82 91 63, www.casald arta.com, doubles €78 incl breakfast), which opened in 1936. Though it has a slightly stuffy atmosphere, with potted ferns and brass

antiques aplenty, it's comfortable enough and the staff are friendly. The eight rooms vary in facilities – some have four-poster beds while others have corner baths – but all are large and decorated with antique-style furniture.

South of Artà, on the PMV403-1 to Son Servera, is the supremely stylish **Son Gener** (Ctra. Son Servera–Arta, km3, 971 18 36 12, www.songener.com, closed 1 Dec-20 Jan, junior suites €250 incl breakfast, restaurant €€€). This 18th-century farmhouse has been transformed by a Mallorcan architect-designer into a light and airy haven of contemporary design, with earthy tones and creamy *marès* stone everywhere. All ten guest rooms are junior suites with their own terraces, and facilities include a pool, spa and restaurant for guests' use.

Resources

Internet
Arta *Café Ciutat, C/Ciutat 26 (971 56 20 86).*
Open 8am-10pm Mon-Thur; 8am-2am Fri, Sat.

Police station
Artà *Plaça Espanya 1 (971 82 95 95).*
Felanitx *C/Ernest Mestre 64 (971 58 22 00).*
Manacor *Avda. del Parc s/n (971 55 00 48/63).*

Post office
Artà *C/Ciutat 26 (971 83 61 27).*
Felanitx *C/Costa i Llobera 32 (971 58 02 52).*
Manacor *Baix Riera 1 (971 55 18 39).*

Getting there

By bus
See p206.

By train
There are 13-14 trains daily from Palma to Manacor (1hr 4mins) via Sineu (48mins) and Petra (56mins).

East Mallorca

East Coast

Little Britain (and Deutschland) on sea.

Torre de Canyamel. *See p203.*

The north-eastern beaches, Capdepera & Cala Ratjada

The wild and largely undeveloped coastline of the north east, between Cap de Ferrutx and Cap des Freu, offers some of the best, and certainly the most secluded beaches in the east. From Artà, head towards Capdepera and almost immediately take a left (north) turn along a steadily rougher and more winding road, through green craggy peaks, to the popular but still wild-feeling **Cala Torta**. Camper vans and cars use the back of the beach as a car park/picnic area/camping ground, but it's big enough to handle it. Cala Torta is a deep horseshoe bay with a fine sand beach backed by dunes and pines; there's also a beach bar that does excellent fish.

Walk over the rocky headland to your left (as you face the sea) to reach **Cala Mitjana**, similar to Torta but a bit smaller and with no bar. Heading straight there by car, it's easier to leave it where the road forks in two – right to Cala Mitjana and left to the narrow inlet of **Cala Estreta**. The latter has no sand, but a deep, beautifully clear natural pool for swimming. Both are a ten-minute walk from the fork, or an uncomfortably potholed drive. If you

want even more isolation, you can continue westwards along the coast to a number of increasingly remote beaches, including **Cala Matzoc, Sa Font Salada** and **S'Arenalet d'Aubarca**. For details on how to reach these idyllic strands, *see p200* **Walk 6**.

Travelling from Artà to Cala Ratjada, you can't miss the dramatically perched 14th-century **Castell de Capdepera**, the focal point of the village of **Capdepera**. A local legend recounts that the citizens, under siege from pirates, placed a statue of the Virgin on the battlements, whereupon the invaders were suddenly driven away by a thick fog.

You can reach the castle by climbing up from the main market square, Plaça de l'Orient (the hairy drive all the way up is only for the foolhardy). Those who don't suffer from vertigo can make a circuit of the crenellated walls (the walkway is narrow and there's no safety rail on the inside), which offer fine views, taking in Menorca to the north-east.

It was from the castle, in 1232, that Jaume I, with a depleted and largely untrained band of men, conquered Menorca without firing a shot. In the dead of night he sent six riders to light 300 fires on the hillsides and along the coast. The Moorish rulers of Menorca were so alarmed and impressed at this apparently mighty army that they surrendered the island and offered themselves as the king's vassals.

There's not much else within the walls to explore beyond the pretty Gothic church of **Nostra Senyora de la Esperança**, but Capdepera makes for a interesting wander. The village's medieval fair takes place over the third weekend of May and involves hog roasts, market stalls, concerts and much pageantry.

From Capdepera a minor road runs north to another fine beach, **Cala Mesquida**, once a smuggling hotspot. The water here is the kind of turquoise you think only exists on postcards, lapping on virgin sand backed by windswept dunes. The cala has, however, been largely swallowed up by a sprawling German-dominated tourist resort, which crowds one side of the bay.

The main resort on this part of the coast is **Cala Ratjada** (12 kilometres/seven and a half miles east of Artà), once a small, charming fishing village until it was picked as one of the first places to be developed for tourism on the island. It's now a German and British-dominated hotspot in season and largely dead out of it. For independent tourists, it holds little appeal, though it has retained some individuality around its little fishing port. From here you can catch a fast boat to Menorca (*see p262*).

The busy town beach, **Platja de Son Moll**, a ten-minute walk south from the port, has

Walk 6 North-east coast

Distance: 9km (5.5 miles). Linear.
Time: 2hrs 50mins.

In truth, there aren't any totally secret beaches left on Mallorca; 30-plus years of mass tourism have seen to that. But there are still some hard-to-access gems that attract only those willing to walk some distance to reach them, which means that they are never crowded and frequently all but deserted. This short walk takes in an invigorating stretch of the rugged and blissfully undeveloped coastline north of Artà before arriving at a couple of such beaches. The walking is relatively easy, though some short but steepish ascents and descents are required (so don't attempt it in the full heat of the summer). Be warned that there are no facilities at these beaches – be sure to bring your own food and water.

To reach the starting point for the walk, take the road from Artà towards Capdepera and Cala Ratjada and, as soon as you've skirted around Artà, turn left where you see a sign pointing the way to Cala Torta. Almost immediately take the next right turn (to Calas Torta, Estreta and Mitjana). Follow this road for ten kilometres (six miles) until it comes to the sea. The first kilometre is well surfaced, but the rest is rough (getting very rough indeed towards the end), but persevere and park your car at the point where the road reaches the sea by a narrow inlet (Cala Estreta) before it sweeps right to arrive at the beach at Cala Mitjana.

On the other side of the inlet you'll see a footpath rising up a low headland. Scramble down and up the other side of the inlet, and follow this path. After around ten minutes you pass through a rusty gate in a wire fence, before walking around a cove and climbing up the next headland, from where you'll see the 16th-century watchtower Torre des Matzoc ahead of you.

The landscapes in this refreshingly virgin part of the island are parched, raw, barren (a series of forest fires has stripped the area of most of its trees) and almost lunar at times, but the sea as it meets the rocks is a translucent, inviting blue – it's certainly a world away from the intensive tourist developments along most of the north and east coasts.

Around 25 minutes after starting out you'll arrive at the beach of Cala Matzoc, which is often seaweed-strewn and, consequently, not that inviting. Continue onwards by climbing up the eroded area towards the front of the far side of the beach and walking through a clump of trees (which provide just about the only shade on the walk).

Ten minutes later you'll reach the watchtower. It's possible to climb up to the top, but the staircase stops short and you'll need to be fairly athletic (and brave) to clamber up the sticks jammed into the walls above it to emerge on the top, where a rusty old cannon has lain for centuries. The views make it worthwhile, though, with the Talaia de Son Jaumell watchtower visible to the east and Talaia Moreia watchtower to the west on the dramatically jutting Cap de Ferrutx; beyond you'll see the Formentor peninsula.

Continue on around the next headland, following a rough path that becomes rockier and more indistinct until it passes through some scrubby trees and emerges high above a long, flattish, lower-lying area of rock. You'll

crystalline water and soft golden sand. It's backed by hotels, bars and restaurants and has all the usual services. Quieter but much smaller is **Cala Gat**, a few minutes' walk from the port in the other direction. Across the headland from Cala Ratjada, **Cala Agulla** is a sweeping curve of white sand lapped by blue water. There are developments (a comfortable distance inland) and it has all the usual services, including beach bars and a restaurant, but its collar of pine-backed dunes gives it that all-important wild air.

Castell de Capdepera

Capdepera (971 81 87 46). **Open** *Apr-Oct* 9am-8pm daily. *Nov-Mar* 9am-5pm daily. **Admission** €2; free concessions. **No credit cards**.

Where to stay & eat

If you're heading for the north-east coast beaches, the best (and only) places to get a bite and a drink are **Bar Cala Torta** on **Cala Torta** (no phone, closed Oct-May, €€), where they grill super-fresh fish and seafood and charge fairly heftily for it, and the stunningly situated **Bar-Restaurante Sa Duaia** (Ctra. Artà–Cala Torta, km8, mobile 651 82 64 16, closed Mon, €€) on the road to the beach (you can't miss the signs). It's a good spot for barbecued meats and the staff are friendly.

Capdepera has a surprisingly decent selection of restaurants. One of the nicest is **Es Castell** (C/Major 47, 971 56 57 30, closed

see the path stretching away below you. Scramble down and follow it through this other-worldly landscape, passing through a rich vermillion seam of rock.

As you round the next headland you pass through a gate in a wire fence. You can spy a building ahead of you in the distance. This stands behind the beach of S'Arenalet d'Aubarca, the farthest point on this walk.

Around 40 minutes after leaving the watchtower, you arrive at the white-sand beach of Sa Font Salada. It's an idyllic spot, and it's easy to while away an hour or two lying here or swimming in the sea. Or you could continue onwards for another ten

minutes to the equally fine, and wider, beach of S'Arenalet d'Aubarca. School kids often stay in the building backing this beach, so you may have more company here.

When you've enjoyed all the R&R you want, retrace your steps along the coast and you should be back at the starting point in around one hour 25 minutes. If you feel in need of refreshment, the Bar-Restaurante Sa Duaia (*see above*) is located a couple of kilometres from the sea, just off the road you came along. Or you can walk over the headland east of Cala Mitjana to the beach of Cala Torta, where there is a bar serving snacks and drinks.

Mon, €), a rustic-looking Chilean-run tapas restaurant, with hugely generous portions of *pa amb oli* slathered with ham, cheese and salad, along with home-made pâté and superb *sobrassada* and honey.

Off the road from Capdepera to Cala Mesquida is one of the more elegant places to stay in the area, **Cases de Son Barbassa** (Ctra. Cala Mesquida, 971 56 57 76, www.son barbassa.com, doubles €66-€92), parts of which are 500 years old. Modern, comfortable rooms are decorated in hues of sand and slate, and the chill-out area around the swimming pool is more reminiscent of a hip and exclusive nightclub than a hotel.

If you want to overnight in **Cala Ratjada**, **Hostal Ca's Bombu** (C/Leonor Servera 86, 971 56 32 03, www.casbombu.com, closed Nov-Easter, doubles €34 incl breakfast) has been here, run by the same family, since 1885; siblings Margarita and Bartomeu now run things. The original guests were artists and intellectuals – one made a bust of the rather fearsome-looking first owner that sits in the lounge. The rooms are simple but have appealing, old-fashioned carved wooden bedsteads, and those in the old building have original 19th-century patterned floor tiles. You can pick your room at the three-star

Ses Rotges (C/Rafael Blanes 21, 971 56 31 08, www.sesrotges.com, closed Nov-Apr, doubles €94 incl breakfast) from its website. All have wooden beams, stone tiles and traditional Mallorcan wooden beds. But do you want stripey or patchwork bedlinen? The Michelin-starred French restaurant (€€€€), under the assured hand of chef Gérard Tétard, has a romantic patio for summer dining.

Other eating options include **El Cactus** (C/Leonor Servera 83, 971 56 46 09, closed Mon in Aug, €€), one of the more stylish spots in town, with white candles in large glass vases, and milk-fed lamb and good fish dishes on the menu. The harbour is a long string of bars and restaurants; try **La Bodeguita** (Passeig América 14, 971 81 90 62, €), which specialises in Mallorcan dishes, with tables overlooking the seafront and a garden out back; choose any five tapas for a very reasonable €6.50.

Canyamel, Cala Millor, Cala Bona & Porto Cristo

Heading south down the coast (though only accessible from the Capdepera–Son Servera road) is **Canyamel**, a small holiday development, named for the sugar cane that used to be grown in the area. A few blocks

View from the mouth of the **Coves d'Artà**. *See p203.*

of holiday chalets and a couple of large hotels face a long sandy beach, with a freshwater *torrent* at one end. The sand is not the finest or whitest, but the atmosphere is more relaxed than at most resorts in the area.

It's also the closest settlement to the **Coves d'Artà** (often signposted in its Castilian form as Cuevas de Artà). There's some debate as to which are the must-see caves on the island, but these undeniably spectacular caverns make a bold bid for supremacy by dubbing themselves the 'ninth wonder of the world'. Guided tours lead you through the thoroughly sanitised cave system, but it doesn't take a huge leap of imagination to envisage the awe felt by French geologist Edouard Martel when he first explored it in 1876. They'd been known about for centuries, however – Jaume I supposedly found 2,000 Moors sheltering inside them after his 13th-century conquest of Mallorca. The caves can also be visited by boat from Cala Millor and Cala Ratjada.

Off the road between Canyamel and Artà is a 13th-century fortified tower, the **Torre de Canyamel**, which can be visited. Impressively preserved, notwithstanding the soot marks from the fire that swept through it 30 or so years ago when farm workers still lived here, it houses antique farming implements, a weaving loom, a kneading trough, old guns and so on.

There's little to distinguish the monster developments of **Cala Millor** and **Cala Bona**, apart from their beaches. Cala Bona has three artificial strands with safe bathing for kids; just north of here, the **Platja d'es Ribell** is a long, unspoilt if slightly unloved-looking stretch of beach. Cala Millor is a two kilometre (one and a quarter mile) strip of hotels, apartments, a promenade and a sandy beach packed with tourists in summer. At least the beach is well serviced and clean. Depressingly, from the beach you can see the wild headland of the nature reserve just to the south, and a sorry contrast it makes.

The virgin, scrubby promontory of **Punta de n'Amer**, with low cliffs rising from clear water, has been a protected area since 1986, and so has avoided the scarring tourist developments that have blighted the coastline on either side of it. A footpath leads from the end of Cala Millor beach to a 17th-century defensive tower and a 21st-century bar.

Continuing south, **Porto Cristo** is set on what must once have been a picturesque inlet, with a narrow beach and a smart little marina. In 1936 Republican troops landed here (Mallorca had been taken over by the Nationalists at the outbreak of the Civil War; Menorca remained loyal to the Republic)

and made rapid gains before running out of steam and ideas just a couple of weeks later. They were pushed back by a Nationalist counter-attack and were forced to evacuate to the mainland.

Approached from Manacor, the town's outskirts – a grid of low-rise apartment blocks – could be those of any small nondescript Spanish town and the inlet is now spanned by an ugly and controversial new bridge. The beach is backed by a small promenade with shops selling beach gear and restaurants selling the ubiquitous pizzas and ice-creams.

In terms of sights, Porto Cristo isn't badly served; there are two major cave complexes. The lesser known is the **Coves d'es Hams** (Cuevas dels Hams in Castilian), accessed from the road to Manacor. Discovered in 1905, these modestly sized but beautiful caves (given fanciful names like 'Milton's Lost Paradise' and 'Fairy Cemetery') are famed for their weird tree-like formations. The guided tours in small groups culminate in a short concert of classical music from musicians in boats floating on an underground lake.

The major tourist attraction in these parts, though (and possibly the best-known sight on the island) is the **Coves del Drac** (or Cuevas del Drac in Castilian). The first thing you have to get over is that these positively seethe with coach parties all day every day and have been totally commercialised. What is amazing is that these astonishing caverns are no less remarkable for the intrusion. Not only is their extent impressive (they stretch for 1.7 kilometres/one mile), but so is the sheer extravagance of their decoration – with weirdly formed and coloured stalagmites and millions of needle-sharp stalactites covering every inch of their roofs. Visitors shuffle along a path for about a kilometre before sitting in a huge natural amphitheatre in front of one of the world's largest underground lakes and, just as in the Coves d'es Hams, watching a water-borne classical music performance. It should be hopelessly corny, but it's really rather lovely.

Close by is the **Acuàrium de Mallorca**, which opened in the mid 1970s, and contains no fewer than 115 tanks of sealife, including some kid-thrilling piranhas.

Acuàrium de Mallorca

C/Gambi 7, Porto Cristo (971 82 09 71). **Open** *Apr-Sept* 11am-6.30pm daily. *Oct-Mar* 11am-3pm daily. **Admission** €5; €2.50 concessions. **No credit cards.**

Coves d'Artà

Ctra. de las Coves s/n, Canyamel (971 84 12 93/ www.cuevasdearta.com). **Open** *Apr-Oct* 10am-7pm daily. *Nov-Mar* 10am-6.30pm daily. **Admission** €8.50; €4 concessions; free under-6s. **No credit cards. Photo** *p202*.

East Mallorca

Coves del Drac

Ctra. de les Coves s/n, Porto Cristo (971 82 07 53).
Open *Mar-Oct* 10am-5pm daily. *Nov-Feb* Guided
tours at 10.45am, noon, 2pm & 3.30pm daily.
Admission €8.50; free under-6s. **No credit cards**.

Coves d'es Hams

*Ctra. Porto Cristo–Manacor, km1 (971 82 09 88/
www.cuevas-hams.com).* **Open** *Summer* 10am-
1.30pm, 2-5.30pm daily. *Winter* 10.30am-5pm daily.
Admission €9.80; free under-12s. **Credit** MC, V.

Torre de Canyamel

Ctra. Artà-Canyamel, km5 (971 84 11 34). **Open**
Apr-Oct 10am-6pm Tue-Sat; 10am-5pm Sun.
Admission €3; €1.50 concessions. **No credit cards**.

Where to stay & eat

Just outside **Canyamel**, **Can Simoneta**
(Ctra. Artà-Canyamel, km8, 971 81 61 10,
www.cansimoneta.com, doubles €235-€290
incl breakfast) is a four-star hotel with all
the charm of a smart *agroturismo*, but with
an unbeatable clifftop position and direct
access to the sea. Its low-key luxury extends
to a swimming pool, seawater baths and
immaculately appointed rooms.

Off the same road is the far more affordable
Na Set Centes (Ctra. Arta–Canyamel, km2.7,
971 83 54 29, www.nasetcentes.com, doubles
€106 incl breakfast), which has three doubles
and one suite, decorated in warm colours and
natural materials; all have their own terraces
and fine views. There's a lovely family feel
to the place, and Granny whips up a wonderful
breakfast of *pa amb oli* with ham, cheese and
her amazing omelette.

Next to the Torre de Canyamel, the **Porxada
de Sa Torre** (971 84 13 10, closed dinner
Sun and all Mon, €€) is a good-value, simple
restaurant serving Spanish standards such
as baked fish, roast chicken and suckling pig.

As accommodation in these parts goes, **Cala
Millor**'s three-star **Hotel Talayot** (C/Son Sard
2, 971 58 53 14, www.hoteltalayot.com, closed
Nov-Feb, doubles €112 half board) is something
of an oasis in a sea of high-rises. It has good-
sized indoor and outdoor swimming pools
and a terrace with sea views.

Porto Cristo is not well served for hotels
and has few decent places to eat. On the
promenade, the **THB Felip Hotel** (C/Burdils
41, 971 82 07 50, www.thbhotels.com, doubles
€122 incl breakfast) feels a bit like a cheap
version of an old-style colonial hotel (it's been
around for over a century), with wicker chairs
and an airy lounge, and balconies for most
of its rooms. Perched on the cliff at the north
end of the beach, **Restaurant Flamingo**
(C/Burdils s/n, 971 82 22 59, closed Nov-mid

Feb, €€) is distinguished by its colourful hand-
painted signs featuring cartoon characters and
its terrace overlooking the water; home-made
fideuà and paella are the highlights of the menu.

By far the classiest place to stay in the area,
however, is located five kilometres (four miles)
south of Porto Cristo, just off the road to Porto
Colom. **Son Mas** (Camí de Son Mas s/n, 971
55 87 55, www.sonmas.com, closed Dec-Jan,
suites €247 incl breakfast) is an immaculate,
tranquil *hotel rural*, centred on a 17th-century
watchtower (containing the perfect, circular
honeymoon suite) and surrounded by a huge
estate of fig, almond, carob and orange trees.
All the rooms are immense junior suites, and all
are decorated in stunning less-is-more chic, with
sandblasted marble floors, huge beds, beamed
ceilings, antique wood furniture, soothing earth
tones and vast terraces. The public areas are
studies in the use of architectural space (the
original mill is incorporated in one of them),
and are warmed by log fires on cold evenings.
There are pools both inside (with massage jets
and a sauna) and outside, and a restaurant for
guests serving a set menu (except Tuesdays).

Porto Colom, Cala d'Or & Porto Petro

The pretty road heading south from Porto
Cristo towards Porto Colom gives no clue
to the sprawling holiday villa horror of the
collection of resorts a couple of kilometres
away on the coast, collectively known as
Cales de Mallorca. Just how wrong priorities
have been in this area becomes evident
if you stumble across the prehistoric village
of **Hospitalet Vell** (signed from the road
towards Cales de Mallorca, then a couple
of hundred metres' walk off to the right). This
is one of the most important talayotic sites
on Mallorca, yet has a (not unattractive) air
of neglect and decay about it (a rusted sign,
in a curious but apt translation, invites visitors
to 'locate the forlornness of the village at the
end of the second century BC'). Hardly anyone
comes here. First settled in the pre-Talayotic
period (and partially reoccupied in Roman and
Moorish times), it preserves its quadrangular
talayot, a number of dwellings and an
impressive chunk of defensive wall.

Porto Colom, 21 kilometres (13 miles) south
of Porto Cristo and 11 kilometres (seven miles)
south-east of Felanitx, is really just one side
of a cluster of small, relatively old-school
(German-favoured) resorts nestled around
a large natural harbour, protected from the Med
by the headlands, Punta de ses Crestes and
Punta de sa Bateria. It was originally developed

Hostal Porto Colom.

as a port for transporting wine from Felanitx to France (before phylloxera destroyed the wine industry in the 1870s; it has recently revived), and there are still some attractive 19th-century villas overlooking the long and winding promenade. The large, calm harbour is home to a colourful mix of local fishing craft and holidaymakers' hobby boats. Cutely painted, flat-fronted cottages mingle with lush villas and modern holiday homes. Many Felanitx residents have holiday properties here, giving the summer festivals, such as the sea-based festival of Mare de Déu del Carme on 16 June, a more local flavour and vibrancy than is often the case in this area. However, most of the hotels and restaurants are German-owned and/or run, and you may find the odd island of haute cuisine in the little town. In fact, the whole harbour is a confusing but intriguing mix-and-match, from modern and flash to cute and historic, from seedy to chic.

Continuing south, you soon come to **Cala d'Or**, a major tourist development stretching across a series of resorts that cluster around a succession of coves and inlets. Each has its marina jammed with yachts and pleasure cruisers, its blocks of white boxy Ibiza-style holiday apartments and hotels, and low-rise bars and restaurants servicing all tastes Brit –

pub grub, pizza, curry, Thai. It's supposed to be a glamorous resort, but although everyone has the leathery tan and gold jewellery badges of conspicuous consumption, there's something a bit Eldorado-tacky about the place.

Porto Petro, neighbouring Cala d'Or to the south, manages to calm the brashness down a bit. It's more of a traditional harbour, with leafy back roads leading down to whitewashed harbour cottages, most of which have now converted into restaurants. The lack of beach means that development has been more contained than further north.

For the enjoyable low-key resorts at Mallorca's south-east tip, *see p188*.

Where to stay & eat

Off the road from Porto Cristo to Porto Colom, inland from Cales de Mallorca, is **Son Josep de Baix** (Ctra. Porto Colom–Porto Cristo, km8.4, 971 65 04 72, www.sonjosepdebaix. com, apartments for 2 €99), an unmissable *agroturismo* with deceptively modern and well-equipped self-catering apartments created in ancient outhouses around a ramshackle farmyard. Amid the flocks of goats, scratching chickens and flowering trees are a secluded pool, a barbecue for guests' use, and several private terraces.

For a small and friendly place to stay south of the harbour in **Porto Colom**, try **Hotel Bahia Azul** (Rda. Crucero Balear 78, 971 82 52 80, www.bahia-azul.de, closed Dec-Mar, doubles €52 incl breakfast), a plain but comfortable spot, run by the German Fecke family and popular with families and young couples. As well as a pool and sauna, this small 15-room hotel overlooking the water also features a diving centre offering courses at all levels. Another keenly priced spot to stay is smart **HPC** or, to give it its full name, **Hostal Porto Colom** (C/Cristófal Colom 5, 971 82 53 23, doubles €30-€70, restaurant €€) on the harbourfront, which combines *hostal*, bar and decent restaurant, serving pizzas, pastas and more traditional Mallorcan grub.

There are two outstanding dining offerings along Porto Colom's waterfront. **Bar Restaurant Florian** (C/Cristófal Colóm 11, 971 82 41 71, closed 5 Nov-10 Dec, €€€) is a crisply furnished restaurant with an outdoor terrace facing the sea. Black-uniformed waiting staff serve creative cuisine, such as turbot poached in olive oil with shellfish couscous and fennel, and shoulder of lamb with a parmesan crust in black bread and balsamic sauce with aubergine *tumbet*. For cheaper snacks, try the lunchtime tapas, such as pickled anchovies and shrimp kebabs. The excellent

East Mallorca

Restaurante Colón (C/Cristófal Colóm 7, 971 82 47 83, closed Wed and Jan-mid Feb, €€€) exudes cool, with elegant white candles in the large stone fireplace, leather sofas in the bar area and smooth service from the smart waiting staff. Dishes include *solomillo* of beef and duck liver, and marinated pig's trotters.

If you haven't got your own luxury yacht to sleep on while moored at **Cala d'Or**, staying at the **Hotel Cala d'Or** (Avda. de Belgica 33, 971 65 72 49, www.hotelcalador.com, closed Nov-Mar/Apr, doubles €112 incl breakfast) is a fine alternative. This lovely 1930s whitewashed villa has beautiful, light and airy lounges with alluringly come-hither sofas. The rooms are slightly less chic, but all are comfortable, smart and clean, with views of the gardens or the sea. The hotel is right next to Cala d'Or's tiny beach, but you can avoid the hordes by swimming in the heated outdoor pool.

A family-oriented hotel in **Porto Petro** is the **Hostal Nereida** (C/Patrons Martina 3, 971 65 72 23, www.hostalnereida.com, closed Nov-Apr, doubles €47-€55 incl breakfast), just back from the harbour, which has decent-sized, no-nonsense rooms, a large swimming pool and garden, table tennis and swings.

At the edge of Porto Petro's furthermost little inlet, you can sit on the first-floor terrace of **Rafael y Flora**'s eponymous restaurant (C/Far 12, 971 65 78 09, closed Nov-Apr, €€) and stuff yourself with perfect paella or sole with ginger and onions. If you're feeling really greedy, start with some of Filipina Flora's oriental/Spanish tapas, such as satay chicken and Mallorcan spinach croquettes. On the edge of the harbour, **Ca'n Martina** (Passeig des Port 56, 971 65 75 17, €€) does a good breakfast, and cakes in the afternoon, but otherwise offers reasonably priced (especially considering its position on the seafront) paella and seafood.

Five kilometres inland from Porto Petro, the town of **Alqueria Blanca** and its surroundings have an abundance of rural lodgings. In the town itself, the **Hotel Son Llorenç** (C/Ramón Llull 7, 971 16 11 61, www.hotelsonllorenc.com, doubles €90-€110 incl breakfast) has eight rooms in a sensitively converted townhouse. Breakfast is served on a charming, flower-filled terrace and there is a small library with a log fire in winter. Keep your eyes peeled on the road from here to Ca's Concos for **Es Pujol** (Camí des Pujols, 971 16 40 65, www.caspagesdespujol.com, doubles €78-€90), a beautifully peaceful house, parts of which date back to the 13th century. There are four double rooms (one with its own kitchen) or the whole house can be rented. As well as a tennis court and small pool, Es Pujol also boasts its own tiny Gothic chapel.

In Alqueria Blanca itself you'll find the area's most upmarket restaurant, located in a pretty *possessió*. **Es Clos** (C/Convento 17, 971 65 34 04, closed lunch and all Mon, €€€€) specialises in a creative fusion that results in dishes like sea bass with spring rolls and a lime and coconut sauce.

Resources

Internet
Porto Cristo *Academia Porto Cristo, C/Sementera 43, Baixos (971 82 26 18)*. Open 9am-1pm, 4-8pm Mon-Fri.

Son Servera *Rótulos, C/Juana Roca 119 (971 56 76 83)*. Open 10am-1pm, 3.30-8.30pm Mon-Sat.

Police station
Cala Millor *C/Molins 27 (971 81 40 76)*.
Cala Ratjada/Capdepera *C/Roses s/n (971 56 54 63)*.

Post office
Cala d'Or *Centre Civic 1 (971 65 94 64)*.
Cala Ratjada *C/Magallanes 29 (971 81 86 22)*.
Capdepera *C/Llum s/n (no phone)*.
Porto Cristo *C/Zanglada s/n (no phone)*.

Tourist information
Cala Millor *OIT, C/Parc de la Mar 2 (971 58 54 09/omitcm@santllorenc.com)*. Open *Apr-Oct* 9am-5pm Mon-Fri. *Nov-Mar* 9am-2pm Mon-Fri.

Cala d'Or *OIT, Avda. Perico Pomar 10 (971 65 74 63)*. Open 8.15am-2.15pm Mon-Fri; 9am-2pm Sat.

Cala Ratjada/Capdepera *OIT, C/Castellets 5 (971 56 30 33)*. Open 9.30am-1.30pm, 3.30-6pm Mon-Fri; 9am-2pm Sat.

Cales de Mallorca *OIT, Passeig de Manacor s/n (971 83 41 44/www.manacor.org)*. Open 9am-4pm Mon-Fri. Closed Nov-Apr.

Porto Colom *OIT, Avda. Cala Marçal 15 (971 82 60 84/turisme@felanitx.org)*. Open *Apr-Oct* 9am-1pm, 4-8pm Mon-Fri; 10am-7pm Sat. Closed Nov-Mar.

Porto Cristo *OIT, C/Bordils 53 baixos (971 81 51 03/turisme@manacor.org)*. Open *May-Oct* 9am-3pm Mon-Fri. *Nov-Apr* 1-5pm Mon-Fri.

Son Servera *OIT, Avda. Joan Servera Camps s/n (971 58 58 64/ma.mintour29@bitel.es)*. Open *May-Oct* 9am-2pm Mon-Sat. *Nov-Apr* 9am-1pm Mon-Fri; 10am-1pm Sat.

Getting there

By boat
Regular ferries run between Cala Ratjada and Ciutadella on Menorca. *See p262.*

By bus
From Palma, there are 5 buses Mon-Fri (3 Sat, 2 Sun) to Cala d'Or, 8 buses Mon-Sat (2 Sun) to Cala Millor, 6 buses Mon-Fri (4 Sat, 3 Sun) to Porto Colom, 2 buses Mon-Sat to Cales de Mallorca, 8 buses Mon-Sat (3 Sun) to Porto Cristo via Manacor, and 4 buses Mon-Sat (2 Sun) to Cala Ragjada via Artà and Capdepera.

Menorca

Parc des Freginal. *See p211.*

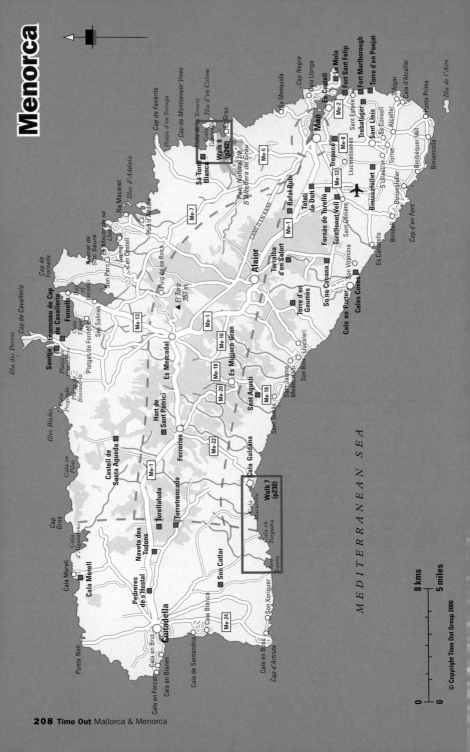

Menorca

MEDITERRANEAN SEA

Walk 8 (p242)

Walk 7 (p230)

8 kms

5 miles

© Copyright Time Out Group 2006

Menorca

Meet Mallorca's laid-back, beguiling little neighbour.

Less than a fifth of the size of Mallorca, Menorca has so far managed to avoid the worst excesses of mass tourism, and is consequently less spoilt than its neighbour. It's true that there are a handful of horror-show holiday resorts of the sort that seem to parody British leisure appetites, but these are self-contained. They are also balanced out, not only by resorts that have managed to limit their environmental and social impact, but also by beaches and coastal areas that are still untouched. Inland, Menorca is still resolutely rural. Dairy and arable farms cover almost the whole of the interior, interspersed with pine forests, areas of unfarmed scrub and marshland, and an extraordinary number of fascinating prehistoric sites. Though urban sprawl and industrialisation is evident around both Maó and Ciutadella, as well as the inland towns of Ferreries and Alaior, it so far represents only a narrow ribbon of grim modernity between rural bliss and old town charm.

MAÓ
Shaped by a history of occupation by Moors, Catalans, British, French and Spanish, the town of Maó sits uneasily beside the huge natural harbour that has made it a site of such strategic importance throughout its 2,000-year existence. Lacking both the usual size or swagger of an island capital, and somehow disjointed from the port that has dictated its fate, Maó is an unusual and intriguing place, with a distinct, idiosyncratic charm.

SOUTH MENORCA
As well as two major fortresses (one now demolished, the other in ruins) and many of Menorca's mysterious prehistoric monuments, the south-east corner of the island is a privileged bastion of pretty villages, holiday villas, gourmet restaurants and attractive beaches. It is also the most densely populated part of the island, particularly around the coast. The interior, in contrast, is cross-hatched by drystone walls, wild olives and holm oaks. Further west along the south coast is the focus for most of the island's beach tourism. Boasting several resorts of varying degrees of intrusion and environmental sensitivity, this is where most of the island's idyllic beaches are found, all of which have fine, creamy white sand and pristine, clear water.

CENTRAL MENORCA
The three main towns in the interior of the island are small, dozy places quietly going about their business (mostly agriculture, cheese- and shoe-making). Neither equipped nor particularly interested in tourism, they are pretty enough spots to wander and soak up the atmosphere.

NORTHERN MENORCA
The wildest, most windswept part of Menorca, the northern coastline is also the most beautiful, an intricate outline of dramatic cliffs and bays with pretty, untouched beaches. Inland, the scenery rises from rolling hills and pine forests in the east to abrupt hillocks of pastureland around the centre before dropping down to the rocky plain of the west.

CIUTADELLA AND WEST MENORCA
Prettier and more welcoming than Maó, Ciutadella is a charming town of old palaces of pink-tinged sandstone, with narrow, cobbled streets and a small, quaint port. The west coast, in contrast, is somewhat rugged, with tiny, overcrowded beaches. It is also home to an almost unbroken strip of holiday resorts, most of them nondescript and unenticing, though a couple are less unpalatable.

The best...

Beaches
See p244 **Top five beaches**.

Hotels
See p223 **Top five agroturismos**.

Museums & sights
Fort Marlborough (p224); **Museu de Menorca** (p214); **Pedreres de s'Hostal** (p257).

Prehistoric monuments
See p260 **Top five prehistoric monuments**.

Restaurants
See p211 **Top five restaurants**.

Things to do
See p237 **Six best things to do**.

Menorca

Maó

Overshadowed by an illustrious maritime past, the Menorcan capital is slowly becoming more than just an ex-naval base.

When two rival towns compete for prime billing, one of them invariably falls shy of the other. In the case of Menorca, Ciutadella was undeniably top dog until the occupying British switched the island capital to Maó (often still referred to by its Castilian name of Mahón) in the 18th century; a fact that still rankles with Ciutadella's inhabitants. Almost 300 years later, Ciutadella still feels more like the coherent, organic town, while Maó continues to have the whiff of a naval base. Its dominant feature is its magnificent, snaking harbour, the second largest in the world after Pearl Harbor, and the reason the maritime Brits were so keen to establish a presence here; it provided the key to naval domination of the western Mediterranean in the 18th century.

The town, impressively arrayed along cliff-tops on the harbour's northern side, may not be as instantly appealing as its rival across the island, but it has a more complex charm, amply repaying exploration of its small squares and narrow streets. These are gradually being smartened up, the old walls are being scrubbed and buffed, and Maó's utilitarian starkness of old is slowly being replaced with a more stylish, contemporary feeling. Maó clearly bears the imprints of the various cultures that have occupied the island over the centuries, particularly the British. Even today it feels more cosmopolitan than its western cousin (though its population is a mere 22,000), both in atmosphere and architecture, though there seems to be a curious mutual ambivalence between town and port, land and sea.

Pilar Alonso statue, **Plaça Colon**. *See p211.*

Sightseeing

The logical place to start a tour of Maó is the **Plaça de s'Esplanada**. Originally the town's parade ground, it was laid out by the British during their second period of occupation (1763-82), and the original barracks still runs along one side of the square. The colonial façade, painted wine red with white window and door frames, sparked off a trend for British colonial architecture throughout the island that is still very much in evidence today. Nowadays the barracks is looking a little shabby, hidden away behind a Franco-era war memorial, a thick hedge and a concrete row of lock-ups serving

snacks, sweets and even British fish and chips. In fact, the square is so cluttered with wretched architecture it is sometimes difficult to appreciate its former charm. At weekends and on summer evenings, though, it is transformed as kids play on the swings among the pine trees, adolescents zoom their scooters around the perimeter roads, and pensioners and holiday-makers fill the café terraces.

To get to the heart of the old town, follow C/Ses Moreres down the hill past the monument to Dr Mathieu Orfila (1787-1853), the father of modern toxicology; the street changes name to Costa de sa Plaça (also known as C/Hannover),

Menorca

and runs past the small, cobbled **Plaça Colón**, with its palm trees and twee statue of the Menorcan singer Pilar Alonso as a young girl.

To the right, C/Àngel runs from the square to Costa d'en Deià, where an arched passage straight ahead leads, unexpectedly, to **Parc d'es Freginal**, a largish, scruffy, pine-filled park hidden away behind the houses; Maó's expat Latin American residents gather here to play volleyball at weekends. Up the hill, at the top of Costa d'en Deià, a large, modern statue of a female nude clutching the masks of comedy and tragedy marks the town's theatre, the **Teatre Principal**, built in 1829.

Back at Plaça Colón, the pedestrianised street continues down to another small, cobbled square, **Plaça de la Constitució**, the administrative heart of Maó. It is dominated by the monolithic edifice of the church of **Santa Maria**, built during the second half of the 18th century on the site of an earlier church erected by Alfons III. The brightly painted interior consists of a single nave beneath a high, Gothic-arched ceiling, with small chapels along each side; there's a fine organ, dating from 1810.

The smaller, ornate building next door is the **Ajuntament** (town hall), built in 1789. Visitors are free to wander in up the stairs, past the statue of St Sebastian, Maó's second patron saint after the Verge de Gràcia (Our Lady of Grace), to look around the council chamber – a rather sombre hall lined with portraits of Spanish dignitaries from the time of the final British handover of the island in 1802 onwards.

Between the town hall and the church, a short alley leads to **Plaça de sa Conquesta**, a large, quiet square containing a statue of Alfons III and one of a number of balconies in Maó to offer great views down over the port. The elegant mansion on the square's north side, **Can Mercadal**, was built by Joan Mercadal in 1761; nowadays it houses the public library. On the opposite side of the square, steps take you down snaking Costa de ses Voltes to the harbour.

Returning to the Ajuntament, C/Sant Roc heads uphill to Plaça Bastió and the **Pont de Sant Roc**, the only surviving medieval gateway into the city. Built under Pere IV in 1359, the impressive structure is almost all that is left of the second city wall, the path of which is traced by C/Rector Mort, C/Bastió, Costa d'en Deià and C/S'Arravaleta.

The narrow white belltower with stained-glass windows beside the Ajuntament is part of the Franciscan convent, founded in 1623, though the tower and most of the chapel date from the end of the 19th century. Access is restricted (unless you're a nun), but the wooden door on the left inside the entrance porch leads to the simple chapel.

From here, C/Isabel II leads off parallel to the port. This is one of the most attractive streets on the island, lined with elegant 18th-century mansions, some featuring Maó's famous bow windows or 'boinders'; a British legacy. **Palau Febrer** (at No.5, about halfway along) is one such mansion; you can see its ground-floor vaulted rooms by visiting the antique furniture shop around the corner (at C/Bonaire 33), which has access to the courtyard with a well at its centre. Since natural water sources on the island are scarce, wells are a ubiquitous feature of Menorcan architecture, both urban and rural, connecting with subterranean water cisterns that store rainwater via elaborate collection systems. They are even present in many talayotic settlements.

On the opposite side of C/Isabel II, another alleyway, Pont des General, leads down long ramps and stairs to the port, via Costa ses General and Costa ses Muret, and offers great views of the ramparts above.

A short way beyond the entrance to this alley is the island's main military headquarters, the **Gobierno Militar**, a small, domestic-looking structure around a courtyard that looks more

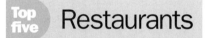

Restaurants

Café Balear
An old Ciutadella favourite, with great seafood and classic Menorcan cuisine served in a traditional family atmosphere. See p251.

C'an Olga
A delightful country restaurant with a flower-filled garden, smack-bang in the middle of the island. Excellent for authentic island cooking. See p237.

Es Cranc
Justifiably famous for its *caldereta de llagosta*, but equally good for plain grilled fish, this celebrated Fornells restaurant is simple and unpretentious. See p245.

Pan y Vino
A meal at this pretty village cottage is rather like dining in somebody's home, with great music and delicious food for the soul. See p225.

Sa Pedrera d'es Pujol
An unusual restaurant that fuses the best of British with avant-garde Asturian cuisine using local produce. See p226.

Menorca

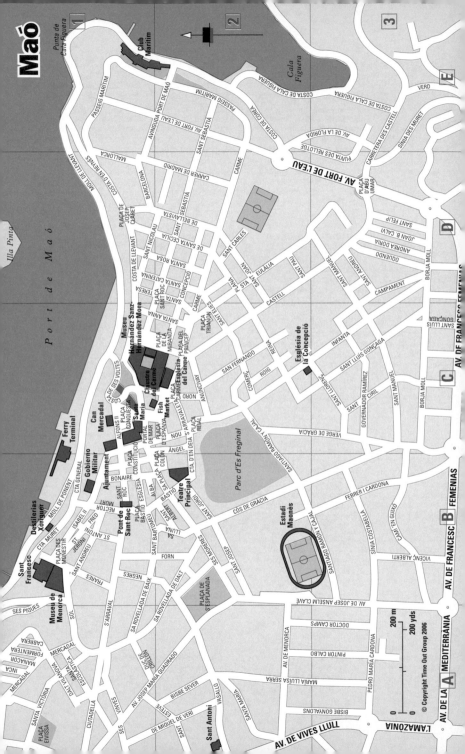

like a converted stable block than a barracks. Originally called the Casa del Rei (King's House), it initially functioned as a fortress at the north-western corner of the ramparts, and was where the governor stayed when he visited from the then capital, Ciutadella. When the capital was moved to Maó in 1722, Governor Richard Kane moved in and had what was once a rather primitive building extended.

C/Isabel II ends at the beautiful, if somewhat worn, red sandstone façade of the church of **Sant Francesc**, built between 1719 and 1792 on the site of an earlier Gothic church. Inside, the church is gloomy and badly in need of restoration, while the murals above the altar give it a black and white cartoon-like feel. The main structure is neo-Gothic, though it has a fine, if faded, baroque altarpiece. Far lighter than the main part of the church is the large, octagonal Chapel of the Immaculate Conception (1745) set into the east wall, complete with cupola and lantern.

The bright, white sandstone cloisters next door form the centrepiece of the **Museu de Menorca** (*see p214*), the largest and most comprehensive museum on the island.

Retracing your steps back to the centre of town, the slight hill beyond Plaça d'Espanya is dominated by the façade of the Carmelite **Església del Carme**, built in 1750, much to the disgust of the town's existing Franciscan community, who held up construction for as long as they could. Next to it, the cloisters (**Claustre del Carme**) have been variously used as prison, law courts and school, and now house the local market, a rather antiseptic affair, with little of the life and colour of most Spanish food markets though it's still a good place to stock up on picnic fodder. More authentic in feel is the little fish market that sits atop a bastion just down from the church. Get there before 1pm if you plan to do any buying.

The exit on the far side of the cloisters leads to Plaça de la Miranda, with more views over the port, and also gives access to the small **Museu Hernández Sanz-Hernández Mora** (*see p214*).

From Plaça d'Espanya, a long flight of steps leads down to the harbour, criss-crossed on its descent by the serpentine **Costa de ses Voltes**. At the harbour you'll often find at least one ferry or cruise ship docked, plus glass-bottomed tourist boats and a long line of restaurants and bars stretching along the waterside. Close to the ferry terminal is the **Destilerías Xoriguer**, within which is made Menorca's Xoriguer gin, one of the more positive aspects of British rule (*see p216* **The British Legacy**).

From the harbour, there is a good view of the naval base and dockyards on the far side of the port, including **Illa Pinta**, an artificial island created by the British. For a closer look at these, and the port's other islands and landmarks, take one of the tourist boats that offer trips around the harbour (such as Yellow Catamarans, *see p214*). These include the **Illa del Rei**, named after Alfons III, who landed and camped here for 12 days before launching his successful conquest of the island in 1287; it's also known as 'Bloody Island', after the now-decaying 18th-century British military hospital built here.

The next island, flat **Illa Plana** or **Illa Quarentena**, was the original quarantine station, until demand in the 18th century necessitated the building of a big hospital for infectious diseases on the larger neighbouring **Illa del Llatzeret**. This has only been an island since 1900, when a canal was cut to provide more sheltered access to the massive **Fortaleza de Isabel II**, more commonly known as **La Mola** (*see p214*), which once guarded the entrance to the port.

The harbour boat trips also give visitors a good view of the gracious British colonial mansion known as the **Golden Farm**. Set high up the hillside on the northern side of the port, the house may have been used (very briefly) by Admiral Nelson during the third British occupation of Menorca (1798-1802), but, alas, was certainly not, as a local legend has it, the scene of love trysts with Emma Hamilton. Look out also for a cute little whitewashed house projecting into the water and accessible only by a jetty – it's informally called 'Little Venice' and is owned by Richard Branson, whose connections with Menorca go back to his childhood.

Another local legend surrounds the origins of mayonnaise. The most likely story is that the chef of the Duc de Richelieu created the sauce in celebration of the French capture of Maó and Fort Sant Felip from the British in 1756. (It was originally spelt 'mahonnaise'.) Local claims that the Duc stole the recipe from the Menorcans are, alas, unlikely to be true.

If you want to pedal your way around Maó and the surrounding area, bikes can be hired for €12 a day from Velo Rent Bike (C/S'Arravaleta 52, 971 35 37 98, www.bikemenorca.com, open 10am-1.30pm, 5-8pm Mon-Fri, 10am-1.30pm Sat).

Alternatively, take to the open seas – one of the best ways of seeing the island – with the Menorca Cruising School (971 35 41 03, www.menorcasailing.co.uk), a reliable and friendly company that offers great-value luxury day sails on board their 36-foot Bavaria yachts with gourmet lunch from €125 per head (maximum of seven people per yacht); the company also runs two- to five-day sailing courses.

Menorca

The imposing edifice of Maó's **Santa Maria** church. *See p211.*

Destilerias Xoriguer

Moll de Ponent 91 (971 36 21 97/www.xoriguer.es).
Open *May-Oct* 8am-7pm Mon-Fri; 9am-1pm Sat.
Nov-Apr 9am-1pm, 4-6pm Mon-Fri. **Admission** free.
Map p212 B1.

Introduced to Menorca during the British occupation, gin has been distilled here ever since, using juniper berries that are imported from around the Mediterranean. The Xoriguer Distillery is really just a glorified shop aimed at tour groups and cruise passengers. Windows at the back look into the distillery, though there's not a great deal to see except a handful of copper stills. On the plus side, you can try various Xoriguer products, as well as the gin itself. In summer, particularly during the festival of Sant Joan, Xoriguer gin is mixed with lemonade, preferably home-made, to create a refreshing *pomada*.

Fortaleza de Isabel II (La Mola)

Ctra de la Mola (mobile 652 80 99 91). **Open**
June-Sept 10am-8pm daily; guided tours 10.30am
& 5.30pm daily. *Oct-May* 10am-2pm daily; guided
tours 10.30am daily. **Admission** €5; free under-12s.
Guided tours €1 per person. **No credit cards.**

Built in the mid 19th century, this extensive fortress guards the northern side of the entrance to Maó harbour. After the Civil War it became notorious as one of Franco's high-security political prisons. The guided tours listed above are in English (booking advisable); audioguides (in English) are an alternative for those wishing to stroll around these impressive fortifications at their own speed.

Museu de Menorca

Plaça des Monastir (971 35 09 55). **Open** *Apr-Oct* 10am-2pm, 6-8.30pm Tue-Sat; 10am-2pm Sun.
Nov-Mar 9.30am-2pm Tue-Fri; 10am-2pm Sat,
Sun. **Admission** €2.40; free-€1.20 concessions.
No credit cards. Map p212 B1.

On the first floor, after a brief but informative video introduction (available in various languages; ask at the desk), there is a collection of artefacts from prehistoric, Roman, Moorish and Catalan Menorca, plus a skeleton of *Myotragus Balearicus*, Menorca's indigenous but long-extinct goat-like mammal – a cheeky chappy with a devilish smile, short horns and eyes mounted in the front of his head (like a chimpanzee), rather than the side (like modern goats and sheep). Upstairs is an extensive collection of maps and paintings, mostly from the 18th and 19th centuries.

Museu Hernández Sanz-Hernández Mora

Plaça Claustre del Carme 5 (971 35 05 97). **Open**
Museum 10am-1pm Mon-Sat. *Library* 10am-1pm
Mon-Fri. **Admission** free. **Map** p212 C1.

This private collection consists of four rooms of furniture, paintings and maps from the 18th, 19th and 20th centuries, with a library on the top floor.

Yellow Catamarans

*Port de Maó, at foot of Costa de ses Voltes (mobile
639 67 63 51).* **Departures** *May-Oct* 10.30am,
11.15am, noon, 12.45pm, 1.30pm, 2.15pm, 3pm (also
3.45pm, 4.30pm June-Sept) Mon-Sat; 10.45am,
12.15pm, 1.45pm Sun. No service Nov-Apr. **Tickets**
€8.50; €4.50 concessions; free under-5s. **Credit** MC,
V. **Map** p212 C1.

Where to eat & drink

Maó prides itself on its seafood, with plenty of fish restaurants along the port, varying considerably in price and quality, as well as other types of Mediterranean and even Asian cuisine. Restaurants in the old town tend to be more individual, with some really excellent places to eat, although the main drag has its fair share of lasagne-and-chips tourist traps. The old town is where most of the cafés are, with several uninspiring bars around Plaça de s'Esplanada – the Café Amadeus is probably the best for coffee and sandwiches – and more attractive places hidden among quiet side streets, while most of the more sophisticated late-night bars are back down in the port.

Old Town

Amatxo

Rovellada de Dalt, Conde de Cifuentes 20 (971 35 38 48). **Open** noon-5pm, 7pm-1am Mon-Sat. **Average** €€. **Credit** AmEx, MC, V. **Map** p212 B2.

While most Basque restaurants are rustic and hearty, Amatxo is cool and minimalist. And the food is excellent – from the interesting Basque-style montaditos (tapas on bread) on the bar to the full-sized meals served at the four tables on the ground floor or in the slightly more formal dining room upstairs. Here traditional dishes are given that nouveau twist – an aperitif of *granizado de gazpacho* (gazpacho sorbet) or hake on a pea sauce (basically a gourmet version of fish and mushy peas) – and the desserts are fabulous.

American Bar

Plaça Reial 8 (971 36 18 22). **Open** *June-Sept* 7am-1am daily. *Oct-May* 7am-10pm daily. **Average** €. **No credit cards**. **Map** p212 C2.

A large, popular French-style café with a pavement terrace and refurbished interior hung with black and white photos that show how characterful it was before the decorators were let loose. It's still popular with locals and tourists of all ages, and serves decent coffee, continental breakfasts, sandwiches and snacks.

Ars Café

Plaça del Príncep 12B (971 36 80 41). **Open** 8.30am-midnight Mon-Sat. Closed Aug. **Average** €. **Credit** AmEx, DC, MC, V. **Map** p212 C2.

With a few notable exceptions, *modernisme* (Catalan art nouveau) more or less passed Maó by. Plaça del Príncep, however, features a couple of attractive *modernista* buildings, including the casino. What was once its 'summer bar' has become the attractive Ars Café, a small, atmospheric café-restaurant offering *torrades* (slices of thick toast smeared with tomato, drizzled with olive oil and topped with cheese, ham, anchovies, etc), sandwiches and interesting salads. The no-choice lunch *menú* is excellent and good value. In summer there are just two, highly coveted tables outside and there's a club/disco in the cellar.

Cristanal y Gradinata

C/Isabel II 1 (971 36 33 16). **Open** 8.30am-3pm, 7.30pm-midnight Mon-Fri; 11am-3pm Sat. Closed 10-30 Sept. **Average** €. **Credit** MC, V. **Map** p212 B1.

A stylish jazz bar with red velvet couches, glass-topped wooden tables, Ella on the sound system and antique radios along the walls. It serves excellent coffee and simple sandwiches, with a short menu of

more elaborate *torrades* and sandwiches available for a couple of hours in the evening.

Café Mirador

Plaça d'Espanya 2 (971 35 21 07). **Open** *June-Oct* 10am-2am Mon-Sat. *Nov-May* noon-midnight Mon-Sat. **Average** €. **Credit** V. **Map** p212 C1/C2.

Halfway up the cliff-side above the port, the easy-going Café Mirador is unique in location, atmosphere and view, and is one of the stalwarts of the Maó scene. Large windows and a summer terrace offer vistas over the ramparts and the harbour. Indigenous masks from around the world add a little colour, as does the music, which is often from similar places. A good range of tapas, sandwiches and salads are available all day.

Ses Palmeras

Plaça Colon 6 (971 36 47 17). **Open** *June-Sept* 7am-8.30pm Mon Sat; 9am 1pm Sun. *Oct May* 7am 5pm Mon-Sat. **Average** €. **Credit** AmEx, MC, V. **Map** p212 B2.

Wherever there's a palm tree, there seems to be a bar called 'The Palm Trees' and Maó is no exception. Ses Palmeras, in the corner of pretty Plaça Colon, is a small place frequented by locals, especially in the morning when it does a brisk trade in decent coffee and delicious bacon and tomato sandwiches. Indeed,

The *modernista* **Café Baixamar**. *See p217.*

it's one of the best places in town for cheap, simple fare with a bargain-priced lunchtime *menú* (not Sundays). Inside, the atmosphere is usually loud and bustling; outside, the tables in the square offer a calm oasis, set a little back from the activity of the town's main pedestrianised street.

La Tropical

C/Sa Lluna 36 (971 36 05 56). **Open** 7.30am-midnight Mon, Tue, Thur-Sun. Closed mid Feb-mid Mar. **Average** €. **Credit** AmEx, DC, MC, V. **Map** p212 B2.

A good, unpretentious Spanish café-restaurant close to Plaça de s'Esplanada and open at all hours of the day for coffee, snacks and more substantial meals, including a hearty set lunch *menú*.

Port

Akelarre

Moll de Ponent 41 (971 36 85 20/www.akelarre jazz.com). **Open** *June-Sept* 8am-4am daily. *Oct-May* 8pm-4am daily. **Admission** €10 incl 1 drink. **No credit cards. Map** p212 B1.

This large, atmospheric former warehouse is the city's leading venue for good quality blues and jazz, with stone arches, a paved floor and the bare rock of the cliff-face dominating the tiny courtyard at the back. At weekends and in summer live music packs the place out, and there's the recent addition of stand-up comedy every Wednesday. All in all, it's Maó's best bet for a grown-up night out.

The British legacy

For 71 of the 94 years between 1708 and 1802 the British ruled Menorca. It was a period of unprecedented European significance for the island and one that hasn't been without its legacies. Perhaps not the least of these is the fondness of British holidaymakers for the island. The Brits make up 29 per cent of foreign visitors to Mallorca, but 60 per cent in Menorca.

The island's most far-sighted Governor, Richard Kane (*see p238* **Local heroes**) introduced numerous innovations and improvements to the island in the first half of the 18th century, the most significant of which was probably the Camí d'en Kane (Kane's Road) between Maó and Ciutadella. Much of the current main road between the towns still follows its course. Defensive works such as Fort Marlborough and 11 coastal watchtowers are more evidence of the British presence.

Kane was responsible for introducing several species of livestock and crop. He brought in apples, still called Pomes d'en Quen, and the ubiquitous Friesian cows to make all that cheese. Later, to feed them, the British also introduced the clover that fills the hedgerows each spring. There are even plums called Prunes de Neversó, after Kane allegedly declared one day, 'I never saw such plums.'

Another legacy is the famous bow windows, or 'boinders' in Menorcan, that adorn many of the elegant townhouses on the island, and the sash technology to open them. There are the door latches too, the kind with a thumb lever on one side of the door, the latch on the other, and so foreign on much of the Continent that even today many guidebooks offer instructions on how to use them.

Not all British contributions to the island were due to official policy. There was a huge garrison stationed on the island, and with prostitution banned and windsurfing still not invented, there wasn't a lot for a homesick sailor to do but drink. And what sailors drank in the 18th century was gin, and plenty of it. So enterprising local tradesmen imported juniper berries from around the Mediterranean and set about distilling gin, as they do to this day (*see p213*).

The Brits also contributed generously to Menorcan vocabulary, and while a lot of it is the language of commerce, carpentry and ship-building (a *tornescrú* is a screwdriver, *moguin* or *mòguini* is mahogany, a *rul* is a ruler) a lot came from less formal sources. When a scuffle breaks out between two or more *mens* (men), or even *bois* (boys), it's called *fàitim*, from 'fight him', the result of which could be an *ull blèc* (black eye), though it's a good idea to patch it up with a *xaquèns* (handshake). Alternatively you could go down to the port and *fer un berguin*, which is to make a deal, but came to mean contracting the services of a prostitute (Kane's ban notwithstanding). You drink from a *moc* (mug) or a *bòtil*, boil water in a *quíter* or *quítel* (kettle), and serve rum, gin, grog, *punx* (punch) or *xèri* (sherry) on your *saidbord* (sideboard). Lower down the ranks, you're a *mitjamen*, from 'midshipman', which is someone foolish, unknown or middle-class – or possibly all three – but if you're an elegant gentleman, you might be a *milord*, married to a *miledi*. Though a *milord* is also a yacht, and a *miledi* can also mean a strange, ugly (British) lady, so clearly not all British imports to the island met with local approval.

Restaurant row down at the port:
Moll de Llevant. *See p216.*

Café Baixamar

Moll de Ponent 17 (971 36 58 96). **Open** *May-Oct*
8am-4am daily. *Nov-Apr* noon-3am daily. **Average** €.
No credit cards. Map p212 B1. **Photo** *p215.*
A friendly, airy *modernista* café with original wood
panelling, an old, ornate bar, marble tables and a
wood-burning stove. Open all day, it's great for a
morning coffee, a late-night drink or anything in
between. An excellent range of salads, snacks and
sandwiches is available all day.

Elefant

Moll de Llevant 106 (971 36 17 08). **Open** phone for
details. **Average** €. **No credit cards. Map** p212 D1.
Painted red, with silk drapes, candles and glittery
knick-knacks, this cosy harbourside lounge has an
Arabic feel to it. It serves a good range of Asian-
inspired vegetarian tapas and has weekend wind-
down sessions on Sunday evenings.

S'Espigó

Moll de Llevant 267 (971 36 99 09). **Open** 1-3.30pm,
8-11.30pm Tue-Sun. Closed Jan. **Average** €€€€.
Credit AmEx, DC, MC, V. **Map** p212 D1.
One of the most respected fish restaurants on the
island, serving classic, simply prepared fresh fish
in an intimate, rather formal setting. The food
is generally excellent, though the service can be a
little wayward at times.

Els Fosquets

Moll de Llevant 56 (971 35 00 58). **Open** *Apr, May*
7.30pm-midnight Thur; 1-3.30pm, 7.30pm-midnight
Fri-Sun. *June-Sept* 7.30pm-midnight Tue-Sun. Closed
Oct-Mar. **Average** €€€. **Credit** V. **Map** p212 D1.
A one-time boathouse dug into the rock, informal
Els Fosquets was one of the first restaurants in the
port, established over a quarter of a century ago.
Despite several changes of ownership, it is still an
institution, renowned for its extremely fresh fish,
cooked simply but very well. The current owners
have retained the basic formula, but added more
adventurous starters and desserts, such as langoustines with mango and chilli, swordfish tartar
with wasabi, and octopus salad. Main courses
depend on the catch of the day, as well as the number of diners: some fish feed a minimum of three.

Itake

Moll de Llevant 317 (971 35 45 70). **Open** 1-3.30pm,
8-11.30pm Tue-Sun. Closed 20 Dec-20 Jan. **Average**
€€. **Credit** AmEx, DC, MC, V. **Map** p212 D1.
Itake is one of Menorca's most idiosyncratic restaurants, from the non-matching crockery and glassware to the mini news-sheet that features the set
lunch menu and the main menu, sprinkled with
anecdotes about the British and French occupations (in Spanish and Catalan). The food is no less
individual, with a whole range of hearty, atypical

Menorca

dishes, including pancakes, brochettes, filled baked potatoes, duck, rabbit stew and grilled vegetables, all served in a friendly, low-key atmosphere.

Jàgaro

Moll de Llevant 334 (971 36 23 90). **Open** *May-Oct* 1-4pm, 8pm-11pm daily. *Nov-Apr* 1-4pm Mon, Sun; 1-4pm, 8pm-midnight Tue-Sat. **Average** €€€. **Credit** AmEx, DC, MC, V. **Map** p212 D1.

A rather eccentric restaurant at the port's south end, Jàgaro feels like a cross between a country kitchen, a conservatory and an artist's studio, full of plants, wickerwork screens and maritime paintings. As well the usual fish and seafood there are unusual additions such as fried sea anemone and sea cucumber, as well as vegetarian paella. When the chef-owner is on form, it can be excellent.

Latitud 40

Anden de Llevant 265 (971 36 41 76). **Open** *May-Oct* 7pm-3am daily. *Nov-Apr* 7pm-3am Mon-Sat. **Average** €€. **Credit** MC, V. **Map** p212 D1.

Wedged between two of the best fish restaurants in Maó, this small bar with a restaurant upstairs is perhaps wise to focus on other things. The food shows influences of French cuisine seen through the prism of an English pub, but is none the worse for it. The bar is one of the few places that is open year round, and the only one that's always busy, thanks to owner Niki's reputation as the host with the most.

La Mar

Moll de Llevant 275 (971 43 65 51). **Open** 7.30pm-1am daily. Closed Jan. **Average** €€. **Credit** MC, V. **Map** p212 D1.

Don't be put off by the canvas director's chairs, wooden deck floor and air of informality. Popular with the yachting crowd, the food here is simple but delicious, consisting of salads, *torrades* and good tapas in a restrained, rather sophisticated atmosphere.

Minerva

Moll de Llevant 87 (971 35 19 95). **Open** 1-3.30pm, 7-11.30pm daily. **Average** €€€. **Credit** AmEx, DC, MC, V. **Map** p212 D1.

Many of the large seafood restaurants along this part of the port are similar in cuisine, quality, decor and price. Minerva's selling point is the floating pontoon moored to the quay, providing the closest view of the port possible (unless you have your own yacht). If you come here in winter and they know your face, you can apparently eat very well. Otherwise it can be something of a lottery, especially in July and August when the restaurant is often bursting at the seams. There are usually two set lunch *menús*.

Il Porto

Moll de Llevant 225 (971 35 44 26). **Open** *Feb-June, Sept, Oct* 1-3.30pm, 7pm-midnight Mon, Tue, Thur-Sun. *July, Aug* 6.30pm-1am daily. Closed Nov-Jan. **Average** €€€. **Credit** AmEx, MC, V. **Map** p212 D1.

It's difficult to miss this large, yellow-hued Italian restaurant, serving a variety of excellent, authentic meat, pasta and pizza dishes, including deliciously

tender lamb, large platters of grilled vegetables and good home-made desserts. The main dining room inside has a maritime feel, with bright wood and large, arched windows out on to the harbourside; next door there's an airier overspill.

La Sirena

Moll de Llevant 200 (971 35 07 40). **Open** *May, June, Sept* 7pm-11pm Mon, Wed-Sun. *July, Aug* 1-4pm, 7pm-midnight daily. **Average** €€. **Credit** AmEx, DC, MC, V. **Map** p212 D1.

A small, homely restaurant offering 'wholefood', with influences as diverse as Central Europe and the Far East. Not exclusively vegetarian.

Varadero

Moll de Llevant 4 (971 35 20 74). **Open** Bar *May-Oct* 9.30am-2am Mon-Sat; 7pm-2am Sun. *Dec-Apr* 11am-11pm Mon-Sat; 11am-5pm Sun. Restaurant *May-Oct* 1-3.30pm, 8-11.30pm Mon-Sat; 8-11.30pm Sun. *Dec-Apr* 1-3.30pm, 8-11pm Mon-Sat; 1-3.30pm Sun. **Average** €€. **Credit** AmEx, DC, MC, V. **Map** p212 D1.

Tucked behind one of the port authority buildings at the foot of Costa de ses Voltes, and with an excellent view along the port as the sun sets, Varadero is uniquely unaffected by the traffic that compromises every other waterside restaurant in Maó – though when the cruise ships moor too close the view is reduced to a wall of painted steel. The small restaurant serves fish and paella, while the terrace is a great place for a quiet drink.

Nightlife

Maó's limited nightlife is quiet as the grave in winter months, but transforms into a right little goer come summer. It also has an increasingly strong jazz scene, with its own festival that starts in April and lasts all summer, featuring live bands in bars and on plaças across town. **Akelarre** (*see p220*) is the best spot for live music, attracting an impressive array of international artists as well as local talent.

Nearby **Sant Climent** (*see p225*) – on the road from Maó to Cala en Porter – is a surprise hub for jazz lovers, and has achieved something of a reputation for its excellent jam sessions (Tuesday nights at the old **Casino** from May to October), which has been known to attract the odd celebrity. As ex-drummer with Pentangle, Terry Cox, who has been living on the island since 1970 puts it: 'It can be excellent, but most importantly it always has a brilliant atmosphere and it's a good place to meet the locals.'

For a more frenzied scene, most of the drinking holes and discos in Maó are scattered along the port. This isn't always convenient, since it's long and snaking, but does make for a good bar hop in the summer months, starting at **Latitud 40** (*see above*) at the easternmost end and working your way back along the Moll de Ponent to the bottom of Costa d'es General. With the exception of **Café Baixamar** (*see p217*) and **Akelarre**, almost nothing moves before midnight. When it does, it really moves, with four hours of frantic activity before compulsory closing time at 4am. There is something for everyone here, including house, ambient, techno, jazz, funk and salsa. **Virtual** (next door to Akelarre) is the latest incarnation of local Latin-themed bars, this time with Dominican tunes – grinding meringue, liquid salsa and buckets of rum punch. Head up the hill on Costa d'es General and the gaggle of bars are of similar stock: **Aura** at No.22 is dark and groovy; **Onda** at No.20 is dark and dingy; **Tse Tse Bar** at No.4 has a more bohemian feel. Do as locals do and hop from one to the other through the night.

Shopping

Most of Maó's shops are concentrated around C/Ses Moreres, Costa de sa Plaça and C/Nou. This is where you will find most of the main clothes, shoe and accessories chains, as well as a few smaller, more individual outlets. In general, though, Maó is not as good a bet for shops as Ciutadella. For locally made goods, including shoes, bags, jewellery and clothes, there are several boutiques interspersed among the restaurants in the port, particularly along Moll de Ponent. These have more character than their counterparts in the old town, and in high season stay open late for the pre- and post-dinner crowd.

For local and foreign cheeses and cured meats, the best place to shop is **J y J** (Plaça d'Espanya 11, 971 36 94 91), which has more variety and better quality produce than the covered market nearby in the Claustre del Carme. The main market, selling mostly shoddy and badly made clothes, is held in Plaça de s'Esplanada every Tuesday and Saturday.

For the obligatory pair of *abarcas* (Menorcan leather sandals with soles made of old car tyres) **S'Avarca de Menorca** (C/Àngel 14, 971 36 63 41) is the oldest factory on the island. If peasant clobber isn't quite your thing, **Jaime Mascaró** (C/Ses Moreres 29, 971 36 05 68), Menorca's poshest shoemaker, offers highly covetable butter-soft leather pumps and stilettos for ladies, and brogues and dress shoes for gents. (The Jaime Mascaró factory shop is just outside Ferreries; *see p238*.)

Where to stay

Menorca's capital has not experienced the designer hotel boom of its big sister Palma, though there are signs that things could soon

Hotel Catalonia Mirador d'es Port. *See p221.*

be changing on the island-that-cool-forgot. For now most of the hotels are either business-bland or basic *hostales* that are fine for a bed but lack soul. If it is boutique chic you're after, you'll need to stay outside town (see particularly the chapter **South Menorca**).

Hotel Capri

C/Sant Esteve 8 (971 36 14 00/www.rtmhotels.com). **Rates** €74-€156 double; €51-€130 apartment per person. **Credit** AmEx, DC, MC, V. **Map** p212 A2.

Conveniently located a few minutes' walk from Plaça de s'Esplanada, the Hotel Capri is a popular and comfortable, mid-range hotel with 75 well-equipped, spacious rooms, almost all with balconies (on to the street or the courtyard at the back.) There's also a small gym, jacuzzi, sun deck and pool with retractable roof, with views over Maó and the surrounding area. Massages and beauty treatments are available. Next door are seven self-catering apartments. The Restaurant Capri downstairs serves excellent pizzas and does a good value lunch menú.

Eurohotel

C/Santa Cecilia 41 (971 36 48 55). **Rates** €57-€103 double. **No credit cards. Map** p212 D2.
One block in from the harbour, this bright, reasonably priced hotel down a quiet side street was refurbished in 1997. Rooms are a little small, and fitted out with all the personality of a corporate-style hotel, but it's clean and comfortable. At the time of writing it was up for sale, though it should remain a hotel.

La Isla

C/Santa Caterina 4 (971 36 64 92). Closed Dec. **Rates** (incl breakfast) €42-€50 double. **Credit** MC, V. **Map** p212 D2.
A modest, 24-room *hostal* above a bar-restaurant of the same name. It's a little bare and dingy, but the owners are friendly and the rooms are clean and quiet, and all have en suite bathrooms.

Jume

C/Concepció 6 (971 36 32 66). Closed 16 Dec-8 Jan. **Rates** (incl breakfast) €44-€50 double. **Credit** MC, V. **Map** p212 C2.
A classic old-style *pensió*, run by a sweet and chirpy old Menorcan couple, with 35 simple but comfortable rooms, all with en suite bathrooms, and a cosy breakfast room. It's not the lap of luxury, but it's not as depressing as some of the other cheaper options in the city and attracts its fair share of budget business travellers.

Hotel Catalonia Mirador d'es Port

Dalt Vilanova 1 (971 36 00 16/www.hoteles-catalonia.com). **Rates** €67-€140 double. **Credit** AmEx, DC, MC, V. **Map** p212 A1. **Photo** *see p220.*
This reasonable mid-range option, located at the western end of the ramparts, close to the Museu de Menorca, has a good view of the port (albeit the more industrial end) from its dining room and terrace. The decor is corporate smart, with lots of blond wood and Scandinavian blues. Rooms are comfortable if unremarkable and most have at least a partial view of the port, as well as looking down on attractive gardens, complete with swimming pool, and the rooftops of the old town.

Hotel Port-Mahón

Avda. Fort de l'Eau 13 (971 36 26 00/www.set hotels.com). **Rates** (incl breakfast) €95-€164 double. **Credit** AmEx, DC, MC, V. **Map** p212 E2.
To relive the days of empire, head for this elegant hotel, a claret-coloured mansion built in English colonial style overlooking the port, with great views from the terrace bar, poolside garden and dining room. By far the nicest hotel in Maó, its appearance is deceptive, dating from 1956 not 1756, but it still manages to recapture a distant colonial splendour.

Posada Orsi

C/Infanta 19 (971 36 47 51). Closed end Dec-end Jan. **Rates** €28-€47 double. **Credit** AmEx, DC, MC, V. **Map** p212 C3.
The best budget option in Maó is this bright, cheerful *hostal*, a perennial favourite close to the market. Rooms are airy and very brightly painted in a variety of bold colours, while upstairs there is a small sitting room and kitchen. Three of the double rooms have en suite bathrooms; otherwise washing facilities are communal, but were given a major overhaul in 2003, with fresh paint and fittings. There's also a cute three-person apartment.

Resources

Internet

Ciber Principal, C/Nou 25 (971 36 26 89). **Open** *June-Oct* 9.30am-10pm Mon-Fri; 11am-2pm, 6-10pm Sat, Sun. *Nov-May* 10am-10pm Mon-Fri; 11am-2pm, 6-10pm Sat, Sun. **Map** p212 C2.
Comunicate, C/Vassallo 22B (971 36 55 11). **Open** 10am-11pm Mon-Sat; 6-11pm Sun. **Map** p212 A2.

Police station

Plaça Constitució 21 (971 36 39 61). **Map** p212 C1.

Post office

C/Bonaire 11 (971 35 66 29). **Map** p212 B1.

Tourist information

Moll de Llevant 2 (971 35 59 52/www.e-menorca.org). **Map** p212 D1.
Maó Airport (971 15 71 15/www.e-menorca.org). **Open** *Feb-Nov* 8am-10pm Mon, Wed-Fri, Sun; 8am-1pm Tue, Sat.

Getting there

For air and sea links to Maó, *see p262.*

By bus

Local buses stop in Maó at Plaça de s'Esplanada, while island-wide services operate from Avda. JM Quadrado. There are 7 buses Mon-Sat and 6 on Sun between Maó and Ciutadella (1hr), via Alaior (20mins), Es Mercadal (30mins) and Ferreries (40mins). Other services from Maó include 26 buses Mon-Sat (20 Sun) to Es Castell (10mins), 13 buses Mon-Sat (12 Sun) to Sant Lluís (10mins), 6 buses daily to Alcaufar (20mins), 3 buses daily to Binibèquer (20mins), 12 buses Mon-Sat (4 Sun) to Sant Climent (10mins), 7 buses Mon-Sat to Cala en Porter (20mins), 5 buses Mon-Sat (4 on Sun) to Cala Galdana (1hr) via Ferreries (40mins), 6 buses Mon-Sat to Son Bou (35mins) via Alaior, 2 buses Mon-Fri (1 on Sat) to Sant Tomàs (40mins), 2 buses Mon-Sat to Fornells (35mins).

Menorca

South Menorca

The best restaurants, the biggest beaches and potloads of prehistory.

Cales Fonts, Es Castell. *See p224.*

Low hills, narrow bays and rugged sandstone cliffs; pint-sized harbours and quaint fishing villages; patchwork wheat fields stitched together with drystone walling – all combine to give the south-eastern corner of the Menorca the flavour of Blighty in miniature. It's a feeling reinforced by the large British expat community who have made this part of the island their (first or second) home. Together with resident wealthy Spaniards, they give this tiny portion of a tiny island an unmistakable whiff of privilege. The south-east is also where you'll find the strip nicknamed by locals the 'golden mile' for its gourmet restaurants and delightful rural hotels and *agroturismos* (working farmhouse hotels). It also boasts a wealth of important prehistoric ruins, which contrast pleasantly with the innumerable white-washed villages that look as though someone has shaken a bag of sugar cubes and let them fall at will across the soft, downy hills.

Further west, the island's longest beaches are backed by purpose-built resorts, and the shoreline rises up into cliffs that are cut by spectacular gorges.

Prehistoric south-east

This part of the island is particularly rich in talayotic settlements (*see p16* **Prehistory primer**). The most impressive in terms of size and conservation is **Trepucó**, situated a kilometre south of Maó. The base of the talayot here is in very good condition, as is the taula precinct, with a particularly tall taula (its support stone has now been replaced by a concrete block). This was once a sizeable settlement, though only a small portion of it has been excavated.

Further south, a kilometre east of Sant Lluís, **Trebalúger** is less well preserved, though it offers good views over the surrounding area. The same distance the other side of Sant Lluís, **Binisafullet** is located in an attractive grove, but is in very poor condition and makes little sense unless you have previously seen a more complete ruin. **So na Caçana**, four kilometres (two and a half miles) west of Sant Climent, is more interesting, with two taula precincts, one of which is sited right next to the talayot.

Menorca

A few minutes' drive north of here on the road to Alaior, **Torralba d'en Salort** is far more complete and impressive, with a tall taula within its sanctuary, two well-preserved talayots, a hypostyle room (a chamber with a roof supported by pillars) and the ruins of several prehistoric buildings (plus an even more ruined 17th-century chapel, providing evidence of continuing use of the site over almost 3,000 years). Archaeological excavations and pathways make the remains more easily comprehensible than on many Menorcan sites, though these, plus the refreshment kiosk/ticket office, take away some of the mystery. The explanatory leaflet you can pick up here is usually, though.

Midway between Maó and Alaior, the two navetas of **Rafal Rubí** stand just north of the main road. Though they are not as well preserved as the Naveta d'es Tudons near Ciutadella, their rural setting is evocative. The northern naveta has an interesting doorway, made from a single stone with a square hole cut into it, including a flange to hold the door itself.

A couple of kilometres back towards Maó, **Talatí de Dalt** (sometimes referred to as simply Talatí), just off the Maó–Ciutadella road, is one of the most comprehensive sites on the island. It has been partially excavated, and a useful explanatory pamphlet is available from the hut at the entrance. Within a lovely bucolic setting, you can wander around the remains of its talayot, taula (with a fallen pillar resting against one end of it), dwellings and defensive wall.

Nearby, on an extremely narrow lane just east of Sant Climent, off the Sant Climent–Maó road, is the talayot of **Torellonet Vell**. Further up this lane are the remains of the basilica of **Fornàs de Torelló**, an early Christian church similar to the one at Son Bou. Little remains of the structure other than its impressive mosaic floor, now enclosed in a huge roofed cage to protect it from the weather, vandals and thieves.

With the exception of Talatí de Dalt and Torralba d'en Salort, all the prehistoric sites mentioned above are open access.

Talatí de Dalt

Ctra. Maó–Ciutadella, km4 (mobile 607 90 08 86/ www.arqueomenorca.com). **Open** 9.30am-sunset daily. **Admission** €3; €2 concessions. **No credit cards.**

Torralba d'en Salort

Ctra. Alaior–Cala en Porter (mobile 696 21 76 64). **Open** *June-Sept* 10am-8pm daily. Closed 1st Sat of mth. *Oct-May* 10am-1pm, 3-6pm Mon-Sat. **Admission** €3; €1.50 concessions. **No credit cards.**

Es Castell & Sant Esteve

In the 18th century, the poor people of **Es Castell**, a couple of kilometres east of Maó, didn't know whether they were coming or going. When British soldiers and their families (during the first period of occupation – 1708-56) built their homes in the lee of the castle of Sant Felip, their settlement was known as Philipstown. During their second period of occupation (1763-82), the British decided to move the town further from the castle to its present site, which they called Georgetown after George III. When the Spanish took over in 1782, they changed the town's name again, to Vilacarlos, after Carlos III. Nowadays, it's simply called 'The Castle', to pre-empt any future changes to its name.

Except there is no castle. With a sense of perverse logic, the Spanish tore the castle down, thinking that if there were no defences

Top five Agroturismos

Until a few years ago there was virtually no classy accommodation on Menorca, but now the *agroturismo* (characterful quality rural accommodation) boom that has characterised Mallorca in the last five or so years has finally reached its smaller neighbour. Here are our pick of the five finest places to stay on the island.

Alcaufar Vell

Built around a Moorish tower, this relaxed, graceful hotel combines sophistication and simplicity. *See p227.*

Biniarroca

An intimate, enjoyably eccentric farmhouse hotel that is a haven of peace, and features a fabulous pool. *See p227.*

Sant Joan de Binissaida

One of the newest kids on the block, this is possibly the finest, friendliest rural hotel on the island, and has excellent food. *See p225.*

Hotel Sant Ignasi

Within easy reach of Ciutadella, Sant Ignasi was one of the first classy spots to stay in Menorca, and has a first-rate restaurant. *See p257.*

Son Triay

The perfect retreat, Son Triay preserves the air of the old family stately home that it remains. *See p234.*

Menorca

the British wouldn't be interested in the island (overlooking the fact that it was the port of Maó that had always been the primary draw). In the event, when the British returned in 1798, they landed at Fornells and Addaia on the north of the island.

Today, Es Castell is an attractive place, built along a regimented grid with a large parade ground at its centre, edged by barracks buildings along the east and west sides. The town hall – a low, red building with a clock tower – is on the northern side, with a small military museum, the **Museu Militar de Menorca**, standing opposite. It contains weapons and various maps from the last three centuries, plus scale models of fortresses and ancient ruins, portraits of British admirals and period furniture.

From the main square, it's a short downhill walk to the picturesque fishing boat-specked little bay of **Cales Fonts**. Edged by restaurants and bars, it's a lovely spot for a stroll, a snack and an evening drink. Boat trips around the port leave from here.

Further west towards Maó is Es Castell's second bay, the narrower, quieter Cala Corb.

The scant remains of **Fort Sant Felip** stand on a headland above the lovely inlet of **Cala Sant Esteve**, a five-minute drive south-east of Es Castell. They can only be visited by guided tour and consist of little more than earth ramparts, though these, especially seen in aerial photographs, show how impressive the whole site would once have been.

This is also the most easterly point of the island (aptly named Sol del Este) and it's well worth shaking yourself out of bed to witness memorable sunrises from here.

A more worthwhile visit than Fort Sant Felip is to **Fort Marlborough**, on the southern side of the inlet, just above the charming village of **Sant Esteve**. This unusual subterranean fortress, built by the British between 1710 and 1726 and named after John Churchill, Duke of Marlborough, is almost entirely below the level of the surrounding hill. An introductory audio-visual show (available in English) gives some good background on the fort and its history, before visitors follow a marked path through the fort's gloomy, claustrophobic and hugely atmospheric rock-hewn tunnels. It suffered two long sieges – by the French in 1756 and the Spanish in 1781 – and an impressive use of life-size figures and sound and light effects make it all too easy to imagine just how scary it would have been inside the fort at such times.

During the sieges the French and Spanish bombarded the fort from the hill just to the south. To prevent any repeat of this, the British built the sturdy **Torre d'en Penjat** on this

hill in 1798; it's sometimes known as **Torre Stuart**, after General Stuart, who ordered its construction.

Fort Marlborough
Cala de Sant Esteve (971 36 04 62). **Open** 10am-1pm, 5-8pm Tue-Sat; 10am-2pm Sun. Closed Jan-Mar. **Admission** €3; €1.80 concessions. **No credit cards.**

Fort Sant Felip
971 36 21 00. **Open** (Guided tour only) *June-Oct* 10am Mon, Thur. *Nov-May* 10am Sat. **Admission** €3; €1.50 concessions. **No credit cards.**

Museu Militar de Menorca
Plaça de s'Esplanada 19, Es Castell (971 36 21 00). **Open** *June-Oct* 11am-1pm Mon-Fri & 1st Sun of mth. *Nov-May* 11am-1pm Mon, Wed, Thur & 1st Sun of mth. **Admission** €3; €1.50 concessions. **No credit cards.**

Where to eat & drink

Most of Es Castell's bars and restaurants are concentrated around traffic-free Cales Fonts, which is a good alternative to Maó for a pleasant waterside meal. Situated in one of the most notable buildings on the bay, **Sa Torre des Sol** (C/Victori 54, 971 36 03 99, www.satorredes sol.com, closed dinner Mon & Sun, €€) is the former home of the local harbourmaster, who controlled maritime traffic from the top of the 18th-century building's tower. The restaurant offers excellent and unusual Menorcan dishes in a smart, contemporary setting.

Miramar (Cales Fonts 15, 971 36 46 43, closed Mon-Fri Dec-Feb and all Mar & Nov, €€) is the oldest and most charismatic restaurant on the bay, and serves good tapas. **Club Náutico** (Camí de Baix 8, 971 38 11 46, €€), above the harbour at the western end, has a great view and is popular with the locals.

In Cala Corb, **Bar Es Cau** (no phone) is where local musicians go to sing and play the guitar. If you just want a glass of wine **Sa Vinya** (Moll d'en Pons 7, 971 35 03 84, closed lunch and all Mon Apr-mid June & Sept, and all Oct-Mar) has the best selection around, including a couple of the island's new, home-grown wines. At the far end of the village, by the roundabout leading to Sant Lluís, **Boomerang Restaurant** (C/San José 47, 971 35 46 15, closed Mon, €€€), in a deep, low-roofed cave, specialises in suckling pig, though you have to book your piglet at least a day in advance.

Where to stay

The choice in Es Castell is between three large, reasonably comfortable chain-style hotels or a very rough local *hostal* off the main square. A further alternative is the lovely **Hotel del**

Almirante in Collingwood House (Puerto de Mahón s/n, 971 36 27 00, www.hoteldel almirante.com, closed Nov-Apr, doubles €72-€92 incl breakfast), halfway between Es Castell and Maó. Built in the 18th century for Admiral Collingwood, much of the original house has been left more or less untouched, so it's a little like staying in a museum, although most of the rooms are in an adjacent modern extension. Unusual and surprisingly inexpensive.

The three large hotels, **Agamenón** (C/Agamenón 16, 971 36 21 50, www.set hotels.com, closed Nov-Apr, doubles €90-€152 incl breakfast), **Barceló Hamilton** (Passeig de Santa Agueda s/n, 971 36 20 50, www.barcelo. com, doubles €72-€110) and **Rey Carlos III** (C/Carlos III 2-4, 971 36 31 00, www.reycarlos iii.com, closed Nov-Apr, doubles €73-€104 incl breakfast) all look out over the harbour, and are comfortable, if a little bland.

Just outside the town, on the road to Sant Lluís, however, are two gems. The splendid **Son Granot** (Ctra. Sant Felip s/n, 971 35 55 55, www.songranot.com, closed Nov-Apr, doubles €128-€220) was built during the first British occupation by Scot Patrick Mackellar and proudly lords it over the surrounding landscape in fine colonial style. The ten beautiful rooms are straight out of an interiors magazine and there's a further room that has been specially adapted for the disabled. A pool and classy restaurant (€€€) are additional attractions.

A more recent arrival on the accommodation scene is the lustrous **Sant Joan de Binissaida** (Camí de Binissaida 108, 971 35 55 98, www.bin issaida.com, doubles €72-€210 incl breakfast), a beautifully renovated farmhouse dating back to 1887. It opened in 2004 and is fast on its way to becoming another gourmet mecca, though you have to stay here to eat. There's a wonderfully welcoming and laid-back atmosphere to the place, which is extended to kids, who are encouraged to lend a hand in the kitchen, feed the farm's various animals and generally have as good a time as their parents. A plush communal living room (which incorporates the tiny altar of the original Chapel of Sant Joan), is well-stocked with back issues of the *New Yorker* and fat reference books. So, with views to die for across unspoiled farmland to the fortress of La Mola and a sapphire sea, an honour bar, and a huge swimming pool edged with snow-white loungers, this fabulous farmhouse is proof that cool has finally found its way to Menorca.

Sant Lluís & Sant Climent

Just south of Maó, **Sant Lluís**, its church standing like a beacon over the surrounding countryside, is a hub for the south-east corner of the island (a signpost just outside the village names four different destinations, all four kilometres away). Like Es Castell, its strict grid plan layout suggests its origins as another garrison town, though a French rather than a British one; it was built by the Duc de Richelieu in the late 1750s, and named after the 13th-century crusading French King Louis IX. It is essentially a two-street town with three windmills, one of which, the Molí de Dalt, still works and houses a small museum of rural tools and machinery. Halfway up C/Comte Lannion, one block over from the main street, there is an interesting donkey-powered well (now unused) opposite No.44. The **Maó Hippodrome** (Ctra. Maó–Sant Lluís 400, 971 36 57 30, €3), halfway between Maó and Sant Lluís, hosts trotting races every Saturday from May to October at 6pm, and every Sunday from November to April at 2pm.

Four kilometres (two and a half miles) south-west of Maó is tiny **Sant Climent**, whose only attraction for visitors is its restaurants and, less obviously, a thriving jazz scene (*see p226*).

Molí de Dalt
C/Sant Lluís 4, Sant Lluís (971 15 10 84). **Open** *May-Nov* 10am-2pm, 6-8pm Mon-Fri; 10am-1pm Sat; 11am-1pm Sun. *Dec-Apr* 10am-2pm Mon-Fri; 10am-1pm Sat. **Admission** €1.20; €0.60 concessions. **No credit cards**.

Where to eat & drink

Sant Lluís has a couple of reasonable restaurants, including **La Rueda** (C/Sant Lluís 30, 971 15 03 49, closed Tue and Nov, €€), a typical village place serving wholesome local food and paella (upstairs) and great tapas (downstairs). Nearby, **La Venta de Paco** (Avda. de sa Pau 158, 971 15 09 95, closed Mon, €€) offers grilled meat and fish in a rustic setting decked with farm tools. However, it is the area just south of Sant Lluís, along a snaking stretch of road through the hamlets of **Torret** and **S'Ullastrar**, that has become known as the 'golden mile' for its culinary clout. Many of the island's best restaurants are located here and it's well worth planning at least one special meal somewhere in the area to enjoy Menorcan cuisine at its finest. In high season, reservations are essential.

Pan y Vino (Camí de la Coixa 3, Torret, mobile 610 31 92 79, closed lunch, all Thur & Fri, all Nov-Apr, €€€) has been around since 1969, when the utterly charming Terry Cox and his wife Jill arrived on the island. Theirs is a fascinating story of the rock 'n' roll years (Terry was drummer for Pentangle and regularly toured with the likes of Bowie, Roy Orbison and Elton John); the odd music

Menorca

industry star has been known to drop by, including Elton and his mum. Jill's cooking is honest, seasonal, local and whatever she's in the mood to produce; maybe prawn ceviche, couscous and lamb, Thai style chicken, with vast mounds of garden-fresh vegetables and home-made puddings – her chocolate cheesecake is a masterpiece. It costs €29 for three courses. Terry, meanwhile, looks after the wine and music from an extensive selection. He is also responsible for the reliable annual restaurant guide *Off the Beaten Track* (for the online version, see www.menorcadining.com).

Small, informal and romantic, **La Caraba** (C/S'Ullastrar 78, 971 15 06 82, closed Sun in June, July & Sept and all Oct-May, €€€) is one of the most appealing places to have a meal in Menorca, offering a short menu of extremely fresh, impressively prepared Menorcan food in a traditional cottage with a small, charming garden.

Another farmhouse – this time modern – houses **Sa Pedrera d'es Pujol** (Caserio de Torret 23, 971 15 07 17, closed Mon, Tue & dinner Sun Nov-Apr, lunch May-Oct & mid Jan-mid Feb, €€€). The main dining room is cosy, with a roaring fire in the winter, while two conservatory-style rooms offer sunlight and privacy for small groups or dinner à deux. In the summer though, most visitors opt for the walled terrace, presided over by a giant dragon tree. Owners Daniel and Nuria offer an impeccable and inspired menu from their home region, Asturias – itself undergoing a boom as a culinary tiger – while maintaining

a strong focus on island staples: succulent beef, *presalé* lamb, vegetables, seafood and cheese.

A pretty wine-red villa in leafy gardens, with wide verandas at the front and back for dining al fresco, is home to **Villa Madrid** (Ctra. S'Uestrá 46, 971 15 04 64, closed Nov-May, €€€€). Inside, the decor is rather self-consciously trendy, as is the food. Interesting combinations of flavours and textures don't always quite work, though the individual ingredients are flawless. It's still a prime spot for a great evening out though.

If you can't get a room at the lovely **Biniarroca** (*see below*, €€€€), you could always just come for dinner to see what you're missing. The only one of Sant Lluís's gourmet restaurants not in the area around S'Ullastrar, Biniarroca is one and a half kilometres (one mile) along the road to Es Castell and serves predominantly French cuisine in a delightful, candlelit atmosphere.

Sant Climent has an inordinate number of restaurants for such a small place, ranging from smart to simple. At the top end of the scale is **Es Molí de Foc** (C/Sant Llorenç 65, 971 15 32 22, closed Jan, all Mon & dinner Sun Feb-May & Sept-Dec, all Mon & lunch Sun June-Aug, €€€), a bright townhouse with beams, stained glass and modern art. The paella is excellent – no surprise, as the owners are from Valencia. The rest of the menu features classic Spanish gourmet cuisine, and is rich and a touch overwrought. At the other end of the scale, the recently refurbished **Casino** (C/Sant Jaume 4, 971 15 34 18, closed Wed and Jan, €€) is

Cova d'en Xoroi. *See p228.*

a typical village restaurant, with an excellent reputation for good, local cuisine and Tuesday jazz nights (May-Oct only). Opposite, **Musupta Cusi** (Sant Climent s/n, mobile 646 67 86 44, closed Nov-Mar and lunch July & Aug, €€) is an attractive, fun English/Hungarian-run restaurant serving up good tapas and nightly live music with allcomers welcome to join in.

There are two English pubs, both authentic in their own way. The **Coach and Horses** (C/Sant Jaume 38, 971 15 33 34, closed evenings Mon & Sun, €) on the high street has a full menu of English-style pub food, with daily specials and a roast on Sundays. For an authentic Menorcan drinking experience, try **Sa Taverna** (no phone) opposite – a fabulous, ramshackle smugglers' den of the kind where pirates hatch plots and get (wooden) legless.

Where to stay

Not far from Sant Lluís are two of Menorca's best rural hotels. **Biniarroca** (Sant Lluís Camí Vell 57, 971 15 00 59, www.biniarroca.com, closed Nov-Apr, doubles €128-€187 incl breakfast) is run by two English women, a painter and an ex-fashion designer, whose combined personal touch can be appreciated at every turn. This is a lovely farmhouse retreat full of nooks and hidden corners, ensuring privacy and tranquillity both inside, where Wiltshire chic meets rural Menorca, and out, where a rampant but carefully planned garden harbours two swimming pools. At the back, a covered sandstone terrace links indoors and out, and is a lovely place to breakfast or dine al fresco.

The simple but elegant rural hotel **Alcaufar Vell** (Ctra. Cala d'Alcalfar, km7.3, 971 15 18 74, www.alcaufarvell.com, closed Jan and Feb, doubles €132-€186 incl breakfast) is a lovely, relaxing place to stay, surrounded by pretty gardens and beautiful sandstone outbuildings. At its heart is a three-storey Moorish tower, subsequently built around to create an imposing manor house with a beautiful 19th-century sandstone façade. Combining rustic simplicity with the right degree of comfort, and with beautiful views over the surrounding area, it's a great place to unwind.

For a more 'authentic' manor house experience, the small rural **Hostal Biniali** (Ctra. S'Ullastrar –Binibèquer 50, 971 15 17 24, www.hostalbiniali.com, closed Nov-May, doubles €125-€146) is simpler and less sophisticated than others in the area. Rooms and furnishings show age and character rather than the influence of an interior designer. Another similar place is the pleasant, quiet **Son Tretze** (C/Binifadet 20, 971 15 09 43, www.hotelmenorca.com, doubles €84-€128), just outside Sant Lluís, close to the windmill.

South-east coast

Almost the entire south-east coastline is taken up by holiday developments of one type or another, from full-blown resorts to estates of private villas. Working from east to west, **S'Algar** is the most built up, with two four-star hotels and several purpose-built estates and villas. The nearest (small) beach is at **Cala d'Alcalfar**, a charming inlet with emerald waters, boathouses built into the side of the cliff and, on its far side, a watchtower guarding the point, surrounded by low vegetation and bare rock.

From here there is a pleasant walk along the old **Camí de Cavalls** (Horse Road), which follows the line of the cliffs to **Punta Prima**, a largish, unappealing resort clustered around a popular sandy beach that looks out to the green and white lighthouse on **Illa de l'Aire**. From here, holiday developments and villas are more or less continuous until you reach **Cap d'en Font** – though happily, for much of the way, the road passes in front of the smug ranks of white houses, giving great views over the rocks out to sea and offering possibilities for clambering down to swim or snorkel.

Binibèquer has a pretty beach, surrounded by a small grove of pine trees and thick shrubs, and protected to the west by fins of rock sharking down into the water, with fine white sand and the most photogenic beach bar on the island, **Los Bucaneros** (no phone).

A little further on, the self-proclaimed 'fisherman's village' of **Binibèquer Vell** is neither a fishing village, nor particularly 'vell' (old). In fact, it's a holiday apartment complex built in 1972 as a composite of Mediterranean architecture (think Greek island church meets North African medina). The result is a higgledy-piggledy heap of whitewashed houses with wooden beams and balconies, clinging together like shipwreck survivors. Pale imitations can be seen throughout the island, from Platges de Fornells to Son Bou, and to seal its fate, it is now an obligatory stop for every bus tour of the island.

West of here, the only sizeable beaches (by Menorcan standards) are **Binissafúller** and **Canutells**, which is like a smaller version of Cala en Porter (*see p228*). There are also some small patches of sand at the end of **Binidalí** and **Biniparratx** coves, both of which are worth the trek, with clear waters and low cliffs, and wild undergrowth threatening the dirt paths that lead down their respective narrow gorges.

Even more rewarding to visit is the magical forked bay at **Cales Coves**. Access is down a very rough dirt road from just outside the development of Son Vitamina, located halfway along the Sant Climent–Cala en Porter road. You can leave your car at the wide tarmacked area just south of the main road and walk down the track off to the right for around 25 minutes to reach the coast. (If you're feeling intrepid, this track is just about negotiable by car.) Cales Coves is home to the largest necropolis on the island, with over 100 prehistoric burial caves carved into the sides of the cliffs, some impossibly high up and hard to reach.

The double bay was used by the Romans, who got their water from a small spring that emerges from the rocks just to the left of the tiny beach. You can still drink from it today and admire a view little changed over the last 2,000 years. It's possible to scramble over the rocks around the right-hand side of the beach to reach the bay's second fork. This is an idyllic spot for a skinny-dip; come early or late enough in the day and you'll have the whole place to yourself. The Romans also constructed a road from here to Porta Magonis (Maó), which doubtless explains why the road to Sant Climent and Maó is the straightest on the island.

The next resort west is **Cala en Porter** (sometimes contracted to Cala'n Porter), at the end of the gorge of the same name. High, steep cliffs create a sheltered, almost rectangular bay with a beach at the end. Small villas and apartments cling to the eastern cliff, with paths and steps leading up to a sprawling, unlovely holiday resort at the top. The other side of the gorge is thankfully untouched, so there are great views over the rugged countryside and down to the sandy bay, where the water is so clear that boats moored there seem to float on air.

Just round the tip of the bay, in the south-facing cliffs, the **Cova d'en Xoroi** is a spectacularly located pirate cave, complete with legend attached (bloodthirsty pirate named Xoroi makes attacks on village, carrying off hapless virgin and somehow disappearing into thin air until improbable fall of snow allows desperate villagers to track footsteps back to the cave and free virgin, while pirate ends it all by jumping into the sea). Nowadays the cave has been turned into a nightclub, which doubles up as a bar/tourist attraction during the day, with fabulous views out to sea, small nooks and low tunnels, and damp patches where water drips through the sandstone. The entrance fee in the daytime is fairly hefty, though it's a pretty memorable experience sipping a cool drink (included in the price) while gazing out to sea from halfway up a cliff, with ambient sounds pulsing through the sound system. If you just want to check out the location, then you can get a pretty good view from the ticket office.

Cova d'en Xoroi

Cala en Porter (971 37 72 36/www.covadenxoroi. com). **Open** *Visits* 10.30am-9pm daily. *Disco* 11pm-5am daily. Disco closed Oct-June. **Admission** *Visits* €5 (incl 1 drink). *Disco* €20-€25. **Credit** MC, V.

Where to eat & drink

There is no shortage of places to eat and drink in the south-east of the island. Essentially one long strip of holiday accommodation, it has the restaurants to match, though quality can vary enormously. In **Cala d'Alcalfar**, the bar-restaurant of the **Hostal Xuroy** (€€, *see p228*) serves fresh fish, grilled meats and snacks on a charming, pine-shaded terrace overlooking the small bay and across to the watchtower, a pleasant stroll away.

Further south, **Son Ganxo** (Urb. Son Ganxo s/n, 971 15 90 75, closed Tue and all Nov, €€), in the development of the same name, seems an unlikely option, but has a sea view from the patio at the back and serves simple but good food, including an excellent *gambas al ajillo* (prawns in oil and garlic), some hefty chunks of meat and an unusual salad with warm garlic dressing. A little further along the coast, on the road between Biniancolla and Cala Torret, **En Caragol** (Marina de Torret s/n, mobile 629 16 50 89, closed Tue and all Nov-Mar, €€) knocks out very good fresh fish, overlooking the rocks and the sea beyond.

Where to stay

In **S'Algar** there are two large hotels, much used by tour operators, the **Hotel S'Algar** (Urb. S'Algar, 971 36 07 00, closed Nov-Mar, doubles €110-€175), which is close to the bay, and its sister operation the **Hotel San Luís** (Urb. S'Algar, 971 15 07 50, ww.salgarhotels. com, closed Nov-Mar, doubles €110-€175) situated further up the hill.

In nearby **Cala d'Alcalfar**, the **Hostal Xuroy** (C/Llevant 1, 971 15 18 20, www.xuroy menorca.com, closed Nov-Apr, doubles €54-€128 incl breakfast) claims to be the oldest hotel on the island and certainly retains some 1950s charm. Most of the rooms have balconies; ask for one with a view of the bay. Be warned, though, that it's often taken over by package groups.

In **Punta Prima**, the five-star apart-hotel **Insotel Club Punta Prima** (971 15 92 00, www.insotel.com, closed Nov-Apr, €83-€384 incl breakfast) dominates the northern edge of town, while just by the beach, the three-star **Xaloc Playa** (C/Major s/n, 971 15 91 20, www.xalocplaya.es, closed Nov-Apr, doubles €58-€156 half board) is usually filled up by the tour operators.

Intrepid explorers are rewarded by the magic of **Cales Coves**. *See p227.*

In **Binibèquer**, the **Binibeca Club** (971 15 10 75, www.eden-hotels.com, closed Nov-Apr, doubles €64-€170 incl breakfast) is an example of postmodernism gone mad: part concrete Aztec bunker, part stone-clad motel. Lucky patrons have a great view of the sea and Binibèquer Vell from their asymmetric pool; from Binibèquer Vell it's an eyesore.

For apartments in **Binibèquer Vell** itself, call **Apartamentos Binivell Park** (971 15 06 08, www.hot-hlghotels.com, closed Nov-Apr, phone for details of prices). For places to hire in **Binibèquer Nou**, closer to the beach, call 971 15 16 18 (www.redorka.com). Further inland, **La Boyera** (Binisafua Roters s/n, 971 38 18 90, www.laboyera.com, closed Nov-May, apartments €39-€120) is a cheaper option, with pleasant bungalows around a pool and a good restaurant.

Alternatively, get away from the developers and decamp to **Binissafullet Vell** (Ctra. Binissafuller 64, 971 15 66 33, www.binissa fullet.com, double €78-€200 incl breakfast). One of Menorca's slowly growing number of *agroturismos*, it has a rustic charm, though the bedrooms are more basic than those of many of its competitors. The real draw is a cosy living room, ample terraces and a good-sized swimming pool. A couple of the rooms have mezzanines, ideal for those travelling with kids. There is also a newly established campsite at **Biniparratx**.

South coast

For beach lovers, the south coast is an idyll. Almost the whole of the southern half of the island consists of soft sandstone, and, consequently, the beaches here all have fine, creamy white sand, while the water is as clear as cut glass, throwing up the kinds of turquoises and emeralds usually only seen in the pages of *National Geographic*. The only viper in this paradise is the sea grass posidonia that gets washed up on the shore, floating in an ankle-tickling band a metre or so wide where the waves break, or piling up in soft walls of gently rotting vegetation on the sand. More inconvenient and unattractive rather than anything else, the sea grass is actually beneficial to the health of the beaches where it is found, preventing them from washing away. In peak season the local authorities usually clear it away from the most popular beaches.

The high, sheer cliffs that rise up south of Sant Climent continue along most of the southern coastline, interrupted only by the stretch from **Son Bou** to **Sant Tomàs**, and then tailing off towards **Cap d'Artrutx** at Menorca's south-western point. Son Bou and Sant Tomàs together share the longest, straightest beaches on the island, separated by a rocky outcrop between Punta de Talis and Punta Rodona.

Walk 7 Cala Galdana to Son Saura

Distance: 14km (9 miles). Linear.
Time: 4hrs.

Some of Menorca's most beguiling beaches are to be found on the totally undeveloped stretch of south-west coast between Cala Galdana and Cala en Bosc. This longish but relatively easy walk takes in a number of them and some wonderful cliff-top scenery, and as it's a linear walk, you can stop at whichever takes your fancy and turn back at any point. It starts at what once must have been one of the island's most paradisical beaches, Cala Galdana, backed by high cliffs, and end point of the stunning Galdana gorge. Alas, some seriously crass overdevelopment has blighted the spot, but the setting is still a treat. If you just want a short, easy walk of an hour or so, then a stroll up the gorge is hugely rewarding. Otherwise…

Park in the big car park just to the right as you cross the bridge from Cala Galdana into Serpentona (by a roundabout). Turn left out of the car park and walk alongside the torrent towards the sea until the road turns sharp right outside the Hotel Audax. Here, keep straight ahead, climbing some steps, ignoring the footbridge to the left, and continuing straight up along a rough track through the trees. Soon you'll have fine views across to the beach and the colossal white hotel that looms over it.

The path climbs, levels, climbs again and levels again as you make your way around the headland. Around ten minutes after setting off you pass through a gap in a stone wall and meet another path coming in from the right by a fire warning sign. Bear to the left, following the now broad track running alongside a drystone wall.

Seven minutes on, the main track swings round to the right, still following the wall, and then splits. Carry on round to the right, climbing up some rocks and keeping the wall on your right. Ignore a path coming in to the left. Eventually the wall peters out. Around 30 minutes after starting you'll come to the top of a long flight of wooden steps. Take these down to the lovely beach of Cala Macarella,

with its decent-sized wedge of golden sand, shallow bay and bar (Cafeteria Susy) to service all your refreshment needs.

Cross the beach close to the waterline. At its far side you'll pass a water culvert to your right and head up a slope, with a stone wall on your right. The path immediately splits. If you take the left branch, you'll be at the barred-off caves you will have seen from the beach, but take the right. You'll find yourself at a locked gate bearing a '*propriedad privada*' sign. By the gate, take the unpromising-looking track to the left, heading upwards through the undergrowth.

After 30 seconds the path splits – take the left branch, and five minutes after leaving Cala Macarella you pass through a gap in a stone wall. The landscape starts to open out now. Ignore a path to the left and carry straight on. A couple of minutes later you reach a T-junction – take the right branch and a minute later you come to the end of a stone wall with a cairn on top. Turn left here in front of the wall, and walk with it on your right as the countryside opens up further (you'll see a stone hut on your left).

Around seven minutes after turning at the cairn-topped wall you go over a path crossroads, and then a gap in a stone wall. You can now see the Talaia d'Artrutx tower ahead of you. Soon you come to another T-junction. Turn right and pass through a gap in a stone wall. Five minutes later, pass over another crossroads (bearing left). The path narrows as you come closer to the cliff edge.

Within ten minutes you'll reach another idyllic beach, Cala en Turqueta. It's actually two small beaches, framed by low cliffs and with a couple of old boathouses the only signs of development.

Walk to the far side of the second beach, and, close to the waterline, you'll see some concrete steps up to a locked door in a building built into the rock. Climb up the narrow rocky path directly to the right of this. The path takes you along the edge of the bay. Just after passing over a broken-down stone wall, you'll find yourself standing above one of the boathouses. A path continues around

West of here the cliffs resume, broken by occasional gorges that harbour small inlets and quiet beaches. The largest and most accessible of these is **Cala Galdana**, a well-protected horseshoe curving between the pine-topped

cliffs on either side, but marred by the high-rise hotel on the beach. Nearby **Cala Mitjana** is smaller and free of hotels. Moving west, the small pirate hideout of **Cala Macarella** is a shortish walk from Cala Galdana, though it is

the bay, but ignore this and head inland on a wider track. There are green and red paint splodges on a rock at this point.

After a minute you'll see a track off to the left – ignore it, but take the next left immediately after it (before the main track veers right). You are now once again following the edge of the bay, but higher up than previously.

Three minutes further on the path forks – take the right branch, and then turn left when you come to another T-junction with a wider track running alongside a stone wall. You're now following a series of green paint spots on rocks. From here there are wonderful views east along the coast as far as the high-rise atrocities at Son Bou. This scrubby headland is also a good place to spot red kites circling over the cliffs. Soon you'll also enjoy coast views to the west as far as Cala en Bosc and Cap d'Artrutx.

When you come to another T-junction with a path running along a wall, again take the left route, still following the green splodges. You'll see the tower to your right now.

Around ten minutes after the last T-junction, you'll reach another lovely beach – Cala d'es Talaier. Cross it and walk up the wide track on its far side. This brings you to a stone wall with a gate (no access) to the right. Turn left down the track, then, a minute later, duck under a tree and go through a gate in a wall. The path forks – take the right, away from the bare rocks by the sea.

Within ten minutes you'll come to a sandy clearing. Go left and you meet the sea at the first of the two beaches of Son Saura – the destination of this walk. This beach is long and sandy, but it's often afflicted by deposits of the sea grass posidonia. At its far end sits a blue-roofed lifeguard station, and beyond this is a second beach – often favoured by nudists. The other things that might catch your eye are a number of old gun emplacements.

Simply retrace your steps to return to Cala Galdana.

Cala Galdana.

also accessible by car from Ciutadella, as are **Cala en Turqueta** and **Son Saura**. As the access roads to these beaches cross private land, landowners usually charge a parking fee during peak periods and sometimes limit visitor numbers. Finally, the coastline ends with a flourish of package hotels and restaurants, ruining the inherent beauty of **Cala en Bosc** (*see p260*) and its natural marina, and nearby **Son Xoriguer**.

Almost every photograph of **Son Bou** features the ruins of an early Christian church in the foreground and miles of virgin beach in the background. It is a shot that evokes wonder at the beauty of the location, a few metres from the water. And it is mendacious to say the least. Just out of shot, almost adjacent to the ruins, rise the twin monoliths of the Sol Milanos Pingüinos hotel, destroying any atmosphere or magic the site must once have had and dominating the landscape, even from several miles away.

It could have been worse. There were plans in the 1970s to build no fewer than 20 hotels here, the theory being that this would concentrate tourism in one spot on the island, and leave everywhere else untouched. This would also have meant draining the large area of marshlands behind the dunes, which is an important stopping point for migrating birds. Fortunately, the plan was shelved, much to the relief of nature lovers, migrating birds and the mosquitoes that enjoy the marsh (and the tourists) to the full. Behind the marshlands, which are impenetrable, the hillside is dotted with villa developments (which spread westwards, merging into the neighbouring resort of **Sant Jaume Mediterrani**). Though hardly inconspicuous, they are certainly less offensive to the eye than a line of tower blocks.

The beach at Son Bou is long and rather narrow. As access is only available at the eastern end, relative calm (and the liberty to sunbathe nude) rewards anyone willing to trudge west, though go too far west and you will find yourself meeting fellow trudgers trudging east from Sant Tomàs, just beyond the rocky outcrop.

The ruins of the early Christian church at Son Bou consist of an outline of low stones that show the precise floor plan of the church, including the location of the altar and three narrow naves. It dates back to the end of the fifth century and is one of six early Christian churches on the island – others have been excavated at Es Fornàs de Torelló (*see p223*), Fornells and on the Illa del Rei, while two more, at Sanitja and on the Illa d'en Colom, have yet to be excavated.

Halfway between Son Bou and Alaior, about a mile down a well-signposted lane, is the largest talayotic village on the island, **Torre d'en Gaumés**. An early example of suburban sprawl, it is spread over a hillside with good views to the coast (and of any marauding invaders sailing in from the south). Remarkable mainly for its size, the individual buildings are in similar condition to others on the island. Key aspects here are the presence of three large talayots. The central talayot has a taula

precinct beside it, although at some point the T-bar was removed and used as a sarcophagus, possibly by the Romans or the Moors, both of whom also inhabited the village. There is a hypostyle chamber with large slabs forming the roof, although whatever filled in the spaces between them has long since disappeared.

The road to **Sant Tomàs** rolls gently down from Es Migjorn Gran through attractive farmland and avenues of tall pines, meeting the coast at the western end of the resort. To the east, a group of hotels, none more than four storeys high, hog the shoreline, their gardens separated from the beach by a pathway, while behind them the hillside is covered with private villas.

To the west stretch various untouched beaches, separated by low rocks and edged with dunes and pine woods. **Platja de Binigaus**, at the western end, where the Binigaus gorge opens out into the sea, is the widest and wildest section, and one of the more accessible nudist beaches on the island.

A farm track on the west side of the gorge heads inland from the remains of a house dug into the rock, past the large meadow where the gorge opens out, and up the west side of the gorge to the farmhouses of Binigaus Nou and Binigaus Vell. The former has an interesting prehistoric hypostyle (pillared) chamber beside it. Along the way you pass two elaborate rain collection systems, which channel the water to large cisterns equipped with a bucket suspended from a pulley.

To get to the huge natural cave, the **Cova dels Coloms**, take either the path at the bottom of the gorge, a couple of hundred metres from the beach, or the path close to the top, soon after Binigaus Nou. Both are clearly signposted. It's worth carrying a torch to explore the dark recesses of this enormous cavern.

Nearby, but difficult to reach from the gorge itself, are the remains of the talayotic settlement at **Sant Agustí**, standing on the eastern clifftop. The easiest access to the site, though, is from the Sant Tomàs–Es Migjorn road. A dirt layby between kilometres eight and nine conceals an unmarked farm road leading to the farmhouse of Sant Agusti Vell. The only indication that you are in the right place is a board 100 metres in from the road telling you to leave your car here, but with no other clues or directions. Continue along the metalled road to the farmhouse, branching off right through the gate and along the stony farm path that passes directly in front of the first outbuildings. Almost a kilometre further on you will come to the next clue: a rubbish bin. The site is a little further along, and well worth the walk: it features two talayots and a taula, as well as subterranean water cisterns. What is particularly interesting is that you can still enter the pillared chamber inside the northernmost talayot, which is supported by a huge, ancient juniper beam.

At first sight, **Cala Galdana**, the next resort to the west after Sant Tomàs, comes as something of a shock: a beautiful horseshoe beach marred by the huge white hotel that stands almost upon it, and by the resort that has sprung up within the natural amphitheatre between the cliffs. Once you get used to the intrusion, though, Cala Galdana is charming and relatively quiet, with a very gently sloping beach that makes it ideal for young children. A tallish outcrop of rock jutting out into the bay, and accessible via a newly constructed bridge, has a bar on it, and gives an alternative view of the bay. Until recently, the outcrop was part of the adjacent hillside, before the connecting rock was dynamited away a couple of years ago so the river that flows down the gorge would run straight into the bay, rather than curling round and taking up too much precious beach. What the planners had not foreseen was that this would allow the ubiquitous posidonia sea grass to be washed straight up the river, trapping dead sea life and filling the area around the new canal with the pungent aroma of rotting fish.

While the resort itself is limited in size because of the natural obstacles on each side, there are plenty of options for walking, mountain biking and sea kayaking nearby. The coastal cliffs harbour numerous caves that can be explored by kayak, especially when there is no wind and the sea is pond-still. It's also a great way of getting to the nearby beaches, including **Cala en Turqueta**, **Cala Mitjana**, **Cala Macarella** and **Son Saura**, all of which are unspoilt. Audax Sports and Nature (Urb. Cala Galdana s/n, 971 15 45 48, www.rtmhotels.com, closed Nov-Apr), beside the Hotel Audax, rents bikes and kayaks, as well as running various types of guided excursions on land and sea.

For a cliff-top walk that takes in many of the best beaches to the west, *see p230* **Walk 7**.

Where to eat & drink

The restaurants in Son Bou, Sant Tomàs and Cala Galdana all cater for tourists, and for the most part the quality is not great. All have beach shacks serving decent snacks – **Es Bruc** (no phone, €) in **Sant Tomàs** is particularly good for fresh, grilled sardines and lovely views (if you turn your back on the concrete hotels) – and bright restaurants serving plastic paella and lacklustre seafood. An exception is **Restaurant Cala Mitjana** (Passeig des Riu 1, 971 15 45 66, closed dinner Sat, Sun and all Nov-Apr, €€) in **Cala Galdana**, with everything

from pizza and salad to grilled meat and very fresh fish. Or head inland to Es Migjorn Gran or Es Mercadal, both of which have some excellent restaurants.

Another alternative, a couple of kilometres south of Ferreries on the road to Cala Galdana, is **El Gallo** (Ctra. Cala Galdana, km1.5, 971 37 30 39, closed Mon and all Dec & Jan, €€), a sizeable old farmhouse serving delicious grilled meat and good paella, or **Es Forn** (Urb. Torres Soli Nou 28, 971 37 28 98, closed Tue, €€€), a couple of kilometres from Son Bou on the Torre Soli Nou road towards Alaior, another venerable farmhouse serving modern cuisine.

None of these resorts are particularly hot on places to go out, but you could try the **Sound House** (no phone) just before the road descends into **Cala Galdana** for drinks and boogie; it's open every night until late in high season. Should you feel the need to escape there's a nice walk from here down through the woods to the beach.

Where to stay

Son Bou has just two hotels, the doubly monolithic **Sol Milanos Pingüinos** (Platja de Son Bou s/n, 971 37 12 00, www.solmelia. com, closed Nov-Apr, doubles €61-€131 incl breakfast) and the **Royal Son Bou** (Platja de Son Bou s/n, 971 37 23 58, www.royalsonbou. com, closed Nov-Mar, doubles €69-€184), which is aimed at families with young children. For apartments, try **Apartamentos Son Bou Gardens** (971 37 12 16, www.menorcarentals. com, closed Nov-Apr, phone for prices).

Sant Tomàs has four hotels and three hotel-like apartment blocks, and all receive large numbers of package tourists. The best is the **Santo Tomas** (Platja de Sant Tomàs s/n, 971 37 00 25, www.sethotels.com, closed Nov-Mar, doubles €94-€238 incl breakfast), a comfortable hotel with balconies overlooking the palm-filled garden and pool, and the beach a few steps away. It also has a small indoor pool and jacuzzi for when Menorcan weather turns grey, as well as sauna and steam rooms, a gym and massages. A close second, and very similar in almost every respect, is the **Sol Menorca** next door (Platja de Sant Tomàs s/n, 971 37 00 50, www.solmelia.com, closed Nov-Apr, doubles €66-€214 incl breakfast), with sea views, a sizeable gym and a decent swimming pool. On the same strip is the **Lord Nelson** (Platja de Sant Tomàs s/n, 971 37 01 25, www.hotelesglobales.com, closed Nov-Feb, doubles €71-€149 half board). For apartments, try the **Hamilton Court** (971 37 00 86, www.hamiltoncourt.com, closed Nov-Apr) or **Mestral & Llebeig** (Urb. Sant Tomàs

Menorca

s/n, 971 37 03 70, www.sethotels.com, closed
Dec-Mar, apartments €74-€164), which also
has some villas to rent.

Cala Galdana has three hotels around
the bay. The immense **Sol Gavilanes** (Urb.
Cala Galdana s/n, 971 15 45 45, www.solmelia.
com, closed Nov-Apr, doubles €64-€225 incl
breakfast) is impossible to miss, being right
on the beach. A better alternative is the **Hotel
Audax** (Urb. Cala Galdana s/n, 971 15 46 46,
www.rtmhotels.com, closed Nov-mid Mar,
doubles €90-€200 half board), on the western
side of the beach, which is far more discreet and
still has a great view of the bay. Further back,
the **Hotel Cala Galdana** (Urb. Cala Galdana
s/n, 971 15 45 00, www.infotelecom.es/galdana,
closed Nov-Apr, doubles €124-€150 incl
breakfast) is a huge, colonial-style mansion.
Up the hill behind the Audax, the **FloraMar**
(Urb. Serpentona, 971 15 45 12, www.comitas
hotels.com, closed Nov-Apr, apartments €45-
€160) has apartments and studios.

A far better option is to head inland a few
kilometres to **Son Triay** (Ctra. Cala Galdana,
km3, 971 55 00 78, mobile 600 07 44 41, www.son
triay.com, cosed Nov-Mar, double €66-€106),
a lovingly restored neo-colonial mansion set in
formal gardens complete with nubile statues and
yet more idyllic rural scenery. Dating back to the
1800s, the current family bought the hourse after
the Civil War and have turned to *agroturismo*
in an attempt to save their heritage. It has just
six large, cool bedrooms in the main house and
two apartments (one old-fashioned with a wood
burning fire and cobbled terrace shaded by
a 200-year old fig tree; the other more modern,
with views over the fields), while the pleasantly
rustic breakfast room, where home-produced
produce is served, has a walk-in fireplace.
There's also a swimming pool and tennis courts.

The only two campsites on the island are close
to the south coast, three kilometres (two miles)
outside Son Bou and Cala Galdana respectively.
Camping Son Bou (Ctra. Sant Jaume, km3.5,
971 37 26 05, 971 37 27 27, www.campingson
bou.com, closed mid Oct-mid Apr, tents €2.75-
€10.75, adults €4.90-€6, bungalows €64-€99,
tent hire €45-€75) has bungalows to hire
and accepts tents and caravans. **Camping
S'Atalaia** (Ctra. Cala Galdana, km4, 971 37
42 32, www.campingsatalaia.com, closed mid
Oct-mid Apr, tents €5.50, adults €5.50) is
reserved for tents only.

Resources

Internet
Cala Galdana *Snack-Bar Alaska, Urb. Cala
Galdana (971 15 45 77).* **Open** *May-Oct* 11am-11pm
daily. Closed Nov-Apr.

Dine at **Sant Joan de Binissaida**. *See p225.*

Police station
Es Castell *Plaça de l'Esplanada 5 (971 36 27 47).*
Sant Lluís *Pla de sa Creu s/n (971 15 17 17).*

Post office
Es Castell *C/Llevant 2 (971 36 71 07).*
Sant Lluís *C/Sant Esteve 14 (971 15 12 87).*

Tourist information
Sant Lluís *OIT, C/Sant Lluís 4 (971 15 10 84).*
Open *Apr-Oct* 10am-2pm, 6-8pm Mon-Sat; 11am-
1pm Sun. *Nov-Mar* 10am-2pm, 6-8pm Mon-Fri; 10am-
1pm Sat.

Getting there

By bus
From Maó, there are 26 buses Mon-Sat (20 Sun) to Es
Castell (10mins), 13 buses Mon-Sat (12 Sun) to Sant
Lluís (10mins), 12 buses Mon-Sat (4 Sun) to Sant
Climent (10mins), 3 buses daily to Binibèquer
(20mins), 7 buses Mon-Sat to Cala en Porter (20mins),
and 6 buses Mon-Sat to Son Bou (35mins), 4 buses
Mon-Fri (3 Sat) to Sant Tomàs (40mins) and 5 buses
daily (4 Sun) to Cala Galdana (1hr) via Ferreries
(20mins). From Ciutadella, there are 7 buses daily (3
Sun) to Cala Galdana (40mins) via Ferreries (not all
stop), 4 buses Mon-Fri (3 Sat) to Sant Tomàs (40mins)
and 1 Mon-Sat to Son Bou (1hr). Note that there are
fewer services to the resorts Nov-Apr.

Central Menorca

Gentle landscapes, sleepy towns and a sprinkling of fine restaurants.

The island's interior is made up of softly undulating pasture-land and copses, bordered by deep green hedgerows sprouting magenta-hued clover and copious other wild flowers during spring and summer. Aside from admiring the scenery there is very little to do or see here, though the three main towns **Alaior**, **Es Mercadal** and **Ferreries** (numbering fewer than 15,000 inhabitants between them) are pleasant enough places for a short wander, and all have at least one unexpected gem in terms of eating. All three are on the main Maó–Ciutadella artery (Me-1), a single carriageway road with occasional stretches of dual carriageway and a couple of long, straight sections useful for overtaking the inevitable trucks and farm vehicles that can slow traffic to a crawl.

If you're not in a particular hurry, though, a far more rewarding drive is along the old **Camí d'en Kane**. This was the original road built by British Governor Richard Kane (*see p238* **Local heroes**) in the early 18th century between Menorca's two main towns. Largely traffic-free, it branches off the Me-7 Maó–Fornells road and then runs parallel to the main highway, bypassing the town of Alaior and rejoining the main Me-1 just before Es Mercadal.

The three central towns also act as gateways to the resorts on the south coast – Son Bou, Sant Tomàs and Cala Galdana respectively (*see chapter* **South Menorca**) – all of which have pretty beaches of fine white sand and turquoise water (and also, alas, intensive tourist development). Equidistant from Es Mercadal, Ferreries and Sant Tomàs, **Es Migjorn Gran** is a village with a couple of decent places to eat, and makes an excellent starting point for exploring the Binigaus gorge and the various natural and prehistoric remains in the area.

Alaior

Perched on a hill around its pretty sandstone church, **Alaior** (12 kilometres/seven and a half miles north-west of Maó) is the largest, but also the quietest, of the towns of the interior, and a focus for local cheese-making. Originally just a quiet maze of narrow streets woven around the church, it has a couple of interesting buildings and an attractive cemetery just outside the town on the Camí d'en Kane. Due

largely to the cheese and shoe-making industries, the town now sprawls southwards in unlovely industrial and housing estates, which are all too visible from the main road.

Standing proudly above the rest of the town, the 17th-century sandstone church of **Santa Eulàlia** is similar in style to the cathedral in Ciutadella; it's desperately gloomy within, thanks to its lack of natural light. Just down the hill from here is Plaça Constitució, a diminutive square, just large enough for a pavement café and the self-important **Casino**, looking like a South American small-town hall. The real town hall is in C/Major, to the right of the pavement café; it's a compact building with a beautiful carved façade, a covered courtyard and a sweeping stone staircase. Almost opposite is **Can Salort**, a 17th-century mansion, similar to those in Ciutadella, which now contains a library and an outpost of the University of the Balearics.

Leading north from the Casino, C/Es Forn contains a number of interesting townhouses and the old Franciscan church of **Sant Didac** (San Diego), with its adjoining monastery. Now used as a cultural centre, it is a large, whitewashed building dating back to 1629, with palm trees in its forecourt giving it a North African flavour. The carved stone doorway features a sculpture of the saint himself; above it is the crest of the Order of St Francis.

To the north of the town is another small chapel, **Sant Pere Nou**, with a small pine-filled park and play area in front. From here, **Es Cós**, the narrow road leading to the walled, cypress-filled cemetery, is remarkable for still being the course for horse races, held during the local festivities, the **Festes de Sant Llorenç**. The continuous drystone walls on either side of the road are topped by a whitewashed step that acts as a single long seat for spectators, while towards the far end, close to the cemetery, is a small tribune for the judges. As architect Joan J Gomila points out in his excellent *Menorca Architecture Guide*, 'the two white lines that mark the path delineate a magical space which, as well as being a racecourse, could perhaps also be a connection between the city of the living and the city of the dead.'

On Camí de Binifabini, the road from Alaior to Addaia, you'll find **Subaida**, a farm with a shop where you can see Menorcan cheese being made.

Sant Didac, Alaior. See p235.

Subaida

Cami de Binifabini s/n (mobile 618 61 46 35/ www.subaida.com). **Open** 9am-3pm Mon-Fri; 9am-1pm Sat. Call in advance to book tours. **Admission** free. *Tours* (incl tasting) €5, €2.50 concessions. **No credit cards**.

Where to eat & drink

There are no hotels and few places to eat and drink in Alaior, the majority of tourists having decamped to Son Bou. The best restaurant is **The Cobblers** (C/San Macario 6, 971 37 14 00, closed lunch Mon-Sat, dinner Sun and end Dec-Apr, €€-€€€), an English-run brasserie in a gorgeous townhouse with exposed beams, arched doorways and, in summer, tables in the airy courtyard; the menu offers the likes of calf's liver, sea bass, mussels and marinated squid.

For something more local, try **C'an Jaumot** (C/San Juan Bautista 6A, 971 37 82 94, closed Sun June-Oct, €), a traditional village restaurant and bar in front of a park full of palms, pines and sycamores just down from the church of Sant Didac. There are two entrances: on one side is the bar, where boisterous labourers indiscriminately share tables and jokes, wolfing down platefuls of hearty food in a smoke-filled backroom; on the other is the more sedate dining room, offering the same hearty food but separate tables.

Es Mercadal & El Toro

Located almost exactly at the centre of the island, **Es Mercadal** (eight kilometres/five miles north-west of Alaior) has always been the place where people stop off on the way to somewhere else, so might perhaps be excused a certain lack of identity and a distinct lack of charm. It is redeemed, just, by a handful of good restaurants, and by its proximity to El Toro, the highest point on the island.

Unfortunately, Es Mercadal's most interesting monument, the **Aljub** or water reservoir (at the western end of the town, a couple of minutes' walk from the town hall) is closed to the public. Built under the orders of the tireless Governor Kane (*see p238* **Local heroes**) in 1735, it was designed to catch rainwater for his parched troops as they marched from one end of the island to the other. Although rather unprepossessing from ground level, it has a surface area of 800 square metres (8,611 square feet), and can store 273,000 litres (60,060 gallons) of water behind walls one and a half metres (five feet) thick. Its key feature is the long, straight staircase (visible through a gate), which is like the proverbial stairway to heaven, topped by a typical Menorcan olive-

Six best Things to do

Take it easy
Visit **Clutadella** (*see p247*), easily the island's most charming town, and eat superlative seafood al fresco on the portside at Café Balear (*see p251*).

I like driving in my car
Drive the relaxing **Camí d'en Kane** (*see p235*), one of the legacies of far-sighted 18th-century British Governor Richard Kane (*see p238* **Local heroes**).

Underwater love
Take the plunge and sample some of the finest **scuba diving** in the Med. No experience required (*see p256* **Dive! Dive! Dive!**).

Out of time
Explore Menorca's unique **prehistory**. Intriguing sites litter the island; for our pick, *see p260* **Top five prehistoric sites**.

Down under
Wander around the island's subterranean tourist attractions: the former quarry-cum-artwork of **Pedreres de s'Hostal** (*see p257*), and the eerie underground castle of **Fort Marlborough** (*see p224*).

Alone again, naturally
Go for an early morning skinny-dip in one of the island's most magical spots, **Cales Coves** (*see p228*), where once Roman ships watered.

wood gate. To the north of the Aljub are various walled allotments, still used for growing fruit and vegetables, while to the south a couple of picturesque streets around the town hall and church attempt to make up for the banality of the rest of the town.

To the east, a steep road snakes up **El Toro**, whose modest summit (357 metres/ 1,171 feet), bristling with a cathedral of telecommunications towers, is visible from most of the island. Beside it, an immense statue of Christ welcomes you to the **Església del Toro**, with its plant-filled courtyard, souvenir shop and snack bar. Much of the church was destroyed by fire and rebuilt during the Civil War, and is now a bright, scrubbed space with interesting tapestries and an ornate gold altarpiece. Next door is the much-rebuilt fortress/barracks block that is all that remains of the stronghold that once stood on this site.

On a clear day you can just about make out the entire coast of Menorca, though it is the Bay of Fornells and Cap de Cavalleria to the north that are most easily distinguished.

Where to stay, eat & drink

There is only one hotel in Es Mercadal, **Hostal Jeni** (Mirada del Toro 81, 971 37 50 59, www.hostaljeni.com, doubles €44-€84 incl breakfast), a bright, spick and span place mostly frequented by business travellers, with bland decor and production-line fittings, though the rooms are comfortable enough. In contrast, Es Mercadal is blessed with more than its fair share of good places to eat. Two of the best, curiously, are run by local men called Crispin, not a common Menorcan name. In fact, they are cousins, named after their common grandfather, though whether the name is another vestige of British occupation is not clear.

N'Aguadet (C/Lepanto 30, 971 37 53 91, €€€) has been in the family since 1936 and is the more classic of the two Crispin eateries, specialising in traditional Menorcan cuisine in a setting that is formal without being starchy. After a 200-year hiatus, Crispin Mariano is also part of a gentle revival of Menorcan viniculture; he currently produces around 10,000 bottles a year of his own red, Ferrer de Muntpalau, almost all of it destined for the restaurant. It's a rather harsh wine that somehow embodies the essence of the island, though it goes well enough with the food. Crispin's sprightly septuagenarian mother still bustles between the tables offering culinary tips, which is perhaps why King Juan Carloo's late father Joan de Borbó often used to slip in unannounced for lunch.

Ca'n Olga (Pont da na Macarrana s/n, 971 37 54 59, closed lunch Wed and all Mon mid Mar-May, lunch daily and all Mon June-Sept, all Oct-mid Mar, €€), smaller, more modern and less formal, is the other Crispin-run restaurant and widely agreed to be one of the best on the island. It also serves excellent Menorcan cuisine, though with wider influences, particularly modern Catalan, French and Basque cooking. The menu changes regularly. In spring and autumn, the restaurant fills the downstairs of a charming cottage, with classical music and lurid, sub-Impressionist paintings on the walls. In summer, though, the dining room moves al fresco to the pleasant, flower-filled garden at the back, which is a lovely spot for a romantic dinner.

It's difficult to miss **Es Molí d'es Racó** (Ctra. Maó–Ciutadella, km21, 971 37 53 92, closed mid Jan-mid Feb, €€), the converted windmill right beside the main road. The

Menorca

Local heroes Richard Kane

No one single person can claim to have done as much for the island of Menorca as its first 18th-century British Lieutenant-Governor and later Governor, **Richard Kane**. Born on the north coast of Ireland in December 1662, Kane was brought up by his mother's family – Presbyterians who had emigrated to Ireland from England a century earlier – following the death of his father Thomas O'Cahan in 1665. Having anglicised his name to make his allegiance to Protestant England clear, Kane's first taste of battle came in 1689, when he helped defend Londonderry against the Catholic King James II. When the siege was relieved, Kane joined the English army, swearing his allegiance to the new King, William of Orange.

For the rest of his life, he was a constant, unswerving servant of the British Crown, a consummate and respected military man who rose to the rank of Colonel before, after 23 years of active service, being rewarded with the prestigious posting to Menorca in 1712.

On arriving on the island he lost no time putting his wide experience to good use. Hard-working and meticulous, he was also compassionate and generous, realising that the welfare of both his troops and the islanders was paramount. Though he was committed to protecting British interests in the Mediterranean (he was twice called to the defence of the British garrison in Gibraltar), Kane was also determined to stamp out the crime, hunger and ignorance that blighted Menorca and to improve its primitive infrastructure.

Maó's magnificent harbour was the key to Menorca's significance to the British, and Kane transferred the centre of Menorcan administration from Ciutadella to Maó, effectively making the latter the capital. The local aristocracy in Ciutadella weren't happy, but the move made economic and strategic sense, and led to the development of Maó – Kane built an aqueduct here, as well as a new town gate, fish and meat markets, and he also paved the streets.

One of his most significant projects was the construction of a proper road between Maó and Ciutadella (the Camí d'en Kane; *see p235*) to replace the existing rough, narrow track. He was also tireless in his efforts to persuade the Menorcans to adopt modern agricultural practices, introducing several new types of livestock and crops to the island.

The list goes on. He had all the public gallows moved from town squares to the outskirts of each town; he shipped any prostitutes and other undesirables back to the mainland; he established fixed fees for lawyers' services; he had stone benches set up at roadsides; he put a duty on brandy to pay for public works; and he ordered the streets and public water cisterns to be cleaned regularly, and built a new cistern in Es Mercadal.

Kane died in 1736 and was buried in the chapel of St Philip's Castle. His tomb and the chapel were lost when the Spanish dismantled the castle in the late 18th century, although a duplicate of his bust was placed in Westminster Abbey in 1742, where it still stands today.

downstairs rooms have been turned into snug dining areas, while outside a vine provides shade for the terrace overlooking the main road. The cheap daily *menú* is popular among local labourers and truck drivers, which is usually a good sign, although the à la carte menu is fairly uninspiring.

Ferreries

The somnolent town of **Ferreries** (eight kilometres/five miles west of Es Mercadal and 16 kilometres/ten miles east of Ciutadella), set among the rolling hills in the centre of the island, probably only registers in most people's minds as the last town on the road to Ciutadella. With just one dull hotel and a handful of bars

and restaurants, the town only really comes alive on Saturday mornings when there is a handicrafts market in the main square, Plaça Espanya. It's a fairly small, dispiriting affair out of season, notwithstanding the odd troupe of adolescents dancing to traditional live folk music. In summer there are many more stalls, many more people, and the dancers wear traditional costume.

Further up the hill is a small square of whitewashed buildings, including the tiny but attractive town hall and the 18th-century church of **Sant Bartomeu**, with its pretty neo-classical belltower (dating from the late 19th century) and doorways picked out in yellow. There are a couple of quiet, attractive bars here, though Plaça Espanya is where the real action is. Nearby, there is a very small natural history and ethnographic museum, the **Centre de la Natura**, which features changing seasonal exhibitions on local animal and plant life and other aspects of Menorca's natural history (those in spring/summer tend to be geared towards tourists, while autumn and winter exhibitions are aimed at schoolchildren). There is also a short stretch of the ancient Ciutadella road, the **Camí Vell** (Old Way) or **Camí Real** (Royal Way), that has been restored and is a pleasant spot for a short stroll – pick up a leaflet from the town hall with a map and points of interest.

On the east side of town is a clutch of factory outlets, the classiest of which is chic shoemaker **Jaime Mascaró** (no phone, open 9.30am-7.30pm Mon-Fri, 4.30-7.30pm Sat).

Just north of Ferreries, **Hort de Sant Patrici** is one of the island's 52 official cheese-makers, producing around 100 cheeses a day. In the morning you can see fresh cheese being made, while in the afternoon the staff tend to the cheese being cured, rubbing it regularly with olive oil. Menorcan cheese, known generically as 'Queso Mahón', comes in fresh, semi-cured and cured varieties; each cheese needs between 30 and 40 litres of milk, which, conveniently, is about how much you get from a cow each day. The place doubles as a cheese museum and also has an interesting sculpture garden. An audio tour is available.

At **Son Martorellet**, on the road south to Cala Galdana, there are twice-weekly Menorcan dressage displays.

Hort de Sant Patrici

Camí Ruma–Sant Patrici s/n (971 37 37 02/ www.santpatrici.com). **Open** *May-Oct* 9am-1.30pm, 4.30-8pm Mon-Sat. *Nov-Apr* 9am-1pm, 4-6pm Mon-Sat. **Admission** free; €6 audio tour. **Credit** AmEx, MC, V. **Photo** *see below.*

Centre de la Natura

C/Mallorca 2 (971 35 07 62/971 37 45 05/ www.gobmenorca.com). **Open** *May-late Oct* 10.30am-1.30pm, 5.30-8.30pm Tue-Sat. *Late Oct-Apr* some afternoons; call for information. **Admission** *May-late Oct* €3; €2 concessions. *Late Oct-Apr* €1. **No credit cards**.

Son Martorellet

Ctra. Cala Galdana, km1.7 (mobile 609 04 94 93/649 53 36 36). **Shows** *May-Oct* 8.30pm, 10pm Tue, Thur. Closed Nov-Apr. **Tickets** €14.50-€16.50; €13-€15 concessions; €5 under-10s. **No credit cards**.

Where to stay, eat & drink

The **Loar** (C/Verge del Toro 2, 971 37 30 30, doubles €38-€117, restaurant €€) is the only hotel, with 17 fairly bland rooms used mostly by business travellers. It also contains one of only a handful of restaurants and offers cheap, wholesome food, including plenty of meat and seafood, and local specialities such as roast

Talk to the hand. **Hort de Sant Patrici**.

kid, courgettes stuffed with seafood and snails with crab. The best restaurant in town and a favourite among island residents is the **Liorna** (C/Dalt 9, 971 37 39 12, www.liorna.com, closed Mon & Tue Nov-mid June and all Jan, €€€); it's a bright, minimalist shrine, which combines classic and more modern Mediterranean cuisine with international influences. **Vimpi** (Plaça Príncipe Juan Carlos 5, 971 37 31 99, €), at the entrance to the village, is a kitsch, very Spanish café-restaurant that serves hearty, good-value tapas, as well as more substantial meals. Alternatively, **El Gallo** (*see p233*) is a 200-year old farmhouse and something of an island institution for its paella and steak melts with Mahon cheese. It is situated just a couple of kilometres down the road to Cala Galdana and is at its most atmospheric for Sunday lunch.

Most of the town's bars are located around the main square, Plaça Espanya, which gets pretty lively on Friday and Saturday nights, when they act as a general meeting point for the local youth. All the bars have tables out on the square, and almost without exception are gloomy and overbearing inside. Far nicer than these are the two bars situated further up the hill: **Bar Can Marc** (no phone) and **Bar Ca'n Bernat** (971 37 31 10) in Plaça de s'Església, the square beside the church.

Es Migjorn Gran

There isn't anything particularly 'gran' ('big') about **Es Migjorn Gran** (six kilometres/four miles south-west of Es Mercadal and south-east of Ferreries). It does have a certain charm, however, with an attractive church, a town hall that looks as if it might have taken over the local stables and a couple of streets of quaint, whitewashed houses highlighted in cornflower blue and buttermilk yellow. Uniquely, the church has a grandfather clock ticking away beside the altar.

For most people, the village is just a staging post on the way to the beach resort of Sant Tomàs (*see p229*), but it's a pleasant enough place to wander, with a friendly atmosphere, a couple of attractive bars and a couple of places to stay and eat. Es Migjorn (as the village is often signposted on the island) is also a possible starting point for walking down the **Binigaus Gorge**, ending up in Sant Tomàs.

Where to stay, eat & drink

58, S'Engolidor (C/Major 3, 971 37 01 93, sengolidor@yahoo.es, closed Nov-Apr, doubles €45-€51, restaurant closed Mon, €€), a converted cottage in the centre of the village, is the best place to stay and eat, with four, cosy and characterful rooms (the best look over the

patio at the back) above a small, eccentric but excellent Menorcan restaurant. The short menu features interesting salads and starters such as *oliaigua* – a fresh tasting tomato and aubergine soup, followed by a couple of meat and fish dishes (stingray with capers, pork with prunes), and is very good value for money. In the summertime bag a table (complete with candelabra) on the flower-filled terrace. The owner also plans to open a small trinket shop within, selling off the excesses of his impressive collection of antiques and island artefacts.

The other place to stay is **Hostal La Palmera** (C/Major 83-85, 971 37 00 23, www.barpalmera.com, doubles €36-€40). Located in the old casino, this simple *pension* has a high, curving staircase located directly above the bar, *modernista* stained glass and an eviscerated theatre at the back. The rooms are cheap but rather spartan, with communal bathrooms and not much of a view.

The other place to eat is **Ca Na Pilar** (Avda. de la Mar 1, 971 37 02 12, closed Nov-Mar, €€), serving local and Mediterranean cuisine in a pretty, rustic restaurant. The focal point for village nightlife (and daylife) is **Bar Peri** (Sa Plaça 1, 971 37 01 15), in the centre of the village.

Resources

Internet
Es Mercadal *Ca'n Internet, Avda. Mestre Gari 48, (971 37 53 59/www.esmercadal.com).* **Open** 10.30am-2pm, 5-10.30pm Tue-Sat; 5-11.30pm Sun.

Police station
Alaior *C/de la Sala s/n (971 37 13 20).*
Ferreries *Plaça de s'Església 1 (971 15 51 77).*
Es Mercadal *C/Major 18 (971 37 52 51).*
Es Migjorn Gran *Plaça de s'Ajuntament (971 37 01 10).*

Post office
Alaior *C/Forn 1 (971 37 19 71).*
Ferreries *Plaça Constitució s/n (971 37 41 00).*
Es Mercadal *C/Lepanto 43 (971 37 53 37).*
Es Migjorn Gran *Plaça de s'Ajuntament (971 37 53 37).*

Getting there

By bus
The 7 buses that run from Monday to Saturday (6 on Sunday) between Maó and Ciutadella stop at Alaior, Es Mercadal and Ferreries. In addition, there are 4 buses daily between Ferreries and Maó (40mins), 7 buses daily between Ferreries and Cala Galdana (20mins), 13 buses Mon-Sat between Alaior and Son Bou (15mins) and 4 buses Mon-Fri (3 on Sat) from Es Migjorn Gran to Sant Tomàs (10mins). Note that there are fewer services to the resorts out of season (November to April).

North Menorca

The untamed shore.

Cap de Favàritx. *See p244.*

Menorca's north coast is the wildest and least developed part of the island. It has virgin beaches of pink, orange and white sands, and therapeutic mud; jagged cliffs and bizarre rock formations carved by the indefatigable Tramuntana wind; and a wild sea – on a dark, blustery day it seems more west coast of Ireland than western Med.

Most of the area is free of development and sparsely served by roads, making it ideal for hikers, bird watchers and those wishing to explore life above and below the waves. A handful of islands scattered off the north-east coast are accessible only by boat and have idyllic desert-island beaches. Also here is the fishing village of **Fornells**, renowned for its lobster, and one of the island's most charming settlements. Aside from the occasional custom-built resort town, the north offers a taste of Menorca before the tourists arrived.

The north-east coast

The road from Maó to Fornells sweeps north-westwards through picturesque farmland, fertile pastures, thick woods and gently rolling hills before reaching the pines and salt flats of the Bay of Fornells. Tributaries branch off to the various villages of the north-east coast. Four kilometres (two and a half miles) north-east of Maó, **Sa Mesquida** has the closest beach to the city (**Cala Mesquida**), sheltered by a rocky outcrop and once protected by a now much-eroded defence tower, built by the British in 1799. In 1781 a combined French-Spanish force landed here to launch their attack on the island.

Further north, the fishing village of **Es Grau** retains much of its charm and is where many Maó families come for the summer. The village lies at the edge of the island's only officially protected nature reserve, **S'Albufera des Grau**, which was dubbed a 'Parc Natural' in 1993 when the island as a whole was declared a UNESCO Biosphere Reserve (a title that means little more than 'what a nice, natural place you have here, please don't change it'). The park includes bays, beaches, farmland (including the winery of **Sa Cudia**, which makes Menorca's first white wine, an excellent 100 per cent malvasia, created with the lobsters of Fornells in mind) and the wetlands of S'Albufera des Grau, and is an important staging post for migratory birds. Three short, well-marked walks lead visitors through different parts of the reserve, one starting at the beach and two more from the visitor centre, a couple of minutes' drive outside the village. There is also a hut in the village car park with information. Excellent free guided tours in Spanish and/or Catalan (but not English) are held every Saturday at 11am, and at other times during peak periods (reservations essential: 971 35 63 02, mobile 609 60 12 49).

This is one of the few places on the island where you can easily follow the old **Camí dels Cavalls** (Horse Path), which used to connect the island's outposts and watchtowers. Beyond the far end of the beach, you can walk to **Cala Tamarells** and **Cala de sa Torreta**, separated by the badly eroded watchtower **Torre del Tamarells**. From Cala de Sa Torreta the path continues inland through meadows and woodland to the farm at **Sa**

Walk 8 Es Grau to Sa Torre Blanca

Distance: 9km (6 miles). Circular.
Time: 2hrs 45mins.

The north-east coast of Menorca contains some of the wildest and most beautiful landscapes on the island. This relatively easy but varied walk starts at the cute little resort of Es Grau and follows the rugged coastline north past countless (often deserted) sandy coves, before turning inland to reach the isolated and little-visited prehistoric site of Sa Torre Blanca, and returning to Es Grau via the northern edge of the Albufera lagoon (*see p241*). There's nowhere to get refreshments along the way, so take a picnic, or start mid-morning if you want to be back in Es Grau in time for a leisurely lunch at one of the resort's waterside bar-restaurants (*see p245*).

Leave your car at the car park by the side of the beach at the edge of Es Grau, and walk around the long, wide arc of sand. At the far end of the beach ignore a sign pointing off to the left to Albufera and climb up the wide rocky path, which gives lovely views back over the bay and the small whitewashed village.

Fifteen minutes after starting the walk, the main path dips down to the left (ignore a lesser path off to the right at this point), and then follows the contours of the densely shrub-packed hillside. On a hot day, the scents of the plants – camomile and rosemary among them – are intoxicating.

The path, now sandy, heads inland through trees (including the most common Menorcan native species, the Aleppo pine), before emerging on to a headland. Ahead of you along the coast you'll see the Torre dels Tamarells, an 18th-century defensive tower. At this point the path splits – ignore the right-hand branch and take the left fork down a rocky path.

After ten minutes you come to a small sandy beach, Cala Tamarells. Climb up the rocks at its far side, and within five minutes you arrive at a stone stile over a wall next to a fire warning sign. (From here, you'll walk in a loop that returns to this spot.) Climb over the stile and head towards the tower. The sandy path zigzags and splits amid the trees and shrubs, but it doesn't matter which branch you take as long as you keep going towards the tower.

In eight or so minutes you'll come to the first of a couple of lovely beaches side by side. If you want to check out the tower, pass them both and climb the rocks to reach the old fortification. If you're not bothered, then walk to the back of the first beach, where you'll come across a dirt track wide enough for a vehicle. Take this, heading roughly in the direction in which you've been walking, with the tower on your right.

Menorca

After five minutes you'll arrive at another azure bay. The track becomes narrower as it meets a stone wall, then widens again as it rises, following the wall, and dipping again as it passes an old cottage. You come to another beach, Cala de Sa Torreta, and follow the path as it bends away from the sea to the left. Almost immediately a wide sandy track crosses the path. Turn right here, through trees, to the back of another bay (with an old boat house visible on its far side), before following the path as it swings inland.

Around eight minutes after leaving the sea, the track heads through a field of thistles and exits by a gateway in a stone wall as it starts to climb. After a further five or so minutes you pass through another stone gateway and immediately see a group of old farm buildings ahead of you.

As you approach you pass through another stone gateway. You'll take the track to the left here on returning from Sa Torre Blanca, which is just a minute's walk away. For now, head straight up to a rusty gate next to a more modern breeze block-built building, and take the path that runs in front of it to the right. This emerges at the small but atmospherically overgrown prehistoric site, complete with taula and ruined talayot. Scramble to the top of the latter for wonderful panoramas of the surrounding countryside.

When you've had your fill of history, return to the spot mentioned earlier, and now turn right on to the track, passing through a wooden gate and returning to open country. Within a few minutes you'll come to two gates. Go through (or climb over) the right-hand one. After a quarter of an hour of walking you'll get your first glimpse of the Albufera lagoon.

Keep following the track as it descends gently through a number of stone gateways and past a stone cattle trough on your left, keeping the lagoon on your right. By this point the track becomes somewhat overgrown, though still easy to follow.

Just as you reach the level of the lagoon, the path curves round to the left. Pass through a double stone gateway with another cattle trough between it and walk steadily upwards, away from the water and back towards the sea.

After five minutes of climbing you again spy the sea and the defensive tower, and start to descend. A further eight or so minutes and you reach a point where the main path bears round to the left before a clump of trees. You take a right here on to a path that is initially somewhat overgrown with rushes and grasses and tricky to make out. This spot is marked by some faint red markings on a rock on the path and also by a small cairn.

Within a minute you're back at the stone stile next to the fire warning sign. From here, retrace your steps back to Es Grau.

Torre Blanca, which has a magnificent taula and the remains of a talayot, made all the more impressive by the tranquillity of the surrounding countryside. For a detailed description of the walk to Sa Torre Blanca, *see p242* **Walk 8**.

From here you can see the lighthouse at **Cap de Favàritx**, a bare, windswept promontory that marks the north-eastern corner of the island. To get there by car, take the recently resurfaced road signed 'Favàritx' from the main Maó–Fornells road, passing through lush farmland that grows increasingly rough and desperate the closer you get to the point. Ignore the 'Propriedad Privada' sign and continue as the road deteriorates. Finally, all vegetation disappears to leave a blasted landscape of stark, desolate black slate, which is especially dramatic in stormy weather. When it's fine, though, there are a couple of nice beaches east of the lighthouse – the nearest is **Cala Presili**, followed by **S'Arenal de Morella** and then the shingly **Platja d'en Tortuga** (Tortoise Beach) – though you need stamina and stout shoes to reach them.

Top five Beaches

Cala en Pilar

It's a long walk from the nearest access point, which makes this pretty beach of reddish-brown sand all the more special. *See p246.*

Cala Pregonda

A short moonwalk across the rugged wastes of Binimel.la, with its red and purple muds and clays, leads you to a small beach with sand like hundreds-and-thousands, protected by jagged outcrops of rock. *See p246.*

Cala en Turqueta

A series of tiny patches of sand and mini-bays, with illicit boathouses and shacks redolent of pirates and smugglers, give this tiny beach its atmosphere of intimacy, exoticism and adventure. *See p233.*

Platja Tortuga

Perched alongside the desolate outcrop of Cap de Favoritx. The only way to get here is to walk or sail, but it's well worth the effort. *See p244.*

Son Bou

The longest beach on the island, with easy access, fine white sand and low dunes. *See p229.*

Between Cap de Favàritx and Fornells, the coast is made up of rocky headlands and sheltered bays of various sizes, including the long, sheltered **Port d'Addaia**, where the English landed in 1798, and which ends in wild salt flats. North-west of here there are various holiday developments of differing degrees of intrusion. Addaia itself has a small, working marina, a defence tower at the tip of the headland and small villas overlooking the bay and across to the featureless but picturesque **Illes d'Addaia** and **Punta de Montgofra**. There's great diving to be had in these parts (*see p256* **Dive! Dive! Dive!**).

Further on, **Na Macaret** consists of private holiday homes and a tiny beach with three palm trees. To the west, **Arenal d'en Castell** is a beautiful horseshoe bay with emerald waters and white sand, though it is dominated by the resort that stretches around it. A couple of quieter beaches, accessible only on foot, can be found to the west at **Es Macar de sa Llosa**. Finally, the grim holiday village of **Son Parc** smears itself through the woods like a virulent weed, emerging from the trees to overlook yet another beautiful white beach, **Arenal de Son Saura**. To escape the crowds, head around the rock at the western edge of the main beach to the small inlet of **Cala Pudent**.

Where to eat & drink

Cap Roig (Urb. Cala Mesquida, 971 18 83 83, closed Mon and all Dec-Mar, €€), at the entrance to **Sa Mesquida**, has wonderful views over the bay and the barren, rocky headlands and a deserved reputation for grilled sardines, prawns and *escopinas* (giant clams usually served raw). Arrive by 1.30pm for lunch as it soon gets jam-packed.

Lovely **Es Grau** has four small bars, three of which are on the waterfront, with great views over the beach and bay. **Es Moll** (Moll Magatzems 17, 971 35 91 67, closed Oct-Mar, €), at the far end of the village, is the quietest and serves delicious home-made snacks and sardines.

Of the three restaurants in **Na Macaret**, **Acuario** (Plaça Macaret s/n, 971 35 98 58, closed Mon and all Nov-Apr, €€) has the nicest view being practically on the beach; it offers tapas and snacks at lunchtime, and a wider selection of more substantial dishes at dinner. **Bar Na Macaret** (C/Moll de Macaret 295, 971 35 80 40, closed dinner Nov-Apr, €€), just behind it, has a pleasant, shady terrace and serves good paella.

In **Arenal d'en Castell**, **Restaurante Alcalde** (Avda. Central s/n, 971 35 80 93, closed Dec-Feb, €€) is good value with a terrace overlooking the beach.

Fornells.

Fornells

The small fishing village of **Fornells** is
justifiably famous for two things: its pretty
location beside the Bay of Fornells and its
seafood restaurants. This is one of the most
charming spots to stay on the island, though
the village itself is no more than a couple
of streets running parallel to the palm-lined
waterfront, with a small walled harbour and a
tiny church. Beyond the village, a rocky
promontory dominates the entrance to the bay
and is topped by the best-preserved watchtower
on the island, built by the English in 1801.

Sheltered from the worst of the Tramuntana
wind, the bay has been strategically important
throughout Menorcan sea-faring history.
Nowadays it provides the perfect place for
sailing and windsurfing. There is nowhere to
swim easily, though, and most people head for
Cala Tirant, just to the west. The short route
leads to a newish resort, **Platges de Fornells**,
while the longer route passes through beautiful
marshlands before arriving at the quieter end.
For watersports, try Windsurf Fornells (C/Nou
33, 971 18 81 50, www.excellence.es/fornells,
closed Nov-Apr).

Where to eat & drink

Fornells is justifiably renowned for its seafood,
most of which comes from the village's own
fleet of small fishing boats. The most famous
dish is *caldereta de llagosta* – spiny lobster
stew (some menus erroneously translate it
as 'crayfish stew') prepared with tomato, onion
and peppers. It was formerly food for poor

fishermen who couldn't afford to eat most of
their catch, which was destined for noblemen's
tables. Lobsters, in contrast, were considered
unworthy fare. Nowadays you practically need
to be a nobleman to afford it – €60 a head is
about the going rate. Much less and the lobster
is likely to be frozen, or the *caldereta* frozen
once cooked, which amounts to the same thing.
Alternatively, *caldereta de marisco* (made with
assorted seafood, rather than just lobster) is
also delicious and only a third of the price.

With one very notable exception, all the
restaurants are along the waterfront and have
similar menus, including fresh fish and paella
as well as *caldereta*. If you want something
more straightforward, both of the *hostales* in the
centre have tapas, *platos combinados* and home
cooking. Alternatively, **Ca Na Marga** (Urb.
Ses Salines 1, 971 37 64 10, ww.canamarga.com,
closed lunch and all Nov-Apr, €) in nearby **Ses
Salines** is a good choice for picky kids, serving
good pizzas and grilled fish and meat.

The only restaurant not on the waterfront,
Es Cranc (C/Escoles 31, 971 37 64 42, closed
Wed Sept-July and all mid Nov-mid Mar, €€€)
deserves its reputation as the best dining spot
in Fornells, and is certainly the place to eat
caldereta, though at peak times (mid July-end
Aug) you need to book at least a week in
advance. In low season there is an excellent set
menu available, offering simple fish dishes
cooked to perfection and delicious desserts.

To avoid the feeding frenzy at the centre
of the village, head for **Es Cranc Pelut**
(Passeig Maritim 98, 971 37 67 43, closed
Tue Sept-July and all Dec-Feb, €€€) at the
southern end of the waterfront, run by Juan

Vicente Flores, who owns an olive grove in his native Andalucia that provides oil for the restaurant, and local chef Diego Coll Petrus, ex-chef at Es Cranc. The specialities are paella, fish, *caldereta de llagosta* and a delicious *caldereta de marisco*, which gets better and better with each serving as the thick, rich sauce cools and deepens in flavour, that are the stars of the show. Don't decline the 'bib' the waiter will proffer you – you'll need it.

Unlike most of the restaurants in Fornells, **Sa Llagosta** (C/Gabriel Gelabert 12, 971 37 65 66, closed Nov-Easter, €€€), in an old cottage in front of the harbour, is small, quiet and intimate, with wooden beams and pretty blue and white decor. A shortish menu features seasonal local dishes as well as a few more modern additions, such as hake with honey and garlic sauce, green risotto with squid, and scorpion fish with shallots.

As an alternative to Menorcan fish and seafood dishes, **Thai Country** (Menorca Country Club, Urb. Platges de Fornells, 971 37 68 60, €) is an opulent affair, decorated with intricate teak wood furniture and Buddhas, and offers some excellent, authentic Thai fare.

Where to stay

There are three *hosteles* in Fornells, all of which offer basic but pleasant accommodation. **S'Algaret** (Plaça S'Algaret 7, 971 37 65 52, www.hostal-salgaret.com, closed Nov-mid May, doubles €50-€82), which also has a restaurant, and **La Palma** (Plaça S'Algaret 3, 971 37 64 87, www.hostallapalma.com, closed end Oct-Mar, doubles €45-€75). are next to each other, opposite the harbour. Both have rooms overlooking their respective swimming pools and also double up as the two main village bars, serving reasonably priced food.

A few metres up the slight hill is **Hostal Fornells** (C/Major 17, 971 37 66 76, www.hostal fornells.com, doubles €61-€120 incl breakfast), which has a little more character. Rooms are priced according to view, the cheapest is a very small interior room with no view, but it's worth splurging on a room overlooking the swimming pool, or the bay. All rooms have bathrooms en suite, air-conditioning, TV, safe and telephone, and the staff are young, friendly and helpful.

One- and two-bedroom apartments, some with a view of the bay, are available at **Can Digus** (C/Vivers s/n, 971 37 65 12, www.candigus.com, apartments €55-€98), which also has its own pool.

If you can't find anywhere in Fornells, **Hostal Port Fornells** (C/d'es Port Fornells s/n, 971 37 63 73, www.hostalportfornells.com, closed late Oct-late Apr, doubles €80-€90), down the road at **Ses Salines**, has simple, clean rooms, half of which look out over the bay.

The north coast to the west of Fornells is the most deserted part of the island. Between Cap de Cavalleria and **Cala Morell**, there is nothing but hilly pastureland and wild beaches at the end of long, rough tracks. **Cap de Cavalleria** is a small, low headland with an unmanned lighthouse and a herd of goats. At the base of the isthmus that connects it to the rest of the island is an optimistic 'eco-museum', **Ecomuseu Cap de Cavalleria**, which displays artefacts from the nearby Roman settlement of **Sanitja**. It's a beautiful spot to visit, though there is little to see as most of the ruins have either been excavated and covered over again, or have yet to be dug up.

The beaches in this part of the island are almost entirely unspoilt, with reddish-brown sand between weather-beaten cliffs. **Platja de Cavalleria** is easy to get to, as is **Platja de Binimel.la** (where you'll find the only place to eat on this stretch of coast; *see p246*), while **Cala Pregonda** is a 20-minute walk from the latter.

Cala en Pilar is also only accessible on foot – there's a car park midway down the side road leading off the main Maó–Ciutadella highway (around km34); from here it's about a three-kilometre (two-mile) walk down to the beach. Alternatively, you can approach it from the side road off the highway between km31 and km32, signed to the **Castell de Sant Agueda**. This ruined Moorish fortress stands atop the island's third highest hill. Built in the tenth century, the fortress was abandoned following Alfons III's conquest of the island and is now little more than an outline, although the medieval track to the top is still in good condition and it's a lovely 45-minute walk through glades of holm oaks up to the peak.

Ecomuseu Cap de Cavalleria

Camí de Sa Cavalleria, Fornells (971 35 99 99/ www.ecomuseodecavalleria.com). **Open** *Apr-June, Oct* 10am-7pm daily. *July-Sept* 10am-8.30pm daily. **Admission** €3; free under-8s. **Credit** MC, V.

Where to eat

The only beach on this coast with any facilities is **Platja Binimel.la**, where you'll find **Restaurante Binimel.la** (971 35 92 75, closed dinner and all Nov-Apr, €€), which specialises in succulent, home-raised roast lamb.

By bus

There are 2 buses Mon-Sat between Fornells and Maó (35mins) and 1 bus Mon-Fri to Es Mercadal (15mins).

Ciutadella & West Menorca

Ignore the dreary resorts, and celebrate the island's most characterful town.

While the charms of Maó, undeniable though they are, might not be immediately apparent, Ciutadella is an instant hit: bright and breezy, it plays the brassy blonde to the island capital's retiring brunette. Ciutadella's attractions are very much on display, and it's difficult not to be seduced by them: elegant mansions of pink-tinged sandstone, narrow cobbled streets, pastel houses with bright shutters and a port that makes up in quaintness what it lacks in size.

It is also becoming increasingly famed for its vibrant Sant Joan festivities around 23 June, when most of the island takes to the streets to feast on hazelnuts, down gallons of the local tipple, *pomada* (Xoriguer gin and lemonade) and watch the *jaleo* (when horseback riders make their steeds rear up on their hind legs and stampede through the crowds).

Inland, the countryside is harsh and rocky, with drystone walls and several interesting prehistoric monuments. The west coast, on the other hand, is home to some of the island's most shocking tour operator resort ghettos.

Ciutadella

Sightseeing

At the heart of the city – if city is a fair description for a town of little more than 20,000 inhabitants, albeit with a cathedral at its centre – are two large, adjoining squares, the one laid-back and bucolic, the other poised and formal. **Plaça de s'Esplanada** is better known as the **Plaça d'es Pins**, with tall pine trees that turn the sandy square into an oasis of shade, filled with park benches, play areas and cafés. Beside it, the **Plaça d'es Born** is an open expanse bordered by buildings straight from a theatre set, including the town hall, theatre and 19th-century palaces. The obelisk at the centre commemorates the bloodthirsty Turkish attack of 1558, which culminated in a three-day rampage of rape, murder and pillage, the razing of the town and the kidnapping of 3,452 men and women to work as galley slaves and courtesans respectively in Constantinople.

The tallest and most arresting building on the Plaça d'es Born is the **Ajuntament** (town hall) in the north-west corner, with an arcaded sandstone façade. Built on the site of the old Moorish Real Alcázar, or royal citadel, the building incorporates references to both Moorish and military architecture. Inside the town hall, a stone stairway leads up to the impressive first floor, where the Gothic council chamber is worth a quick visit. Round the back, the remains of the old **Governor's Palace** can still be visited (9am-1pm daily, free) to give a better idea of the building's military past.

A road beside the town hall leads down to the port, while on its other side, a balustrade overlooking the port tops all that is left of the city's medieval ramparts, which were demolished at the end of the 19th century and replaced by the wide avenues that now circumscribe the old town. Looking up from the port, though, these ramparts still give a good idea of the Ciutadella's one-time defences.

Alongside them, on the square's north side, is the late 19th century **Teatro d'es Born** (Plaça d'es Born 20, 971 48 44 84). To the right of the theatre, C/Sa Muradeta leads to the Bastió de sa Font, a blind stone edifice built in 1677 as part of the town's defences (and doubling up as a warehouse for storing tithes). Nowadays it contains the small but interesting **Museu Municipal de Ciutadella**. Below here is the Pla de Sant Joan, a sandy area at the end of the port where jousting games take place during the Festes de Sant Joan in June.

Back in the Plaça d'es Born, the eastern side of the square is taken up by three palaces, all built in the 19th century. To the left as you face them is the **Palau Torresaura**, the most impressive of the three, with a fine neo-classical façade, complete with two triple-arched, double-height galleries that were added later to bring the building in line (physically and architecturally) with the **Palau Salort** next door. These days you have to screw up your eyes and ignore the ground-floor shops selling tourist trinkets to see it at its best.

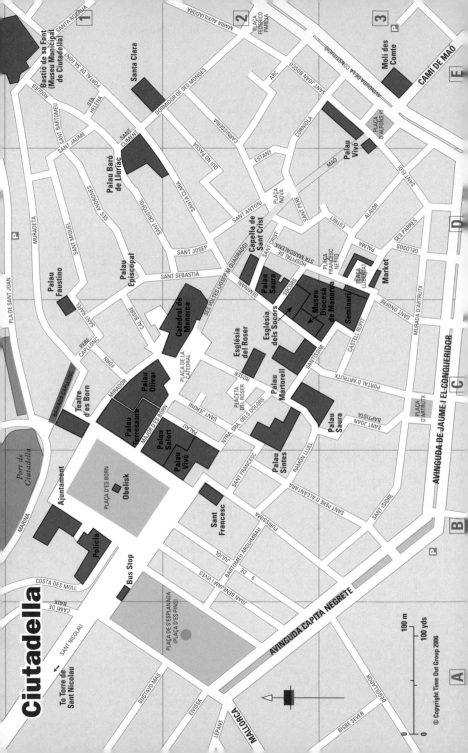

In the south-east corner of the square stands the large, simple church of **Sant Francesc**, most of which was built at the end of the 16th century (1583-1607) to replace the one that had been destroyed (with its adjoining monastery) during the Turkish sacking of the city in 1558. The sedate, unadorned main façade dates from the 19th century. The site of the monastery, which was active until 1835, is now hidden beneath the modern monstrosity of the post office.

Between the Palaus Torresaura and Salort, pedestrianised C/Major d'es Born leads up past yet another palace, the 17th-century (with an 18th-century façade) **Palau Olivar**, to the **Catedral de Menorca**, a beautiful, monolithic hulk of a building of creamy-pink sandstone that changes colour throughout the day as the sun moves across the sky.

Next to the cathedral's south entrance, a wooden door leads to the pleasant, plant-filled courtyard of the **Palau Episcopal**, which gives a different perspective of the cathedral and the three subsequent side chapels. Also of interest is the bakery opposite, where bread and Menorcan 'pasties' are baked in a wood-fired oven, concealed behind the guillotine-like oven door behind the counter.

Just to the south of the cathedral, down C/del Roser, is the elaborately carved entrance of the **Església del Roser**, a small, pretty baroque church built at the beginning of the 18th century, which has now been converted into an exhibition hall. The red sandstone façade is one of the most ornate on the island, despite being badly damaged by erosion.

Back in Plaça de la Catedral, the square narrows, leading to the charming C/Ses Voltes, an arcaded pedestrianised street with low, whitewashed arches; it's best seen at night, when the surrounding shops have packed away their wares and the arches can be fully appreciated.

At the start of C/Ses Voltes, C/d'es Seminari leads south to the dilapidated Renaissance **Església del Socors**, built between 1619 and 1670. Beside it, and now housing the seminary and the **Museu Diocesà de Menorca**, is the Augustine monastery, added in the mid 17th century, with airy cloisters that offer a good view of the church's two belltowers. The Diocesan Museum itself fills five small rooms around the courtyard, giving a rapid tour of Menorcan history that complements the Museu Municipal de Ciutadella.

Directly behind the seminary, and now tucked in beneath its walls, is the small but quaint marketplace in Plaça de la Llibertat, a charming square with tall arcades and a fish market (looking rather like a fish tank) in the middle.

Meanwhile, Ses Voltes continues east through pretty Plaça Nova before reaching Plaça d'Alfons III, more usually referred to as Plaça de ses Palmeres (on account of the palm trees). Standing above the square is the town's only remaining windmill, the **Molí des Comte**, with a handicraft centre beside it and the atmospheric **Bar El Molí** (971 38 33 08) occupying the ground floor. The windmill marks the start of the Maó road, and can be visited by appointment.

The windmill's geographical and architectural mirror image, the **Torre de Sant Nicolau**, stands on the low cliffs at the western tip of Ciutadella, guarding the mouth of the port at the end of Passeig Sant Nicolau. Built in the 17th century, it is the most elegant of the island's watchtowers and, although there is little to see inside, the view from the roof is excellent. The rocks around its base were used as defences during the Civil War. Nearby is a statue to Admiral David Glasgow Farragut (1801-70), son of a Ciutadella emigrant, hero of the American Civil War and the first four-star admiral of the US Navy.

On the port in Ciutadella there are a couple of places for aspiring seadogs to get their hands on a boat. Anything from a small dinghy (no licence required) to swish powerboats can be rented from Mestral Rent a Boat and Boat Trips (Moll Comercial 46-48, 971 38 14 85, mobile 619 67 30 39, www.menorcadigital.com/mestral.htm, €90-€250 per day). Proper sail boats can be rented from Arrayan (Apdo. Correos 366, mobile 649 82 90 72, www.velero arrayan.com, €390-€2,400). There are also tourist boat trips to be had from the port.

Bikes can be hired from Velos Joan (C/Sant Isidre 32-34, 971 38 15 76, €7 per day, map p248 B3).

Catedral de Menorca

Plaça de la Catedral (971 38 07 39). **Open** 8.30am-1pm, 6-9pm daily. See note below. **Admission** free. **Map** p248 C2.

From the outside, the lower half of the cathedral appears as a single, unadorned base, supporting an upper half of buttresses and stained-glass windows – though once inside it becomes clear that there are, in fact, shrines between each of the support columns. Following the Turkish raid of 1558, the lower parts of the buttresses were encased in stone to guard against future attack. Originally one of four chapels ordered by Alfons III to celebrate his conquest of the island, work started in 1303 under Jaume II on the site of an existing mosque, and incorporated the mosque's minaret as the belltower. The south entrance, facing C/Roser, retains its original Gothic portal, while at the main entrance, the original west doorway is now hidden behind a neo-classical entrance that was added at the beginning of the 19th

Menorca

century, perhaps to celebrate the church's newly awarded status as a cathedral in 1795. Inside, the cathedral consists of a single Gothic nave flanked by small chapels, although three other slightly larger chapels have been added along the left-hand side over the centuries. The Capilla de las Ánimas (Chapel of the Souls) is one of Menorca's most impressive examples of the baroque.

Note that at the time of writing the cathedral was being renovated until some time in 2006 and opening times are unpredictable during this period.

Museu Diocesà de Menorca

C/Seminari 7 (971 48 12 97). **Open** 10.30am-1.30pm Tue-Sat. Closed end Oct-Apr. **Admission** €2.50; €1.20-€1.80 concessions; free under-7s. **No credit cards. Map** p248 C2.

The Diocesan Museum contains various talayotic artefacts and bones, human skulls that show evidence of early experiments in trepanning, a single skull of the extinct but still grinning local goat-like *Myotragus Balearicus*, and Roman jars and jewellery. There is also a room dedicated to religious paraphernalia and another to the paintings of Pere Daura y Garcia, a sub-Cézanne with only a tenuous link to Menorca.

Museu Municipal de Ciutadella

Plaça de sa Font s/n (971 38 02 97/www.ciutadella. org/museu). **Open** 10am-2pm Tue-Sat. **Admission** €2.06; free-€1.03 concessions. Free to all Wed. **No credit cards. Map** p248 E1.

This absorbing little museum focuses on the history of the city and the island, particularly from prehistoric times until its integration with the Crown of Aragón in 1287.

Palau Salort

C/Major d'es Born 9 (971 38 00 56). **Open** 10am-2pm Mon-Sat. Closed Nov-Apr (except groups of ten or more). **Admission** €2.50; €1.20 concessions; free under-8s. **No credit cards. Map** p248 C2.

Where to eat & drink

Restaurants and bars are scattered throughout the old town and along the port, which is lined with seafood restaurants of varying quality. The port is also where most of the nightlife can be found, though it generally doesn't get going until midnight. There is a preponderance of pizzerias and the usual

Ciutadella. *See p247.*

Menorca

tourist-oriented snack bars in the centre of town, and you have to search a little to find something a bit better.

All of the seafood restaurants along the port have outside terraces, a few feet from the moored yachts. Offering almost identical menus, including fresh fish, meat and pricey *caldereta de llagosta* (spiny lobster stew), they are very tourist-oriented and most offer set *menús* in the region of €15. Remember, though, that you get what you pay for, and here you're paying for the setting as much as anything. Remember too that the ubiquitous grilled salmon is not indigenous to the Mediterranean.

Of the port places, **Sa Figuera** (C/Marina 99, 971 38 21 12, closed dinner mid Nov-Apr and 1mth Dec-Jan, €€€) is probably the most reliable spot, offering a range of set menus from €15 to €50. If it's kitsch cuisine you're after, then **Es Forat** (Passeig del Port s/n, 971 48 08 30, closed lunch Sun and all Oct-Apr, €€€) won't disappoint, with its romanticised paintings of horses hanging on the stone walls above the tables on the terrace. Next to that,

Corb Marí (C/Marina 43, 971 38 42 93, €€) is smaller and much less formal, with a few tables in its cavern. **Triton** (Moll Comercial 55, 971 38 00 02, open year round, €) is a fisherman's caff nestling among the tourist-luring restaurants alongside the port. It serves unexceptional snacks, sandwiches and tapas all day, but you can just come for a drink and enjoy the view. Most of the locals, though, head for **Café Balear** (*see below*).

Café Balear

Passeig de Sant Joan 15 (971 38 00 05). **Open** *June-Sept* 1-4pm, 7.30pm-midnight Mon-Sat. *Oct, Dec-May* 1-4pm, 7.30pm-midnight Tue-Sat; 1-4pm Sun. Closed Nov. **Average** €€-€€€. **Credit** AmEx, DC, MC, V. **Map** p248 C1.

Ask anyone in Ciutadella where to find the best fish and they unanimously name Café Balear, at the inland end of the port, between the bridge and the bastion. Classical in decor and cuisine, but none the worse for it in either case, this is where the locals come for simply prepared local fish caught by the restaurant's own fishing boats. The set lunch *menú* is excellent, featuring house specialities and

Menorcan and Spanish staples. In summer, either reserve a table inside or queue up along the quayside for one outdoors (reservations are not taken for the terrace).

Cas Ferrer

Portal de sa Font 16 (971 48 07 84). **Open** *Sept-Feb, Apr-mid July* 1-3.30pm, 8pm-midnight Tue-Sat. *Mid July-Aug* 8pm-midnight Mon, Sun;1-3.30pm, 8pm-midnight Tue-Sat. Closed Mar. **Average** €€€€. **Credit** MC, V. **Map** p248 E1.

It would be easy to overlook this small restaurant, tucked away near the bastion. The old blacksmith's, complete with forge, anvil and bellows, has been refurbished with taste and restraint to create a charming, intimate warren of rooms with original beams and tiles. The food is a mix of gourmet influences and is perhaps a little self-conscious and eager to please, while not always quite hitting the mark. Nevertheless, it's a welcome break from the identi-fish restaurants in the port and has an excellent reputation among island residents.

La Guitarra

C/Dolors 1, Bajos (971 38 13 55). **Open** 12.30-3.30pm, 7-11.30pm Mon-Sat. Closed Feb. **Average** €€. **Credit** DC, MC, V. **Map** p248 C2.

A discreet doorway leads to a flight of steps down to a vaulted stone cellar, where this atmospheric restaurant offers homely food. The lunch menu can be a little too homely quality-wise, but the €32 main evening menu of traditional Menorcan tapas: *frito Menorquín* (mixed, fried fish) and *embutidos* (a selection of local sausages) followed by the ubiquitous *caldereta de llagosta* is actually good value. There's also a much cheaper, lunchtime *menú*.

El Horno

C/d'es Forn 12 (971 38 07 67). **Open** 7pm-midnight daily. Closed Dec-Mar. **Average** €€. **Credit** AmEx, DC, MC, V. **Map** p248 C1.

A small, friendly restaurant in an old cellar close to the Plaça d'es Born, with a varied menu of French staples at very reasonable prices.

El Imperi

Plaça d'es Born s/n (no phone). **Open** varies. **No credit cards**. **Map** p248 B1.

A deserving classic, open day and night in the corner of Plaça d'es Born, El Imperi simply oozes character, from the wonderful beamed bar with marble tables to the stone arches of the back room and the pretty courtyard beyond. It's a great place for watching the comings and goings of folk about town, and sells excellent hot sandwiches and pies for a cheap lunch.

El Jardí

C/Sant Isidre 33 (971 48 05 16). **Open** phone for details. **Average** €€-€€€. **No credit cards**. **Map** p248 B3.

Brand new, and built around a pretty terrace shaded by a giant umbrella pine, El Jardí is an oasis in the heart of the old town and a peaceful retreat for

new wave *menorquí* cooking. Expect dishes like duck confit with fig carpaccio and rum, and slow-roasted goat kid and *sepia* (cuttlefish) noodles.

Look al Plaça

Plaça de la Llibertat 1 (971 38 58 67). **Open** *Apr-Oct* 9am-midnight daily. *Nov-Mar* 9am-2pm, 5-10pm Mon-Sat. **No credit cards**. **Map** p248 D3.

There are various small bars clustered around the market; this one's a real treat. Small, simple and laid-back, it is open all day and evening, and offers decent music, delicious coffee and plenty of tables on the pavement outside. Tapas are also served in the summer.

Oristano

Borja Moll 1 (971 38 41 97). **Open** 6pm-1am Thur-Sun. Closed Dec-Mar. **Average** €. **Credit** MC, V. **Map** p248 B1.

The pizzas here, cooked in a wood-fired oven and deliciously thin and crisp, have a deserving reputation. Other items on the menu should be treated with circumspection. A pleasant building overlooking the port, but somewhat lacking in atmosphere.

Pa amb Oli

C/Nou de Juliol 4 (971 38 36 19). **Open** noon-5pm, 7.30pm-1am Mon-Sat. **Average** €€. **Credit** MC, V. **Map** p248 B2.

Inadvertently kitsch, from the perplexed bull and stag heads to the artificial barrels, and with gruesome displays of red meat to greet you, Pa amb Oli is actually reasonably good and, surprisingly, one of the better options for vegetarians. There's a selection of grilled vegetable dishes on offer, alongside (literally) all the grilled meats, hams, cheeses and seafood. Unpretentious and friendly, though not especially cheap, it is rightly popular with the locals.

Restaurante Anny's

Avda. Conqueridor 71 (971 38 46 67). **Open** *June-Oct* 8am-midnight Mon-Sat. *Nov-May* 8am-midnight Mon-Sat; 8am-5pm Sun. **Average** €€. **Credit** MC, V. **Map** p248 C3.

If you can manage to ignore the laminated signs outside and the faux-rustic decor inside – somewhat ubiquitous in Ciutadella – Anny's is friendly and offers tasty, good-value food. Generous portions and competent, unfussy cuisine attract the locals in ravenous hordes, as does a good value lunchtime *menú*. Low-ish ceilings and wide tables combine to boost noise levels beyond comfort during peak times and, together with rather bright lighting, make this a place to come for a good hot meal rather than a good hot date.

Restaurante Pizzeria Roma

C/Sant Pere d'Alcantara 18 (971 38 47 18). **Open** 7pm-1am daily. **Average** €€. **No credit cards**. **Map** p248 B2.

With a pleasant pavement terrace spilling on to the narrow streets of the old quarter, this is a good bet for a pizza or bowl of pasta, and handy for late-night pickings.

La Taberna

Port de Ciutadella (no phone). **Open** 1pm-late daily.
Average €-€€. **No credit cards. Map** p248 B1.
Decked with fishing nets, this converted boathouse
opened as a restaurant 25 years ago and continues
to run its own two fishing boats. It serves spanking fresh fish and elaborate seafood tapas at a frac-
tion of the price of Café Balear. It may not have the
latter's sophistication but it's fun to watch the
small lobster boats come in (approximately
between 12.30pm and 1pm) and unload their catch
as you eat.

La Torre de Papel

Camí de Maó 46 (mobile 676 33 66 99). **Open** 9am-
midnight Mon-Sat; 5pm-midnight Sun. **No credit
cards. Map** p248 E3.
A small, charming and slightly radical bar-cum-
bookshop, with plenty of second-hand books that
say a lot about local (and national) reading habits;
the English section is all airport novels and historical romances, the French section full of poetry
and philosophy.

Nightlife

Ciutadella is no Ibiza, although at weekends
and during the summer there are a dozen or
so bars and clubs clustered around the Pla de
Sant Joan at the inland end of the port, offering
a variety of musical styles and venues from
pop to techno by way of lounge, jazz, funk
and rock, and terraces for open-air chillouts.
Handily, they are concentrated around an area
the size of a teenager's midriff, which makes
flitting from one to the other instant, effortless
and enjoyable. **Jazzbah** (Pla de Sant Joan 3,
971 48 29 53, open June-Sept 11pm-6am daily,
Oct-May 11pm-6am Fri, Sat) is the classiest
spot, attracting a crowd as good-looking
as the club itself, which has several terraces,
high-priced drinks and some very good live
jazz music (it's probably the most reliable
big-night-out in town).

There is also a handful of small, smart late-
night bars on Baixada Capllonc, the slope that
runs from the town down to the port: **Cactus
Bar** (No.15, mobile 662 06 02 28) is German-
run and the only proper cocktail bar on the
port, with a gigantic terrace for drinks; **Es
Vaporet** (No.14, no phone) is a little more
upbeat and lively; at the bottom of the hill,
cave-like **Sa Clau** (C/Marina 93, 971 38 48
63, www.saclau.com, closed mid Sept-mid
May Mon-Thur, Sun and all mid Dec-mid Jan)
is a miniscule jazz bar that could easily
be a pirate's lair and certainly makes up in
atmosphere what it lacks in size. But the place
that really gets the party started is **Martin's
Bar** (no phone), gay-orientated, loud and
proud, and great fun.

Shopping

The centre of Ciutadella sometimes feels like
an outdoor themed shopping arcade. Most of
the shops can be found along Ses Voltes and
the streets that run off it, particularly its
extension C/Maó and C/Santa Clara, which has
several interesting boutiques. For local shoes,
especially *abarcas*, the leather sandals with car
tyre soles (check the sides of the soles – if they
are made from genuine tyres, they have a wire
thread running through them) try **Xoquins**
(Baixada Capllonc 14, 971 38 00 97) on the
ramp leading down to the port from C/de
Sa Muradeta, behind the Teatre d'es Born;
it sells the genuine tyre variety as well as
the more modern kind.

Ciutadella scores higher for food than
fashion and the local produce makes great
gifts. For local cheese, cured meat and wine,
there are several small grocers around the
marketplace, all of which have a good
selection. **Ca na Riera** (Hospital Santa
Magdalena 7, no phone) is chaotic but very
good. **Ca'n Padet** next door (Plaça Francesc
Netto s/n, 971 38 00 91) is less atmospheric
but better organised. **Moll Pastisseria
Bomboneria** (C/Maó 8, 971 38 40 81 and
C/Roser 1, 971 38 10 85) sells wonderful
artisan preserves including Figat de Menorca
(fig jam), home-cured *alcaparras* (capers)
and *amargos* (sweet almond cakes). For wine,
Xoriguer gin and other local concoctions,
Ses Industries (C/Santa Clara 4, 971 38 28
82) is small but irresistible. A more select list
of wines and cheeses can be found at **La
Bodega** (C/Santissim 14, 971 48 02 84), which
is part-deli, part-wine bar, serving wine by
the glass plus various cheese and cured meat
tapas. Not to be missed either is the **Horno
Montaner** (C/Obispo Torres 11, 971 38 08 32),
the oldest continuing functioning bakery
on the island (the Montaner family has had
it for five generations, though the house
it's located in is at least 400 years old) and
the old-fashioned bread oven has become
an attraction in itself. It's excellent for picnic
fodder: home-made bread, cheese and meat
pies and sweet pastries.

Where to stay

Ciutadella is not especially well served for
accommodation; there are a few reasonable
places, but nowhere outstanding.

Hostal Paris

C/Santandria 4 (971 38 16 22). **Rates** (incl
breakfast) €36-€60 double. Closed Oct-Apr.
Credit MC, V.

Run by a Basque woman, this youthful, laid-back *hostal* is ideal for solo travellers. Of the 13 brightly painted rooms, the six singles all have sunny balconies facing west. Most of the doubles look out on to the main road south, which can get quite busy in high season, and only two rooms have en suite bathrooms.

Hostal Residencia Ciutadella
C/Sant Eloi 10 (971 38 34 62). **Rates** €45-€95 double. **Credit** MC, V. **Map** p248 D3.
It's easy to miss this large, old-fashioned hotel right in the old town, just off Plaça Alfons III. Rooms are reasonably comfortable, spick and span and excellent value, and many of them look out on to the narrow street. The hotel is open all year round and there is a traditional family restaurant on the ground floor.

Hostal Residencia Menurka
C/Domingo Savio 6 (971 38 14 15/www.menurka. com). **Rates** (incl breakfast) €40-€78 double. **Credit** MC, V.
A simple, family-run *pensión* with 21 rooms, close to the bus station and a few minutes' walk to the old town. Internal rooms are dim and a little noisy; external ones are quiet, bright and spacious, and some have a balcony.

Hotel Balear
Camí de Maó 178 (971 48 23 41). **Rates** (incl breakfast in high season) €42-€72 double. **Credit** MC, V. **Map** p248 E3.
This 16-room hotel on the road out of Ciutadella is a touch inconvenient, but it is friendly, with clean, comfortable en-suite rooms, making it a reasonable budget option – if you don't mind the ten-minute walk to the centre of town.

Hotel Esmeralda
Avda. Sant Nicolau 171 (971 38 02 50/www.mac-hotels.com). **Rates** €35-€53 double. Closed Nov-Apr. **Credit** AmEx, MC, V. **Map** p248 off A1.
A large, modern-looking hotel overlooking Castell de Sant Nicolau and the sea filled almost exclusively with package tourists. There is a small surcharge for rooms facing the sea, but it's well worth paying the extra – the view is fantastic.

Hotel Geminis
C/Josepa Rossinyol 4 (971 38 46 44/www.hotel geminismenorca.com). **Rates** (incl breakfast) €45-€86 double. Closed 10 Dec-end Feb. **Credit** MC, V. **Map** p248 off E3.
A pastel-pink building down a quiet side street just outside the old town, the Geminis is light, bright and friendly. Half the rooms look out on to a small swimming pool and the overgrown garden next door, complete with palm trees. The other half look out on to the street. Comfortable sofas are strewn around the bar and reception.

Hotel Hesperia Patricia
Passeig de Sant Nicolau 90-92 (971 38 55 11/ www.hoteles-hesperia.es). **Rates** €75-€161 double. **Credit** AmEx, DC, MC, V. **Map** p248 off A1.

The largest non-seasonal hotel in Ciutadella is comfortable, close to the port and convenient for the centre of town, a five-minute walk away. Though slightly corporate in style, it attracts a combination of holidaymakers as well as business travellers.

Hotel Madrid
C/Madrid 60 (971 38 03 28/www.menorcadigital. com/hoteles.htm). **Rates** (incl breakfast) €67-€73 double. Closed Nov-Apr. **Credit** MC, V. **Map** p248 off A1.
Set in the quiet residential area on the Ciutadella headland, not far from the seafront, this hotel has pleasant rooms, though some are a little cramped. There is a reasonably sized pool in the garden and a snack bar downstairs. Some of the 22 rooms are block-booked by tour operators, but others are reserved for independent clients.

Hotel Playa Grande
C/Obispo Juano 2 (971 38 24 45/www.grupo andria.com). **Rates** (incl breakfast) €72-€120 double. Closed 15 Dec-15 Jan. **Credit** MC, V.
Located in Ciutadella's city centre this large, corporate-style chain hotel does not quite overlook the ironically named beach (it's miniscule) from which it takes its name, though many of the rooms have balconies from which can be seen a little sand and water, just.

Hostal Sa Prensa
Plaça de Madrid s/n (971 38 26 98). **Rates** €35-€70 double. Closed 1mth in winter. **No credit cards**. **Map** p248 off A1.
Close to Castell de Sant Nicolau, four of the rooms here have great views of the sea from their generous balconies and are usually booked up several months in advance. The other three have no balcony and look out on to drab apartment blocks.

Oasis
C/Sant Isidre 33 (971 38 21 97). **Rates** (incl breakfast in high season) €36-€48. Closed 16 Oct-31 Mar. **No credit cards**. **Map** p248 B3.
This small, simple *pensión* really is an oasis, hidden away in the middle of the old town, but opening out into a bright, peaceful courtyard filled with flowers. The bedrooms are quite small and simply furnished, with old-fashioned fittings, but are nevertheless clean and comfortable.

Resources

Internet
Café Internet, Plaça d'es Pins 37 (971 38 42 15/ www.elcafenet.net). **Open** *June-Oct* 9am-1am Mon-Sat. *Nov-May* 9am-11pm Mon-Sat. **Map** p248 A2.

Police station
Ajuntament, Plaça d'es Born 15 (971 38 07 87). **Map** p248 B1.

Post office
Plaça d'es Born 9 (971 38 00 81). **Map** p248 B1.

Cala Morell. *See p259.*

Dive! Dive! Dive!

'The Med's dead', or so they say when it comes to diving. Not so around Menorca. Riddled with caves and grottoes, and with a thriving underwater flora and fauna community and gin-clear waters giving visibility of up to 30 metres (100 feet), the island is rightly nicknamed the 'Caribbean of the Mediterranean', a premier dive destination for a seemingly endless variety of superb sites to suit every level of diver. If you've never dived before, it's an ideal place to give it a go. All the dive shops offer 'try dives', which allow even uncertified people to pop in a regulator and poke about underwater with a trained instructor at your side. It's safe, easy and well worth it as a testing ground if you're considering taking a PADI Open Water Course.

On the west coast, Cala en Blanes may seem like the Blackpool of Menorca on terra firma, but below the waves it's a different story. The guys at **7 Fathoms** are loads of fun and have a knack of making even the most reticent of divers comfortable in the water. Hence 90 per cent of their business comes from try dives. But they are also an excellent choice if you're into more challenging or technical diving, being the only school that covers all the accessible wrecks

on the island, including the spectacular Francisquita – a fully intact cargo ship sitting at 50 metres (164 feet) deep.

The most popular sites on this stretch of coast include Slipway (a good one for try dives), where close encounters with octopus are likely, and, if you're very, very lucky, the elusive sea horse may also come out to play. For more experienced divers, Grand Canyons is an underwater labyrinth snaking its way through the reef, and Punta d'en Forcat, at a depth of 24 metres (79 feet), offers some top-class wall diving, particularly good for spotting larger deep-water fish like sun fish and John Dory.

In the nature reserves of the north-east coast, **Ulmo Diving** offers more than 60 sites. Among them, and a must-do for advanced divers, is its combo day-trip comprising two boat dives. First is the Malakoff wreck – a British-built steamer that made her final voyage in 1928. With depths of up to 40 metres (131 feet), she is now an exceptional artificial reef providing one of the most memorable dive sites in the western Mediterranean. Your second tank takes in the spectacular, fairytale cavern at Pont d'En Gil. Ulmo is also a good bet when choppy water prevents diving further south. Try to get

Tourist information

OIT (Oficina d'Informació Turística), Plaça Catedral 5 (971 38 26 93/www.e-menorca.org). **Open** *May-Oct* 9am-8.30pm Mon-Sat. *Nov-Apr* 9am-1pm, 5-7pm Mon-Fri; 9am-1pm Sat. **Map** p248 C2.

OMIT (Oficina Municipal d'Informació Turística), Plaça des Pins (971 48 41 55). **Open** *June-Sept* 9am-1pm, 6-8pm Mon-Sat. *Jan-May, Oct-Dec* 9am-1pm Mon-Fri.

West interior

The area around Ciutadella is rich in prehistoric remains. All are within easy cycling distance of the town, and a tour of them makes for an excellent day or half-day excursion through beautiful countryside.

Seven kilometres (four miles) south of the town, on the way to Son Saura, is Menorca's largest prehistoric settlement, **Son Catlar**. It's hard to make out most of its internal structure beyond four talayots and a taula (without its T stone), but its outstanding feature is an 870-metre (2,854-foot) encircling defensive wall studded with defensive towers

– the only one of its kind to survive in its entirety on Menorca.

Accessed by minor roads, some of the islands's finest beaches lie south of here: **Son Saura**, **Cala en Turqueta** and **Cala Macarella**. For a walk from Cala Galdana that takes in all three, *see p230* **Walk 7**).

Off the main Ciutadella to Maó highway are two interesting sites. The most photographed of all the island's prehistoric remains is the **Naveta d'es Tudons**, close to the road, situated around five kilometres (three miles) east of Ciutadella. This superbly preserved burial monument, used between 1200 and 750 BC, consists of two large compartments one on top of the other. When it was excavated and restored in the 1950s, it was found to contain the remains of more than 100 people and a wide variety of burial objects; these are now displayed in the island's museums.

A further three kilometres (two miles) east is the far less frequently visited and romantically overgrown site of **Torrellafuda**, which sits in lovely countryside, bathed in sunlight and

something in at Swiss Cheese – a hollow reef on the north coast consisting of tunnels and chasms, chimney stacks, blow holes and craters to wriggle through. Great fun for confident divers. Ditto Cormorant Rock, an underwater island at 28 metres (92 feet), strewn with gigantic marble-shaped boulders and teeming with fish.

At the south-east end of the island, **S'Algar Diving** does up to eight boat dives a day, and is a good choice for more nervous divers (try dives take place mainly in the pool and the sandy bay). It also has a rich variety of sites. Coral galleries – the Chelsea Flower Show of the underwater world – are fringed by lacy mermaid's veils, while vibrantly coloured violet aeolit (an ornate, slug-like coral) looms out of crevasses and sink holes, in striking contrast to the fields of yellow cup corals carpeting the roofs of the grottoes.

More experienced divers will get a kick out of the world-famous Cathedral Cavern, a vast cave with a dramatic turquoise entrance and boulder-strewn floor – it gives the impression of having stumbled across a giant's abandoned game of marbles. Funnels is a good all-round dive offering a little bit of everything – two caves interlinked by a passageway and good flora and sealife. The mysterious Moon Pool stretches 90 metres (295 feet) back into a cave accessible by torchlight. Another interesting dive is the Statue of the Virgin Mary at San Esteban, which is a small statuette placed underwater in the 1960s by a Menorcan diver in memory of shipwrecked sailors. A shoal of around 200 Mediterranean barracuda patrol the site, making for a memorable dive.

All the diving schools listed below are open from Easter through to the end of October. Prices below include all equipment.

S'Algar Diving

Passeig Marítim, S'Algar (971 15 06 01/ www.salgardiving.com). **Prices** try dive €72; 1 boat dive €55; 6 boat dives €306; PADI Open Water Course €495.

7 Fathoms Dive Centre

Local 6, Parcela 410, C/Canal, Calas Picas, Ciutadella (971 38 87 63/www.7fathoms. com). **Prices** try dive €55; 1 boat dive €37; 6 boat dives €187; PADI Open Water Course €420.

Ulmo Diving

Zona Comercial, Addaia (971 35 90 05/ www.ulmodiving.com). **Prices** try dive €70; 1 boat dive €57; 5 boat dives €160; PADI Open Water Course €460.

birdsong. Here you'll find a huge talayot, a couple of taulas and the remains of houses, plus fragments of the encircling wall.

Nearby, but only accessible from the road running parallel and to the south of the main highway (known as the Camí Vell), is the small site of **Torretrencada**, which contains a fine taula (with a rib carved down the back of the main pillar, rather than a separate supporting stone) and rock-cut burial chambers. It's a five-minute walk from the car park.

Back towards Ciutadella on the Camí Vell, just a couple of kilometres outside the town, is perhaps Menorca's strangest attraction, the **Pedreres de s'Hostal**. In 1994 an organisation called Lithica was set up with the aim of preserving Menorca's sandstone quarries as centres for 'cultural activities and scenic attraction'. Those at Pedreres de s'Hostal are a mixture of 200-year-old hand-hewn pits and some more modern mechanical extraction quarries. A pleasant path runs through the old and new pits. Partly overgrown with fragrant trees and shrubs, and with birds of prey hovering above, the older part is less regular and marked by hand tools. The newer area is far bigger, deeper and more dramatic and imposing – it looks almost like an immense contemporary art installation. Weird and rather wonderful. Al fresco concerts are held here during the summer.

Pedreres de s'Hostal

Camí Vell, km1 (971 48 15 78/www.lithica.com). **Open** *May, Sept, Oct* 9.30am-sunset daily. *June-Aug* 9.30am-2.30pm, 4.30pm-sunset daily. *Nov-Apr* 10am-1pm Mon-Fri; 10am-5pm Sat, Sun. **Admission** €3; concessions €1.50-free. Free to all Nov-Apr. **No credit cards**.

Where to stay & eat

Two of the loveliest places to stay on the island lie between Ciutadella and Cala Morell. **Hotel Sant Ignasi** (Ctra. Ciutadella–Cala Morell s/n, 971 38 55 75, www.santignasi.com, closed 9 Dec-9 Jan, €110-€220 double), a couple of kilometres from Ciutadella, comes straight from the pages of a design magazine, with its

Menorca

mustard yellow colonial façade and elegant rooms, each one different – all very 'designer rural'. If you can afford it, it's a wonderfully peaceful place to stay, with nice gardens, a pool and the excellent **Es Lloc** restaurant (phone to check opening times, closed Oct-Mar, €€€€) next door. The food is stylishly presented Mediterranean cuisine, with just a handful of starters followed by three meat and three fish dishes. Nouveau-fiddling is kept to a minimum (a foam here, an emulsion there), and the results are delicious. The hotel and restaurant are located up a very long, very narrow rural lane off the Ciutadella- to Cala Morell road.

For some rural peace and quiet, the 500-year-old **Biniatram** farmhouse (Ctra. Ciutadella–Cala Morell, km6, 971 38 31 13, www.biniatram.com, doubles €55-€115) can't be beaten. Close

enough to Ciutadella for a night on the town, yet just a kilometre from the coast and set in acres of farmland. It has a pool, tennis court and large, baronial sitting room, as well as a kitchen for self-catering, plus a couple of self-contained apartments. All rooms have TVs and air-conditioning. Pleasant walks wind through the fields to the beach at **La Vall**. Be warned though: there is talk of various schemes (restaurant, campsite, concerts, mini-golf) that could wreck the idyll if they ever come to pass.

The north-west & west coasts

The only development on the western part of the north coast is at **Cala Morell**, built around a small, pretty bay between high cliffs, with a sizeable but not overbearing estate of holiday

Punta Nati. *See p260.*

apartments. Isolated as it is, the settlement has a somewhat, not unattractive, forlorn atmosphere, and some wonderfully colourful rock formations. It is also the site of an interesting prehistoric necropolis, also known as **Cala Morell**, of 15 caves dug from the rock.

East of here lies the pretty bay and pleasant beach of **Cala d'Algairens**, also known as **La Vall**. It's a better, bigger beach than that at Cala Morell and remains undeveloped, though you have to pay to use the car park. On the road here from Ciutadella, you pass the medieval defence tower at **Torre d'en Quart** and go through the pine woods of **Son Àngel**. Here, those with an equine bent can hire horses from **Cavalls Son Àngel** (call Toni or Catalina on mobiles 609 83 39 02 or 649 48 80 98 or email cavallssonangel@yahoo.es).

At its western end, Menorca drops down into a flat, rough plain that ends abruptly in low cliffs, as if the land has been snapped off by divine forces and hurled into the sea; this is the place for romantic sunsets. From the lighthouse at Punta Nati in the north-west corner down to its counterpart at Cap d'Artrutx in the southwest, there are no more than half a dozen narrow rocky inlets, the largest being the port of Ciutadella. The rest are now dominated by holiday resorts, from Cala en Blanes in the north down to Cala en Bosc and Son Xoriguer just round the corner in the south.

English-dominated ghetto **Cala en Blanes**, just north of Ciutadella, is a depressing encampment of hotel-apartments built around leisure complexes filled with English pubs. It's a miserable place, especially as the two 'beaches', **Cala en Forcat** and **Cala en Brut**, are nothing more than pocket handkerchiefs of sand less than a dozen metres across at the end of their respective inlets. The beach of Cala en Blanes itself, surrounded by independent villas, is slightly larger and a lot more pleasant, with a herd of elephant-footed palms clustered around its landward end. Trotting races take place at the **Torre del Ram** racetrack in Cala en Blanes every Sunday from April to November.

From here, the road back to Ciutadella passes along the top of the low cliffs, in front of a diverse line-up of interesting villas, some a century old. North of Cala en Blanes the coastline is wild, rocky and almost entirely devoid of human habitation. For lovers of the romantically barren, it's well worth driving up to the **Punta Nati** lighthouse and clambering about on the rocks above the crashing waves. This is also where you can see some of the best examples of *ponts* and *barracas*, the stone cattle shelters that look like ancient dwellings but actually date from the mid 19th century (*see* **p16 Prehistory primer**). The former are usually oblong, while the latter are circular pyramids, with a single entrance and a bare interior, with a stone lintel that sometimes has the construction date carved into it.

South of Ciutadella, the inlets at **Cala de Santandria** and **Cala Blanca** are slightly larger and much nicer than their counterparts to the north. Both are surrounded by villas, with a couple of hotels and snack bars on or overlooking the beach. From Cala Blanca the road runs a mile inland, through attractive grazing land neatly separated into plots by drystone walls and dotted with pine copses and the occasional farmhouse. Alternatively,

a beautiful but rugged coastal path leads over the top of the cliffs, with great views inland and out to sea.

Around the tip of **Cap d'Artrutx**, with its unprepossessing lighthouse, the beaches of **Cala en Bosc** and **Son Xoriguer** are stunning, with fine white sand, turquoise waters and more of the low cliffs that dominate this end of the island. Unfortunately, this is another package holiday ghetto and although the hotels are no more than a few storeys high, they still cover every inch of land here. The once attractive natural lagoon at Cala en Bosc is now a malodorous marina, lined with more British pubs and restaurants catering to package tours.

Where to stay

Almost every hotel on the west coast is the preserve of package tours, and none can be recommended. You're better off staying in Ciutadella and making forays to the coast, or try lovely **Biniatram**, just outside Cala Morell (*see p258*).

Getting there

By bus

Buses to and from Ciutadella leave from Plaça del Pins. There are 7 buses Mon-Sat and 6 on Sun between Ciutadella and Maó (1hr), via Ferreries (20mins), Es Mercadal (30mins) and Alaior (40mins). Other services from Ciutadella include 7 daily buses (3 on Sun) to Cala Galdana (40mins) via Ferreries, 3 buses Mon-Fri (2 Sat) to Sant Tomàs (40mins) and 1 bus Mon-Sat to Son Bou (1hr). There are also hourly buses along the west coast from Cala en Forcat (via Ciutadella) to Cala Blanca and Cap d'Artrutx (25mins). Note that there are fewer services on some routes Nov-Apr.

Top five Prehistoric monuments

Cala Morell
This complex of burial chambers dug into the sides of a gully, with steps, platforms and pillars, is unique on the island. Clambering visitors have left their mark, but it remains a fascinating place. *See p246.*

Naveta d'es Tudons
The best-preserved burial naveta on the island, standing like an upturned boat close to the main road out of Ciutadella. *See p256.*

Son Catlar
A prehistoric village circumscribed by a long defensive wall of large rocks that remains

more or less intact and gives the place a unique feel, bringing its past alive. *See p256.*

Talatí de Dalt
A large settlement with several ruined chambers and huts, as well as a talayot and taula, which give a good idea of the layout of a prehistoric Menorcan village. *See p223.*

Trepucó
Located just south of Maó, the talayot and taula here are among the biggest and best preserved on the island. *See p222.*

Menorca

Directory

Features

Sóller. *See p124.*

Directory

Getting There & Around

Arriving & leaving

By air

Log on to www.aena.es for information on all Spanish airports and live departure and arrival details.

Maó airport, Menorca

971 15 70 00/airport tourist office 971 15 71 15
Menorca's international airport is four kilometres (two and a half miles) south-west of Maó.

From mid May to October, a bus service runs from the airport to Maó bus station from 5.55am to 10.25pm every 30 minutes (plus 11.15pm and 12.15am) daily. From November to mid May, services run from 6.10am to 10.40pm every 30 minutes Monday to Friday; hourly at weekends and public holidays.

From mid May to October, services from Maó bus station to the airport run from 5.45am to 10.15pm every 30 minutes daily. From November to mid May, buses run from 6am to 10.30pm every 30 minutes Monday to Friday, and hourly from 6am to 10.30pm at weekends and on public holidays.

A single fare is €1.50. For details, phone 902 07 50 66 or Torres bus company on 971 38 64 61 or the airport tourist office on 971 15 71 15.

A taxi into Maó shouldn't cost more than €12.

Palma airport, Mallorca

971 78 90 00/airport tourist office 971 78 95 56
Son Sant Joan airport lies eight kilometres (five miles) east of Palma. It's a huge, sprawling place, with all the facilities you'd expect in an international airport, which seems ghostly quiet out of season and heaving during the summer, when most of its ten million or so annual visitors fly in. Expect long walks from the arrivals gates.

Bus No.1 runs between the airport and the bay-side Passeig Marítim via Plaça Espanya every 15 minutes from around 6am to around 2.15am every day. The single fare is €1.85. For details, phone 971 43 10 24.

A taxi will cost around €22 to the city centre. There are fixed-rate taxi fares to other places on the island.

Airlines

Below are listed the major airlines flying to Palma and Maó. Some only offer charter flights and may have a reduced timetable or no service out of the summer season.

Air Berlin *UK 0870 738 8880/ www.airberlin.com*
London Stansted to Palma.

Air Scotland *UK 0141 222 2363/ www.air-scotland.com*
Glasgow to Palma.

bmi British Midland
UK 0870 607 0555/Palma 971 78 94 75/78 92 69/www.flybmi.com
London Heathrow, Aberdeen, Belfast, Dublin, Durham Tees Valley, Edinburgh, Glasgow, Leeds Bradford and Manchester to Palma.

bmibaby
UK 0870 264 2229/Spain 902 10 07 37/www.bmibaby.com
Birmingham, Cardiff, Durham Tees Valley, Nottingham East Midlands and Manchester to Palma.

Britannia
UK 0800 000747/Palma 971 78 77 34/www.britanniaairways.com
London Gatwick, Stansted, Luton and 19 other UK airports to Palma, and 14 other UK airports to Maó.

EasyJet
UK 0905 821 0905 (premium rate)/Spain 902 29 99 92/Palma 971 78 76 58/www.easyjet.com
London Stansted, Gatwick and Luton, Belfast, Bristol, Liverpool and Newcastle to Palma, and Gatwick and Bristol to Maó.

Excel Airways
UK 0870 169 0169/www.xl.com
London Gatwick, Manchester and Newcastle to Palma and Maó, and Glasgow to Palma.

First Choice
UK 0870 850 3999/Palma 971 78 79 47/www.firstchoice.co.uk/flights
London Gatwick, Luton and Stansted, Manchester and 14 other UK airports to Palma and Maó.

flybe
UK 0871 700 0535/www.flybe.com
Birmingham and Exeter to Palma.

flyglobespan
UK 0870 556 1522/ www.flyglobespan.com
Edinburgh and Glasgow to Palma.

GB Airways/British Airways
UK 0870 850 9850/Spain 902 11 13 33/Palma 971 26 51 88/26 51 74/Maó 971 15 70 25/www.gb airways.com/www.ba.com
London Gatwick to Palma and Maó, and Palma to Maó and Ibiza.

Iberia
UK 0870 609 0500/Spain 902 40 05 00/Maó 971 36 90 15/www.iberia.com
London Gatwick to Palma, and Palma to Maó.

Jet2
UK 0871 226 1737/Spain 902 02 00 51/Palma 971 78 95 80/www.jet2.com
Leeds Bradford to Palma.

Monarch
UK 0870 040 5040/Spain 91 414 15 00/Palma 971 78 95 80/Maó 971 36 38 00/15 70 87/www.flymonarch.com
Scheduled flights from Manchester to Palma and London Luton to Maó. Chartered flights from Dublin, London Gatwick, Luton and Stansted, and six other UK airports to Palma. London Gatwick and Luton and six other UK airports to Maó.

My Travel
UK 0870 238 7777/Palma 971 78 79 38/www.mytravel.com
London Gatwick, Luton, Stansted and 18 other UK airports to Palma, and 14 other UK airports to Maó.

Thomsonfly
UK 0870 190 0737/Spain 91 414 14 81/www.thompsonfly.com
Bournemouth, Coventry and Doncaster/Sheffield to Palma.

By boat

Baleària

Information & reservations Spain 902 16 01 80/Palma 971 40 53 60/ www.balearia.com
Baleària operates both standard and high-speed passenger and car ferries between Barcelona and Valencia and the Balearics.

From Barcelona, there is a daily service to Ciutadella on Menorca (3hrs 45mins), going on to Alcúdia on Mallorca (5hrs 30mins; 1hr from Ciutadella to Alcúdia), and three slow ferries a week to Maó (9hrs). From Dénia, a twice-daily service runs to Palma via Ibiza (5hrs or 8hrs 45mins; 2hrs or 4hrs from Palma to Ibiza).

Between Mallorca and Menorca, ferries run daily between Alcúdia and Ciutadella (1hr) and three times a week (from July to September only) between Alcúdia and Maó (1hr 30mins).

Single passenger tickets from mainland Spain to the Balearics are €54 (standard ferry) and €75 (high-speed ferry). Single fares between Mallorca and Menorca are €51, and €36-€51 between Palma and Ibiza. Online booking available.

Cape Balear

Information Spain 902 10 04 44/ www.capebalear.es
Cape Balear runs a twice daily passenger service (with an extra service on Fridays and Sundays from July to September) between Cala Ratjada on Mallorca and Ciutadella on Menorca (1hr). Fares are €60 one way. Online booking available.

Iscomar

Information & reservations Spain 902 11 91 28/www.iscomar.com
Iscomar operates twice daily (once daily Sat, Sun, with an extra service on Saturdays from mid June to September) car and passenger ferries between Alcúdia on Mallorca and Ciutadella on Menorca (2hrs 30mins), as well as a daily passenger service between Barcelona and Palma (8hrs 30mins) and six boats a week between Valencia and Palma (9hrs). Online booking available.

A single passenger fare between Alcúdia and Ciutadella is €39; between Barcelona and Palma is €29; between Valencia and Palma €25.

Trasmediterranea

Information & reservations 902 45 46 45/www.trasmediterranea.es
Trasmediterranea runs a wide range of services from Barcelona and Valencia to the Balearics on both high-speed and standard passenger and car ferries. There are daily departures in high season from Barcelona to Palma (3hrs 45mins or 7hrs) and six a week during high season to Maó (8hrs). During the summer, daily services run from Valencia to Palma (6hrs or 7hrs 15mins) and one a week (on Saturdays) to Maó (14hrs). There's a weekly ferry every Sunday between Palma and Maó (5hrs 30mins), as well as a twice daily service between Palma and Ibiza (2hrs).

Fares between mainland Spain and the Balearics start at €52.50 (standard ferry) and €73 (high-speed ferry) one way. A single fare between Palma and Maó is €33. Online booking available.

Public transport

For information on all forms of transport on, and to, the Balearics, see **tib.caib.es**.

Bus

Mallorca is well served by buses, which offer the easiest means of getting around the island if you don't have your own transport. Many of those running to and from tourist areas only offer limited services out of season.

The main companies operating bus services are: **Empresa Municipal de Transportes Urbanos de Palma** (971 21 44 44, www.emtpalma.es), which has more than 20 routes in and around Palma; **Autocares Levante** (971 81 80 76, www.autocareslevante.com) runs airport transfers and excursions; **Autocares Mallorca** (971 54 56 96, www.autocaresmallorca.com) offers 11 routes covering most of Mallorca.

Buses are the only form of public transport on Menorca. As in Mallorca, services to resort areas are more frequent in high season. **Transportes Menorca** (971 36 04 75, www.transportesmenorca.net) is the main operator; its website shows timetables. Other operators include **Torres Allés Autocares** (971 38 64 61, www.e-torres.net) and **Autocares Norte** (971 36 66 00, www.autocares-norte.com).

For details of specific routes, see **Getting there** at the end of individual chapters.

Train

On Mallorca there are two rail lines. The picturesque old narrow-gauge Palma to Sóller railway now exists largely for tourists. *See p64* **All aboard!** Locals are far more likely to use the Palma to Inca line (run by SFM: 971 75 22 45), which has stops at Marratxí, Santa Maria del Camí, Consell, Binissalem and Lloseta. In 2003 its extension to Manacor via Sineu was reopened, 26 years after it had been closed down. Another branch line extends from Inca to Llubí, Muro and Sa Pobla. In Palma, the stations for both lines are in Plaça d'Espanya.

Menorca has no rail services.

Driving

Driving (on the right) on the islands is straightforward enough. You'll rarely encounter a serious traffic jam outside Palma (though the busy cross-Mallorca routes and the Maó–Ciutadella road on Menorca are largely single carriageways and you can get stuck behind slow-moving traffic). The main problem you are likely to encounter will be parking (*see p264*).

Car rental

Renting a car is cheap compared to the rest of Europe. There's lots of competition, so it pays to shop around. The local firms tend to be cheaper than the big international names, but make sure you check about hidden extras. At Palma airport, in particular, there's a huge choice of companies and you should be able to find the cheapest compact car for around €130 a week all-inclusive.

One of the cheapest brokers in Spain is **CarJet** (902 12 00 09, www.carjet.com), which is notable for its no extras policy that means extra drivers, car seats and damage excess are all included in the price. Another competitively priced broker is **Holiday Autos** (UK 0870 400 4461, www.holidayautos.com).

Avis *www.avis.es*
Toll-free number from the UK 0870 606 0100
Palma airport 971 78 91 87
Palma city, Passeig Marítim 16 (971 73 07 20/73 07 35)
Maó city, Moll de Ponent 61 (971 36 47 78)
Europcar *www.europcar.com*
Palma airport 971 78 91 35
Palma city, Passeig Marítim 19 (971 45 52 00)
Maó city, Sant Jaume Centro Comercial (971 37 84 11)

Directory

THE WORLD'S YOUR OYSTER

Hertz *www.hertz.es*
Palma airport 971 78 96 70
Palma city, Passeig Marítim 13
(971 73 47 37/73 23 74)
Maó airport 971 35 40 92
Maó city, C/Son Cremat 10 (971 36 15 12)

National-Atesa *www.atesa.es*
Palma airport 971 26 60 01
Palma city, Passeig Marítim 25
(971 45 66 02)
Maó airport 971 36 62 13

Driving tips

● Do not expect other drivers to allow you into a lane in busy city traffic. You need to wait for a gap, and then go for it with conviction.
● Do not hold back from using your horn – it is not regarded as offensive in Spain.
● It's not obligatory for cars to stop at zebra crossings.

Fuel

There's no shortage of petrol stations on the islands, and the majority still have attendants to fill your car for you. Almost all hire cars take unleaded petrol (*sense plom/sin plomo*).

Legal requirements

● In order to drive in Spain you'll need a valid driving licence and third-party motor insurance. Theoretically, all valid UK licences should be accepted; but, in fact, older non-photocard licences and Northern Ireland licences issued prior to 1 January 1991 do not conform to the EU model and may cause confusion. Drivers from the US and other non-EU countries should obtain an international driving permit.
● The minimum age at which you may drive a temporarily imported car or motorcycle (over 75cc) is 18. Most rental companies require the driver to be at least 21 years old and to have held a full driving licence for at least a year. Drivers under 25 often have to pay a supplementary charge.

● The minimum age for hiring a scooter (up to 49cc) is 16; no driving licence is required. For motorbikes over 250cc drivers must hold a driving licence and be aged 21 or over.
● Severe penalties, including fines and the withdrawal of your driving licence, may be enforced if the level of alcohol in your bloodstream is found to be 0.05 per cent or above. Fines are issued on the spot and can be steep; always ask for an official receipt.
● Seatbelts are compulsory for front and rear seat occupants, if fitted. Children under 12 cannot travel as front seat passengers unless a suitable restraint system is used.
● By law you must carry a fluorescent warning triangle, which must be set up on the hard shoulder some way behind the car if you break down. You must also carry a spare set of headlight bulbs.

Motorbikes/scooters

Scooters are fine for pottering along the coast, but you'll need something more powerful to explore the mountains.
Helmets are compulsory. Speed limits are enforced on an ad hoc basis. The police are hot on headlights, which should be set on half-beam at all times.
There are motorbike rental places all over the islands, including:
Rent A Bike *C/Joan Miró 330D, San Augustín, Palma (971 40 18 21)*

Parking

The Spanish drive everywhere and there are never enough parking spaces, particularly in Palma. Most towns and villages have an *aparcament* (car park), which is often free. If you park illegally, expect a fine (*multa*).

Roads & tolls

The most reliable map is Michelin's Balears/Baleares

(map 579), but get an up-to-date version as roads are constantly being built, rebuilt and reclassified.
The islands' only toll is through the Sóller tunnel on Mallorca.

Road classifications

Roads are prefixed PM or C, but the letters bear little relation to their size or quality. For example, the four main *autopistas*, all of them on Mallorca, are prefixed PM, but so are many of the secondary roads. C roads are the equivalent of main roads, and may be single or dual carriageways. PM V is the only other prefix you might spot. These roads are generally tiny and often winding. The number of numerals after the letter is a clue to the road's size – generally, the more numerals, the narrower the road.
Note that the ring road around Palma is known as the Via de Cintura.

Signs

● *cedeixi el pas/cede el paso* – give way
● *vosté no té prioritat/usted no tiene la prioridad* – you don't have the right of way
● *sentit únic/unico sentido* – one way
● *canvi de sentit/cambio de sentido* – a junction that allows you to change direction
● *recordi/recuerde* – remember (warning)

Speed limits

On major roads and motorways the speed limit is 120km/h (75mph), though many local drivers don't seem to take much notice of this. The minimum speed on motorways is 60km/h (37mph). In urban areas the speed limit is 50km/h (31mph); on other roads it is 90km/h (56mph).

Directory

Where to Stay

Mallorca is blessed with a vast number of places to stay. The package crowds stick to the coasts, while inland you can find small, boutique-style hotels with designer prices, and *casas rurales*: former farmhouses or private residences turned into accommodation. If designer luxury is your thing, you'll revel in a greater concentration of classy hotels on the island than anywhere else in Spain.

Menorca is lagging some way behind its bigger neighbour, with the boutique and *agroturismo* boom only just starting to make its presence felt. Pickings are fewer for those on a budget, with standard resort hotels often offering the keenest prices but little character.

Prices compare favourably to those in much of Europe, but accommodation in the Balearics is notably more expensive than in much of the rest of Spain.

Book ahead in high season (mid June to mid September). Many of the hotels in the coastal resorts are likely to be block-booked by tour operators months ahead, and finding a room on spec in July and August can be nigh on impossible. There shouldn't be problems at other times of the year, except during Semana Santa (Easter Week).

Many hotels have mid-season rates too, which generally run from March to mid June and mid September to the end of October. Some accommodation – particularly hotels in resorts – closes between late November and January. Low season prices (from November to February) can be considerably cheaper than those during summer, and it's possible to find some great bargains.

Most places will display the tariff at reception and also behind the door of your room.

It is unlikely that you will ever be ripped off, but there is always a *libro de reclamaciones* (complaints book) at reception.

The **Spanish National Tourist Office (SNTO)** publishes the *Guía de Hoteles, Campings y Apartamentos*, which is available from the major tourist offices and SNTO office abroad (*see p277*). It lists every officially recognised place to stay on the islands, and prints prices in both high and low seasons, together with symbols denoting facilities available.

Value-added tax, known as IVA, will be added to your bill at the rate of seven per cent. **Always check whether IVA is included in the quoted room price.** Breakfast (*desayuno*) may or may not be included in the rate.

Reis de Mallorca (www.reisdemallorca.com) and the **Small Hotel Company** (www.smallhotelcompany.com) represent some of the more interesting Mallorcan hotels; each has around 30 hotels and *fincas* on their books. **In this guide we have added IVA to prices for accommodation.** Bear in mind, however, that although the prices were correct at the time of writing, most of the establishments raise their rates each year.

Agroturismos & rural hotels

Turismo rural or *agroturismo* is the Balearics government's way of getting more tourists away from the coast and into the countryside. There has been a significant growth in this area in recent years.

The Balearic government divides the accommodation into three different types:

● **Agroturismo** – farms and country estates offering a maximum of 11 bedrooms.
● **Hotel rural** – generally more upmarket places with 12 or more bedrooms.
● **Turismo de interior** – renovated historic houses in towns and villages.

The **Associació Agroturisme Balear** (Avda. Gabriel Alomar i Villalonga, Palma, 971 72 15 08, www.topfincas.com) publishes an annual guide, *Fincas y pequeños hoteles*, to rural accommodation on both islands; their excellent website lists around 100 *agroturismos* with lots of photos. Nine *fincas* have broken away from the association and maintain their own website (www.fincaturismo.com). Menorca's fledgling *agroturismos* and *hoteles rurales* can be found on the **Menorca Rural** website (www.menorca-rural.com).

Camping

Very few people camp on Mallorca and Menorca, and there are only three official campsites. On Mallorca: **Club Nautico San Pedro**, Cala dels Camps–Colònia de San Pere, near Artà (971 58 90 00, closed mid Sept-May). On Menorca: **Camping Son Bou** and **Camping S'Atalaia** (for both, *see p234*). You can camp elsewhere, but it's important to use your judgement – city centres, private farmland and tourist beaches are off-limits; if you camp here you are liable for a fine.

Casa huéspedes, fondas & camas

You don't often see the letters 'CH' (*Casa huéspedes*), but they signify basic accommodation, often not much more than a room in someone's house. You'll be lucky to have a sink and are likely to be sharing the bathroom with the owners. *Fondas*, denoted by 'F', are of a similar quality. The sign '*Camas*' indicates that the homeowner rents beds for the night.

Hostales & pensiones

These are a rarity on the islands, with just a handful in Palma and the odd one in larger inland towns. *Hostales* (and *hostal-residencias*) are graded in the same way as hotels, with one or two stars. Most offer simple rooms with en suite facilities at reasonable prices. Some have a restaurant or café attached and most are family-run. '*Residencia*' simply means that no meal other than breakfast is served.

There is little difference between a *hostal* and a *pensión*, although *hostales* perhaps have the edge in terms of quality. At the simplest level, a *pensión* (*pensió* in Catalan) is going to be pretty basic – you may be offered a cell of a room with just a bed and a dock off a noisy stairwell. *Pensiones* are also graded with one or two stars, but there's very little difference between the categories.

Hotels

Few of the international chains have a presence on the islands, but there is no shortage of Spanish hotel groups. They include the upmarket chains **AC** (www.ac-hoteles.com) and **Sol Meliá** (www.solmelia.com), mid-market **NH** (www.nh-hoteles.com), **Husa** (www.husa.es) and **Riu** (www.riu.com).

The Balearic government has banned any new hotels of fewer than three stars and is trying to upgrade the remainder, so you'll find the majority of places to be three-star and up. However, there are a handful of one- and two-star places, and in all categories you'll find that standards are generally high.

There are five grades of hotel, ranging from one star to five stars; the appellation 'GL' beside the five stars means that the hotel is '*Gran Lujo*' ('grand luxury'), which is even posher than five stars. The stars correspond to the hotel's facilities, size of room, whether it has a lift, etc, but do not reflect levels of services, atmosphere or location.

At the one-star level, expect a simple room, usually with en suite shower and little else. At this level there is not much difference between a one-star and a decent *hostal*, and often you may be paying more simply for a phone in the room. At two stars you are likely to find all rooms en suite with certain facilities, such as TV, minibar and perhaps air-conditioning and/or heating. From three stars up you can expect all mod cons, maid service, often a café or restaurant and perhaps even a swimming pool. Four- and five-star hotels are as you would expect worldwide, with prices to match, although it's worth noting that four stars does not guarantee a pool.

'HA' denotes Apartment-Hotels, which are graded from one to four keys and offer self-catering facilities. These are very good value if you are travelling as a family and plan on spending more than a few days on the islands.

Monasteries

These offer simple accommodation, often in stunning surroundings and at very low prices. See the individual chapters for details. You can obtain a full list (*Ermites i santuaris*) from tourist offices.

Refugios

There are a handful of mountain refuges dotted around the serras at strategic points along trails, offering spartan accommodation, simple food and cheap prices.

Villa rental

Renting a villa is hugely popular on Mallorca and Menorca and there is a vast number and range of properties to choose from. Among the companies offering villas are:

James Villa Holidays
From the UK 0870 055 6688/ www.jamesvillaholidays.co.uk
Almost 200 villas on Mallorca, most in the Pollença area, and around 180 on Menorca, the majority on the south coast. All have pools.

Mallorca Farmhouse Holidays
From the UK 0118 947 3001/from outside the UK +44 118 947 3001/ www.mfh.co.uk
More than 100 Mallorcan farmhouses, villas and apartments.

MNK Villas
902 36 99 02/www.mnkvillas.com
Country houses, villas, townhouses and apartments on Menorca.

Owners Direct
www.ownersdirect.co.uk
Around 370 villas and houses on Mallorca and 165 on Menorca, direct from their owners.

Villa Retreats
From the UK 0870 013 3979/from outside the UK +44 1625 586586/ www.villaretreats.com
More than 40 villas and apartments on Mallorca and 13 on Menorca.

Youth hostels

There are just two youth hostels on Mallorca, one in S'Arenal (Albergue Playa de Palma, C/Costa Brava 13, 971 26 08 92, amateu@tjove.caib.es, closed Nov-Jan, €9-€14 per person) and the other is just outside Alcúdia (Albergue de la Victoria, Ctra. Cabo de Pinar, km4.9, 971 54 53 95, 971 54 55 42, lavict oria@tjove.caib.es, closed Oct-Jan, €9-€14 per person). For more details, see the website www.reaj.com.

Sport & Activity Holidays

The Balearics are a paradise for the sporty and lovers of activity holidays. As islands, inevitably the emphasis is on watersports, and in particular sailing, but on land you can take part in a wealth of sports and activities. For a full list get hold of the booklet Sports Facilities from tourist offices.

Activity holidays

A number of companies offer all-in adventure holidays to Mallorca. One of the best is **Tall Stories** (Brassey House, New Zealand Avenue, Walton-on-Thames, Surrey, KT12 1QD, from the UK 01932 252 002, www.tallstories.co.uk), which runs one-week multi-sport trips in northern Mallorca, featuring coasteering (scrambling, abseiling and climbing around the coast), sea kayaking, snorkelling, diving, canyoning and sailing.

Other good companies include **Explore** (1 Frederick Street, Aldershot, Hampshire, GU11 1LQ, from the UK 0870 333 4001, www.explore.co.uk), which organises week-long walking holidays in the Tramuntana mountains, and **Headwater** (The Old School House, Chester Road, Castle, Northwich, Cheshire, CW8 1LE, from the UK 01606 720 033, www.headwater.com) , which offers cycling and walking trips. **Balearic Discovery** (C/Jaime Solivellas 11, Selva, 971 87 53 95, www.balaeric discovery.com) tailor-makes holidays that include caving, ballooning, canyoning, cycling, deep-sea fishing, diving, riding and parapenting (leaping off the side of a mountain).

Cycling

Cycling is very popular on the islands, particularly in the flat interior and, for the more adventurous, the mountains of Mallorca's Serra de Tramuntana. In the east, the Serra de Llevant's lower peaks are less challenging and more accessible for the novice. There are a number of marked cycle routes on Mallorca. Menorca's flatter terrain makes it less challenging for the serious cyclist, but offers some lovely routes to small coves and bays. Be warned: cycling in the high summer heat is inadvisable.

For further information and route maps contact the **Federación Balear de Ciclismo** (C/Francesc Fiol i Juan 2, 1, 17A, Palma, 971 75 76 28, www.fcib.org), or get hold of the *Guia del Ciclista* map from tourist offices. The website www.baleares.com/tourist.guide/cycling/cycling. htm details eight circular cycling routes on Mallorca.

There are bike rental places all over the islands, including **Velo Sport Team Mallorca** (971 58 05 41, www.velosport mallorca.com), which can deliver bikes anywhere on Mallorca. (Call in advance.)

Golf

Golf is big business in Mallorca, and growing – more than 50,000 British golfers played the island's 17 courses in 2004. (There's also one course on Menorca – with proposals for another two currently being considered.) A further four courses are under construction – at Majoris, Puntiro, Son Vida and Santa Ponça.

Book tee times well in advance during the official season (October to May), and during the summer aim for an early tee. Wear a decent pair of shorts/trousers and a collared shirt (ladies too). Most courses don't ask to see a handicap certificate but it's something you should have just in case (Golf Andratx does like to see them). Most courses have clubs for hire and there are several driving ranges. If you're new to the game, there are good academies at the Marriott and Son Vida.

For reservations and further information see www.mallorcaonline.com, www.allspaingolf.com and www.magoco.com.

Golf Alcanada
Ctra. del Faro s/n, Port d'Alcúdia (971 54 95 60/www.golf-alcanada.com). **Green fees** (9/18 holes) €45/€75.
Opened in 2003, and designed by Robert Trent Jones Sr and Jr, this challenging course is the closest to a links course you'll find on the island, with magnificent views.

Golf Pollença
Ctra. Palma–Pollença, km49.3, Pollença (971 53 32 16/www.golf pollensa.com). **Green fees** (9/18 holes) €36/€58.
Expect good fairways, lots of sand, a couple of lakes and wonderful views to the coast.

Golf de Poniente
Ctra Cala Figuera s/n, Calvià (971 13 01 48/www.ponientegolf.com). **Green fees** (9/18 holes) €45/€74.
The 18 holes, opened in 1978, were designed by J Harris. Don't believe other guides that suggest that this is the island's toughest course; it's not.

Golf Santa Ponça I
Urbanización Santa Ponça, Calvià (971 69 02 11/www.habitatgolf.es). **Green fees** (9/18 holes) €40/€70.
Opened in 1992 and designed by Jose Gancedo, this is a good course for less confident golfers, with generous flat fairways and no dramatic rough.

Golf Son Parc
Urbanización Son Parc, Es Mercadal (971 18 88 75/971 35 90 59/ www.clubsonparc.com). **Green fees** (14 holes) €55.
Extended in the past few years from nine to 14 holes, with the final four holes due to be completed by summer 2006. So far the only course on Menorca.

Golf Son Termens
Ctra. S'Esglaieta, km10, Bunyola (971 61 78 62/www.golfsontermens). **Green fees** (9/18 holes) €42/€70.

This fabulous course is set at the foot of the Serra de Tramuntana and offers wondrous views. It's a hard walk, so lazy golfers should hire a buggy.

Marriott Hotel & Golf Resort

Llucmajor (971 12 92 00/ www.marriotthotels.com/pmigs). **Green fees** (9/18 holes) €38/€68 (€42 twilight fee). NB 9 holes only available 9-9.30am or late afternoon. The East is the older course and the West benefits from some creative landscaping. Perfect for golfers who don't enjoy uphill fairways and elevated tees.

Pula Golf

Ctra. Son Servera–Capdepera, km3, Son Servera (971 81 70 34/ reservas@pulagolf.com). **Green fees** (18 holes) €84.
Not easy for beginners, Pula Golf has plenty of challenging narrow fairways and small greens. Smart dress a must.

Real Golf de Bendinat

Urb. Bendinat, C/Campoamor s/n, Calvià (971 40 52 00/www.real golfbendinat.com). **Green fees** (18 holes) €67 (€48 twilight fee).
Good golfing along pine-lined fairways, with beautiful views across the Bay of Palma.

Son Vida Golf

Urbanización Son Vida, Palma (971 79 12 10/www.golfsonvida.com). **Green fees** (9/18 holes) €42/€75.
This excellent, varied course was the first on Mallorca when it opened in 1964.

Vall d'Or Golf

Ctra. Porto Colom–Cala d'Or, km7.7, S'Horta (971 83 70 68/ www.valldorgolf.com). **Green fees** (18 holes) €71.50 (€44.60 twilight fee).
An excellent, challenging course, facing south across Porto Colom and Cala d'Or, which offers plenty for all abilities. Several uphill fairways and elevated greens.

Horse riding

Horse riding is popular on both islands, and there are numerous stables and schools where you can hire a horse for trekking. Most schools offer ponies for kids, guides for tours and schooling for the rusty or novices. Both islands are criss-crossed with bridle paths, but the terrain varies enormously. The Serra de Tramuntana's lower slopes and those of the Serra de Llevant offer the best terrain for trekking on Mallorca. Menorca's flatter landscape lends itself to easy riding, particularly on the Camí de Cavalls bridle path.

For general information and a list of all riding clubs on the islands, contact the **Federació Hípica de les Illes Balears** (Recinto Ferial d'Es Mercadal, Menorca, 971 15 42 25, www.fhib.org).

Llevant Riding Club

C/Aurora 5A, Manacor, Mallorca (mobile 610 42 71 86).

Mallorca Riding School

Real Club Escola Equitació de Mallorca, Ctra. de Sóller, km 12.2, Bunyola, Mallorca (971 61 31 57).

Son Molina Riding Centre

Ctra. de Sóller, km 12.2, Bunyola, Mallorca (971 61 37 39).
Offers riding for the handicapped.

Alaior Riding School

Es Cos s/n, Alaior, Menorca (971 37 82 43).

Ciutadella Riding Club

Camino Caracol s/n, Ciutadella, Menorca (971 48 26 21/clubhipic ciutadella@hotmail.com).

Sailing & watersports

For many visitors, this is what Mallorca and Menorca are all about. Mallorca alone has 20,000 berths available in 30 marinas; Menorca has six marinas. For information on the marinas, get hold of a copy of the leaflet *España Nautica: Baleares* from tourist offices.

Some of the biggest yachts in the world berth here, including that of the King of Spain, who times his annual visit for August's **Copa del Rey** (King's Cup), the most prestigious Mediterranean sailing event in the calendar. Menorca runs a number of regattas year-round, including the most prestigious, the **Almirante Ferragut de Snipes National Trophy**, organised by four local clubs.

There are countless sailing clubs on both islands and spots where you can rent a boat for a day or longer.

The **Escuela Nacional de Vela de Calanova** (Avda. Joan Miró 327, Palma, 971 40 25 12, calanova.caib.es) and **Sail & Surf Pollença** (Passeig Sara Legui 134, Pollença, 971 86 53 46, www.sailsurf.de) are the top sailing schools on the islands. The latter also offers surfing for beginners. The **Federación Balear de Vela** (Balearics Sailing Federation, C/Joan Miró 327, Palma, 971 40 24 12, www.federacionbalear vela.org) has information about sailing in the islands.

Scuba diving

The diving off Mallorca is not spectacular. Expect the usual Mediterranean topography of granite boulders and seaweed, with sparse marine life – the odd octopus, moray eel and some local fish species. Perhaps the best spot is around the island of Sa Dragonera off the south-west tip, where the water is crystal clear. There is the odd wreck around the island, mainly in the Bay of Palma.

Menorca, however, is a completely different story, and offers some of the finest diving in the Med (*see p256* **Dive! Dive! Dive!**). The best time to go is late in the high season – mid August and September – when the sea has warmed sufficiently and you'll find temperatures of up to 25 degrees centigrade.

There are dive centres in almost all the resorts on the island (see individual chapters). For more information, contact the **Federación Balear de Actividades Subacuáticas** (Polideportivo Son Moix, Camí La Vileta 40, 971 28 82 42, www.fbdas.com); its Menorcan branch is at C/Andronas, Ciutadella (971 31 58 15).

Directory

Resources A-Z

Addresses

These are written street first, number second. In other words: C/Palma 7. Apartment addresses are written according to the floor and which side of the block the flat is on, and may be written in Catalan or Castilian, so 'dcha' = *dreta/derecha* (right); 'izda' = *esquerra/izquierda* (left); 'cto' = *centre/centro* (centre). 'Piso 1° dcha' would therefore translate as 'first-floor flat on the right'. The odd moniker s/n stands for '*sin número*', or 'no number'. *Código postal* is the five-figure postcode and should always be included.

Most Spanish street names are preceded by '*Carrer*' ('*Calle*' in Castilian), meaning 'street', often abbreviated to 'C/' and not marked at all on many street maps. We've used the following common abbreviations in addresses in this guide: Avda. = *avinguda* (Catalan)/*avenida* (Castilian) (avenue), and Ctra. = *carretera* (road). Other common words that you may come across in either Catalan or Castilian are *passeig/paseo* (boulevard), *passatge/pasaje* (alley, passageway) and *placeta/plazuela* (small square).

Addresses outside of towns are often designated by a kilometre mark. For example, 'Ctra. Palma–Manacor, km4' means 'at the 4km mark on the Palma to Manacor road.

Age restrictions

The minimum legal age for smoking and drinking is 16. The age of consent for both hetero- and homosexuals is just 13, one of the lowest in Europe. To drive a car or motorbike/scooter above 125cc you need to be 18; to drive a scooter up to 50cc you must be 14; to drive one up to 125cc you must be 16.

Attitude & etiquette

The Spanish are far more tactile than northern Europeans; the common greeting between members of the opposite sex and between two women is a kiss on both cheeks. Personal space is much less guarded than in the UK or USA, so do not be fazed if you find someone crowding you or bumping into you without apologising. However, the Balearics have been welcoming and dealing with the foibles of foreigners for so long that you're unlikely to be subject to any sort of significant culture shock.

Children

The Spanish love children – so much so that they take them with them wherever they go, at almost any time of day or night. Do not be surprised to see a baby asleep in a pushchair in a bar at 1am. The Spanish are also much less strict about keeping control of their kids than northern European parents. Bars and restaurants will bend over backwards to look after children or babies, even if they have no special facilities or kids' menus, and almost all hotels are happy to accommodate children at reduced rates. *See p95* **The best stuff for kids**.

Consumer

The Govern de les Illes Baleares has a freephone number (900 16 60 00, 8.30am-2pm Mon-Fri, operators speak English) dedicated to consumer issues and its website (www.caib.es) contains details of offices around the islands (five on Mallorca, one on Menorca) that can offer consumer help and advice (see http://web2.caib.es/pcnfront/do/serveis/xarxa).

Some staff speak English at the main offices: Passeig des Born 17, Palma, Mallorca (971 17 62 62/63); Avda. Josep M Quadrado 17, Maó, Menorca (971 36 04 26).

Consulates

British Consulate
Plaça Major 3D, Palma, Mallorca (971 71 24 45/971 71 60 48/ www.fco.gov.uk). **Open** 9am-2pm Mon-Fri.

Travel advice

For up-to-date information on travel to a specific country – including the latest news on safety and security, health issues, local laws and customs – contact your home country government's department of foreign affairs. Most have websites packed with useful advice for would-be travellers.

Australia
www.dfat.gov.au/travel

Canada
www.voyage.gc.ca

New Zealand
www.mft.govt.nz/travel

Republic of Ireland
www.irlgov.ie/iveagh

UK
www.fco.gov.uk/travel

USA
www.state.gov/travel

British Consulate

SA Casa Nova, Camí de Biniatap 30, Es Castell, Menorca (971 36 78 18/ www.fco.gov.uk). **Open** 9.30am-1.30pm Mon-Fri.

US Consular Office

Edificio Reina Constanza, C/Porto Pi 8, 9th floor, Palma (971 40 37 07). **Open** 10.30am-1.30pm Mon-Fri.

Customs

There are no restrictions on the import/export of duty-paid goods into Spain from any other EU country, provided the goods are for personal consumption only. Amounts qualifying as personal consumption are as follows. (If you import more than these amounts, you may be asked to prove that the goods are solely for you.)

● up to 800 cigarettes, 400 small cigars, 200 cigars or 1kg loose tobacco.
● 10 litres of spirits (over 22% alcohol), 90 litres of wine (under 22% alcohol) or 110 litres of beer.

If you are travelling into Spain from outside the EU, the limits are as follows.

● 200 cigarettes, 100 small cigars, 50 cigars or 250g loose tobacco.
● 1 litre of spirits (over 22% alcohol) or 2 litres of wine and beer (under 22% alcohol).
● 50g perfume.
● 500g coffee, 100g tea.

Disabled

The main towns and the resorts are fairly well geared up for disabled travellers, but rural areas are not. Many new buses are of the low-floor type, and wheelchairs should be available at most train stations. Many of the major car hire companies offer specially adapted cars for hire. Disabled parking bays are denoted by a blue wheelchair sign.

Most public buildings and monuments, certainly in the cities, have disabled access and facilities by law. This also applies to larger hotels, but smaller places are unlikely to be equipped for disabled visitors. Larger restaurants and service stations in tourist areas will also have disabled access, but in smaller villages facilities are scarce. Most toilets, outside of the resorts and big hotels, are similarly unadapted.

Organisations

Get a list of wheelchair-friendly accommodation and useful tips about Mallorca and Menorca for disabled visitors before you go from Spanish National Tourist Offices around the world. For your nearest office, *see p277* **Tourist information**.

ASPROM

C/Pascual Ribot 6A, Palma (971 28 90 52/asprom@asprom.es).
This is the main association on Mallorca for people with disabilities, and can offer basic information on accessibility by phone or via email.

Holiday Care Service

7th Floor, Sunley House, 4 Bedford Park, Croydon CRO 2AP (from UK 0845 124 9971/from outside UK 00 44 208 760 0072/ www.holidaycare.org.uk).
Provides information on travel for the disabled; its Mallorca factsheet (£2.50) has lots of useful details on wheelchair accessibility around the island and can be ordered online.

Drugs

Tolerance towards soft drugs has become stricter since the heady days of the late 1980s when it was perfectly acceptable to smoke in parks, public spaces and many bars and cafés. Today, you might see people smoking joints (*porros*) in certain areas such as El Terreny in Palma, but it's not as commonplace. Cannabis possession is illegal in Spain and can result in a fine and a possible court appearance. If you are found in possession of any other drugs, you are looking at big fines and a prison sentence.

Electricity & gas

Spain operates on a 220V, 50-cycle AC grid and uses two-pin plugs. You will need an adaptor if you are bringing British electrical appliances with you. Visitors from the USA will need to bring an adaptor and a transformer to use appliances from home.

Emergencies

The general 24-hour emergency number is **112**. Multilingual operators can then co-ordinate the necessary police, fire or ambulance services.

Gay & lesbian

There's not much of a scene outside Palma (*see p83*) and, in season, Magaluf.

For information (though only if you speak Spanish/ Catalan), contact:

Ben Amics

C/Conquistador 2 Principal, 07001 Palma (971 71 56 70, 6-9pm Thur only/www.benamics.com).
This is the Balearic gay and lesbian association. Their website is only in Catalan and Castilian.

Health

All travellers are strongly advised to take out comprehensive travel health insurance that will cover medical costs and repatriation, if required. Visitors can obtain emergency care through the public health service. EU nationals are entitled to free basic medical attention if they have the European emergency health card, also known as the EU health insurance card. This card replaced the E111 form and is valid for one year. Contact the health service in your country of residence for details. For non-emergencies, it's usually quicker to use private travel/ medical insurance rather than the state system.

Directory

For further information about health matters visit the Balearic government website (www.caib.es).

Accident & emergency

In a serious medical emergency requiring an ambulance, call the general emergency number 112. For lesser injuries, pharmacists are highly knowledgeable and can offer advice. *See below.*

Contraception

Condoms (*condons/preservativos*) can be bought from pharmacies and vending machines in the toilets of some bars. The female contraceptive pill (*la píndola/la píldora*) can be bought at most pharmacies without prescription, but women travellers are advised to bring their own supply with them. Local doctors are also able to write prescriptions for female contraceptive pills, and you'll usually need a prescription to get the morning-after pill (*la píndola del dia seguent/la píldora del día siguiente*). If you want a pregnancy test, ask a pharmacist for a 'Predictor' (a brand name, but the word everyone uses).

Doctors & dentists

Medical treatment covered by the European emergency health card (EU health insurance card; see the introduction to the Health section above) is only provided by practitioners within the Spanish national health service at a participating surgery (*consultori metge/consultorio*), health centre (*centre sanitari/centro sanitario*) or hospital clinic (*ambulatori/ambulatorio*). If you require treatment, you will need to have your card available to show to the doctor. Anyone without such a card who gets medical treatment in

Spain (including all non-EU visitors) will need a doctor's signature in order to make an insurance claim.

In Spain doctors, health centres and hospitals have separate surgery times for private patients. If you are asked to pay for treatment, be aware that you are not being treated under the national health service and your emergency health card will not be accepted. If you need to call out a doctor in an emergency, make it clear you have an EU emergency health card and that you want to be treated under the EU arrangements.

Note that dental treatment is not usually available free of charge and you are unlikely to be able to claim the costs unless you have comprehensive travel health insurance.

Hospitals

Hospital Manacor
Ctra. Manacor–Alcúdia s/n (general 971 84 70 00/ emergencies 971 84 70 60/ http://fundacion.hospitalmanacor.org).

Hospital Son Llàtzer
Ctra. Palma–Manacor, km4 (871 20 20 00/www.hsll.es).

Hospital Son Dureta
C/Andrea Doria 55, Palma (971 17 50 19/www.hsd.es).

Hospital Verge del Toro
C/Barcelona 3 (971 15 77 00/ www.smen.org).

Opticians

You can get a replacement pair of spectacles or order new contact lenses at any opticians (*optica*) as long as you have your prescription with you.

Pharmacies & prescriptions

Farmàcies/farmacias, denoted by an illuminated green cross, can be found in most villages and all towns and cities.

Pharmacists are highly knowledgeable and will often be able to save you a trip to the doctor. Pharmacies are usually open 10am to 2pm and 5pm to 8pm Monday to Saturday, but also operate a rota system so there is always one in the vicinity that is open 24 hours, as listed at the back of the local paper under '*Farmàcies de guàrdia*'.

Holders of an EU health insurance card will pay 40 per cent less than the full price for a prescription; other visitors must pay full prescription charges.

STDs, HIV & AIDS

Spain has the highest number of AIDS cases and deaths in the EU, according to UN statistics. Most cases are caused by the use of infected needles by drug abusers, rather than by sexual contact. However, this is largely confined to mainland Spain, particularly in the big cities and the south. The Spanish national AIDS helpline can provide further information in English (freephone 900 11 10 00, www.fase.es).

Helplines

Alcoholics Anonymous
mobile 616 08 88 83/ www.alcoholicos-anonimos.org
There are regular meetings held in English in Mallorca, but none currently in Menorca.

Narcotics Anonymous
902 11 41 47/www.na-esp.org/ engnaesp@yahoo.es
The email address above is for queries from English speakers. There are currently no English-language meetings, but Ibiza-based Sandy (mobile 690 15 28 82) can help out.

ID

You are meant to carry some form of ID with you at all times in Spain; the Spanish have identity cards but a passport is ideal for most foreign visitors. If you are stopped by the police and are not carrying valid ID, you will probably get a warning, although you may be liable to an on-the-spot fine. This is, however, very rare. Valid ID (passport) is essential when you're checking into a hotel, hiring a car, changing or paying with travellers' cheques and collecting poste restante.

Insurance

All travellers should take out personal travel insurance to cover trip cancellation, emergency medical costs and loss or theft of baggage, money or travellers' cheques. Don't forget to add on 'dangerous sports' cover if you're planning on horse riding, scuba diving, etc. Keep a record of your policy number and the emergency telephone number with you at all times.

Internet

There is usually an internet café or at least a *locutori/ locutorio* offering internet access in most towns and resorts and in some villages. See the listings under 'Resources' in the individual chapters of this guide. For useful websites on Mallorca and Menorca, *see p282*.

Legal help

Consulates (*see p270*) can help tourists in emergencies, and can provide a list of English-speaking lawyers/interpreters.

Libraries

Municipal libraries are open 9am to 9pm Monday to Friday and 9am to 2pm on Saturday.

Lost property

If you lose something in your hotel, report it to the staff. If you lose something on public transport or in the street, go to your nearest police station. See the listings under 'Resources' in each chapter.

Maps

All tourist offices supply free local maps. If you're planning on driving, get the Michelin Baleares map (no.579). The Spanish Cycling Federation publishes cycling route maps on its website (www.rfec.com).

Media

Newspapers & magazines

In Spain newspapers and magazines are sold from *quioscos/kioscos* – kiosks on the street.

The Spanish press is largely serious and pretty dry; you won't find anything equivalent to the British tabloids. The biggest seller on a national level, with a circulation of about 400,000, is the left-of-centre *El País*, which has the best foreign coverage and political analysis. The regional edition has a daily Baleares section inside. *El Mundo* and *Diario 16* are both good centrist alternatives, while *ABC* is solidly conservative and reactionary.

The islands have a couple of good local papers: *Diario de Mallorca*, which is a serious tabloid, and *Ultima Hora*, which is a bit more populist. Its English equivalent is the *Majorca Daily Bulletin* (www.majorcadailybulletin.es), which keeps expat residents updated on local and UK news, and includes an extensive classified section.

Mallorca Reporter is a surprisingly good weekly free paper, distributed in various resorts, which has news, features and classifieds.

The glossy English language mag *Island Life* (www.islandlifemallorca.com) carries features on everything from cool new hotels to celebs living on the islands.

The free fortnightly Spanish-language *Youthing* publication has listings guides to gigs and youth-slanted events all over the island. It's available from many bars, music shops, etc.

Otherwise, most British and US newspapers are available the same day in the larger towns (many print a Spanish edition on Mallorca), and the following day in villages.

Celebrity gossip is confined to the magazines – in fact, Spain pioneered the genre with the sycophantic glitz of *!HOLA!*.

Parents should note that Spain's laissez-faire attitude towards pornography means that you will often find hard-core porn magazines within easy reach of children.

Radio

The Spanish are avid radio fans; you'll hear radios blaring out in bars, cafés, buses and taxis. **Radio Nacional de España** is the main public broadcaster, with four stations. The main commercial broadcaster is **SER** (Sociedad Española de Radiofusión), which controls four networks: SER, a news network and music channels. There are an enormous number of talk radio-style stations with endless discussions about current affairs, including **Onda Cero**.

The best pop stations are **Cadena Cuarenta Mallorca** and **Cadena 100**, which plays about two Spanish songs to every three British or American ones and is littered with ad breaks. **Radio Clasical** is a relaxing alternative. The local stations include **Ultima Hora Radio 98.8 FM**, **Somràdio** (in Catalan) and **Radio Balear**. You'll also find a few English channels including **Sunshine Capital Radio**, which is on the same frequency as its namesake in London – 95.8 FM.

Television

Spanish television is poor, but you'll find it dominating almost every bar or café you visit. There are five main channels, which pump out an endless diet of tacky game shows, talk shows, hilariously dreadful imported *telenovelas* (soaps) from South/Central America and badly dubbed American movies. The only redeeming feature is the news coverage.

The local TV channel in Mallorca is **Canal 4** (Palma). **TVE** (Televisión España) has a Balearic outpost in Palma, broadcasting in Catalan and Castilian; **m7 Televisió de Mallorca**, also in both languages, is another Mallorca-specific channel.

In most three-star and above hotels you should be able to get **BBC World** and **CNN**. Cable channel **Canal Plus** offers premium sport and music.

Money

Spain's currency is the **euro**. Each euro (€) is divided into 100 cents (¢), known as *céntims/céntimos*. Notes come in denominations of €500, €200, €100, €50, €20, €10 and €5. Coins come as €2, €1, 50¢, 20¢, 10¢, 5¢, 2¢ and 1¢. Euro travellers' cheques are widely accepted.

Banks & ATMs

You will find a bank in even the tiniest rural community. Banks invariably offer better rates of exchange than bureaux de change. For opening hours, *see below*.

Almost every bank has an ATM (Automated Teller Machine) that can be used to withdraw cash. ATMs accept most credit cards, as well as debit cards that display the Cirrus symbol; they're usually the most convenient way to get hold of local currency. For both credit and debit cards you will need a valid PIN number in order to withdraw money. Your card issuer is likely to charge you a fee for using an ATM while abroad.

Credit cards

Credit cards, especially MasterCard and Visa, will be accepted in all major hotels and many upmarket restaurants on the islands, as well as in supermarkets and petrol stations. However, smaller shops, bars, *hostales* and restaurants in rural areas will often not have credit card facilities. Note too that many places will be reluctant to accept AmEx due to the cost to the retailer. If your card has a Maestro symbol on it, you can use it in major department stores and hotels.

Natural hazards

In summer beware of the strength of the sun. In the mountains watch out for rockfalls, flash flooding and getting caught up in a snowfall in the winter.

Opening hours

Banks

Opening hours are 9am to 2pm Monday to Friday. Banks in towns and cities are also open 9am-1pm on Saturdays from October to April.

Bars & cafés

Bars and cafés usually open at lunchtime and stay open until midnight or 1am. However, some cafés may open as early as 5.30am or 6am, depending on their clientele. *Bares de copa*, where the emphasis is more on drinking than eating, rarely open before 7pm and may continue serving until 4am. *Discoteca-bars* start later still and often do not close until after dawn (*madrugada*) at 6/7am. Note that few bars and cafés have strict closing times.

Museums & monuments

Opening hours vary, although a siesta period in the afternoon is not uncommon. Many sights are also closed on a Monday.

Restaurants

Restaurants are generally open from 1/2pm until 4/5pm and again from 8/9pm until midnight or 1am at weekends. In tourist areas UK opening hours are more common. Note: most restaurants have a *día de descans/descanso* (rest day), usually Monday or Wednesday. Away from the coast they may close for the summer holidays in August (*tancat per vacances/ cerrado por vacaciones*).

Post offices

Correus/correos are open from 8am to noon and again from 5pm to 7.30pm, although the ones in big cities do not close in the afternoon. Some offices are also open on Saturdays.

Shops

Most shops are open from about 9.30/10am until 1/2pm, when they close for a siesta until 5pm. In the evening they stay open until 8pm. Some smaller shops, such as bakers (*forn de pa/panadería*) and greengrocers (*fruiteria/ frutería*), will open much earlier at 7/8am, and department stores and supermarkets stay open all day, sometimes until 10pm.

Police & crime

There are three types of police in Spain: the Guàrdia Urbana, the municipal police, operate on a city or town level, directing traffic and dealing with intra-urban crime; the Policía Nacional, who wear brown uniforms, patrol the areas outside the cities; while the green-uniformed paramilitary Guàrdia Civil spend most of their time on highway patrol handing out speeding tickets.

Postal services

There is usually just one post office (*correus/correos*) per urban area, often characterised by endless queues; so if you are only after stamps (*segells/sellos*), you are better off going to a tobacconist (*estanc/estanco*), recognisable by its brown and yellow *tabacs/tabacos* sign. They also sell phonecards. For opening times, *see p274*.

Stamps for letters or postcards up to 20g within Spain are €0.28, €0.53 within the EU and €0.78 for other international destinations. Post can take days just to go to the next town. Airmail within Europe takes at least five days, but often longer, and it will take at least ten days to a destination outside Europe.

Poste restante

Poste restante is available at any post office. Letters should be addressed to the recipient at '*Llistat de correus*'/'*Lista de correos*'. You will need your passport to collect your post. American Express offers the same service.

Public holidays

The Spanish enjoy more public holidays than any other European. On Mallorca and Menorca there are also holidays specific to the islands and local fiestas (*see chapter* **Festivals & Events**). If a holiday falls midweek, the Spanish will often take the following day(s) as holiday too, turning it into a long weekend or *pont/puente* (bridge).

On public holidays, banks, post offices and public buildings close down and many museums operate Sunday opening times. Note too that many Spaniards take the whole of August off as holiday and that many restaurants and shops away from the resorts will close for the whole month.

The following are public holidays on both islands:

1 Jan *Cap d'Any/Día de Año Nuevo* (New Year's Day)
6 Jan *Epifanía del Senyor/Día de Los Reyes Magos (Epifanía del Señor)* (Epiphany)
1 Mar *Dia de les Illes Balears/Día de las Islas Baleares* (Balearics Day)
19 Mar *Dia de Sant Josep/San José* (St Joseph's Day)
13 Apr 06/5 Apr 07 *Dijous Sant/ Jueves Santo* (Maundy Thursday)
14 Apr 06/6 Apr 07 *Divendres Sant/Viernes Santo* (Good Friday)
1 May *Festa del Treball/Día del Trabajo* (Labour Day)
15 Aug *Assumpció/Día de la Asunción* (Assumption)
12 Oct *Día de la Hispanidad* (Spanish National Day)
1 Nov *Tots Sants/Todos los Santos* (All Saints' Day).
6 Dec *Dia de la Constitució/ Constitución* (Constitution Day)
8 Dec *Immaculada Concepció/Inmaculada Concepción* (Immaculate Conception)
25 Dec *Nadal/Navidad* (Christmas Day)
26 Dec *Segona Feste de Nadal/Día de San Esteban* (Boxing Day)

Religion

Although officially a Catholic country, as elsewhere in Europe Spain's church-going is dominated by the older generation. It is also worth noting that many religious festivals on the islands, such as Semana Santa (Easter Week), are as much about civic pride and spectacle as they are about religious devotion.

Safety & security

Serious crime is rare on the islands. If you are unlucky, call the general emergency line 112.

The only type of crime you are likely to be the victim of is petty crime, such as bag-snatching or pickpocketing, particularly in Palma. Another common crime involves cutting handbag straps or camera straps (especially around the cathedral in Palma).

For this reason you should take reasonable precautions when you're out and about:

● Don't flash around wads of cash or, indeed, carry a lot of cash on your person; lock it in your hotel safe instead.
● Conceal cameras and any other valuables.
● Keep a firm hold of your handbag both when walking along and when sitting in a café or restaurant, especially outside. (A good tip is to slip the strap of your bag under your chair leg.)

Theft from hotel rooms is more common in cities in the lower-end establishments. Again, it generally tends to be opportunistic, so don't leave valuables lying around when you leave your room. Either put them in the safe or give them to the hotel reception for safe-keeping.

Cars are vulnerable when parked or in stationary traffic with the window open, when scooter riders can snatch belongings from the passenger seat, though this is rare. Overnight, try and park in a hotel garage or a patrolled public garage.

If you are the victim of a theft, head straight to the nearest police station to report it (see under 'Resources' in each chapter). You're unlikely to ever see your possessions again, but you'll need the police report in order to make an insurance claim. Be warned: outside the main tourist areas the police often don't speak English, and the form-filling (which is likely to be in Spanish) takes ages.

If you have your passport stolen, contact your nearest consulate (*see p270*).

Smoking

Cigarettes in Spain – both international and local brands – are very cheap by UK standards and attitudes towards lighting up are easygoing. The only places you'll find no-smoking areas are on public transport and in the airports. If you are a non-smoker, some hotels have designated no-smoking floors and some smarter restaurants have designated no-smoking areas.

Study

If you want to learn Spanish in Spain, your best resource is to check out the **Instituto Cervantes** website (eee.cervantes.es). This provides a full list of the various courses on offer and a description of the places where they are run.

The Palma-based **Universitat de les Illes Balears** (information office 971 17 29 39, 17 27 42, www.uib.es) was founded in 1978 in an attempt to prevent a mass migration of bright local youngsters to the mainland; it now has 15,000 students. In addition to a wide range of degree courses, it also offers Spanish courses for foreigners (www.uib.es/en/courses).

It operates the **Erasmus** student exchange scheme, as part of the EU's Socrates programme to help students move between member states. Interested students should contact the Erasmus co-ordinator at their home college. Information is available in the UK from the **UK Socrates-Erasmus Council**, Rothford, Giles Lane, Canterbury, Kent, CT2 7LR (01227 762712, www.erasmus.ac.uk).

Tax

Value-added tax (IVA) at seven per cent is included in the price of all consumer goods and will be added on to the total bill in hotels and restaurants. (Be aware that it is often not included in initial quotes for rates in hotels.) IVA is non-recoverable for EU citizens. Visitors residing outside the EU should pick up a form at the airport and keep all receipts in order to get an IVA refund.

Telephones

The Spanish telephone network is efficient and fairly cheap to use. Telephone numbers in Mallorca and Menorca consist of nine digits. The area code for the Balearics is 971, which is followed by six digits. You always need to dial the area code, even when you are on the islands.

Freephone calls are prefixed with 900, cheap rate calls are prefixed with 902 and premium rates are prefixed with 906. Any number starting with a 6 will be a mobile.

International calls

When calling Mallorca or Menorca from abroad, you need to dial the international access code (0011 from Australia; 00 from Ireland, New Zealand and the UK; 011 from the USA and Canada), followed by the country code for Spain (34), followed by the nine-digit number.

To make a call abroad from Mallorca and Menorca, dial 00 (the international access code) plus the international country code, area code and number. Remember to omit the initial 0 from the area code unless you are calling the United States.

International country codes: Australia 61; Canada 1; Ireland 353; New Zealand 64; South Africa 27; United Kingdom 44; United States 1.

Mobile phones

Most European mobile phones (*telefons mòbils/telefonos moviles*) work in Spain (once you have set them up for roaming), but be warned that even if you are making a local call you will be charged at international roaming rates. You will also be charged for incoming calls. Contact your service provider for details. US handsets are not GSM-compatible and will not work

in Europe. If you plan on being on the islands for more than a few weeks, you might be better off buying a pay-as-you-go package when you arrive.

Mobile phone shops include **Linea Móvil** C/Francisco Sancho 2A, Palma (971 29 12 04, www.ono.es).

Spanish service providers
Amena *1474*
Moviline *1435*
Movistar *1485*
Vodafone *607 12 30 00*

Public phones

It's much cheaper to make a call from a phone box than a hotel. There are plenty of phone boxes in towns and villages; most will take coins (you'll need a fistful) and phonecards (*tarja telefónica/tarjeta telefonica*). Phonecards are the simplest option and can be bought at most *quioscos/kioscos* (kiosks) and *estancs/estancos* (tobacconists), as well as from phone shops. Many bars have payphones.

To make a call from a public phone: lift the receiver, insert the card or coins, then dial the number (not forgetting the area code). If you wish to make another call and you have change left, press the 'R' button and dial the next number rather than hanging up the receiver.

You can also make calls from *locutoris/locutorios*, which are small rooms full of phone booths where you sit down to talk and then pay for your call at the end. These often double up as internet cafés and you can also send faxes. Faxes may also be sent from hotels and stationery shops (*papereries/papelerías*).

Operator services

In most phone boxes operator services will be denoted by little buttons with signs on the main phone panel. You will usually have to insert a coin even to make a free call, although it will be returned when you hang up.

Note that English is not commonly spoken by Spanish phone operators; none of the following is in English.

Useful numbers
National operator *1009*
Operator for calls to EU *1008*
International operator *1005*
Directory enquiries *11811*
International directory enquiries *025*
Weather reports *906 36 53 65*
Speaking clock *093*

Time

Spain is an hour ahead of Greenwich Mean Time and six ahead of Eastern Standard Time. Clocks go back in the last week of October and forward in the last week of March.

Tipping

Spaniards aren't tippers and rarely do more than round up bills. In smarter restaurants you may find a service charge of ten per cent is added to the bill. It's not obligatory, and don't feel you have to pay it if you're not happy with the service you've received. In tourist areas, however, there's a greater expectation of tipping in restaurants. You are not expected to tip at a bar. Taxi drivers expect a small tip for longer journeys. Hotel staff don't rely on tips to supplement their wage and will not expect them. Having said that, it is perfectly acceptable to reward particularly good service.

Toilets

Toilets (*serveis/servicios*) are generally of a good standard, except in the older bars or restaurants in rural areas. They are much less private than in the UK or USA, with usually just one door rather than two giving on to the facilities. Public toilets are

fairly rare, but most bars will be happy to let you use their facilities. They are also known as aseos, *banys/baños* or *lavabos*, and are usually denoted by 'S' for ladies (*senyores/señoras*), and sometimes 'D' (*dones/damas*) or 'M' (*mujeres*), and 'C' for gentlemen (*cavallers/caballeros*). Sometimes, however, you'll find an 'S' on both doors, denoting *senyores/señoras* and *senyors/señores*.

Tourist information

Despite the enormous number of tourists who visit the islands, Mallorca and Menorca have just a small network of turismos run by the **Conselleria de Turisme**, confined chiefly to the tourist areas (for details see the relevant area chapters under 'Resources').

Tourist office staff are usually helpful and will often speak a little English. As well as supplying (usually free) maps and pamphlets with information on the local area, they can also help you find accommodation and provide you with lists of hotels and restaurants.

In the larger towns *turismos* open throughout the day and at weekends. In villages they often close for siesta and at weekends. Out of season, village and resort *turismos* may operate to a winter timetable with reduced hours, or close altogether.

If there is no actual tourist office in the place you are visiting, try the Ajuntament (town hall), which should be able to supply you with basic information and maps.

For tourist information before you leave your own country, contact the local **Spanish National Tourist Office**:

Canada *2 Bloor Street West, Suite 3402, Toronto, Ontario M4W 3E2 (416 961 3131/4079/www.tour spain.toronto.on.ca).*

UK *PO Box 4009, London W1A 6NB (020 7486 8077/www.tour spain.co.uk).*
USA *8383 Wilshire Boulevard, Suite 960, Beverly Hills, CA 90211 (323 658 7188/www.okspain.org); Water Tower Place, Suite 915 East, 845 North Michigan Avenue, Chicago, IL 60611 (312 642 1992); 1395 Brickell Avenue, Miami, FL 33131 (305 358 1992); 666 Fifth Avenue, 35th floor, New York, NY 10103 (212 265 8822).*

Visas & immigration

If you are a citizen of the EU, Norway, Iceland, the USA, Japan, Canada, Australia or New Zealand, you do not need a visa to enter Spain and stay for 90 days. All other nationals should contact their local Spanish consulate for information. Regulations do change, so all visitors should check with their local Spanish consulate for the latest information prior to travelling.

To stay longer you need to obtain a *permiso de residencia* (residency permit) at a police station and prove that you can support yourself financially. If you have found employment within this time, your employer will often sort out the red tape for you (*see p278* **Working**).

Weights & measures

Spain uses the metric system.

Conversions
1 kilometre (km) = 0.62 miles
1 litre (l) = 1.76 UK pints/2.12 US pints
1 gram (g) = 28 ounces
1 kilogram (kg) = 2.2 pounds
(9/5 Celsius temperature) +32 = temperature in Fahrenheit

When to go

The Balearics enjoy a Mediterranean climate with a year-round average temperature of 21°C in Mallorca on the coast and 20°C

Directory

in Menorca, and an average of more than 300 days of sunshine throughout the year. For average monthly temperatures, *see below* **Weather**.

The best time to visit the islands is in the spring, when the blossom and wildflowers are out, the sun is not too fierce and the fiesta season is just beginning. At this time, prices (except during Easter Week) are still low, but the weather is often warm enough to enjoy a beach holiday. Inland, however, it can still be a bit damp and cold, especially in the mountains, so come prepared.

From mid June prices and temperatures rise steeply, and by July and August the islands are a furnace, with temperatures regularly hitting the mid 40s.

By mid September high season is officially over and prices and temperatures start to fall. This is also a good time to visit as the fine, mild weather often stretches into late October.

November to February is officially winter, and many hoteliers and restaurants choose to close for a few months. It can snow during this period, especially in the high mountains, and it gets very cold in towns like Valldemossa. This is also a

rainy season, and sudden downpours after months of near drought can lead to flash floods and rock falls.

Women

The Balearics (and Catalunya in general) have probably the most enlightened attitudes to women in Spain, and you are unlikely to encounter any more harassment than you would at home. Women encounter few problems travelling solo; you may be approached if you are on your own in a bar or café, but if you make it clear that you are not interested, you are likely to be left alone. Sex crimes are very rare.

Working

Queries regarding residency and legal requirements for foreigners working in Spain can be addressed to the Ministry of Interior's helpline on 900 150 000 (there are English-speaking operators). Its website (www.mir.es) lays out the regulations in force on these matters (not in English).

It's a great deal easier for EU citizens to find (legal) work in the Balearics than those from non-EU countries. By far the

easiest and most usual way of finding work on the islands is working on yachts, both taking them out with their owners in season and keeping them polished and well maintained while they languish in the harbour. Your best bet is to simply turn up at any port or marina and ask around.

Close second is as an English teacher. It's also a great way to meet locals and learn Spanish yourself. The majority of *academias de inglés* are based in Palma and Maó, but you will also find them in some smaller towns and villages. You do not even have to speak Spanish to become an English teacher (many schools prefer it, in fact, if you don't), but most want you to be qualified in TEFL (Teaching English as a Foreign Language). Many of the bigger English language institutions, such as Wall Street and Opening, advertise in the UK in the British Council newspaper and sometimes in the job sections of the national newspapers. Many will also have a website.

You may also find seasonal work in bars and restaurants, particularly in the English-dominated resorts such as Santa Ponça and Magaluf.

Weather

	Av daily max temp °C/°F	Av daily min temp °C/°F	Av monthly hrs of sunshine	Av monthly rainfall mm/in	Average humidity %
Jan	14.9/58.8	3.4/38.1	5.3	37/1.5	79
Feb	15.3/59.5	3.9/39.0	5.5	34/1.3	77
Mar	16.7/62.1	4.4/39.9	6.2	36/1.4	75
Apr	18.8/65.8	6.3/43.3	7.2	39/1.5	74
May	22.8/73.0	10.0/50.0	8.8	30/1.2	71
June	27.3/81.1	14.2/57.6	10.2	14/0.6	67
July	30.7/87.3	17.0/62.6	10.7	10/0.4	65
Aug	30.6/87.1	17.6/63.7	10.0	20/0.8	69
Sept	27.6/81.7	15.6/60.1	7.4	50/2.0	75
Oct	23.2/73.8	12.0/53.6	6.6	63/2.5	78
Nov	18.7/65.7	7.4/45.3	5.6	47/1.9	79
Dec	15.9/60.6	5.0/41.0	5.0	44/1.7	80

Vocabulary

The official language of the Balearics is Catalan (*català*), of which *mallorquí* and *menorquí* are dialects. Though every Spanish native on the islands will speak Castilian Spanish, Catalan is the mother tongue of the majority. It was banned under Franco, and for many is a badge of pride, identity and independence. You might find that some locals will prefer to speak to you in English rather than Castilian. Most of the road signs, street names, etc, that you'll see on the islands will be written in Catalan.

There are differences between the Catalan spoken in the Balearics and that of the Barcelona region (one of the more obvious is the use of the articles es, sa, ses rather than el, la, els, les), but most of them are fairly minor. The information given below is standard Catalan. The most interesting linguistic quirk is the appearance of corrupted anglicisms in *menorquí*, dating from the period of British occupation in the 18th century (*see p216* **The British legacy**)

English is widely spoken in holiday areas and on the coast but less so in the interior, where if you take an interest and learn a few phrases, it is likely to be appreciated.

For food and menu terms, *see chapter* **Food & Drink**.

Catalan

Pronunciation

In Catalan, as in French but unlike in Spanish, words are run together, so *si us plau* (please) is more like 'sees-plow'.

à at the end of a word (as in Francesc Macià) is an open 'a' rather like 'ah', but very clipped

ç, and **c** before an 'i' or an 'e', are like a soft 's', as in 'sit'; **c** in all other cases is as in 'cat'

e, when unstressed as in *cerveses* (beers), or Jaume I, is a weak sound like the second 'e' in 'centre'

g before 'i' or 'e' and **j** are pronounced like the 's' in 'pleasure'; **tg** and **tj** are similar to the '**dg**' in 'ba**dg**e'

g after an 'i' at the end of a word, as in *puig*, is a hard 'ch' sound, as in 'wat**ch**'; **g** in all other cases is as in '**g**et'

h is silent

ll is somewhere between the 'y' in 'yes' and the '**lli**' in 'mi**lli**on'

l.l, the most unusual feature of Catalan spelling, has a slightly stronger stress on a single 'l' sound, so *para**l.l**el* sounds similar to the English 'para**ll**el'

o at the end of a word is like the '**u**' sound in 'fl**u**'; **ó** at the end of a word is similar to the 'o' in 'tomat**o**'; **ò** is like the 'o' in 'h**o**t'

r beginning a word and **rr** are heavily rolled; but at the end of many words are almost silent, so *carrer* sounds like 'carr-ay'

s at the beginning and end of words and **ss** between vowels are soft, as in 'sit'; a single **s** between two vowels is a 'z' sound, as in 'la**z**y'

t after 'l' or 'n' at the end of a word is almost silent

x at the beginning of a word, or after a consonant or the letter 'i', is like the '**sh**' in 'shoe', and at other times as in 'e**x**pert'

y after an 'n' at the end of a word or in **nys** is not a vowel but adds a nasal stress and a y-sound to the 'n'

Useful expressions

hello *hola*; **goodbye** *adéu*; **hello** (when answering the phone) *hola, digui'm*

good morning, good day *bon dia*; **good afternoon, good evening** *bona tarda*; **good night** *bona nit*

please *si us plau*

very good/great/OK *molt bé*

thank you (very much) *(moltes) gràcies*; **you're welcome** *de res*

Do you speak English? *Parla anglés?*; **I'm sorry, I don't speak Catalan** *Ho sento, no parlo català*; **I don't understand** *No entenc*; **Can you say it to me in Spanish, please?** *M'ho pot dir en castellà, si us plau?*

What's your name? *Com se diu?*

Sir/Mr *senyor (sr)*; **Madam/Mrs** *senyora (sra)*; **Miss** *senyoreta (srta)*

excuse me/sorry *perdoni/disculpi*; **excuse me, please** *escolti* (literally 'listen to me')

OK/fine *val/d'acord*

How much is it? *Quant és?*

Why? *Perquè?*; **When?** *Quan?*; **Who?** *Qui?*; **What?** *Què?*; **Where?** *On?*; **How?** *Com?*; **Where is...?** *On és...?*; **Who is it?** *Qui és?*; **Is/Are there any...?** *Hi ha...?/ N'hi ha de...?*

very *molt*; **and** *i*; **or** *o*; **with** *amb*; **without** *sense*; **enough** *prou*

I would like... *Vull...* (literally, 'I want'); **How many would you like?** *Quants en vol?*; **I don't want** *No vull*; **I like** *M'agrada*; **I don't like** *No m'agrada*

good *bo/bona*; **bad** *dolent/a*; **well/badly** *bé/malament*; **small** *petit/a*; **big** *gran*; **expensive** *car/a*; **cheap** *barat/a*; **hot** (food, drink) *calent/a*; **cold** *fred/a*

something *alguna cosa*; **nothing** *res*; **more** *més*; **less** *menys*; **more or less** *més o menys*

nothing at all/zilch *res de res* (said with both 's's silent)

toilet *el bany/els serveis/el lavabo*

open *obert*; **closed** *tancat*

entrance *entrada*; **exit** *sortida*

price *preu*; **free** *gratuit/de franc*; **change, exchange** *canvi*

to rent *llogar*; **(for) rent, rental (de)** *lloguer*

Getting around

a ticket *un bitllet*; **return** *d'anada i tornada*; **card expired** (on metro) *títol esgotat*

left *esquerra*; **right** *dreta*; **here** *aquí*; **there** *allí*; **straight on** *recte*; **at the corner** *a la cantonada*; **as far as** *fins a*; **towards** *cap a*; **near** *a prop*; **far** *lluny*; **Is it far?** *És lluny?*

Time

In Catalan, quarter- and half-hours can be referred to as quarters of the next hour (so, 1.30 is two quarters of 2.00).

now *ara*; **later** *més tard*; **yesterday** *ahir*; **today** *avui*; **tomorrow** *demà*; **tomorrow morning** *demà pel matí*; **morning** *el matí*; **midday** *migdia*; **afternoon** *la tarda*; **evening** *el vespre*; **night** *la nit*; **late night** (roughly 1-6am) *la matinada*

At what time...? *A quina hora...?*; **in an hour** *en una hora*; **at 2** *a les dues*; **at 1.30** *a dos quarts de dues/a la una i mitja*; **at 5.15** *a tres quart de sis/a las cinc i quart*; **at 22.30** *a vint-i-dos-trenta*

Numbers

0 *zero*; 1 *u, un, una*; 2 *dos, dues*; 3 *tres*; 4 *quatre*; 5 *cinc*; 6 *sis*; 7 *set*; 8 *vuit*; 9 *nou*; 10 *deu*; 11 *onze*; 12 *dotze*; 13 *tretze*; 14 *catorze*; 15 *quinze*; 16 *setze*; 17 *disset*; 18 *divuit*; 19 *dinou*; 20 *vint*; 21 *vint-i-u*; 22 *vint-i-dos, vint-i-dues*; 30 *trenta*; 40 *quaranta*; 50 *cinquanta*; 60 *seixanta*; 70 *setanta*; 80 *vuitanta*; 90 *noranta*; 100 *cent*; 200 *dos-cents, dues-centes*; 1,000 *mil*; 1,000,000 *un milló*

Days, months, seasons

Monday *dilluns*; Tuesday *dimarts*; Wednesday *dimecres*; Thursday *dijous*; Friday *divendres*; Saturday *dissabte*; Sunday *diumenge*

January *gener*; February *febrer*; March *març*; April *abril*; May *maig*; June *juny*; July *juliol*; August *agost*; September *setembre*; October *octobre*; November *novembre*; December *desembre*

spring *primavera*; summer *estiu*; autumn/fall *tardor*; winter *hivern*

Spanish

Pronunciation

c before an 'i' or an 'e' and z are like 'th' in 'thin'; c in all other cases is as in 'cat'

g before an 'i' or an 'e' and j are pronounced with a guttural 'h' sound that doesn't exist in English – like 'ch' in Scottish 'loch', but much harder; g in all other cases is as in 'get'

h at the beginning of a word is normally silent

ll is pronounced almost like a 'y'

ñ is like 'ny' in 'canyon'

a single r at the beginning of a word and rr elsewhere are heavily rolled

Stress rules

In words ending with a vowel, 'n' or 's', the penultimate syllable is stressed. In words ending with any other consonant, the last syllable is stressed. An accent marks the stressed syllable in words that depart from these rules: eg *estación, tónica*.

Useful expressions

hello *hola*; hello (when answering the phone) *hola, diga*; good morning, good day *buenos días*; good afternoon, good evening *buenas tardes*; good evening (after dark), good night *buenas noches*;

goodbye/see you later *adiós/ hasta luego*

please *por favor*; thank you (very much) *(muchas) gracias*; you're welcome *de nada*

Do you speak English? *¿Habla inglés?*; I don't speak Spanish *No hablo castellano*; I don't understand *No entiendo*; Speak more slowly, please *Hable más despacio, por favor*; Wait a moment *Espere un momento*

What's your name? *¿Cómo se llama?*

Sir/Mr *señor (sr)*; Madam/Mrs *señora (sra)*; Miss *señorita (srta)*

excuse me/sorry *perdón*; excuse me, please *oiga* (the standard way to attract someone's attention, politely; literally 'hear me')

OK/fine (to a waiter) that's enough *vale*

Where is...? *¿Dónde está...?*; Why? *¿Porqué?*; When? *¿Cuándo?*; Who? *¿Quién?*; What? *¿Qué?*; Where? *¿Dónde?*; How? *¿Cómo?*; Who is it? *¿Quién es?*; Is/Are there any...? *¿Hay...?*

very *muy*; and *y*; or *o*; with *con*; without *sin*

open *abierto*; closed *cerrado*; What time does it open/close? *¿A qué hora abre/cierra?*

pull (on signs) *tirar*; push *empujar*

I would like... *Quiero...*; How many would you like? *¿Cuántos quiere?*; How much is it? *¿Cuánto es?*; I like (it) *me gusta*; I don't like (it) *no me gusta*

good *bueno/a*; bad *malo/a*; well/ badly *bien/mal*; small *pequeño/a*; big *gran, grande*; expensive *caro/a*; cheap *barato/a*; hot (food, drink) *caliente*; cold *frío/a*; something *algo*; nothing *nada*; more/less *más/menos*; more or less *más o menos*

Do you have any change? *¿Tiene cambio?*

price *precio*; free *gratis*; discount *descuento*; to rent *alquilar*; (for) rent, rental *(en) alquiler*

Getting around

airport *aeropuerto*; railway station *estación de ferrocarril*

entrance *entrada*; exit *salida*

car *coche*; bus *autobús*; train *tren*; a ticket *un billete*; return *de ida y vuelta*; bus stop *parada de autobus*; the next stop *la próxima parada*

Excuse me, do you know the way to...? *¿Oiga, señor/señora/etc, sabe cómo llegar a...?*

left *izquierda*; right *derecha*; here *aquí*; there *allí*; straight on *recto*; to the end of the street *al final de*

la calle; as far as *hasta*; towards *hacia*; near *cerca*; far *lejos*

Accommodation

Do you have a double/single room for tonight/one week? *¿Tiene una habitación doble/para una persona/para esta noche/una semana?*

We have a reservation *Tenemos reserva*; an inside/outside room *una habitación interior/exterior*; with/without bathroom *con/sin baño*; shower *ducha*; double bed *cama de matrimonio*; with twin beds *con dos camas*; breakfast included *desayuno incluido*; air-conditioning *aire acondicionado*; lift *ascensor*; pool *piscina*

Time

now *ahora*; later *más tarde*; yesterday *ayer*; today *hoy*; tomorrow *mañana*; tomorrow morning *mañana por la mañana*; morning *la mañana*; midday *mediodía*; afternoon/evening *la tarde*; night *la noche*; late night (roughly 1-6am) *la madrugada*

At what time...? *¿A qué hora...?*; at 2 *a las dos*; at 8pm *a las ocho de la tarde*; at 1.30 *a la una y media*; at 5.15 *a las cinco y cuarto*; in an hour *en una hora*

Numbers

0 *cero*; 1 *un, uno, una*; 2 *dos*; 3 *tres*; 4 *cuatro*; 5 *cinco*; 6 *seis*; 7 *siete*; 8 *ocho*; 9 *nueve*; 10 *diez*; 11 *once*; 12 *doce*; 13 *trece*; 14 *catorce*; 15 *quince*; 16 *dieciséis*; 17 *diecisiete*; 18 *dieciocho*; 19 *diecinueve*; 20 *veinte*; 21 *veintiuno*; 22 *veintidós*; 30 *treinta*; 40 *cuarenta*; 50 *cincuenta*; 60 *sesenta*; 70 *setenta*; 80 *ochenta*; 90 *noventa*; 100 *cien*; 200 *doscientos*; 1,000 *mil*; 1,000,000 *un millón*

Days, months, seasons

Monday *lunes*; Tuesday *martes*; Wednesday *miércoles*; Thursday *jueves*; Friday *viernes*; Saturday *sábado*; Sunday *domingo*

January *enero*; February *febrero*; March *marzo*; April *abril*; May *mayo*; June *junio*; July *julio*; August *agosto*; September *septiembre*; October *octubre*; November *noviembre*; December *diciembre*

spring *primavera*; summer *verano*; autumn/fall *otoño*; winter *invierno*

Further Reference

Books

There are surprisingly few books in print in English on Mallorca and Menorca (there is, for instance, no dedicated account of Mallorcan history currently available). A number of the books listed below are either out of print or only available on the islands.

Mallorca

Abulafia, David
A Mediterranean Emporium: the Catalan Kingdom of Mallorca
A detailed dissection of independent Mallorca during the Middle Ages, concentrating on its role in trade in the western Mediterranean.

Alcover, Mossèn Antoni
Folk Tales of Mallorca
This enormous compendium of island folk stories was gathered by a 19th-century priest.

Bennison, Vicky
The Taste of a Place: Mallorca
Excellent culinary guide to the island and its cuisine, including recommended restaurants, markets, shops and recipes.

Brawn, David & Ros
Discovery Walking Guides
The Brawns produce a series of excellent walking guides to various different areas of Mallorca (and also Menorca).

Carr, Raymond
Spain: A History
In the absence of a dedicated history of Mallorca, this is the best short survey of the history of the country as a whole; it touches on the Balearics.

Carrigan, Henry L
Romancing God: Contemplating the Beloved
A short introduction to the life of scholar, linguist, poet and missionary Ramón Llull.

Catoir, Barbara
Miró on Mallorca
Catalan artist Joan Miró always held Mallorca in special affection (his mother was a native and it was his permanent home from the mid 1950s until his death). This book focuses largely on the techniques and themes of Miró's later works, many inspired by the piercing blue light of his adopted island.

Crespí-Green, Valerie
Sunflower Guides: Mallorca
Containing more than 20 detailed walks on the island, plus suggestions for six driving tours and picnics.

Graves, Lucia
A Woman Unknown
A compelling memoir of life in Francoist Mallorca and Catalonia by the daughter of Robert Graves. In beautifully measured prose it tells the story of a woman caught between two cultures, and of the unsung lives of many of the quietly heroic women she came into contact with during that period.

Graves, Robert
Majorca Observed
The poet's thoughts and fancies on his adopted island just as the first waves of mass tourism were breaking upon the shores he thought of as his own. Though snobbish at times, it's an interesting portrait of a society on the cusp of monumental change.

Graves, Tomás
Bread & Oil: Majorcan Culture's Last Stand
Still resident in Deià, to where his father Robert moved in 1929, son Tomás is a passionate supporter of traditional Mallorcan culture, and this absorbing and idiosyncratic exploration of the classic Mallorcan peasant dish of *pa amb oli* (bread and oil) is also part autobiography and part cultural history of the island during the last few decades.

Graves, Tomás
Tuning Up At Dawn: A memoir of music and Majorca
Published in 2004, this is Graves' affectionate portrait of the island, its history and the central role that music has played in his life. Better written and with a more general appeal than *Bread & Oil*, it's particularly interesting when dealing with Deià's bohemian past and the many colourful characters who have passed through the village over the year.

Graves, William
Wild Olives
Another book by another son of Robert Graves, this account is chiefly concerned with the author's childhood, his difficult relationship with his father and their less than harmonious family life.

Hearl, Graham & King, Jon
A Birdwatching Guide to Mallorca
The island is a favourite haunt of twitchers, and this is the best guide available to what you can see and where.

Heinrich, Herbert
Twelve Classic Hikes through Mallorca
There are a far wider range of quality guides to Mallorca in German than in English; this translation details some superb walks in the Serra de Tramuntana.

Jeffries, Roderic
An Enigmatic Disappearance
This is one of Jeffries' Inspector Alvarez series of detective novels, set on Mallorca.

Kerr, Peter
Snowball Oranges/Mañana Mañana/ Viva Mallorca!/A Basketful of Snowflakes
Enjoyable if predictable accounts of the author's attempts to set up a new life in south-west Mallorca in the *Year in Provence/Driving over Lemons* style.

Könemann (publisher)
Majorca: Culture and Life
This large-format picture-packed book by German publisher Könemann is by far the best and most comprehensive general introduction to the island.

Rusiñol, Santiago
Majorca: The Island of Calm
Possibly the best known book by the Catalan writer and humourist, this series of vignettes on subjects such as 'The men of Palma' and 'Eulogy of the ensaimada' now seems somewhat dated and rather cloying in style, but it is still an intriguing document of an early 20th-century Mallorca that four decades of mass tourism have long since eradicated. Available in English on Mallorca.

Sand, George
A Winter in Majorca
Sand's notorious demolition of the Mallorcans, sparked by the miserable winter (1838-39) she spent in Valldemossa with her children and companion Frédéric Chopin is, ironically, widely available throughout the island in a number of different editions. Though she was unimpressed by the islanders, she loved the scenery, and the book remains a highly entertaining and valuable (if biased) account of an isolated agricultural society.

Scott, George
The Bloody Bhokara
Written by the co-owner of Scott's Hotel in Binissalem, this enjoyable crime fiction romp provides plenty of interesting background detail on expat life on the island along the way; its follow-up is *The Chewed Caucasian*.

Seymour, Miranda
Robert Graves: Life on the Edge
A detailed but rarely dynamic account of Graves's long life and turbulent relationships. The book was written with the full co-operation of Graves's family.

Villalonga, Llorenç
The Dolls' Room
Published in the 1950s, this sharply observed portrayal of the declining fortunes of the 19th-century Mallorcan nobility was written by one of the island's best-known authors.

West, Gordon
Jogging Round Majorca
This easygoing, entertaining account of the author's slow progression around the island in the 1920s paints a fascinating portrait of a Mallorca before mass tourism.

Menorca

Amics del Museu de Menorca
Guide of Menorca: Historical and Natural Patrimony
This haltingly translated island guide produced by the Museu de Menorca contains lots of interesting details that you won't find in most other guidebooks.

Ansell, Rodney
Sunflower Guides: Menorca
Contains more than 20 detailed walks on the island, plus various suggestions for driving tours and picnics.

Gregory, Desmond
Minorca, the Illusory Prize: History of the British Occupation of Minorca between 1708 and 1802
An expensive, exhaustive, academic survey of the 18th century British occupations of the island.

Laurie, Bruce
The Life of Richard Kane: Britain's First Lieutenant-Governor of Minorca
Overview of the life of the most influential foreigner in Menorca's history. Pricey.

Marti, Rev Fernando
History of Menorca
Though dated in some respects (it was published in the late 1970s) and idiosyncratic in style, this is a treasure trove of facts, figures and stories on the island, covering everything from Menorcan surnames to ancient rock paintings and the shoe industry.

Mata, Micaela
Conquests and Reconquests of Menorca
There's a heavy pro-Catalan bias to this exploration of Menorca between the 13th and 18th centuries. Nevertheless, it's full of interesting

detail, particularly regarding the devastating pirate attacks on the island during the 16th century, and the British and (brief) French occupations of the 18th century. The book is easiest to find in Maó and Ciutadella.

Ramos, Enric
The Birds of Menorca
This excellent title provides a detailed description of all the species of birds recorded in Menorca. Reader-friendly and full of handsome illustrations.

Websites

a2zMallorca
www.a2smallorca.com
Heaps of information on just about every subject and every town and village on the island.

Ajuntament de Palma
www.a-palma.es
Palma city council website. Good listings for public libraries, bus timetables and all things municipal, and has a useful interactive street finder and city map.

Beaker Pages
www.arrakis.es/~rinord
Amateur-looking but fascinating site dedicated to the islands' prehistoric past.

Consell Insular de Menorca
www.emenorca.org
The island council's website, with a handy events and activities search facility as well as useful opening hours.

Digame
www.digame-online.com
Online guide to Mallorcan events, from exhibitions to theatre to club nights.

Discover Menorca
www.discovermenorca.co.uk
Located in the UK, this agent rents villas on the island as well as arranging travel insurance and car hire. It also offers useful information on activities and guided tours.

Govern de les Illes Balears
www.caib.es/kfcont.htm
Official Balearic government website with useful links, including a directory of local products and tourist information.

Fauna Ibérica
http://faunaiberica.org
Conservation-led guide to the islands' native fauna. In Spanish only.

hot-maps
www.hot-maps.de
www.hot-maps.de/europe/spain/ balearen/palma_de_mallorca/homede. htm
German site with access to a detailed interactive map of Palma.

Illes Balears
www.visitbalears.com
Official tourist office site for the Balearics, with everything from the weather to what's on.

Magalluf-Palmanova/ Santa Ponsa.com
www.magalluf-palmanova.com
www.santa-ponsa.com
Listings for everything from bookies to lawn bowls in Mallorca's party capital, and its slightly more sedate near neighbour.

Majorca Daily Bulletin
www.majorcadailybulletin.es
Online version of the English-language paper.

MallorcaWeb
www.mallorcaweb.com/eng
General Mallorca search engine.

Menorca Private Owners
www.villanet.co.uk
An independent organisation run by villa owners who want to rent their properties direct to holidaymakers.

Menorca The Guide
www.menorca-net.co.uk
Free registration to an online guide with information on everything from the biosphere, beaches, car hire and accommodation to learning Spanish.

Minorca
www.islandofminorca.info
An updated e-book version of David Wilson Taylor's detailed 1970s guide to Menorca's history and culture.

PuertoPollensa.com
www.puertopollensa.com
Guide to the resort of Port de Pollença (Puerto Pollensa).

Sollernet.com
www.sollernet.com
Guide to the town of Sóller and sister resort Port de Sóller.

Spain for Visitors
http://spainforvisitors.com
A useful resource with cultural information.

Think Spain
www.thinkspain.com
A comprehensive website covering travel and accommodation to useful local news and the environment.

STRIANET
http://nibis.ni.schule.de/~trianet/ mallorca/physic3.htm
If you like graphs, you'll enjoy this educational site that delves beneath the tourist tat to look at the physical character of the Balearics.

Ultimate Guide to Menorca
www.ultimateguide-menorca.com
Good all round guide to the island.

VisitMenorca.com
www.visitmenorca.com
Website of the Menorca Hotel Association with an online search facility.

Index

Note: page numbers in **bold** indicate section(s) giving key information on topic; *italics* indicate photos.

Menorca, continued

General, continued

Advertisers' Index